D1716694

Contents

The Wire

The Wire

Crime, Law, and Policy

Adam M. Gershowitz
Professor, William & Mary Law School

Carolina Academic Press
Durham, North Carolina

Gershowitz, Adam M.
 The wire : crime, law, and policy / Adam M. Gershowitz.
   pages cm
 Includes bibliographical references and index.
 ISBN 978-1-61163-196-8 (alk. paper)
 1. Criminal justice, Administration of--United States. 2. Wire
(Television program) I. Title.

  KF9223.G47 2013
  364.973--dc23

                       2012051838

Carolina Academic Press
700 Kent Street
Durham, North Carolina 27701
Telephone (919) 489-7486
Fax (919) 493-5668
www.cap-press.com

Printed in the United States of America

This book has not been endorsed or authorized by HBO or the creators of *The Wire*.

To Laura, for letting me watch and discuss The Wire *incessantly*

Summary of Contents

Table of Cases

Page numbers in *italics* refer to primary cases.

Preface

"Whatever it was, they don't teach it in law school."[1]

— Assistant State's Attorney Rhoda Pearlman, reacting to
how the prosecution had just lost a huge trial.

Criminal law professors have described *The Wire* as "the greatest television series ever made."[2] The show offers brilliant character development and a gripping drama, but it also does much more. *The Wire* highlights crucial legal and policy issues that are unfortunately absent from the law school curriculum.

On a doctrinal level, *The Wire* introduces us to the law of wiretapping, which is not covered in many criminal procedure courses. It also shows us the law of drug possession—a crime that is responsible for more than a quarter of the United States' prison population,[3] but which is almost never carefully analyzed in first-year criminal law classes.

The Wire also forces us to dig deeper into issues that are only addressed superficially in traditional law school classes. For instance, every criminal procedure student learns about informants when studying probable cause and the Fourth Amendment. But students are rarely asked to think hard about the benefits given to informants in charge reductions and sentencing discounts. And little attention is paid to the terrible harm that snitching can have on the informants and their communities. Most law students never consider, for example, in what circumstances police should be allowed to rely on juvenile informants and what protections they should afford to those children before sending them back into schools or onto the street.

The Wire also asks us to grapple with major public policy issues that drive the criminal justice system, but which are not suited to the case method that dominates most law school classes. For instance, should drug use be legalized, decriminalized, or simply ignored in some areas? Does the media have undue influence in directing the police toward certain neighborhoods and pushing arrests for certain types of crimes? Do officers manipulate the information in police reports in order to increase their clearance rates and improve crime statistics? Do states do an adequate job of helping prisoners to reintegrate into society after release? Although these issues are typically absent from most criminal law and procedure classes, they are front and center in *The Wire*.

Finally, *The Wire* deals with core legal issues, such as searches and seizures and confessions that are covered in law school classes, but forces us to confront them from a different perspective. Rarely do students take a step back to think about whether the police

---

1. *The Wire*, Season 5, Episode 7, at 53:15 minutes.
2. Susan A. Bandes, *And All the Pieces Matter: Thoughts on The Wire and the Criminal Justice System*, 8 Ohio St. J. Crim. L. 435, 445 (2011).
3. William J. Sabol et al., Bureau of Justice Statistics Bulletin: Prisoners in 2008, at 2 (2009), available at http:// bjs.ojp.usdoj.gov/content/pub/pdf/p08.pdf, at 37 App. Tbl 15.

consider the Supreme Court's Fourth and Fifth Amendment jurisprudence to be legitimate. Even more rarely do students consider whether the police actually understand the search and seizure and confession rules that the Supreme Court asks them to comply with. And while there is a body of scholarship questioning whether the Supreme Court's criminal procedure jurisprudence is biased as a whole against the poor and minorities, it is unusual for students to focus on that big picture question as opposed to becoming mired in the thicket of Fourth and Fifth Amendment rules themselves. *The Wire* brilliantly shows us the bigger picture.

For all of these reasons, *The Wire* is a perfect vehicle for thinking about the most important criminal justice issues of our generation. The goal of this textbook is to supplement *The Wire* with the doctrinal law that applies to the wiretapping, drug possession, search and seizure, confession, sentencing, and other criminal law and procedure issues in the series. The book also seeks to offer a balanced analysis of the big-picture policy questions—such as drug legalization, prisoner reentry, resource allocation, media influence, police honesty, crime statistic manipulation, police brutality, and the use of informants—raised by the show. These are certainly not the only criminal law issues raised by *The Wire*. I have chosen these topics both for their importance as well as their absence from many traditional law school classes. By looking to cases, statutes, government reports, non-profit position papers, law review articles, and *The Wire* itself, students can see a fuller picture of the criminal justice system and its dysfunctions.

———

Because a textbook based on a television show is unconventional, a note on formatting is in order. Throughout the book, I have primarily excerpted cases, articles and other sources that address key issues raised by *The Wire*. Thereafter, in many of the notes, I have pointed to scenes from the series that encapsulate the issues or raise interesting discussion points. Because the scenes are sometimes lengthy I have cited to the beginning of the scenes, not the exact moment when a quote is spoken. For example, early in the book I encourage readers to watch *The Wire*, Season 1, Episode 5, at 11:20 minutes in order to consider a comment made by Stinger Bell. The scene begins at 11 minutes and 20 seconds into the episode, although Stringer's quote does not occur until about one minute later.

———

I have discussed *The Wire* with more people than I can count. I am sure I have forgotten many of them, but for helpful suggestions I wish to express my gratitude to Susan Bandes, Jeff Bellin, John Blevins, Zack Bray, David Dow, Brandon Garrett, Laura Killinger, Lee Kovarsky, Alex Kreit, Richard Leo, Nancy Leong, Paul Marcus, Michael O'Hear, Ellen Podgor, Michael Rich, Eli Silverman, Christopher Slobogin, Sandy Guerra Thompson, and Ron Turner. I also wish to thank Andrew Dao, Sarah Samuel, Courteney Taylor, Courtney Walsh, and Katherine Witty for helpful research assistance.

Acknowledgments

I gratefully acknowledge the authors and publishers of the following works for granting permission to reproduce excerpts in this book:

Barbara Armacost, *Organizational Culture and Police Misconduct*, 72 Geo. Wash. L. Rev. 453 (2004). Reprinted with permission of the George Washington Law Review and the author.

Mary Sue Backus & Paul Marcus, *The Right to Counsel in Criminal Cases: A National Crisis*, 57 Hastings L.J. 1031 (2006). Reprinted with permission of the Hastings Law Journal and the authors.

Susan Bandes, *Patterns of Injustice: Police Brutality in the Courts*, 47 Buff. L. Rev. 1275 (1999). Reprinted with permission of the Buffalo Law Review and the author.

Sara Sun Beale, *The News Media's Influence on Criminal Justice Policy: How Market Driven News Promotes Punitiveness*, 48 Wm. & Mary L. Rev. 397 (2006). Reprinted with permission of the William & Mary Law Review and the author.

Craig M. Bradley, *Two Models of Fourth Amendment Law*, 83 Mich. L. Rev. 1468 (1985). Reprinted with permission of the author.

William Bratton, *Cutting Crime and Restoring Order: What America Can Learn From New York's Finest,* Heritage Foundation Lecture, Oct. 15, 1996. Reprinted with permission of The Heritage Foundation.

Andrea L. Dennis, *Collateral Damage? Juvenile Snitches in America's "Wars" on Drugs, Crime, and Gangs*, 46 Am. Crim. L. Rev. 1145 (2009). Reprinted with permission of the American Criminal Law Review and the author.

Steven B. Duke, *Drug Prohibition: An Unnatural Disaster*, 27 Conn. L. Rev. 571 (1995). Reprinted with permission of the Connecticut Law Review and the author.

John A. Eterno & Eli B. Silverman, *The New York City Police Department's Compstat: Dream or Nightmare?* 8 International Journal of Police Science & Management 218 (2006). Reprinted with permission of the International Journal of Police Science and Management and the authors.

Adam M. Gershowitz, *An Informational Approach to the Mass Imprisonment Problem*, 40 Ariz. St. L.J. 47 (2008). Reprinted with permission of the Arizona State Law Journal and the author.

Adam M. Gershowitz, & Laura R. Killinger, *The State (Never) Rests: How Excessive Prosecutor Caseloads Harm Criminal Defendants*, 105 Nw. U. L. Rev. 261 (2011). Reprinted with permission of the authors.

Nancy Gertner, *A Short History of American Sentencing: Too Little Law, Too Much Law, or Just Right?*, 100 J. Crim. L. & Criminology 691 (2010). Reprinted with permission of the Northwestern University School of Law, The Journal of Criminal Law and Criminology, and the author.

Harry J. Holzer & Steven Raphael, *Employment Barriers Facing Ex-Offenders*, Urban Institute (2003). Reprinted with permission of the Urban Institute.

Peggy Fulton Hora & Theodore Stalcup, *Drug Treatment Courts in the Twenty-First Century: The Evolution of the Revolution in Problem-Solving Courts*, 42 Ga. L. Rev. 717 (2008). Reprinted with permission of the Georgia Law Review and the authors.

Richard A. Leo, *Inside the Interrogation Room*, 86 J. Crim. L. Criminology 266 (1996). Reprinted with permission of the Northwestern University School of Law, The Journal of Criminal Law and Criminology and the author.

Steven Levitt & Sudhir Alladi Venkatesh, *An Economic Analysis of a Drug-Selling Gang's Finances*, 115 Quarterly Journal of Economics 755 (2000). Reprinted with permission of the Quarterly Journal of Economics.

Marc Mauer & Ryan S. King, The Sentencing Project, Uneven Justice: State Rates of Incarceration by Race and Ethnicity (2007). Reprinted with permission of The Sentencing Project and the authors.

William R. Montross & Patrick Mulvaney, *Virtue and Vice: Who Will Report on the Failings of the American Criminal Justice System?*, 61 Stan. L. Rev. 1429 (2009). Reprinted with the permission of the Stanford Law Review and the authors.

Alexandra Natapoff, *Snitching: The Institutional and Communal Consequences*, 73 U. Cin. L. Rev. 645 (2004). Reprinted with permission of the University of Cincinnati Law Review and the author.

Alexandra Natapoff, *Underenforcement*, 75 Fordham L. Rev. 1715 (2006). Reprinted with permission of the Fordham Law Review and the author.

Michael M. O'Hear, *Federalism and Drug Control*, 57 Vand. L. Rev. 783 (2004). Reprinted with permission of the Vanderbilt Law Review and the author.

Police Executive Research Forum, Is the Economic Downturn Fundamentally Changing How We Police? (2010). Reprinted with permission.

Nino Rodriguez & Brenner Brown, Vera Institute of Justice, *Preventing Homelessness Among People Leaving Prison* (2003). Reprinted with permission.

Christopher Slobogin, *Testilying: Police Perjury and What To Do About It*, 67 U. Colo. L. Rev. 1037 (1996). Reprinted with permission of the University of Colorado Law Review and the author.

William J. Stuntz, *The Distribution of Fourth Amendment Privacy*, 67 Geo. Wash. L. Rev. 1265 (1999). Reprinted with permission of the George Washington Law Review.

Urban Institute, Understanding the Challenges of Prisoner Reentry: Research Findings From the Urban Institute's Prisoner Reentry Portfolio (2006). Reprinted with permission of the Urban Institute.

Steven Wisotsky, *Drug Facts Don't Matter: A Brief Comment on Drug Prohibition: An Unnatural Disaster*, 27 Conn. L. Rev. 639 (1995). Reprinted with permission of the Connecticut Law Review and the author.

The Wire

Chapter I

The Reality of Life in the Drug Trade

A. Introduction

Before jumping into the law of *The Wire*, it is worth pausing to consider the non-legal issues posed by the show. What is life like for the young men in America's urban neighborhoods who end up embroiled in "the game"? How much formal education do they have? Are the dealers themselves addicted to drugs? What are the chances of finding a job that pays above minimum wage in their neighborhood? As you read the materials below, consider whether you think *The Wire* offers a realistic portrayal of the choices afforded to poor urban youth.

B. Education, Drug Use, and Prison Populations

"What ... you want to go to school for? What you want to be? An astronaut, a dentist, a paid lawyer ...?"[1]

—Bodie

You need not be a social scientist or a policymaker to realize that a solid education is crucial for thriving in a global economy in which manufacturing jobs are disappearing. And you also don't have to be an expert in demography to know that the people who end up in jail and prison typically have attained far less education than the rest of society. Similarly, it should be obvious to most observers that drug addiction and drug use are common among those who are incarcerated. The key question is how strong the correlation is. Of those incarcerated, how little education and how much drug use are we talking about?

---

1. *The Wire*, Season 4, Episode 3, at 12:25 minutes.

Caroline Wolf Harlow, Bureau of Justice Statistics, Special Report: Education and Correctional Populations
1–10 (2003)[2]

About 41% of inmates in the Nation's State and Federal prisons and local jails in 1997 and 31% of probationers had not completed high school or its equivalent. In comparison, 18% of the general population age 18 or older had not finished the 12th grade.

Between 1991 and 1997, the percent of inmates in State prison without a high school diploma or GED remained the same—40% in 1997 and 41% in 1991. Of inmates in State prisons, 293,000 in 1991 and 420,600 in 1997 had entered prison without a high school diploma, a 44% increase.

* * *

Correctional populations less educated than the general population

Correctional populations—including State and Federal prison inmates, local jail inmates, and probationers—differ substantially in educational attainment from persons 18 and older in the general civilian noninstitutional population.

Correctional populations report lower educational attainment than do those in the general population. An estimated 40% of State prison inmates, 27% of Federal inmates, 47% of inmates in local jails, and 31% of those serving probation sentences had not completed high school or its equivalent while about 18% of the general population failed to attain high school graduation.

* * *

Jail inmates and the general population reported why they dropped out of school

Approximately 1 in 6 jail inmates dropped out of school because they were convicted of a crime, sent to a correctional facility, or otherwise involved in illegal activities.

Over a third of jail inmates and a sixth of the general population said the main reason they quit school was because of academic problems, behavior problems, or lost interest. About a fifth of jail inmates and two-fifths of the general population gave economic reasons for leaving school, primarily going to work, joining the military, or needing money.

* * *

Minority State prison inmates were less likely than whites to have a high school diploma or GED

Minority State inmates were generally less educated than their white peers. About 44% of black State prison inmates and 53% of Hispanic inmates had not graduated from high school or received a GED compared to 27% of whites in State prisons.

Minorities were less likely than whites to have attended college or some other institution of higher learning. About 1 in 10 blacks and 1 in 13 Hispanics had studied beyond high school compared to 1 in 7 whites. Minorities were also less likely than whites to have earned a high school diploma or a GED: 26% of blacks and 17% of Hispanics, compared to 30% of whites, had a high school diploma; 30% of blacks and Hispanics passed the GED compared to 43% of whites.

* * *

---

2. Editor's Note: All tables and charts have been omitted.

Inmates raised without two parents less likely to have a high school diploma or a GED

State prison inmates who grew up in homes without two parents, with an incarcerated parent, or on welfare or in subsidized housing were less likely than other inmates to have obtained a high school diploma/GED or attended a postsecondary institution.

A larger percentage of State prison inmates who were raised by a single parent or other adult, including relatives, friends, or other adults, compared to those who lived in a two-parent household, failed to obtain a high school diploma or pass the GED; 43% of inmates raised by one parent, 47% by others, and 34% by both parents did not complete a high school diploma/GED.

Inmates who reported that a parent had been incarcerated were less likely to have completed 11th grade at most, compared to inmates who did not have a parent serve time in a correctional institution (43% versus 39%). Among inmates with an incarcerated parent, twice as many received a GED as their final educational achievement as received a high school diploma (34% versus 16%).

An estimated 47% of inmates who reported that they had either received welfare or lived in publicly-supported housing and 35% who received no government aid did not finish high school. Those who received public assistance were likely to obtain a GED as their highest level of attainment; 30% received a GED compared to 16% with a high school diploma.

* * *

47% of drug offenders did not have a high school diploma or a GED

Almost half of State prison inmates serving their sentence for selling or using illegal drugs had not graduated from high school or passed the GED. About 4 in 10 inmates serving a sentence for a violent or property offense had not finished high school. Violent offenses include homicide, sexual assault, robbery, and assault, and property crimes include burglary, larceny/theft, motor vehicle theft, and fraud. An estimated 42% of those in prison for a public-order offense — primarily weapons, obstruction of justice, and violations of supervised release — did not complete high school or its equivalent.

Inmate unemployment before admission varied with education

Approximately 38% of inmates who completed 11 years or less of school were not working before entry to prison. Unemployment was lower for those with a GED (32%), a high school diploma (25%), or education beyond high school (21%). About 20% without a high school diploma, 19% with a GED, 14% with a high school diploma, and 13% with training beyond high school were not looking for work.

* * *

Notes and Questions

1. Roughly 40% of the incarcerated population lacks a high school diploma or GED. Is this a cause or an effect problem when it comes to involvement in crime?

2. What type of job can a convicted felon without a high school diploma or GED get upon release from prison? Perhaps more worrisome, what kind of job can someone with no criminal history get in the United States today if they lack a high school diploma or GED?

3. The study indicates that 1 in 6 inmates dropped out of school because they became embroiled in the criminal justice system. Should jails and prisons have an obligation to provide GED education to inmates? Should a mandatory condition of release be completion of a GED? While many states have education programs for prisoners, education is mandatory in less than half of states, and only about 10 states require participation in a GED program. And while GED participation is a factor in parole decisions in many states, completion of a GED is not a requirement for release in any jurisdiction. *See* Anna Crayton & Suzanne Rebecca Neusteter, *The Current State of Correctional Education*, Urban Institute 4 (March 2008) (available at http://urban.org/projects/reentry-roundtable/upload/Crayton.pdf).

4. Watch *The Wire*, Season 1, Episode 5, at 11:20 minutes, in which Stringer Bell says he suspects there is a snitch in D'Angelo's crew. Stringer tells D'Angelo not to pay his employees. When D'Angelo protests that his crew will quit if they are not paid, Stringer replies "[do you think they'll say] let me quit this game here and go to college?... They're not gonna walk." Is this a fair assessment?

5. Also consider *The Wire*, Season 1, Episode 6, at 1:30 minutes. In that scene, Wallace, who is only sixteen years old, wakes up a group of boys in his apartment to get them to school on time. He sends them off to school with a juice box and a bag of potato chips for lunch. Wallace is the closest thing to a parent or adult guardian these children have. Do these children have any chance of graduating from high school or will they all end up involved in the drug game?

6. The problem is bigger than simply absentee parents. In poor neighborhoods, schools are underfunded and the students have even greater needs. *See* James E. Ryan, *Schools, Race, and Money*, 109 Yale L.J. 249, 285 (1999). Professor Ryan references the New Jersey Supreme Court:

> Unfortunately, obstacles to a thorough and efficient education are present not only in the schools themselves, but also in the neighborhoods and family conditions of poor urban children. With concentrated poverty in the inner-city comes drug abuse, crime, hunger, poor health, illness, and unstable family situations. Violence also creates a significant barrier to quality education in city schools where often just getting children safely to school is considered an accomplishment. Those conditions further contribute to grave discipline problems and high dropout rates.

Abbott v. Burke, 693 A.2d 417, 433 (N.J. 1997).

7. Watch *The Wire*, Season 4, Episode 4, at 15:50 minutes. Bubbles brings Sherrod — a homeless boy who has missed the last three years of school — to re-enroll in middle school. When Bubbles asks why Sherrod will be starting in eighth grade, Vice Principal Donnelly responds: "Social promotion. We don't have the resources to repeat grade levels, and we feel to place the older children in the younger classes is unfair to teachers who are responsible for maintaining order." Is social promotion as rampant in Baltimore as it appears in *The Wire*? An actual member of the board of education argues that it is not. *See* Kalman R. Hettleman, *The Truth About Policy on Social Promotion*, Balt. Sun, Sept. 18, 2006. Other Maryland politicians disagree. *See* Sara Neufeld, *City Schools Shun Test for Grade Promotion*, Balt. Sun, Sept. 8, 2006.

8. How hard does the education system work to keep students in school? Watch *The Wire*, Season 4, Episode 4, at 22:40 minutes. Mrs. Donnelly hires Cutty to find students who are on the class roll but have not shown up. She cannot hire Cutty as a truant officer because there has not been funding for truant officers for twenty years, so she must

get creative and label him a custodian. Later, it becomes clear that Cutty is only supposed to bring each truant to school once per month so that the school can count the students as enrolled and receive state funding. According to the *Baltimore Sun*, about 7.5% of Baltimore students are habitually truant, meaning they miss more than 20% of school days. For the worst offenders, the Office of Attendance and Truancy actually files criminal charges against the parents and seeks to have them locked up. *See* Erica L. Green, *When Students Don't Go To School, Parents Go To Jail*, BALT. SUN, Apr. 24, 2011. Do any of these policies make sense?

Christopher J. Mumola & Jennifer C. Karberg, Bureau of Justice Statistics Special Report: Drug Use and Dependence, State and Federal Prisoners, 2004
2–8 (2006)[1]

* * *

Overall drug use by State prisoners unchanged from 1997; methamphetamine use rose

A third of State inmates said they had committed their current offense while under the influence of drugs. Over half used drugs in the month before the offense, and more than two-thirds had used drugs regularly at some time in their lives. These figures were unchanged from 1997.

Marijuana remained the most common drug used by State prisoners. Forty percent of State prisoners reported using marijuana in the month before their offense, and 15% said they had used marijuana at the time of the offense. All measures of marijuana use were within 1% of 1997 estimates.

Reported use of cocaine or crack cocaine in the month before the offense fell from 25% of State prisoners in 1997 to 21% in 2004, while use at the time of offense fell from 15% to 12%.

Over the same period, the use of heroin and other opiates fell slightly on all measures. Use of hallucinogens (including ecstasy) in the month before the offense rose slightly from 4% to 6%.

State prisoner reports of stimulant use went up on all measures. Stimulant use in the month before the offense increased from 9% in 1997 to 12% in 2004, and use at the time of offense rose from 4% to 7%.

The increases in the use of stimulants were attributable to the rising use of methamphetamines. Use of methamphetamines in the month before the offense increased from 7% to 11%, and use at the time of the offense rose from 4% to 6%.

Overall drug use by Federal prisoners rose; cocaine/crack use declined

Across all measures of use, Federal prisoners reported higher levels of prior drug use from 1997 to 2004. An estimated 26% of Federal inmates reported using drugs at the time of the offense, up from 22% in 1997. Drug use in the month before the offense rose to 50% of Federal prisoners, up from 45% in 1997.

During the period, marijuana use among Federal prisoners in the month before the offense rose from 30% to 36%. Stimulant use in the month before the offense grew slightly,

---

1. Editor's Note: All Tables and charts have been omitted.

due to methamphetamines which rose from 7% to 10%. Use of hallucinogens in the month before the offense rose from 2% to 6%.

Heroin or other opiate use among Federal prisoners remained stable. In both years 3% of inmates committed their crimes while using heroin or other opiates. Depressant use was also unchanged.

The percentage of Federal prisoners who reported prior use of cocaine-based drugs dropped between 1997 and 2004. Use of cocaine or crack in the month before the offense fell slightly from 20% to 18%, and use at the time of the offense fell from 9% to 7%. No other drug types displayed a decline in prior use during this period.

* * *

1 in 4 violent offenders in prison committed their offenses under the influence of drugs

Nearly three-quarters (72%) of drug offenders in State prison reported drug use in the month before their offense. Property offenders (64%) were more likely than violent and public-order offenders (50% of each) to have used drugs in the month before the offense. Burglary (68%), robbery and larceny (67% of both) offenders reported the highest levels of drug use in the month of the offense.

Drug offenders (44%) were most likely to have committed their crimes while using drugs, followed by property offenders (39%). About a quarter of both violent (28%) and public-order (25%) offenders reported drug use at the time of their offense. Inmates serving time for sexual assault (17%) and aggravated assault (24%) were least likely to commit their crimes while under the influence of drugs.

An estimated 59% of Federal offenders held for drug trafficking reported using drugs in the month before their offense, followed by 57% of those held for robbery and 54% for weapons. About a quarter of Federal inmates (26%) committed their crimes while under the influence of drugs, led by trafficking (34%) and robbery (29%) offenders. Federal fraud offenders (9%) were the least likely to commit their crimes while under the influence of drugs.

* * *

1 in 3 property offenders in State prisons report drug money as a motive in their crimes

Fewer than a fifth (17%) of all State prisoners said they committed their crimes to get money for drugs. By the type of offense, drug money as a motive in the offense varied widely. About 1 in 3 property offenders reported drug money as a motive, followed by about 1 in 4 drug offenders. Violent offenders (10%) and public-order offenders (7%) were least likely to report that they committed the offense to get money for drugs.

Among Federal inmates the overall percentage who committed their offense to get money for drugs (18%) was similar to State prisoners. A quarter of Federal drug offenders, 15% of violent offenders, and 11% of property offenders said they committed their crimes for drug money.

53% of State and 45% of Federal prisoners met criteria for drug dependence or abuse

More than half of State prisoners (53%) said they experienced symptoms consistent with drug dependence or abuse in the 12 months prior to their admission to prison. Seventeen percent reported symptoms that met the criteria for drug abuse only....

State and Federal prisoners were more likely than other adults in the U.S. resident population to meet the criteria for drug dependence or abuse.... [Two percent] of U.S. adult residents were dependent on or abusing drugs in the last 12 months.

* * *

Half of drug dependent or abusing inmates in State prisons reported three or more prior sentences

Nearly half (48%) of State prisoners meeting the DSM-IV criteria for drug dependence or abuse were on some form of criminal justice status (probation, parole, or escape) at the time of their arrest, compared to 37% of other State inmates. Federal inmates meeting the DSM-IV criteria (30%) were slightly more likely to have been on a criminal justice status at the time of arrest than other Federal inmates (25%).

Drug dependent or abusing inmates in State prisons were more likely than other prisoners to have a prior offense (84% compared to 68%). More than half (53%) of drug dependent or abusing State prisoners reported at least three prior sentences; a third (32%) of other State prisoners had three or more prior sentences.

1 in 7 drug dependent or abusing inmates in State prison were homeless in year before admission

Drug dependent or abusing inmates were more likely than other inmates to report troubled personal backgrounds, including experiences of physical or sexual abuse, homelessness, unemployment, parental substance abuse, and parental incarceration.

Drug dependent or abusing inmates in State prisons (14%) were twice as likely as other inmates (6%) to report being homeless during the year before admission to prison. They also reported lower levels of employment in the month prior to admission (68% compared to 78% of other inmates).

While growing up, 12% of drug dependent or abusing State prisoners received public assistance, 45% lived in single-parent homes, and 41% had a substance-abusing parent. By comparison, 31% of other inmates received public assistance, 39% lived in single-parent homes, and 24% had a substance-abusing parent.

* * *

Notes and Questions

1. The Bureau of Justice Statistics study above is based on interviews of more than 18,000 inmates at more than 400 state and federal prisons.

2. When you read that 1 in 3 incarcerated property offenders committed their crimes to pay for drugs, what do you think? Does this suggest we should legalize or decriminalize drugs? Does it suggest to you that we should provide more treatment programs?

3. Although many of the drug dealers in *The Wire* never themselves take drugs, some do become addicted. For instance, after providing information that leads to a brutal murder, sixteen-year-old Wallace ceases to be a reliable dealer and turns to drugs himself. Watch *The Wire*, Season 1, Episode 9, at 25:00 minutes. Do you think Wallace would have become a drug user if he had not been in the game to start with?

C. Minimum Wage for Drug Dealers?

Drug dealing is tough work. It comes with no health insurance, no retirement plan, and a high risk of death. Why do it, then? Surely it must be the money. After all, drugs are not regulated, they are not taxed, and their clientele is often addicted and in desperate need of scoring them. Dealers must therefore be making money hand-over-fist by selling illegal drugs, right? For a few at the top of the pyramid, drug dealing may make them rich. But for the average drug dealer the reality is much less lucrative, and the idea of getting rich is nothing more than a pipe dream. Consider an infamous economic study of how a drug gang is organized and how it pays its members.

Steven Levitt & Sudhir Alladi Venkatesh, *An Economic Analysis of a Drug-Selling Gang's Finances*
115 Quarterly Journal of Economics 755 (2000)[1]

Street gangs have a long history in American cities. Until recently, gangs were organized primarily as social peer groups. Any economic activities were of secondary importance. The last two decades, however, have given rise to a dramatic transformation in street gangs.... When crack became widely available in the mid-1980s, sold in small quantities in fragmented street-corner markets, street gangs became the logical distributors. The potential profit in drug dealing dwarfed that previously available to gangs through other criminal channels. As a consequence, gangs became systematically involved in the distribution of various narcotic substances including heroin and crack-cocaine.

* * *

... In this paper we are able to directly analyze for the first time a wide range of economic issues related to gangs and drug distribution. We do so through the use of a unique data set containing detailed financial information over a recent four-year period for a now-defunct gang. These data were maintained by the leader of the group as a management tool for tracking the gang's financial activities and for monitoring the behavior of gang members. Updated monthly, the data include breakdowns of costs and revenues into major components, as well as information on the distribution of profits as wages to gang members at different levels of the hierarchy. Information on both price and quantity is included. These financial data are supplemented with information on the numbers of violent deaths, injuries, and arrests of gang members over this period, as well as interviews and observational analysis of the gang. While the data suffer from important limitations and a number of potential biases (which appear below), they nonetheless represent a substantial improvement on previously available information.

Using these data, we analyze the extent to which the individual and collective actions of gang participants can reasonably be characterized as emanating out of economic maximization. We address three different issues in this regard. First, we examine the economic returns to drug dealing relative to legitimate labor market activities. The higher the returns to drug selling, the more likely it is that the economic aspects of the gang are paramount. We then consider the causes and consequences of gang wars. Finally, we analyze the risk trade-offs made by gang members and whether these can be reconciled with optimizing decision making.

A number of insights emerge from the paper. Street-level sellers appear to earn roughly the minimum wage. Earnings within the gang are enormously skewed, however, with high-level gang members earning far more than their legitimate market alternative. Thus, the primary economic motivation for low-level gang members appears to be the possibility of rising up through the hierarchy.... The average wage in the gang (taking into

---

1. Editor's Note: All internal citations and footnotes have been omitted.

account all levels of the hierarchy) is perhaps somewhat above the available legitimate market alternatives, but not appreciably higher.

Gang wars are costly, both in terms of lost lives and lost profits. Almost all of the deaths of drug sellers are concentrated in war periods. Moreover, the violence keeps customers away. This negative shock to demand is associated with a fall of 20–30 percent in both the price and quantity of drugs sold during fighting, and the drug operation becomes far less profitable. In spite of this, the gang discussed in this paper fights with rivals roughly one-fourth of the time....

Finally, drug selling is an extremely dangerous activity. Death rates in the sample are 7 percent annually. Given the relatively low economic returns to drug selling noted above, the implied willingness to accept risk on the part of the participants is orders of magnitude higher than is typically observed in value of life calculations. This suggests either that gang members have very unusual preferences, that the ex post realization of death rates was very different than the ex ante expectation, systematic miscalculation of risk, or the presence of important noneconomic considerations.

Based on these findings, we conclude that even in this gang—one of the most economically sophisticated and successful gangs—the decision making of members is difficult (but not impossible) to reconcile with that of optimizing economic agents. Certainly, economic considerations play an important role in the decisions of members and the activities of the gang. However, we find that social/nonpecuniary factors are likely to play an important role as well. Of course, all of these conclusions are based on the analysis of a single gang's experience. The degree to which these results are broadly generalizable remains an open question.

* * *

I. THE GANG AND THE SOCIAL, ECONOMIC, AND COMPETITIVE ENVIRONMENT IN WHICH IT OPERATES

The gang for which we have data is located in an inner-city neighborhood in a large, industrial American city.... Residents of the area are almost exclusively African-American (over 99 percent), as are all of the gang members.... Unemployment rates for males in 1990 were over 35 percent—six times higher than the national average. In addition, over 40 percent of males were not in the labor force. The female unemployment rates are roughly half of the male unemployment rate.

Children in the neighborhood experience high probabilities of adverse economic circumstances. Over half of the children were below the poverty line at the time of the 1990 census. More than three-quarters of all children live in single-parent families, and 60 percent are in families that receive public assistance.

Median family income is $15,077 annually, less than half of the national average. A small fraction of the census tract is public housing, although the immediate neighborhood in which the gang operates does not include any large-scale public-housing complexes. Roughly half of adults in the community do not have a high-school diploma. Only one in twenty residents has a degree from a four-year college, compared with one in five Americans generally.

* * *

The organizational structure of the gang ... is simple compared with most firms of comparable size. The top-level of the organization is made up of what we broadly denote the "central leadership." This body is chaired by four to six individuals with responsibility for devising the long-term strategies of the multistate organization, and maintaining relationships with suppliers and affiliates in other regions of the country. The central leadership also includes approximately twelve persons who are responsible for collecting dues, overseeing recruitment of new members, allocating punishments, and serving as liaisons to the community. Roughly one-third of these leaders are imprisoned at any given time. The next tier in the organization is a group of "local gang leaders" with specific territorial responsibility for one or more localized gang. In the organization we study, there are roughly 100 of such gang leaders. Reporting in to each gang leader are three "officers." The "enforcer" is responsible for ensuring the safety of group members, the "treasurer" manages the liquid assets of the group, and the "runner" performs the risky task of transporting large quantities of drugs and money to and from the supplier. Reporting to the enforcer are the "foot soldiers" who serve as street-level drug sellers and from whose ranks future officers and leaders arise. Foot soldiers are typically 16–22 years of age, although potentially much older. At the periphery of the gang is a "rank-and-file" member pool who span all ages (the age range in the group we study is 14 to 40) and who have little formal responsibility for drug selling. Rank and file, unlike foot soldiers and higher gang members, pay dues to the gang, in return receiving protection, status, and a reliable supply of drugs for those who deal independently.

* * *

The data that we have are for just one gang within the larger organizational structure. That gang is overseen by a local gang leader, and has one enforcer, one treasurer, and one runner at any given point in time. The number of foot soldiers ranges between 25 and 75 over the period examined, and there are 60 to 200 rank and file. At any given point in time, roughly one-fourth of the males aged 16–22 in the neighborhood are foot soldiers.

The geographic … landscape in which the gang operates is … a twelve-square block area bordered by major thoroughfares on all sides. Most of the drug-dealing is conducted along the edges of the territory on or near one of the major streets. The gang sells perhaps 30 percent of the drugs to those living within the twelve-block area — most of the remaining purchasers come from a relatively limited geographic range. In this particular area, few buyers come from the suburbs.

* * *

II. DATA AND DESCRIPTIVE STATISTICS

The data set contains detailed financial information on the activities of the gang described above on a monthly basis for a recent four-year period. The data were originally maintained by the leader in control of the gang, and they were updated each month by the enforcer, who compiled the information by hand. The data end abruptly with the arrest of the gang leader and other officers. Shortly thereafter, the gang, weakened by these arrests and beset by infighting, was overpowered by rivals, its turf divided between enemy gangs. The gang we study is no longer in operation. Most of the former gang members have since abandoned drug dealing. The person who supplied us the data is a former gang member with ties to the gang that tracked the data (although he was not necessarily directly affiliated with this particular group). Our informant, after serving a prison sentence, now holds a full-time job in the legitimate sector. For obvious reasons, we have accommodated his request to remain anonymous.

* * *

… Of the 48 months spanned by our sample, six months of data are missing. Averages are calculated based only on those months for which data are available. All dollar values are converted into 1995 dollars…. Revenues are broken down into three sources: proceeds from drug sales (almost exclusively crack-cocaine), dues from gang members, and "street taxes," i.e., money extorted from individuals (and occasionally companies) conducting business on the gang's turf. Examples of those required to pay street taxes would include grocery store owners, gypsy cabs, people selling stolen goods, and those providing services such as auto or plumbing repair. Average monthly revenue from all sources for the gang rose from $18,500 to $68,400 over the period examined....

Although the revenue numbers may appear low, "back-of-the-envelope" calculations suggest that they are reasonable. Using these revenue figures and average dollars per sale of $10, we estimate that the number of sales per hour by a drug-selling team ranges from five to twelve over the sample. That frequency of sale is consistent with self-reports of the participants as well as recent observational data we have collected in similar neighborhoods.

In the original data, the nonwage costs are broken down into six categories: costs of drugs sold, payments to higher levels of the gang, weapons, payments to mercenary fighters (nongang members who are hired for short periods of time to help fight in gang wars), funeral costs and payments to families of the deceased, and miscellaneous expenses.

The greatest nonwage expenditure of the gang was the regular tribute payment to higher levels of the gang. Such payments amount to almost 20 percent of total revenues. Expenditures related to drugs comprise the next largest nonwage cost component, accounting for 15 percent of total revenue, and almost 25 percent of drug sales. The price paid by the gang to obtain powder cocaine, which is subsequently transformed into crack by the gang for resale on the street, declines roughly 35 percent over the sample period, reflecting a citywide decline in the price of bulk cocaine. Surprisingly, there appears to be substantial imprecision in the measurements used in these bulk drug transactions.

Standard units such as kilograms and pounds are not used by the gang (although the supplier does use such units). Quantities instead described in various "street" units that we are able to only roughly translate into kilograms. Thus, we report our results in an artificial unit ("bags") that approximates the standard quantity in which street sales occur, rather than in kilograms. While this choice of units is essentially arbitrary, it has the attractive feature of roughly capturing the number of sales made by the gang in a month. A bag contains an extremely small quantity of crack-cocaine (e.g., a few pebbles) and typically sells for about $10 on the street. By our calculations, between 10,000 and 15,000 bags can be produced from one kilogram of powder cocaine, making the street value of a kilogram of pure cocaine converted into crack between $100,000 and $150,000.

* * *

Another important expenditure item is for mercenary fighters known as "warriors" whom the gang hires on a retainer basis to fight in wars. Fees for warriors are roughly $2000 per person per month of service. The warriors have various duties including guarding areas where drugs are sold, occupying front-line positions on the gang's turf, and performing drive-by shootings. The use of hired warriors declines at the end of the sample as the gang increasingly chose to use internal resources (foot soldiers) for fighting rather than contracting-out this task. This decision on the part of the gang appears to be linked in part to its difficulty in controlling the expanded turf, over which the gang had no inherent legitimacy. The original territory was much easier to defend because the gang's roots were in their original neighborhood and the "original" gang members continued to reside there....

Funerals and related expenses such as compensating victims' families are costly to the gang. Typically, for a foot soldier who is killed, the gang pays $5000, or approximately three years of foot-soldier wages, to his family for compensation and funeral services. Such payments are viewed as extremely important by the gang leaders, both to maintain community support for the gang and, because in the words of one gang leader, "You got to respect family." Interestingly, when the gang expanded, members conscripted from the former rival outfit were treated much less generously than were those who belonged to the original gang.

The purchase of weapons, at a cost of $300–$400 per month, is initially a relatively small component of gang costs. Expenditure on weapons increases dramatically in the final year, both due to increased fighting, and because the gang reduced its reliance on outside warriors, choosing instead to defend itself. Combined with miscellaneous expenses, all of these nonwage costs total to just less than 50 percent of revenues.

The remainder of the revenues are distributed as wages to gang members, or are retained by the gang leader as profits. The earnings of the gang members involved with drug distribution is the focus of the next section.

III. THE ECONOMIC RETURNS TO DRUG SELLING IN THE GANG

In this section we attempt to measure the economic return to selling drugs in the gang. We begin with the "official" data reported in the gang's books. Later, we incorporate "off-the-books" sources of income as well.

An individual's rank within the gang is of critical importance for his personal remuneration. The local gang leader is the residual claimant on drug profits.... [T]he gang leader retains between $4,200 and $10,900 a month as profit, for an annual wage of $50,000–130,000. This value is well above what leaders could hope to earn in the legitimate sector given their education and work experience. For instance, a former leader of a rival gang is now employed in the legitimate sector at an annual salary of $16,000. His legitimate sector wage may be lower than it otherwise would have been, however, due to his intervening years spent in prison.

The officers each earn roughly $1000 per month. This wage is relatively constant, although in war periods reductions sometimes occur. These tasks are generally full-time jobs (in the sense that the people who perform them would be unlikely to be concurrently employed in the legitimate sector, although they may not strictly involve 40 hours of work per week). The standard of living associated with holding these jobs is only slightly higher than a full-time minimum wage job.

This gang is unusual in that foot soldiers for the most part received a flat wage. Compensation was not directly linked to the volume of sales. Their wage depended both on the number of shifts in which they distributed crack and on their position within their drug-selling team. Crack was sold in teams of six foot soldiers, with a team leader, a carrier who delivers the goods, two laborers who package the goods, make change, etc., and a lookout. Wages were highest for the team leader and lowest for the lookout who is typically an entry level foot soldier.

Our monthly data, however, are not broken down to that level of detail. The only information we have is total wages paid to all foot soldiers in a month. Based on field notes recorded at the time, we have a reasonably accurate assessment of the number of shifts that were taking place, other gang-related activities that required the participation of foot soldiers, and the number of active foot soldiers. By combining this information with total foot-soldier wages, we are able to construct estimates of monthly earnings per foot soldier and an hourly wage.

* * *

Official monthly payments to each foot soldier are low: only $200 per month or less until the final year. Based on observation and discussion with the gang leader, we estimate that the typical foot soldier worked four four-hour shifts per week selling drugs, and performed approximately four hours of other tasks for the gang, for a total of twenty hours of work per week. Hours worked per person appear to have stayed relatively constant over time. The increased demand for labor by the gang was accomplished through an expansion of the number of foot soldiers from approximately 25 at the beginning of the time period to over 60 in the final year. Based on these estimates of hours worked, the hourly wage earned by the typical foot soldier was below the federal minimum wage.

While these foot-soldier wages are strikingly low, there are both theoretical arguments and corroborating empirical evidence in support of these numbers. From a theoretical perspective, it is hardly surprising that foot-soldier wages would be low given the minimal skill requirements for the job and the presence of a "reserve army" of potential replacements among the rank and file.... Empirically, the behavior of the foot soldiers suggests that they are not well off financially. First, gang members below the level of gang leaders live with family because they cannot afford to maintain a separate residence. Second, many foot soldiers also hold low-paying jobs in the legitimate sector, typically working as service-sector employees in shopping malls and fast-food restaurants, performing physical labor such as demolition, or working in small local businesses like dry cleaners or grocery stores. We estimate that 75–80 percent of the foot soldiers are employed in the legitimate sector at some point over the course of a year. Job tenure, however, is generally quite low, so that perhaps only 40–50 percent of the foot soldiers are employed in the legitimate sector at any given point in time....

* * *

Given the enormous gap between the wages of the foot soldiers and those higher up in the gang, the most reasonable way to view the economic aspects of the decision to join the gang is as a tournament, i.e., a situation in which participants vie for large awards that only a small fraction will eventually obtain. Gang members themselves appear to be keenly aware of this, as evidenced by the following quote from a foot soldier: "You think I wanta be selling drugs on the street my whole life? No way. But I know these n_____ [above me] are making more money, and it's like, people don't last long doing this s___. So you know, I figure I got a chance to move up. But if not, s___, I get me a job doin' something else."

* * *

IV. CAUSES AND CONSEQUENCES OF GANG WARS

Due to the illicit nature of the drug trade, gangs do not have access to legally enforceable contracts or property rights. The illegality of drug selling also makes advertising difficult. As a consequence, violence emerges both as a primary tool with which disputes are resolved (both within the gang and across gangs)....

... During gang wars, there is an easily discernible reduction in street activity and public loitering, and typically a heightened police presence.... Over the period we study, there are seven episodic gang wars lasting for a total of twelve months, or roughly one-quarter of our sample....

* * *

... [D]rug revenues fall almost in half in war months. The quantity of drugs sold falls 29 percent, and price falls 25 percent....

During gang wars, net profits are actually slightly negative.... A month of fighting costs the gang leader over $10,000 on average in short-run profits....

* * *

A final feature to note with respect to gang wars is the steep increase in foot-soldier wages during wars in the early part of the sample.... [F]oot-soldier wages are almost 70 percent higher during gang wars. The increase in foot-soldier wages appears to be a clear example of compensating differentials. As one foot soldier put it at the time: "Would you stand around here when all this s___ [shooting] is going on? No, right? So if I gonna be asked to put my life on the line, then front me the cash, man. Pay me more 'cause it ain't worth my time to be here when [the gangs are] warring."

* * *

V. THE DANGERS OF DRUG SELLING AND THE WILLINGNESS OF GANG MEMBERS TO ACCEPT RISK

* * *

... The per-person likelihood of death ranges from 1 to 2 percent a month during gang wars and the transition period.... Gang members who were active for the entire four-year period had roughly a one in four chance of dying. Furthermore, there was an average of over two nonfatal injuries (mostly gunshot, but some due to knives or fists) per member, and almost six arrests. The risks associated with selling drugs in this sample are astonishing. By comparison, homicide victimization rates for black males aged 14–17 in the United States are roughly 1 in 1000 per year, about 1/80 the rate we observe in this sample. Even among rank and file of this gang (those affiliated with the gang, but not actively engaged in the drug trade), homicide rates are only about 1 in 200 annually in our sample.

* * *

VI. CONCLUSION

This paper provides the first detailed analysis of the financial activities of an entrepreneurial street gang. The data imply that for this gang drug dealing is not particularly lucrative, yielding average wages only slightly above those of the legitimate sector. Hourly wages for those on the lowest rung of the gang hierarchy are no better than the minimum wage. The wage structure within the gang is highly skewed, however, so that the more reasonable way to measure the economic rationale for gang participation is in the context of a tournament. Gang wars are extremely costly in terms of injuries, death, and profits. Nonetheless, fighting takes place over roughly one-fourth of the sample. The willingness to accept a risk of death among gang members appears to be extremely high.

Taken as a whole, our results suggest that even in this financially sophisticated "corporate" gang, it is difficult (but not impossible) to reconcile the behavior of the gang members with an optimizing economic model....

Our results provide general guidance as to possible public policy interventions that might be useful for combating gang violence. The fact that most foot soldiers are simultaneously employed by the gang and in the legitimate sector suggests that gang participation may be sensitive to improvements in outside opportunities. That suggests a possible role for job-market interventions aimed at high-risk youths. However, given the tournament structure of the gang and the symbolic value attached to the upward mobility, minor changes in the immediate economic returns to foot soldiers do not appear paramount in determining gang involvement. Thus, it seems unlikely that such a policy by itself could be successful.

An alternative approach to reducing the attractiveness of gang involvement is to lower the profitability of the organization. One way to do this would be to substantially increase punishments and enforcement against drug purchasers. This would put downward pressure on both the price and quantity of drugs sold. A very different strategy is drug legalization. Faced with competition from legal sources of drugs, the gang's market would evaporate. Without profit to fight over, gang violence would likely return to precrack levels. Of course, the adverse consequences of either draconian punishment of drug users or legalization might be severe and need to be weighed against any benefits associated with reduced gang violence.

* * *

Notes and Questions

1. Watch *The Wire*, Season 2, Episode 9, at 1:20 minutes in which Bodie's group and a rival drug gang have a shoot-out in broad daylight in a fight over territory. Now consider the financial data that Levitt and Venkatesh present in their article. Are you stunned to learn that the average drug dealer risks arrest, serious bodily injury, and death for less than minimum wage?

2. Early in *The Wire*, D'Angelo Barksdale explains the game of chess to his crew. The description quite clearly applies to the drug trade as well:

D'Angelo:	These right here, these are the pawns. They like the soldiers. They move like this, one space forward only. Except when they fight, then it's like this. And they like the front lines, they be out in the field.
Wallace:	So how do you get to be the king?
D'Angelo:	It ain't like that. See, the king stay the king, a'ight? Everything stay who he is. Except for the pawns. Now, if the pawn make it all the way down to the other dude's side, he get to be queen. And like I said, the queen ain't no bitch. She got all the moves.
Bodie:	A'ight, so if I make it to the other end, I win.
D'Angelo:	If you catch the other dude's king and trap it, then you win.
Bodie:	A'ight, but if I make it to the end, I'm top dog.
D'Angelo:	Nah, yo, it ain't like that. Look, the pawns, man, in the game, they get capped quick. They be out the game early.
Bodie:	Unless they some smart-ass pawns.

The Wire, Season 1, Episode 3, at 11:50 minutes. Is Bodie's optimistic assessment consistent with the tournament theory that Levitt and Venkatesh lay out to explain why drug dealers work in a terribly dangerous environment for less than minimum wage?

3. Three seasons later, Bodie has a very different take on his prospects:

Bodie:	I been out there since I was 13. I ain't never fucked up a count, never stole off a package, never did some shit that I wasn't told to do. I been straight up. But what come back? Hmm? You'd think if I get jammed up on some shit they'd be like, "A'ight, yeah. Bodie been there. Bodie hang tough. We got his pay lawyer. We got a bail." They want me to stand with them, right? But where the fuck they at when they supposed to be standing by

us? I mean, when shit goes bad and there's hell to pay, where they at? This game is rigged, man. We like the little bitches on the chessboard.

McNulty: Pawns.

The Wire, Season 4, Episode 13 at 40:30 minutes. For a wonderful discussion of how D'Angelo's chess theme permeates all aspects of *The Wire* (not simply the drug dealers themselves), see Susan A. Bandes, *And All the Pieces Matter: Thoughts on The Wire and the Criminal Justice System*, 8 Ohio St. J. Crim. L. 435 (2011).

4. Watch *The Wire*, Season 1, Episode 13, at 51:10, 53:50, and 58:30 minutes, which shows the sentencing hearing for the Barksdale gang. Avon Barksdale gets a maximum of seven years, while his underlings received tougher sentences of fifteen and twenty years. Does this scene show that the tournament theory is nothing more than a fantasy? Does the king always stay the king? Do the pawns always stay the pawns?

5. At the end of Season 1, D'Angelo Barksdale also offers an interesting perspective on being born into a drug gang:

> You all don't get it. You grow up in this shit ... All my people been in — my father, my uncles, my cousins. It's just what we do. You just live with this shit [pointing to pictures of murder victims] until you can't breathe no more. I swear to god I was courtside for eight months and I was freer in jail than I was at home.

The Wire, Season 1, Episode 13, at 21:20 minutes. D'Angelo does not manage to get out. Is there anything the police and prosecutors could have done differently?

6. Even if a child isn't born into a drug family like the Barksdales, they may be inundated with the drug environment. Watch *The Wire*, Season 3, Episode 3, at 26:15 minutes. As Detective Bunk is investigating a dead body on the street, we can hear children playing in the background. At the end of the scene, the camera pans to the children — they are clearly under ten years of age — and Bunk sees them role playing a violent drug shootout. One child starts to yell "It's my turn to be Omar." Is it likely that these children will end up embroiled in the drug game?

7. If gang wars are so costly — both in lives and lost profits — why do they occur so often? Watch *The Wire*, Season 1, Episode 3, at 1:00 minutes, in which D'Angelo tries to get his crew to be less aggressive:

> The game ain't got to be played like that, yo. You can't tell me this shit can't get done without people beating on each other, killing each other, doing each other like dogs. And without all that you ain't got Five-0 down here on our backs every five minutes, throwing us around.... You think Five-O care about [people] getting high? In the projects? Man, Five-O be down here about the bodies, yo. That's what they be down here about, the bodies.

Why don't dealers listen to D'Angelo's advice? Levitt and Venkatesh suggest that the answer is an agency problem in which foot soldiers make a name for themselves by being tough and senior management of the gang is unable to control those underlings. Is there any way around this problem, short of legalizing drugs?

8. In their conclusion, Professors Levitt and Venkatesh consider but quickly reject the idea that foot soldiers could be coaxed out of the drug trade if there were more (and better) legitimate employment opportunities. They conclude that the tournament model and the prospect, no matter how remote, of becoming a high-ranking and well-paid gang member outweighs any legitimate employment that might pay them marginally more

than their current foot soldier wages. Are Levitt and Venkatesh correct to reject this option so quickly? Are foot soldiers so irrational that they will accept less money to work under terribly dangerous conditions just out of the hope (which they acknowledge to be unlikely) that they will rise to the top of the drug gang? In answering, consider the scene from *The Wire*, Season 2, Episode 7, at 1:00 minute, in which Bodie buys flowers for D'Angelo's funeral and asks for the arrangement to be in the shape of the project towers. Are drug dealers' identities so wrapped up in their work in the drug trade that it would be unthinkable for them to do anything else?

9. While working on his doctoral dissertation, Professor Venkatesh spent a tremendous amount of time in a Chicago housing project interacting with gang leaders. He recounts his experience in an incredible book that details the inner-workings of the gang. *See* SUDHIR VENKATESH, GANG LEADER FOR A DAY: A ROGUE SOCIOLOGIST TAKES TO THE STREETS (2008). Although some of the individuals who sell drugs eventually leave the gang, the book paints a bleary picture for the prospect of getting out of the gang and into the legitimate workforce.

10. In their conclusion, Levitt and Venkatesh also suggest in passing that one way to limit gang activity would be to punish drug purchasers more harshly. Do you think drug purchasers are currently punished lightly or harshly? More specifically, what do you think the average punishment is for a defendant caught with a small amount of crack that is consistent with personal use?

11. *Does anything ever change?* Watch the final scene of Season 1 of *The Wire*, Episode 13, at 1 hour and 1:00 minute. Dealers are still selling drugs on the corners. Bubbles and Johnny are still stealing to pay for drugs. Stringer Bell is still making a tremendous amount of money. Does anything really change? Watch the final montage scene from Season 2 of *The Wire* as well. Do you get the same feeling—that in spite of all the work of Lieutenant Daniels and his unit—everything remains exactly the same as it was at the start of the season?

Chapter II

The Law of *The Wire*(tap)

"The case is in the phones, though we're going to need a Title III to take a look at them."[1]

—Detective Lester Freamon

A. Introduction

Criminal Procedure students typically spend an entire semester focusing on the Fourth and Fifth Amendment protections guaranteed to criminal defendants. Yet, defendants also have important protections created by statutes and local rules. Not surprisingly, the legal doctrine that receives the most attention early in *The Wire* is the detailed set of statutory rules governing wiretapping. In the federal system these rules are often referred to as Title III, based on their location in the governing federal statute. All fifty states have their own wiretapping statutes, which are usually very similar to Title III. The materials below introduce a brief history and overview of Title III and the Maryland wiretapping law presented in *The Wire*.

B. Overview of the Statutory Rules Governing Wiretaps

Wiretaps give law enforcement access to the most private information about suspects: conversations with friends, loved ones, and business partners. And the suspects have no idea that they are being listened to. What rules should law enforcement have to follow to qualify for a wiretap? Is the level of suspicion higher than we demand for ordinary evidence gathering? And are the standards for wiretaps in state cases markedly different than the rules that govern federal cases?

---

1. *The Wire*, Season 5, Episode 9, at 4:15 minutes.

Davis v. State

21 A.3d 181 (Md. Ct. Spec. App. 2011)

Moyland, J.,

* * *

The appellant, Tyrone Davis, was found guilty in the Circuit Court for Montgomery County by Judge Terrance J. McGann, sitting without a jury, of the possession of marijuana with the intent to distribute. He was sentenced to five years imprisonment. After his pretrial motion to suppress evidence because of an alleged violation of the Maryland Wiretapping and Electronic Surveillance Act had been denied by Judge Michael J. Algeo, the appellant proceeded to trial on an agreed statement of facts, preserving his right to appeal from the denial of his suppression motion.

A Solitary Contention

The appellant's single contention is that the Montgomery County Police violated Maryland Code, Courts and Judicial Proceedings Article, § 10-408(c)(3) when they "intercepted a phone call made by the appellant ... and that, as a result, not only the contents of the ... interception but all derivative evidence flowing therefrom must be suppressed pursuant to § 10-405."

The Year of Decision: 1967–68

Some brief background is necessary to give context to the contention. In 1967, the United States Supreme Court, in *Berger v. New York,* 388 U.S. 41 gave off ominous warnings that state statutes authorizing the investigative use of either wiretapping or electronically enhanced eavesdropping, at least as most of those state statutes then stood, might fail to pass Fourth Amendment muster. The typical state statute, it was strongly suggested, would have difficulty in satisfying, *inter alia,* the Fourth Amendment's probable cause requirement, its particularity requirement, and its minimization requirement. The very length of the routinely authorized eavesdropping or wiretapping, the Supreme Court intimated, might turn a single warrant, in effect, into a series of open-ended general warrants. Within six months of the *Berger* decision, *Katz v. United States,* 389 U.S. 347 (1967), confirmed that the Fourth Amendment applies to the seizure of intangible conversation even without the necessity of some physical intrusion into a protected area....

Both to effectuate, completely and immediately, the protections that were the concern of *Berger* and *Katz,* but also to preserve wiretapping and electronic eavesdropping as effective law enforcement weapons, when properly constrained, Congress enacted "Title III" of the Omnibus Crime and Safe Streets Acts of 1968, now codified as 18 U.S.C., § 2510-2521. Title III is a comprehensive scheme setting out in meticulous detail the careful steps that must be taken by law enforcement officials before a judge will authorize a wiretap or the use of a "bugging" device. Title III also provided that the use of either technique by state law enforcement would be, *ipso facto,* illegal unless the state in question enacted its own implementing statute, fully satisfying all of Title III's requirements. The implementing state statute could be more protective of citizens' rights than Title III, but it could never be less so....

By ch. 692, sec. 3, of the Acts of 1977, Maryland enacted an implementing statute, now codified in Courts and Judicial Proceedings Article, §§ 10-401 through 10-414. As Chief Judge Robert Murphy noted in *Mustafa v. State,* 591 A.2d 481 (1991):

> The Maryland Act was modeled on the federal act and closely tracks its provisions; however, the Maryland legislature has made some of the provisions of the State Act more restrictive than the federal law (Emphasis supplied).

The Maryland Act followed the federal act, and with two exceptions, is essentially indistinguishable from it. In *Fearnow v. Chesapeake & Potomac Telephone Co. of Md.*, 655 A.2d 1 (1995), Judge Harrell wrote for this Court:

> It is clear through both legislative history and case precedent that *the federal wiretap statute ... served as the guiding light for the Maryland Act. Therefore, we read the acts in pari materia, so as to obtain the legislative intent of the language.*

(Emphasis supplied; citations omitted).

In *Adams v. State*, 406 A.2d 637 (1979), Judge Chasanow pointed out the two minor respects in which the Maryland law is more restrictive than its federal counterpart. Under the federal law, an interception will be lawful if either party to a conversation consents to its being overheard and recorded. In Maryland, by contrast, such an interception is lawful only if both parties give consent. *See Mustafa v. State*, 591 A.2d 481 (1991). The distinction is between one-party consent and two-party consent. The closely related second distinction is that in Maryland one-party consent, as an exception to the general Maryland rule, may be enough for the investigation of certain specially designated crimes. Under Title III, one-party consent will always be sufficient no matter what the crime.... In almost every other respect, the two acts essentially track each other.

⁺ ⁺ ⁺

Notes and Questions

1. Are you surprised that the Maryland Wiretapping statute almost identically tracks the federal Title III? States, of course, are free to provide greater criminal procedure protection to their residents than the federal constitution and federal statutes require. Do states often do this however? Scholars generally believe that the answer is no. *See, e.g.*, Robert F. Williams, *State Courts Adopting Federal Constitutional Doctrine: Case-by-Case Adoptionism or Prospective Lockstepping*, 46 WM. & MARY L. REV. 1499 (2005). Yet in some surprising instances, states offer dramatically greater protections to criminal defendants than required by the U.S. Constitution. *See* Adam M. Gershowitz, *Is Texas Tough on Crime But Soft on Criminal Procedure?* 49 AM. CRIM. L. REV. 31 (2012) (documenting how Texas affords criminal defendants greater protections of search and seizure, confessions, jury trial rights, and a host of other matters than is constitutionally required); David A. Harris, *Addressing Racial Profiling in the States: A Case Study of the "New Federalism" in Constitutional Criminal Procedure*, 3 U. PA. J. CONST. L. 367 (2001) (finding a "mixed bag" in independent state responses to racial profiling).

2. One party consent: Watch *The Wire*, Season 5, Episode 10, at 47:00 minutes, in which Prosecutor Pearlman plays a recording of defense attorney Maurice Levy arranging by phone to buy secret grand jury documents. The recording was made after a corrupt official was caught and agreed to make a recorded phone call to Levy. When the tape is played, the otherwise unflappable Levy appears very uncomfortable. Why didn't Pearlman and her colleagues need a wiretap to make this recording?

3. What are the other requirements imposed on investigators under Title III and the Maryland Act? Read carefully the excerpt below from Maryland's wiretapping statute.

Maryland Wiretapping and Electronic Surveillance Act
Md. Code, Courts and Judicial Proceedings, § 10-408

Applications for interception in writing

(a)(1) Each application for an order authorizing the interception of a wire, oral, or electronic communication shall be made in writing upon oath or affirmation to a judge of competent jurisdiction and shall state the applicant's authority to make the application. Each application shall include the following information:

(i) The identity of the investigative or law enforcement officer making the application, and the officer authorizing the application;

(ii) A full and complete statement of the facts and circumstances relied upon by the applicant, to justify his belief that an order should be issued, including:

1. Details as to the particular offense that has been, is being, or is about to be committed;

2. Except as provided in paragraph (2) of this subsection, a particular description of the nature and location of the facilities from which or the place where the communication is to be intercepted;

3. A particular description of the type of communications sought to be intercepted; and

4. The identity of the person, if known, committing the offense and whose communications are to be intercepted;

(iii) A full and complete statement as to whether or not other investigative procedures have been tried and failed or why they reasonably appear to be unlikely to succeed if tried or to be too dangerous;

(iv) A statement of the period of time for which the interception is required to be maintained. If the nature of the investigation is such that the authorization for interception should not automatically terminate when the described type of communication has been first obtained, a particular description of facts establishing probable cause to believe additional communications of the same type will occur thereafter;

(v) A full and complete statement of the facts concerning all previous applications known to the individual authorizing and making the application, made to any judge for authorization to intercept wire, oral, or electronic communications involving any of the same persons, facilities or places specified in the application, and the action taken by the judge on each application; and

(vi) Where the application is for the extension of an order, a statement setting forth the results thus far obtained from the interception, or a reasonable explanation of the failure to obtain the results.

* * *

Additional testimony or documentary evidence

(b) The judge may require the applicant to furnish additional testimony or documentary evidence in support of the application.

Grounds for ex parte interception order

(c)(1) Upon the application the judge may enter an ex parte order, as requested or as modified, authorizing interception of wire, oral, or electronic communications within the territorial jurisdiction permitted under paragraphs (2) and (3) of this subsection, if the judge determines on the basis of the facts submitted by the applicant that:

(i) There is probable cause for belief that an individual is committing, has committed, or is about to commit a particular offense enumerated in § 10-406 of this subtitle;

(ii) There is probable cause for belief that particular communications concerning that offense will be obtained through the interception;

(iii) Normal investigative procedures have been tried and have failed or reasonably appear to be unlikely to succeed if tried or to be too dangerous; and

(iv) There is probable cause for belief:

1. That the facilities from which, or the place where, the wire, oral, or electronic communications are to be intercepted are being used, or are about to be used, in connection with the commission of the offense, or are leased to, listed in the name of, or commonly used by this person in accordance with subsection (a)(1) of this section; or

2. That the actions of the individual whose communications are to be intercepted could have the effect of thwarting an interception from a specified facility in accordance with subsection (a)(2) of this section.

* * *

Contents of ex parte interception orders

(d)(1) Each order authorizing the interception of any wire, oral, or electronic communication shall specify:

(i) The identity of the person, if known or required under subsection (a)(2) of this section, whose communications are to be intercepted;

(ii) The nature and location of the communications facilities as to which, or the place where, authority to intercept is granted, if known;

(iii) A particular description of the type of communication sought to be intercepted, and a statement of the particular offense to which it relates;

(iv) The identity of the agency authorized to intercept the communications, and of the person authorizing the application; and

(v) The period of time during which the interception is authorized, including a statement as to whether or not the interception shall automatically terminate when the described communication has been first obtained.

(2) An order authorizing the interception of a wire, oral, or electronic communication, upon request of the applicant, shall direct that a provider of wire or electronic communication service, landlord, custodian or other person furnish the applicant forthwith all information, facilities, and technical assistance necessary to accomplish the interception unobtrusively and with a minimum of interference with the services that the service provider, landlord, custodian, or person is according the person whose communications are to be intercepted. Any provider of wire or electronic communication service, landlord, custodian or other person furnishing the facilities or technical assistance shall be compensated therefor by the applicant for reasonable expenses incurred in providing facilities or assistance.

Duration of interception

(e)(1) An order entered under this section may not authorize the interception of any wire, oral, or electronic communication for any period longer than is necessary to achieve the objective of the authorization, nor in any event longer than 30 days. The 30-day period begins on the earlier of the day on which the investigative or law enforcement officer first begins to conduct an interception under the order or 10 days after the order is entered.

(2) Extensions of an order may be granted, but only upon application for an extension made in accordance with subsection (a) of this section and the court making the findings required by subsection (c) of this section. The period of extension shall be no longer than the authorizing judge deems necessary to achieve the purposes for which it was granted and in no event for longer than 30 days.

(3) Every order and extension thereof shall contain a provision that the authorization to intercept shall be executed as soon as practicable, shall be conducted in such a way as to minimize the interception of communications not otherwise subject to interception under this subtitle, and must terminate upon attainment of the authorized objective, or in any event in 30 days.

(4) In the event the intercepted communication is in a code or foreign language, and an expert in that foreign language or code is not reasonably available during the interception period, minimization may be accomplished as soon as practicable after the interception. An interception under this subtitle may be conducted in whole or in part by federal, State, or local government personnel, or by an individual operating under a contract with the State or a political subdivision of the State, acting under the supervision of an investigative or law enforcement officer authorized to conduct the interception.

Reports to issuing judge

(f) Whenever an order authorizing interception is entered pursuant to this subtitle, the order shall require reports to be made to the judge who issued the order showing what progress has been made toward achievement of the authorized objective and the need for continued interception. The reports shall be made at the intervals the judge requires.

Recording of contents of intercepted communications

(g)(1) The contents of any wire, oral, or electronic communication intercepted by any means authorized by this subtitle, if possible, shall be recorded on tape or wire or other comparable device. The recording of the contents of any wire, oral, or electronic communication under this subsection shall be done in the way as will protect the recording from editing or other alterations. Immediately upon the expiration of the period of the order, or extensions thereof, such recordings shall be made available to the judge issuing such order and sealed under his directions. Custody of the recordings shall be wherever the judge orders. They may not be destroyed except upon an order of the issuing or denying judge and in any event shall be kept for ten years. Duplicate recordings may be made for use or disclosure pursuant to the provisions of subsections (a) and (b) of § 10-407 of this subtitle for investigations. The presence of the seal provided for by this subsection, or a satisfactory explanation for the absence thereof, shall be a prerequisite for the use or disclosure of the contents of any wire, oral, or electronic communication or evidence derived therefrom under subsection (c) of § 10-407 of this subtitle.

(2) Applications made and orders granted under this subtitle shall be sealed by the judge. Custody of the applications and orders shall be wherever the judge directs. The applications and orders shall be disclosed only upon a showing of good cause before a judge of competent jurisdiction and shall not be destroyed except on order of the issuing or denying judge, and in any event shall be kept for 10 years.

(3) Any violation of the provisions of this subsection may be punished as contempt of the issuing or denying judge.

(4) Within a reasonable time, but not later than 90 days after the termination of the period of an order or extension of an order, the issuing judge shall cause to be served on the persons named in the order, and on the other parties to intercepted communications as the judge may determine in the judge's discretion is in the interest of justice, an inventory which shall include notice of:

(i) The fact of the entry of the order;

(ii) The date of the entry and the period of authorized interception; and

(iii) The fact that during the period wire, oral, or electronic communications were or were not intercepted.

(5) The judge, upon the filing of a motion, shall make available to the person or the person's counsel for inspection portions of the intercepted communications, applications, and orders pertaining to that person and the alleged crime.

(6) On an ex parte showing of good cause to the judge, the serving of the inventory required by this subsection may be postponed. The periods of postponement may not be longer than the authorizing judge deems necessary to achieve the purposes for which they were granted and in no event for longer than 30 days. No more than three periods of postponement may be granted. Any order issued extending the time in which the inventory notice is to be served must be under seal of the court and treated in the same manner as the order authorizing interception.

Disclosures relating to intercepted communications prior to use as evidence

* * *

Motions to suppress by aggrieved persons

(i)(1) Any aggrieved person in any trial, hearing, or proceeding in or before any court, department, officer, agency, regulatory body, or other authority of this State or a political subdivision thereof, may move to suppress the contents of any intercepted wire, oral, or electronic communication, or evidence derived therefrom, on the grounds that:

(i) The communication was unlawfully intercepted;

(ii) The order of authorization under which it was intercepted is insufficient on its face, or was not obtained or issued in strict compliance with this subtitle; or

(iii) The interception was not made in conformity with the order of authorization.

* * *

Notes and Questions

1. Sub-section 10-408(c)(1)(i) above notes that a wiretap order cannot issue unless it is for a crime enumerated in 10-406. That portion of the statute (not excerpted above) specifies that wiretaps are limited to gathering evidence for murder, kidnapping, rape, child pornography, gambling, drug dealing, and about a dozen other serious crimes. Why would the list of possible crimes giving rise to a wiretap be so limited?

2. Watch *The Wire*, Season 2, Episode 7, at 45:00 minutes. The detectives discuss applying for a wiretap but Prosecutor Pearlman quickly advises them that prostitution is

not a ground for which a wiretap can issue under Maryland law. Is there a way that the officers could have gotten around this restriction?

3. Do the wiretap rules apply when one party to a conversation consents to the recording? Watch *The Wire*, Season 1, Episode 10, at 30:50 minutes, in which Proposition Joe sets up a "parlay" between Omar and Stringer Bell to negotiate a truce. Unknown to Stringer, Omar is wearing a wire and the conversation is being recorded and listened to by the officers. Do the officers need to follow the wiretap rules and procure a warrant to do this?

4. Can undercover police sell drug dealers a disposable phone that is already wiretapped? In Season 3, the officers are stymied because the Barksdale gang only uses disposable cell phones. The wireless provider takes nearly a week to respond to a subpoena request and by that time the drug dealers have disposed of their phones and acquired new ones. Detective Freamon hatches a plan to cut out the middleman and sell the phones directly to the drug dealers, thus ensuring a longer wiretap period before the dealers dump their cell phones. Prosecutor Pearlman explains that there is no precedent for such a wiretap, but she convinces Judge Phelan to authorize it anyway. Watch *The Wire*, Season 3, Episode 10, at 33:20 minutes. Is this legal?

5. Watch *The Wire*, Season 3, Episode 11, at 12:55 minutes. The officers need Stringer Bell's cell phone number to connect him to the drug conspiracy, but they cannot get it through their wiretap. So, the officers use a "triggerfish" device, which mimics a cell phone tower to determine a cell phone's number and location. A triggerfish requires a Pen/Trap order from a judge, but it is not yet clear whether more rigorous Fourth Amendment protections would also apply. *See* William Curtiss, *Triggering a Closer Review: Direct Acquisition of Cell Site Location Tracking Information and the Argument for Consistency Across Statutory Regimes*, 45 Colum. J. L. Soc. Probs. 139 (2011). Some lower courts and one leading Fourth Amendment expert, Professor Orin Kerr, take the position that historical cell-site data is not protected by the Fourth Amendment's warrant requirement. *See* Orin Kerr, Are Historical Cell-Site Data Protected Under the Fourth Amendment After *United States v. Jones*, available at http://www.volokh.com/2012/03/04/are-historical-cell-site-data-protected-under-the-fourth-amendment-after-united-states-v-jones/.

C. Qualifying for a Wiretap: Demonstrating Necessity

"I thought I knew what paperwork was. But what you all go through to listen to someone else's phone calls …"[1]

— Port Officer Beatrice Russell

A crucial issue in wiretapping cases, and one that is explored in detail in *The Wire*, is whether the police have justification to qualify for a wiretap in the first place. For most searches, police need probable cause before conducting the search. That is certainly true for wiretaps. Yet, to get a wire, the police also need to demonstrate something further — that the wiretap is truly necessary, rather than merely convenient. The necessity element takes on great importance during Seasons 1 and 2 of *The Wire* and is portrayed as a major

---

1. *The Wire*, Season 2, Episode 8, at 12:20 minutes.

obstacle to stopping Avon Barksdale's drug ring and investigating the illegality on the docks. As you read the cases below and become familiar with the legal requirements for establishing necessity, ask yourself whether *The Wire* accurately portrays the law or whether it exaggerates the obstacles police face.

United States v. Willock

682 F.Supp.2d 512 (D. Md. 2010)

WILLIAM D. QUARLES, JR., District Judge.

On February 21, 2008, the grand jury returned a 20 count indictment against Michelle Hebron, Sherman Pride, Ronnie Thomas, and others. All the defendants were charged in Count One with Conspiracy to Participate in a Racketeering Enterprise. Pride was charged in Count Two with Conspiracy to Distribute and Possess with the Intent to Distribute Controlled Substances....

* * *

Motion to Suppress Electronic Surveillance....

1. Background

In November 2006, the Baltimore City Police Department ("BPD") and the Bureau of Alcohol, Tobacco, Firearms, and Explosives ("ATF") began an investigation of drug trafficking by the [Tree Top Pirus ("TTP"), a subset of the Bloods gang]. From August 2007 to February 2008, the Circuit Court for Baltimore City authorized wiretaps of cellular telephones of alleged TTP members Kevin Gary, Sean Frazier, and Jerrod Fenwick. In August 2007 and October 2008, the Circuit Court authorized interceptions on the "A-Line" and "J-Line," cellular telephones used by Gary.... [One of the defendants has moved to suppress] arguing that the J-Line affidavits did not establish probable cause or the exhaustion of normal law enforcement techniques.

2. Analysis

"When a state court authorizes a wiretap, state wiretapping law should govern the admissibility of wiretap evidence in federal court." *United States v. Bullock,* 2000 WL 84449, *4 (4th Cir. Jan. 27, 2000). Because Maryland law is identical to federal law on the subjects of probable cause and exhaustion, "whether [the Court] analyzes this case under state or federal law is of little consequence." *Id.* Section 10-408 of the Courts and Judicial Procedure Article of the Maryland Code authorizes a wiretap when the applicant shows (1) probable cause for belief that an individual is committing, has committed or is about to commit an enumerated offense; (2) probable cause for belief that particular communications concerning the offense will be obtained through such interception; (3) that normal investigative procedures have been tried and have failed or appear to be unlikely to succeed or are too dangerous; and (4) probable cause for belief that the facilities from which the communications are to be intercepted are being used in connection with the commission of such offense. Md. Code Ann., Cts. & Jud. Proc. § 10-408.

a. Probable Cause

"The probable cause required for issuance of a wiretap order is the same as that which is necessary to obtain the issuance of a search warrant." *United States v. Talbert,* 706 F.2d 464, 467 (4th Cir.1983)....

The A-Line and J-Line affidavits show that Gary was a member of the TTP, an organization involved in drug-trafficking in Maryland. The A-Line affidavit described telephone conversations between Gary and Steve Willock, alleged leader of the TTP, about various TTP matters, including plans for Gary's travel to contact TTP members in Compton, California.[10] Gary's "MySpace" webpage indicated his affiliation with the TTP, including his residence in "Pirumore, Maryland" and praise for the "Piruettes," (*i.e.,* female TTP members).

The A-Line affidavit also described Gary's arrangements to sell heroin and his sale of crack cocaine to a confidential informant ("CI-206") whom Gary and other TTP members had accepted as a fellow Blood. CI-206, who had learned Gary's cell phone number—the A-Line number—at a July 8, 2007 TTP meeting, called Gary to arrange the heroin deal.

The A-Line affidavit also cited Dialed Number Recording ("DNR") Data for August 3, 2007 to August 19, 2007 showing more than 7,100 direct connect "activations" of the A-Line cell phone—more than 400 per day—suggesting "commercial" use of the phone. Finally, the A-Line affidavit documented Gary's criminal record, including a 2001 conviction for possession with intent to distribute cocaine and heroin. The A-Line affidavit established probable cause to believe that (1) Gary was engaged in the sale of controlled dangerous substances in violation of Maryland law and (2) communications concerning Gary's drug sales would be intercepted on the A-Line.

The J-Line affidavit states that CI-206 reported that Gary had discarded the A-Line cell phone and began using the J-Line phone in early October 2007. The affiants compared outgoing calls on the A-Line and J-Line and found 26 common numbers, suggesting that Gary had used both lines. DNR data on the J-Line for October 1, 2007 to October 28, 2007 showed 9,930 activations—354 per day—suggesting "commercial" use. The A-Line affidavit and this information established probable cause that (1) Gary was violating Maryland's drug laws and (2) communications about his drug sales would be intercepted on the J-Line.

b. Exhaustion

Like its federal counterpart, § 10-408(c)'s exhaustion requirement was enacted "to make doubly sure that the statutory authority [to wiretap] is used with restraint and only where the circumstances warrant ... surreptitious interception." *Salzman v. State,* 430 A.2d 847, 853 (Md.Ct.Spec.App.1981). "[T]he exhaustion requirement's basic purpose is to assure that wiretapping is not ... routinely employed as the initial step in [a] criminal investigation." *Id.* Thus, "[t]he affidavit must demonstrate ... that normal investigative procedures have been tried and failed, or they are unlikely to be successful, or that their use is too perilous to the investigators." *Id.*

Law enforcement "need not exhaust every conceivable investigative possibility before seeking a wiretap order." *Id.* Rather, "the exhaustion requirement is to be tested in a practical and common sense fashion." *Id.* Although the Government cannot show exhaustion "through a mere boilerplate recitation of the difficulties of gathering useful evidence," *United States v. Oriakhi,* 57 F.3d 1290, 1298 (4th Cir.1995), the burden on the Government is "not great," and courts should be wary of reading the requirement in an overly restrictive manner lest they unduly hamper the investigative powers of law enforcement agents. *United States v. Smith,* 31 F.3d 1294, 1297 (4th Cir.1994).

The J-Line affidavit met the exhaustion requirement. The affidavit detailed specific obstacles to the investigation:

---

10. The conversations took place while Willock was incarcerated in Hagerstown, Maryland and were recorded pursuant to Maryland Division of Corrections policy. * * *

[T]he goals and objectives of this investigation are to develop evidence sufficient to identify, locate, arrest and convict … the criminal confederates of the CDS trafficking organization in which GARY is involved … [and to] identify the organization's suppliers and the means by which the organization obtains and receives CDS, and to determine where the organization stores CDS and how it processes and launders CDS proceeds.

The affiants noted that although two confidential informants had been useful in obtaining evidence about Gary's drug sales, they had not learned the TTP's sources of supply, methods of distribution, stash house locations, or the manner of concealment and laundering of CDS proceeds. As the TTP prided itself on its violence,[11] the affiants believed it was too dangerous to have the informants press Gary for this information.

The affidavit demonstrated that the introduction of an undercover officer was unlikely to succeed. According to the informants, Gary balked at meeting people who were not affiliated with the Bloods. And even if the informants were able to introduce an undercover officer, it was unlikely that the officer would gain information not already available to the informants. The TTP's violence also counseled against using an undercover officer.

The affidavit demonstrated that cooperation of TTP associates was unlikely, and attempts to interview them would compromise the investigation. Similarly, the execution of search warrants at TTP members' homes could prompt the TTP to suspend operations and cause the targets to dispose of monitored phones. The TTP was a small, tightly knit group. The arrests of top-level members Jerrod Fenwick and Shonn Eubanks may have increased the TTP's vigilance for law enforcement. Approaching other targets or their associates or executing multiple search warrants would have been dangerous and could have caused the destruction of evidence. Witness interviews were also unlikely to succeed because the potential witnesses were implicated in CDS distribution and/or feared for their safety.

Grand jury subpoenas were also unlikely to succeed. The potential witnesses were themselves TTP members. Those witnesses would have likely asserted the Fifth Amendment privilege against self-incrimination before the grand jury. As the State's Attorney for Baltimore City had decided that no TTP member would receive immunity, the testimony of these witnesses could not be compelled.

Surveillance of Gary was unlikely to succeed. Because of the arrests of Fenwick and Eubanks, Gary was "maintaining a very low profile at his mother's house." Physical surveillance of Gary was thus unlikely to reveal TTP suppliers and the means by which the TTP received CDS, where CDS was stored, and how the TTP processed and laundered CDS proceeds. Placing GPS tracking devices on Gary's cars would have risked compromising the investigation because of Gary's "extreme[ ] aware[ness] of law enforcement's efforts to discover his illegal activity." Because Gary used more than one vehicle-and the vehicles he used were used by others-the value of GPS tracking was outweighed by the risk of exposing the investigation.

Finally, although telephone toll records (*i.e.,* DNR data) on the J-Line had been helpful, the call data did not reveal the identities of many of the callers. The affiants believed that listening to the telephone conversations was necessary to learn those identities.

---

11. Gary had boasted to CI-206 that in 2005, TTP was responsible for 75% of Baltimore's 300 murders.

Viewed in a practical, commonsense fashion, the affidavit adequately informed the Baltimore City Circuit Court judge of the difficulties involved in using conventional law enforcement techniques and why those techniques were unlikely to achieve the goals of the investigation. The J-Line Order was based on probable cause and the exhaustion requirement had been satisfied. Thomas's motion to suppress the wiretap will be denied.

* * *

Notes and Questions

1. The court in *Willock* concludes that the police were entitled to seek a wiretap because they exhausted other available options. The court uses the wrong terminology however. The key question is whether the wiretap was a necessity, not solely whether the officers exhausted other options. *See* CLIFFORD S. FISCHMAN & ANNE T. MCKENNA, WIRETAPPING AND EAVESDROPPING: SURVEILLANCE IN THE INTERNET AGE § 8.71 (3rd ed. 2010) (explaining that when analyzing necessity it is "less often and less accurately" referred to as exhaustion).

2. Were you convinced by the court's explanation for why the wiretap was necessary? Although it is somewhat unfair to pick apart the officer's rationales one piece at a time, rather than reading their explanation under a totality of the circumstances, do you nevertheless find some of the explanations lacking? Is it the case that officers could not use a GPS device because a suspect was "extremely aware of law enforcement's efforts" to investigate him? What about the assertion that a suspect could not be surveilled in person because he maintains "a very low profile at his mother's house"? Couldn't police make these types of assertions for almost any suspect?

Salzman v. State
430 A.2d 847 (Md. Ct. Spec. App. 1981)

LOWE, Judge.

In January of 1978 Baltimore County Police began an investigation into what was believed to have been the largest illegal drug operation ever investigated by State law enforcement officials. The investigation concluded in the indictments of some twenty individuals, spread throughout four different counties, who were involved on various levels in an operation which dealt with literally tons of marijuana, a quantity of cocaine and methaqualone, and so much United States currency that cash exchanges by members of the group were calibrated by the suitcase full....

Police were first alerted to the operation on January 6, 1978, when one Victor Tomich went to the Baltimore County Police Headquarters and confessed to a larceny he had committed some nine days previously. Tomich related that he had removed approximately $100,000 in cash and a bag of marijuana from a safe in the home of appellants Paul and Marcia Blinken. After explaining that he and his wife, Mindy Tomich (the sister of Marcia Blinken), lived in a house trailer on the Baltimore County property of Paul and Marcia Blinken, Victor divulged to the police that Paul and Marcia Blinken, along with Paul Blinken's brothers Neal and Jeffrey and one of their cousins (later identified as appellant Bruce Salzman), were operating a large-scale illegal drug conspiracy.

From this initial meeting and two subsequent interviews with Victor and Mindy Tomich, it was learned that the Blinkens ran what was described as a "corporation" dealing in illegal drugs, with members of the corporation residing and operating throughout the State. The Tomichs had personally observed bales of marijuana, suitcases full of methaqualone, and quantities of cocaine stored at the home of Paul and Marcia Blinken. They had further seen these drugs delivered to and used and distributed at the Blinkens' residence. Among other personal observations by the Tomichs were (1) the sale of cocaine by Paul Blinken, (2) firearms carried by Paul Blinken, (3) frequent drug deliveries and traffic in and out of Paul and Marcia Blinken's home, and (4) drug use at the residence of Jeffrey Blinken. Mindy Tomich further informed the police that on one occasion in 1974 Paul Blinken had arranged for her to pick up two suitcases full of marijuana at his father's house in Florida. Upon her return with the drugs, she was paid $500 by Paul Blinken for her efforts.

A five-week investigation by Baltimore County Police detectives ensued, and on February 24, 1978 Victor and Mindy Tomich along with three Baltimore County Police detectives personally appeared before Judge Frank E. Cicone in the Circuit Court for Baltimore County and submitted a detailed affidavit which served as the basis for an application by the State's Attorney for Baltimore County for an order authorizing a wiretap on the telephone of appellants Paul and Marcia Blinken. Judge Cicone issued the order....

Based on the information obtained from the Tomichs and on a number of intercepted telephone conversations couched in carefully coded language and interpreted by experts as being drug related, search warrants were ultimately obtained and executed on April 28, 1978 and May 1, 1978 for the premises and vehicles of Bruce Salzman, Jeffrey Blinken, and Paul and Marcia Blinken. The police seized 229 pounds of marijuana with an approximate street value of $145,920, 2 grams, 700 milligrams of cocaine with a significant purity of 95%–100%, and assorted drug paraphernalia from Paul and Marcia Blinken's; 400 pounds of marijuana with an estimated street value of $180,000, one ounce of cocaine with an approximate street value of $2,000, and 500 quaalude tablets with an approximate street value of $1,000 from the truck and residence of Bruce Salzman, plus $598,000 in cash found in the trunk of an unlicensed Mercedes Benz parked within the Salzman curtilage; five and one-half pounds of marijuana having an estimated street value of $2,475, two ounces of cocaine with an approximate street value of $4,000, 123 quaalude tablets with a street value of $246 and $101,595 in cash packets of $1,000 per wrapper from the residence of Jeffrey Blinken; and approximately two tons of marijuana plus three vehicles fictitiously registered, from the group's warehouse in Anne Arundel County.

* * *

... All [of the defendants] were convicted on various violations of the laws relating to controlled dangerous substances.

* * *

All four appellants contend that the police failed to exhaust normal investigative procedures before seeking wiretap authorizations and that therefore the wiretaps were obtained in violation of applicable federal and state statutes. Section 10-408(a)(3) of Maryland's wiretap and electronic surveillance statute, Md.Cts. & Jud.Proc.Code Ann. ss 10-401 10-412, and its federal counterpart s 2518(1)(c) of Title III of the Omnibus Crime Control & Safe Streets Act of 1968, 18 U.S.C. ss 2510–2520, (hereinafter Title III), set forth the identical requirement that every application for an ex parte order authorizing wiretap interception must demonstrate:

… whether or not other investigative procedures have been tried and failed or why they reasonably appear to be unlikely to succeed if tried or to be too dangerous.

The Title III preconditions for obtaining wiretap authority, and particularly the exhaustion requirement (18 U.S.C. s 2518(1)(c)) after which Maryland's s 10-408(a)(3) is modeled, were established by Congress "to make doubly sure that the statutory authority (to wiretap) be used with restraint and only where the circumstances warrant the surreptitious interception of wire and oral communications." United States v. Giordano, 416 U.S. 505 (1974). Specifically, the exhaustion requirement's basic purpose is to assure that wiretapping is "not … routinely employed as the initial step in criminal investigation." Id.…

The State, however, need not exhaust every conceivable investigative possibility before seeking a wiretap order. Rather, the exhaustion requirement is to be tested in a "practical and common sense fashion," Bell v. State, 429 A.2d 300 at 302, since its purpose is "simply … to assure that wiretapping is not resorted to where traditional investigative techniques would suffice." United States v. Kahn, 415 U.S. 143, 153 n. 12 (1974)…. "Merely because a normal investigative technique is theoretically possible, it does not follow that it is likely. What (the exhaustion) provision envisions is that the showing be tested in a practical and common sense fashion." Calhoun, 367 A.2d 40. Consequently, the State "need not prove to a certainty that (normal investigative) techniques will not succeed if as stated in the statute (they) 'reasonably appear to be unlikely to succeed.'"

* * *

Applying the pragmatic approach to the first Baltimore County affidavit, it is clear that the exhaustion requirement was met. Contrary to appellants' contention that it merely contained "boiler-plate verbiage," the 34-page affidavit outlined with great detail the investigative procedures that the police had unsuccessfully attempted to use, and why the efforts had failed in light of the objectives, which included identification of the alleged conspiracy's sources of supply and higher-echelon figures.

Intermittent stationary surveillance of Paul Blinken's home and place of business over a five-week period had predictably failed to reveal identities of any "higher-ups," sources of supply, or coconspirators; telephone toll records and informant tips, indicated that Paul Blinken was associated with known and convicted narcotics law violators, but were not sufficient to prove a criminal conspiracy or to identify sources of supply; a check on criminal arrest records rendered no information; requests to the Tomichs to introduce undercover agents to Paul Blinken were fruitless because the Tomichs refused, explaining that Blinken only dealt with old friends and associates; intermittent mobile surveillance of Paul Blinken proved futile and rendered no evidence; the Tomichs' access to Paul and Marcia Blinken's house had been curtailed since the disappearance of the Blinkens' money from their safe; and inquiries to other reliable police informants for information on Paul Blinken or any of his co-conspirators met with negative results.

Besides detailing the above unsuccessful efforts, the police set forth an exhaustive list in their affidavit to Judge Cicone outlining why other investigative techniques "reasonably appear(ed) to be unlikely to succeed if tried or to be too dangerous." A "blind buy" (i. e., an attempt to purchase drugs from the Blinkens without prior introduction) appeared likely to fail in light of the Tomichs' information that Paul Blinken only sold to long-time associates (moreover, a "blind buy" would not aid in identifying sources of supply or "higher-ups"); because the Blinken house was in an isolated area of Baltimore County, long-term stationary surveillance would likely be detected and would fail at any rate to reveal sources of supply and "higher-ups"; infiltration of the conspiracy appeared impossible since Paul Blinken dealt only with long-term associates; execution of a search and seizure warrant would not aid in determining co-conspirators; and further checks of toll records, implementation of a "pen register," or electronic eavesdropping of conversations between the Blinkens and the Tomichs (with the permission of the Tomichs) all appeared unlikely to reveal sources of supply and higher-echelon figures in the suspected conspiracy. In sum, it was clear from the information set forth in the affidavit, that normal investigative procedures would "reasonably" be unlikely to succeed. The February 24, 1978 original application for wiretap authorization in Baltimore County more than met the exhaustion requirement.

* * *

[Convictions Affirmed.]

Notes and Questions

1. Does it seem realistic to you that the police investigation in *Salzman* began when a man walked into a police station and confessed to stealing $100,000 from his brother-in-law? Are you at all suspicious that the police shaded the truth from the beginning?

2. Given that the informant Victor Tomich told police that Paul, Marcia, Neal, and Jeffrey "were operating a large-scale illegal drug conspiracy" was there really a need for a wiretap in this case? If the conspiracy was operating out of the defendant's house, couldn't the police have procured a simple search warrant to look for further information? Was the court too quick to assume that visual surveillance, a pen register, or further use of the Tomich as informants would be useless in acquiring other valuable information? Put simply was a wiretap truly necessary?

3. How does *The Wire* portray the necessity standard for acquiring a wiretap in Baltimore? For example, watch *The Wire*, Season 1, Episode 4, at 43:25 minutes in which Detectives McNulty, Freamon, and Greggs explain that to get a wiretap they must prove "nothing else works." Also consider *The Wire*, Season 2, Episode 8, at 6:30 minutes, in which the officers try to convince Prosecutor Pearlman that the port investigation involves drugs and thus qualifies for a wiretap. Before agreeing to seek a wiretap, Pearlman presses the officers on whether they could acquire the information through informants or surveillance.

4. Watch *The Wire*, Season 1, Episode 5, at 5:00 minutes, in which the officers present their affidavits and Judge Phelan authorizes the wiretap. Notice how much paperwork was produced and must be signed to support the wiretap application.

5. In light of the courts' decisions in *Salzman* and *Willock*, does it seem that *The Wire* does an accurate job describing the burdens on law enforcement to qualify for a wiretap?

D. Executing a Wiretap: Minimization and Progress Reports

As the materials above indicate, investigators can obtain a wiretap when they have probable cause and when they can demonstrate necessity. What happens after the judge issues the wiretap though? Can law enforcement officers listen to everything, or are some conversations off limits? Does anyone supervise the officers to ensure they are executing the wiretap in compliance with the statutory rules and the judge's order? The cases below address these questions.

United States v. Fauntleroy

800 F. Supp.2d 676 (D. Md. 2011)

BENSON EVERETT LEGG, District Judge.

This is a drug conspiracy case. On June 16, 2010, a federal grand jury returned a twelve-count indictment that charged 22 defendants, including Dione Fauntleroy, Jr., with conspiring to distribute controlled substances. Fauntleory, Jr., has filed several motions.... For the reasons stated herein, the Court will, by separate Order of even date DENY the [motions]....

* * *

On March 25, 2010, Judge Timothy Doory of the Baltimore City Circuit Court approved an application submitted by the Baltimore City Police and the DEA for a wiretap on telephone numbers identified as the A-line and the B-line. The A-line was believed to be used by Defendant Roger Ford. The B-line was believed to be used by Defendant Travis Stanfield. Later in the investigation, subsequent wiretap orders were obtained for the C-line (believed to be used by Fauntleroy, Jr.), the D-line (believed to be used by Robert Campbell), the E-line (also believed to be used by Robert Campbell), the F-line (believed to be used by Damian Jackson), and the G-line (believed to be used by Fauntleroy, Jr.).

* * *

... Fauntleroy, Jr., asserts that the officers monitoring telephone calls in this case failed to minimize their interception of non-pertinent information as required by the wiretap orders. Title 18 U.S.C. § 2518(5) requires wiretap orders to include a directive that the order be executed "in such a way as to minimize the interception of communications not otherwise subject to interception." The minimization requirement is satisfied if the reviewing court finds that, in light of all of the facts and circumstances, "the agents have shown a high regard for the right of privacy and have done all they reasonably could to avoid unnecessary intrusion." *United States v. Tortorello*, 480 F.2d 764, 784 (2d Cir.1973).

The wiretap orders issued by Judge Doory contained a directive of the type required by 18 U.S.C. § 2518(5), and enumerated with specificity the subject matter that was fair game for interception. The instructions issued to all monitoring agents repeated the standard contained in the wiretap orders, and instructed the agents that all intercepted calls could be monitored for an initial period of two minutes "for the purpose of identifying the parties to the conversation and determining whether said conversation is criminal in nature or constitutes evidence of the offenses under investigation." If, after the initial two-minute period, the monitoring agent designated the conversation as non-pertinent to the investigation, interception would have to be terminated. The instructions further authorized spot monitoring or spot checking, meaning that the monitoring agent would be permitted to reactivate the interception of a call initially designated non-pertinent "every thirty (30) to sixty (60) seconds or so to determine if the parties or the nature of the conversation have changed to those covered in the order. LISTEN JUST LONG ENOUGH TO GET THE GIST OF THE CONVERSATION." The agent was instructed to use his or her judgment as to when and for how long to spot check, based on several factors. These factors include the "parties to the conversation, precise relationship of the parties, the length of the relationship, the number of contacts between the parties, present status of the investigation, [and the] past conduct of the parties."

Fauntleroy, Jr., first argues that "[t]wo minutes on its face is unreasonable when privacy rights are at issue." The Court disagrees. Taking into consideration the complexity of the alleged conspiracy, the number of individuals involved, and the coded language that has become a fixture of communication in the world of illegal drugs, two minutes is a reasonable time in which to make an initial determination as to pertinence. *See United States v. Quintana,* 508 F.2d 867, 874 (7th Cir.1975) ("[l]arge and sophisticated narcotics conspiracies may justify considerably more interception than would a single criminal episode. This is especially so where, as here, the judicially approved purpose of the wiretap is not so much to incriminate the known person whose phone is tapped as to learn the identity of far-flung conspirators and to delineate the contours of the conspiracy.").

Gone are the days when drug dealers discussed business by phone in a straightforward manner. Today's recorded conversations are replete with code words and code phrases intended to veil the speaker's meaning. For a reviewing court, the import of a call often becomes evident only by deconstructing the transcript with the assistance of expert testimony. In fact, the very abstruseness of the conversation raises legitimate suspicion. If the target of a wiretap is calling the gas and electric company about a bill, minimization is not a difficult task. When the target is talking to another suspect, however, and using language susceptible of multiple meanings, the monitoring agents are justified in listening longer and more closely.

Fauntleroy, Jr., then turns to statistical analysis of the call logs for the A-, B-, and C-lines in an attempt to show that the monitoring agents intercepted more of the conversations than necessary or permissible. For example, as to the A-line, this analysis purports to show that only 35% of the total duration of non-pertinent calls was minimized, and that 3,545 calls not designated either pertinent or non-pertinent were not minimized at all. The latter point ignores, most notably, the fact that the vast majority of undesignated calls lasted in the neighborhood of 40 seconds, and so would never have been minimized whether pertinent or not. As to the total duration, the statistics for the A-line reveal that the average non-pertinent call lasted 8:02, of which 2:51 was minimized. Subtracting the initial 2-minute period discussed above, this leaves an average of 3:11 for spot monitoring.

While this may seem somewhat high, dealing in averages for thousands of calls that run the full range between hang-ups and lengthy conversations presents obvious difficulties, and the Court must exercise great care before substituting its own *ex post* judgment for that of the monitoring agents. "It is all well and good to say, after the fact, that certain conversations were irrelevant and should have been terminated. However, monitoring agents are not gifted with prescience and cannot be expected to know in advance what direction a conversation will take." *United States v. LaGorga,* 336 F.Supp. 190, 196 (W.D.Pa.1971). What is most telling is that Fauntleroy, Jr., has not identified a single discrete call that he contends was monitored more than necessary. Based on the evidence presented, the Court is unable to conclude that such monitoring constituted a failure to minimize as required by the issuing court's order.

For these reasons, the Motion to Suppress Evidence Obtained by Electronic Surveillance and Interception by Wire and Fruits of Wiretapping must be denied.

* * *

Notes and Questions

1. Watch *The Wire*, Season 1, Episode 6, at 10:30 minutes. In this scene, Freamon and Greggs explain to the other officers that they cannot simply listen to the wiretap. Rather, they must know that one of the targets of their investigation is talking on the payphone before they can listen. At least one officer must therefore physically observe the tapped phone to see whether a target is using it before the other officers can monitor the call. Officer Herc is exasperated by all of the work necessary before they can even listen to a call.

2. For an example of the minimization problem, Watch *The Wire*, Season 1, Episode 9, at 21:30. Officers Herc and Carver listen to the wiretap and hear one of the targets (Poot) engaged in phone sex, a non-pertinent topic that the officers should not be listening to. Detective McNulty explains to them "you know you're supposed to shut down after ninety seconds if it's non-pertinent." Immediately afterward, Poot makes incriminating statements about the drug gang. Carver confidently proclaims, "[it's] pertinent now, right." McNulty responds "well it is if you can explain while we're still on the line after ten minutes [of phone sex]. You gotta justify that."

Calhoun v. State

532 A.2d 707 (Md. Ct. Spec. App. 1987)

GILBERT, Chief Judge.

In this appeal we once again visit an inhabitant of the world of the stealthy and surreptitious — the wiretap. We are here asked whether the Maryland Wiretap and Electronic Surveillance Law commands the principal prosecuting attorney personally to make progress reports to the judge who issued the order and whether the periodical submission of the wiretap logs to the issuing judge satisfies the Act's requirement of a progress report.

Roy Edwin Calhoun does not challenge his culpability, probable cause for issuance of the wiretap order, or the sufficiency of the evidence. He does not even voice objection to the lengthy term of imprisonment he faces. Instead, as can be seen from the issues posited to us, Calhoun rests his appeal on what he perceives to be procedural defects in the execution of the surveillance.

Calhoun was indicted and tried in both Baltimore County and Baltimore City. In the county he was sentenced to terms totaling fifty-five years. The term meted to him in the Circuit Court for Baltimore City was twenty years concurrent with the previous sentence. Both cases were consolidated on appeal.

The evidence to convict Calhoun was derived principally from telephone wiretaps. On four separate occasions the State's Attorney for Baltimore County applied for the issuance of a wiretap order. Each application was supported by the appropriate affidavit, signed and sworn to by two detectives of the Baltimore County Police Department's narcotics unit. The wiretap orders were issued by Judge James S. Sfekas of the Circuit Court for Baltimore County. Pursuant to Md.Cts. & Jud.Proc. Code Ann. § 10-408(f), all of the orders directed that progress reports be made to the judge by "the Baltimore County Police Department, the applicant, or a duly sworn Assistant State's Attorney for Baltimore County." The reports were to show what progress was being "made toward achievement of the authorized objectives" as well as the necessity, if any, "for continued interception...." The wiretap orders commanded that the progress reports be made to the issuing judge, no later than every seventy-two hours. The orders were, however, completely silent as to the mode of reporting.

During the period of surveillance, which continued from June 17 to August 14, 1985, Judge Sfekas received timely reports from the police. The progress reports that were submitted to Judge Sfekas consisted of updates from the wiretap logs. Those logs were records of the date and time of each telephone call received or made, as well as the telephone number called, if initiated from the tapped phone. The logs also contained a summary of the intercepted conversations. Notations were made in the log as to the pertinence of each intercepted call. If the progress report was submitted in person by the police officer, the judge was shown the logs and informed relative to any pertinent calls. When the report was made to Judge Sfekas by telephone, the police officer read the logs to the judge but did not comment on the content. Until the wiretap was terminated, the judge, at the end of each progress report, advised the reporting police officer to continue the interceptions.

The two questions Calhoun presents to us relate to compliance with Md. Cts. & Jud. Proc. Code Ann. § 10-408(f). That section of the Code states:

> Whenever an order authorizing interception is entered pursuant to this subtitle, the order shall require reports to be made to the judge who issued the order showing what progress has been made toward achievement of the authorized objective and the need for continued interception. The reports shall be made at the intervals the judge requires.

I.

Calhoun initially contends that the wiretap authorization order is defective because it permits law enforcement officials other than the State's Attorney to make the mandated progress report. Progress reports are an essential precondition for obtaining valid intercept authority. The legislatively required progress report is an integral part of the intercept stage and, therefore, strict compliance with it is necessary. Section 10-408(f) is, however, silent regarding the identity of the person who must provide the progress report to the issuing judge.

The appellant ... argues that the progress reports necessitated by § 10-408(f) must be made by the State's Attorney personally and not by a designated assistant or the police. That argument is bottomed on analogizing the progress report to the application for the wiretap order or to the request for postponement of notice to the suspect. The "Wiretap Act" specifically provides in § 10-406 that the application for an order to wiretap must be made by "[t]he Attorney General, State Prosecutor or any State's Attorney." The same requirement applies to the postponement of notice to the persons whose conversations had been intercepted.

We think the analogy employed by Calhoun falls short because progress reports, although mandated by the statute, are vested, insofar as the manner of report is concerned, in the absolute discretion of the issuing judge. The reports may be either oral or written, as the judge directs. The period of time covered by the report and the frequency of the reports are for the issuing judge to decide. Since the purpose of the report are solely to apprise the judge from time to time as to the progress that is being made toward the achievement of the objective of the electronic surveillance, we perceive no reason why one of the police officers who is actually engaged in the surveillance cannot make the progress reports to the issuing judge. Indeed, the officer is in a much better position to inform the judge, firsthand, about the progress of the surveillance than is the principal prosecuting attorney, who ordinarily would not have personal knowledge of the progress of the surveillance but must rely upon information received from the surveillance team. The principal prosecutor's reports to the judge, of necessity, would be grounded on second or thirdhand information. The statute does not require the principal prosecutor to make the progress reports personally to the issuing judge. There is nothing in the statute that directs the judge to receive secondhand information from the principal prosecutor when firsthand data is available through the police members of the surveillance team.

* * *

We now make explicit what we have heretofore made implicit, and we hold that § 10-408(f) permits the issuing judge to specify the identity of the reporting agent for the requisite progress reports, and that designation may include the law enforcement officers who are members of the surveillance team.

II.

Calhoun next assails the adequacy of the progress reports that were made by the police to the issuing judge. The progress reports consisted of logs kept by the surveillance team. The logs, we are informed by the transcript of the testimony, contained a summary of each intercepted conversation and the telephone number dialed from the tapped telephone, as well as the date and time of the interception. Calhoun avers that the reports were deficient because the reporting agents presented the issuing judge with the logs, leaving him to draw his own conclusions as to the progress that was being made toward the achievement of the objective of the investigation and the need for continued interception.

Under the federal statute, 18 U.S.C. § 2518(6), progress reports are not mandated, but the issuing judge may require them. The Maryland statutory counterpart, § 10-408(f), as we have seen, compels progress reports. In *Baldwin v. State, supra,* we explained the purpose of progress reports:

> Section 10-408(f) was enacted so as to *assure* the public that notwithstanding the issuance of a wiretap order, its use would be, insofar as possible, controlled by a neutral authority, the issuing judge, and that it would continue no longer than necessary so as to minimize the intrusion into the privacy of others.

413 A.2d at 255 (emphasis added). Under the federal statutory scheme, the issuing judge *may* require progress reports, but in Maryland the issuing judge *must* demand them. The particulars of the reports in both instances are left to the discretion of the issuing judge.

A defendant may attack the reporting aspects of a wiretap investigation on various grounds. To instantiate: an accused may assail the facial validity of the wiretap order on the basis that it does not contain a provision for progress reports, *Baldwin, supra,* or specify the reporting intervals, *Salzman, supra.* He may also challenge whether the judge-ordered reports were actually made to the issuing judge. *Pearson v. State,* 452 A.2d 1252 (1982).

Defendants may not, however, inquire into the mental processes by which the issuing judge determined whether to continue or terminate a surveillance. Defendants may not ask the issuing judge to explain why he or she continued a surveillance, and they may not ask another judge to review the progress reports and second-guess the issuing judge's continuing of a surveillance.

Although § 10-408(f) mandates that there be progress reports, the reports themselves are merely tools to assist the issuing judge in his overall supervision of the interception process. The reports, under Maryland law, are discoverable solely to ascertain that they exist and were not shams.[3]

JUDGMENTS AFFIRMED.

---

3. There can be no question but that Judge Sfekas actively supervised the wiretap investigation. Twice he personally visited the wiretap plant site. On at least six other occasions, he initiated contact

Notes and Questions

1. Notice how the Maryland wiretap statute is more restrictive than Title III because it requires, rather than permits, progress reports. *Compare* 18 U.S.C. § 2518(6) with Md. Cts & Jud. Proc. Code Ann. § 10-408(f).

2. When you initially watched *The Wire*, did it seem unusual to you that Detective McNulty and Prosecutor Pearlman had to meet with Judge Phelan to discuss the wiretap? For an illustration watch *The Wire*, Season 1, Episode 7 at 6:05 minutes. Why did these meetings occur?

3. Did the meetings with Judge Phalen seem strangely informal? Although Maryland's wiretapping statute requires progress reports, does *Calhoun v. State* signal that such reports need not be particularly formal or detailed? In the scene mentioned in note 2 above, Prosecutor Pearlman and Detective McNulty spend approximately thirty seconds telling the judge about the crimes committed by the Barksdale organization and the legitimate businesses being used to launder the money. The judge asks no probing questions and barely glances at any documentation (instead using his time to criticize McNulty's spelling ability). The judge says, "there's more than enough indication of progress to justify continued intercepts. I'll sign an order for thirty more days on all taps and phones." *See id* at 7:15 minutes. Does this seem like much of a progress report to you?

4. Finally, consider again the opening quote to this chapter, where Lester Freamon instructed the younger officers to seize the cell phones of drug dealers because "the case is in the phones, though we're going to need a Title III to take a look at them." *The Wire*, Season 5, Episode 9, at 4:15 minutes. Detective Freamon's statement is correct for real-time monitoring of cell phones. But is it correct when officers arrest a drug dealer and find a cellphone on his person? Many courts have held that police can conduct warrantless searches of text messages, call histories, photographs, and other data found on cell phones when the search is conducted incident to arrest. For an overview of this emerging area of law, see Adam M. Gershowitz, *Password Protected? Can a Password Save Your Cell Phone From a Search Incident to Arrest*, 96 Iowa L. Rev. 1125 (2011); Adam M. Gershowitz, *The iPhone Meets the Fourth Amendment*, 56 UCLA L. Rev. 27 (2008).

---

with the investigating officers for updates. While on vacation he telephoned for updates. The progress reports by the police constituted only a part of Judge Sfekas's diligent supervision.

Chapter III

The Crime of *The Wire*

A. Introduction

Through five seasons of *The Wire*, viewers are exposed to a lot of crime. The series depicts more than four-dozen murders. Politicians engage in blatant fraud, money laundering, and campaign finance violations. Union officials participate in racketeering. There is also a significant amount of theft, solicitation, armed robbery, assault, bribery, perjury, and prostitution. But, of course, none of these crimes are the heart of *The Wire*. The story centers around drugs and the wide-ranging conspiracies to distribute those drugs. The materials below examine the law of narcotics possession and distribution as well as conspiratorial liability.

B. Possession of a Controlled Substance

When interviewed about *The Wire*, David Simon and many of the cast members say the story is about Baltimore, rather than any particular character. To the extent *The Wire* focuses on a particular aspect of the criminal justice system though, it is the sale and use of illegal drugs, primarily heroin. When police catch an individual with a small amount of drugs on his person or in his car (assuming a valid search was conducted) the legal issues are simple. The defendant will be guilty of possession of a controlled substance, and the severity of the charge will depend on the quantity. In other situations, however, the legal questions surrounding drug charges are much more complex. What if — as often happens in *The Wire* — the corner boys keep the drugs nearby but not on their person? What if multiple people are in close proximity to the drugs and none admits to ownership? When drugs are in the stash-house, are the guards outside the front and back doors guilty of possession just like someone who was holding the drugs inside the house? When police find a large quantity of drugs, how do prosecutors prove that the defendant intended to distribute the drugs rather than consume them for personal use? Are there laws that punish kingpins like Avon Barksdale and Marlo Stanfield more stiffly than run-of-the-mill corner boys? And when is the quantity of drugs enough for federal officials to become involved? *The Wire* offers visual depictions of all of these problems, but very few actual legal answers. The materials below attempt to clarify these issues.

1. Constructive Possession by Proximity

In Re K.A.

682 N.E.2d 1233 (Ill. App. Ct. 2nd Dist. 1997)

Justice COLWELL delivered the opinion of the court:

The State filed a second supplemental delinquency petition against the respondent, K.A., seeking to have him adjudicated a delinquent minor and made a ward of the court pursuant to the Juvenile Court Act of 1987. The petition alleged that K.A. had committed the following offenses: unlawful possession of a controlled substance for knowingly and unlawfully possessing less than 15 grams of a substance containing cocaine; unlawful delivery of a controlled substance for knowingly and unlawfully possessing with the intent to deliver less than one gram of a substance containing cocaine; unlawful possession of a controlled substance for knowingly and unlawfully possessing more than 15 but less than 100 grams of a substance containing cocaine; and unlawful delivery of a controlled substance for knowingly and unlawfully possessing with the intent to deliver more than 15 but less than 100 grams of a substance containing cocaine. The trial court subsequently issued an order of adjudication finding K.A. to be a delinquent minor for committing the charged offenses ... K.A. appeals.

* * *

Testimony at the adjudicatory hearing revealed the following facts. Detective Joe Vincere testified that at approximately 12:10 p.m. on November 1, 1994, several members of the Rockford police department metro narcotics unit executed a search warrant at 313 South Fourth Street. The building at that address was a two-story dwelling containing three or four apartments. The search warrant was executed in a lower apartment.

Detective Vincere knocked on the rear door of the apartment and announced his office. He received no verbal response but heard some type of movement within. At that point, an officer used a battering ram to force open the door.

Detective Vincere was the first officer to enter the apartment. Detective Vincere immediately observed K.A. and Myron Taylor running in the living room toward the front door. K.A. exited the apartment behind Myron but stopped on command after about 40 yards. Myron continued running, was caught, and was returned to the apartment.

Detective Vincere estimated that, when he first observed K.A. and Myron, they were between one foot to three feet away from a McDonald's box under which cocaine was later discovered and five to six feet away from a closet in which cocaine was later discovered in a hole in the floor. The closet was located between the kitchen and the living room.

Detective Vincere testified that K.A. and Myron told him at the scene that they were visiting the apartment. Detective Vincere also testified that K.A. later told him that Myron had told him to go to the apartment the evening before the raid and that he had arrived at the apartment at about 11:45 a.m. to smoke a joint and listen to some music. K.A. explained that he ran because he was afraid. K.A. denied any knowledge of narcotics within the apartment.

Detective Vincere also testified that no cannabis was recovered in the apartment or on K.A. In addition, Detective Vincere admitted on cross-examination that no scales or cutting agents were recovered and that K.A. did not have a key to the apartment.

Detective Vincere further testified to the condition of the interior of the apartment. The apartment contained some McDonald's boxes in a garbage bag, an empty refrigerator, no furniture, except for a kitchen chair and some cushions, and no clothing. He did not recall observing any type of device to play music. He did not observe any indications that someone was staying in the apartment on a regular basis and no documents were located regarding the tenancy of the apartment.

Detective Vincere also testified that the apartment had been raided on three previous occasions within the last four months. The apartment was also under surveillance earlier in the morning prior to the November 1, 1994, raid. K.A. was never observed on any of the prior occasions or on the morning of the raid. Different people were present in the apartment on each occasion.

According to Detective Vincere, the rear door of the apartment was in bad condition from the previous raids. Although the door could be shut and locked, it was not very sturdy, meaning that anyone could enter the apartment through that door.

Detective Mark Welsh's testimony corroborated Detective Vincere's testimony regarding the interior of the apartment. According to Detective Welsh, the apartment was basically vacant of any furniture, food, or clothing, and it appeared no one lived there. He did not observe any machine capable of playing music. Detective Welsh did observe garbage, such as McDonald's boxes, around the apartment.

Detective Welsh also testified that he found a McDonald's box opened up and facing down in the living room. Under the box, Detective Welsh found 10 corners of clear plastic bags which contained an off-white, rock-like substance later identified as cocaine. In a hole in the floor of the closet, Detective Welsh also found two bags, each tied in a knot and containing several smaller corners of clear plastic bags with an off-white, rock-like substance later identified as cocaine. The closet was located between the kitchen and the living room about six to eight feet from the McDonald's box. There were a total of 87 smaller corners of plastic bags.

* * *

In the kitchen cupboards, Detective Welsh observed a large quantity of plastic bags with the corners cut off. The narcotics found in the apartment were wrapped in what appeared to be corners cut from plastic bags. Detective Welsh did not observe any drug paraphernalia, nor did he find any cannabis within the apartment or on K.A. or Myron.

Detective Welsh searched K.A. and found $140 in United States currency in his front pant pocket. K.A.'s mother testified that a few days before November 1, 1994, she gave K.A. $140 so he could buy some clothes.

K.A. testified that Myron told him to go to the apartment and that he arrived at about 11:45 a.m. K.A. knocked on the front door and Myron let him in. Myron was already in the apartment when K.A. arrived. K.A. spent most of his time in the living room without looking around the apartment. K.A. observed a television, some cushions, a boom box, some tapes, and some garbage in the apartment.

K.A. testified that he was listening to music for about 15 minutes when he heard an unusual sound coming from the back door. K.A. then observed the back door caving in and when he turned around he saw Myron unlocking and running out the front door. K.A. then followed Myron out the front door but stopped on command of the police.

K.A. did not think that Myron lived at the apartment but thought one of Myron's relatives lived in the apartment. K.A. testified that he had never been to the apartment before.

* * *

To establish the elements of unlawful possession of a controlled substance, the State must prove the defendant's knowledge of the possession of the controlled substance and that the controlled substance was in the defendant's immediate and exclusive control. Possession may be actual or constructive.

In the instant case, K.A. was clearly not in actual possession of a controlled substance, and the State does not make such a claim. Rather, the State contends that K.A. was in constructive possession of a controlled substance. Constructive possession exists without actual personal present dominion over a controlled substance, but with an intent and capability to maintain control and dominion. Constructive possession may be inferred from the defendant's exclusive control of the premises where narcotics were found. Once it is established that narcotics were found on premises under the defendant's control, it may be inferred that the defendant had the requisite knowledge and possession for a conviction of possession of a controlled substance, absent other facts and circumstances that might leave a reasonable doubt as to guilt in the minds of the jury.

Here, the narcotics were found in the apartment occupied by K.A. during the raid. The mere presence in the vicinity of contraband, however, cannot establish constructive possession. Nonetheless, where other circumstantial evidence is sufficiently probative, proof of proximity combined with inferred knowledge of the presence of contraband will support a finding of guilt on charges of possession.

In the instant case, there is a reasonable doubt, in light of the evidence when viewed as a whole, that the apartment where the drugs were found was under K.A.'s exclusive control. As a result, it cannot be inferred that the narcotics were in his constructive possession.

The record contains no evidence to prove that K.A. owned, rented, or resided in the apartment where the narcotics were found. One way to prove the necessary control over the premises is to show that the defendant lived there. The State presented no evidence of rental receipts, utility bills, or clothing to show that K.A. lived in the apartment. Additionally, K.A. denied residing at the apartment, and Detective Vincere admitted the police were unable to find proof of tenancy for the apartment. Proof of residency, however, "has little if any relevance to the issue of control" when the dwelling is a "drug house." *See People v. Lawton,* 625 N.E.2d 348 (Ill. App. 1993).

A drug house is a dwelling not used primarily as a residence but instead as a center for the packaging and distribution of drugs, and typically it contains very little or no furniture, appliances, food, or clothing. Detectives Vincere and Welsh both testified that the apartment contained very little furniture besides a chair and some cushions, no food, and no clothing. Neither observed any type of device to play music despite K.A.'s testimony that the apartment also contained a television and a radio. It appeared to both detectives that no one lived in the apartment. Thus, K.A. was present in a drug house at the time of the raid. As a result, the fact that K.A. did not own, rent, or reside in the apartment is not fatal to a finding that he controlled the apartment and therefore constructively possessed the drugs found therein.

Even though residence is not a major factor in determining control of a drug house, the State must still prove the defendant's control over a drug house to establish constructive possession....

In this case, however, the State did not present any evidence of K.A.'s fingerprints on the narcotics or on any drug paraphernalia in the apartment. There was no evidence of drug paraphernalia, and the State presented no testimony to characterize the cut plastic bags as drug paraphernalia. In addition, there was no evidence of cocaine residue or any other drugs on K.A. Furthermore, the police never found a key to the apartment and there was no evidence that K.A. admitted owning a key to the apartment. In fact, K.A. testified that Myron was already in the apartment and let K.A. into the apartment when he arrived. Finally, the narcotics were not in plain sight; they were concealed. Detective Welsh testified that the narcotics under the McDonald's box and in the hole in the closet could not be seen.

* * *

In addition, the State presented no evidence to prove that K.A. was ever present at the apartment on any other prior occasion or that he frequently visited the apartment....

The State also presented no evidence to establish that K.A. kept any personal belongings in the apartment or that K.A. was attempting to dispose of the narcotics.

K.A. was also not present at the apartment for a significant amount of time prior to the raid. At most, K.A. was present in the apartment for 25 minutes, and he could have been present for as little as 15 minutes.

Moreover, K.A. was not alone when the police executed the search warrant. Myron was also present during this raid. In addition, Detective Vincere testified that the apartment was basically available to anyone since the rear door was so fragile and other people did access the apartment as evidenced by the presence of different people during each of the prior raids.

* * *

Finally, K.A. did not admit that he possessed or controlled the apartment. On the contrary, K.A. specifically told Detective Vincere that he did not reside at the apartment, that Myron told him to go to the apartment, and that he was there to smoke a joint and listen to some music. In addition, K.A. testified that he thought a relative of Myron's lived at the apartment.

The only factors tending to show K.A.'s control of the apartment are too weak when viewed in light of the overall circumstances. For example, even though K.A. was present when the police executed the search warrant, presence alone is insufficient to prove control over premises. In addition, K.A. was in possession of $140, but his mother testified that she gave him the money. Finally, although K.A. fled from the scene, flight may only be considered along with other factors tending to establish guilt; flight by itself is not sufficient to establish guilt.

In sum, the record shows that the State only proved that K.A. was present in a drug house where the police found drugs and that K.A. fled the apartment. In light of the overall circumstances of this case, the State failed to prove beyond a reasonable doubt that K.A. exercised control over the apartment. Therefore, the State failed to prove K.A.'s possession of the narcotics beyond a reasonable doubt.

* * *

Notes and Questions

1. Do you believe K.A.'s story? Do you think he was involved in the distribution of drugs? What else could he plausibly be doing in the apartment (particularly if there was no device to play music, as he contended he was there for)?

2. Do you believe K.A.'s mother that the $140 in his pocket was to buy clothes? Watch *The Wire*, Season 4, Episode 2, at 29:40 minutes. After Detective Carver approaches juveniles near a stolen car, everyone flees. Eventually, an officer spots Randy running in an alley and stops him. The officer searches Randy and pulls $200 out of his front pocket. Marlo Stanfield had given the $200 to Randy to buy loyalty among the neighborhood kids, but Randy does not admit that he got the money from Marlo. Instead, he claims: "my foster mother gave me that to buy school clothes with." The officer does not believe Randy. Would you have believed him? Consider again K.A.'s mother's story that the $140 in K.A.'s pocket was to buy clothes. Do you believe her? Does she have an incentive to lie?

3. The court states the rule that proximity to drugs, without evidence of anything further, typically is not enough for constructive possession. Is this a good rule? Have you ever been present at a party where drugs were openly being consumed? Should you be guilty of possession if you fail to leave the party promptly? Is there a difference between being at a party where drugs are present and being in a known drug house that is not used by anyone as a residence and has as its primary purpose the distribution of drugs?

4. What if the police had found a very large amount of drugs hidden in the house? Would that change your opinion about whether K.A. was guilty of constructive possession?

Cottman v. State
886 A.2d 932 (Md. Ct. Spec. App. 2005)

KENNEY, J.

Nathaniel Cottman, Jr., appellant, was convicted in the Circuit Court for Baltimore County of distribution of cocaine, conspiracy to distribute cocaine, and possession of cocaine. Appellant was sentenced, as a repeat offender, to ten years' incarceration without the possibility of parole, for the distribution conviction. The remaining convictions were merged for sentencing purposes.

* * *

For the following reasons, we shall affirm appellant's convictions.

FACTUAL AND PROCEDURAL HISTORY

In the early morning hours of August 14, 2002, appellant and Ms. Benson were arrested following the completion of a drug deal with Earnest Moore, an undercover Baltimore County Police Detective....

Detective Moore, a member of the Essex Community Drug and Violence Interdiction Team, was the State's only witness. At approximately 5:45 on the morning of August 14, 2002, he was wearing "undercover clothes" and driving an unmarked sport utility vehicle on Dartford Road in Essex. He witnessed several individuals leaning against a car parked in front of 1614 Dartford Road. A woman, later identified as "Ms. Benson," shouted: "Hey, come here." Detective Moore pulled his vehicle to the curb and Benson, along with a male Detective Moore identified as appellant, approached.

Benson stood next to the driver's window. Appellant stood at the driver's mirror and leaned toward the driver's window, approximately two to three feet from Detective Moore. Benson asked Detective Moore whether he was a police officer, and he replied that he was not. Appellant then inquired: "Are you sure you're not police?" Detective Moore repeated his denial. Benson asked Detective Moore if he had been drinking, and lying, Detective Moore claimed that he had. Benson smelled his breath, and said, "Yeah, he's all right." Appellant walked to the front of the police vehicle and looked up and down the street. Detective Moore said that "lookouts" "commonly traveled with drug dealers in that area," and during drug transactions, "will keep a lookout to try to identify any police that are in the area." According to Detective Moore, appellant's actions were consistent with a drug dealer's lookout.

While appellant was standing at the front of the vehicle, Benson asked Detective Moore what he wanted. Detective Moore responded that he wanted $20 worth of cocaine, and Benson retrieved a small bag of cocaine from her mouth. She exchanged the bag for a $20 bill Detective Moore presented. During the transaction, Detective Moore saw appellant's face for "20 seconds, maybe at the most."

As he drove away, Detective Moore witnessed Benson and appellant walk together toward the group in front of 1614 Dartford Road. He notified the surveillance units working with him that he had made a drug purchase and described appellant and Benson. Two to three minutes later, he returned to Dartford Road and walked to where appellant and Benson were being detained. Detective Moore identified both as the individuals involved in the earlier transaction. At trial, Detective Moore again identified appellant and testified that he had no doubt regarding his identification.

Incident to his arrest, appellant was searched, but no drugs or money was found. The substance in the bag Benson gave to Detective Moore was later analyzed and found to contain 0.2 grams of cocaine. Appellant stipulated that the substance in the bag was cocaine, and the drugs were admitted into evidence.

* * *

The circuit court found Detective Moore's testimony "very credible," and concluded that appellant had aided and abetted the distribution of drugs and found him guilty of distribution of cocaine, conspiracy to distribute cocaine, and possession of cocaine....

DISCUSSION

* * *

II.

Appellant ... contends that the evidence was insufficient to sustain his convictions.... [He maintains that] the State "failed to prove that the male subject exercised the requisite dominion and control over the cocaine to justify any rational trier of fact in concluding that he 'possessed' the cocaine at issue."

* * *

Appellant claims that, even if Detective Moore's testimony is credited, the evidence, viewed in the light most favorable to the State, merely demonstrated that appellant was present at the scene at the time the sale occurred. Because there was no evidence that he held the cocaine or the money, or otherwise directed Benson, the evidence was insufficient to permit a rational trier of fact to conclude that he exercised dominion or control over the cocaine.

In response, the State asserts that, although the cocaine was produced from Benson's mouth, there was sufficient evidence presented from which "it could be inferred ... that this was Benson's and [appellant's] method of concealing their cocaine before it was distributed to their buyers." Therefore, the State maintains, there was sufficient evidence for a rational trier of fact to find that appellant was in constructive possession of the cocaine. Alternatively, the State contends that "a determination by this Court that the evidence was insufficient to show that [appellant] possessed the cocaine at issue would not require reversal of [appellant's] convictions for distribution of cocaine or conspiracy to distribute cocaine. [Appellant's] conviction for distribution was based on an aiding and abetting theory."

* * *

"Under Maryland law, one may commit an offense as either a principal in the first degree, or a principal in the second degree." *Evans v. State,* 855 A.2d 291 (2004). The actual perpetrator of a crime is termed the first degree principal. "[O]ne who encourages, aids, abets, or assists the active perpetrator in the commission of the offense, is a guilty participant, and in the eye of the law is equally culpable with the one who does the act." *Grandison v. State,* 506 A.2d 580 (1986). "'A second degree principal must be either actually or constructively present at the commission of a criminal offense and aid, counsel, command, or encourage the commission of that offense.'" *Owens* [*v. State*], 867 A.2d 334 (2005).... A principal in the second degree, "in the eye of the law[,] is equally culpable with the one who does the act." *Grandison,* 506 A.2d 580.

A person's mere presence at the scene of the crime is not sufficient to establish that he or she participated in the crime. It is, nonetheless, "an important element" in determining whether that person participated in the crime.

A. Distribution of Cocaine Conviction

In *McMorris v. State,* 338 A.2d 912 (1975), this Court upheld a conviction for distribution of heroin of the person who brokered and directed a sale of heroin between an undercover police officer and another individual. In so doing, we reasoned that, "[a]lthough appellant was not shown to have been in actual possession of the drug, he was an aider and abettor in its distribution and thus responsible as a principal in the second degree." *Id.* at 912.

Here, the circuit court credited Detective Moore's testimony that appellant acted as the "lookout" during the drug sale. Appellant stood next to Benson when she inquired into whether Detective Moore was a police officer. After Detective Moore denied being an officer, appellant again queried the prospective purchaser in order to be "sure" that he was not a police officer, and after further checking, Benson assured appellant that Detective Moore was "all right." Not until then did the sale begin, and not until then did appellant walk to the front of Detective Moore's vehicle. This evidence supports an inference that appellant knew of the presence of the drugs and of the impending sale; otherwise, appellant would have had no reason to question Detective Moore or act as a "lookout." Under these circumstances, a reasonable fact finder could conclude that appellant encouraged and assisted Benson in the distribution of cocaine.

B. Possession of Cocaine Conviction

Based on the arguments presented in their respective briefs, it appears that both appellant and the State presume that a defendant cannot be convicted of possession of controlled dangerous substances under an aiding and abetting theory. Although it appears to be a matter of first impression in Maryland, the majority of courts addressing the issue have concluded that nothing in statutes criminalizing possession of controlled dangerous substances precludes the application of general accomplice liability law.

We find *Bullock v. United States,* 709 A.2d 87 (D.C.1998), instructive. In that case, police observed the activities of three men on a street in a "high drug area." One of the suspects, Bullock, handed a bundle of packets to another suspect, Davis. Davis secreted the packets at the base of a nearby tree. Afterwards, the third suspect, Rawlinson, approached Davis and the two engaged in a conversation. Although the surveilling officer could not hear what was said, Davis gestured towards the tree and Rawlinson nodded in response.

During the surveillance, Rawlinson directed a passerby to Davis, who thereafter appeared to sell the pedestrian drugs from the stash. For approximately the next hour, Davis appeared to engage in five or six more drug transactions with pedestrians. After each sale, Davis reportedly gave the proceeds to Bullock, who lingered in a nearby alley. The officer also witnessed the three men confer with one another in a group.

The surveilling officer ordered the arrest of the three suspects. Incident to his arrest, $115 was found in Bullock's pockets, and the arresting officers uncovered two small cellophane bags containing heroin at the base of the tree. No drugs or money were found on Rawlinson. At trial, in addition to the testimony of the surveillance officer and the evidence obtained at the arrest scene, an expert testified regarding the operation of "open-air drug enterprises." The expert explained that such drug enterprises typically consist of a "runner" that "solicit[s] potential customers and direct [s] them to the 'holder,' who supervised the supply of drugs." A jury convicted Bullock of distribution of heroin and both Bullock and Rawlinson were convicted of possession of heroin with intent to distribute.

On appeal, considering Rawlinson's challenge to his conviction for possession with intent to distribute, the District of Columbia Court of Appeals initially noted that "Rawlinson's case was submitted to the jury under two alternative theories, as a principal and as an aider and abettor." *Id.* at 93. With regard to the constructive possession theory, the Court determined that "the jury could infer that Rawlinson knew the location of the stash and that he shared both the ability and intent to exercise dominion and control over the stash by the tree." *Id.* Alternatively, the *Bullock* Court reasoned that "the same evidence was sufficient to sustain Rawlinson's conviction under an aiding and abetting theory." *Id.* According to the District of Columbia Court of Appeals, to be convicted of aiding and abetting possession with intent to distribute, "the government must prove that (1) someone committed the [possession with intent to distribute] offense as a principal and (2) appellant knowingly assisted or participated in the principal's offense." *Id.* at 94. The court concluded that there was sufficient evidence that either Davis or Bullock possessed the heroin, and that "the jury could infer from the government's evidence that Rawlinson knowingly assisted or participated in the [possession with intent to distribute] by acting as a runner." *Id.*

In the instant case, as in *Bullock,* there was sufficient evidence to sustain appellant's conviction for possession of cocaine under either an aiding and abetting theory or a constructive possession theory. Maryland Code (2002), §5-601(a)(1) of the Criminal Law Article ("C.L."), makes it a crime to "possess or administer to another a controlled dangerous substance, unless obtained directly or by prescription or order from an authorized provider acting in the course of professional practice[.]" C.L. §5-101(u) defines "possess," in relevant part, as "to exercise actual or constructive dominion or control over a thing by one or more persons." The Court of Appeals has explained that "[t]o prove control, the '"evidence must show directly or support a rational inference that the control over the prohibited ... drug in the sense contemplated by the statute, *i.e.,* that [the accused] exercised some restraining or direct influence over it."'" *White v. State,* 767 A.2d 855 (2001). Moreover, "'[k]nowledge of the presence of an object is normally a prerequisite to exercising dominion and control.'" *Id.* . . . .

Possession need not be exclusive, but may be joint. It is also not necessary that the drugs be on appellant's person for him to possess them. In cases where two or more people were charged with the possession of contraband in a home or vehicle, we have relied upon the following factors in determining whether there was joint possession:

> (1) the proximity between the defendant and the contraband, (2) the fact that the contraband was within the view or otherwise within the knowledge of the de-

fendant, (3) ownership or some possessory right in the premises or the automobile in which the contraband is found, or (4) the presence or circumstances
from which a reasonable inference could be drawn that the defendant was participating with others in the mutual use and enjoyment of the contraband.

Hall [*v. State*], 705 A.2d 50 (1998).

Here, the evidence was clearly sufficient to establish that appellant assisted Benson in
selling cocaine to Detective Moore. Appellant was always in close proximity to Benson,
who physically transported the cocaine in her mouth. The circumstances permit the reasonable inference that the existence and the purpose of the cocaine was within appellant's
knowledge, and that he was participating with Benson in the sale. To be sure, appellant,
by engaging in the determination of the prospective buyer's good faith, and by acting as
a "lookout" during the sale, assisted Benson in distributing the cocaine, but his presence
also served to protect Benson's physical possession of the drugs prior to the sale. Therefore, the evidence was sufficient to sustain appellant's conviction for possession of cocaine as a second degree principal.

* * *

Alternatively, a rational trier of fact could have concluded that appellant, along with Benson, constructively exercised dominion and control over the cocaine. Appellant approached
Detective Moore's vehicle with Benson and stood next to her immediately prior to the sale.
As discussed above, his knowledge of the presence of the cocaine can be inferred from his
question posed to Detective Moore. Although no money or drugs were found on appellant
incident to his arrest, it is a rational inference that appellant had "earned" some portion of
the proceeds from the sale or other consideration by acting as a lookout and protecting both
Benson and the drugs, such that he shared in the mutual use and enjoyment of the cocaine.
His concern that Detective Moore might be a police officer and his acting as a lookout during the transaction permits an inference that appellant exercised a restraining influence over
the cocaine. In other words, he could halt the sale in the event that he sensed police involvement or intervention. Viewing the evidence, and the inferences derived therefrom, in
the light most favorable to the prosecution, we are persuaded that a reasonable fact finder
could have found that appellant was in constructive joint possession of the cocaine.

* * *

The evidence was, therefore, sufficient to sustain each of appellant's convictions.

* * *

———————

Notes and Questions

1. Do you understand the difference between a theory of criminal liability based on constructive possession and one based on aiding and abetting?

2. Are you convinced by the court's argument in the alternative that Cottman "constructively exercised dominion and control over the cocaine"? Wasn't the cocaine in Benson's
mouth the entire time? How could Cottman have exercised any control over the cocaine?

3. Does the *Bullock* case (described by the court in *Cottman*) resemble the open-air
drug markets portrayed in *The Wire*?

4. Watch *The Wire*, Season 1, Episode 3, at 44:00 minutes in which Omar breaks into
a stash house and takes drugs from under the kitchen sink in an apartment. Which char-

acters from the Barksdale gang were in constructive possession of the heroin before Omar arrived? Certainly the young boys sitting in the stash house who knew the location of the heroin were in constructive possession. But what about Bodie and the crew he was running in the courtyard? Would prosecutors be able to prove that they were in constructive possession?

5. Watch *The Wire*, Season 4, Episode 3, at 11:15 minutes. Three men want to buy drugs. Bodie points them toward Little Kevin, who takes their money and signals to Michael across the street so that Michael will know how much each man paid. Michael then runs into an alley to get the drugs and serves the drugs around the corner. Obviously, Michael is in possession of the drugs because he is holding them. Could a prosecutor demonstrate that Bodie and Little Kevin were in constructive possession though? Are they in physical proximity to the drugs?

6. Can a defendant be in constructive possession of narcotics if the drugs are intercepted just before the defendant would have acquired them? Consider a situation where a correctional officer reviews incoming mail and sees a postcard addressed to an inmate. Upon closer inspection, the officer notices that the mail is actually two postcards glued together with a small amount of cocaine in the middle. The officer seizes the cocaine before the mail is delivered to the prisoner. Is the defendant guilty on a theory of constructive possession? *See* In re Rothwell, 78 Cal. Rptr. 3d 723 (Cal. App. 4th Dist. 2008).

7. What if Cottman had no idea what amount of drugs Benson was hiding in her mouth? What if the quantity was very large and thus carried a huge sentence? Could Cottman be punished to the same extent as Benson if he had no idea of the quantity? The next case addresses this question.

2. Drug Quantity: Issues with Mens Rea and Adulterants

Whitaker v. People
48 P.3d 555 (Colo. 2002)

Justice HOBBS delivered the Opinion of the Court.

A jury convicted the defendant, David Whitaker, of possessing with intent to distribute over 1,000 grams of methamphetamine, a schedule II controlled substance, and importing methamphetamine into Colorado. Whitaker claimed that his conviction should be reversed because the trial judge did not instruct the jury to apply the mens rea of "knowingly" to both the quantity and the importation of the drug. The court of appeals upheld Whitaker's conviction. We agree.

We hold that the General Assembly, in section 18-18-405, did not intend to apply a culpable mental state to the quantity of drugs the defendant distributed, manufactured, dispensed, sold, or possessed....

I.

On January 14, 1998, David Whitaker was a passenger on a Greyhound bus en route from Los Angeles, California to Denver, Colorado. The bus stopped in Grand Junction, Colorado for routine service and to change drivers. Passengers were required to leave the bus during this stop. After the passengers had reboarded, three Grand Junction Police Department officers entered the bus, identifying themselves as police officers. Two of the officers began talking to each of the bus passengers, including Whitaker.

The officers testified that Whitaker appeared nervous while talking to them. When asked about his luggage, Whitaker told the police that he had none. The officers pointed to a black bag near Whitaker and asked if it was his. Whitaker responded that it was not his bag, but said he had placed his jacket and a few other items inside it because no one else appeared to be using it. Whitaker then consented to a search of the bag. The officers discovered 8.8 pounds of uncut methamphetamine contained in several duct tape covered packages inside the bag.

The prosecution charged Whitaker with several drug offenses. At trial, Whitaker argued that he did not possess the drugs and did not know that the packages of drugs were in the bag. The defense did not dispute the facts that the bag contained 8.8 pounds of methamphetamine and that the drugs came across Colorado's state lines via the Greyhound bus. The jury convicted Whitaker of possessing 1,000 grams or more of a schedule II controlled substance with intent to distribute and importation of a schedule II controlled substance. The trial court sentenced him to twenty years in state prison.

The court of appeals affirmed Whitaker's conviction and sentence.... It held that the prosecution need not prove that Whitaker "knowingly" imported the controlled substance, nor that the defendant "knew" the drugs weighed more than 1,000 grams....

* * *

II.

We hold that the General Assembly, in section 18-18-405, did not intend to apply a culpable mental state to the quantity of drugs the defendant distributed, manufactured, dispensed, sold, or possessed. We also hold that importation under Colorado's special offender statute, section 18-18-407, does not include a mens rea requirement. The jury found beyond a reasonable doubt that the defendant possessed the drug quantity specified by section 18-18-405(3)(a)(III), and imported the drugs across state lines as specified by section 18-18-407(1)(d). Accordingly, we uphold Whitaker's conviction and sentence.

A.
Section 18-18-405 and Quantity of Drug

* * *

... Section 18-18-405(3)(a)(III) defines the required sentence for a defendant convicted of unlawful distribution, manufacturing, dispensing, sale or possession of 1,000 grams or more of a schedule I or II controlled substance.[3]

Whitaker argues that the quantity of drugs contained in section 18-18-405(3)(a)(III) is an essential element of the crime of possession with intent to distribute, and the mens

---

3. Section 18-18-405(3)(a)(III), 6 C.R.S. (2001), provides:

(3)(a) Except as otherwise provided in section 18-18-407 relating to special offenders, any person convicted pursuant to paragraph (a) of subsection (2) of this section for knowingly manufacturing, dispensing, selling, distributing, possessing, or possessing with intent to manufacture, dispense, sell, or distribute, or inducing, attempting to induce, or conspiring with one or more other persons, to manufacture, dispense, sell, distribute, possess, or possess with intent to manufacture, dispense, sell, or distribute an amount that is or has been represented to be:

...

(III) One thousand grams or one kilogram or more of any material, compound, mixture, or preparation that contains a schedule I or schedule II controlled substance as listed in section 18-18-203 or 18-18-204 shall be sentenced to the department of corrections for a term greater than the maximum presumptive range but not more than twice the maximum presumptive range provided for such offense in section 18-1-105(1)(a).

rea contained in section 18-18-405(1)(a), "knowingly," must apply to it. However, whether the quantity of drugs involved in the offense requires a mens rea is a matter of statutory interpretation. "Our fundamental responsibility in interpreting a statute is to give effect to the General Assembly's purpose and intent in enacting the statute." *Empire Lodge Homeowners' Ass'n v. Moyer*, 39 P.3d 1139, 1152 (Colo.2001). "If the plain language of the statute clearly expresses the legislative intent, then the court must give effect to the ordinary meaning of the statutory language. Likewise, the court should avoid interpreting a statute in a way that defeats the obvious intent of the legislature." *Pediatric Neurosurgery, P.C. v. Russell*, 44 P.3d 1063, 1068 (Colo.2002). We must read the statute as a whole, construing each provision consistently and in harmony with the overall statutory design, if possible.

Here, section 18-18-405(1)(a) defines the offense, and the provisions of 18-18-405(2), (3), (5) and (6) set forth the applicable punishment levels.[4] This statutory structure demonstrates the General Assembly's intent to separate sentencing factors, such as drug type and quantity, from the elements of the crime. Section 18-18-405(3)(a) does not prescribe drug quantity as an element of the offense, nor does it require proof of a culpable mental state in regards to it....

Although section 18-18-405(1)(a) requires the prosecution to prove that the defendant "knowingly" distributed, manufactured, dispensed, sold or possessed the controlled substance, nothing in the statute's language suggests that the prosecution must show that the defendant "knew" the actual weight of the drugs under section 18-18-405(3)(a). To the contrary, section 18-18-405(3)(a) triggers the level of punishment upon proof that the drug quantity involved in the offense was "an amount that is or has been represented to be" the amount specified by subsections (I), (II), or (III) thereunder....

The statute thereby sets forth the drug quantity separately from the elements, with no *mens rea* requirement and with the apparent design of separating the applicable punishment from the creation and definition of the offense.

Any amount of drugs, even less than a usable quantity, can support a conviction under 18-18-405(1)(a). The quantity of drugs turns on objective standards and requires no inquiry into the defendant's state of mind.

The underlying purpose of section 18-18-405(3) is to punish more severely those offenders who deal with large quantities of controlled substances. The legislature's choice to do so is within its prerogative. Section 18-18-405(3)(a) does not create an additional element for the underlying substantive offense; rather, it defines circumstances that, if proven beyond a reasonable doubt, may require a sentence greater than the presumptive minimum contained in section 18-1-105(1)(a), 6 C.R.S. (2001).

* * *

Accordingly, we affirm the judgment of the court of appeals upholding Whitaker's conviction and sentence.

———————

4. Subsection (1) defines the elements of the offense covered by this statute. Subsection (2) defines the level of felony to be applied based upon the type of drug involved in the offense. Subsection (3) defines the required sentence for offenses involving various large quantities of drugs. Subsection (5) works to apply subsection (3) to those defendants who commit a section 18-18-405 offense two or more times within six months and the violations involve an aggregate amount of at least 25 grams of a controlled substance. Subsection (6) requires revocation of the offender's driver's license upon conviction.

Notes and Questions

1. Most other courts to confront the question have reached the same conclusion as *Whitaker*: Prosecutors must prove that the defendant knew he possessed drugs, but they do not need to show mens rea as to the quantity. *See* Richard Singer, *The Model Penal Code and Three Two (Possibly Only One) Ways Courts Avoid Mens Rea*, 4 Buff. Crim. L. Rev. 139 (2000). In one prominent decision—People v. Ryan, 626 N.E.2d 51 (1993)—the court concluded that prosecutors must demonstrate knowledge of the weight of the drugs. The New York legislature promptly overturned the decision. *See* William J. Stuntz & Joseph L. Hoffman, Defining Crime 378 (2011).

2. In *The Wire*, did runners and lookouts like Wallace have any idea how large the stash was that they were helping to sell? Were they in constructive possession of the entire stash? Were they criminally responsible for the entire stash under an accomplice liability theory?

3. Watch *The Wire*, Season 1, Episode 7, at 9:30 minutes. The police officers make a plan to catch Stinkum when he brings $40,000 worth of drugs to the courtyard for the "re-up." When the police try to pull over Stinkum's vehicle he flees and eventually a passenger in the vehicle—a low-level drug runner—jumps out of the vehicle and tries to get away with the drugs. After a chase, the police eventually capture him. Do you think the runner had any idea what quantity of drugs was in the package he jumped out of the vehicle with?

4. Is it fair to hold runners and lookouts responsible for the full amount of drugs in the package if they had no idea of the quantity? Do those involved in the drug trade willingly take the risk of a large quantity because they know they are engaged in illegal behavior generally?

United States v. Berroa-Medrano

303 F.3d 277 (3rd Cir. 2002)

FUENTES, Circuit Judge.

This case requires us to consider what constitutes a "mixture or substance containing a detectable amount" of a controlled substance for purposes of sentencing. Pursuant to a plea agreement, defendant Juan Berroa-Medrano ("Berroa") pled guilty to a single count of conspiracy to distribute heroin, but reserved the right to challenge at sentencing the weight of the heroin in question. At sentencing, although one of the two packages Berroa admitted to distributing contained mostly drug cutting agents and only trace amounts of heroin, the court used the total weight of the two packages as the basis to sentence Berroa to a 100-month prison term. On appeal, Berroa challenges the sentence on the grounds that the court improperly considered the gross weight of the two packages, about 1 kilogram, rather than the net weight of the heroin itself. Because we conclude that the District Court was entitled to consider the entire weight of any mixture or substance that contained a trace amount of heroin, we affirm.

I.
A.

The facts of this case are fairly straightforward. Berroa entered into an agreement with his co-defendant Mustafa Alabed to sell an undetermined amount of heroin to an individual who was actually a confidential informant. On October 28, 1997, the informant, equipped with a wireless transmitter, met with Alabed to arrange for the purchase of one kilogram of heroin.

The informant and Alabed met inside Alabed's carpet store in Philadelphia, and then, to complete the transaction, walked across the street to a building that Alabed was renovating. Inside the building, the two men met Berroa, who was holding a cereal box. Berroa handed the box to the informant, who opened it and found that it contained two separately wrapped packages, one large and one small, each containing an off-white substance that appeared to be heroin. The informant inspected the packages without removing the contents, and returned the box to Berroa, asking the defendants whether the heroin was from the same batch as a sample that had been given to him earlier in the day by Alabed. Alabed assured him that it was. The informant left the building, ostensibly to retrieve the payment for the heroin, but instead informed the drug enforcement agents of what had transpired. When he informed them that he believed Berroa was carrying a gun, the agents decided to wait for backup. Before backup arrived, however, Berroa fled the scene.

Once the backup officers arrived, Alabed was arrested and the cereal box containing the two packages of off-white powder was seized. The larger of the packages, which was approximately the size and shape of a kilo of heroin, was field-tested by the agents with negative results for the presence of heroin. However, the smaller package, which was on top of the larger one inside the cereal box, field-tested positive for heroin. The smaller package contained slightly more than one ounce of off-white powder. Subsequent laboratory analysis disclosed that the larger package weighed slightly less than one kilogram (983.9 grams) and was comprised almost exclusively of procaine and lidocaine, common heroin cutting agents. The lab also determined that the larger package contained traces of heroin, but the purity of the drug could not be determined due to its small quantity. The smaller package, weighing 32 grams, contained a similar mix of cutting agents, but with heroin detected at a purity of 3%.

B.

On December 3, 1997, a federal grand jury indicted Berroa ... and charged him with conspiracy to distribute heroin in violation of 21 U.S.C. § 846; distribution of heroin in violation of 21 U.S.C. § 841(a)(1) and 18 U.S.C. § 2; and distribution of heroin near a school in violation of 21 U.S.C. §§ 860(a) and 841(a)(1)....

On February 22, 1999, Berroa pled guilty, pursuant to a written plea agreement, to a single count of a superseding information charging distribution of heroin.... Berroa's plea agreement contained a provision stating that the parties "have not agreed on the quantity of drugs on which the defendant's sentence should be calculated under[the relevant sentencing guidelines], and reserve their right to present their respective positions to the Court and Probation Department."

On May 2, 2001, the District Court sentenced Berroa. The District Court concluded that under the United States Sentencing Guidelines, the entire contents of each package must be included in calculating Berroa's sentence. The court therefore determined that Berroa's offense conduct involved more than one kilogram of heroin, and that, accordingly, Berroa's sentencing guideline range was 168–210 months. However, because of the unusually low purity of the drug, the court granted Berroa a downward departure under U.S.S.G. § 2D1.1(b)(6), and sentenced him to 100 months imprisonment, 5 years supervised release, and a fine of $2,500. Berroa timely appealed.

In this case, the Government acknowledged the District Court's discretion to depart downward based on low purity and does not challenge the exercise of the Court's discretion in this regard on appeal. Accordingly, we need not reach this issue here.

* * *

III.
A.

The District Court calculated Berroa's sentence using the Drug Quantity Table, subsection (c) of U.S.S.G. § 2D1.1. Application Note (A) of the "Notes to Drug Quantity Table" provides that, "[u]nless otherwise specified, the weight of a controlled substance set forth in the table refers to *the entire weight of any mixture or substance containing a detectable amount of the controlled substance*" U.S. Sentencing Guidelines Manual § 2D1.1(c), cmt. n.A. (emphasis added). The language is derived from the mandatory minimum sentence provision of the statute under which Berroa was convicted. Section 841(b) provides minimum penalties for anyone violating § 841(a), including "100 grams or more *of a mixture or substance containing a detectable amount of heroin*" 21 U.S.C. § 841(b)(1)(B)(i) (emphasis added). The District Court examined this language and determined that, under the circumstances of Berroa's case, it was required to include the combined weight of both packages in calculating Berroa's sentence. The judge commented that, although it was "unusual" in his experience that a lab was "unable to determine the purity of [the drug in question,]" he could not "ignore [that] ... [t]here was a detectable amount of a [controlled] substance" in the larger package....

The District Court was not without precedent in deciding to include the entire contents of the larger, highly adulterated package in sentencing Berroa. For example, this Court recently determined that, even when a drug contains a very slight amount of a controlled substance, the entire package must count toward a defendant's sentence. *See United States v. Butch*, 256 F.3d 171, 177–80 (3d Cir.2001) (instructing that the District Court must include the gross weight of Endocet pills in calculating a defendant's mandatory minimum sentence under § 841(b), even though the controlled substance (oxycodone) in the pills was merely 0.8% of the total weight of the pills); *see also United States v. Touby*, 909 F.2d 759, 772–73 (3d Cir.1990) (holding that the entire weight of 100-gram slab of Euphoria must be considered by sentencing court, even though the controlled substance only comprised 2.7% of the total weight); *United States v. Buggs*, 904 F.2d 1070, 1077, 1079–80 (7th Cir.1990) (upholding sentence under § 841(b) for mixture containing 1.2% heroin). Nevertheless, Berroa attempts to distinguish his case by arguing that an immeasurably small "trace" of a controlled substance, together with an overwhelming amount of cutting agent, is neither a "mixture" nor a "substance," either as those terms are commonly understood or as intended by the statute or the Sentencing Guidelines.

The Supreme Court has observed that since the terms "mixture" and "substance" have "not been defined in the statute or the Sentencing Guidelines and [have] no distinctive common-law meaning," they should be "construed ... to have their ordinary meaning." *Neal v. United States*, 516 U.S. 284, 289 (1996) (citing *Chapman v. United States*, 500 U.S. 453, 461–62, (1991)). In Chapman, the Supreme Court analyzed a provision of the Comprehensive Drug Abuse Prevention and Control Act, 21 U.S.C. § 841, *et seq.*, that calls for a mandatory minimum sentence of five years for the distribution of any "mixture or substance" containing LSD that weighed one gram or more. *Chapman* 500 U.S. at 455, (quoting 21 U.S.C. § 841(b)(1)(B)(v)). The question before the Court was whether, for sentencing purposes, the weight of LSD should also include the blotter paper that is routinely sold with LSD. *Id.* at 458. The *Chapman* court reasoned that, because the LSD was "diffused among the fibers of the paper ... [and] cannot be distinguished from the blotter paper nor easily separated from it," the entire package constituted a mixture, and therefore, the total weight of the blotter paper along with the absorbed LSD must be considered under the statute. *Id.* at 462.

Like the LSD and blotter paper in *Chapman*, the traces of heroin in the package used to sentence Berroa were diffused within the procaine and lidocaine, and the heroin could neither be distinguished nor easily separated from the contents of the package. Thus, the entire contents of the larger of the two packages used to sentence Berroa appears to satisfy the criteria identified by the *Chapman* court for identifying a "mixture" or a "substance."

Nevertheless, Berroa attempts to distinguish his case from *Chapman* by relying on this court's decision in *United States v. Rodriguez*, 975 F.2d 999 (3d Cir.1992). In *Rodriguez*, the defendants had taped a thin layer of cocaine (approximately 65 grams) over a much heavier block of boric acid (approximately 3 kilograms) and, attempting to pass the entire package off as 3 kilograms of cocaine, sold this block to undercover government agents as a "gag bag."[6] This Court held that, unlike the blotter paper/LSD mixture in *Chapman*, the sentencing court in *Rodriguez* should have excluded the weight of the boric acid, and only considered the weight of the much lighter cocaine in calculating the defendant's base offense level under U.S.S.G. § 2D1.1. *Rodriguez*, 975 F.2d at 1007.

Berroa argues that, like the defendants in *Rodriguez*, he did not actually intend to sell a kilo of heroin to the informant, but rather meant to "rip him off" by selling him a highly diluted "gag bag." He claims that the immeasurably small amount of heroin in the larger package proves this intent. Therefore, he concludes that as in *Rodriguez*, the sentencing court should not consider the weight of the non-controlled substances in calculating his sentence.

However, Berroa's reading of this Court's holding in *Rodriguez* is too narrow. In *Rodriguez*, this Court placed as much emphasis on the plain meaning of the term "mixture," in the context of that case, as it did on the intent of the seller. The *Rodriguez* court observed that, unlike the circumstances in *Chapman*, in their case: 1) the boric acid and the cocaine remained distinct although in close proximity; 2) the boric acid was not being used as a cutting agent; 3) the boric acid, being highly toxic, was not intended to be consumed; and, 4) the boric acid did not facilitate the distribution of cocaine. Relying on these characteristics, we concluded that the combination of cocaine and boric acid did not constitute a "mixture or substance" as contemplated by the Sentencing Commission in promulgating § 2D1.1, and that the clear intent of the seller was to use the cocaine "only to effectuate the scam by masking the identity of the boric acid blocks." *Id.* at 1006.

Berroa's case is clearly distinguishable. First, the trace of heroin in the larger package was not "distinct although in close proximity," but instead was inextricably combined with the procaine and lidocaine. Second, while Berroa may argue that the procaine and the lidocaine in the larger package were not truly used as cutting agents but simply used to trick the buyer into buying a "gag bag," procaine and lidocaine are among the most common cutting agents for street heroin. Indeed, we note that this Court and other courts of appeals have upheld sentences for distribution of a controlled substance where procaine and/or lidocaine were part of the "cut." *See, e.g., United States v. Agee*, 597 F.2d 350, 352 (3d Cir.1979) (upholding conviction for sale of heroin that had been diluted with "quinine, procaine and reducing sugar"); *United States v. Nelson*, 499 F.2d 965, 966 (8th Cir.1974) (affirming conviction for distribution of heroin "laced with procaine and lactose, the latter two being cutting powders"). Furthermore, neither one of these common cutting agents is toxic, and each is regularly "consumed" by the purchasers of heroin in the normal course of using the drug. Finally, the presence of the procaine and lidocaine was intended to "facilitate the sale of[a controlled

---

6. "Gag bag" is street parlance for a highly diluted or completely fake container of drugs.

substance]," since pure heroin would likely be toxic to most any user. Clearly, the larger package for which Berroa was sentenced was a "mixture" according to the *Rodriguez* standards.

Alternatively, Berroa argues that, even if the larger package constituted a "mixture or substance," it was not a "consumable," "marketable," or "ingestible" mixture of the type that numerous courts have determined that Congress and the Guidelines intended to punish. Berroa attempts to draw an analogy between these cases and his own by emphasizing, once again, the immeasurably small portion of controlled substance that was included in the larger bag in his case. He argues that this is not a "marketable" mixture since it is highly unlikely that such a disproportionately low ratio of drugs to "cut" was ever intended to be consumed or ingested, and that therefore, the *entire* weight of the larger bag should have been excluded in calculating his sentence under § 841(a)(1).

We disagree. In analyzing the cases upon which he relies, Berroa ignores the single factor that was common to the determination of each: that in order for the substance in question to be marketable, ingestible, and/or consumable, either the distributor or the dealer first had to separate the controlled substance from the additional material....

Conversely, common cutting agents such as procaine and lidocaine are added to heroin specifically to facilitate its use by addicts—thereby improving its ingestibility—and to increase its profitability for dealers and distributors—thereby enhancing its marketability. Because it was aware of this, Congress "clearly intended [that a] dilutant, cutting agent, or carrier medium be included in the weight of [drugs like heroin and cocaine] for sentencing purposes" even though "[i]n some cases, the concentration of the drug is very low." *Chapman*, 500 U.S. at 459–60. In *Chapman*, the Supreme Court noted that "Congress adopted a 'market-oriented' approach to punishing drug trafficking, under which the total quantity of what is distributed, rather than the amount of pure drug involved, is used to determine the length of the sentence." *Id.* at 461. The Court observed that "Congress did not want to punish retail traffickers less severely, even though they deal in smaller quantities of the pure drug, because such traffickers keep the street markets going." *Id.* The Court further explained that Congress "intended the penalty for drug trafficking to be graduated according to the weight of the drugs in whatever form they were found-cut or uncut, pure or impure, ready for wholesale or ready for distribution at the retail level." *Id.* Thus it is clear that a small amount of controlled substance combined with common cutting agents is a "marketable mixture" and the weight of the entire mixture must be included for sentencing purposes. We find that Congress' "market-oriented approach" to punishing drug trafficking clearly implicates Berroa's larger package that included a large quantity of procaine and lidocaine and only a trace of heroin.

* * *

Accordingly, we hold that the traces of heroin disclosed during lab testing in this case, although in amounts too small to determine its purity within a mixture, constitute a detectable amount, and that the District Court did not err when it included the entire weight of the larger package in calculating Berroa's sentence under U.S.S.G. § 2D1.1.

IV.

For the foregoing reasons, the judgment of the District Court is affirmed.

Notes and Questions

1. For an example of a gag bag, which contains little or no pure controlled substance, watch *The Wire*, Season 1, Episode 9, at 17:30 minutes. After stealing drugs from the Barksdale gang, Bubbles and Johnny realize that the drugs are actually just baking soda.

2. A "gag bag" brings to mind the mistake of fact and impossibility cases that many students review in first-year criminal law courses. For instance, imagine that D attempts to sell cocaine but mistakenly distributes a bag of baking flour. Students learn (or at least hopefully learn) that D cannot be convicted of the target offense because he has not actually distributed cocaine. However, D can be convicted of attempted distribution because, if the facts had been as D believed them, he would have distributed cocaine. Since we would punish D for attempt, does it thus make perfect sense to say that defendants like Berroa should be held responsible for the full weight of the mixture, even if the package contains virtually no controlled substance? Before you answer, consider how most criminal statutes punish attempt crimes compared to the punishment for completing the target offense.

3. We need not travel the difficult attempt and impossibility route, because under Maryland law, distributing a gag bag is a separate crime itself. Watch *The Wire*, Season 1, Episode 11, at 37:10 minutes, where Sovino, a member of the Barksdale gang, turns himself in after the shooting of Detective Greggs. He claims that when Detective Greggs was shot that he was only trying to sell baking soda, not actual heroin. His defense attorney tells prosecutors "the best you can do is 286b." The defense attorney is referencing Md. Code Art. 27 § 286b, which has since been updated and moved to Md. Code, Criminal Law § 5-617. Under that provision, "[a] person may not distribute, attempt to distribute, or possess with intent to distribute a noncontrolled substance that the person represents as a controlled substance." In *The Wire*, the attorneys mention that the maximum penalty was three years and a $5,000 fine, but under the new version of the statute, a defendant now faces up to five years and a $15,000 fine.

4. Although *Berroa* is an extreme example, it states the general rule, which is that drug quantity includes adulterants, dilutants, or cutting agents. A person can therefore be held liable for a large quantity of a controlled substance even though the substance itself is minimal. Does the rule described in *Berroa* make sense? When drugs have been heavily watered down to primarily be cutting agents with a trace of narcotics, is it fair to punish the defendant for the entire weight of the mixture?

5. Courts do occasionally reject the complete weight rule discussed in *Berroa*. For instance, in United States v. Jackson, 115 F.3d 843, 848 (11th Cir. 1997), the court held that the entire weight of a package containing 99% sugar and 1% cocaine could not be counted because the package was not sufficiently integrated to be a "mixture." The court explained:

> Here, the package contained 1104.4 grams of sugar, and 10 grams of cocaine. The chemist testified that the package was probably constructed so that "the cocaine present was originally contained in an area at the surface of the block." Although tests for cocaine on the powder in the package were positive, tests on several lumps of the sugar were negative. The chemist said that it would be impossible to determine the extent of the mixing that occurred during the analysis and repackaging. There was testimony from the chemist and the police officer that the cocaine, as packaged, was not marketable, was not worth more than $100, and probably would not have been detectable if mixed with the sugar. Although the cocaine and sugar are not easily distinguished, sugar is commonly used as a cutting agent, and the sugar was "consumable." The sugar was not used as a

cutting agent but was used to trick a purchaser into thinking it was cocaine. And … it does not seem possible that the sugar, which comprised over 99 percent of the weight of contents of the package could have been used to cut the cocaine without rendering the resulting mixture unmarketable.

* * *

The evidence establishes that the contents of the package was not a mixture. Jackson should have been sentenced based on the ten grams of cocaine. We, therefore, hold that the district court erred in basing Jackson's sentence upon the weight of the entire unmarketable package....

Berroa cited to *Jackson* in arguing that he should not be held responsible for the entire weight of the package. The court (in an omitted portion of the opinion) rejected any reliance on *Jackson* because the sentencing guidelines indicate that "the presence of 'any detectable amount' of a controlled substance requires a sentencing court to consider the entire weight of the mixture." *Berroa*, 302 F.3d at 284–85. Which court — *Berroa* or *Jackson* — is correct?

3. Possession with Intent to Distribute

United States v. Hunt
129 F.3d 739 (5th Cir. 1997)

EMILIO M. GARZA, Circuit Judge:

Latarsha Hunt appeals her conviction for possession of cocaine base with intent to distribute in violation of 21 U.S.C. § 841(a)(1). Finding insufficient evidence to support the verdict, we reverse, vacate the sentence, and remand for sentencing on the lesser included offense of simple possession.

I

A confidential informant told police that marijuana was being sold out of 832 Arthur Walk, which police identified as property leased to Hunt. Executing a search warrant on those premises, police officers discovered a brown paper bag containing marijuana on a coffee table in the living room along with loose tobacco and cigar labels on the floor. In addition, they found a loaded handgun under the couch. In Hunt's bedroom, they discovered 7.998 grams of cocaine base (or "crack") and a razor blade on a plate on the top of a dresser. The cocaine was broken into one large rock and several smaller pieces. Hunt, Dashanta Burton, who is a friend of Hunt's, and an unidentified male juvenile were present when the police entered the house. Hunt was standing near the front door when police entered, and, according to the testimony of the officers, did not appear to be expecting the police.

Detective Ruben Rodriguez testified that the cocaine was worth about $200, an amount that could be doubled depending on how it was cut, and that it was a distributable amount. Furthermore, he stated that each of the smaller rocks would be "a lot of crack for a crack head" and that the rocks are available in sizes smaller than that size. Brian Cho, a forensic drug analyst, stated that the amount of cocaine base he usually receives for testing is around 100 to 200 mg per submission, usually in the form of one small rock.

Detective Rodriguez also stated, however, that a cocaine base addict may smoke close to $500 worth in one day. He explained that although a junkie who had a rock as big as the largest one "would be in heaven," it would produce only a three-second high. When questioned about the razor blade that was found with the cocaine, he testified that a razor blade is necessary to cut the cocaine base, either for distribution or, as he conceded on cross-examination, for personal use (i.e., to fit in a smoking device).

When questioned about drug paraphernalia, Detective Rodriguez testified that crack users will smoke from homemade crack pipes, which can be made from objects such as broken car antennas, aluminum cans, and aluminum foil. The officers did not find any smoking devices, such as a smoke pipe, and, according to Detective Rodriguez, this indicated that no crack cocaine smokers were present. Furthermore, in his opinion, the tobacco and cigar wrappings they found were evidence of "blunts" being sold out of Hunt's house. He explained that blunts are made by taking the tobacco out of cigars and replacing it with marijuana and that "primos" are made by adding crack cocaine to the marijuana. He stated that in the area of town where Hunt's house was located, marijuana and crack are usually sold hand in hand, "like a little drug store." On recross, however, he stated that "primos" are one way that cocaine users smoke cocaine.

Hunt testified that she arrived at home just before the police officers and that she had not yet entered her bedroom, where the police officers found the cocaine. She admitted that she used marijuana, but claimed she did not "indulge" in crack cocaine. She said she knew the marijuana was in the house, but denied knowledge of the cocaine being there. She also denied allegations that she had ever sold drugs. She said she had given a key to the house to Burton, who was also living in the house, and that Burton had obtained the marijuana for a "get-together" they were going to have with a few friends that night. She also admitted she owned the gun, but denied owning the tobacco. Wendy Wilson, Hunt's neighbor and friend, testified that she had never seen Hunt use or deal crack cocaine.

Hunt was indicted under § 841(a)(1) for possession of cocaine base with intent to distribute. The first trial resulted in a hung jury. During the first and second trials, neither the government nor the defendant requested that the lesser included offense of possession be submitted to the jury. Moreover, neither the government nor Hunt challenged the instructions at trial or on appeal. In the second trial, the jury returned a verdict of guilty.

II

On appeal, Hunt contends that the evidence is insufficient to support the jury's verdict regarding the element of intent to distribute. She does not contend that the evidence was insufficient to support possession. In reviewing a challenge to the sufficiency of the evidence in a criminal case, we will affirm a conviction if a rational trier of fact could have found that the evidence established the essential elements of the offense beyond a reasonable doubt....

To establish a violation of 21 U.S.C. § 841(a)(1), the government must prove the knowing possession of a controlled substance with the intent to distribute. The elements of the offense may be proved either by direct or circumstantial evidence.

Intent to distribute may be inferred solely from the possession of an amount of controlled substance too large to be used by the possessor alone. On the other hand, a quantity that is consistent with personal use does not raise such an inference in the absence of other evidence.

Hunt contends that the 7.998 grams of crack cocaine that the police discovered in her house is insufficient as a matter of law to infer intent, and we agree. Although the government introduced testimony that this amount is a distributable amount and that the individual rocks may be larger than those that Detective Rodriguez believes are usually smoked or that Cho, the forensic analyst, usually tests, the testimony also indicated ... that this amount was also consistent with personal use. In particular, Detective Rodriguez testified that a crack cocaine user may smoke, in one day alone, close to $500 worth, an amount that exceeds even the highest value he assigned to the cocaine found in Hunt's house. Furthermore, at oral argument, the government conceded that "the amount alone, by itself, is not sufficient" to support an inference of intent to distribute.

We must therefore examine the other evidence to determine whether it, in conjunction with the quantity of cocaine found, suffices to establish the requisite intent to distribute. *See United States v. Munoz,* 957 F.2d 171, 174 (5th Cir.1992) (noting that even a small quantity of cocaine is sufficient to infer intent when augmented by the presence of evidence such as distribution paraphernalia or large quantities of cash). As with the quantity of drugs, however, "[p]araphernalia that could be consistent with personal use does not provide a sound basis for inferring intent to distribute." *United States v. Skipper,* 74 F.3d 608, 611 (5th Cir. 1996). As evidence of intent to distribute, the government points to the razor blade, the absence of smoking pipes or other such instruments, the evidence of blunts, the gun, and Hunt's testimony. In *Skipper,* the government similarly argued that a straight-edged razor and the absence of smoking paraphernalia suggested the intent to distribute. We held that, even viewed in the light most favorable to the government, the evidence was insufficient to prove intent beyond a reasonable doubt. The same conclusion is warranted here. Detective Rodriguez testified that although a razor blade is needed to cut crack cocaine for distribution, it is also needed to cut the cocaine for personal use. Furthermore, even though Rodriguez testified that the evidence of blunts indicated drug sales, he also said that the evidence indicated use, namely, the smoking of cocaine in the form of primos. Because this evidence is also consistent with personal use, we do not believe it provides a sound basis for inferring that Hunt intended to distribute the cocaine.

The government also points to the gun found under her couch as evidence of Hunt's intent to distribute. We have often recognized that guns are tools of the trade in the drug business. *See United States v. Martinez,* 808 F.2d 1050, 1057 (5th Cir.1987). In *United States v. Lucien,* 61 F.3d 366, 375 (5th Cir.1995), the government argued that three guns that were found in the defendant's apartment were evidence that he was distributing cocaine base. In response, we noted that "[a]lthough we do not discount the prevalence of guns in drug trafficking, we do not place undue weight on the presence of the guns in this case because [the defendants] could have untold reasons, nefarious and otherwise, for keeping guns in the apartment." *Id.* at 375–76; *see also United States v. Gibbs,* 904 F.2d 52, 59 (D.C.Cir.1990) (stating that "[w]hile the presence of weapons may be a factor in considering whether the defendants intended to distribute the cocaine, the mere presence of weapons is not, in and of itself, dispositive of such intent"). The reasoning in *Lucien* applies with equal force to this case. Hunt's gun was found in her residence, under a couch, and not with the cocaine. Furthermore, Hunt made no move toward the gun when the police entered, and she admitted when asked that she did have a gun in the house. This evidence can be contrasted with cases in which a weapon was found in a more incriminating context. *See, e.g., United States v. Harrison,* 55 F.3d 163, 165 (5th Cir.) (noting that loaded .22 caliber pistol and ammunition were found next to 49.32 grams of cocaine base in dresser drawer); *United States v. Perez,* 648 F.2d 219, 220–21 (5th Cir. Unit B June 1981) (noting that when defendant noticed police observing him feeding bales of marijuana on conveyor belt to boat, he ran into house and was apprehended as he reached toward a shelf on which there were two loaded weapons). Unconnected with any such circumstances, however, the gun is no more probative of distribution of drugs than of other, non-nefarious purposes for which one may keep a gun. We therefore cannot affirm Hunt's conviction based on the presence of the gun.

The government also argues that the jury could have rejected Hunt's testimony that she had no knowledge of the cocaine and that Hunt's denial of use of cocaine necessitates a conclusion that the cocaine was kept on the premises for distribution. On appeal, however, Hunt does not challenge the jury's finding that she possessed the cocaine. Furthermore, although denial of personal consumption may be a factor in inferring intent to distribute in certain circumstances, we have stated that a defendant's "denial of guilt itself should not be permitted to become evidence of guilt." *United States v. Sutherland,* 428 F.2d 1152, 1157 (5th Cir.1970). Accordingly, we reject the government's argument that Hunt's denial of use leads to the inference that she intended to distribute the crack.

When we have concluded that the evidence presented at trial was sufficient to support an inference of intent to distribute, we have pointed to evidence that is not as equally probative of possession as of distribution. *See, e.g., United States v. Lucien,* 61 F.3d 366, 376 (5th Cir. 1995) (over $1200 cash, three weapons, and a plastic bag with several aluminum foil packets); *United States v. Pigrum,* 922 F.2d 249, 251 (5th Cir.1991) (two sets of scales, coffee cup containing a test tube, cutting agent); *United States v. Onick,* 889 F.2d 1425, 1430-31 (5th Cir.1989) (drug paraphernalia, particularly 4,063 empty gelcaps, and testimony that dealers package drugs in these gelcaps for street distribution); *United States v. Prieto-Tejas,* 779 F.2d 1098, 1101 (5th Cir.1986) (value of cocaine between $2,200 and $9,000). We do not, however, see any evidence in this case, viewed individually or collectively, that is more probative of distribution than of possession. We therefore hold that a reasonable jury could not conclude beyond a reasonable doubt that Hunt intended to distribute the cocaine. We accordingly reverse Hunt's conviction for possession with intent to distribute.

* * *

… We therefore remand the case with instructions to enter a judgment of guilt of simple possession under 21 U.S.C. § 844(a) and to sentence Hunt for that offense.

* * *

Notes and Questions

1. Do you think the Fifth Circuit panel reached the correct decision? The jury heard testimony that Hunt was in possession of nearly eight grams of crack, a razor blade, a gun, and that the crack was broken into several rocks and that there was no pipe present to smoke it with. Couldn't a rational jury have concluded that Hunt had an intent to distribute?

2. The Department of Justice did not petition for a writ of certiorari to have the Supreme Court of the United States reverse the Fifth Circuit. If the Court had heard the case though, how do you think they would have voted? Can you imagine Chief Justice Rehnquist, Justice Scalia, or Justice Thomas concluding that there was insufficient evidence to support a distribution charge? How about Justice O'Connor or Justice Kennedy?

3. What quantity of crack cocaine would police have to discover (absent any other factors, such as scales, razor blades, or individually wrapped small baggies) for a court to safely conclude that there was an intent to distribute? Put differently, if police had found only ten grams of crack cocaine, could a jury fairly infer that the defendant had an intent to distribute? How about twenty grams of crack cocaine? We typically think of crack users as down-on-their luck addicts who must beg, steal, or prostitute themselves to get money for their next fix. But is it possible that some crack addicts plan ahead and purchase a larger quantity of crack for personal use that they simply spread over a week rather than a single day?

4. Throughout *The Wire*, Omar Little robs stash houses and walks away with large quantities of drugs. If police stopped Omar right after he robbed drug dealers, could

Omar be charged with possession with intent to distribute based on the large quantity of drugs? How would he disprove the distribution charge?

5. How about two friends sharing drugs? In the first three seasons of *The Wire*, Bubbles and his friend Johnny Weeks work together to buy drugs. If Bubbles spends $15 to buy three hits of drugs and shares one of the hits with Johnny, is Bubbles guilty of distribution? Would it matter if Johnny gave Bubbles $5 toward the purchase before Bubbles approached the corner boys to purchase the drugs?

State v. Wilkins

703 S.E.2d 807 (N.C. App. 2010)

HUNTER, ROBERT C., Judge.

Kendrick Wilkins ("defendant") appeals from a judgment entered after a jury found him guilty of felonious possession of marijuana with intent to sell or deliver ("PWISD"). Defendant argues that the trial court erred in denying his motion to dismiss the charge. After careful review, we vacate defendant's sentence and remand for resentencing upon a conviction of possession of a controlled substance.

Background

The evidence at trial tended to establish the following facts: On 17 January 2008, defendant was driving a brown Ford Crown Victoria along Raleigh Road in Rocky Mount, North Carolina. Defendant was driving to his mother's house after purchasing cigars at a convenience store. Defendant passed by Rocky Mount Police Officer T.J. Bunt ("Officer Bunt"), who recognized the Crown Victoria as the car typically driven by Rico Battle ("Battle"). Officer Bunt knew that there were several outstanding warrants for Battle so he activated his blue lights and pulled over the Crown Victoria. When Officer Bunt approached the car, he noticed that defendant was the only occupant of the car and that he was wearing a hat and sunglasses. Officer Bunt testified that when he knocked on the driver's side window, defendant "kind of turned … away" and "refused to open" the window or the car door. Officer Bunt then opened the driver's side door, and, upon being asked his name, defendant identified himself as Kendrick Wilkins. Officer Bunt knew that there were outstanding warrants for defendant, and after confirming the existence of the warrants, Officer Bunt arrested defendant.

Upon searching defendant subsequent to the arrest, Officer Bunt discovered a small plastic bag inside of defendant's pocket, which contained three smaller bags. Each of the three bags was "tied off" at the top and contained a substance Officer Bunt believed to be marijuana. The substance was later weighed and determined to be 1.89 grams of marijuana. Defendant testified that he purchased the marijuana for personal use and that typically marijuana can be bought in "nickel" or "dime" bags for $5.00 to $10.00 each.

During the pat down, Officer Bunt also found $1,264.00 in cash separated into 60 $20.00 bills, one $10.00 bill, nine $5.00 bills, and nine $1.00 bills. At trial, defendant testified that approximately $1,000.00 of the cash recovered was for a cash bond that his mother gave to him and the remaining $264.00 was from a check he had cashed. Defendant testified that he was carrying cash because he was "on the run" and if he were arrested the bail bondsman would not accept a check. Defendant was charged with PWISD.

At trial, the jury was instructed on PWISD and misdemeanor possession of marijuana. The jury found defendant guilty of PWISD. Defendant was determined to be a record level III for sentencing purposes and the trial court sentenced defendant to a suspended sentence of 6 to 8 months imprisonment. Defendant was placed on 36 months of supervised probation. Defendant timely appealed to this Court.

Discussion

Defendant's sole argument on appeal is that the trial court erred in denying his motion to dismiss the PWISD charge. We agree.

* * *

Defendant was charged with PWISD pursuant to N.C. Gen. Stat. § 90-95(a)(1) (2009). "While intent [to sell or deliver] may be shown by direct evidence, it is often proven by circumstantial evidence from which it may be inferred." *State v. Nettles*, 612 S.E.2d 172 (2005). "[T]he intent to sell or [deliver] may be inferred from (1) the packaging, labeling, and storage of the controlled substance, (2) the defendant's activities, (3) the quantity found, and (4) the presence of cash or drug paraphernalia." *Id.* at 176. "Although 'quantity of the controlled substance alone may suffice to support the inference of an intent to transfer, sell, or deliver,' it must be a substantial amount." *Id.*

In the present case, only 1.89 grams of marijuana was found on defendant's person, which alone is insufficient to prove that defendant had the intent to sell or deliver. Accordingly, we must examine the other evidence presented in the light most favorable to the State.

The State points to the fact that the marijuana seized from defendant was separated into three smaller packages. Officer Bunt testified that marijuana is typically sold "in bags in different sizes." Based on his training and experience, Officer Bunt believed that each bag of marijuana found in defendant's pocket would sell for between $5.00 and $10.00 each. "The method of packaging a controlled substance, as well as the amount of the substance, may constitute evidence from which a jury can infer an intent to distribute." *State v. Williams*, 321 S.E.2d 561, 564 (1984). The State has not pointed to a case, nor have we found one, where the division of such a small amount of a controlled substance constituted sufficient evidence to survive a motion to dismiss. Moreover, the 1.89 grams was divided into only three separate bags. While small bags may typically be used to package marijuana, it is just as likely that defendant was a consumer who purchased the drugs in that particular packaging from a dealer. Consequently, we hold that the separation of 1.89 grams of marijuana into three small packages, worth a total of approximately $30.00, does not raise an inference that defendant intended to sell or deliver the marijuana.

In addition to the packaging, we must also consider the fact that defendant was carrying $1,264.00 in cash.... Upon viewing the evidence of the packaging and the cash "cumulatively," we hold that the evidence is insufficient to support the felony charge. Had defendant possessed more than 1.89 grams of marijuana, or had there been additional circumstances to consider, we may have reached a different conclusion; however, given the fact that neither the amount of marijuana nor the packaging raises an inference that defendant intended to sell the drugs, the presence of the cash as the only additional factor is insufficient to raise the inference.

... Defendant possessed a very small amount of marijuana that was packaged in three small bags and he had $1,264.00 in cash on his person. The evidence in this case, viewed in the light most favorable to the State, indicates that defendant was a drug user, not a drug seller.

... Consequently, we vacate defendant's sentence and remand for entry of a judgment "as upon a verdict of guilty of simple possession of marijuana."

Vacated and Remanded.

Notes and Questions

1. Courts typically consider the individual wrapping of drugs to be evidence of an intention to distribute. *See, e.g.*, Bowers v. State, 394 S.E.2d 141 (Ga. App. 1990) (finding an intent to distribute based solely on possession of four individually wrapped baggies of crack). Why wasn't the individual wrapping of the marijuana sufficient to draw that inference in *Wilkins*?

2. How about the large amount of cash found on Wilkins? Isn't that also evidence that he was involved in the sale of drugs? Have you ever walked around town for an extended time period with more than $1,000 in cash in your pocket? Should it matter what type of denominations the bills were and whether they were neatly folded or crumpled in Wilkins's pocket?

3. Although the court does not stress the value of the marijuana, do you think the fact that Wilkins was only caught with about $30 in drugs on his person is what proved fatal to the State on appeal? Doesn't the small amount of individually wrapped drugs, coupled with the $1,264 in cash cut the other way though? In other words, couldn't a jury have drawn the inference that the reason for the small quantity of drugs is because Wilkins had already sold most of his supply, thus explaining the $1,264 in cash?

4. With respect to the money, Wilkins claimed that he had a lot of cash because he was on the run and would need it to pay his bail bondsman. Is this story credible? If you find it outlandish, does it make you more likely to believe that the money was from selling drugs?

Jones v. State

695 S.E.2d 665 (Ga. App. 2010)

BLACKBURN, Judge.

Following a jury trial, Charles Jones appeals his conviction on various drug-related counts.... We hold that the evidence sufficed to show Jones possessed the drugs in question with an intent to distribute same....

... [T]he evidence shows that on April 15, 2006, Jones (a hip-hop artist) and his associates were exiting a concert arena to enter a limo when nearby youths fired guns at them. Jones's group dove into the limo and returned gunfire, and the limo eventually began to drive away. With drawn weapons, police stopped the limo before it could exit the arena grounds, and despite commands from police to submit peacefully, Jones and an associate exited the limo and fled, with officers in hot pursuit. Ignoring police demands to stop, Jones ran down a hill until caught by a security guard, who wrestled the resisting Jones to the ground. Police officers (assisted by a police dog) arrived and subdued Jones, placing him in handcuffs.

A search of Jones's person revealed that in one front pocket of his pants was a container of sixteen tablets of methamphetamine (weighing in the aggregate 4 to 5 grams), four small baggies of marijuana (weighing in the aggregate 2.7 grams), and $393 in cash in various denominations. A subsequent search of the limo seat from which Jones fled revealed two guns in that seat, and an officer testified that he saw a firing pin from one of those guns at Jones's feet before he exited the vehicle. At trial, evidence showed that the arena grounds as well as the place of Jones's apprehension were within 1,000 feet of an adjacent public housing project.

Jones was charged with possession of marijuana with intent to distribute (Count 1), possession of methamphetamine with intent to distribute (Count 2), possession of methamphetamine (Count 3), possession of marijuana with intent to distribute within 1,000 feet of public housing (Count 4), possession of methamphetamine with intent to distribute within 1,000 feet of public housing (Count 5), possession of a firearm during the commission of a crime (Count 6), attempt to injure a police dog (Count 7), and possession of a firearm by a convicted felon (Count 8). A jury found him guilty on the first five counts, acquitting him of Counts 6 and 7; the court subsequently entered a directed verdict of not guilty on Count 8. At sentencing, the trial court merged Count 3 into Count 2. Following the denial of Jones's motion for new trial, in which he asserted ineffective assistance of counsel, Jones appeals.

* * *

Jones challenges the sufficiency of the evidence on two grounds. First he claims that no evidence showed he intended to distribute the marijuana and methamphetamine found on his person. Second, he claims that no evidence showed he knew he was within 1,000 feet of public housing. Both arguments lack merit.

Evidence showed Jones intended to distribute the drugs. "To support a conviction for possession with intent to distribute, the [S]tate is required to prove more than mere possession." *Helton v. State* [609 S.E.2d 200 (2005)]. However, "[n]o bright line rule exists regarding the amount or type of evidence sufficient to support a conviction for possession with intent to distribute." *Cotton v. State* [686 S.E.2d 805 (2009)]. Rather, the State "may show intent to distribute in many ways, including expert testimony that the amount of contraband possessed was inconsistent with personal use, evidence showing the manner of packaging, and the possession of certain amounts or denominations of currency." *Helton*, 609 S.E.2d 200. "Moreover, even if not formally admitted as an expert, a police officer may give his opinion as to whether the amount or value of the contraband is consistent with distribution, if the [S]tate lays a foundation for the opinion by eliciting testimony about the officer's experience and training in drug enforcement." *Haywood v. State* [689 S.E.2d 82 (2009)].

Here, some evidence showed Jones's intent to distribute the marijuana and methamphetamine found on his person. In the same pocket of Jones, police found a large amount of cash in various denominations and a large amount of each of the drugs (2.7 grams of marijuana and sixteen individual tablets of methamphetamine), with the marijuana packaged in four small baggies as if for resale; police also found guns in the limo where Jones had sat with a firing pin at his feet. A friend of Jones testified that Jones had not personally smoked marijuana since his youth some years ago. Finally, a police officer trained and experienced in the illegal drug distribution industry testified that the amount and packaging of the drugs indicated that Jones possessed these drugs with an intent to distribute them. Accordingly, the evidence sufficed to sustain the conviction of Jones on the four counts requiring a showing that he intended to distribute the methamphetamine or marijuana.

* * *

Judgment affirmed.

Notes and Questions

1. Do you agree that there is sufficient evidence to convict Jones of intent to distribute both methamphetamine and marijuana? Is it possible that there was sufficient evidence

of intent to distribute one drug, but not the other and that the court failed to separate the sufficiency inquiry for each count?

2. What constitutes "a large amount of cash," which the court argues is one factor suggesting drug distribution? The court obviously believed $393 was a large amount of money to have on one's person. Is that correct though? In some neighborhoods, most legitimate transactions are conducted by cash, rather than credit cards or debit cards. Could $393 have been Jones's money for a week's worth of groceries, rent, and other legitimate transactions? Also, couldn't he have just been paid in cash for the musical performance he had just finished?

3. Notice that the prosecutors in *Jones* introduced testimony from "a police officer trained and experienced in the illegal drug distribution industry … that the amount and packaging of the drugs indicated that Jones possessed these drugs with an intent to distribute them." Is this a proper subject of expert testimony? How does the police officer have any idea whether Jones in particular was planning to distribute the drugs? Is the expert testimony just pure speculation, or are trained narcotics officers in a position to offer valuable evidence to juries?

4. Is 2.7 grams of marijuana a lot? Is it plausible to conclude that Jones would have consumed the 2.7 grams for personal use? Couldn't he have purchased four bags of marijuana because he considered the amount in a single bag to be too little? Isn't it also possible he would be traveling a long distance to his next musical performance and had simply bought marijuana in bulk to take with him?

5. The court says that Jones was a hip-hop artist, traveling with associates in a limousine. Is it reasonable to believe that a musician traveling with an entourage will have more drugs for personal use than an average drug user would have? If he gives the drugs to his entourage, even if he does it for free, that would be distribution, wouldn't it?

6. In addition to the marijuana, Jones was also found in possession of sixteen tablets of methamphetamine. Does the possession of two different types of drugs make it more or less likely that he was dealing the drugs?

7. Can you reconcile the decision upholding Jones's conviction with the North Carolina court's decision overturning Wilkins's conviction? Wilkins was in possession of three bags of marijuana weighing 1.89 grams, as well as $1,264 in cash. Jones was in possession of four bags of marijuana weighing 2.7 grams of marijuana, as well as $393 in cash. On these facts, can you say that Wilkins should be not guilty of distribution while Jones is guilty? Is the difference between the two cases that there were two guns in Jones's car?

4. Drug Kingpins

Maryland Code, Criminal Law, § 5-613

Drug Kingpin

"Drug kingpin" defined

(a) In this section, "drug kingpin" means an organizer, supervisor, financier, or manager who acts as a coconspirator in a conspiracy to manufacture, distribute, dispense, transport in, or bring into the State a controlled dangerous substance.

Drug kingpin conspiracy; penalty

(b)(1) A drug kingpin who conspires to manufacture, distribute, dispense, transport in, or bring into the State a controlled dangerous substance in an amount listed in § 5-612 of this subtitle is guilty of a felony and on conviction is subject to imprisonment for not less than 20 years and not exceeding 40 years without the possibility of parole or a fine not exceeding $1,000,000 or both.

(2) A court may not suspend any part of the mandatory minimum sentence of 20 years.

(3) The person is not eligible for parole during the mandatory minimum sentence.

* * *

Maryland Code, Criminal Law § 5-612
Volume Dealer

Unlawful amounts

(a) A person may not manufacture, distribute, dispense, or possess:

(1) 50 pounds or more of marijuana;

(2) 448 grams or more of cocaine;

(3) 448 grams or more of any mixture containing a detectable amount of cocaine;

(4) 50 grams or more of cocaine base, commonly known as "crack";

(5) 28 grams or more of morphine or opium or any derivative, salt, isomer, or salt of an isomer of morphine or opium;

(6) any mixture containing 28 grams or more of morphine or opium or any derivative, salt, isomer, or salt of an isomer of morphine or opium;

(7) 1,000 dosage units or more of lysergic acid diethylamide;

(8) any mixture containing the equivalent of 1,000 dosage units of lysergic acid diethylamide;

(9) 16 ounces or more of phencyclidine in liquid form;

(10) 448 grams or more of any mixture containing phencyclidine;

(11) 448 grams or more of methamphetamine; or

(12) any mixture containing 448 grams or more of methamphetamine.

Aggregation of amounts

(b) For the purpose of determining the quantity of a controlled dangerous substance involved in individual acts of manufacturing, distributing, dispensing, or possessing under subsection (a) of this section, the acts may be aggregated if each of the acts occurred within a 90-day period.

* * *

———————

Notes and Questions

1. Is Avon Barksdale covered under the drug kingpin statute? The primary drug sold in *The Wire* is heroin. Is heroin clearly covered by § 5-612?

2. How about other key figures in the Barksdale organization? Is Stringer Bell a kingpin for purposes of Maryland Code, Criminal Law, § 5-613? Is D'Angelo Barksdale?

3. Notice how § 5-612 allows for the aggregation of sales over a 90-day period. After having watched Season 1 of *The Wire*, is it possible that Bodie, Poot, or even Wallace might qualify as a kingpin under the Maryland statute? If they do, does that make sense? Do you think the legislators who drafted the statute would have intended for Bodie, Poot, or Wallace to qualify as kingpins?

5. Across the Street but Worlds Apart: State versus Federal Drug Prosecutions

Michael M. O'Hear, Federalism and Drug Control
57 Vanderbilt Law Review 783 (2004)

* * *

The Evolution of Federal Drug Policy

Since its origins nearly a century ago, federal drug policy has emphasized enforcement and reflected strong legalist tendencies. Yet, also from the beginning, influential voices have characterized drug abuse as a medical problem that is suitable for treatment, either to supplement or supplant criminal justice responses. Thus, the history of federal drug policy has been marked by a series of successive enforcement and treatment initiatives, some originating from within the federal policymaking establishment and some from states and local communities.

* * *

A. 1914–1968: The Other Prohibition

Like the nation's well-known, unsuccessful experiment with alcohol prohibition, federal antidrug policies emerged from the Progressive Era of the early twentieth century. After a few preliminary statutes of more modest scope, in 1914 Congress enacted its most ambitious early drug law, the Harrison Act, which banned the distribution of opiates (including morphine and heroin) and cocaine outside medical channels. This law followed earlier state and local efforts to regulate such drugs, and represented, in part, an effort by the medical profession to gain greater control over the distribution of pharmaceuticals at a time when opiate-based patent medicines were widely available without prescription.

Although medical professionals supported passage of the Harrison Act, conflicts soon developed between drug enforcement agents and many of the doctors who treated drug addicts. The Treasury Department, charged with enforcing the Harrison Act, concluded that physicians could not legally employ maintenance therapies as part of a treatment regimen. The Department equated maintenance, which involves the continued administration of drugs in order to help addicts avoid withdrawal symptoms, with drug trafficking, and began to prosecute physicians employing maintenance therapies for Harrison Act violations. While some lower courts initially rejected the Department's broad interpretation of the Act, the Supreme Court endorsed the prohibition on maintenance in 1919. Subsequent federal prosecutions resulted in the incarceration of some physicians and the closure of all public drug treatment clinics established by states and cities. Consequently, community-based treatment options for addicts essentially dried up during the interwar years. * * *

Meanwhile, despite the national abandonment of alcohol prohibition, Congress not only maintained, but actually expanded the drug prohibition laws with passage of the Marihuana Tax Act of 1937. As with opiates, the federal government did not develop an interest in marijuana regulation until after earlier efforts at the state and local level. Reacting to lurid stories associating marijuana with violence and sex crimes, El Paso, Texas adopted the nation's first marijuana ban in 1914. Twenty-nine states followed suit over the next 17 years, and one (Louisiana) formally petitioned the federal government for a nationwide ban. The federal law enforcement establishment reacted coolly to the proposal at first, but, for reasons that have been the subject of some debate, later lobbied vigorously and successfully for federal legislation.

Overall, the period from the 1930s to the 1960s was marked both by a pronounced emphasis on criminal punishment as the preferred response to drug use and by relatively low levels of middle-class drug use, especially outside of urban areas. Proposals for more treatment-oriented drug policies were met with "vitriolic" attacks from federal officials.

B. 1969–1980: Making War on Drugs

Despite the enactment of important criminalization statutes in 1914 and 1937, drug enforcement generally had limited political salience (and budgetary resources) before the 1960s, when drug use first became prevalent among middle-class young people. Reacting to this development, Richard Nixon elevated the status of drug abuse as a national political issue in 1968, arguing on the campaign trail that drugs were "decimating a generation of Americans." Building on this rhetoric, in 1969, shortly after taking office, Nixon declared a national "war on drugs." His administration launched high-profile enforcement initiatives, particularly targeting the heroin trade, and increased federal antidrug expenditures from $86 million in 1969 to nearly $800 million in 1974. His administration also oversaw the creation of the federal Drug Enforcement Administration ("DEA") in 1973.

Despite Nixon's strong rhetoric and emphasis on law enforcement, the legalist paradigm did not necessarily dominate federal drug policy in the 1970s. The nation's most notoriously strict drug laws, which included long mandatory minimum sentences for drug offenders, were not adopted by Congress, but by the state of New York. Moreover, inspired by the success of pioneering treatment programs in New York City and Illinois, the Nixon Administration supported major drug treatment initiatives, including methadone maintenance programs for heroin addicts. With financial assistance from a Nixon-created agency, the National Institute on Drug Abuse, many cities witnessed the return of the sorts of community-based drug treatment clinics that the federal government had stamped out in the 1920s. Federal support of treatment continued through the administration of Jimmy Carter, who also publicly endorsed the decriminalization of marijuana.

C. 1981–2000: Escalating the War — The Triumph of Enforcement

Soaring drug use by middle class teenagers prompted a backlash by angry parents. A grassroots "parents' movement" in the late 1970s exerted pressure on Washington for tougher policies. These efforts ultimately led to an unprecedented escalation of the war on drugs in the 1980s. During this time period, as drug control became entrenched as a preeminent domestic policy issue, federal interest in treatment and receptivity to the public health paradigm diminished considerably.

Ronald Reagan, who emphasized the drug issue during the 1980 election, received the enthusiastic support of the parents' movement. Once in office, he declared a renewed "war on drugs." The federal antidrug budget accordingly grew to nearly $6 billion by 1987. The Reagan Administration's position on drug policy received its most familiar articulation in First Lady Nancy Reagan's "just say no" campaign of the mid-1980s — a blunt articulation of the legalist view that drug use is a morally wrong choice, not a manifestation of a disease. With the emphasis on law enforcement, antidrug publicity, and new international interdiction programs, treatment received little consistent support from Washington.

The defining moment in the federal war on drugs may have come with enactment of the Anti-Drug Abuse Act of 1986. Responding to the public furor over the cocaine-related death of college basketball star Len Bias, Congress adopted new mandatory minimum sentences of five and ten years for dealing crack cocaine (also known as "cocaine base"), depending on the quantity of crack involved. The law resulted in substantially greater penalties for crack offenses than for powder cocaine offenses. For instance, convictions involving 50 grams of crack result in the same ten-year minimum as convictions involving 5000 grams of powder cocaine, a ratio that has led commentators to refer to the crack provisions as the 100:1 law. A 1988 amendment made crack penalties even tougher, broadening the applicability of the five-year minimum from trafficking to mere possession.

These crack penalties are difficult to justify under any paradigm other than legalism. The mandatory minimum sentences impose substantial costs, not just on the convicted offenders, but also on society more generally in the form of incarceration costs, the fragmentation of families and communities, the difficulty of reintegrating long-time inmates back into the community, and demoralization of the judiciary. Demonstrable benefits are few. Yet, the penalties have been retained because any decrease in sentences would, in the words of a Senate Republican leader, "send[ ] the wrong signal to young people" — hearkening back to what Professors Zimring and Hawkins referred to as the "central inflexibility" of the legalist paradigm. The boundaries between licit and illicit substances, once demarcated, must be vigorously enforced, and those who choose to step on the wrong side of that border merit strict punishment.

By some measures, the war on drugs reached its peak in the mid- to late-1980s. Drugs remained salient on the national political stage throughout the 1990s, however, and the federal antidrug budget continued its growth to nearly $20 billion by 1998—more than 200 times greater than when Richard Nixon began his campaign against drugs.

With the change from a Republican to a Democratic Administration in 1993, reform proponents saw an opportunity for new directions in drug policy, but, after launching a half-hearted and unsuccessful treatment-oriented initiative, the Clinton Administration returned to the dominant policies of the 1980s. The Administration did support a modest reduction in crack penalties, but also proposed countervailing increases in the penalties for powder cocaine. A Republican-dominated Congress nonetheless rejected the Clinton proposal out of a desire to hold the line on crack sentences. New laws reflecting the legalist perspective included the 1998 Drug Free Student Loans Act, which denies aid to college students who have so much as a misdemeanor conviction "under any Federal or State law involving the possession or sale of a controlled substance."

D. Federal Policy in the Twenty-First Century

In February 2003, the Bush Administration promulgated the latest version of the National Drug Control Strategy, a comprehensive, congressionally mandated statement of the federal government's drug policies and plans. Taking the Strategy at face value, a reader might conclude that Washington has moved a considerable distance away from the staunch legalism of the 1980s and towards the public-health paradigm. The Strategy identifies "healing America's drug users" as one of its three "national priorities." To that end, it discusses at length the "key lessons" offered by the "public health model." The Strategy takes pains to contradict characterizations of federal drug policy as "punitive," and purports to demonstrate that America, in contrast to decriminalizing European nations, has the "genuine public health approach." The Strategy touts President Bush's proposal to increase federal funding for treatment by $600 million over the next three years. Enforcement receives comparatively muted treatment.

Despite the Strategy's emphasis on the public-health model, in most respects federal drug policy has remained very much on the legalist course set in the 1980s. The federal drug control budget, including the law enforcement component, continues to grow. Federal mandatory minimum sentences remain in place. After a brief downward trend in the early 1990s, the annual number of arrests for drug violations has increased, ultimately setting a record in 2001 (the most recent year for which data is available).

Indeed, upon closer inspection, the Strategy itself seems far less committed to the public-health model than it might appear at first blush. First, the Strategy does not encompass alcohol or tobacco; instead, it targets only illicit substances. Second, the Strategy defines its goals exclusively in terms of reduced drug usage, without regard to more conventional public-health objectives such as reducing the number of drug overdose deaths and babies born addicted to drugs. The Strategy's purpose thus seems to be reduction of drug use per se (the legalist goal), rather than reduction of the harms resulting from drug use (the public-health goal)....

*   *   *

b. Direct Enforcement

The federal government also advances its policy agenda by directly enforcing (i.e., through its own agents) the federal drug laws. Direct enforcement is arguably the least important, albeit perhaps the most visible, mechanism of federal policy control. Due to resource constraints, the federal government can only investigate, prosecute, and incarcerate a small percentage of drug offenders. In 2000, for instance, state institutions held more than 250,000 prisoners convicted of drug crimes, while federal institutions held just over 73,000. To be sure, federal enforcement resources have been growing rapidly, leading to a more than doubling of the number of federally incarcerated drug offenders between 1990 and 2000. Yet, the true significance of direct enforcement as a tool of federal control rests not simply in the volume of cases prosecuted, but in the way that the limited federal enforcement resources are targeted.

First, the federal government has targeted conduct that is permissible under state law, with the objective of preventing states from implementing policies that contravene federal preferences. An early precedent was the federal prosecution of public treatment clinics in the 1920s. A contemporary example is the prosecution of medical marijuana cases, such as the Rosenthal case.

In the same vein, when a state does criminalize conduct that is prohibited under federal law, but imposes more lenient penalties, federal agents overcome this lenience by prosecuting drug offenders in federal court. Indeed, federal prosecutors have systematically done so at various times in New York City and Washington, D.C. Moreover, under prevailing interpretations of the Double Jeopardy Clause, when there is a state prosecution, federal agents can wait to see if the sentence imposed in state court is satisfactorily punitive before deciding whether to bring federal charges for the same conduct. In short, federal officials often focus their resources on those sorts of cases in those particular locales that would likely produce little or no punishment in state court, thereby bringing those locales into greater alignment with the more punitive federal preferences. Though federal enforcement resources are limited, federal control is advanced by strategically targeting the most significant deviations from federal norms.

Second, federal enforcement resources are leveraged through cooperation with state and local law enforcement agencies. While the nature of these cooperative arrangements is detailed below, the basic functioning of the "cooperation multiplier" bears particular note in this context. In general, one of the great weaknesses of federal law enforcement lies in the lack of personnel at the street level; federal agents do not, as a rule, walk a beat. Instead, federal agencies like the FBI and DEA traditionally specialize in the most technically sophisticated law enforcement techniques, such as electronic surveillance, sting operations, and following a convoluted money trail. Cooperative arrangements with local police help federal agencies compensate for their traditional limitations, effectively providing the federal government with a street-level presence. Important leads uncovered by state and local agents can be relayed to federal agents for joint or federal-only investigation. Drug offenders nabbed by state and local agents can be referred to federal prosecutors. In sum, the federal government gets to have it both ways: federal law enforcement agencies remain small, elite, and specialized, and federal prosecutors are referred a more than ample supply of drug cases.

Third, given an ample supply of referrals but significant budgetary limitations [on] their offices, federal prosecutors can selectively prosecute only those cases that maximize the impact of federal law. This may mean, as noted above, prosecution of cases in which state law deviates most from federal, such as the medicinal marijuana cases. Additionally, federal prosecutors may try to take only the highest-profile cases. State prosecutors have long been suspicious of federal prosecutorial tendencies in this direction, and recent empirical work supports these suspicions. A comparison of state and federal prison inmates convicted of drug crimes finds that the federal inmates tend to have more "human capital": they are older, more successful in the aboveground economy, and are more likely to have the resources required to hire a private attorney. This evidence is consistent with the view that federal prosecutors target high-profile cases.

Federal emphasis on high-profile drug cases likely magnifies the bully-pulpit phenomenon discussed above. Media attention provides a public forum for the articulation and judicial validation of federal drug policy preferences. High-profile federal cases also reinforce the view that the federal government is responsible for handling drug issues, thereby diminishing state and local accountability.

Fourth, federal preferences for tougher drug penalties are even felt in cases prosecuted in state court. Most criminal cases, wherever prosecuted, are resolved by way of plea bargaining, not trial. In order to gain more leverage in plea bargaining, state prosecutors may use the threat of referral to federal authorities for prosecution under harsher federal law. To the extent that such threats may be credibly made (which probably varies from jurisdiction to jurisdiction), the "market rate" for bargained drug pleas in state court should rise considerably.

A defendant who refuses to comply with prosecutorial expectations may suffer draconian consequences. Thus, for instance, in a Pennsylvania case, a drug defendant rejected a state plea offer requiring a four-year prison term. Following his plea rejection, federal prosecutors agreed to prosecute him in federal court, where he ultimately received a life sentence. Such cases serve as an example to other state defendants and thus help to extend the influence of federal law.

* * *

Notes and Questions

1. One problem that occurs throughout *The Wire* is the federal government's lack of interest in the Barksdale (and later, Stansfield) drug organization. For example, watch *The Wire*, Season 1, Episode 13 at 27:40 minutes. After hearing about the Barksdale case, the federal agents decline to get involved because the FBI has been directed to focus on counter-terrorism and organized crime. Two seasons later, watch *The Wire*, Season 3, Episode 9, at 28:55 minutes, when FBI agents give a similar explanation for declining the case and say that "ghetto drug stuff just doesn't rate." Given Professor O'Hear's description of the power of federal narcotics law enforcement, does it ring true to you that the FBI and federal prosecutors were never interested in offering significant help or taking over the investigation? Might it be, as Professor O'Hear suggests, that federal prosecutors are typically interested in high-profile drug cases, rather than run-of-the-mill inner-city drug trafficking?

2. While it is comparatively rare for the federal government to get involved in drug cases, when the FBI and other federal agents show up, their presence can be quite intimidating. Watch *The Wire*, Season 3, Episode 9, at 28:25 minutes. Lieutenant Daniels and his detail are not able to get the wireless company to give them information fast enough to tap the disposable cell phones being used by the Barksdale gang, so they call in the FBI. Prosecutor Pearlman explains: "They're only half scared of us. But a visit from the feds, you all have profile enough to push them." Why are corporations and criminals so much more afraid of the federal government? Is it that the feds have superior resources? Is it that the punishment in federal cases is much stiffer? Or is it something else?

3. Professor O'Hear's article was published in 2004. Is the federal government's power in the drug war waning? Over the last few years, states have shown much greater interest in allowing medical marijuana, even though it still violates federal law. The federal government has begun to back down from its threat to prosecute medical marijuana users. In 2009, the Department of Justice issued a memorandum seemingly cautioning against prosecution in such cases. *See* Department of Justice, Memorandum for Selected United States Attorneys on Investigations and Prosecutions in States Authorizing Medical Use of Marijuana (Oct. 19, 2009) (the "Ogden Memo") (explaining that prosecutors "should not focus federal resources in your States on individuals whose actions are in clear and unambiguous compliance with existing state laws providing for the medical use of marijuana"). Yet, in a clarifying memorandum sent less than two years later, the Department of Justice made clear that it would rigorously prosecute marijuana cases, including those which were characterized as a low priority under the 2009 memorandum. *See* Department of Justice, Guidance Regarding the Ogden Memo in Jurisdictions Seeking to Authorize Marijuana for Medical Use (June 29, 2011).

4. Watch *The Wire*, Season 3, Episode 11, at 5:40 minutes. Mayor Royce is very interested in the crime reduction resulting from Hamsterdam. He wants to continue the experiment, but his political advisors strongly pressure him to shut it down. Delegate Watkins explains that the Department of Justice will come down hard on the city if it learns about Hamsterdam. Are general federalism concerns and respect for state independence different in the drug context? Put differently, has the federal government scared state and local politicians into uniformity rather than allowing states to act as "laboratories of democracy?" *See* New State Ice Co. v. Liebmann, 285 U.S. 262, 311 (1932) (Brandeis, J., dissenting).

5. The War on Drugs is the classic criminal justice example of the dispute between federal and state authority, but it is by no means the only one. There are many other in-

stances in which more than one governmental agency is potentially responsible for the same episode of criminal conduct. Season 2 of *The Wire* vividly portrays this problem with respect to the thirteen dead women found in the shipping container. Although there is no colorable claim that the federal government should be involved, there is still a dispute as to which division of Maryland law enforcement should handle the case. Colonel Rawls does not want to take responsibility for the bodies and works hard to foist them onto the Maryland State Police. Watch *The Wire*, Season 2, Episode 2, at 27:25 minutes. After McNulty is able to prove the time of death, it becomes far more likely that the victims died in the jurisdiction of the Baltimore Police Department. Rawls then attempts to claim that the case should go to Anne Arundel County, Baltimore County, the Coast Guard or anyone except his agency. *See id.* at 33:00 minutes. Ultimately, the Baltimore Police Department accepted responsibility, but who would have made the final decision on which jurisdiction was responsible if Colonel Rawls and the other law enforcement agencies all refused to take the bodies?

What Sentence Would Avon Barksdale Have Received in Federal Court?[1]

After hundreds of hours of visual and electronic surveillance, Lieutenant Daniels and his team finally acquire enough evidence to charge Avon Barksdale. The closing scenes of Season 1 of *The Wire* demonstrate a number of important points about the criminal justice system. First, while it is easy for the police to target low-level street dealers, it is much harder to build a case against the leaders of an illegal operation who talk behind closed doors and never themselves touch the drugs, guns, or dirty money. Second, when police do build a case against a high-level drug trafficker they often have to contend with high-priced and effective criminal defense lawyers who will make it tough to win at trial. Third, by virtue of being at the top of the organizational pyramid, defendants like Avon Barksdale know figuratively (and sometimes literally) where the bodies are buried. They have valuable information to turn over to law enforcement in exchange for a lighter sentence. The difficulty in winning a case based on wiretaps and facing a high-powered attorney, coupled with the allure of clearing other cases off the books, makes it irresistible for prosecutors to plea bargain. The closing scenes of Season 1 of *The Wire* thus beautifully illustrate why prosecutors are willing to cut a deal in which the mastermind of an enormous criminal conspiracy pleads guilty to a single count of drug possession and receives a sentence of only seven years. In short, Avon Barksdale gets an incredibly favorable deal given the extent of his criminal activity.

What *The Wire* fails to demonstrate (and, in fairness, what it really cannot demonstrate given the storyline) is how much Avon Barksdale also benefitted by being prosecuted in state court, rather than federal court. Although federal prosecutors might have been eager (though perhaps not as eager as state prosecutors) to agree to a plea bargain, they would have had much greater leverage to seek a higher sentence. As explained below, the exact charge Avon Barksdale plead guilty to in a local Baltimore circuit court would have resulted in a much tougher sentence if it had been adjudicated in a Baltimore federal court.

---

1. Editor's Note: This excerpt contains spoilers from Seasons 1, 2, and 3 of *The Wire*.

Avon Barksdale pleaded guilty to one count of possession with intent to distribute one kilogram of heroin, and he agreed to a maximum sentence of seven years. Under the Federal Sentencing Guidelines, Barksdale's sentence would be determined by a combination of his base offense level (the seriousness of his crime and other relevant conduct) and criminal history. Because he insulated himself so well from his organization's criminal activity, Barksdale had no prior convictions and would thus have the lowest criminal history category—Category I.

To determine Barksdale's base offense level, we would begin with the crime of conviction—possession with intent to distribute one kilogram of heroin. Section 2D1.1 of the Federal Sentencing Guidelines sets a base offense level of 32 for possession of this quantity of heroin. That does not end the matter, however. The Guidelines look at a host of other factors to determine whether the base offense level should be moved upward or downward. For example, Barksdale would receive a two-level reduction for "acceptance of responsibility" which is awarded as a matter of course to defendants who plead guilty. *See* Federal Sentencing Guidelines § 3e1.1.[2] Barksdale's guilty plea would therefore move his base offense level down to 30. But that is where the good news would end for him. Section 3B1.1 of the Guidelines imposes a four-level increase for the "organizer or leader of a criminal activity that involved five or more participants or was otherwise extensive." This would bring Barksdale's base offense level to 34.

It is possible, though uncertain, that other provisions of the Guidelines would apply as well. Section 5K2.18 allows for upward departures if the defendant is involved in a violent street gang, although this provision is rarely invoked. More common is § 5K2.21, which authorizes a judge to increase a sentence for dismissed or uncharged conduct. This means a court could take into consideration other crimes Barksdale committed even if the government cannot prove them beyond a reasonable doubt.

If a judge were to invoke §§ 5K2.18 and 5K2.21, Barksdale's base offense level would almost certainly be higher than 34. On the other hand, a capable defense lawyer might be able to convince prosecutors to agree to a lower base offense level. But a defense attorney's negotiating position is limited because Congress has imposed a mandatory minimum sentence of ten years for possession of one kilogram of heroin. *See* 21 U.S.C. § 841. As such, it is reasonable for us to assume that Barksdale will be sentenced based on a base offense level of 34. As noted above, because Barksdale had no prior conviction, his Criminal History Category would be I. Look at the sentencing table on the following pages and find the intersection of those two axis.

As you should see, under the Federal Sentencing Guidelines, Barksdale's sentencing range is 151 to 188 months, the equivalent of 12½ to 15⅔ years. As you may have learned in your criminal procedure class, the Supreme Court's decision in United States v. Booker, 543 U.S. 220 (2005) rendered the Guidelines advisory. After *Booker*, federal judges are free to depart from the Guidelines so long as the departure is reasonable. The possibility therefore exists that a judge could impose a below guideline sentence. Yet, in roughly 85% of cases since *Booker*, federal judges have declined to impose sentences below the Guide-

---

2. In an illustration of how complicated the Guidelines can be, § 3e1.1 contemplates the possibility of a three-level reduction for some defendants if they accept responsibility at a particularly early stage of the case. Given the timing of his acceptance of responsibility, Barksdale would not qualify for this more significant reduction. In any event, the three-level departure requires a motion from the government, which prosecutors would have been unlikely to make in Barksdale's case.

CRIMINAL HISTORY CATEGORY & CRIMINAL HISTORY POINTS						
OFFENSE LEVEL	I	II	III	IV	V	VI
	0 or 1	2 or 3	4, 5 or 6	7, 8 or 9	10, 11 or 12	13 or More
1	0–6	0–6	0–6	0–6	0–6	0–6
2	0–6	0–6	0–6	0–6	0–6	1–7
3	0–6	0–6	0–6	0–6	2–8	3–9
4	0–6	0–6	0–6	2–8	4–10	6–12
5	0–6	0–6	1–7	4–10	6–12	9–15
6	0–6	1–7	2–8	6–12	9–15	12–18
7	0–6	2–8	4–10	8–14	12–18	15–21
8	0–6	4–10	6–12	10–16	15–21	18–24
9	4–10	6–12	8–14	12–18	18–24	21–27
10	6–12	8–14	10–16	15–21	21–27	24–30
11	8–14	10–16	12–18	18–24	24–30	27–33
12	10–16	12–18	15–21	21–27	27–33	30–37
13	12–18	15–21	18–24	24–30	30–37	33–41
14	15–21	18–24	21–27	27–33	33–41	37–46
15	18–24	21–27	24–30	30–37	37–46	41–51
16	21–27	24–30	27–33	33–41	41–51	46–57
17	24–30	27–33	30–37	37–46	46–57	51–63
18	27–33	30–37	33–41	41–51	51–63	57–71
19	30–37	33–41	37–46	46–57	57–71	63–78
20	33–41	37–46	41–51	51–63	63–78	70–87
21	37–46	41–51	46–57	57–71	70–87	77–96
22	41–51	46–57	51–63	63–78	77–96	84–105
23	46–57	51–63	57–71	70–87	84–105	92–115
24	51–63	57–71	63–78	77–96	92–115	100–125
25	57–71	63–78	70–87	84–105	100–125	110–137
26	63–78	70–87	78–97	92–115	110–137	120–150
27	70–87	78–97	87–108	100–125	120–150	130–162
28	78–97	87–108	97–121	110–137	130–162	140–175
29	87–108	97–121	108–135	121–151	140–175	151–188
30	97–121	108–135	121–151	135–168	151–188	168–210
31	108–135	121–151	135–168	151–188	168–210	188–235

32	121–151	135–168	151–188	168–210	188–235	210–262
33	135–168	151–188	168–210	188–235	210–262	235–293
34	151–188	168–210	188–235	210–262	235–293	262–327
35	168–210	188–235	210–262	235–293	262–327	292–365
36	188–235	210–262	235–293	262–327	292–365	324–405
37	210–262	235–293	262–327	292–365	324–405	360–LIFE
38	235–293	262–327	292–365	324–405	360–LIFE	360–LIFE
39	262–327	292–365	324–405	360–LIFE	360–LIFE	360–LIFE
40	292–365	324–405	360–LIFE	360–LIFE	360–LIFE	360–LIFE
41	324–405	360–LIFE	360–LIFE	360–LIFE	360–LIFE	360–LIFE
42	360–LIFE	360–LIFE	360–LIFE	360–LIFE	360–LIFE	360–LIFE
43	LIFE	LIFE	LIFE	LIFE	LIFE	LIFE

lines. *See* Douglas A. Berman & Paul J. Hofer, *A Look at Booker at Five*, 22 FED. SENT. R. 77 (Dec. 1, 2009). And given the extent of Barksdale's criminal enterprise — the enormous amounts of drugs, the murders, the use of children to peddle his product — the possibility of a below Guidelines sentence is very unlikely. Assuming a judge imposed the middle of the Guideline range, Barksdale would have received a sentence of 169.5 months or slightly over 14 years. Put simply, Barksdale probably would have received a sentence that was twice as long in federal court as the 7 years he received in state court.

The longer front-end sentence is not the end of the story however. There is a major divide between how some states and the federal system handle early release of prisoners. As we learn in Season 2 of *The Wire*, Avon Barksdale cuts a favorable deal with prison authorities and is paroled after serving only 26 months of his seven-year sentence. *See The Wire*, Season 3, Episode 5, at 30:30 minutes. This would not happen in the federal system. Pursuant to the Sentencing Reform Act of 1984 (which adopted the Federal Sentencing Guidelines), Congress abolished parole. Thus, Barksdale would not have any chance of being paroled early in the federal system. The best Barksdale could hope for is to have his sentence reduced for good behavior. Under 18 U.S.C. § 3624(b), federal prisoners are permitted to earn up to 54 days each year for good behavior that will be deducted from their sentences. The Bureau of Prisons uses a complicated formula to make good time calculations and arguably inmates who behave exceptionally can end up with less than the statutory prescribed 54 days per year of credit. *See* Barber v. Thomas, 130 S. Ct. 2499 (2010). Nevertheless, let us assume that Barksdale receives the maximum credit and shaves 756 days off of his sentence. His 14-year sentence would then drop to about 12 years of actual incarceration.

At the end of the day, the comparison between Barksdale's case being handled in federal versus state court is stark. While he served just over 2 years following his state conviction, a federal conviction probably would have added another decade of incarceration, and possibly more.

C. Conspiracy

Conspiracy has been called "the darling of the modern prosecutor's nursery." Harrison v. United States, 7 F.2d 259, 263 (2d. Cir. 1925). In some years, more than one-quarter of federal criminal defendants are charged with conspiracy. *See* Raphael Prober & Jill Randall, *Federal Criminal Conspiracy*, 39 AM. CRIM. L. REV. 571, 572 n.9 (2002). Prosecutors love conspiracy charges because they allow for flexible venue locations, very favorable evidentiary rules for admissions by other parties, and the ability to hold large and lengthy joint trials that conserve resources. *See* WAYNE R. LaFAVE, CRIMINAL LAW § 12.01 (4th ed. 2003). Moreover, while prosecutors might not wish to admit it, conspiracy trials provide the possibility for guilt-by-association to seep into the jury's mind. *See* Paul Marcus, *Criminal Conspiracy Law: Time to Turn Back From an Ever Expanding, Ever More Troubling Area*, 1 WM. & MARY BILL RTS. J. 1, 7–8 (1992). And, of course, proving conspiracy is much easier than demonstrating an attempt or a completion of the target offense. Prosecutors need only demonstrate an agreement to commit a crime and possibly some very minor overt act toward that goal. But that is not the only reason prosecutors love conspiracy charges. As the famous decision of Pinkerton v. United States demonstrates below, conspiracy charges provide prosecutors with even further benefits.

Pinkerton v. United States
328 U.S. 640 (1946)

Mr. Justice DOUGLAS delivered the opinion of the Court.

Walter and Daniel Pinkerton are brothers who live a short distance from each other on Daniel's farm. They were indicted for violations of the Internal Revenue Code. The indictment contained ten substantive counts and one conspiracy count. The jury found Walter guilty on nine of the substantive counts and on the conspiracy count. It found Daniel guilty on six of the substantive counts and on the conspiracy count....

A single conspiracy was charged and proved. Some of the overt acts charged in the conspiracy count were the same acts charged in the substantive counts. Each of the substantive offenses found was committed pursuant to the conspiracy....

* * *

It is contended that there was insufficient evidence to implicate Daniel in the conspiracy. But we think there was enough evidence for submission of the issue to the jury.

There is, however, no evidence to show that Daniel participated directly in the commission of the substantive offenses on which his conviction has been sustained, although there was evidence to show that these substantive offenses were in fact committed by Walter in furtherance of the unlawful agreement or conspiracy existing between the brothers. The question was submitted to the jury on the theory that each petitioner could be found guilty of the substantive offenses, if it was found at the time those offenses were committed petitioners were parties to an unlawful conspiracy and the substantive offenses charged were in fact committed in furtherance of it.

Daniel relies on United States v. Sall, 116 F.3d 745 (3rd Cir. 1940). That case held that participation in the conspiracy was not itself enough to sustain a conviction for the substantive offense even though it was committed in furtherance of the conspiracy. The court held that, in addition to evidence that the offense was in fact committed in furtherance of the conspiracy, evidence of direct participation in the commission of the substantive offense or other evidence from which participation might fairly be inferred was necessary.

We take a different view. We have here a continuous conspiracy. There is here no evidence of the affirmative action on the part of Daniel which is necessary to establish his withdrawal from it.... And so long as the partnership in crime continues, the partners act for each other in carrying it forward. It is settled that 'an overt act of one partner may be the act of all without any new agreement specifically directed to that act.' Motive or intent may be proved by the acts or declarations of some of the conspirators in furtherance of the common objective. A scheme to use the mails to defraud, which is joined in by more than one person, is a conspiracy. Yet all members are responsible, though only one did the mailing. The governing principle is the same when the substantive offense is committed by one of the conspirators in furtherance of the unlawful project. The criminal intent to do the act is established by the formation of the conspiracy. Each conspirator instigated the commission of the crime. The unlawful agreement contemplated precisely what was done. It was formed for the purpose. The act done was in execution of the enterprise. The rule which holds responsible one who counsels, procures, or commands another to commit a crime is founded on the same principle. That principle is recognized in the law of conspiracy when the overt act of one partner in crime is attributable to all....

A different case would arise if the substantive offense committed by one of the conspirators was not in fact done in furtherance of the conspiracy, did not fall within the scope of the unlawful project, or was merely a part of the ramifications of the plan which could not be reasonably foreseen as a necessary or natural consequence of the unlawful agreement. But as we read this record, that is not this case.

Affirmed.

Mr. Justice RUTLEDGE, dissenting in part.

The judgment concerning Daniel Pinkerton should be reversed. In my opinion it is without precedent here and is a dangerous precedent to establish.

Daniel and Walter, who were brothers living near each other, were charged in several counts with substantive offenses, and then a conspiracy count was added naming those offenses as overt acts. The proof showed that Walter alone committed the substantive crimes. There was none to establish that Daniel participated in them, aided and abetted Walter in committing them, or knew that he had done so. Daniel in fact was in the penitentiary, under sentence for other crimes, when some of Walter's crimes were done.

* * *

The court's theory seems to be that Daniel and Walter became general partners in crime by virtue of their agreement and because of that agreement without more on his part Daniel became criminally responsible as a principal for everything Walter did thereafter in the nature of a criminal offense of the general sort the agreement contemplated, so long as there was not clear evidence that Daniel had withdrawn from or revoked the agreement. Whether or not his commitment to the penitentiary had that effect, the result is a vicarious criminal responsibility as broad as, or broader than, the vicarious civil liability of a partner for acts done by a co-partner in the course of the firm's business.

Such analogies from private commercial law and the law of torts are dangerous, in my judgment, for transfer to the criminal field....

* * *

———————

Notes and Questions

1. What is the legal rule adopted by the *Pinkerton* case?

2. Does the *Pinkerton* doctrine provide for liability that is too far ranging? Aren't conspirators being held liable for the actions of others under a simple negligence theory? Shouldn't courts disfavor liability when an individual is not personally aware (i.e. at least reckless, as opposed to negligent) that a crime is occurring?

3. Some states, as well as the Model Penal Code, have rejected the *Pinkerton* doctrine because it allows for liability that is too far-ranging. *See* Neal Katyal, *Conspiracy Theory*, 112 YALE L.J. 1307 (2003).

4. Watch *The Wire*, Season 3, Episode 5, at 27:00 minutes, in which all the members of the "Co-Op" meet to discuss how to maximize profit without violence. Stringer Bell runs the meeting like a traditional business meeting and follows the Roberts Rules of Order. At the end of the scene, Stringer walks over to a lower-level drug dealer and asks him what he's doing. The young man responds that he's taking notes, as required by the Roberts Rules of Order. Stringer is furious and asks "[are] you taking notes on a criminal ... conspiracy?" While the scene shows that some criminals are dumb enough to broadcast that they are involved in a conspiracy, most are smart enough not to say so. In the absence of explicit evidence how do we prove conspiracy?

5. *All the pieces matter*: In considering the answer to question 4 above, watch *The Wire*, Season 1, Episode 6 at 21:30 minutes. After Bodie makes a call to Stinkum on a payphone, Officer Pryzbylewski marks the call as non-pertinent because there was no drug talk on the call. Detective Freamon quickly corrects him.

Freamon: They used codes to hide their pager and phone numbers. And when someone does use a phone they don't use names. And if someone does use a name, he's reminded not to. All of that is valuable evidence.

Prez: Of what?

Freamon: Conspiracy.

Prez: Conspiracy?

Freamon: We're building something here, Detective. We're building it from scratch. All the pieces matter.

What Other Crimes Might Avon Barksdale Be Guilty Of?

"Three or four years ain't enough ... Not for Avon Barksdale."[1]

— Rhonda Pearlman, Assistant State's Attorney

As you know, prosecutors agreed to allow Avon Barksdale to plead guilty to a single count of possession with intent to distribute heroin in exchange for a seven-year prison term. The decision deeply angered Detective McNulty and many of his colleagues, who saw Avon as a drug kingpin responsible for numerous murders, assaults, and even the attempted murder of a police officer. If Detective McNulty had his way, prosecutors would

———————

1. *The Wire*, Season 1, Episode 13, at 52:50 minutes.

have thrown the book at Avon Barksdale and charged every offense under the sun. An interesting question is therefore what charges prosecutors could have brought if they followed the McNulty approach? Specifically, what crimes in Season 1 of *The Wire* could be connected to the drug conspiracy and Avon Barksdale?

For example, Watch *The Wire*, Season 1, Episode 1, at 45:00 minutes. In the beginning of the scene, a drug addict named Johnny Weeks unsuccessfully tries to buy $30 worth of drugs by folding two fake $10 bills inside of a real $10 bill. He has used this trick before and the drug dealers are watching for this type of ploy. When the buy starts to go bad, Johnny runs away and the drug dealers give chase. Bodie is ready to kill Johnny for stealing from the gang. D'Angelo Barksdale, who is in charge of the drug crew, ignores Bodie and listens to Johnny apologize for trying to steal. Without saying anything, D'Angelo turns his back on Johnny and walks away without giving any instructions. Bodie and the other drug dealers then savagely beat Johnny.

Although Avon Barksdale has never met Johnny, was not present at the scene, and certainly did not order the beating, can he be charged with aggravated assault? Is the beating of Johnny in furtherance of the drug conspiracy? When you run a drug dealing operation is it reasonably foreseeable that addicts will try to steal from your gang? And if it is foreseeable that addicts will try to steal, is it foreseeable that the response of the dealers working the corner will be to brutally beat those who have attempted to steal? Is Avon Barksdale guilty under *Pinkerton*? What if Bodie had gotten his way and the dealers had killed Johnny for his transgression? Would it be reasonably foreseeable that drug dealers would kill an addict for stealing $20 worth of drugs?

The answers to these questions are tricky and depend on the jurisdiction where the case is prosecuted. That caveat aside, it is plausible that Avon Barksdale could be held liable even if he never ordered the beating of Johnny or even met the individuals who committed the assault. As Professor Joshua Dressler has explained:

> To be regarded as a co-conspirator, a person does not need to know the identity, *or even the existence*, of every other member of the conspiracy, nor must she participate in every detail or event of the conspiracy. It follows, therefore, that a prosecutor's theory of conspiracy is not fatally flawed solely because one party to the alleged agreement never communicated with certain other members. However, to be a co-conspirator, a defendant must have a general awareness of both the scope and objective of the enterprise; in general, there must be a community of interest [among the parties] or reason to know of each other's existence.

Joshua Dressler, Understanding Criminal Law § 29.07[D] (4th ed. 2006) (internal quotations omitted).

Assuming Avon Barksdale's liability reaches down as far as the individual drug dealers on the corners, he faces an enormous number of possible charges. Putting aside criminal charges in which Avon was a direct participant (such as solicitation to commit murder and money laundering), consider the crimes he is guilty of simply under basic conspiracy law:

- Conspiracy: Generally, the conspiracy charge does not merge with the target offense. This means that in a drug distribution conspiracy, prosecutors are free to charge, convict, and punish the defendant for *both* conspiracy and the completed offense of drug distribution. *See* Paul Marcus, *Re-Evaluating Large Multiple Defendant Prosecutions*, 11 Wm. & Mary Bill Rts. J. 67, 71 (2002).

- Multiple Counts of Possession With Intent to Distribute: Season 1 of *The Wire* depicts dozens of drug deals by Avon Barksdale's employees. Each sale of drugs is a separate offense for double jeopardy purposes because it is a separate transaction. Barksdale could thus be prosecuted for each drug deal, either in a single trial or in consecutive proceedings. *See* Blockburger v. United States, 284 U.S. 299 (1932).

- Multiple Counts of Aggravated Assault: In addition to the beating on Johnny Weeks discussed above, numerous other assaults are carried out by Barksdale's drug crews. In the federal system and states that have adopted the *Pinkerton* doctrine, Avon is potentially responsible for all of these offenses.

- Witness Tampering: In the very first episode of *The Wire*, D'Angelo Barksdale is on trial for murder. One of the corroborating witnesses, Nakeesha Lyles, changes her story and testifies that she is unable to identify D'Angelo. Stringer Bell is in the courtroom and it is apparent that someone in Barksdale's gang has intimidated Lyles into changing her story. Avon Barksdale likely orchestrated this crime, but even if had no direct involvement, he may be guilty under the *Pinkerton* doctrine because the witness tampering is in furtherance of maintaining the drug conspiracy and reasonably foreseeable.

- Murder: Avon Barksdale's drug gang commits numerous murders in Season 1 of *The Wire*. At the outset, D'Angelo was on trial for a murder committed in the towers. After that trial, the gang kills William Gant (who testified against D'Angelo) and Nakeisha Lyles (who changed her story and refused to testify against D'Angelo). Later in the season, after Omar Little and his partners, steal the stash, the Barksdale gang murders both of Omar's partners. At the end of Season 1, Avon's trusted hitman, Wee-Bey Brice, confesses to killing Orlando Blocker (who owned the club Avon used) and Little Man (who had assisted in killing Orlando). As with the crimes outlined above, these murders are both foreseeable and in furtherance of the drug dealing conspiracy, thus making Avon Barksdale liable under *Pinkerton* even if he did not directly participate.

- Attempted Murder: During the murder of Orlando Blocker, Wee-Bey and Little Man unexpectedly encounter Detective Greggs and shoot her as well. Greggs survives, thus creating an attempted murder charge. Obviously, it was not Barksdale's intent to kill Detective Greggs, as he did not even know who she was. But because it might have been foreseeable that someone else could have been present during the hit on Orlando and that the gang would shoot that person, Avon Barksdale may be liable under the *Pinkerton* doctrine for the attempted murder charge as well.

Chapter IV

The Fourth Amendment in the Real World

A. Introduction

Almost no criminal procedure topic has attracted as much attention as the Fourth Amendment. From *Law and Order* to *CSI*, search and seizure issues are all over television. Criminal procedure professors spend an enormous amount of time teaching students the doctrinal law of the Fourth Amendment. And there's a lot to teach. There are different standards for traffic stops, sobriety checkpoints, full-scale arrests and dozens of exceptions to the warrant requirement. When class is over, many professors head back to their offices to write law review articles attempting to show whether the doctrine is right, where it has gone wrong, and what unifying theories might explain or debunk current Fourth Amendment jurisprudence.

At this point in your legal career, you are probably already familiar with a lot of Fourth Amendment jurisprudence. However, there are some Fourth Amendment questions that receive relatively little attention in law school classes and legal literature. The first question—which often gets lost in the maze of legal doctrine—is whether the police officers who are responsible for complying with the Fourth Amendment actually understand the law they are supposed to be applying. A second question that also lurks beneath the surface is whether the Court's Fourth Amendment jurisprudence benefits primarily the wealthy at the expense of the poor. In other words, does the Court's focus on homes as opposed to the rights of individuals in vehicles or on the street inadvertently protect the wealthy while leaving the less affluent more exposed to prosecution in the criminal justice system? Finally, is the Court operating in a fantasy world by believing that the police actually comply with the Fourth Amendment rules? Do officers take the law seriously, or do they only comply with the Fourth Amendment's requirements when they think they are likely to find evidence that can be used against the defendant? This chapter attempts to answer these questions by looking beyond and beneath the Fourth Amendment rules traditionally covered in introductory criminal procedure courses.

B. Do the Police Understand the Fourth Amendment Rules?

Professor Akhil Amar famously compared Fourth Amendment jurisprudence to a "sinking ocean liner — rudderless and badly off course." Amar, *Fourth Amendment First Principles*, 107 HARV. L. REV. 757, 759 (1994). The Supreme Court has adopted dozens of exceptions to the warrant requirement and criminal procedure students can spend an entire semester trying to understand Fourth Amendment doctrine. While a small percentage of law enforcement officers are attorneys who have sat through a semester of criminal procedure, most learn only limited Fourth Amendment doctrine in police academy courses. Do police understand the Fourth Amendment rules they are supposed to be following? And does the law have to be this difficult?

Craig M. Bradley, Two Models of Fourth Amendment Law
83 Michigan Law Review 1468 (1985)

The fourth amendment is the Supreme Court's tarbaby: a mass of contradictions and obscurities that has ensnared the "Brethren" in such a way that every effort to extract themselves only finds them more profoundly stuck. In 1971 Justice Harlan called for "an overhauling" of fourth amendment law, but this has not occurred. Instead, the Court has simply continued to struggle with the same problems, finding "solutions" which sow ever more litigation and confusion. More than a decade ago, Professor Weinreb cited the fact that in the preceding five Terms (1968–69 to 1972–73) the Court had rendered sixteen major opinions interpreting the fourth amendment, illustrating that the "body of fourth amendment doctrine ... is unstable and unconvincing." In the past five Terms (1979–80 to 1983–-84) the Court has decided thirty-five cases involving the fourth amendment. In seven of these there was no majority opinion. In the seventeen cases decided in the last two years, the Supreme Court has never reached the same result as all lower courts and has usually reversed the highest court below, rendering a total of sixty-one separate opinions in the process. Thus it is apparent that not only do the police not understand fourth amendment law, but that even the courts, after briefing, argument, and calm reflection, cannot agree as to what police behavior is appropriate in a particular case. What policeman (or judge or law professor) could say confidently what the proper scope of a search incident to arrest is, or how far the authorities may go in detaining a suspected drug smuggler at an airport?

Professor LaFave recently engaged in the game, so dear and familiar to fourth amendment scholars, of demonstrating that the nine search and seizure decisions rendered in the 1982–83 Term were illogical, inconsistent with prior holdings and, generally, hopelessly confusing. While opinions that lend themselves to this sort of demolition are wonderful grist for law professors' mills, they do little to advance the purposes of the amendment: "to safeguard citizens from rash and unreasonable interferences with privacy" by giving the police clear-cut rules to follow. The Court's failure to provide such rules leads not only to the exclusion of evidence in cases involving the guilty, but also to intrusions upon the rights of both the innocent and the guilty by police who, faced with incomprehensibly complex rules, either ignore them or, in their efforts to follow them, make mistakes which lead to evidentiary exclusion.

Contributing to the Court's difficulties in this area is the exclusionary rule, but it is not solely to blame. Until the establishment of the "good faith" exception to the exclusionary rule last Term, the rule's operation was simple: if evidence was unconstitutionally obtained it was (always) inadmissible in the prosecutor's case-in-chief. There was no confusion surrounding the operation of the rule. The only difficulty arose in the first step of the exclusionary process—determining whether the evidence was constitutionally obtained. However, the fact that a negative conclusion on this question led to the unpalatable result of excluding valid (and frequently vital) evidence against a person who was probably a criminal undoubtedly influenced this determination. As will be demonstrated, the Court is loathe to declare searches unconstitutional, with the concomitant evidentiary exclusion, in cases where the police have essentially acted reasonably, even if they have not exactly conformed to existing Supreme Court doctrine. The result is that the Court strives to justify such police behavior by stretching existing doctrine to accommodate it. Herein lies the inherent contradiction, and source of confusion, in fourth amendment law: The Court tries on the one hand to lay down clear rules for the police to follow in every situation while also trying to respond flexibly, or 'reasonably,' to each case because a hardline approach would lead to exclusion of evidence. Since the rules are not clear and since, even if they were, it is virtually impossible to lay down a rule that anticipates all potential cases, the police engage in behavior that does not conform to the rules but that strikes the Court as having been essentially reasonable. Given the Court's predilection for clearcut rules, however, simply declaring such conduct 'reasonable' and leaving it at that is not enough. Instead, the Court offers a detailed explanation as to how the police behavior really did conform to the old rule (and in so doing, changes the contours of the old rule), or creates a new rule to justify the behavior. Naturally, such a holding spawns new litigation, which leads to a new opinion, which leads to a new rule, etc.

Fourth amendment critics rank in rows, and it has been repeatedly pointed out that individual cases are inconsistent with each other or that whole chunks of doctrine, such as the automobile exception or the plain view exception, are either misconceived, too broad, or too narrow. But these critics all play the Court on its own field, simply arguing as tenth Justices that the doctrines should be tinkered with in different ways than the Court has done. This Article, in contrast, suggests that current fourth amendment law, complete with the constant tinkering, which it necessarily entails, should be abandoned altogether. Instead, there are two, and only two, ways of looking at the fourth amendment which will provide the police with reasonably coherent direction as to how they must proceed and the courts with a consistent basis for decision.

The two models, briefly, may be called the 'no lines' and the 'bright line' approaches. Model I, no lines, uses tort law as a guide in proposing that the hopeless quest of establishing detailed guidelines for police behavior in every possible situation be abandoned. It suggests that the Court adopt the following view of the fourth amendment: A search or seizure must be reasonable, considering all relevant factors on a case-by-case basis. If it is not, the evidence must be excluded. Factors to be considered include, but are not limited to, whether probable cause existed, whether a warrant was obtained, whether exigent circumstances existed, the nature of the intrusion, the quantum of evidence possessed by the police, and the seriousness of the offense under investigation. This model enjoys support from the history of the fourth amendment and is (roughly) the current practice in Germany and other European countries. Moreover, in most cases it reflects the result, though not the reasoning, of current Supreme Court cases.

The second model may be as shocking at first glance to 'law and order' advocates as the first model is to civil libertarians. It is, basically, that the Supreme Court should actually enforce the warrant doctrine to which it has paid lip service for so many years. That is, a warrant is *always* required for *every* search and seizure when it is practicable to obtain one. However, in order that this requirement be workable and not be swallowed by its exception, the warrant need not be in writing but rather may be phoned or radioed into a magistrate (where it will be tape recorded and the recording preserved) who will authorize or forbid the search orally. By making the procedure for obtaining a warrant less difficult (while only marginally reducing the safeguards it provides), the number of cases where 'emergencies' justify an exception to the warrant requirement should be very small.

These models are the only two possibilities because they are the only two ways of dealing with fourth amendment problems that do not force the Court into the clear rule/flexible response dilemma. Model I, by presenting an unabashedly *unclear* rule that provides no guidelines, will never have to be modified to suit an unusual fact situation. While not an ideal solution, it will, it is argued, work considerably better than the present system where the Court purports to set forth clear rules but does not actually do so. Model II presents a clear rule which can be lived with. If the Court required a modified, easily obtainable warrant to be used in all but true emergencies, the police would know what is expected of them and would be able to conform their conduct to the requirement of the law, much as they have accommodated their behavior to the *Miranda* requirements. Any other approach which tries to set forth rules which the Court is unwilling to enforce strictly will necessarily become mired in exceptions and modifications (with resultant confusion) as has occurred in the current law.

I. THE PROBLEM

As indicated, the fundamental problem with fourth amendment law is that it is confusing. It fails to inform the police how to behave and to inform the lower courts of the basis for the exclusionary decision. This failure is the result of the Court's attempt to pursue a compromise between considering cases flexibly, on the grounds of the reasonableness of police behavior, and setting forth clear rules, which, if the police fail to follow them, will lead to evidentiary exclusion. The Court purports to set forth clear rules while actually adjusting them constantly to accommodate each new fact situation. Confusion in the law is not unique to the fourth amendment, of course, but it is a particularly serious problem in this area because the exclusionary remedy for fourth amendment violations does not make whole the criminal defendant whose rights have been violated—nothing can 'unsearch' his house—and does nothing at all for an innocent victim of an illegal search who derives no benefit from evidentiary exclusion. Thus, it is not a 'remedy' in the ordinary sense. If police are confused about the law and therefore perform illegal searches, the prosecution suffers loss of evidence (in many cases, if the police had understood the law they could have conformed their conduct to it) and society suffers violations of the civil rights of its citizens. Moreover, unlike other areas of law, which can be contemplated at leisure by judges and lawyers, fourth amendment law is supposed to instruct police how to act in the heat of enforcement of the criminal laws. Consequently, in criminal procedure it is uniquely imperative that the police be informed of simple, straightforward principles by which to guide their behavior.

At the heart of both the fourth amendment and the clear rule/flexible response dichotomy is the warrant 'requirement'—so often espoused and so rarely enforced by the Court. Recently, in *United States v. Ross*, the Court, quoting an earlier, unanimous opinion, reaffirmed its commitment to the search warrant:

> The Fourth Amendment proscribes all unreasonable searches and seizures, and it is a cardinal principle that 'searches conducted outside the judicial process, without prior approval by judge or magistrate, are *per se* unreasonable under the Fourth Amendment—subject only to a few specifically established and well-delineated exceptions.'

In fact, these exceptions are neither few nor well-delineated. There are over twenty exceptions to the probable cause or the warrant requirement or both. They include searches incident to arrest (exceptions to both); automobile searches (exception to warrant requirement); border searches (both); searches near the border (warrant and sometimes both); administrative searches (probable cause exception); administrative searches of regulated businesses (warrant); stop and frisk (both); plain view, open field seizures and prison 'shakedowns' (both, because they are not covered by the fourth amendment at all); exigent circumstances (warrant); search of a person in custody (both); search incident to nonarrest when there is probable cause to arrest (both); fire investigations (warrant); warrantless entry following arrest elsewhere (warrant); boat boarding for document checks (both); consent searches (both); welfare searches (both, because not a 'search'); inventory searches (both); driver's license and vehicle registration checks (both); airport searches (both); searches at courthouse doors (both); the new 'school search' (both); and finally the standing doctrine which, while not strictly an exception to fourth amendment requirements, has that effect by causing the courts to ignore fourth amendment violations.

As anyone who has worked in the criminal justice system knows, searches conducted pursuant to these exceptions, particularly searches incident to arrest, automobile and 'stop and frisk' searches, far exceed searches performed pursuant to warrants. The reason that all of these exceptions have grown up is simple: the clear rule that warrants are required is unworkable and to enforce it would lead to exclusion of evidence in many cases where the police activity was essentially reasonable.

By its continued adherence to the warrant requirement in theory, though not in fact, the Court has sown massive confusion among the police and lower courts. The automobile cases are paradigmatic of this trend. In *Carroll v. United States*, the Court upheld a warrantless search of a car that prohibition agents had stopped with probable cause sixteen miles outside of Grand Rapids, Michigan. The Court did not consider the possibility of holding the car while one of the agents went for a warrant. Instead it recognized that the mobility of a vehicle, in contradistinction to a house or store, made it impracticable 'to secure a warrant because the vehicle can be quickly moved out of the locality or jurisdiction in which the warrant must be sought.' However, the Court added that 'in cases where the securing of a warrant is reasonably practicable, it must be used.'

In *Chambers v. Maroney*, the Court dealt with a case in which a car had been seized by the police, its occupants arrested, and the car driven to the police station where it was searched without a warrant. While on the facts of *Chambers* it certainly would have been 'practicable' to obtain a warrant, the Court obviously considered the police activity reasonable anyway. It therefore relied on the 'cars are different from houses' language in *Carroll* to posit an exception to the warrant requirement in cases involving automobile searches. Thus the 'auto exception' grew to accommodate police behavior which, though violative of both the general warrant requirement and the express 'practicability' holding of *Carroll*, seemed reasonable to the Court. . . .

* * *

In an effort to give 'clear rules' to the police while maintaining a degree of flexibility, the Court has failed on both counts. Each 'clear rule' has left unanswered questions, which have turned it into an unclear rule. Yet the application of these rules as if they were bright line rules ('you can search cars without a warrant') leads to injustices in many cases — either the injustice of allowing governmental intrusions into areas where one reasonably expects privacy or that of excluding evidence based on 'technicalities' where the police have tried to follow the unclear rules. . . .

* * *

… Certainly the primary focus of attention should be on clarifying the rules rather than making them increasingly unclear by focusing attention on penalties and exceptions. The Models that follow attempt to accomplish this.

II. MODEL I

Model I, no lines, demands only that searches be reasonable, based upon a consideration of the *facts* of each individual case. In determining the factual question of reasonableness, the Court should consider not only whether there was a warrant, probable cause, or exigent circumstances, but also such factors as the nature of the intrusion (*i.e.*, was it a search for private papers or narcotics, a search of a house or of a barn, etc.), the strength of the evidence possessed by the police, the dangerousness of the defendant, and the seriousness of the crime. Given the long tradition of the warrant and probable cause requirements, the presence or absence of these factors should probably be the most important, but not necessarily the controlling, elements. A lesser intrusion, such as a seizure of evidence in a fenced field behind the defendant's house, would be unlikely to require a warrant, whereas a search of a house probably would. Yet, as discussed above, one can conceive of a case where the suspect's expectation of privacy in his field is so clearly announced, or the need to search a house so great, that rules developed in other cases would not be applicable. Consequently, fixed criteria such as 'warrant requirement,' the 'exigent circumstances exception,' and the 'open fields doctrine' should be avoided. Rather, each case must be evaluated on its own facts, recognizing that, because no two cases will have completely identical facts, prior decisions may only be indicative but not dispositive of future cases. This model is drawn from European criminal procedure and American tort law. It frankly recognizes that it gives no guidance to police as to how to behave, beyond admonishing them to act reasonably, because such guidance is inherently impossible to give....

* * *

… 'Reasonable' police behavior should not depend on their ability to conform to a complex set of rules as they are currently required to do. It makes no sense to say that, because it was reasonable for a policeman to search a car in one case without a warrant, an 'automobile exception' is now created whereby if police follow the rules (*i.e.*, have probable cause) they can always search cars without warrants. The richness of the facts of each search renders it impossible to create a rule in one case that will be readily applicable to all later cases. Yet all of the exceptions to the warrant requirement previously noted were created in just this way. An example will show how a case-by-case approach can help to eliminate the irrational results that the present system requires.

Suppose the police have a certain amount of evidence that a crazed murder suspect armed with a submachine gun is at his summer cottage with a captive. Because they contemplate an arrest in a house, a warrant based on probable cause is normally required. The police, not sure of the precise definitions of either of the following terms, conclude that they have 'probable cause' and 'exigent circumstances' and consequently they enter without a warrant and arrest the suspect. On the motion to suppress the court concludes that the police were absolutely right about exigent circumstances — this was a true emergency. However, they were wrong about probable cause — they did not actually have enough (whatever 'enough' is after *Illinois v. Gates*) to conclude that the suspect was at the summer house.

Since, under the current rules, the exigent circumstances do not affect the issue of probable cause (only the need for a warrant if probable cause is otherwise established), the submachine gun and any other evidence seized incident to the arrest as well as, possibly, any statements made by the suspect at the time of arrest must be excluded. In order to avoid this distasteful result, the courts will be tempted to tinker with the definition of probable cause, stretching it, just a little more, to accommodate this case. To simply examine all relevant factors and conclude that here the police acted reasonably seems far more sensible.

* * *

To be sure, Model I will require that the fourth amendment be read somewhat differently than it has been in the past. The first phrase, forbidding unreasonable searches and seizures, will take over, rendering the requirement that warrants must issue on probable cause less important since warrants would no longer be a precondition of reasonableness....

Because the warrant requirement is largely a sham anyway, a detailed historical justification for doing away with it hardly seems necessary. The more important inquiry is whether such a proposal would prove workable. A compelling argument for Model I can be found in German practice where such an approach is used successfully, generating far less litigation and controversy than the American system. Under the German system, the question of the reasonableness of the search as such is not relevant, there being no precise equivalent to the fourth amendment. However, when the question of whether to admit or exclude seized evidence is considered, a balancing or reasonableness test is employed in virtually every case. The fact that the search may have violated the rules for searches set forth in the Code of Criminal Procedure is only one factor to be considered. More important is whether the intrusion on the defendant's privacy (whether caused by the search for the evidence or its use in court) is *proportional* to the seriousness of the offense, *i.e.*, a case-by-case balancing test is applied. Thus, an individual's diary was excluded from evidence in a perjury case even though it was properly seized because the case did not warrant such a serious intrusion (the exposure of the diary's contents in court) into the private sphere of the individual. However, the court noted that the result might have been different in a murder case. In another case the court refused to issue an order to take spinal fluid from a suspect in a misdemeanor case to determine his possible insanity, despite the fact that such a taking was authorized by the Code of Criminal Procedure. The court reasoned that such a drastic intrusion was out of proportion to the seriousness of the crime.

If the Supreme Court were to opt for Model I, infinite flexibility, then it would not have to decide whether recreational vehicles (RVs) are subject to the 'automobile exception' or what the scope of a search incident to arrest might be. The infinite variety of possibilities which each search presents makes it impossible to declare with confidence that RVs or automobiles or boats or suitcases are or are not entitled to the protection afforded by a warrant in every case. It may even happen that if police are enjoined to think about the facts of each case and act appropriately, rather than to follow an incomprehensible set of rules, they will prove capable of exercising more judgment than had previously been believed.

What are the advantages and disadvantages of Model I? The most obvious advantage is that it will extract the Court from the tarbaby of fourth amendment law. While an occasional decision on a lower court's determination of reasonableness may be in order, the Supreme Court will generally find it unnecessary to involve itself in decisions that are unique to the facts of each case. To free the Court from a series of decisions that has brought it both disruption and a degree of disrepute is no small gain. Furthermore, exclusionary law can be restored to the common sense proposition that evidence obtained unreasonably must always be excluded and evidence obtained reasonably should always be admitted. Such a rule makes far better sense than the rather bizarre rule established recently in *Leon* that if an unreasonable search is performed reasonably then the evidence will be admissible anyway.

The second, and greater, advantage is that evidence will neither be excluded *nor admitted* due to legal technicalities. A minor error by the police in drafting or executing a warrant or in assessing whether adequate cause exists for an automobile search will probably not lead to exclusion, at least in more serious cases. But such legal technicalities as the 'automobile exception,' the 'open fields doctrine' or 'standing' which currently prohibit exclusion, even in the face of gross violations of individual expectations of privacy in particular cases, need not stand in the way of exclusion due to unreasonableness.

The principal disadvantage of Model I is that warrants may be used less if they are not strictly required. As pointed out, however, they are not really strictly required or frequently used now....

The other major argument against Model I is that the police, given no guidelines, will be hopelessly confused, and trial courts will render decisions dependent largely on the predilections of the individual judge. On the contrary, enjoining the police to use their common sense and judging them by that standard, while not an ideal guideline, seems more likely to produce sensible responses than does a set of fictitious rules and vague exceptions that the Supreme Court itself, not to mention the cop on the beat, cannot consistently apply or understand. Moreover, the decisions of the courts will at least be based upon a comprehensible standard, which goes farther down the road to 'justice' than the current vehicle. A judge's personal opinion as to 'reasonableness,' subject to appellate review, is more likely to produce a sensible result than is his personal opinion as to whether a recreational vehicle is an automobile, or a chicken house part of an open field, from which flows, mechanically, his decision that certain police conduct was 'reasonable' or not.

* * *

III. MODEL II

Model I is founded on a belief that the officials charged with operating our criminal justice system — the police and the courts — will be better off if enjoined to act reasonably and reviewed on that basis, than if, as under the current arrangement, they are expected to obey a set of incomprehensible rules. This view flies in the face of the Supreme Court's recent criminal procedure jurisprudence which assumes that giving more or less exact guidelines to the police is the overriding function of the Court's decisions. If the Court and the legal community at large cannot give up this long held view of criminal procedure law, then it is necessary to develop a rule which really does give guidance to the police and the courts. That is, a simple, easily obeyed rule that will actually apply in most cases. Model II will accomplish this by requiring a warrant in all but genuine emergencies but by allowing the warrant to be granted orally on the basis of an oral (telephoned or radioed) submission, provided only that the submission be tape recorded so that its sufficiency can later be tested at a motion to suppress....

Model II proposes that a warrant truly be *required* except when absolutely prevented by an emergency. This means twenty-four-hour-a-day availability of magistrates (assuming the police want to search twenty-four hours a day). It means that before searching an automobile, the police must radio in for a warrant. In short, Model II does for the fourth amendment what *Miranda v. Arizona* did for the fifth: it establishes a relatively simple, straightforward rule that can be applied in virtually every case. Just as in fifth amendment cases, there would be litigation as to whether or not the rule were applicable at all (*i.e.*, 'is this a search?' vs. 'is this a custodial interrogation?') but far less confusion than at present. Also, just as with *Miranda*, the declaration of such a rule by the Court would lead to much hair-tearing and teeth-gnashing by police, who would complain that they were being 'handcuffed.' But the police could get used to radioing for permission before conducting a search, just as they have gotten used to 'reading the rights' before questioning a suspect. The advantage of knowing that they must act according to fixed guidelines in most circumstances and of knowing that their plan of action, having been approved by the magistrate, is appropriate and will virtually always render the evidence admissible, will soon outweigh their temporary feeling of being hamstrung by legal rules.

To be sure, in terms of protection of individual rights, a traditional written warrant is better than an oral one. The traditional warrant procedure forces the police to take more time and to be more careful. It allows the magistrate an opportunity to deliberate and to be sure that everything is in its proper place. But it is precisely this deliberativeness that is the downfall of the present system. The written warrant requirement of the eighteenth century simply cannot apply to most police-citizen encounters in the highly mobile twentieth century. It is this cumbersomeness that has led the Court to declare so many exceptions to the warrant 'requirement.' It is time to take advantage of such technological advances as readily portable two-way radios (including wrist radios) and tape recorders to bring the warrant requirement up to date.

Will it work? Consider first the exceptions to the current warrant requirement discussed earlier. Unless Model II can eliminate many of these exceptions, the light it provides will not be worth the candle. But it will readily be seen that it can. Searches incident to arrest, for example, can be eliminated as an exception to the warrant and probable cause requirements. All arrests must necessarily entail a frisk for weapons which does not depend on probable cause and therefore cannot be subject to a warrant requirement. However, searches of the 'area within the immediate control' of the suspect should only be performed after probable cause has been called in to the magistrate. (If there is no probable cause why should an arrest justify such a search?) Similarly, the automobile exception can be scrapped. When a car is stopped on the highway and the occupants arrested, as in *Chambers v. Maroney*, there is no reason not to call for judicial approval before searching the car. Even if the occupants have not been arrested, the normal case will not present an emergency of such immediacy that calling for judicial authorization is precluded. Finally, many warrantless searches currently justified under the 'exigent circumstances' exception need no longer be performed without a warrant since circumstances so 'exigent' as to prevent the police from radioing for a warrant will rarely occur. For example, in *Warden v. Hayden*, the classic exigent circumstances case, once the police had chased Hayden into his house they could have surrounded the house and stopped for the five minutes or less that it would have required to describe the situation to the magistrate over the radio and receive his authorization before entering.

* * *

Such an exercise may seem unduly restrictive of effective police work. Since it goes against police nature to cease pursuit of a suspect to observe the niceties of criminal procedure, it will undoubtedly mean that, at first, Model II will lead to more, not less, exclusion of evidence. However, once the police realize that warrant use will be rewarded *and* that warrantless searches will be penalized by automatic exclusion of evidence, they will quickly learn to adhere to the Model II requirements.

Certainly there was a time when one could have reasonably argued that to deny the authorities the use of thumb screws and, later, rubber hoses went so much against 'police nature' that it was futile to try to forbid such practices. Yet today the police seem to get along well enough without these aids and have even gotten used to informing suspects of their legal rights before questioning. They could similarly get used to obtaining magisterial authorization before searching, so long as the process did not substantially interfere with their ability to do a good job. This warrant requirement, with its emergency exception, is designed to be quick enough not to interfere with legitimate police activities, yet demanding enough to check abuses of the rights of the citizenry. Indeed, such a system might prove very attractive to police. Unlike the *Miranda* warnings, which tend, however ineffectively, to interfere with what the police are trying to do (get confessions from suspects), a warrant requirement is a neutral higher authorization that should make a functionary in a hierarchical police organization comfortable. If the magistrate authorizes the search, the policeman cannot be criticized for conducting it. If the magistrate refuses the search, the policeman cannot be criticized for not searching. Much of the uncertainty that currently plagues police would thus be eliminated.

If such a readily enforceable warrant requirement were adopted, the Court might be tempted to expand the fourth amendment's coverage. As discussed, a search of an 'open field' frequently intrudes on areas in which people have a reasonable expectation of privacy. Yet the Court has excluded open field searches from the coverage of the fourth amendment, presumably to reduce the burdens that would be placed on law enforcement by a contrary holding. Since it would be a simple matter for police to radio for a warrant before searching open fields, the Court could feel more free to restore 'reasonable expectation of privacy' as the test of fourth amendment protected interests and require warrants for all searches of 'fields' which bear indications that they are private property from which the public is excluded.

Model II is necessarily limited to 'probable cause' searches because searches that are not based on probable cause could not be subject to a warrant requirement unless the Constitution, which requires that 'no warrants shall issue, but upon probable cause,' were amended. Thus, border searches, driver's license checks, and car inventory searches, which are not based on probable cause, and which principally serve other societal interests than the discovery of the evidence of crime, must necessarily remain free of any warrant requirement. Similarly, stop and frisk encounters on the street, which are based not on probable cause but upon a reasonable suspicion that a suspect is 'armed and dangerous,' must be excepted both because a probable cause warrant could not issue under the current standards for stop and frisk and because the 'armed and dangerous' requirement implies an emergency such that the policeman would not have time to radio for authorization before dealing with such a suspect.

* * *

CONCLUSION

Fourth amendment law, to be effective in limiting inappropriate police behavior while at the same time allowing for effective law enforcement, must be a coherent and relatively simple doctrine that a policeman can readily understand and apply. No one could seriously argue that the current law even remotely approaches this ideal. On the contrary, it is so full of fictitious rules and multifaceted exceptions (and exceptions to those exceptions) that the most that could be said of anyone's grasp of the doctrine is that 'he sees where most of the problems are.' The two models suggested in this Article can each be summed up in a single terse command that every policeman can understand: 'Act reasonably!' or 'Get a warrant whenever you can!' Model I may seem a shocking and unacceptable solution to civil libertarians; Model II, to law and order advocates. But both groups, as well as those in between, would agree that strong solutions are necessary if a workable doctrine is to be developed. The Court's efforts to tread a tightrope between two extremes have resulted in a morass of confusion that can satisfy nobody. In discussing these models I have endeavored to show that they are *neutral* proposals which will have some benefits for law enforcement, for defendants, and for public perception of the exclusionary process, which is currently regarded as erratic and irrational. If the Court does not embrace one of these solutions, it is destined to sink ever deeper into the mire of contradiction and confusion.

Notes and Questions

1. Is the current state of Fourth Amendment law as dire as Professor Bradley portrays? Police officers conduct millions of stops, arrests, and searches every year. Do officers by-and-large do a better job understanding and complying with Supreme Court precedent than Professor Bradley suggests?

2. Consider the Supreme Court's decision in Illinois v. Wardlow, 528 U.S. 119 (2000), which was decided well after Professor Bradley's article. In *Wardlow*, the Supreme Court held that unprovoked flight from the police in a high crime neighborhood creates reasonable suspicion to believe criminal activity is afoot. What is a high crime area? Would almost any neighborhood portrayed in *The Wire* fall into this category? How are officers supposed to know which neighborhoods are high crime? Would it be best to define high crime neighborhoods statistically by using computer programs that analyze crime data and provide a map of crime hot spots? *See* Andrew Guthrie Ferguson, *Crime Mapping and the Fourth Amendment: Redrawing "High Crime" Areas*, 63 HASTINGS L.J. 179 (2011).

3. Even more recently, consider Arizona v. Gant, 556 U.S. 332, 335 (2009), in which the Supreme Court overruled longstanding precedent and held that police can only search the passenger compartment of a vehicle incident to arrest if the arrestee is unsecured or if it is "reasonable to believe the vehicle contains evidence of the offense of arrest." What does the latter half of the Court's test mean? If an officer arrests a drunk driver on his way home from the bar, is it reasonable to believe evidence of that crime will be found in the vehicle? Are police able to determine in advance when a search incident to arrest complies with the *Gant* standard?

4. In his Model I, Professor Bradley proposes the elimination of hard-and-fast rules and instead asks officers to act reasonably. Is this a plausible solution given the vast power wielded by police officers? Can we trust Officer Pryzbylewski to act reasonably in Season 1 of *The Wire*? Recall that in Season 1, Episode 2, at 7:00 minutes, Pryzbylewski accidentally shot his gun in the office because he didn't realize he had left a round in the chamber. Pryzbylewski had previously shot up an undercover police car with his personal gun and lied about it claiming that a sniper shot the car. *See The Wire*, Season 1, Episode 2, at 10:00 minutes. And, of course, remember that he showed up drunk in the towers late at night and assaulted a juvenile, causing the boy to lose his eye. *See The Wire*, Season 1, Episode 2, at 44:45 minutes. With this track record can we simply trust Officer Pryzbylewski to act reasonably in complying with the Fourth Amendment? On the other hand, if Officer Pryzbylewski is unwilling to follow police department rules about discharging his weapon, use of force, and telling the truth, is he likely to comply with a detailed set of Fourth Amendment rules?

5. In *The Wire*, Season 4, Episode 5, at 41:45 minutes, three officers set up a surveillance camera in a public park to watch a drug gang. Later in Episode 5, at 46:20 minutes,

the officers sit in a van near the park and watch the video of the drug gang doing business in the park. Detective Sydnor asks Detective Herc: "Is this legal? I mean intercepting what they're saying?" What is the answer to the officer's question? If you are not sure, how are the officers supposed to know if the tactic is permissible?

Shamaeizadeh v. Cunigan
338 F.3d 535 (6th Cir. 2003)

MOORE, Circuit Judge,

Plaintiff-Appellant Dr. Ali Shamaeizadeh ("Shamaeizadeh") appeals the district court's grant of summary judgment for Defendants-Appellees with respect to Shamaeizadeh's § 1983 claims and his state law malicious prosecution claim. On March 14, 1994, the Richmond Police Department received a call reporting the burglary of Shamaeizadeh's residence ("the residence"). An officer responded to the call and searched the residence for the burglar. The officer then called for assistance and conducted a second search with one of his supervisors. After discovering evidence of drug paraphernalia during the second search, the two officers called narcotics experts to the scene to participate in a third search. Based on the evidence discovered, the officers secured and executed two search warrants for the residence. Shamaeizadeh was indicted for federal drug violations....

* * *

I. FACTS AND PROCEDURE

Shamaeizadeh owned a one-story house with a basement, located at 121 Millstone Drive, Richmond, Kentucky. He occupied the main floor of the residence with his fiancée, Theresa Schmitt ("Schmitt"), and rented the basement to Brian Reed ("Reed") and Joe Ford ("Ford"). All four residents of the house regarded the basement as a separate apartment.

On March 14, 1994, Schmitt placed an emergency call to the Richmond Police Department, reporting a possible burglary of the residence. Officer Mark Wiles ("Wiles") was dispatched and arrived five minutes later. Schmitt met Wiles at the front door, invited him into the residence, and walked into the kitchen. She told Wiles that she had left the back door open for her cats, and then had passed out on the kitchen table after taking muscle relaxants and consuming a beer. When Schmitt awoke, she noticed that her room key was missing from her pocket. She went into another room and, while she was there, someone allegedly reentered the house and broke the glass top of the kitchen table. Wiles observed broken glass on the kitchen floor.

Schmitt asked Wiles to search the residence with her, and he proceeded to walk through the main floor of the residence. Wiles discovered a locked door, but did not attempt to open it because Schmitt said that it was Shamaeizadeh's room and that Shamaeizadeh kept it locked when he was away. Wiles also discovered a broken door, which led to the basement. He did not examine the broken door because Schmitt said she had kicked it open to use the telephone a few days earlier. Wiles later said that during this search he detected the odor of growing marijuana.

After searching the main floor of the house, Wiles moved onto a deck overlooking the backyard and searched the rear of the premises. Meanwhile, Schmitt entered the basement through the broken door, walked out through the back door of the basement apartment, and met Wiles in the backyard. Explaining that the occupants of the basement apartment were away on spring break, she asked Wiles to check the basement. Wiles proceeded to search the basement.

During his search, Wiles noticed that the basement contained several rooms. Many of the doors were locked, and Wiles did not attempt to open them. He did smell what he thought was growing marijuana. After walking through the basement, Wiles called Assistant Chief of Police Wayne Grant ("Grant") because he believed he needed the assistance of a supervisor.

Wiles and Schmitt returned to the kitchen and waited for Grant to arrive.[1] Schmitt never asked Wiles to leave. While they were waiting, Schmitt told Wiles that she believed the "government" was the burglar. Wiles was thus inclined to discredit Schmitt's allegations of burglary. When Grant arrived, Wiles briefed him about his activity thus far. Schmitt participated in the conversation, informing the officers that she would retrieve a key for the locked doors in the basement.

Wiles and Grant then conducted a second search of the basement apartment. They did not ask Schmitt's permission to conduct the search. When they entered the basement, Wiles again smelled what he suspected was marijuana. The officers discovered small marijuana cigarette butts, known as "roaches," in an ashtray. They also found boxes of fluorescent light bulbs under the apartment stairway and observed fluorescent lighting in one of the locked rooms turn on and off intermittently. They suspected that the fluorescent lighting was being used to grow marijuana because it is often used for that purpose. Schmitt arrived with a ring of keys, but none of them fit the locked doors.

Wiles and Grant then called Assistant Chief of Narcotics Bill Jesse ("Jesse"). They related their observations to him and requested the assistance of an officer experienced in detecting narcotics. Jesse dispatched Sergeant Joel Cunigan ("Cunigan") to the scene. Cunigan arrived at 9:20 p.m., approximately the same time that Wiles's immediate supervisor, Sergeant Sam Manley ("Manley"), arrived. Wiles and Grant briefed Cunigan and Manley on the situation. Then all four officers conducted a third search of the basement apartment. They did not explicitly ask Schmitt's permission to conduct the third search, but Schmitt participated in the walk-through of the basement.

When the officers entered the basement during the third search, Cunigan smelled a strong odor that he believed to be growing marijuana. The officers discovered a hemostat; rolling papers; a plastic bag of what was suspected to be marijuana, but was actually catnip; and a bag containing a variety of pills. At this point, they advised Schmitt of her rights. Schmitt stated her belief that Reed and Ford were growing marijuana in their basement apartment. According to Schmitt, although she never saw marijuana, the scent was so strong that she covered her vents to avoid it, particularly at nighttime.

Cunigan called a state prosecutor and submitted a sworn affidavit in support of his application for a search warrant. A state court judge issued a warrant for the search and seizure of "[a]ny and all illegally possessed controlled substances including marijuana, both growing and processed, and any drug paraphernalia, also any and all illegally possessed prescription drugs."

At 11:19 p.m., Cunigan returned to the residence with other officers and an agent from the Drug Enforcement Agency to execute the search warrant, conducting a fourth search of the residence. The officers forcibly opened locked doors in the basement apartment, finding and seizing 393 marijuana plants and various pieces of growing equipment. In addition to the drugs and drug paraphernalia, the officers indicated that they seized "assorted paper records, receipts, bank records, insurance records, tax papers, personal ledgers, jewelry."

---

1. Shamaeizadeh conceded at oral argument that, at some point prior to the second search, Schmitt informed Wiles that she believed that some of the other occupants of the house were growing marijuana.

On March 15, 1994, Detective John Telek ("Telek") signed an affidavit in support of a second warrant to search the house and two vehicles found there. According to the warrant, Telek was permitted to search for the following items:

1. Any and all illegally possessed controlled substances to wit: Marijuana and any drug paraphernalia;

2. Any and all tax records or documents reflecting the income and/or sources of income of any of the above named persons[;]

3. Any documents reflecting the purchase of drug paraphernalia including the receipts for grow lights, potting soil, fertilizer, plant pots, fans[.]

Shamaeizadeh claims that this search warrant was drafted in an attempt to cover up the illegal seizure of items during the execution of the first warrant.

Upon the recommendation of the local Commonwealth Attorney and a representative of the United States Attorney for the Eastern District of Kentucky, the Richmond Police Department turned over the evidence and prosecution of this matter to the United States government. Shamaeizadeh, Reed, and Ford were arrested and indicted for federal drug-law violations under 21 U.S.C. §§ 841(a)(1) and 846 and 18 U.S.C. §§ 2 and 924(c)(1). Shamaeizadeh was also charged with renting the basement apartment for the purpose of unlawfully manufacturing, storing, or distributing marijuana under 21 U.S.C. § 856....

Shamaeizadeh, Reed, and Ford moved to suppress the evidence seized pursuant to the first warrant. At the suppression hearing, Cunigan and Wiles, the only officers directly involved in Shamaeizadeh's criminal prosecution, testified. The magistrate judge concluded that Wiles's initial warrantless search of the residence was constitutional due to exigent circumstances, but found the second and third warrantless searches unconstitutional. The magistrate judge recommended that Cunigan's affidavit be redacted to reflect only the information obtained as a result of the initial search and through conversations with Schmitt. He then concluded that the redacted affidavit provided probable cause to search the main floor of the residence for illegal drug activity, but not probable cause to support a warrant for the basement. The magistrate judge therefore recommended suppressing the evidence seized from the basement, and the district court adopted this recommendation. The government appealed the district court's decision to suppress the evidence, and the Sixth Circuit affirmed. The government then moved to dismiss the indictment, and the district court granted the motion.

Shamaeizadeh brought a § 1983 action against the City of Richmond, the Richmond Police Department, and five individual police officers-Cunigan, Wiles, Manley, Telek, and Grant-for damages caused by the illegal searches and Shamaeizadeh's subsequent prosecution....

* * *

II. ANALYSIS

* * *

A. Shamaeizadeh's Standing to Challenge the Basement Searches

[The court concluded that Shamaeizadeh lacked a reasonable expectation of privacy in the basement apartment that he had rented to others and therefore lacked standing.]

* * *

B. Qualified Immunity

According to the doctrine of qualified immunity, "government officials performing discretionary functions generally are shielded from liability for civil damages insofar as their conduct does not violate clearly established statutory or constitutional rights of which a reasonable person would have known." *Harlow v. Fitzgerald,* 457 U.S. 800, 818 (1982)....

* * *

The officers contend that the second and third searches were constitutional because either (1) Schmitt gave continuing consent for the searches, (2) exigent circumstances were present, or (3) the plain view doctrine applied. If any of these exceptions to the Fourth Amendment warrant requirement apply, the searches were constitutional.

a. Consent

Consent from an individual whose property is to be searched or from a third party who possesses common authority over the premises validates a search that would otherwise be considered unreasonable and unconstitutional. However, even when a search is authorized by consent, "the scope of the search is limited by the terms of its authorization." *Walter v. United States,* 447 U.S. 649, 656 (1980). The Supreme Court has explained that "the scope of a suspect's consent under the Fourth Amendment" turns on what "the typical reasonable person [would] have understood by the exchange between the officer and the suspect[.]" *Florida v. Jimeno,* 500 U.S. 248, 251 (1991). As long as an officer has an objectively reasonable belief that the search was within the course of consent, the search is valid....

The officers suggest that we should conclude that Schmitt provided continuing consent which authorized all three warrantless searches.[5] The police contend that, as a historical matter, once consent is granted in Kentucky, it must be expressly revoked. Some states have recognized a principle of continuing consent, which allows officers to execute subsequent, closely-related searches in the absence of an objection because the absence of objection permits an inference that the initial consent continued. *See, e.g., State v. Luther,* 663 P.2d 1261, 1263 (1983); *Phillips v. State,* 625 P.2d 816, 818 (Alaska 1980). But even if we were to recognize a principle of continuing consent that might extend throughout three separate searches closely related in time and purpose, the second and third searches exceeded the scope of Schmitt's initial consent.

The officers could not have had an objectively reasonable belief that the second and third searches were within the course of Schmitt's consent. Schmitt clearly consented to Wiles's first search of the premises when she asked him to search for an intruder. But the officers do not assert that Schmitt explicitly consented to the second or third search. In fact, they

---

5. Although they did not press the issue in their brief, the officers also suggested at oral argument that all three warrantless searches were actually components of a single constitutional search. This court has recognized "that a single search warrant may authorize more than one entry into the premises identified in [a] warrant, as long as the second entry is a reasonable continuation of the original search." *United States v. Keszthelyi,* 308 F.3d 557, 568 (6th Cir. 2002). Although we have not previously applied *Keszthelyi* in the context of a search justified on grounds other than a warrant, it is clear that regardless of the source of authority for a search, a search ends when subsequent entries into the identified premises are not reasonable continuations of the original search. Thus, if the first search was constitutional because Schmitt consented to it, the search ended when it exceeded the scope of her consent to the officer's search for a possible intruder. Similarly, if the first search was constitutional because there were exigent circumstances that search ended when the officers began to search for drugs rather than a burglar. The fact that Wiles called in additional officers with drug experience suggests that the searches for drugs and drug paraphernalia were new searches, rather than reasonable continuations of the constitutional search for a burglar.

admit that they did not expressly request her consent when additional officers arrived to search the residence and that they do not recall Schmitt expressly articulating any such consent of her own volition. Schmitt's request that Wiles search the residence for a burglar does not objectively indicate consent for Wiles to call in a supervisor and execute a second search or for Wiles and a supervisor to call in officers with more experience in detecting drugs to execute a third search. Because the second and third searches exceeded the scope of Schmitt's consent, they were unconstitutional.

b. Exigent Circumstances

The officers also maintain that the second and third searches were constitutional because they were executed under exigent circumstances. Warrantless entries are permitted under exigent circumstances, which "exist where there are real immediate and serious consequences that would certainly occur were a police officer to postpone action to get a warrant." *Ewolski v. City of Brunswick,* 287 F.3d 492, 501 (6th Cir. 2002). As with the consent exception to the warrant requirement, we measure exigent circumstances by a standard of objective reasonableness, asking "whether the facts are such that an objectively reasonable officer confronted with the same circumstances could reasonably believe that exigent circumstances existed." *Id.* Exigent circumstances typically exist in one of three situations: officers are in hot pursuit of a suspect, a suspect represents an immediate threat to officers and the public, or "immediate police action [is] necessary to prevent the destruction of vital evidence or thwart the escape of known criminals." *Hancock v. Dodson,* 958 F.2d 1367, 1375 (6th Cir. 1992).

No one contests that Wiles's initial search of the residence was conducted in the face of exigent circumstances. Wiles was dispatched to investigate a possible burglary and believed the burglar might still be present in the residence. The officers now claim that the second and third searches were necessary because the burglar may have been hiding behind locked doors. However, at the suppression hearing in the federal criminal trial, Wiles testified "that he called for backup not because he suspected that a burglary had occurred or because he suspected that a burglar may still be present in the residence, but because when he walked into the downstairs portion of the residence he smelled what he suspected to be growing marijuana." Moreover, Wiles's present claim that he sought backup for the purpose of looking for a possible intruder is inconsistent with the officers' decision to search the entire residence again, rather than simply to investigate the locked rooms that Wiles had been unable to enter. Most importantly, the fact that the officers called in narcotics experts to conduct the third search drastically undercuts the officers' claim that the possible presence of an intruder created exigent circumstances justifying a third search. These facts are such that an objectively reasonable officer could not have reasonably believed that there were exigent circumstances.

The officers' suspicion that marijuana was being grown in the residence also failed to create new exigent circumstances justifying a search. During the second and third searches, the officers were not in hot pursuit of a suspect, threatened by a suspect, or attempting to thwart the escape of a known criminal. The only arguable exigent circumstance in this context was a possible need to prevent the destruction of vital evidence. But the officers cannot argue that they were attempting to prevent the destruction of vital evidence because they were not even certain of what evidence they were searching for at the time — the second and third searches were fishing expeditions for evidence of a drug crime. Thus, new exigencies did not arise to justify the second and third searches.

Because the exigencies justifying the first search did not continue and because new exigencies did not arise to justify the second and third searches, we cannot conclude that exigent circumstances justified the otherwise unconstitutional searches.

c. Plain View

Finally, the officers maintain that their warrantless second and third searches of the residence were justified by the plain view doctrine because drug paraphernalia was in plain view during the second and third searches.... Although the plain view doctrine would likely have justified Wiles's seizure of immediately incriminating drug paraphernalia during the first search, it clearly cannot justify the second and third searches. For the exception to apply, an officer seizing an item in plain view must be "lawfully located." Because the officers were not lawfully in the residence during the second and third searches, the plain view doctrine cannot serve to constitutionalize an otherwise improper search....

* * *

... A reasonable officer therefore could not have objectively considered the consent or exigencies purportedly justifying the warrantless search to have extended beyond Wiles's initial search of the residence.... [W]e must conclude that the officers' second and third warrantless searches violated a clearly established constitutional right of which a reasonable person would have known....

Therefore, we reverse the district court's grant of summary judgment on this issue, and we conclude that the officers are not entitled to summary judgment on Shamaeizadeh's § 1983 claims pertaining to the second and third searches either on the merits or on grounds of qualified immunity. In fact, we conclude that the second and third searches were unconstitutional.

* * *

CONCLUSION

For the reasons explained above, we REVERSE the district court's grant of summary judgment with respect to the second and third warrantless searches....

Notes and Questions

1. Are you surprised that the court concluded the second and third searches were so clearly unconstitutional that the police officers were not even entitled to qualified immunity? Were the officers' actions here clearly in violation of the Fourth Amendment's consent and exigency doctrines?

2. If you were the officer who answered a burglary call, found the occupant acting strangely, smelled marijuana in multiple locations, and encountered locked bedrooms that the 911 caller refused to open, what steps would you have taken?

3. When the occupant accompanied the officers on the second and third searches in the basement, was it logical for the officers to conclude that she was giving continuing consent, or should they have realized the first grant of consent had ended? How were the officers supposed to know that the Sixth Circuit would reject a claim of continuing consent?

4. Do you think the officers knew they were violating the Fourth Amendment and were purposefully trying to skirt the rules?

5. Watch *The Wire*, Season 1, Episode 10, at 19:20 minutes and at 21:00 minutes. In these scenes, the officers listen to a phone call between a gang member in the drug zone and a man out in the suburbs. The officers piece together that the suburban man is the person who delivers the re-up. After hearing the call, Detective Sydnor follows the suburban man from a pay phone to a home. Detective Sydnor sees the man enter a modest

and ordinary looking house that has multiple video cameras positioned around the exterior of the house. How many modest suburban homes have video cameras around the outside of the home? When we add the cameras to the phone call, does that create enough for probable cause to search the house? If not, how much more evidence would you need before you think a judge should issue a warrant? If yes, are there exigent circumstances to justify a search of the house without a warrant because the drugs could be moved at any time? If you don't feel confident in the answers to these questions, how are the police supposed to know what to do?

C. Does Fourth Amendment Doctrine Protect Average People or Just the Wealthy?

The Wire documents the life of the urban poor. With the exception of high-level leaders of the drug gangs — for instance, Avon Barksdale, Stringer Bell, and a handful of others — most of the main characters have virtually no privacy to speak of. Young men live in close quarters in dilapidated apartment buildings, business is conducted in heavily trafficked courtyards, and phone calls are made in outside common areas. In large part, this is a function of the open-air drug markets that the main characters work in. But even law-abiding citizens in these neighborhoods experience a lack of privacy. And ordinary citizens are occasionally (or perhaps often) mistaken for criminals and subjected to police detentions and searches. Does the Fourth Amendment protect the urban poor, or has the Supreme Court made Fourth Amendment protection a haven for the affluent?

1. Houses versus Apartments

Kyllo v. United States
533 U.S. 27 (2001)

Justice SCALIA delivered the opinion of the Court.

This case presents the question whether the use of a thermal-imaging device aimed at a private home from a public street to detect relative amounts of heat within the home constitutes a "search" within the meaning of the Fourth Amendment.

I

In 1991 Agent William Elliott of the United States Department of the Interior came to suspect that marijuana was being grown in the home belonging to petitioner Danny Kyllo, part of a triplex on Rhododendron Drive in Florence, Oregon. Indoor marijuana growth typically requires high-intensity lamps. In order to determine whether an amount of heat was emanating from petitioner's home consistent with the use of such lamps, at 3:20 a.m. on January 16, 1992, Agent Elliott and Dan Haas used an Agema Thermovision 210 thermal imager to scan the triplex. Thermal imagers detect infrared radiation, which virtually all objects emit but which is not visible to the naked eye. The imager converts radiation into images based on relative warmth — black is cool, white is hot, shades of gray connote relative differences; in that respect, it operates somewhat like a video camera showing heat images. The scan of Kyllo's home took only a few minutes and was performed from the passenger seat of Agent Elliott's vehicle across the street from the front of the house and also from the street in back of the house. The scan showed that the roof over the garage and a side wall of petitioner's home were relatively hot compared to the rest of the home and substantially warmer than neighboring homes in the triplex. Agent Elliott concluded that petitioner was using halide lights to grow marijuana in his house, which indeed he was. Based on tips from informants, utility bills, and the thermal imaging, a Federal Magistrate Judge issued a warrant authorizing a search of petitioner's home, and the agents found an indoor growing operation involving more than 100 plants. Petitioner … unsuccessfully moved to suppress the evidence seized from his home.…

* * *

II

The Fourth Amendment provides that "[t]he right of the people to be secure in their persons, houses, papers, and effects, against unreasonable searches and seizures, shall not be violated." "At the very core" of the Fourth Amendment "stands the right of a man to retreat into his own home and there be free from unreasonable governmental intrusion." *Silverman v. United States,* 365 U.S. 505, 511 (1961). With few exceptions, the question whether a warrantless search of a home is reasonable and hence constitutional must be answered no.

On the other hand, the antecedent question whether or not a Fourth Amendment "search" has occurred is not so simple under our precedent. The permissibility of ordinary visual surveillance of a home used to be clear because, well into the 20th century, our Fourth Amendment jurisprudence was tied to common-law trespass. Visual surveillance was unquestionably lawful because "'the eye cannot by the laws of England be guilty of a trespass.'" *Boyd v. United States,* 116 U.S. 616, 628, (1886) (quoting *Entick v. Carrington,* 19 How. St. Tr. 1029, 95 Eng. Rep. 807 (K.B.1765)). We have since decoupled violation of a person's Fourth Amendment rights from trespassory violation of his property, but the lawfulness of warrantless visual surveillance of a home has still been preserved. As we observed in *California v. Ciraolo,* 476 U.S. 207, 213 (1986), "[t]he Fourth Amendment protection of the home has never been extended to require law enforcement officers to shield their eyes when passing by a home on public thoroughfares."

… In assessing when a search is not a search, we have applied somewhat in reverse the principle first enunciated in *Katz v. United States. Katz* involved eavesdropping by means of an electronic listening device placed on the outside of a telephone booth—a location not within the catalog ("persons, houses, papers, and effects") that the Fourth Amendment protects against unreasonable searches. We held that the Fourth Amendment nonetheless protected Katz from the warrantless eavesdropping because he "justifiably relied" upon the privacy of the telephone booth. As Justice Harlan's oft-quoted concurrence described it, a Fourth Amendment search occurs when the government violates a subjective expectation of privacy that society recognizes as reasonable. We have subsequently applied this principle to hold that a Fourth Amendment search does *not* occur—even when the explicitly protected location of a *house* is concerned—unless "the individual manifested a subjective expectation of privacy in the object of the challenged search," and "society [is] willing to recognize that expectation as reasonable.".…

The present case involves officers on a public street engaged in more than naked-eye surveillance of a home. We have previously reserved judgment as to how much technological enhancement of ordinary perception from such a vantage point, if any, is too much. While we upheld enhanced aerial photography of an industrial complex in *Dow Chemical,* we noted that we found "it important that this is *not* an area immediately adjacent to a private home, where privacy expectations are most heightened," 476 U.S., at 237 (emphasis in original).

III

... While it may be difficult to refine *Katz* when the search of areas such as telephone booths, automobiles, or even the curtilage and uncovered portions of residences is at issue, in the case of the search of the interior of homes—the prototypical and hence most commonly litigated area of protected privacy—there is a ready criterion, with roots deep in the common law, of the minimal expectation of privacy that *exists,* and that is acknowledged to be *reasonable.* To withdraw protection of this minimum expectation would be to permit police technology to erode the privacy guaranteed by the Fourth Amendment. We think that obtaining by sense-enhancing technology any information regarding the interior of the home that could not otherwise have been obtained without physical "intrusion into a constitutionally protected area," constitutes a search—at least where (as here) the technology in question is not in general public use. This assures preservation of that degree of privacy against government that existed when the Fourth Amendment was adopted. On the basis of this criterion, the information obtained by the thermal imager in this case was the product of a search.

The Government maintains, however, that the thermal imaging must be upheld because it detected "only heat radiating from the external surface of the house," The dissent makes this its leading point, contending that there is a fundamental difference between what it calls "off-the-wall" observations and "through-the-wall surveillance." But just as a thermal imager captures only heat emanating from a house, so also a powerful directional microphone picks up only sound emanating from a house-and a satellite capable of scanning from many miles away would pick up only visible light emanating from a house. We rejected such a mechanical interpretation of the Fourth Amendment in *Katz,* where the eavesdropping device picked up only sound waves that reached the exterior of the phone booth. Reversing that approach would leave the homeowner at the mercy of advancing technology—including imaging technology that could discern all human activity in the home. While the technology used in the present case was relatively crude, the rule we adopt must take account of more sophisticated systems that are already in use or in development....

The Government also contends that the thermal imaging was constitutional because it did not "detect private activities occurring in private areas." It points out that in *Dow Chemical* we observed that the enhanced aerial photography did not reveal any "intimate details." 476 U.S., at 238. *Dow Chemical,* however, involved enhanced aerial photography of an industrial complex, which does not share the Fourth Amendment sanctity of the home. The Fourth Amendment's protection of the home has never been tied to measurement of the quality or quantity of information obtained. In *Silverman,* for example, we made clear that any physical invasion of the structure of the home, "by even a fraction of an inch," was too much, 365 U.S., at 512, and there is certainly no exception to the warrant requirement for the officer who barely cracks open the front door and sees nothing but the nonintimate rug on the vestibule floor. In the home, our cases show, *all* details are intimate details, because the entire area is held safe from prying government eyes. Thus, in *Karo, supra,* the only thing detected was a can of ether in the home; and in *Arizona v. Hicks,* 480 U.S. 321 (1987), the only thing detected by a physical search that went beyond what officers lawfully present could observe in "plain view" was the registration number of a phonograph turntable. These were intimate details because they were details of the home, just as was the detail of how warm — or even how relatively warm — Kyllo was heating his residence....

Limiting the prohibition of thermal imaging to "intimate details" would not only be wrong in principle; it would be impractical in application, failing to provide "a workable accommodation between the needs of law enforcement and the interests protected by the Fourth Amendment," *Oliver v. United States,* 466 U.S. 170, 181 (1984). To begin with, there is no necessary connection between the sophistication of the surveillance equipment and the "intimacy" of the details that it observes — which means that one cannot say (and the police cannot be assured) that use of the relatively crude equipment at issue here will always be lawful. The Agema Thermovision 210 might disclose, for example, at what hour each night the lady of the house takes her daily sauna and bath — a detail that many would consider "intimate"; and a much more sophisticated system might detect nothing more intimate than the fact that someone left a closet light on. We could not, in other words, develop a rule approving only that through-the-wall surveillance which identifies objects no smaller than 36 by 36 inches, but would have to develop a jurisprudence specifying which home activities are "intimate" and which are not. And even when (if ever) that jurisprudence were fully developed, no police officer would be able to know *in advance* whether his through-the-wall surveillance picks up "intimate" details — and thus would be unable to know in advance whether it is constitutional.

⋆　⋆　⋆

We have said that the Fourth Amendment draws "a firm line at the entrance to the house," *Payton,* 445 U.S., at 590. That line, we think, must be not only firm but also bright — which requires clear specification of those methods of surveillance that require a warrant. While it is certainly possible to conclude from the videotape of the thermal imaging that occurred in this case that no "significant" compromise of the homeowner's privacy has occurred, we must take the long view, from the original meaning of the Fourth Amendment forward.

⋆　⋆　⋆

Where, as here, the Government uses a device that is not in general public use, to explore details of the home that would previously have been unknowable without physical intrusion, the surveillance is a "search" and is presumptively unreasonable without a warrant.

⋆　⋆　⋆

[The dissenting opinion of Justice Stevens, joined by the Chief Justice, Justice O'Connor, and Justice Kennedy, is omitted.]

Notes and Questions

1. To what extent is Justice Scalia (and the other members of the *Kyllo* majority) willing to protect privacy in the home over other areas?

2. Does it make sense to afford Fourth Amendment protection to the temperature in a home because the lady of the house might be taking her sauna, while offering minimal Fourth Amendment protection in vehicles and other areas?

3. Does the decision in *Kyllo* encourage police to devote their attention to courtyards and open air drug markets like those portrayed in *The Wire* because those areas retain less Fourth Amendment protection than homes?

4. The Court often speaks of the Fourth Amendment protecting homes. But does *Kyllo* actually signal protection for *middle-class* houses, rather than other types of homes? Do apartments with shared walls carry less Fourth Amendment protection than traditional stand-alone houses? The next case considers that question.

State v. Benton

536 A.2d 572 (Conn. 1988)

CALLAHAN, Associate Justice.

The defendant was charged in an information with four counts of violating the state dependency producing drug law and one count of possession of drug paraphernalia in a drug factory situation....

The defendant appealed to the Appellate Court, claiming that the trial court erred in failing to suppress evidence that had been gathered as a result of a wiretap on his telephones and a subsequent search of his apartment by the police....

On his appeal to the Appellate Court, the defendant's principal claim was that the affidavit in support of the state's application to the wiretap panel contained references to conversations that emanated from his apartment in a two family duplex house located at 200 Westfield Avenue in Bridgeport. Those conversations, he argued, were illegally overheard by an eavesdropping police officer in violation of the defendant's rights under the fourth amendment to the United States constitution. He contended, therefore, that they could not be cited in the affidavit and that, without those conversations, there was insufficient probable cause to justify the issuance of the wiretap order. Information gathered as a result of the wiretap was later used as a principal component of probable cause in an affidavit employed to obtain the search warrant for the defendant's apartment. The defendant argued that any evidence that had resulted from the wiretap and the search warrant should have been suppressed as "fruit of the poisonous tree." *Wong Sun v. United States,* 371 U.S. 471, 488 (1963).

... On petition, we granted certification limited *solely* to the following question: "Were the defendant's rights under the fourth amendment to the United States constitution violated by [the trial court's] failure to suppress statements overheard without the use of any aural enhancement device, by a police officer stationed in an apartment adjacent to that of the defendant?"....

The conversations in question were overheard by a detective who was assisting in an investigation of the defendant's alleged participation in illegal narcotics activity. On the evening of January 6, 1984, at the time he overheard the conversations, the detective was in the apartment adjacent to that of the defendant for the specific purpose of maintaining a surveillance of the defendant. It is unquestioned that he was there with the express permission of the tenant of that adjacent apartment. While there, intermittently, over a period of some three hours, from a distance not closer than twelve to eighteen inches to the common wall dividing the two apartments, the detective overheard incriminating conversations. It is undisputed that the detective did not employ electronic aids or sensory enhancing devices of any kind and that the conversations were heard with the "naked ear."

The general rule is that what a government agent perceives with his or her unaided senses, when lawfully present in a place where he or she has a right to be, is not an illegal search under the fourth amendment. Since *Katz v. United States,* 389 U.S. 347, 351(1967), it is clear that "the Fourth Amendment protects people, not places." The protection that the fourth amendment affords "people," however, generally requires a reference to "place" to determine what degree of privacy can be expected and whether that expectation is one society is prepared to recognize as reasonable.

Persons, such as the defendant, residing in an apartment, or persons staying in a hotel or motel have the same fourth amendment rights to protection from *unreasonable* searches and seizures and the same *reasonable* expectation of privacy as do the residents of any dwelling. That right honors the justifiable expectation that if their conversations are conducted in a manner undetectable outside their room or residence by the electronically unaided ear they will not be intercepted. The shared atmosphere and the nearness of one's neighbors in a hotel or motel or apartment in a multiple family dwelling, however, diminish the degree of privacy that one can reasonably expect or that society is prepared to recognize as reasonable. The occupant of any such facility who speaks in tones discernible to a neighbor or to a neighbor's invitee who may be expected to be only inches away on the other side of a common wall does not have an objectively reasonable expectation that what is said will not fall on alien ears.

Conversations carried on in any type of residence, or anywhere for that matter, in a tone audible to the unaided ear of a person located in a place where that person has a right to be, and where a person can be expected to be, are conversations knowingly exposed to the public. Conversations knowingly exposed to the public are not within the penumbra of fourth amendment protection. The type of dwelling is inconsequential except insofar as its physical attributes increase the vulnerability of its occupants to eavesdropping by the unaided ear.

The simple fact is that we "do not live in a vacuum." *United States v. Mankani,* 738 F.2d 538, 542 (2d. Cir. 1984). One who is insensitive to his surroundings and indiscriminate in his conversation bears the risk of being overheard by an eavesdropper. "'It is the kind of risk we necessarily assume whenever we speak.'" *Hoffa v. United States,* 385 U.S. 293, 303 (1966). "Eavesdropping from a place where [an] officer has a right to be is a long-accepted technique of crime detection, not outlawed by the Fourth Amendment. If [the defendant] had talked loud enough to be overheard his expectation of privacy would be gone." *United States v. Martin,* 509 F.2d 1211, 1214 (9th Cir.).

The defendant believes that a different rule should apply to multiple family dwellings in general and duplex apartments in particular. We find it difficult to quarrel with the overwhelming weight of authority which we think dictates a different result.

The judgment of the Appellate Court is affirmed.

[The concurring opinion of Justice Healey is omitted.]

––––––––––

Notes and Questions

1. How much less Fourth Amendment protection do residents have in duplexes, row-houses, or apartments compared to stand-alone houses? Can you think of any characters in *The Wire*—besides the police officers, judges, and attorneys—who live in traditional homes that would be afforded the maximum privacy protection available under the Fourth Amendment?

2. Watch *The Wire*, Season 1, Episode 10, at 10:20 minutes. Detective McNulty is looking for Wallace in the hopes of using him as an informant. McNulty is able to walk right into Wallace's apartment complex (which is legal) and his apartment (which is illegal). He is also able to overhear conversations as he walks outside in the back of the apartments. Does Wallace have any Fourth Amendment privacy?

3. The court notes in *Benton* that the officers heard the incriminating statements while standing at least twelve to eighteen inches from the common wall. Would the police have been acting lawfully if they had to place their ears directly against the wall? What if the officers needed to use an amplification device? After *Kyllo*, would your answer turn on whether the amplification device is widely available to the public?

4. Watch *The Wire*, Season 1, Episode 12, at 33:30 and 37:30 minutes. The police want to see and hear what is going on in Avon Barksdale's office but they do not have enough information to get a warrant. Instead, they go to the abandoned office space next door, drill a hole through the wall, and insert a camera. Is this a Fourth Amendment violation? Would your answer be different if the police didn't drill a hole and just listened through the wall? What if they attached a device to the wall of the abandoned office that amplified the sound coming from Avon Barksdale's side of the wall?

5. Does it make sense that police can listen through a wall of a neighboring home without any Fourth Amendment regulation, but that they cannot stand across the street and point a thermal imaging device at a home without a warrant? Can you imagine a theory of the Fourth Amendment that more equitably distributes privacy rights?

2. The Reality of Fourth Amendment Protection on the Street

State v. Dillon

2005 WL 1910749, Ohio App. 10 Dist.

SADLER, J.

On March 29, 2004, defendant-appellant, Dean A. Dillon ("appellant"), was indicted by a Franklin County Grand Jury for possession of cocaine in violation of R.C. 2925.11, a felony of the fifth degree. On the date of his scheduled trial, a hearing was conducted on appellant's motion to suppress evidence obtained as a result of his arrest. Appellant's motion to suppress was denied and a jury convicted appellant of the charge in the indictment. Appellant now appeals....

The facts adduced at the suppression hearing consist of the following. Columbus Police Officer Jason Ayers ("Ayers") testified that on November 24, 2004, he was working with his partner, Officer Greg Seevers ("Seevers") in a marked police paddy wagon. That evening, Ayers communicated with Columbus Police Officer Chapman ("Chapman") on the police radio, during which Chapman told Ayers he had lost track of an individual he had been observing in the area of Wilcox and High Street who Chapman believed was acting suspiciously. Ayers testified Chapman provided a general description of the man to him.

As the officers were patrolling the Short North and The Ohio State University campus area, they observed a man, later identified as appellant, walking westbound in the middle of Tompkins Street. According to Ayers, appellant failed to use the sidewalks available on both sides of the street. Ayers testified his attention was initially drawn to appellant because he was walking in the middle of the road, and that he did not know at the time appellant was the man Chapman had described as acting suspiciously. The officers concluded appellant had just committed the offense of walking in an adjacent roadway, in violation of Columbus City Code 2171.05. As the officers approached appellant to issue a citation, he immediately ran in the opposite direction between the houses on Tompkins

Street. The officers drove through an alley in pursuit of appellant, and witnessed him fall while attempting to run up an embankment. Thereafter, Ayers and Seevers were able to detain him.

According to Ayers, appellant informed the officers he had no identification on his person. Ayers testified regarding his attempt to identify appellant:

> * * *I began a verbal identification process asking him his name and date of birth. He gave me the name Gearheart with a date of birth of—I think it was 1972. Every time we ask somebody their name and date of birth, immediately after the date of birth, I ask the suspect how old they are. He said he was 25. There is a five-year discrepancy there between the date of birth that he gave and the age that he gave. Asked him again. He changed the spelling of the last name. It was G-a-r-h-e-a-r-t, I believe. He changed it to G-e-a-r-h-e-a-r-t and gave a date of birth with the year ending in '72, I believe, which is still inconsistent. He said he was 29. The second date of birth would have actually made him 31. I again explained the inconsistencies to Mr. Dillon. He changed the date of birth again to 1971, which again would have made him 32 and not 25 like he had initially stated.

Because the officers were unable to verify appellant's identification in order to issue him a traffic citation, he was arrested. Subsequent to his arrest, a search of appellant's person revealed narcotics and drug paraphernalia in his jacket pocket.

* * *

Appellant testified at the suppression hearing on his own behalf. He testified a gentleman, unbeknownst to him as Chapman, was following him in a brown van and "staring at [him] in a real peculiar way." Because the man continued to follow him, appellant confronted him because he thought he was a homosexual. Thereafter, appellant walked away from the man, and cut through an alleyway. As he entered the alleyway, appellant heard the roar of engines, and "when the lights came on, there were five or six police officers with their guns drawn on [him]." Defendant testified the officers ordered him to lie down. When the officers approached him, "they" put their knee in his back and asked if he had any drugs or weapons. The officers performed a pat down search for weapons, didn't find any, and then "manipulat[ed] his pockets and pull[ed] everything out of his pockets." Appellant testified he "assumed that they found a baggy or whatever that had drugs in it" in the jacket he was wearing. Thereafter, the officers arrested him.

Appellant testified he was never asked for identification prior to his arrest. After he was placed in the paddy wagon, appellant testified an officer accosted him with derogatory remarks, and threatened him for "[making] him mess up his uniform." At that point, Ayers approached him, and appellant identified himself as James H. Gearheart.

* * *

... [A]ppellant argues the court erred in denying his motion to suppress evidence. In particular, appellant contends the officers *caused* him to commit a jaywalking violation, and impermissibly used that violation as probable cause to detain and arrest him.

* * *

In this case, the officers testified they attempted to stop appellant because he committed a jaywalking offense. A law enforcement officer may stop an individual when he has reasonable suspicion that criminal activity is afoot. *Terry v. Ohio* (1968), 392 U.S. 1. Reasonable suspicion is present when an officer is able to identify specific facts that, when taken together with rational inferences from those facts, would warrant a person of reasonable caution in the belief that an individual being stopped is committing a crime. *Florida v. J.L.* (2000), 529 U.S. 266.

* * *

Columbus City Code Section 2171.05 provides "(a) Where a sidewalk is provided and its use is practicable, it shall be unlawful for any pedestrian to walk along and upon an adjacent roadway." In the instant matter, the officers testified they observed appellant walking in the middle of Tompkins Street when sidewalks were readily available on both sides of the street. Because this violation transpired in the officers' presence, they attempted to detain appellant for the purpose of issuing a jaywalking citation. As the officers approached him, appellant ran in the opposite direction.

Appellant testified that he "cut through an alleyway" instead of walking towards Chapman, who was stopped in his van at a stop sign on Tompkins Street. Appellant did not address where he walked on Tompkins Street to reach the alleyway, and therefore did not refute the officers' allegations that he was jaywalking on the date of the incident. Based on the evidence presented, we find the officers had reasonable suspicion to stop appellant for jaywalking.

We next consider whether the officers violated the Fourth Amendment when they asked appellant for identification during the stop. Once a police officer obtains reasonable suspicion a person may be involved in criminal activity, the officer may stop the person for a brief time and take additional steps to further investigate. *Hibel v. Sixth Judicial Dist. Ct. of NV* (2004), 542 U.S. 177. The officer's action must be justified at its inception, and "'reasonably related in scope'" to the circumstances that initially justified the interference. In the ordinary course of an investigation, a police officer is free to ask a person for identification without implicating the Fourth Amendment.

In this case, the officers testified appellant ran from them as they attempted to issue him a citation for jaywalking. After he was detained, appellant provided at least two versions of his last name and conflicting dates of birth. R.C. 2935.26 provides "when a law enforcement officer is otherwise authorized to arrest a person for the commission of a minor misdemeanor, the officer shall not arrest the person, but shall issue a citation, unless * * * the offender cannot or will not offer satisfactory evidence of his identity." Moreover, the Ohio Supreme Court has held that the making of an unsworn, false, oral statement to a public official with the purpose to mislead, hamper or impede the investigation of a crime is punishable conduct within the meaning of R.C. 2921.13(A)(3) (falsification) and 2921.31(A) (obstructing official business). We conclude the officers' inquiry of appellant's identity was justified and reasonable, and appellant's responses provided justification for his arrest. Thus, the officers did not violate the Fourth Amendment rights when they asked him for identification, and when they lawfully arrested him.

We now turn to the final issue raised by the fourth assignment of error, which is whether Ayers and Seevers were justified in performing the search incident to arrest. A law enforcement officer may conduct a search incident to a lawful arrest under a well-established exception to the Fourth Amendment warrant requirement. In conducting a search incident to a lawful arrest, the police may conduct a full search of the arrestee's person. That search is not limited to the discovery of weapons, but may include evidence of a crime as well. In this case, because the officers executed a valid *Terry* stop of appellant, and lawfully arrested the search incident to an arrest was proper. Thus, Ayers and Seevers did not violate appellant's Fourth Amendment rights by searching appellant following the arrest.

* * *

We now turn to appellant's argument that his arrest was invalid because the officers were acting at the direction of Chapman, and therefore had no probable cause to arrest him. The United States Supreme Court has held the subjective intentions of law enforcement officers play no role in probable cause analysis. *Whren v. United States* (1996), 517 U.S. 806, 812. In this case, we have previously determined that the officers were justified in arresting appellant for reasons independent from their communication with Chapman. Therefore, appellant's theory that an officer's ulterior motive of investigating unrelated criminal activity invalidates an arrest otherwise based on probable cause is without merit.

* * *

Judgment affirmed.

_____

Notes and Questions

1. Whose side of the story—the officers or the defendant—do you believe? Will courts typically believe the story of the arresting officers rather than the defendant?

2. Does it make sense that police can conduct a full-custody arrest for the crime of jaywalking? If your answer is yes, does it make sense that police can conduct a full search incident to arrest of everything on a person following an arrest for jaywalking? In City of Lago Vista v. Atwater, 532 U.S. 318 (2001), a police officer stopped a mother who was driving her children home because she was not wearing a seatbelt. The officer took Atwater into custody and conducted a search incident to arrest but found no contraband. Atwater subsequently sued the police department under the federal civil rights statute, 42 U.S.C. § 1983. Even though the crime of failure to wear a seatbelt was a low-level misdemeanor that carried no possibility of jail time and just a monetary fine, the Supreme Court refused to forbid a custodial arrest. Unless state law is more restrictive, police officers in the United States are thus free to arrest defendants for any offense in the criminal code and search the arrestee (and possibly his automobile) incident to arrest.

3. Do you think the police officers were really interested in Dillon because he was jaywalking? Or did the officers have a hunch (in other words, a gut feeling but less than probable cause) that Dillon had drugs on him? If the officers took the time to stop Dillon because they hoped to find drugs, rather than because of the jaywalking, should that matter? As the opinion notes, the Supreme Court's decision in *Whren v. United States*, 517 U.S. 806 (1996) made the subjective intent of the officer irrelevant in assessing whether the police acted properly. Rather, a unanimous Court held in *Whren* that as long as the police have an objectively valid basis for stopping an individual, their actual motivations for the stop are irrelevant.

4. Watch *The Wire*, Season 4, Episode 1, at 55:15 minutes. An officer comes upon an intoxicated man drinking late at night on a public park bench. The man is mayoral candidate Tommy Carcetti, and the officer declines to arrest or even ticket Carcetti. Would the officer have been so flexible and accommodating if the man on the park bench were poor, unconnected, or a racial minority? Should officers have this much discretion? Will broad police discretion inevitably be used to the detriment of the poor and minorities?

5. How many different crimes can police point to when deciding to arrest someone? In most states, the answer is hundreds and in the federal system there are more than 3,000 criminal offenses. *See* William J. Stuntz, *The Pathological Politics of Criminal Law*, 100

MICH. L. REV. 505, 513–15 (2001). How many different crimes has Tommy Carcetti committed by drinking on the park bench in Season 4, Episode 1?

6. Think about the combined information in notes 1 through 5 above. Police are permitted to arrest defendants for hundreds of crimes, including jaywalking and failure to wear a seatbelt. The officers' personal reasons for conducting arrests are irrelevant as long as they can point to a law that has been violated. And the officers can search everything on an arrestee's person, including digging through their pockets and opening any packages, even if the arrest is for a low-level misdemeanor. In the urban world of *The Wire*—where Maryland law forbids jaywalking, littering, and other quality of life offenses—does that mean police have the power to arrest and search practically anyone on the street for drugs if the officers simply watch and wait for them to commit a minor legal infraction? Consider Detective McNulty's explanation to a patrol officer:

> Let me tell you a little secret. Patrolling officer on his beat is the one true dictatorship in America. We can lock a guy up on a humble, we can lock him up for real, or we can say fuck it, pull under the expressway and drink ourselves to death. And our side partners will cover it. So no one, and I mean no one, tells us how to waste our shift.

The Wire, Season 4, Episode 10, at 30:15 minutes.

7. Would it be possible to alter Fourth Amendment doctrine to take into consideration the severity of the crime? When dealing with less serious crimes should police have less authority to arrest and search? For a compelling argument that courts consider the severity of the offense when determining the reasonableness of the police action, see Jeffrey Bellin, *Crime-Severity Distinctions and the Fourth Amendment: Reassessing Reasonableness in a Changing World*, 97 IOWA L. REV. 1 (2011).

State v. Rollins
922 A.2d 379 (Del. 2007)

STEELE, Chief Justice:

A New Castle County grand jury indicted the defendant-appellee Arthur Rollins, on the following charges: possession of cocaine with intent to deliver, distribution of cocaine within 1000 feet of a school, and possession of drug paraphernalia. Rollins filed a motion to suppress evidence police seized from his person claiming that the police did not have a reasonable articulable suspicion to detain and search him.... A Superior Court judge granted Rollins's motion to suppress.... [W]e reverse and remand.

FACTS AND PROCEDURAL HISTORY

Officers Witt and Fossett were patrolling in a vehicle at approximately 1:20 p.m. on August 8, 2005 in the Riverside area of Wilmington. The officers knew that the large courtyard near Riverside Apartment Projects bordered by East 26th and 27th Streets, Bowers Street, and Claymont Street was a high drug sales area. In order to surprise anyone in the courtyard engaging in drug transactions, they drove their vehicle over the curb and into the courtyard. There were a fairly large number of people there and one woman yelled "five-O"[1] in the direction of defendant-appellee Rollins. The officers then observed Rollins put his right hand in his pocket, then withdraw it and begin to walk away from them. Witt drove the police car near Rollins and asked him to come over to the car. Fos-

---

1. This is a common phrase that is used to refer to police.

sett grabbed Rollins by the arm and brought him to the car because the officers believed that Rollins "looked like he was looking for a way out." The officers patted Rollins down for weapons but found none. According to the officers' testimony, Fossett asked Rollins "if he had anything that he wasn't supposed to," and Rollins said, "no." Fossett then asked Rollins if he could search his pockets; however, there is a dispute about whether Rollins agreed that the police could search his pockets.[3] Fossett then searched Rollins's pockets and found cocaine in the right front pocket of Rollins's trousers. The officers then arrested him.

* * *

DISCUSSION
Reasonable and Articulable Suspicion to Stop

* * *

On appeal, the State contends that the Superior Court judge erred when he granted Rollins's motion to suppress because the police did have a reasonable articulable suspicion to stop Rollins. The State contends that the trial judge erred in his evaluation of the police officers' assessment of the reasonable articulable suspicion standard because he considered each fact in isolation rather than looking at the totality of the circumstances.

... "In *Terry v. Ohio,* the United States Supreme Court held that a police officer may 'detain an individual for investigatory purposes for a limited scope and duration, but only if such detention is supported by a reasonable and articulable suspicion of criminal activity.'" The stop is only justified, however, if 'specific and articulable facts ... together with rational inferences" suggest that a suspect is involved in criminal activity.

... The United States Supreme Court has made it clear that courts should evaluate the reasonable articulable suspicion standard under the totality of the circumstances, rather than examining each factor in isolation. Both the U.S. Supreme Court and this Court have recognized that "[i]n some instances ... lawful and apparently innocent conduct may add up to reasonable suspicion if the detaining officer articulates 'concrete reasons for such an interpretation.'" "The totality of the circumstances, as viewed through the eyes of a reasonable, trained officer in the same or similar circumstances, must be examined by both the trial judge and appellate court to determine if reasonable suspicion has been properly formulated."

The State has identified several factors that, when considered together, the State believes justify the *Terry* stop. The police were patrolling in an area that was well known for drug sales. As the police entered the courtyard in their patrol car, a woman shouted a warning that police were nearby in Rollins's direction. This prompted Rollins to look up, turn away, and quickly insert and remove his hand from his pocket. He then began to walk away from the officers. We must consider the totality of those factors in order to determine whether the police had a reasonable articulable suspicion that Rollins was engaged in criminal action in order to detain Rollins.

The first factor to consider is that the neighborhood was well known as a high drug area. Officer Witt testified that based on his 11 years of experience and approximately 350 drug arrests, he knew the courtyard to be a location for drug sales. He testified that

---

3. Rollins testified at his suppression hearing that he did not consent to the search but the officers testified that he did consent. The Superior Court judge never reached the issue of consent because he found that the police did not have a reasonable suspicion to stop Rollins in the first place.

the courtyard is an ideal place for drug sales because there drug dealers can easily see the police approach and the courtyard presents multiple avenues of escape. In *Wardlow,* the United States Supreme Court noted, "[O]fficers are not required to ignore the relevant characteristics of a location in determining whether the circumstances are sufficiently suspicious to warrant further investigation." In *United States v. Johnson,* the Court considered a high crime area to be a factor in its reasonable suspicion analysis. Following *Wardlow,* the Court in *Johnson* noted, "While obviously insufficient by itself to amount to reasonable suspicion, the 'fact that the stop occurred in a high crime area is among the relevant contextual considerations in a Terry analysis.'"

Next, we will consider the bystander's warning shout of "five-O" directed to Rollins. The Appellate Court of Connecticut, in *State v. Williamson,* considered a police warning as a factor in analyzing whether the police had reasonable articulable suspicion to stop a defendant. In *Williamson,* the officer "observed that, upon his and other officers approach on the night of the incident, the defendant, after hearing someone yell 'police' or some other word of alert, began running . . ." The Court noted that "[w]hile the police had no more than a generalized suspicion of illegal contact when they approached the [site of the incident], that suspicion became specific and focused on the defendant when he ran into the restaurant in response to the warnings that police had arrived." We likewise conclude that the focused warning shout "five-O" contributed to the police officers' reasonable suspicion that Rollins might be engaged in criminal activity.

Next we will consider Rollins's insertion and removal of his hand in his pocket when he saw the officers approaching. In *United States v. Johnson,* police observed a parked car with two passengers in a high narcotics area. The officers saw a young woman lean into the passenger's window and hand Johnson an object that they could not identify. As the police approached the vehicle, the woman walked away. One officer saw Johnson make a "shoving down motion." The court noted that Johnson's "furtive gestures after the officer's display of authority contributed to the officer's reasonable suspicion." Rollins furtive gestures can similarly be considered for the purpose of determining reasonable articulable suspicion.

The final factor is that Rollins walked away from the officers. As this Court noted in *Cummings v. State,* "merely leaving the scene upon the approach, or the sighting, of a police officer is not, in itself and standing alone, suspicious conduct," however, it may be considered as a factor in the totality of the circumstances. Although Rollins walked away as the officers approached him rather than run away, he nevertheless appeared to be intent on evading the police after the woman gave him a warning that police were in the area.

Although it is possible that each factor, in isolation, could indicate seemingly innocent behavior, when we examine these facts under the totality of the circumstances, we find that the police had a reasonable articulable suspicion that Rollins may be engaged in criminal activity. They were, therefore, justified in detaining him and conducting a *Terry* pat down or frisk for their own protection.

Scope of the Terry Stop

[The court concluded that the officers exceeded the scope of a valid *Terry* frisk because they went beyond a pat down and instead conducted a full search of his picket. The court remanded for factual findings as to whether Rollins' consented to that search.]

* * *

Notes and Questions

1. Do you agree with the Delaware Supreme Court that under the totality of the circumstances there was reasonable suspicion to stop Rollins for suspected drug activity?

2. As *The Wire* demonstrates, the residents of poor urban areas, particularly young people, often distrust the police. Studies show that the poor believe they are likely to be subjected to wrongful arrest, unconstitutional searches, and police brutality. *See* Andrew E. Taslitz, *Respect and the Fourth Amendment*, 94 J. Crim. L. & Criminology 15 (2003). In light of this, was there good reason for Rollins to walk away from the police when they arrived in the courtyard?

3. Regardless of whether you think police had reasonable suspicion to stop Rollins, would you agree that the Court's decision signals a very low level of suspicion necessary to conduct a *Terry* stop? If police observe the courtyard of a housing complex for long enough, will they eventually be able to point to suspicious movements by practically everyone in the courtyard?

William J. Stuntz, The Distribution of Fourth Amendment Privacy
67 George Washington Law Review 1265 (1999)

Fourth Amendment law protects individual privacy, when it does so, by barring the police from seeing or hearing certain things in certain ways unless they have a sufficiently good reason. In general, the more harm to privacy the investigative tactic causes, the better the reason must be. Thus, police officers can see behavior on the street with no justification at all; they can inspect a pedestrian's jacket pocket based on reasonable suspicion that the pocket might contain a weapon coupled with reasonable suspicion of some criminal activity; they can conduct a thorough search of a car only given probable cause to believe the car contains evidence of crime (a higher standard than reasonable suspicion); they can search a private home only if they have both probable cause and a warrant obtained in advance of the search. It seems plausible to assume that houses are more private than cars, which are more private than jacket pockets, which are more private than public movements on the street. If so, the law affords a kind of graded protection to individual privacy.

The literature in this area is full of criticism, but no one criticizes that. It is common to complain that the law protects privacy too little, and a few of us have argued that it should protect other things—the interest in being free from unjustified police violence, for example—more. But there seems to be fairly widespread agreement on the twin propositions that (1) Fourth Amendment law should protect privacy, and (2) the protection should tend to increase as the privacy invasion increases. Indeed, to state these two propositions is to state the obvious.

These obvious propositions may be wrong. Begin with the central problem of late-twentieth-century American criminal justice: it seems biased, both against the poor and against blacks. Between 1980 and 1992, the fraction of defendants who received appointed counsel went from just under half to four-fifths. Although this is not a precise measure of the proportion of poor defendants, it is at least suggestive. In the early 1970s, the ratio of white to black inmates was approximately three to two; today blacks outnumber whites. This shift coincided with an unparalleled growth in the inmate population, from about 325,000 in 1970 to over 1.8 million in 1998. These are complex phenomena; contrary to much of the rhetoric about them, they are not primarily the product of simple bigotry or malice. Some portion of these phenomena may even reflect improvements in the quality of law enforcement. But these numbers do suggest a system ever more focused on, and ever more punitive toward, the crimes of poor people and black people. Even if that focus is to some degree justified—punishing criminals creates benefits as well as costs for the communities from which the criminals come—it must send some destructive messages to residents of communities that see a large fraction of their young men imprisoned, a fate that remains rare for residents of other sorts of communities. It would be foolish, perhaps reprehensible, for a society with patterns of criminal punishment like these not to worry a great deal about the distributive effects of the rules and practices of its criminal justice system.

If so, we should worry about Fourth Amendment law, and in particular the way that law defines and protects privacy. Fourth Amendment law makes wealthier suspects better off than they otherwise would be, and may make poorer suspects worse off. And Fourth Amendment law heightens the tendency of the police to target the kinds of drug markets that prevail in poor black neighborhoods. These tendencies operate at the margin; their precise effects are unknown, and probably unknowable. Still, it is plausible to believe that Fourth Amendment law has contributed to the creation of a prison population increasingly dominated by blacks punished for crack offenses.

Fourth Amendment law has these tendencies for two reasons. The first goes to the nature of the interest being protected. Privacy, in Fourth Amendment terms, is something that exists only in certain types of spaces; not surprisingly, the law protects it only where it exists. Rich people have more access to those spaces than poor people; they therefore enjoy more legal protection. That is not true of some other interests Fourth Amendment law protects. Thus, to the extent the law focuses on privacy rather than, say, the interest in avoiding police harassment or discrimination, it shifts something valuable—legal protection—from poorer suspects to wealthier ones.

The second reason is probably more important. When the Fourth Amendment limits the use of a police tactic like house searches, it does two things: it raises the cost of using that tactic, and it lowers the relative cost of using other tactics that might be substitutes. Different kinds of crimes require different kinds of police tactics to ferret them out. Raising the cost of some tactics and lowering the cost of others thus means raising the cost of investigating some kinds of crimes and lowering the cost of investigating others. Different crimes are committed by different classes of criminals. As it happens, the kinds of crimes wealthier people tend to commit require greater invasions of privacy by the police to catch perpetrators. By raising the cost of the tactics that most intrude on privacy, Fourth Amendment law lowers the cost of other tactics, and those are the tactics that are most useful in uncovering the crimes of the poor.

* * *

I. Privacy's Bias

In Fourth Amendment law, privacy has a positive definition: the kind of privacy protection citizens have vis-a-vis the police is tied to the kind of privacy the same citizens have with one another. That kind of privacy can be bought, so that people who have money have more of it than people who don't. It follows that people who have money have more Fourth Amendment protection than people who don't. One might solve this problem by giving privacy a normative definition, by deciding what privacy protection people ought to have vis-a-vis the government, without regard to the distribution of privacy in society. But the solution works only if one fundamentally changes what one means by "privacy." Under any definition that focuses on the interest in keeping certain spaces and activities secret, protecting privacy will tend to advantage wealthier suspects at the expense of poorer ones.

The proper place to start is with the law's definition. Most of Fourth Amendment law is devoted to the regulation of searches, and searches are defined as anything agents of the government do that infringes a reasonable expectation of privacy. As every criminal procedure class learns, if the key to that definition is the word "expectation," the definition is circular. People expect what they think will happen, and what they think will happen is a function of what has happened in the past. By altering its behavior, the government can change how people expect it to behave. Thus, if the government is bound only to respect people's expectations, it is not bound at all, for it can easily condition the citizenry to expect little or no privacy.

So if it is to have any bite, Fourth Amendment privacy protection must be tied to something other than what people expect from the police. The law's solution is to tie its protection to what people expect from one another. People define, in their ordinary interactions with each other, the kinds of things they do and don't want to keep secret; once that private space has been so defined, the police should be required to respect it. This sounds like a brilliant idea, a way to permit the law to develop and adapt to changing circumstances without having judges pull their own intuitions about privacy out of thin air.

Two Supreme Court decisions from the early 1980s capture this idea. In United States v. Knotts, the police used an electronic tracking device to follow the movements of a suspect along the public streets. Knotts posed two issues: Can the police track public movements, and can they do so by the use of (what were then) high-tech tracking devices? The Court dismissed the second issue with a wave of the hand, saying that if tracking devices became a serious danger it could reassess the situation, but until then the rule would be the same whether the police tracked the suspect by a beeper or by a pair of eyes in a police car. As for the first issue, the Court held that the police could observe movements in public without any Fourth Amendment justification, because any member of the public might have observed the same thing. Because Knotts's travels were public to the world, they were public to the police.

In United States v. Karo, decided the next year, the police used a similar tracking device to follow several drums of chemicals into a private house; they continued to use the device to "observe" the movements of the chemicals within the house. As in Knotts, tracking the drums' movements in public was not a search. Tracking them once inside the house, though, was a different story. Because ordinary citizens could not have observed those movements, neither could the police, unless they complied with the rules governing house searches.

The principle that underlies Knotts and Karo — absent some special justification, the police can see and hear only those things that the rest of us can see and hear — has wide application; it is not too much to call it the defining principle of Fourth Amendment doctrine. Eavesdropping on telephone conversations is a "search." Overhearing a conversation on the street isn't. Jumping over a backyard fence to look around is a "search." Viewing the same yard from an airplane window isn't. Hiding in the bushes just outside the house and looking in the living room window is a "search." Standing in the street and peering through the open curtains into the living room isn't. The pattern is clear enough: the police can infringe privacy in ways that anyone else might infringe it, but not (meaning, again, not without special justification) in ways that differ from the sorts of things ordinary people might do. All these results seem designed to take the privacy people have, and use it to define the privacy that the police cannot invade without some good cause.

* * *

... [F]or all its contradictions, the law retains a substantial degree of coherence. The things and places people keep secret from one another are surely more private, and hence their discovery more harmful to privacy, than the things and places people expose to the world. And among the places where people maintain their privacy, a hierarchy exists. Homes really are more private than other places; cars and containers we carry around are private, but less so than homes; clothing less so still. These propositions are not perfectly true, but the law must deal in generalizations, and they are good generalizations.

Perhaps because they are good generalizations, they have a substantial class bias. Consider how Fourth Amendment protection works in four major spheres: home, job, car, and street. Save for a small homeless population, rich and poor alike have homes. But the homes of the rich are larger and more comfortable, making it possible to live a larger portion of life in them. Privacy follows space, and people with money have more space than people without. People with more money are more likely to live in detached houses with yards; people with less money are more likely to live in apartment buildings with common hallways. Because others can hear (sometimes smell) from the hallway what goes on inside apartments, the police can too. My neighbors cannot freely surround my house to hear what is happening inside; consequently, neither can the police. The open fields doctrine reduces this gap slightly, by allowing the police to walk about on large tracts of privately owned land without any Fourth Amendment justification. But the reduction is slight, for open fields are just that—fields, not yards.

One finds a similar distributive tilt in the workplace. A police search of an enclosed office requires probable cause and a warrant. Consent of the employer is not enough. People who work on assembly lines or shop floors or hotel kitchens do not have offices; they share their work space with many others. When that space is open to the public, the police can see what it holds without justification. When that space is open only to employees, the police may need the consent of the employer, but not the consent of the suspected employee. In practice, probable cause and warrants are never needed.

With cars, the tilt is less substantial: one can enjoy as much, or as little, privacy in an old Chevrolet as in a new Lexus. Still, a substantial slice of the urban poor (in some cities, the urban middle class as well) use public transportation in place of cars. Fourth Amendment law treats passengers on subways and buses no differently than pedestrians on the street. And pedestrians receive less Fourth Amendment protection than drivers.

Which leads to the fourth sphere, the street. As with transport, there are two divides here: between cities and everyplace else, and between richer and poorer. Street life is mostly an urban phenomenon. It is also mostly a phenomenon of the lower and lower-middle classes. Again, poorer people have less comfortable homes; it is natural to want to spend less time, and do less, in them. Other forms of entertainment are more costly than sitting on a front stoop or wandering the streets and talking to friends. So among urban residential neighborhoods, one finds more pedestrian traffic in poorer neighborhoods than in wealthier ones.

And Fourth Amendment law makes it easy for police to stop and search pedestrians. Police can approach anyone and ask questions with no justification at all; as long as the encounter is no more coercive than any police-citizen encounter must be, it is deemed consensual, notwithstanding the fact that such conversations rarely seem optional to the suspect. That power is terribly important, for it gives the police the authority to initiate street encounters at will. The Supreme Court's decision in Whren v. United States has attracted a lot of criticism, because it permits the police to use traffic violations as a justification for stopping cars when the real reason for the stop lies elsewhere. Traffic violations are sufficiently common that, if this authority were used widely enough, automobile stops could become effectively unregulated. In an odd way, Whren shows how broad police authority over pedestrians is, for Whren does no more than narrow the gap between Fourth Amendment protection for drivers and the rules for police-pedestrian encounters. The police can, after all, already "stop" pedestrians without cause, given that every street encounter is functionally a stop.

The general picture is clear enough. Fourth Amendment privacy is unequally distributed; it more closely resembles the right to buy political advertisements, which is useful only to those with money, than the right to vote, which almost all adult citizens share. Privacy, as Fourth Amendment law defines it, is something people tend to have a lot of only when they also have a lot of other things.

The temptation is to blame this feature of Fourth Amendment law on privacy's definition. By tying the definition of "searches" to the kind of privacy people actually have, the doctrine naturally tends to favor some classes of people over others, for people who have more privacy also have more, period. The solution, one might think, is a less positive, more normative definition of privacy. Ask not what privacy we actually have with each other; rather, ask what privacy we ought to have with the police. If rich and poor deserve the same level of privacy protection from the police, perhaps the law can simply give it to them.

That task is harder than it sounds. If by "privacy" one means the interest in not being observed (seen or heard), it is impossible. The problem is that, in general, the harm from being observed declines steeply with the addition of each new observer. If my wife and I have conversations that we wish to share only with each other, it is a real injury to each of us for a third party to listen in. If we live in an apartment building where our neighbors hear all our conversations because the walls are so thin, the addition of one more pair of ears is not particularly harmful. The point is not that poor people don't care about privacy; they surely do. Rather, the point is that, much of the time, the police don't take privacy (in the Fourth Amendment sense of the word) away from poor people, because those people have already lost it, and one cannot lose it twice. However the law of police searches is defined, if its goal is to protect against the harm of being observed, it will give most of its protection to people who can afford lives that allow limited observation. That excludes the urban poor.

Note: the urban poor, not simply the poor. People who live outside cities tend to have cars whatever their income level. People in trailer parks live in places that afford almost as much privacy as detached houses. It is poor people in cities who tend to live in large apartment buildings, to travel by bus or subway, and because of a combination of income and concentrated population, to spend more time on the street than do people in other places. This urban-nonurban divide creates another divide. Poverty in America is not exclusively an urban phenomenon. Poverty among certain population groups in certain parts of the country is almost exclusively an urban phenomenon. Poor whites are dispersed; they do not live in close proximity to large numbers of other poor whites. Poor blacks are more likely to live in cities, surrounded by other poor blacks. If the law is tilted against the urban poor, it is bound to have a racial tilt as well.

∗ ∗ ∗

II. Privacy and the Cost of Policing

The gist of the last section is this: The police are subject to different standards when they search people in different kinds of neighborhoods. In one kind of neighborhood, police investigations involve entry into houses, cars, and offices; in another, apartments, buses, and shop floors. In the first kind of neighborhood, street encounters are not very useful to the police, because little street traffic exists. In the second kind, street traffic and hence police-citizen encounters on the street are much more common. The law is formally the same for everyone, but a little prodding exposes a serious wealth effect in the degree of privacy protection it provides.

That ought to sound troubling enough, but the problem is actually worse. Notwithstanding the crime drop of the past eight years, we live in a high-crime society. In a high-crime society, police cannot seriously investigate all offenses; they must pick and choose. Anything that makes one set of crimes more expensive makes another set cheaper: the cost that matters most is relative. That holds especially true in a society that invests heavily in policing drug markets. The nature of those markets is such that, in well-off neighborhoods, transactions are likely to take place in private dwellings through arranged meetings; in poorer neighborhoods, transactions take place on the street. Fourth Amendment law makes it much harder to police the former, and thereby pushes police to focus ever more on the latter.

A. Fourth Amendment Rules as Taxes

The essential idea is a commonplace in legal theory, though as yet it has not penetrated the law and literature of criminal procedure. Sensible legal regulation of, say, automobile design has two kinds of effects. First, it produces safer cars by making unsafe ones more costly to manufacturers: unsafe cars might lead to fines or large damages bills. Second, it produces fewer cars by making automobile design generally—not just unsafe design—more costly. Engineers must be trained to comply with the legal standards, lawyers must review particularly troubling design questions, and so forth. The second effect is less obvious than the first, but no less certain. With rare exceptions, anytime one raises the price of anything, one gets less of it. And regulation does raise the price of regulated activities, if only because regulated actors must invest in learning the regulations and complying with them. In this way, legal regulation acts as a tax, a mechanism for making some activities more expensive relative to their substitutes. If the law makes cars more expensive while the cost of train and air travel remains level, there will be some shifting, at the margin, from the first kind of transportation to the other two. That is a part of what regulating automobile safety does.

Almost all legal regulation is like this. It raises the quality of the regulated activity (assuming the regulation is sensible) and, at the same time, lowers the quantity of the regulated activity. Both effects are important, and the mix of the two will vary according to context. Still, the presence of both effects is nearly universal. And the second effect, the effect on activity level, tends naturally to produce some substitution, a shifting of resources from one activity to another.

These points apply as much to regulating police investigation as to regulating automobile safety. Consider house searches. Fourth Amendment law requires, as a precondition to searching a dwelling, probable cause to believe the dwelling contains evidence of crime, plus either the authorization of a neutral magistrate in advance of the search or a showing that obtaining a magistrate's approval was not feasible. Obviously, these rules make for better house searches. A police officer with no more than a hunch that cocaine can be found in my basement will not likely look for it there. His hunch alone will not support a warrant, and without a warrant any cocaine he finds will be suppressed. This state of affairs should lead the officer to gather more evidence, which will either permit him to get a warrant or lead him to discard his hunch. The result is that officers will tend to search houses like mine when, but only when, they have good reason to believe they will find cocaine, or something similarly serious. This is the usual Fourth Amendment story;

its essence is the law's tendency to produce better quality searches. The same rules also produce fewer searches. Warrants are costly to the police: they require both paperwork and hours hanging around a courthouse waiting to see the magistrate. Gathering evidence from informants and witnesses about whose basement contains cocaine is likewise costly. Both the warrant and probable cause requirements, then, make house searches considerably more expensive for police than those searches would be absent those requirements. The rules function as a tax, payable in police time rather than money. When a police officer decides to search a house or apartment, he must first spend several hours performing tasks that the law says are prerequisites to such a search. As I will explain in the next section, one will not necessarily see fewer house searches than in a world with no legal regulation. But that is the natural tendency—here as elsewhere, if you tax a given kind of behavior, you will probably see less of it.

Less of one kind of behavior usually means more of another. Tax work and you may get more leisure; tax airplane tickets and you may see more highway traffic. So too, if Fourth Amendment law acts as a tax on policing in general, if it simply makes all criminal investigation more costly, the likely result is less policing and more of something else the government might do. But Fourth Amendment law doesn't work that way. Some police tactics are wholly unregulated, some are regulated lightly, and a few, like house searches, are regulated fairly heavily. In a world like that, a world where the law taxes some kinds of policing more than others, the likely substitutions will occur within policing, not outside it, as the police shift time and energy away from more expensive (because more highly taxed) tactics and toward cheaper ones. Street stops are much less regulated than house searches. That may lead to more of the former and fewer of the latter.

The conditions under which this pattern might hold are explored in the next section. If it does hold, Fourth Amendment law not only changes the mix of police tactics, it pushes the police away from wealthier suspects and toward poorer ones. Fourth Amendment law protects privacy more than it protects anything else. For reasons discussed in Part I, protecting privacy means protecting different classes of people differently; in particular, it means protecting the urban poor less than others. Consequently, Fourth Amendment law raises the cost of policing some neighborhoods relative to others, and the line that best separates the two kinds of neighborhoods is concentrated poverty.

To be sure, Fourth Amendment law does not produce this effect by itself. Even in a world with no Fourth Amendment, policing wealthy neighborhoods would be more costly than policing poor neighborhoods. Street stops and frisks take as little as one or two minutes; house searches take much longer. Approaching every passenger on a city bus may occupy half an hour; stopping the same number of cars to ask each driver a few questions would take twice as long. More important, the political costs of these different types of investigation differ substantially. Searching every house on a middle-class block in order to crack a drug ring would be politically risky even if it were legally possible. When it comes to blanket street stops in poor urban neighborhoods, the political risks must be manageable, for those stops happen. To put it another way, the cost of investigating wealthier suspects is intrinsically higher than the cost of investigating poorer ones. That cost gap is produced not by Fourth Amendment law, but by social fact.

Yet Fourth Amendment law makes the gap larger than it otherwise would be. House searches may be intrinsically more expensive than street stops, but Fourth Amendment law makes them more expensive still. Automobile stops may be more difficult than "working the buses" for reasons wholly apart from the law, but Fourth Amendment doctrine exaggerates the difference by protecting the privacy of people in cars more than it protects the privacy of bus passengers. As a rough generalization, it seems fair to say that wherever the cost gap is small, the law makes it larger. If differences in cost matter at the margin, that must lead to less intrusive police investigation of middle- and upper-class suspects, and may lead to more intrusive investigation of their lower-class counterparts.

Interestingly, where the cost gap is already largest, where the relevant police tactic is already very expensive without legal regulation, Fourth Amendment law tends to leave it alone. Consider two examples of investigative tactics that are extremely intrusive of individual privacy yet receive no Fourth Amendment protection at all: high-end undercover agents and stakeouts. Most undercover agents do little more than propose a drug buy and then make the bust if and when the transaction takes place. Some undercover agents, however, do much more. They infiltrate suspects' lives, and thus monitor a wide range of conversations and transactions that are closed to public scrutiny. This amounts to sustained spying, and no greater privacy intrusion exists than spies who pose as close friends and associates. Stakeouts are less intrusive, because they involve spying from a distance rather than up close. But stakeouts sometimes do involve monitoring the movements of a given suspect or all who deal with him over an extended period of time—roughly the equivalent of being stalked.

Yet Fourth Amendment law, the one body of law that more than any other seems concerned with protecting that kind of privacy interest, places no limits on these tactics. Undercover-agents-as-spies require no Fourth Amendment justification; the theory is that any contacts the agent has with the suspect are consensual and hence not a "search" or "seizure." Stakeouts—observing the comings and goings of residents of and visitors to a private home, sometimes over a period of days—likewise require no Fourth Amendment justification. Here the idea is that everything the police can see, others can see as well. The intensive nature of the observation, the difference between noticing someone and watching them, plays no role in the analysis.

Why so little regulation of such obviously intrusive tactics? One reason may be their cost. Undercover-agents-as-spies require enormous amounts of police time and entail serious risk for the agents. Stakeouts involve less risk but likewise require very large investments of police time and energy. Precisely because these tactics are so costly, police must be careful not to use them too often. For tactics like these, Fourth Amendment restrictions are not terribly important, since cost alone limits police abuse.

That is not true of house searches or street stops, or any of the range of tactics that police routinely use to catch drug and street-crime offenders. All these tactics cost police time and energy; some cost more time and energy than others; none is unaffordable. It seems reasonable to suppose that those cost differences affect the way police allocate their time and personnel. Fourth Amendment law alters the cost differences. The consequence is that policing the rich is more costly than it otherwise would be. Policing the poor is, relatively speaking, much less so.

B. The Effect of Police Resource Constraints

How Fourth Amendment rules actually shape police behavior depends critically on the ratio of serious crimes to police officers. Given a low ratio—few crimes, many officers—regulating any particular police tactic is likely to lead the police to use that tactic more sparingly, or perhaps better. Use of other police tactics in other investigations will likely be unaffected.

* * *

Around 1961 American crime rates began to rise steeply. Between that year and 1971, the number of serious non-drug felonies almost trebled, while the population rose thir-

teen percent. Growth in police departments was modest. In 1962, there were 1.9 law enforcement employees per 1000 inhabitants of American cities; by 1972 that number had
risen only to 2.4. As the growth in non-drug felonies abated in the 1970s, drug markets
exploded, giving already strapped police departments another large class of crimes to investigate (about which more later). We quickly went from a society with very favorable
crime-to-police ratios to one where those ratios were very unfavorable.

In that kind of society, spillover effects may be much larger. Where there are more
crimes than the police can investigate, the police must, by definition, choose which crimes
to investigate. Anything that makes investigating some crimes more expensive will tend
to drive police toward other crimes, in the same way that making airplane travel more expensive will drive passengers to trains or cars. Fourth Amendment law raises the cost of
investigating middle- and upper-class crime. That will tend to drive police away from
those crimes, and toward the crimes of the poor.

For that proposition to hold, four things must be true. First, search and seizure law must
raise the cost of investigating the crimes of relatively wealthy criminals more than the
crimes of relatively poor ones. It does, for reasons explored in the preceding section. As
we will see shortly, the effect is particularly pronounced for drug crime. Second, the police must be resource-constrained; that is, they cannot afford to go after everyone. That
too is true, and not just in the obvious sense that we all live in a world of scarcity. Between
1972 and 1991, the ratio of FBI index crimes to population rose forty-nine percent, during the same period the ratio of police officers to population rose just ten percent. Remember
that in the decade before 1971, index crimes trebled while law enforcement personnel
grew by about a quarter. These numbers do not reflect the large additional burden of
drug markets. In 1971, drug cases were a small part of state criminal justice systems, com-
prising less than five percent of criminal charges. By 1990, one-third of all felony convictions
were in drug cases. Between 1968 and 1988, drug arrests more than quintupled. Even
given the eighteen percent decline in index crimes from 1991 to 1998, these numbers suggest very severe resource constraints—much more severe than in the early 1970s, which
were in turn much more severe than in the early 1960s.

Third, police must have some significant interest in catching richer criminals. (If going
after middle-class cocaine dealers is politically unthinkable, Fourth Amendment regulation will make no difference—the police will ignore middle-class dealers no matter what
the law does.) This is far more controversial, but it is probably correct. Wealthier criminals are both more rare and more prominent than poorer ones, so their capture and conviction is likely to generate more favorable publicity. And the social cost of wealthier
criminals is likely to be borne by wealthier citizens, who presumably have some political
clout that would lead the police to seek to protect their interests. In short, though going
after richer criminals has its costs, it also has benefits.

* * *

Which leads to the fourth assumption: that police respond to changes in the cost of
policing. If the cost of pursuing wealthier suspects is high enough relative to poorer suspects, the police will leave the former alone and concentrate on the latter. We see evidence of this phenomenon in the behavior of local police. Local police forces do make large
numbers of fraud arrests, but the frauds tend to be of the blue-collar sort: passing bad
checks and the like. Paradigmatic white-collar crimes are generally left to the federal authorities. Substantive criminal law does not command this result; on the contrary, the
range of federal white-collar criminal law covers conduct almost all of which violates state
criminal statutes as well. Local police leave white-collar crime to the federal authorities

because the opportunity cost of white-collar cases is simply too high. In the time it takes to investigate and prosecute a given fraud case, police and prosecutors might get several burglars, assorted car thieves, and a few felony assaults. If police could do all of these things and still pursue the fraud, they would presumably do so. But if they cannot, the value of the foregone street crime cases is too great to bear, absent some unusual public demand that the fraud defendant be caught and convicted.

Of course, these factors can be more or less strong for different crimes at different times and places. But the point remains: by raising the cost of investigating some crimes but not others, search and seizure law can, under some plausible sets of circumstances, push police away from the now-more-expensive crimes and toward the cheaper ones. To see how likely that possibility is, and how problematic, one must look at the nature of contemporary drug markets and how those markets are policed.

C. Policing Drug Markets

For most crimes, allocation of policing is done by criminals. Political pressure demands that police try to solve murders; where the murders take place determines where (and how) the police investigate. The same is true, to varying degrees, of a range of serious violent and theft offenses. The police rarely have the option of simply ignoring armed robberies or felony assaults; some investigation of such crimes tends to be a political necessity. As for where the investigations happen and whom they target, those things are determined more by where crimes occur than by police choice.

Drugs are different. Because the criminal behavior is consensual, the police do not receive reports of crimes when they happen. In order to catch the criminals, the police must seek them out; they must look for the crime, not merely respond to it. Because the criminal transactions involve goods or services that many people want, there are a lot of crimes: the number of cocaine purchases each year is vastly higher than, say, the number of car thefts. That means the police cannot hope to ferret out every drug transaction, or even a large fraction of them. Selectivity, choosing which crimes to go after — or, rather, where to look for them — is essential. And again, the police, not the criminals, are doing the choosing.

The range of police choice is large, because illegal drug markets operate in all sorts of neighborhoods and cater to all sorts of customers. This is always true of vice crimes. Gambling and prostitution, alcohol in the 1920s and drugs today, all cut across social class and ethnic affiliation. This too distinguishes drugs, and vice generally, from other sorts of criminal behavior. A lot of crime is class-bound: there are very few white-collar robbers, and equally few blue-collar embezzlers. Not so with drugs. Though illegal drug use is much more common in some communities than others, it nevertheless is fairly common in communities of all sorts. Poor urban neighborhoods and wealthy suburbs alike have drug markets.

Not that drug markets look the same everywhere. In poor city neighborhoods, crack is typically sold on the street. In the suburbs, dealers sell cocaine powder through individual deliveries, arranged meetings, and telephone transactions. The reason for this common pattern is simple. In illegal markets as in legal ones, individualized transacting is costly. Mass marketing of the sort offered by a floating street market is much more efficient. But street markets have a cost of their own: the police can more easily identify them. This produces the following pricing pattern: In poor neighborhoods where dealers sell drugs on the street, monetary prices are low and the risk of arrest and punishment is relatively high; in wealthier areas with more discreet transacting procedures, monetary prices are much higher but the risk of police intervention is lower. Buyers in poor neighborhoods are likely to find the low-price-high-risk package attractive, if only because the other package is unaffordable. Some middle-class buyers will find it attractive too, which is why sub-urbanites making drive-through purchases are a regular feature of some urban crack markets. But other upscale customers will tend to prefer to spend more to reduce the risk of police intervention.

Note that the division between street markets in poor neighborhoods and more individualized transactions elsewhere flows naturally from policing—different transacting procedures and different prices track different risks of arrest. That hardly seems surprising: police can more easily catch drug dealers who do business on the street than those who do business on the phone or behind closed doors. But this difference in the cost of policing different sorts of drug markets depends heavily on the law, on the way Fourth Amendment doctrine forces the police to internalize some sorts of costs but not others.

Consider the kinds of tactics police are likely to use when attacking these two types of drug markets. When going after street markets, police tend to do two sorts of things: they engage in a lot of street stops, "sweeps," and the like; they also use undercover buy-and-busts. Each of these tactics is cheap, in the sense that neither requires much police time or effort. Street stops can go forward with little or no advance investigation. Responding to a few visual cues—age, sex, race, location, and company (who else is in the vicinity)—is perfectly feasible, and the cues are available from quick on-the-spot observation. Meanwhile, the stops themselves consume little time, so the police have no strong incentive to ration them carefully. The same is basically true of buy-and-busts. The undercover agent pretends to buy; the seller either sells or doesn't. Again, police select targets based on minimal information, and the tactic does not consume much police time and energy.

All of which is to say that policing street markets is indeed cheap—for the police. But there are other costs to these tactics, costs borne not by police officers but by innocent citizens of the targeted neighborhoods. Large numbers of street stops based on fairly casual cues mean large numbers of bad stops as well as good ones. (By "good" and "bad" I mean nothing more than stops that either do or don't correctly identify participants in the drug trade.) This imposes a very substantial cost on young men present in places where drug deals are known to take place. The same point holds of mistaken buy-and-busts, which work only if the undercover agent looks and acts like a buyer. When the target of the buy-and-bust turns out not to be a seller, the effect of the undercover agent on the community's street life is no different than the effect of a real buyer publicly seeking drugs. Both the real buyer and the fake one send the signal that those who engage in drug transactions own the street.

Now consider the kinds of police tactics that must be used against more upscale drug markets. Because those markets are more secretive, the police must do more work to get inside them, making heavy use of both informants and undercover agents—but not the kind of undercover agents involved in buy-and-busts. Undercover agents who penetrate upscale markets consume a lot of police man-hours; they also expose themselves to real danger, for they are constantly at risk of being discovered. Generating and maintaining informants is cheaper, but not cheap, for the informants are really undercover agents themselves; they frequently are on the public payroll, and they often require a significant amount of police management in order to provide useful information. Finally, in order to exploit such information, the police often must search dwellings or other enclosed structures for the drugs. Searches of closed structures usually require warrants. And warrants usually mean effort and delay—hours spent preparing the relevant papers and sitting around a courthouse waiting for a magistrate to act on the application.

These tactics impose heavy costs on the police. Interestingly, they probably impose very low costs on innocent citizens. Informants are usually reliable, as shown by the data on warrants obtained through informants' tips. Undercover agents who infiltrate criminal enterprises produce very good information. And searches pursuant to warrants are astonishingly successful: a leading study of the issue shows a success rate in excess of eighty percent.

The two sets of police tactics are mirror images of each other. One is cheap for the police but relatively expensive for the local citizenry; the other is expensive for the police and cheap for the citizenry. If the police internalized both sorts of cost, we would probably still see an emphasis on drug markets in lower-class neighborhoods. But the emphasis would be weaker than it is now.

Of course, Fourth Amendment law has a large effect on this calculation, because Fourth Amendment law determines what costs the police need to take into account. Searches of private dwellings require serious justification — probable cause, not some lesser standard — adjudicated by a neutral magistrate before the search takes place. Wiretaps and other sorts of electronic eavesdropping also require serious justification and ex ante review. These privacy-based restrictions make it impossible for the police to do dragnet-style investigations of upscale drug markets; they must instead use tactics that involve extensive information-gathering as a prerequisite to searching for and seizing drugs.

The rules for street encounters, also privacy-based, are much more forgiving. Those encounters are generally deemed consensual if the officer refrains from physical force and puts his commands in the form of questions. Even when consent is absent, the law of street stops holds that the police may briefly detain people based on some suspicion of crime, but much less than probable cause. The lax definition of consent makes it easy for the police to initiate street encounters based on very little suspicion, for the law says that they need none. Often the search that nails the suspect is itself "consensual," and thus requires no advance information-gathering at all. Even where the encounter falls outside the generous bounds of consent, the rule for street stops means the police need no more than the information they can obtain through quick observation. To a significant degree, the law forces the police to investigate upscale criminal markets in ways that minimize the costs to bystanders, while giving a green light to very different tactics in downscale markets.

Notice how the law's tilt is tied to its focus on protecting privacy. House searches and telephone taps are serious privacy intrusions. Consequently, they are heavily regulated. They are also the tactics police must use if they are to attack middle-class drug networks. Street stops and sweeps can be very intrusive indeed, but the privacy intrusion is not as great as in house searches; the law accordingly regulates these tactics much more lightly. And these are the tactics police must use when attacking crack markets in poor urban neighborhoods.

So policing urban crack markets is cheaper than policing suburban markets in cocaine powder, and Fourth Amendment law makes that cost gap substantially larger than it otherwise might be. What effect is that likely to have on where police go to look for drugs, and on whom they arrest? The answer depends on local circumstances, but at the very least, Fourth Amendment law probably changes the mix of drug arrests — if it were easier to target middle-class whites, more middle-class whites would likely be arrested, prosecuted, and punished, and the prison population would be less heavily tilted toward poor blacks.

The effect may well be more serious than that. At current levels of crime in general and drug crime in particular, police in most cities will operate at capacity, meaning that any given drug investigation will be a substitute for some other investigation — if not this buy-and-bust, that one; if less attention to this neighborhood, more to that one. Were it cheaper to attack middle-class drug markets, police resources might well be drawn toward those markets, and away from markets in poorer neighborhoods. Which would mean not only a more middle-class pool of drug defendants, but a whiter one as well, given the high concentration of blacks in poor urban neighborhoods. If this possibility is right, Fourth Amendment law is in no small measure responsible for the drug war's enormous racial tilt, and for the consequently growing racial tilt in our nation's majority-black prison population.

* * *

II. Evaluating Fourth Amendment Privacy

* * *

Privacy is a good and important thing; infringing it is bad. Perhaps that is enough reason to have a Fourth Amendment whose chief purpose is to protect privacy. But the Fourth Amendment is the primary source of legal regulation of the police, and in our time and place privacy is a very strange thing to focus on when regulating the police. The targets of police searches and seizures tend to be relatively poor. Privacy is an interest whose importance grows with one's bank account, or one's square footage. Partly because most suspects are poor, most searches and seizures take place on the street, far from the world of bedroom closets and telephone conversations. Privacy is not much at stake in street encounters, so Fourth Amendment law has little to do with those encounters. Which means Fourth Amendment law, the body of law that most regulates the police, regulates very little when it comes to what the police do most.

There is something very wrong with this picture. As it is currently structured, Fourth Amendment law focuses its attention on an interest that is at the periphery of policing, not at the core. It focuses its protection on people who, it would seem, can likely protect themselves reasonably well without the need of judicial intervention. In the process, it may make another set of people, people who cannot so easily protect themselves against police abuse, worse off. It is hard to see how this can be a good state of affairs.

All of which suggests that Fourth Amendment law protects the wrong people because it protects the wrong interest. Perhaps it is time to think about search and seizure cases not in terms of the strength of different defendants' privacy interests, but in terms of the kinds of interests that matter most to the kinds of suspects police target most. That might mean less constitutional regulation—orienting search and seizure law around police coercion and harassment would be hard, and developing workable rules might be impossible. At the least, it would mean less protection for middle-class homeowners. But then, less constitutional regulation might not be a bad thing, given that constitutional regulation does not seem to be advancing the cause of fairer, and more fairly distributed, policing. And in a criminal justice system like ours, protecting middle-class homeowners hardly seems like a priority.

———————

Notes and Questions

1. What is Professor Stuntz's key point about the distribution of privacy under the Fourth Amendment?

2. Is Professor Stuntz correct that the Fourth Amendment's warrant requirement offers little protection? Throughout *The Wire*, how often do you see the Baltimore police making use of search or arrest warrants? When they do seek warrants, is it for items and places that are typically used by the wealthy?

3. Watch *The Wire*, Season 1, Episode 8, at 15:55 minutes. After seeing members of the Barksdale drug gang hand a bag into a towncar that had pulled over on the street, the officers follow the car. Eventually, they pull over the car and see the driver trying to hide the bag under the front passenger seat. The officers arrest the driver, retrieve the bag, open it and find a large amount of cash inside. As a matter of current Fourth Amendment jurisprudence, the officers' actions are perfectly constitutional. Does that make sense to you? Should the police have been required to get a warrant to stop the car? How about to search for the bag inside the car? Should they be required to procure a warrant before opening the bag? Or does the officers' warrantless searching seem perfectly reasonable? If the officers' actions seem reasonable under the circumstances, does that suggest that Professor Stuntz oversells his case?

4. Is Stuntz correct to assert that the police are drawn to poor neighborhoods because of the violence and the political focus on murder cases and other crimes catalogued by the FBI's Uniform Crime Reports?

5. Consider the scenes in *The Wire*, Season 4, Episode 5, at 41:45 minutes and 46:20 minutes where the officers set up a surveillance camera in the park without a warrant in order to observe a drug gang. Also watch *The Wire*, Season 2, Episode 7, at 14:50 minutes and 16:35 minutes in which the officers put a bug in a tennis ball and leave it on the street to listen to drug transactions. Is all of this warrantless surveillance constitutional? If so, does this lack of privacy on the street prove Stuntz correct?

6. Watch *The Wire*, Season 1, Episode 10, at 38:50 minutes, in which the officers dress as garbage workers and covertly take two black trash bags from outside the suburban stash house. The officers have no warrant. The Supreme Court has upheld such searches. *See* California v. Greenwood, 486 U.S. 35 (1988). In considering Professor Stuntz's article, how do you interpret this scene? Does it cast doubt on his position that Fourth Amendment jurisprudence favors the affluent, because police are able to get information from a suburban home without a warrant or even having to show probable cause? Or does it support his larger point because the officers had to create an elaborate ruse and still could not get beyond the curb of the house?

7. Watch *The Wire*, Season 1, Episode 12, at 39:40 minutes. After figuring out that D'Angelo Barksdale is about to make a drug run to New York, the officers attach a tracking device to the underside of his rental car. Was this constitutional? At the time *The Wire* aired in 2002, the answer was seemingly yes. *See* United States v. Knotts, 460 U.S. 276 (1983) (upholding visual surveillance based on a beeper in a chemical container being transported in a vehicle). Recently, however, in United States v. Jones 132 S.Ct. 945 (2012), the Supreme Court ruled, albeit based on divided rationales, that the physical installation and long-term use of a GPS tracker on a vehicle without a warrant violated the Fourth Amendment. Now that GPS technology is ubiquitous and seemingly inexpensive for police departments, is the Supreme Court's decision consistent with Professor Stuntz's position?

8. Professor Stuntz is not the only criminal procedure expert to assert that Fourth Amendment jurisprudence dramatically disfavors the poor. For another excellent assessment, *see* Christopher Slobogin, *The Poverty Exception to the Fourth Amendment*, 55 Fla. L. Rev. 391 (2003).

D. Do the Police Actually Follow the Fourth Amendment Rules or Do They Try to Circumvent or Ignore The Rules?

The primary rationale for excluding illegally seized evidence is to deter the police from violating the Fourth Amendment. The Supreme Court has spent a lot of time and ink to define the scope of Fourth Amendment protection and to set forth when evidence should be suppressed. But do the police really follow these rules? There are a few possible responses to that question. One possibility is that police academies teach police the law and officers then do their best to scrupulously follow the Court's precedents to avoid suppression of evidence. Another possibility is that police learn the Supreme Court's rules and then, either through training sessions or informal discussions amongst themselves, figure out how to circumvent the rules the Court has created. Still another possibility is that police ignore the rules if they think they won't be caught, but follow the rules when they expect to find incriminating evidence and think they won't be able to shade the events that occurred. Which of the three categories does the next case fall into?

Murray v. United States
487 U.S. 533 (1988)

Justice SCALIA delivered the opinion of the Court.

* * *

I

... Based on information received from informants, federal law enforcement agents had been surveilling petitioner Murray and several of his co-conspirators. At about 1:45 p.m. on April 6, 1983, they observed Murray drive a truck and Carter drive a green camper, into a warehouse in South Boston. When the petitioners drove the vehicles out about 20 minutes later, the surveilling agents saw within the warehouse two individuals and a tractor-trailer rig bearing a long, dark container. Murray and Carter later turned over the truck and camper to other drivers, who were in turn followed and ultimately arrested, and the vehicles lawfully seized. Both vehicles were found to contain marijuana.

After receiving this information, several of the agents converged on the South Boston warehouse and forced entry. They found the warehouse unoccupied, but observed in plain view numerous burlap-wrapped bales that were later found to contain marijuana. They left without disturbing the bales, kept the warehouse under surveillance, and did not reenter it until they had a search warrant. In applying for the warrant, the agents did not mention the prior entry, and did not rely on any observations made during that entry. When the warrant was issued—at 10:40 p.m., approximately eight hours after the initial entry—the agents immediately reentered the warehouse and seized 270 bales of marijuana and notebooks listing customers for whom the bales were destined.

Before trial, petitioners moved to suppress the evidence found in the warehouse. The District Court denied the motion, rejecting petitioners' arguments that the warrant was invalid because the agents did not inform the Magistrate about their prior warrantless entry, and that the warrant was tainted by that entry. The First Circuit affirmed, assuming for purposes of its decision that the first entry into the warehouse was unlawful....

II

The exclusionary rule prohibits introduction into evidence of tangible materials seized during an unlawful search, and of testimony concerning knowledge acquired during an unlawful search. Beyond that, the exclusionary rule also prohibits the introduction of derivative evidence, both tangible and testimonial, that is the product of the primary evidence, or that is otherwise acquired as an indirect result of the unlawful search, up to the point at which the connection with the unlawful search becomes "so attenuated as to dissipate the taint," *Nardone v. United States,* 308 U.S. 338, 341(1939).

Almost simultaneously with our development of the exclusionary rule, in the first quarter of this century, we also announced what has come to be known as the "independent source" doctrine....

The dispute here is over the scope of this doctrine. Petitioners contend that it applies only to evidence obtained for the first time during an independent lawful search. The Government argues that it applies also to evidence initially discovered during, or as a consequence of, an unlawful search, but later obtained independently from activities untainted by the initial illegality. We think the Government's view has better support in both precedent and policy.

Our cases have used the concept of "independent source" in a more general and a more specific sense. The more general sense identifies *all* evidence acquired in a fashion untainted by the illegal evidence-gathering activity. Thus, where an unlawful entry has given investigators knowledge of facts *x* and *y,* but fact *z* has been learned by other means, fact *z* can be said to be admissible because derived from an "independent source." This is how we used the term in *Segura v. United States,* 468 U.S. 796, 104 S.Ct. 3380, 82 L.Ed.2d 599 (1984). In that case, agents unlawfully entered the defendant's apartment and remained there until a search warrant was obtained. The admissibility of what they discovered while waiting in the apartment was not before us, but we held that the evidence found for the first time during the execution of the valid and untainted search warrant was admissible because it was discovered pursuant to an "independent source."

* * *

As the First Circuit has observed, "[i]n the classic independent source situation, information which is received through an illegal source is considered to be cleanly obtained when it arrives through an independent source." *United States v. Silvestri,* 787 F.2d 736, 739 (1986). We recently assumed this application of the independent source doctrine (in the Sixth Amendment context) in *Nix v. Williams.* There incriminating statements obtained in violation of the defendant's right to counsel had led the police to the victim's body. The body had not in fact been found through an independent source as well, and so the independent source doctrine was not itself applicable. We held, however, that evidence concerning the body was nonetheless admissible because a search had been under way which would have discovered the body, had it not been called off because of the discovery produced by the unlawfully obtained statements. This "inevitable discovery" doctrine obviously assumes the validity of the independent source doctrine as applied to evidence initially acquired unlawfully. It would make no sense to admit the evidence because the independent search, had it not been aborted, would have found the body, but to exclude the evidence if the search had continued and had in fact found the body. The inevitable discovery doctrine, with its distinct requirements, is in reality an extrapolation from the independent source doctrine: *Since* the tainted evidence would be admissible if in fact discovered through an independent source, it should be admissible if it inevitably would have been discovered.

Petitioners' asserted policy basis for excluding evidence which is initially discovered during an illegal search, but is subsequently acquired through an independent and lawful source, is that a contrary rule will remove all deterrence to, and indeed positively encourage, unlawful police searches. As petitioners see the incentives, law enforcement officers will routinely enter without a warrant to make sure that what they expect to be on the premises is in fact there. If it is not, they will have spared themselves the time and trouble of getting a warrant; if it is, they can get the warrant and use the evidence despite the unlawful entry. We see the incentives differently. An officer with probable cause sufficient to obtain a search warrant would be foolish to enter the premises first in an unlawful manner. By doing so, he would risk suppression of all evidence on the premises, both seen and unseen, since his action would add to the normal burden of convincing a magistrate that there is probable cause the much more onerous burden of convincing a trial court that no information gained from the illegal entry affected either the law enforcement officers' decision to seek a warrant or the magistrate's decision to grant it. Nor would the officer *without* sufficient probable cause to obtain a search warrant have any added incentive to conduct an unlawful entry, since whatever he finds cannot be used to establish probable cause before a magistrate.

* * *

III

To apply what we have said to the present cases: Knowledge that the marijuana was in the warehouse was assuredly acquired at the time of the unlawful entry. But it was also acquired at the time of entry pursuant to the warrant, and if that later acquisition was not the result of the earlier entry there is no reason why the independent source doctrine should not apply. Invoking the exclusionary rule would put the police (and society) not in the *same* position they would have occupied if no violation occurred, but in a *worse* one.

* * *

The ultimate question, therefore, is whether the search pursuant to warrant was in fact a genuinely independent source of the information and tangible evidence at issue here. This would not have been the case if the agents' decision to seek the warrant was prompted by what they had seen during the initial entry, or if information obtained during that entry was presented to the Magistrate and affected his decision to issue the warrant....

* * *

Accordingly, we vacate the judgment and remand these cases to the Court of Appeals with instructions that it remand to the District Court for determination whether the warrant-authorized search of the warehouse was an independent source of the challenged evidence in the sense we have described.

It is so ordered.

[The dissenting opinions of Justice Marshall and Justice Stevens are omitted]

————————

Notes and Questions

1. When the officers entered the warehouse the first time without a warrant, was that a flagrant violation of the Fourth Amendment or was it a close call that could have fallen under the exigency exception?

2. If officers are trained to comply with the Fourth Amendment, why didn't they wait for the warrant before entering?

3. Justice Scalia takes the view that an independent source exception will not lead the police to search first and get a warrant second because they would not want to risk suppression of any evidence found during the first search? Does this seem correct to you? Doesn't the independent source doctrine, as well as the Court's inevitable discovery decision in Nix v. Williams, 467 U.S. 431 (1984), give police an incentive to search illegally because the evidence is unlikely to be suppressed?

4. Police are permitted to use anonymous informants as the basis for probable cause. *See* Illinois v. Gates, 462 U.S. 213 (1983). Doesn't the independent source exception therefore encourage police to search illegally first to find incriminating information and then attribute that information to an anonymous informant in order to get a search warrant? And, if police use that scheme, won't the fake informant always give an accurate tip, thus making him more reliable and more likely to be accepted by judges the next time the police use this ruse? *See* Craig M. Bradley, *Murray v. United States: The Bell Tolls for the Search Warrant Requirement*, 64 Ind. L.J. 907, 918 (1989).

5. Officers Herc and Carver use a scheme like the one outlined in note 4 when they attribute information to a fake informant named Fuzzy Dunlop. Watch *The Wire*, Season 2, Episode 8, at 22:15 minutes in which Officer Herc pays his cousin to allow his picture and social security number to be used as an informant named Fuzzy Dunlop. Officer Herc relies on the fake informant throughout the series, even lying to his lieutenant about having received a confidential tip from Fuzzy Dunlop rather than admitting the information came from an unauthorized surveillance camera. Watch *The Wire*, Season 4, Episode 6, at 5:45 minutes.

6. Does the scenario in *Murray* seem similar to the plot from the last season of *The Wire*, in which the officers use an illegal wiretap to find a drug supply warehouse and then later write a legitimate warrant application for that warehouse? In particular, watch *The Wire*, Season 5, Episode 9.

7. Are courts too deferential to police officers in drug cases? Narcotics officers often testify in suppression hearings that a suspect fit a drug profile or that furtive movements indicated a drug hand-off, even if the officer did not actually see drugs or money change hands. And courts typically accept this testimony and deny suppression motions. *See, e.g.*, Williams v. State, 981 A.2d 46, 56 (Md. Ct. Spec. App. 2009) (finding probable cause for an arrest based on the testimony of a narcotics officer who had "observed thousands and thousands of street distribution methods" even though officer never saw the drugs or the money change hands). How can courts be sure the officers are telling the truth in cases like this?

8. In confession cases, there is sometimes a preliminary question about whether police had authority under the Fourth Amendment to bring the suspect into custody in the first place. Watch *The Wire*, Season 1, Episode 2, at 25:00. Detectives McNulty and Bunk have arrested D'Angelo Barksdale and are about to interrogate him when Lieutenant Daniels arrives:

Lt. Daniels: What do you have to connect him to the dead witness?

McNulty: Not a thing.

Lt. Daniels: Then why did you pick him up?

McNulty: Press him. See what kind of flex he shows.

Rather than being upset at the unlawful arrest (and the interrogation that will be fruit of the poisonous tree), Lieutenant Daniels allows the detectives to go forward with the interrogation.

9. The tactic employed by the police in *Murray* is clever. On the other hand, watch *The Wire*, Season 3, Episode 1, at 7:50 minutes. The officers conduct a drug raid and are aware that one runner will take off as a decoy in an effort to lead the police away from the other dealers. The officers specifically say they will not fall for this trick. Yet, when the runner picks up a plastic garbage bag, the officers give chase. And as soon as they do, the dealers pick up the actual stash of drugs and walk away. Are the officers in this scene just as stupid as the officers in *Murray* were clever? By and large, do you think the police are more or less intelligent than most people assume?

United States v. Amato
2006 WL 800799 (S.D.N.Y. 2006)

SWAIN, J.

On December 8, 2005 [at a suppression hearing].... the Court determined, *inter alia*, that "the search [of Defendant's vehicle, during which a firearm was seized,] was conducted only after police officers observed Defendant making unusual movements, and after an officer had observed a pistol through the window of the car."

Following the Court's December 8 Order, the Court granted Defendant's request to submit an additional videotape purporting to show that, even with the aid of a flashlight, it was not possible for a police officer to have seen a pistol through the rear passenger side window of the Defendant's vehicle on the night of his arrest. Finding the videotape inconclusive, the Court determined that it was necessary to view the vehicle itself after dark. On January 25, 2006, at approximately 5:30 p.m., the Court and counsel inspected the Mountaineer with the aid of a flashlight of the type the officer had testified he had used to look through the windows of the vehicle on the night of the arrest....

At a conference held on February 16, 2006, the Court made the following findings of fact on the record, based on its inspection of the vehicle ... (1) on January 25, 2006, it was not possible to see through the rear passenger side windows of the Mercury Mountaineer after dark with the aid of a Maglight flashlight; and (2) the Court's visual inspection is consistent with ... [an expert's] finding that the windows in their present condition transmit only 3% of light. The Court identified a single material factual issue remaining with regard to Defendant's suppression motion: "Was the level of tinting of the rear passenger side window of Amato's vehicle on the night of his arrest the same as the current level of tinting on the window?" Noting that the record included only the police officer's testimony, a copy of the tinting receipt and representations of counsel concerning the condition of the vehicle on the night of the arrest, the Court allowed the parties a final round of evidentiary submissions on this discrete issue.

On March 10, 2006, the defense served and submitted affidavits from Amato's brother and from an employee of the window tinting company attesting to the aftermarket application of the current level of tint to the vehicle windows on June 14, 2004 (several months prior to Amato's arrest) and representing that the tint has not been altered since that time. The affidavits were accompanied by documentation of the original factory level of tint, to which additional tint had been applied. The Government proffered no further evidence and did not request an opportunity to cross-examine either witness.

DISCUSSION

The relevant findings set out in the December 8 Order were based primarily upon the testimony of New York City Police Officer Sean Lynch ("Lynch"). Lynch had testified that, while he was looking through the rear passenger side window of Amato's vehicle with his flashlight, he "noticed a firearm ... sticking out of the pouch behind the driver's seat." Officer Lynch further testified that he was "[r]ight up next to the vehicle" as he was looking through the window. The Court had also considered a videotape made by the defense in support of its contention that it was impossible for Officer Lynch to have been able to see through the tinted car windows. However, it was not clear from the videotape whether a person could have seen through the tinted windows with the aid of a flashlight. Accordingly, the Court found that the Government had met its burden of proof and denied Defendant's motion.

The Court's own inspection of the vehicle and the subsequent testimonial and documentary evidence give the lie to Lynch's testimony. The Court was not able to see through the rear passenger side window, which was heavily tinted black, with or without the aid of a flashlight. Even when the flashlight was held against the window, it did not illuminate the rear seating area within the car. The flashlight also neither illuminated the rear of the front passenger seat nor the pouch located on the rear of the front passenger seat. Indeed, one could not see the pouch.

The uncontroverted additional evidentiary proffers are sufficient to establish that the level of tint observed by the Court was the same as that which was on the vehicle's windows at the time of Amato's arrest. It was thus impossible for Officer Lynch to have observed the gun through the window of the vehicle. The Government has not, in light of the totality of the evidence of record, carried its burden of demonstrating by a preponderance of the credible evidence that the subsequent search of the vehicle, in which the gun was found in the pouch located behind the driver's seat, was supported by probable cause. The December 8 Order is vacated to the extent it denied Defendant's motion to suppress the physical evidence seized from the vehicle, and Defendant's suppression motion is hereby granted.

SO ORDERED.

Notes and Questions

1. Judge Swain seemingly accuses the officer of lying when she says that the "testimonial and documentary evidence give the lie to Lynch's testimony." This is unusual. Judges are often reluctant to say officers have lied, even when they disbelieve police officers and suppress evidence. *See* Benjamin Weiser, *Police in Gun Searches Face Disbelief in Court*, N.Y. TIMES, May 12, 2008 (quoting highly regarded federal judge John Gleeson as saying that he is reluctant to even imply that officers have lied). Notice however that Judge Swain did not publish her decision suppressing the evidence.

2. How difficult is it for judges to catch police lying? In *The Wire*, Season 3, Episode 7, at 12:40 minutes, Detective Freamon explains to the other officers how acquiring one of the drug dealers' disposable cell phones would enable the police to figure out the leadership and structure of the drug gang. Later in that episode, at 32:00 minutes, McNulty and other officers pull over a vehicle in order to pat down one of the drug dealers, grab his cell phone, and replace it with a different phone. Of course, switching the cell phone is unconstitutional because police had no lawful reason to seize the phone. If the officers testified though that they found the disposable cell phone on the ground or in the trash, would a judge ever know that they were lying? Would a judge believe the testimony of a drug dealer over the officers?

3. Although it is difficult to find many written judicial opinions concluding that officers lied about how they acquired evidence, does that mean the practice of police lying is rare? Is the number of written decisions a fair representation of how police officers

comply with the Fourth Amendment? If prosecutors dismiss cases because they believe officers lied about complying with the Fourth Amendment, will there be any written record of the prosecutors' conclusions?

4. Watch *The Wire*, Season 5, Episode 8, at 23:45 minutes. Detective Sydnor explains to other officers how to conduct surveillance of Marlo Stansfield and his gang. At the end of the explanation he says: "None of what we do here is necessary for court. So rest easy on that." Does *The Wire* show us that the police carefully follow one set of rules when they want to make a big bust that will stick and another set of rules for smaller "rip and run" cases where it is less important if the bust sticks or if they have no interest in acquiring evidence? Watch *The Wire*, Season 2, Episode 9, at 12:25 minutes. After an innocent child is killed in the crossfire from a drug shoot-out, officers descend on the area and arrest every young black man in sight to show that the police department is responsive to violence. The officers have no individualized probable cause for any of the arrests. When one arrestee protests "I'm clean" an officer responds "well what are you doing in the pit then?" Implicitly, the officer acknowledges arresting the man unlawfully simply because he was found in a high crime area. Also consider *The Wire*, Season 4, Episode 9, at 37:30 minutes and 48:40 minutes. Detective Herc and his colleagues harass Marlo's crew in an effort to recover a missing surveillance camera. In the first scene, the officers stop and frisk gang members and break their property. In the second scene, they conduct a traffic stop and search the vehicle. In both instances, the officers lack reasonable suspicion to believe criminal activity is afoot and certainly lack probable cause for the search. Do you think Detective Herc knows he is violating the Fourth Amendment? If so, do you think he cares? If he is not seeking to arrest anyone in Marlo's gang is there anything to deter him from violating the Fourth Amendment? Is it remotely possible that Marlo or his colleagues would file a complaint with the police department or initiate a federal civil rights lawsuit?

5. The *New York Times* article cited in note 1 makes clear that police officers are rarely punished, even if judges conclude that the officers blatantly lied. Are there real repercussions for officers who simply hassle or arrest suspects to get information? Other than the prospect of evidence being suppressed, do officers really face any penalties for disregarding clear Fourth Amendment rules? Is the suppression of evidence actually punishment?

6. Is it possible for police to comply with the Fourth Amendment and successfully fight the drug war? One writer for *The Wire* described the problem like this:

> By the time a cop chases a kid across an open courtyard, the kid was inside the tower taking the stairs three at a time. By the time that same officer followed up the stairwell, bolts would begin locking on doors, the drugs would disappear, and both the suspect and contraband could be in one of a hundred apartments on more than a dozen floors.

Rafael Alvarez, The Wire: Truth Be Told 50 (2009). Would the officers have probable cause for each apartment? If not, are they simply supposed to walk away from the scene? Do you think most officers would do so?

Chapter V

Interrogation:
The Law and the Reality

A. Introduction

Confessions are the most valuable piece of evidence against a defendant. When a suspect has confessed, prosecutors are more willing to charge high, and juries find confessions to be more persuasive than even eyewitness identifications. Yet, the problems with confessions are legion. Police officers sometimes engage in overly aggressive tactics in order to procure confessions. These tactics range from misrepresenting the *Miranda* rules, to ignoring the *Miranda* doctrine altogether, to threatening suspects who refuse to consent, to actual physical violence. Even when police have behaved perfectly properly, suspects still occasionally confess to crimes they did not commit. As with Fourth Amendment jurisprudence, a key question is therefore whether the Supreme Court's Fifth Amendment rules actually help criminal suspects.

This chapter begins by asking whether the infamous *Miranda* doctrine, which has now been in place for nearly fifty years, actually helps average criminal defendants or whether it sets up rules that only benefit the very sophisticated. If the *Miranda* rules, as well as the rules against coerced confessions, are potentially helpful to suspects, we next must consider whether the police in fact follow those rules or whether they simply ignore them when they are inconvenient. A related question is whether, when police are presented with rules that would seemingly stand in the way of getting a confession, the officers are clever enough to technically comply with the rules while still getting incriminating admissions from suspects? Finally, in a world of ubiquitous technology, is there a better way to make sure that police comply with the rules while not completely handcuffing law enforcement? Would recording interrogations be feasible and would it solve the manipulation and police brutality that repeatedly occurs in *The Wire* and (hopefully less often) in police stations across the United States?

B. Does the *Miranda* Doctrine Offer Any Protection to the Unsophisticated?

Perhaps no other criminal procedure decision has generated as much controversy as *Miranda v. Arizona*. In *Miranda*, the Supreme Court focused on the unfairly coercive atmosphere of many police interrogations and mandated that suspects be warned of certain rights and that police terminate interrogations when suspects decide to remain silent or ask for a lawyer. The *Miranda* Court believed that these rules would put suspects on a more even playing field. To critics, the Court's decision was egregious judicial activism that sided with dangerous criminals rather than public safety. Yet, contrary to the criticism that the sky would fall as a result of *Miranda*, the police have arguably benefitted in the long run. As you read the materials below, ask yourself whether the *Miranda* doctrine provides any helpful protection to unsophisticated criminal defendants. At the same time, ask yourself whether any of the dire predictions of *Miranda* critics have come true. In short, is it possible that the *Miranda* majority over-estimated the benefits for criminal defendants while critics under-estimated the benefits that law enforcement would gain from the decision?

Miranda v. Arizona

384 U.S. 436 (1966)

Mr. Chief Justice WARREN delivered the opinion of the Court.

The cases before us raise questions which go to the roots of our concepts of American criminal jurisprudence: the restraints society must observe consistent with the Federal Constitution in prosecuting individuals for crime. More specifically, we deal with the admissibility of statements obtained from an individual who is subjected to custodial police interrogation and the necessity for procedures which assure that the individual is accorded his privilege under the Fifth Amendment to the Constitution not to be compelled to incriminate himself.

* * *

Our holding will be spelled out with some specificity in the pages which follow but briefly stated it is this: the prosecution may not use statements, whether exculpatory or inculpatory, stemming from custodial interrogation of the defendant unless it demonstrates the use of procedural safeguards effective to secure the privilege against self-incrimination. By custodial interrogation, we mean questioning initiated by law enforcement officers after a person has been taken into custody or otherwise deprived of his freedom of action in any significant way. As for the procedural safeguards to be employed, unless other fully effective means are devised to inform accused persons of their right of silence and to assure a continuous opportunity to exercise it, the following measures are required. Prior to any questioning, the person must be warned that he has a right to remain silent, that any statement he does make may be used as evidence against him, and that he has a right to the presence of an attorney, either retained or appointed. The defendant may waive effectuation of these rights, provided the waiver is made voluntarily, knowingly and intelligently. If, however, he indicates in any manner and at any stage of the process that he wishes to consult with an attorney before speaking there can be no questioning. Likewise, if the individual is alone and indicates in any manner that he does not wish to be interrogated, the police may not question him. The mere fact that he may have answered some questions or volunteered some statements on his own does not deprive him of the right to refrain from answering any further inquiries until he has consulted with an attorney and thereafter consents to be questioned.

1.

The constitutional issue we decide in each of these cases is the admissibility of statements obtained from a defendant questioned while in custody or otherwise deprived of his freedom of action in any significant way. In each, the defendant was questioned by police officers, detectives, or a prosecuting attorney in a room in which he was cut off from the outside world. In none of these cases was the defendant given a full and effective warning of his rights at the outset of the interrogation process. In all the cases, the questioning elicited oral admissions, and in three of them, signed statements as well which were admitted at their trials. They all thus share salient features—incommunicado interrogation of individuals in a police-dominated atmosphere, resulting in self-incriminating statements without full warnings of constitutional rights.

An understanding of the nature and setting of this in-custody interrogation is essential to our decisions today. The difficulty in depicting what transpires at such interrogations stems from the fact that in this country they have largely taken place incommunicado. From extensive factual studies undertaken in the early 1930's, including the famous Wickersham Report to Congress by a Presidential Commission, it is clear that police violence and the 'third degree' flourished at that time. In a series of cases decided by this Court long after these studies, the police resorted to physical brutality—beatings, hanging, whipping—and to sustained and protracted questioning incommunicado in order to extort confessions. The Commission on Civil Rights in 1961 found much evidence to indicate that 'some policemen still resort to physical force to obtain confessions.' The use of physical brutality and violence is not, unfortunately, relegated to the past or to any part of the country. Only recently in Kings County, New York, the police brutally beat, kicked and placed lighted cigarette butts on the back of a potential witness under interrogation for the purpose of securing a statement incriminating a third party.

* * *

Again we stress that the modern practice of in-custody interrogation is psychologically rather than physically oriented. . . . Interrogation still takes place in privacy. Privacy results in secrecy and this in turn results in a gap in our knowledge as to what in fact goes on in the interrogation rooms. A valuable source of information about present police practices, however, may be found in various police manuals and texts which document procedures employed with success in the past, and which recommend various other effective tactics. These texts are used by law enforcement agencies themselves as guides. It should be noted that these texts professedly present the most enlightened and effective means presently used to obtain statements through custodial interrogation. By considering these texts and other data, it is possible to describe procedures observed and noted around the country.

The officers are told by the manuals that the 'principal psychological factor contributing to a successful interrogation is privacy—being alone with the person under interrogation. . . .

To highlight the isolation and unfamiliar surroundings, the manuals instruct the police to display an air of confidence in the suspect's guilt and from outward appearance to maintain only an interest in confirming certain details. The guilt of the subject is to be posited as a fact. The interrogator should direct his comments toward the reasons why the subject committed the act, rather than court failure by asking the subject whether he did it. Like other men, perhaps the subject has had a bad family life, had an unhappy childhood, had too much to drink, had an unrequited desire for women. The officers are instructed to minimize the moral seriousness of the offense, to cast blame on the victim or on society. These tactics are designed to put the subject in a psychological state where his story is but an elaboration of what the police purport to know already—that he is guilty. Explanations to the contrary are dismissed and discouraged.

* * *

The interrogators sometimes are instructed to induce a confession out of trickery. The technique here is quite effective in crimes which require identification or which run in series. In the identification situation, the interrogator may take a break in his questioning to place the subject among a group of men in a line-up. 'The witness or complainant (previously coached, if necessary) studies the line-up and confidently points out the subject as the guilty party. Then the questioning resumes 'as though there were now no doubt about the guilt of the subject.' . . . .

* * *

From these representative samples of interrogation techniques, the setting prescribed by the manuals and observed in practice becomes clear. In essence, it is this: To be alone with the subject is essential to prevent distraction and to deprive him of any outside support. The aura of confidence in his guilt undermines his will to resist. He merely confirms the preconceived story the police seek to have him describe. Patience and persistence, at times relentless questioning, are employed. To obtain a confession, the interrogator must 'patiently maneuver himself or his quarry into a position from which the desired objective may be attained. When normal procedures fail to produce the needed result, the police may resort to deceptive stratagems such as giving false legal advice. It is important to keep the subject off balance, for example, by trading on his insecurity about himself or his surroundings. The police then persuade, trick, or cajole him out of exercising his constitutional rights.

* * *

It is obvious that such an interrogation environment is created for no purpose other than to subjugate the individual to the will of his examiner. This atmosphere carries its own badge of intimidation. To be sure, this is not physical intimidation, but it is equally destructive of human dignity. The current practice of incommunicado interrogation is at odds with one of our Nation's most cherished principles—that the individual may not be compelled to incriminate himself. Unless adequate protective devices are employed to dispel the compulsion inherent in custodial surroundings, no statement obtained from the defendant can truly be the product of his free choice.

* * *

III.

* * *

It is impossible for us to foresee the potential alternatives for protecting the privilege which might be devised by Congress or the States in the exercise of their creative rule-making capacities. Therefore we cannot say that the Constitution necessarily requires adherence to any particular solution for the inherent compulsions of the interrogation process as it is presently conducted. Our decision in no way creates a constitutional straitjacket which will handicap sound efforts at reform, nor is it intended to have this effect. We encourage Congress and the States to continue their laudable search for increasingly effective ways of protecting the rights of the individual while promoting efficient enforcement of our criminal laws. However, unless we are shown other procedures which are at least as effective in apprising accused persons of their right of silence and in assuring a continuous opportunity to exercise it, the following safeguards must be observed.

At the outset, if a person in custody is to be subjected to interrogation, he must first be informed in clear and unequivocal terms that he has the right to remain silent. For those unaware of the privilege, the warning is needed simply to make them aware of it—the threshold requirement for an intelligent decision as to its exercise. More important, such a warning is an absolute prerequisite in overcoming the inherent pressures of the interrogation atmosphere. It is not just the subnormal or woefully ignorant who succumb to an interrogator's imprecations, whether implied or expressly stated, that the interrogation will continue until a confession is obtained or that silence in the face of accusation is itself damning and will bode ill when presented to a jury. Further, the warning will show the individual that his interrogators are prepared to recognize his privilege should he choose to exercise it.

* * *

The warning of the right to remain silent must be accompanied by the explanation that anything said can and will be used against the individual in court. This warning is needed in order to make him aware not only of the privilege, but also of the consequences of forgoing it. It is only through an awareness of these consequences that there can be any assurance of real understanding and intelligent exercise of the privilege. Moreover, this warning may serve to make the individual more acutely aware that he is faced with a phase of the adversary system—that he is not in the presence of persons acting solely in his interest.

The circumstances surrounding in-custody interrogation can operate very quickly to overbear the will of one merely made aware of his privilege by his interrogators. Therefore, the right to have counsel present at the interrogation is indispensable to the protection of the Fifth Amendment privilege under the system we delineate today. Our aim is to assure that the individual's right to choose between silence and speech remains unfettered throughout the interrogation process. A once-stated warning, delivered by those who will conduct the interrogation, cannot itself suffice to that end among those who most require knowledge of their rights. A mere warning given by the interrogators is not alone sufficient to accomplish that end. Prosecutors themselves claim that the admonishment of the right to remain silent without more 'will benefit only the recidivist and the professional.' Even preliminary advice given to the accused by his own attorney can be swiftly overcome by the secret interrogation process. Thus, the need for counsel to protect the Fifth Amendment privilege comprehends not merely a right to consult with counsel prior to questioning, but also to have counsel present during any questioning if the defendant so desires.

The presence of counsel at the interrogation may serve several significant subsidiary functions as well. If the accused decides to talk to his interrogators, the assistance of counsel can mitigate the dangers of untrustworthiness. With a lawyer present the likelihood that the police will practice coercion is reduced, and if coercion is nevertheless exercised the lawyer can testify to it in court. The presence of a lawyer can also help to guarantee that the accused gives a fully accurate statement to the police and that the statement is rightly reported by the prosecution at trial.

An individual need not make a pre-interrogation request for a lawyer. While such request affirmatively secures his right to have one, his failure to ask for a lawyer does not constitute a waiver. No effective waiver of the right to counsel during interrogation can be recognized unless specifically made after the warnings we here delineate have been given. The accused who does not know his rights and therefore does not make a request may be the person who most needs counsel....

* * *

Accordingly we hold that an individual held for interrogation must be clearly informed that he has the right to consult with a lawyer and to have the lawyer with him during interrogation under the system for protecting the privilege we delineate today. As with the warnings of the right to remain silent and that anything stated can be used in evidence against him, this warning is an absolute prerequisite to interrogation. No amount of circumstantial evidence that the person may have been aware of this right will suffice to stand in its stead. Only through such a warning is there ascertainable assurance that the accused was aware of this right.

If an individual indicates that he wishes the assistance of counsel before any interrogation occurs, the authorities cannot rationally ignore or deny his request on the basis that the individual does not have or cannot afford a retained attorney. The financial ability of the individual has no relationship to the scope of the rights involved here. The privilege against self-incrimination secured by the Constitution applies to all individuals. The need for counsel in order to protect the privilege exists for the indigent as well as the affluent. In fact, were we to limit these constitutional rights to those who can retain an attorney, our decisions today would be of little significance. The cases before us as well as the vast majority of confession cases with which we have dealt in the past involve those unable to retain counsel. While authorities are not required to relieve the accused of his poverty, they have the obligation not to take advantage of indigence in the administration of justice....

In order fully to apprise a person interrogated of the extent of his rights under this system then, it is necessary to warn him not only that he has the right to consult with an attorney, but also that if he is indigent a lawyer will be appointed to represent him. Without this additional warning, the admonition of the right to consult with counsel would often be understood as meaning only that he can consult with a lawyer if he has one or has the funds to obtain one. The warning of a right to counsel would be hollow if not couched in terms that would convey to the indigent — the person most often subjected to interrogation — the knowledge that he too has a right to have counsel present. As with the warnings of the right to remain silent and of the general right to counsel, only by effective and express explanation to the indigent of this right can there be assurance that he was truly in a position to exercise it.

Once warnings have been given, the subsequent procedure is clear. If the individual indicates in any manner, at any time prior to or during questioning, that he wishes to remain silent, the interrogation must cease. At this point he has shown that he intends to exercise his Fifth Amendment privilege; any statement taken after the person invokes his privilege cannot be other than the product of compulsion, subtle or otherwise. Without the right to cut off questioning, the setting of in-custody interrogation operates on the individual to overcome free choice in producing a statement after the privilege has been once invoked. If the individual states that he wants an attorney, the interrogation must cease until an attorney is present. At that time, the individual must have an opportunity to confer with the attorney and to have him present during any subsequent questioning. If the individual cannot obtain an attorney and he indicates that he wants one before speaking to police, they must respect his decision to remain silent.

This does not mean, as some have suggested, that each police station must have a 'station house lawyer' present at all times to advise prisoners. It does mean, however, that if police propose to interrogate a person they must make known to him that he is entitled to a lawyer and that if he cannot afford one, a lawyer will be provided for him prior to any interrogation. If authorities conclude that they will not provide counsel during a reasonable period of time in which investigation in the field is carried out, they may refrain from doing so without violating the person's Fifth Amendment privilege so long as they do not question him during that time.

If the interrogation continues without the presence of an attorney and a statement is taken, a heavy burden rests on the government to demonstrate that the defendant knowingly and intelligently waived his privilege against self-incrimination and his right to retained or appointed counsel....

An express statement that the individual is willing to make a statement and does not want an attorney followed closely by a statement could constitute a waiver. But a valid waiver will not be presumed simply from the silence of the accused after warnings are given or simply from the fact that a confession was in fact eventually obtained....

Whatever the testimony of the authorities as to waiver of rights by an accused, the fact of lengthy interrogation or incommunicado incarceration before a statement is made is strong evidence that the accused did not validly waive his rights. In these circumstances the fact that the individual eventually made a statement is consistent with the conclusion that the compelling influence of the interrogation finally forced him to do so. It is inconsistent with any notion of a voluntary relinquishment of the privilege. Moreover, any evidence that the accused was threatened, tricked, or cajoled into a waiver will, of course, show that the defendant did not voluntarily waive his privilege. The requirement of warnings and waiver of rights is a fundamental with respect to the Fifth Amendment privilege and not simply a preliminary ritual to existing methods of interrogation.

* * *

Mr. Justice HARLAN, whom Mr. Justice STEWART and Mr. Justice WHITE join, dissenting.

I believe the decision of the Court represents poor constitutional law and entails harmful consequences for the country at large. How serious these consequences may prove to be only time can tell. But the basic flaws in the Court's justification seem to me readily apparent now once all sides of the problem are considered.

* * *

At the outset, it is well to note exactly what is required by the Court's new constitutional code of rules for confessions. The foremost requirement, upon which later admissibility of a confession depends, is that a fourfold warning be given to a person in custody before he is questioned, namely, that he has a right to remain silent, that anything he says may be used against him, that he has a right to have present an attorney during the questioning, and that if indigent he has a right to a lawyer without charge. To forgo these rights, some affirmative statement of rejection is seemingly required, and threats, tricks, or cajolings to obtain this waiver are forbidden. If before or during questioning the suspect seeks to invoke his right to remain silent, interrogation must be forgone or cease; a request for counsel brings about the same result until a lawyer is procured....

While the fine points of this scheme are far less clear than the Court admits, the tenor is quite apparent. The new rules are not designed to guard against police brutality or other unmistakably banned forms of coercion. Those who use third-degree tactics and deny them in court are equally able and destined to lie as skillfully about warnings and waivers. Rather, the thrust of the new rules is to negate all pressures, to reinforce the nervous or ignorant suspect, and ultimately to discourage any confession at all. The aim in short is toward 'voluntariness' in a utopian sense, or to view it from a different angle, voluntariness with a vengeance.

* * *

What the Court largely ignores is that its rules impair, if they will not eventually serve wholly to frustrate, an instrument of law enforcement that has long and quite reasonably been thought worth the price paid for it. There can be little doubt that the Court's new code would markedly decrease the number of confessions. To warn the suspect that he may remain silent and remind him that his confession may be used in court are minor obstructions. To require also an express waiver by the suspect and an end to questioning whenever he demurs must heavily handicap questioning. And to suggest or provide counsel for the suspect simply invites the end of the interrogation.

* * *

Mr. Justice WHITE, with whom Mr. Justice HARLAN and Mr. Justice STEWART join, dissenting.

* * *

The rule announced today will measurably weaken the ability of the criminal law to perform these tasks. It is a deliberate calculus to prevent interrogations, to reduce the incidence of confessions and pleas of guilty and to increase the number of trials. Criminal trials, no matter how efficient the police are, are not sure bets for the prosecution, nor should they be if the evidence is not forthcoming. Under the present law, the prosecution fails to prove its case in about 30% of the criminal cases actually tried in the federal courts. But it is something else again to remove from the ordinary criminal case all those confessions which heretofore have been held to be free and voluntary acts of the accused and to thus establish a new constitutional barrier to the ascertainment of truth by the judicial process. There is, in my view, every reason to believe that a good many criminal defendants who otherwise would have been convicted on what this Court has previously thought to be the most satisfactory kind of evidence will now under this new version of the Fifth Amendment, either not be tried at all or will be acquitted if the State's evidence, minus the confession, is put to the test of litigation.

* * *

In some unknown number of cases the Court's rule will return a killer, a rapist or other criminal to the streets and to the environment which produced him, to repeat his crime whenever it pleases him. As a consequence, there will not be a gain, but a loss, in human dignity. The real concern is not the unfortunate consequences of this new decision on the criminal law as an abstract, disembodied series of authoritative proscriptions, but the impact on those who rely on the public authority for protection and who without it can only engage in violent self-help with guns, knives and the help of their neighbors similarly inclined. There is, of course, a saving factor: the next victims are uncertain, unnamed and unrepresented in this case.

Nor can this decision do other than have a corrosive effect on the criminal laws as an effective device to prevent crime. A major component in its effectiveness in this regard is its swift and sure enforcement. The easier it is to get away with rape and murder, the less the deterrent effect on those who are inclined to attempt it. This is still good common sense.

If it were not, we should posthaste liquidate the whole law enforcement establishment as a useless, misguided effort to control human conduct.

And what about the accused who has confessed or would confess in response to simple, noncoercive questioning and whose guilt could not otherwise be proved? Is it so clear that release is the best thing for him in every case? Has it so unquestionably been resolved that in each and every case it would be better for him not to confess and to return to his environment with no attempt whatsoever to help him? I think not. It may well be that in many cases it will be no less than a callous disregard for his own welfare as well as for the interests of his next victim.

* * *

[The dissenting opinion of Justice Clark is omitted.]

———————

Notes and Questions

1. It has been over 45 years since *Miranda* was decided. Does the Court's vision for interrogations in any way resemble the way they are conducted in *The Wire*?

2. In dissent, Justices Harlan and White painted a bleak picture of how *Miranda* would hinder interrogations and allow the guilty to go free. In viewing *The Wire*, do you have the impression that *Miranda* has impeded the police from procuring confessions?

3. The majority made clear that *Miranda* did not require "each police station must have a 'station house lawyer' present at all times to advise prisoners." If the Court's goal was to protect the unsophisticated from a coercive environment, wouldn't it have been preferable for the Court to have mandated a station house lawyer rather than the reading of certain rights?

4. Does the *Miranda* doctrine offer any practical protection for criminal defendants? Watch *The Wire*, Season 2, Episode 9, at 29:45 minutes, in which two detectives are interrogating Bodie after a child was killed during a drug gang shootout. The officers lie to Bodie and falsely tell him that his fingerprints are on one of three weapons connected to the crime. When Bodie asks the detectives which gun has his prints on it, they point to the wrong gun, thus confirming to Bodie that they are lying. If Bodie hadn't outsmarted the police however, would the *Miranda* doctrine have prevented the detectives from such blatant lying?

5. Consider the same scene discussed in note 4. During the middle of the interrogation, Bodie says, "where that lawyer at, man?" Although we don't see the beginning of the interrogation, it would seem that the officers read Bodie his *Miranda* rights and that he invoked his right to counsel. Does this prove that the *Miranda* rights are helpful to suspects (even if the police flagrantly violate them)? Or is it possible that Bodie invoked his right to counsel not because the officers read him the *Miranda* rights but instead because he is a repeat player in the criminal justice system and therefore more sophisticated than the average suspect? In the article below, Professor Richard Leo begins to answer this question.

Richard A. Leo, Inside the Interrogation Room
86 Journal of Criminal Law & Criminology 266 (1996)

I. Introduction

The "gap problem"—the gap between how law is written in the books and how it is actually practiced by legal actors in the social world—has been an ongoing concern to legal scholars at least since the advent of Legal Realism in the 1930s, and has been the focus of countless empirical studies associated with the Law and Society Movement since the 1960s. Nevertheless, the gap in our knowledge between legal ideals and empirical realities remains as wide as ever in the study of police interrogation. Recognizing the source of the gap problem in 1966, the Miranda Court wrote that "interrogation still takes place in privacy. Privacy results in secrecy and this in turn results in a gap in our knowledge as to what in fact goes on in the interrogation room." Linking the gap problem to the secrecy of interrogation, the Miranda Court emphasized the absence of first-hand knowledge of actual police interrogation practices, issuing a clarion call for empirical research in this area. Regrettably, this call has gone almost entirely unheeded in the three decades following the influential Miranda opinion. Although law libraries are overflowing with doctrinal analyses of appellate court cases, there exist no contemporary descriptive or analytical studies of routine police interrogation practices in America. If, as William Hart has written, "no law-enforcement function has been more visited by controversy, confusion and court decisions than that of the interrogation of criminal suspects," then it is not only surprising but also disturbing to note just how little we know about everyday police interrogation practices in America.

To be sure, since 1966 there have been a few experimental studies of the social psychology of confessions, several early evaluative studies of the judicial impact of the controversial Miranda decision on confession and conviction rates, and a few socio-linguistic or "conversational" analyses of individual police interrogation transcripts. But unlike their English counterparts, American scholars have almost altogether ignored or avoided the empirical study of police interrogation practices and criminal confessions. In legal scholarship, there have been no empirical studies of police interrogation practices since the late 1960s. Instead, law professors, lawyers, and law students have created a formidable law review literature that focuses almost entirely on the doctrinal and ethical aspects of interrogation and confession case law, rather than on the routine activities of legal actors and institutions. Since traditional legal scholarship is based on an analysis of leading cases—which are unrepresentative of the larger universe of court cases and thus may depict atypical police practices as the norm—this literature is by itself both narrow and misleading. In short, we know scant more about actual police interrogation practices today than we did in 1966 when Justice Earl Warren lamented the gap problem in Miranda v. Arizona.

This Article … will attempt to fill in some of the gaps in our knowledge of routine American police interrogation practices by describing and analyzing the characteristics, context, and outcome of interrogation and confession in ordinary criminal cases that are not likely to make the published record on appeal.... [It is] based on nine months (more than 500 hours) of fieldwork inside the Criminal Investigation Division (CID) of a major, urban police department I shall identify by the pseudonym "Laconia,"[13] where I contemporaneously observed 122 interrogations involving forty-five different detectives. In addition, I viewed thirty videotaped custodial interrogations performed by a police department I shall identify by the pseudonym "Southville"[14] and another thirty video taped interrogations performed by a police department I shall

---

13. In 1990 Laconia had a population of 372,242—approximately 43% black, 28% white, 15% Hispanic, and 14% Asian/Pacific Islander. In 1992 there were 58,668 Part I offenses in Laconia (10,140 violent crimes and 48,546 property crimes), an official crime rate of 123 per 1,000 members of the population.

14. In 1993 Southville had a population of 121,064. Fifty-one percent of Southville's residents were white, 24% Hispanic, 15% Asian, and 10% black. In 1993 there were 8,505 Part I offenses in

identify by the pseudonym "Northville."[15] For each interrogation, I recorded my observations qualitatively in the form of fieldnotes and quantitatively with a forty-seven question coding sheet. Thus, my field research represents a more general, multi-faceted and methodologically diverse study of the history and sociology of police interrogation in America.

This Article takes the reader inside the interrogation room to understand the characteristics, context, and outcome of contemporary police interrogation practices in America. It is the only study to do so in more than twenty-five years, and the first ever to do so in any sustained, explicit, or comprehensive manner. I hope to reorient much of the research and discourse on police interrogation practices in legal scholarship from its near exclusive doctrinal (or "law-on-the-books") focus to a more empirically-grounded (or "law-in-action") perspective, which I believe is necessary to inform the legal, ethical, policy, and theoretical debates in the study of criminal procedure.

* * *

II. Methodological Caveat: Observer Effects and the Problem of Bias

Participant observation may be the ideal method to get as close as possible to the phenomena the researcher intends to analyze and understand. This has been one of the underlying methodological assumptions in my empirical study of American police interrogation practices. However, the problem of studying naturally occurring data confronts the participant observer. Consequently, the participant observer cannot control the parameters of his research nor the effects of his behavior on the research subjects.

It is a methodological truism that the field researcher inevitably influences the environment in which he participates during the very process of observation. These so-called "observer effects" may "contaminate" the data that the participant observer seeks to collect. In the context of my research, my presence may have altered the behavior of the detectives during the custodial interrogations I observed....

I do not believe that my presence in the interrogation room significantly altered the behavior of the detectives I observed. Although I will never know the true effect of my presence, I offer the following observations. First, I sometimes put my ear to the door and listened to those interrogations from which I was purposely excluded, and each time the Miranda warnings were given properly. Nor did I overhear any threats or promises. Conversely, I occasionally observed behavior inside the interrogation room—such as yelling, table pounding, or highly aggressive questioning—that straddled the margins of legality. After one such interrogation, one of the two interrogating detectives informed me that he could be fired if I reported his behavior to the Captain.... I viewed a few interrogations that were clearly "coercive" by the standards of contemporary appellate courts. In one of these interrogations, the primary detective ignored the suspect's repeated invocations of his Miranda rights to silence and counsel, though ultimately the detective failed to convince the suspect to talk. After the interrogation session, the detective asked me what I thought he could have done differently to elicit admissions. When I responded that it did not matter since any subsequent confession would have been suppressed by the court, the detec-

---

Southville (1,298 violent crimes and 7,207 property crimes), and official crime rate of 70.3 per 1,000 members of the population.

15. By the end of 1993 Northville had a population of 116,148. Forty-six percent of Northville's residents were white, 21% Asian, 20% black, and 11% Hispanic. In 1993 there were 9,360 Part I crimes in Northville (1,613 violent crimes and 7,747 property crimes), an official crime rate of 80.78 per 1,000 members of the population.

tive casually replied that neither one of us would have remembered the Miranda violations in court. That one of the detectives could so naturally assume that I would perjure myself to advance the cause of crime control is, I think, good evidence that my presence, at least in some instances, had little effect on the interrogation practices I was observing.

Second, the more time I spent inside the CID, the more the detectives became accustomed to my presence. As I became part of the "furniture" inside the Laconia Police Department (LPD), the detectives frequently treated me as one of their own. They would, for example, describe their cases to me by penal code sections or their actions by police codes or jargon, apparently forgetting that I did not know what they meant. In addition, many of the detectives shared with me explicitly confidential information about their co-workers or superiors, information whose exposure could have damaged their reputations, if not their careers, within CID. At the same time, detectives told me of their own indiscretions and sometimes questionable behaviors, for which they could have been administratively sanctioned, and in some instances held civilly liable, had I publicly revealed their confidences....

Third, I interviewed prosecutors and public defenders who were knowledgeable of LPD custodial interrogation practices. They agreed with my general descriptions of police interrogation practices at LPD, confirming that the methods and techniques I observed were representative of what they knew of interrogation methods at LPD from their daily cases as well. Significantly, the public defenders—the most strident ideological critics of police in an adversarial system of criminal justice—generally spoke respectfully of custodial interrogation practices at LPD, agreeing that detectives rarely engage in any illegalities during custodial questioning. Nevertheless, despite these comments, and although I established high levels of trust with the LPD detectives and sometimes even felt literally invisible during the interrogations, inevitably my presence must have exerted some effect on their behavior.

That I tended to be (but was not always) excluded from the more serious cases raises the general methodological issue of bias, and more specifically the problem of the representativeness of my data within LPD and the generalizability of my findings beyond LPD. In field studies, the researcher can overcome these problems only in degrees. I was unable to select randomly those cases whose interrogations I observed for three reasons. First, I had no control over those interrogation from which some detectives chose to exclude me. Second, even in those cases in which I was allowed to attend the interrogation, the suspect had sometimes posted bail and left the jail prior to any custodial questioning. A class bias that is naturally present in the practice of interrogation at LPD was therefore inevitably present in my data. Third, occasionally circumstances conspired to provide me with a choice over which interrogations I would attend. Although sometimes hours would pass during which no interrogations would occur, at other times multiple interrogations would be occurring simultaneously. To correct for the inherent biases in my data, I always requested to sit in on the interrogation of the most serious cases available to me. Nevertheless, the 122 interrogations I observed contemporaneously were still not entirely representative of the general category of interrogations occurring within LPD.

In addition, I attempted to correct for the bias against serious cases in the data I collected in my non-participant observations of sixty videotaped interrogations at the Southville and Northville Police Departments. I specifically requested videotapes of interrogations in the more serious felony crimes, especially homicide, rape, and assault, from these two departments. Observing the videotaped interrogations of two other police departments served as a check on any idiosyncratic interrogation practices at LPD. Certainly the interrogation practices at LPD, which has been generally regarded as one of the most professional police departments in America during the last three decades, are not representative of the interrogation practices of all police departments in America. Nevertheless, observing the interrogation practices of two other police departments was one way I attempted to redress the intrinsic limitations of the case study method.

III. The Context and Outcome of Police Interrogation: Exploring the Data

In all the interrogations I observed, both contemporaneously at LPD as well by videotape at the Southville and Northville Police Departments, I coded for a number of independent variables (e.g., class, race, gender, and social distance between the suspect and victim, strength of evidence against the suspect, and prior conviction record of the suspect) and a number of dependent variables (e.g., whether suspect waived/invoked Miranda, length of interrogation, outcome of interrogation, and ultimate case disposition)....

... Slightly more than one-third (35%) of the interrogations were conducted in an interrogation room located inside the jail; the remaining (65%) were conducted in the interrogation rooms located inside the CID. In the large majority of interrogations (69%), one detective questioned the suspect; in the remaining interrogations (31%), two detectives conducted questioning. The primary detective was typically white (69%), though not infrequently African-American (19%) or Hispanic (12%); when present, the secondary detective was also white most of the time (65%) and African-American some of the time (19%). There was less variation in the gender of the detectives: virtually all (over 90% of the primary and 86% of the secondary detectives) were men. Most of the primary detectives had been police officers for between ten and twenty years (62%) and detectives for one to five years (61%); most secondary detectives had also been police officers for ten to twenty years (68%) but detectives for only zero to three years (54%).

The typical suspect in my sample was a young, lower or working class, African-American male. Although the age range spanned from the middle teens to the late sixties, approximately two-thirds (66%) of the suspects were less than thirty years old. More than 87% of the suspects were from the lower or working class; almost 12% were middle class; and only 1% were upper middle class. Sixty-nine percent of the suspects were African-American, 14% were white, 13% were Hispanic, and the remaining 4% were either Asian or Native American. Thus, more than 85% of the suspects in my sample were minorities. As with the detectives who interrogated them, virtually all the suspects were male (more than 90%).

* * *

All the interrogations I observed were for felony offenses. A frequency distribution of these offenses, divided into five categories, is listed below in Table 1.

Table 1 Frequency Distribution of Type of Crime

Type of Crime	Freq.	Percent
Theft	9	4.95%
Burglary	21	11.54
Robbery	78	42.86
Assault	44	24.18
Homicide	22	12.09
Other	8	4.40
Total	182	100.00

Table 2 Frequency Distribution of Suspect's Response to Miranda Warnings

Suspect's Response to Miranda Warnings	Freq.	Percent
Waived	136	74.73%
Changed to Waive	1	0.55
Invoked	36	19.78
Changed to Invoke	2	1.10
Not Applicable	7	3.85
Total	182	100.00

* * *

… In 33% of the cases in my sample, the strength of the evidence against a suspect prior to an interrogation was weak (highly unlikely to lead to charging); in 32% of the cases the strength of the evidence was moderate (probably likely to lead to charging); and in 35% of the cases it was strong (highly likely to lead to charging). In 13% of the cases in my sample, the suspect did not have a prior criminal record; in 29% of the cases, the suspect had a misdemeanor record; and in 58% of the cases, the suspect had a felony record. Not surprisingly, almost 90% of the suspects interrogated were repeat players with prior criminal records.…

The formal interrogation process must, of course, be preceded by the well-known Miranda warnings. Table 2 lists the frequency distribution for suspect's responses to Miranda.

In seven (almost 4%) of the cases I observed, the detective did not provide any Miranda warnings because the suspect technically was not "in custody" for the purpose of questioning. Therefore, in these seven cases the detectives were not legally required to issue Miranda warnings. With the exception of these cases, the detective(s) read each of the fourfold Miranda warnings verbatim from a standard form prior to virtually every interrogation I observed. A suspect might respond in one of four ways: waiving his rights, invoking them, or changing his initial response either to a waiver or an invocation. As Table 3 below indicates, 78% of my sample ultimately waived their Miranda rights, while 22% invoked one or more of their Miranda rights, thus indicating their refusal to cooperate with police questioning.

If a suspect chooses to waive his Miranda rights, the custodial interrogation formally begins. If a suspect chooses to invoke one or more of his Miranda rights, typically the detective terminates the interrogation and returns the suspect to jail (if he was under ar-

Table 3 Frequency Distribution of Suspect's Ultimate Response to Miranda

Whether Suspect Waived or Invoked	Freq.	Percent
Waived	137	78.29%
Invoked	38	21.71
Total	175	100.00

Table 4 Frequency Distribution of Tactics Employed Per Interrogation

Number of Interrogation Tactics Used by Detectives per Interrogation	Freq.	Percent	Cumulative Percentage
0	2	1.31%	—
1	8	5.23	99%
2	19	12.42	93
3	17	11.11	81
4	16	10.46	70
5	16	10.46	59
6	16	10.46	49
7	19	12.42	39
8	10	6.54	26
9	11	7.19	20
10	9	5.88	12
11	5	3.27	7
12	3	1.96	3
15	2	1.31	
Total	153	100.00	

rest). However, in seven (4%) of the cases I observed, the detectives questioned suspects even after receiving an invocation. In each of these cases, the detective(s) informed the suspect that any information the suspect provided to the detective could not and therefore would not be used against him in a court of law. The detective told the suspect that the sole purpose of questioning was to learn "what really happened." Of course, what the detectives knew and did not tell the suspect was that although the prosecution could not use such evidence as part of its case-in-chief, any information the suspect provided to the detective nevertheless could be used in a court of law to impeach the suspect's credibility, and indirectly incriminate the suspect if he chose to testify at trial. In the remaining thirty-one cases in which the suspect invoked his Miranda rights at some point during questioning (82% of all cases in which a suspect invoked a Miranda right), the detective(s) promptly terminated the interrogation.

In any session in which the detective questioned a suspect beyond the Miranda warnings (whether or not a suspect invoked), I coded for twenty-five potential interrogation techniques. Table 4 lists the frequency distribution for the total number of tactics employed by detectives during each interrogation. The number of tactics a detective employed per interrogation ranged from zero (e.g., the suspect spontaneously confessed or the detective did not genuinely try to elicit a confession) to fifteen. The cumulative percentage figure represents the percentage of interrogations in which detectives used at least that many interrogation tactics.

The detectives employed a median of 5 and a mean of 5.62 tactics per interrogation. Clearly, however, the detectives used some interrogation tactics more frequently than others. Table 5 below lists each of the twenty-five tactics, and the frequency of their use during the interrogations I observed.

Table 5 Types of Interrogation Tactics and Their Frequency

Type of Interrogation Tactic	No. of Cases in Which Tactic Used	% of Cases in Which Tactic Used
TACTICS USED MOST OFTEN		
Appeal to the suspect's self-interest	134	88
Confront suspect with existing evidence of guilt	130	85
TACTICS USED OFTEN		
Undermine suspect's confidence in denial of guilt	66	43
Identify contradictions in suspect's story	65	42
Any Behavioral Analysis Interview questions	61	40
Appeal to the importance of cooperation	56	37
Offer moral justifications/psychological excuses	52	34
Confront suspect with false evidence of guilt	46	30
Use praise or flattery	46	30
Appeal to detective's expertise/authority	45	29
Appeal to the suspect's conscience	35	23
Minimize the moral seriousness of the offense	33	22
TACTICS USED LEAST OFTEN		
Touch suspect in a friendly manner	17	11
Invoke metaphors of guilt	15	10
Minimize the facts/nature of the offense	9	6
Refer to physical symptoms of guilt	7	5
Exaggerate the facts/nature of the offense	6	4
Yell at suspect	5	3
Exaggerate the nature/purpose of questioning	3	2
Exaggerate the moral seriousness of the offense	3	2
Accuse suspect of other crimes	2	1
Attempt to confuse the suspect	1	1
Minimize the nature/purpose of questioning	1	1
Good cop/Bad cop routine	1	1
Touch suspect in an unfriendly manner	0	0

As Table 5 indicates, there is great variation in the distribution of the interrogation tactics I observed. A couple of the tactics were used in virtually all of the cases, several others were used in approximately one-third to one-half of the cases, a couple were used in approximately one-fifth of the cases, a few others were used only sparingly, and others virtually not at all. If a portrait of the typical interrogation emerges from the data, it involves a two-prong approach: the use of negative incentives (tactics that suggest the suspect should confess because of no other plausible course of action) and positive incentives (tactics that suggest the suspect will in some way feel better or benefit if he confesses). In my sample, detectives typically began the interrogation session by confronting the suspect with some form of evidence, whether true (85%) or false (30%), suggesting his guilt and then attempting to undermine the suspect's denial of involvement (43%), while identifying contradictions in the suspect's alibi or story (42%). But detectives relied on positive incentives as well, most often by appealing to the suspect's self-interest (88%), but also by frequently offering the suspect moral justifications or psychological excuses (34%), using praise or flattery (30%), minimizing the moral seriousness of the offense (22%), appealing to the importance of cooperation with legal authorities (37%) or appealing to the detective's expertise (29%), or appealing to the suspect's conscience (22%). In approximately 90% of the interrogations I observed, the detective confronted the suspect with evidence (whether true or false) of his guilt and then suggested that the suspect's self-interest would be advanced if he confessed.

Of course, the interrogations in my sample also varied by length, ranging from literally seconds (when the suspect invoked before the detective even introduced himself) to four and one-half hours. Table 6 shows the frequency distribution of the length of the interro-

Table 6 Length of Interrogation Only Where an Interrogation Occurred

Length of Interrogation	Freq.	Percent	Cum.
Less Than 30 Minutes	53	34.64%	34.64%
31–60 Minutes	56	36.60	71.24
1–2 Hours	32	20.92	92.16
More Than 2 Hours	12	7.84	100.00
Total	153	100.00	

gations for those cases in which the detective chose to question a suspect (i.e., excluding the twenty-nine cases in my data in which the suspect invoked his Miranda rights, and the detective terminated all questioning). As Table 6 indicates, more than 70% of the interrogations in my sample lasted less than an hour, and only 8% lasted more than two hours.

The outcome of an interrogation is, of course, the most important aspect of questioning from the perspective of the police, and potentially the most important aspect of a case from the perspective of the suspect. In each interrogation, I coded for one of four possible outcomes: the suspect provided no information to the police that they considered incriminating (whether or not the suspect invoked); the suspect provided some information that police considered incriminating (whether or not intentionally) but did not directly admit to any of the elements of the crime; the suspect admitted to some, but not all, of

Table 7 Outcome of Interrogations

Suspect's Response to Interrogation	Freq.	Percent
No Incriminating Statement	65	35.71%
Incriminating Statement	41	22.53
Partial Admission	32	17.58
Full Confession	44	24.18
Total	182	100.00

the elements of the crime; and the suspect provided a full confession to the detectives. Table 7 displays the frequency distribution for the outcome of the interrogations in my sample.

* * *

… The issue of coercive questioning has been the fundamental concern of the appellate courts that have traditionally regulated police interrogation procedures in America.…

To operationalize the concept of "coercion," I attempted to capture those set of police behaviors and interrogation practices that contemporary appellate courts generally tend to label as "coercive." Thus, I coded any interrogation in my sample as "coercive" if at least one of the following ten conditions were present during the interrogation:

(1) The detective failed to read the Miranda warnings;

(2) The suspect was not permitted to invoke his Miranda rights;

(3) The detective touched the suspect in an unfriendly manner;

(4) The suspect was in obvious physical or psychological pain (whether or not related to the detective's actions);

(5) The detective threatened the suspect with physical or psychological harm;

(6) The detective promised the suspect leniency in exchange for an admission of guilt;

(7) The detective deprived the suspect of an essential necessity (such as water, food, or access to a bathroom);

(8) The detective's questioning manner was unrelenting, badgering or hostile;

(9) The interrogation lasted an unreasonable amount of time (more than six hours); or

(10) The suspect's will appeared to be overborne by some other factor or combination of factors.

Although some may disagree with where or how I chose to draw the line between coercive and non-coercive interrogations, I believe that I erred on the side of ruling as "coercive" questioning methods that many contemporary trial and appellate courts would otherwise deem to be non-coercive and thus, my criteria for coercive tactics generally resolve any doubts in favor of the suspect, not the police. Nevertheless, in my sample of 182 custodial interrogations, police questioning methods in only four (or 2%) of the cases rose to the level of "coercion" according to these criteria.

Since four is too small a number to warrant any statistical analysis, I can only quali-tatively describe the patterns, if any, I observed in these cases. All four cases involved the use of psychologically coercive methods; none involved the use of physically coercive methods. In one interrogation, detectives questioned a heroin addict who was quite ob-viously experiencing extremely painful withdrawal symptoms. While the detectives did noth-ing to contribute to the suspect's agony, they intentionally questioned him during the second day of his incarceration when they knew his withdrawal symptoms would be most acute. Although the police arrested the suspect on probable cause for felony gun posses-sion, the detectives considered him a potential, not an actual, suspect in their robbery case. The detectives questioned him as if he were an informant, promising to release him just as soon as he provided them with information about a couple of robberies. Shortly thereafter, the police released the suspect from custody without charging him. In another case I coded as "coercive," two detectives employed the "good cop-bad cop" routine on a young gang member who witnessed a violent gang beating. As one detective kindly promised to release him from custody if he named the perpetrators of the assault, the other detective angrily threatened to provide the prosecutor with incriminating infor-mation that would send the suspect to prison. The suspect provided the detectives with the information they desired and was subsequently released without charge.

In another case, an alleged violent armed robbery by an individual with a long crim-inal record who had been recently released from prison, the detectives failed to acknowledge the suspect's repeated invocation of silence in response to the initial Miranda admonition. After repeatedly trying to talk the suspect out of waiving his Miranda rights, the detec-tives terminated their questioning after approximately five minutes. The suspect, against whom strong eyewitness evidence existed, was eventually charged by the prosecutor. The last instance of a "coercive" interrogation in my sample involved a suspect who police ar-rested for selling drugs and offered an explicit promise of leniency if he became an informant and provided names of more highly placed drug dealers. The suspect refused to turn state's witness, and received a four year prison sentence instead.

* * *

IV. The Context and Outcome of Police Interrogation: Analyzing the Data

* * *

A. A SUSPECT'S RESPONSE TO MIRANDA AND ITS EFFECTS

Despite the passing of almost thirty years since their judicial creation, the Miranda warnings remain one of the most controversial issues in American criminal justice, even as Miranda has become settled doctrine in the appellate courts, standard policy in police departments, and a household word in American popular culture. The con-ventional wisdom in legal and political scholarship is that virtually all suspects waive their rights prior to interrogation and speak to the police. However, as we saw above, almost one-fourth of my sample (22%) exercised their right to terminate police ques-tioning, while 78% of the suspects chose to waive their Miranda rights. Nevertheless, one might expect that certain individuals are more likely to waive their rights than oth-ers. Indeed, the Warren Court in Miranda speculated that underprivileged suspects were less likely to comprehend or exercise their constitutional rights to silence and counsel than their more advantaged counterparts. Though I tested for twelve social, legal and case-specific variables, the only variable that exercised a statistically signifi-cant effect on the suspect's likelihood to waive or invoke his Miranda rights was whether

Table 9 Suspect's Response to Miranda by Prior Criminal Record

Suspect's Prior Record	Whether Suspect Waived or Invoked		
	Waived	Invoked	Total
None	22	2	24
	91.67%	8.33%	100.00%
Misdemeanor	42	5	47
	89.36%	10.64%	100.00%
Felony	72	31	103
	69.90%	30.10%	100.00%
Total	136	38	174
	78.16%	21.84%	100.00%

a suspect had a prior criminal record. As Table 9 above indicates, while 89% of the suspects with a misdemeanor record and 92% of the suspects without any record waived their Miranda rights, only 70% of the suspects with a felony record waived their Miranda rights. Put another way, a suspect with a felony record in my sample was almost four times as likely to invoke his Miranda rights as a suspect with no prior record and almost three times as likely to invoke as a suspect with a misdemeanor record. This result confirms the findings of earlier studies, as well as the conventional wisdom among the detectives I studied, who complained that ex-felons frequently refuse to talk to them as a matter of course. The more experience a suspect has with the criminal justice system, the more likely he is to take advantage of his Miranda rights to terminate questioning and seek counsel.

* * *

E. THE EFFECT OF CONFESSIONS ON CASE PROCESSING

What happens to suspects who incriminate themselves during interrogation? What effect does providing incriminating statements, admissions, and confessions in the interrogation room have on the likelihood that a suspect will subsequently be charged and convicted? The process through which a suspect's case is resolved? The severity of sentencing? Is it true, as critics have argued, that once a suspect confesses to police his case is largely over; in effect, the rest of the judicial process is mostly form rather than substance?

This study suggests that confessions may well be the most damning and persuasive evidence of criminal guilt, a finding that confirms the beliefs of many detectives and prosecutors, as well as the outcome of mock jury experiments. Incriminating statements provided to police during interrogation cast a long shadow over the defendant's fate within the criminal justice system. Suspects who provide incriminating information to detectives are significantly more likely to be treated differently at every subsequent stage of the criminal process than those suspects who do not provide incriminating information during interrogation. As Table 16 at right indicates, suspects in my sample who incriminated themselves during interrogation were 20% more likely to be charged by prosecutors (p<.006); 24% less likely to have their cases dismissed (p<.000); 25% more likely to have their cases resolved by plea bargaining (p<.001); and 26% more likely to be found guilty

Table 16 The Effect of Providing Incriminating Statements on Case Processing

Stage of Criminal Process	Percentages	CHI2
Whether Suspect Charged		.006*
Successful Interrogation	76%	
Unsuccessful Interrogation	56	
Whether Suspect's Case Was Dismissed		.001*
Successful Interrogation	29	
Unsuccessful Interrogation	53	
Whether Suspect's Case Resolved		.001*
By Plea Bargaining		
Successful Interrogation	52	
Unsuccessful Interrogation	27	
Whether Suspect Was Convicted		.001"
Successful Interrogation	69	
Unsuccessful Interrogation	43	
Severity of Sentence Received		.012*
NONE		
Successful Interrogation	33	
Unsuccessful Interrogation	57	
LOW SENTENCE (Less than One Year)		
Successful Interrogation	43	
Unsuccessful Interrogation	21	
MEDIUM SENTENCE (One to Five Years)		
Successful Interrogation	19	
Unsuccessful Interrogation	18	
LONG SENTENCE (More than Five Years)		
Successful Interrogation	13	
Unsuccessful Interrogation	13	

and thus convicted (p<.001). Suspects who incriminated themselves during interrogation were also significantly likely to receive more punishment following their conviction (p<.012). These findings confirm the view of many criminal justice professionals that what happens during police interrogation will be fateful for the subsequent processing of the suspect's case in the criminal justice system.

* * *

V. Conclusion: Closing the Gap

I began this Article by pointing to the familiar contrast between how law is written in the books and how it is actually practiced by legal actors in the social world, arguing that the gap in our knowledge between legal ideals and empirical realities remains as wide as ever in the study of American police interrogation....

This study offers a number of findings with important academic, legal, and policy implications. For example, the Miranda Court lamented the tactics advocated in police interrogation training manuals and texts for exploiting the weaknesses of criminal suspects and threatening to overbear their rational decision-making capacity. Yet this study indicates that these techniques—undermining a suspect's confidence in his denial of guilt, offering moral justifications for his behavior, and confronting suspects with fabricated evidence of their guilt, to name but a few—appear to be exceedingly common in contemporary American police interrogations. In addition, this study suggests that detectives have become increasingly successful at eliciting incriminating information from custodial suspects in the last thirty years; that one in five custodial suspects invokes his or her constitutional right to avoid cooperating with custodial police questioning; that most of the suspects who invoke their Miranda rights to silence or counsel have prior criminal records; that very few everyday police interrogations are "coercive" by contemporary judicial standards; that the overwhelming majority of everyday police interrogations last less than one hour; and that suspects who provide incriminating information to detectives are significantly more likely to be treated differently at every subsequent stage of the criminal process (from charging to sentencing) than their counterparts who do not. These findings confirm the view of many criminal justice professionals that what happens inside the interrogation room exerts a fateful effect on the processing of a defendant's case at every subsequent stage in the criminal justice system.

* * *

Notes and Questions

1. Professor Leo does not identify the "major, urban police department" where he gathered his data, although we know from its size of roughly 370,000 residents that is a city smaller than Baltimore, which has a population of about 600,000 people. Do you wonder whether the mostly professional conduct Professor Leo describes is the norm, or whether the reality in most major cities is closer to how Baltimore police are portrayed in *The Wire*?

2. Were you surprised by Professor Leo's finding that 22% of suspects invoked their *Miranda* rights? If so, did that number seem higher or lower than you expected?

3. One of the more striking findings in Professor Leo's study is that a suspect with a felony conviction was "almost four times as likely to invoke his *Miranda* rights as a suspect with no prior record and almost three times as likely to invoke as a suspect with a misdemeanor record." The explanation for this would seem to be that suspects who are nervous and lack experience with the criminal justice system will not fully understand the protections *Miranda* affords them, even if an officer reads them, whereas experienced suspects will have learned from prior mistakes. Consider the case of D'Angelo Barksdale. In *The Wire*, Season 1, Episode 2, at 26:00 minutes, Detectives McNulty and Bunk interrogate D'Angelo for the first time and play on his heartstrings. They describe a hard-working man who was murdered and even show D'Angelo pictures of the victim's children (although the pictures

are actually of Bunk's children). When D'Angelo still refuses to confess, the officers trick him into writing an apology letter to the victim's children (which, of course, amounts to an inculpatory statement even if it is not on official police stationary). In short, an inexperienced D'Angelo is tricked by Bunk and McNulty. Fast-forward to Season 1, Episode 12, at 43:10 minutes when D'Angelo is interrogated a second time. Putting aside the flagrant *Miranda* violations committed by the officers during the interrogation, how much more sophisticated is D'Angelo during his second interrogation?

Det. McNulty:	Remember me.
D'Angelo:	Lawyer.
Lt. Daniels:	Easy. We're just getting started.
D'Angelo:	Lawyer, [expletive].
Det. McNulty:	Okay, so you are hard. Guess what, I could give a [expletive].
D'Angelo:	You. I'm tired of your games. What, you want me to write a letter or some [expletive] like that.
Lt. Daniels:	No game we need to run. You're popped with a kilo of uncut [heroin].
Det. McNulty:	Not that you messed up. I mean, you did everything right: speed limits, turn signals, working taillights. The question you've got to ask is how'd those troopers know to pull you over? Someone else [expletive]. You follow me? But it's you they're going to blame and you that's going to do the jolt.
D'Angelo:	Lawyer.
Det. McNulty:	Well that will be Levy, right? He's getting paid by your Uncle. Oh yeah, he's looking out for your interests.
D'Angelo:	More than you. Listen. I ain't saying another damn thing to nobody but my lawyer.

Ledbetter v. Edwards

35 F.3d 1062 (6th Cir. 1994)

BOGGS, Circuit Judge,

The State of Ohio appeals from the district court's decision ... to issue a writ of habeas corpus on behalf of Russell Ledbetter. For the reasons set forth below, we reverse....

I

Ledbetter had been indicted by an Ohio grand jury on one count of kidnapping, one count of abduction, one count of robbery, one count of theft, and two counts of having a weapon while under disability. The kidnapping, theft, and robbery charges were tried by jury in July 1988, and resulted in the jury finding Ledbetter guilty of abduction with respect to the kidnapping count, and guilty of robbery and theft. He was sentenced in November 1988, and the Ohio Court of Appeals affirmed the judgment in October 1989. The Supreme Court of Ohio dismissed his appeal, without opinion, in February 1990. He then brought this habeas case, pursuant to 28 U.S.C. § 2254.

The charges against Ledbetter arose from the events surrounding the abduction of Nancy Clark from the parking lot of the Eastgate Mall in Clermont County, Ohio on May 14, 1987. Clark arrived at the mall shortly after 5:00 p.m. that day, driving alone in a 1987 Voyager van. As she was parking, she noticed "a greenish-yellow car that [she] pulled up right behind." She saw a man "slumped down" in the driver's seat of the car watching her through the outside rear-view mirror.

Clark went into the mall for approximately fifteen minutes. When she returned to her van, she noticed that the greenish-yellow car was no longer parked in front of her vehicle. Rather, the car was now parked to her right. No one was in that car. Clark began to drive out of the parking lot. As she turned onto the access road, a man arose from behind her seat and grabbed her around the neck. The man told Clark "not to stop and that he had a gun and if [she] didn't do what he said he would shoot [her]." He later threatened her with a knife and told her that he had a friend watching.

Clark was extremely "excited" and scared, fearing that she might be killed. She tried to get a good look at her abductor so that she would be able to later identify him if she "live[d] through this." Clark saw the man in the rear-view mirror. Although she primarily saw the section of the man's face above his mouth, she saw enough of his face below his mouth to discern that he had a few days' growth of facial hair. When the man saw that Clark was gazing at him, he "slapped the mirror down" with his free hand. At that point, Clark realized that the man did not have a weapon within easy access.

Clark continued driving. Soon she reached an intersection, pulled in front of another car, and "popped the clutch." Her abductor was thrown off balance, enabling her to escape from the van. As she darted out, she looked back in an effort to see her abductor one more time. She saw the man restart the van, reach out and shut its door, and drive away. Clark testified that she again saw the man's face briefly when she looked back at him.

Clark stated that her abductor had been wearing black mesh "biker gloves" and a black thermal underwear shirt. She testified that "[h]e was not cleanly shaven, but he did not have a heavy beard, I would say maybe two or three days growth with a mustache." Clark stated that the man's most distinctive features were his eyes and nose. What she remembered "most of all" was that the man's eyes were "kind of offset" and his nose "was bridged."

At 9:30 p.m., approximately four and a half hours after the incident occurred, a police officer came to Clark's home with a photographic array of five persons that included a picture of Ledbetter with a beard. Clark looked at the pictures for approximately ten minutes and was unable to identify anyone positively. However, she did indicate to the officer that one picture captured characteristics of her abductor. Nevertheless, she explained that she was "sorry," but she "didn't feel good about making a positive ID because of the beard." That is, she was sure that her abductor had only a few days' facial growth. The police officer then told Clark that the photograph toward which she had inclined was that of Ledbetter, the suspect.

Four days later, the police presented Clark with another photographic array. This time, the array included a picture of Ledbetter without a beard. Clark looked at the pictures for less than two minutes and identified the Ledbetter photograph as that of her abductor. Later, at trial, Clark identified him in person.

* * *

Five weeks later, at around 12:00 midnight, Ledbetter was arrested at his sister's residence. Detective McMillan of the Union Township Police Department advised him of his *Miranda* rights, reading from a card. Ledbetter was cooperative. He was then transported to the Union Township police station, where McMillan questioned him in an interview room. Detective Zinser was present as an observer. Prior to the interview, Ledbetter was again informed of his *Miranda* rights from a Notification of Rights Form, and he was given a copy of the form to follow as the rights were read to him. As McMillan went through each of the rights, Ledbetter wrote his initials next to each portion. He then signed the waiver of his rights. He did not indicate at any time that he did not understand his rights or that he wished to have an attorney present.

The interrogation began at 12:25 a.m. and continued for approximately three hours. However, the police tape-recorded only the final half hour of the interview. Officer McMillan explained:

> [I]t's a matter of how the interview is being conducted. What you try to do is establish a bond of trust between you and the offender. By turning on the tape recorder it kind of puts him on notice and generally speaking a suspect would not be too cooperative with the officer and would hold back on certain information. It's more a threat to the offender than it is to anything else.
>
> ....
>
> ... I've known Mr. Ledbetter for a period of time, and we've always had a rapport, and so in order not to jeopardize that rapport, I told [him] I wanted to just sit down and have a talk with him and we would discuss some things. And after I obtained the confession I decided to reduce it down to a tape recorded statement.

Before Ledbetter gave his tape-recorded confession, he was advised a third time of his *Miranda* rights.

During the unrecorded portion of the interview, Ledbetter apparently began his side of the conversation by claiming that he had been somewhere else ... at the time that the alleged abduction took place. Detective McMillan then employed various psychological tactics and misrepresentations to convince Ledbetter to confess his involvement. First, Detective McMillan showed Ledbetter two enlarged photographs of a latent fingerprint that the officer claimed had been recovered from the victim's van, and a fingerprint that had allegedly been obtained from Ledbetter, together with a chart indicating that a fingerprint expert had made a "14 point comparison" between the latent and the identified fingerprints. In fact, the fingerprints were not Ledbetter's, and no expert had made any such comparison. When he was informed of the purported fingerprint evidence, Ledbetter responded that he did not understand how his prints could have come from the van. However, he conceded for the first time that he "may have been up in the mall area."

Detective McMillan also falsely told Ledbetter that the female victim and two other witnesses had identified him from a photographic array. In fact, no witness had identified him. Detective McMillan would later admit that the information he had presented to Ledbetter about his having been identified from photographic arrays had been a "blatant lie."

Finally, McMillan told Ledbetter that the victim was waiting outside the interview room, prepared to identify her assailant. In fact, Clark was not at the police station. Instead, McMillan set up a female dispatcher to stand in front of a two-way mirror that could be seen from the interview room. The office lights were turned on and the blinds on the mirror were opened so that Ledbetter would see, from his vantage point inside the interview room, a woman's silhouette appearing at the window. McMillan left the interview room and returned approximately fifteen minutes later. He told Ledbetter that the victim had observed him through a mirror, that she had made a positive identification, and that she was sure that Ledbetter was the person who had abducted her. At that point, Ledbetter "broke down in tears and started crying, said he was sorry for the way it happened, the way it had taken place, that he wanted to come clean and he wanted to make a new start for himself."

Ledbetter confessed just before 3:00 a.m.... Ledbetter's confession was introduced as evidence against him at trial.

According to the detectives, during the entire interview, Ledbetter never showed a reluctance to talk, nor did he indicate that he wanted an attorney present. When Ledbetter was informed of his *Miranda* rights for a third time, immediately prior to giving his recorded confession, he indicated that "[i]t would be nice" to have an attorney present. The detectives further emphasized that, during the interview, Ledbetter was allowed to obtain food, drinks, and cigarettes, and to go to the bathroom. McMillan insisted that a "whole rapport" between him and the suspect had developed during the interview.

Based on the totality of the circumstances under which Ledbetter's confession was elicited, the district judge adopted the magistrate judge's Report and Recommendation ("R & R") and agreed that a writ of habeas corpus should be issued....

II

The Fifth Amendment prohibits the prosecution's use of a defendant's compelled testimony. *Oregon v. Elstad,* 470 U.S. 298, 306–07 (1985). The Due Process Clause of the Fourteenth Amendment also prohibits the admission of coerced confessions procured by means "so offensive to a civilized system of justice that they must be condemned." *Miller v. Fenton,* 474 U.S. 104, 109 (1985). An admission is deemed to be coerced when the conduct of law enforcement officials is such as to overbear the accused's will to resist. *Beckwith v. United States,* 425 U.S. 341, 347–48 (1961).

An involuntary confession may result from psychological, no less than physical, coercion by law enforcement officials. *Arizona v. Fulminante,* 499 U.S. 279, 285–89 (1991). However, not all psychological tactics are unconstitutional. In determining whether a confession has been elicited by means that are unconstitutional, this court looks at the totality of the circumstances concerning "whether a defendant's will was overborne in a particular case." Factors to consider in assessing the totality of the circumstances include the age, education, and intelligence of the accused; whether the accused has been informed of his constitutional rights; the length of the questioning; the repeated and prolonged nature of the questioning; and the use of physical punishment, such as the deprivation of food or sleep. *Schneckloth v. Bustamonte,* 412 U.S. 218, 226 (1973).

* * *

In this case, in examining the totality of circumstances that surrounded the interrogation of Ledbetter, the magistrate judge ... identified various factors that could support a finding that Ledbetter's confession had been offered voluntarily. Thus, voluntariness could be upheld based on the facts that: (1) no physical punishment or threats had been used; (2) Ledbetter had not been deprived of physical necessities, such as food and drink, and had been allowed to go to the bathroom; (3) the interrogation had not been unduly lengthy in duration; (4) Ledbetter had been informed of his *Miranda* rights on three different occasions during the night of his interrogation; (5) he had clearly indicated that he understood his rights and did not appear to be under the influence of drugs or alcohol or otherwise unable to comprehend those rights; (6) he had not expressed reluctance to talk; and (7) he had not requested the presence of an attorney.

However, the district court found that, despite those circumstances, other circumstances contributed to an atmosphere of coercion, "particularly in light of the impact of the staged victim identification": (1) the interrogation had occurred from midnight into the early morning hours; (2) the portion of the interrogation during which the police had engaged in trickery had not been recorded; (3) insufficient evidence had been proffered at trial regarding Ledbetter's intelligence, education, or experience in dealing with the criminal justice system; and (4) no attorney had been present to offset the deception employed by the police officers.

... In this case, the district court was concerned that the questioning of Ledbetter had extended from midnight through 3:00 a.m. However, [in another case] this court expressly approved the overnight interrogation of [a defendant], who was questioned much longer, until 6:00 in the morning, and whose confession made him death-eligible. Second, the district court in this case was concerned that only a portion of the police interrogation of Ledbetter had been tape-recorded. However, this court expressly approved [another defendant's] interrogation, even though only one hour of those conversations was taped. Third, the district court was concerned that insufficient evidence had been proffered at trial regarding Ledbetter's prior experience with the criminal justice system. However, the record before that court included the opinion of the Ohio Court of Appeals, which explicitly found that:

> [A]ppellant *is an adult with experience in the criminal law process.* Appellant was in command of his mental faculties and was not subject to an unreasonable interrogation. In addition, the record is devoid of any indication of physical abuse or harsh conditions. Therefore, the totality of the circumstances establishes that appellant's statements were completely voluntary and of his own volition.

This state court finding has not been shown to be erroneous by convincing evidence. Thus, it must be presumed to be correct.

Finally, the district court was concerned that no attorney had been present during the police conversations with Ledbetter. However, he had been apprised of his *Miranda* rights three separate times; yet he did not formally request an attorney. Recently, in *Davis v. United States,* 512 U.S. 452 (1994), the Supreme Court held that "if a suspect makes a reference to an attorney that is ambiguous or equivocal in that a reasonable officer in light of the circumstances would have understood only that the suspect *might* be invoking the right to counsel, our precedents do not require the cessation of questioning.... Rather, the suspect must unambiguously request counsel." In *Davis,* a suspect said to his questioners during an interrogation, "Maybe I should talk to a lawyer." The Court held that such a statement was too ambiguously worded to require that questioning cease. Here, Ledbetter's statement that "[i]t would be nice" to have an attorney was even more ambiguous.

Schneckloth teaches that the key issue is whether a confession arises from the defendant's will being overborne.... A defendant's will is not overborne simply because he is led to believe that the government's knowledge of his guilt is greater than it actually is.

In light of the totality of the circumstances, we hold that the district court committed error in adopting the legal analysis of the magistrate judge. A careful look at this case in the light of the *Schneckloth* factors shows that Ledbetter had prior experience with the criminal justice system and was sufficiently intelligent to appreciate the lessons of that experience; had been amply notified of his constitutional rights; had been questioned for a reasonable amount of time; and had been allowed the necessary creature comforts that *Schneckloth* anticipates. Therefore, we hold that Ledbetter's confession was obtained by means of legitimate law-enforcement methods that withstand constitutional scrutiny.

* * *

IV

For the foregoing reasons, we REVERSE the decision of the district court to issue a writ of habeas corpus for the petitioner-appellee.

Notes and Questions

1. Do you agree with the magistrate and district judge that the trickery here was sufficient to overcome Ledbetter's will, or is the appellate court correct that the interrogation was not coercive?

2. As you learned in your introductory criminal procedure course, police must comply with two separate sets of interrogation rules: (1) the *Miranda* doctrine; and (2) the prohibition against involuntary or coerced confessions. Although the doctrines are analyzed separately, the *Miranda* doctrine is designed to effectuate the protection against coerced confessions. In other words, the *Miranda* warnings are intended to even the playing field between the police and the suspect and protect against unfair coercion. Did *Miranda* help to do that here? The police read Ledbetter his rights three times, but he waived those rights each time. And when Ledbetter said, "it would be nice" to have an attorney, the court correctly recognized that such a statement does not amount to an invocation of *Miranda*. In light of this, did the *Miranda* doctrine really afford any useful protection or assistance to Ledbetter?

3. On the flipside of note 2, does the fact that Ledbetter received and waived his *Miranda* rights three separate times make it easier for the court to conclude that his confession was voluntary and thus not coerced? In other words, even though *Miranda* was intended to effectuate the protection against involuntariness, does it actually result in a weakened involuntariness analysis by courts? When police comply with the letter (although not necessarily the spirit) of *Miranda*, are courts more lax in enforcing the prohibition against coerced confessions? For a sampling of cases on this issue, see Paul Marcus, *It's Not Just About Miranda: Determining the Voluntariness of Confessions in Criminal Prosecutions*, 40 Val. U. L. Rev. 601, 636–637 (2006).

4. Putting aside the current legal rules and whether the court decided Ledbetter correctly, ask yourself whether the police *should* be allowed to engage in such blatant manipulation and lying in order to procure a confession.

5. Watch the very first scene of *The Wire*, Season 5, Episode 1. Detective Bunk Moreland and his partner conduct a polygraph examination by using an office photocopier. The suspect is taped to the photocopier and another officer pretends to study the copy machine to determine whether the suspect is lying. When the copy machine prints outs a pre-loaded piece of paper with the word "false" on it, the suspect believes he is caught and confesses. Is the suspect's confession voluntary or coerced? Was it coercive when the officers—immediately before using the photocopier—lied to the suspect about his accomplice already having confessed? Is it coercive when combined with the photocopier tactic?

6. Is the photocopier ruse too ridiculous to even believe? The creator of *The Wire* reports that it really happened in both Baltimore and Detroit. *See* David Simon, Homicide: A Year on the Killing Streets 204 (1991).

7. For one more over-the-top tactic, consider People v. Smith, 150 P.3d 1224, 1238 (Cal. 2007). In that case, officers used a "Neutron Proton Negligence Intelligence Test"

on the defendant to determine whether his hands showed gunshot residue. The "test" consisted of spraying Smith's hands with soap and then patting them with a paper towel. The court concluded that the tactic was not so coercive as to be unconstitutional. Yet, what rational person could believe the officers were doing anything other than lying? Does the size of the lie make the police tactic more or less acceptable? Following the polygraph on the photocopier, Detective Bunk Moreland tells his partner, "the bigger the lie, the more they believe." *The Wire*, Season 5, Episode 1, at 3:30 minutes. Is that true?

C. Do the Police Follow the Interrogation Rules?

In the previous chapter, we considered whether the police really follow the search and seizure rules set forth by the Supreme Court. The same question should be asked of the Court's interrogation doctrine. With respect to *Miranda*, the answer at first blush appears clear. The police consistently read the *Miranda* warnings, often advising the same suspect of his rights three or four times in a single interrogation. But this is not much of a sacrifice for police when most suspects immediately waive their rights. The difficult question is whether police comply with *Miranda* after suspects have invoked their rights to silence or an attorney. Perhaps more importantly, behind closed doors do the police comply with the prohibition against coerced confessions, or do they use force or the threat of force to procure confessions? While police use of torture, physical violence, and threats of force are certainly less common than they were fifty years ago, the question still remains, how often do they occur? As you read the cases below, consider first whether the police are complying with the Fifth Amendment and second whether you think these cases are representative of how most police officers conduct themselves.

Brewer v. Williams
430 U.S. 387 (1977)

Mr. Justice STEWART delivered the opinion of the Court.

* * *

I

On the afternoon of December 24, 1968, a 10-year-old girl named Pamela Powers went with her family to the YMCA in Des Moines, Iowa, to watch a wrestling tournament in which her brother was participating. When she failed to return from a trip to the washroom, a search for her began. The search was unsuccessful.

Robert Williams, who had recently escaped from a mental hospital, was a resident of the YMCA. Soon after the girl's disappearance Williams was seen in the YMCA lobby carrying some clothing and a large bundle wrapped in a blanket. He obtained help from a 14-year-old boy in opening the street door of the YMCA and the door to his automobile parked outside. When Williams placed the bundle in the front seat of his car the boy "saw two legs in it and they were skinny and white." Before anyone could see what was in the bundle Williams drove away. His abandoned car was found the following day in Davenport, Iowa, roughly 160 miles east of Des Moines. A warrant was then issued in Des Moines for his arrest on a charge of abduction.

On the morning of December 26, a Des Moines lawyer named Henry McKnight went to the Des Moines police station and informed the officers present that he had just received a long-distance call from Williams, and that he had advised Williams to turn himself in to the Davenport police. Williams did surrender that morning to the police in Davenport, and they booked him on the charge specified in the arrest warrant and gave him the warnings required by Miranda v. Arizona, 384 U.S. 436. The Davenport police then telephoned their counterparts in Des Moines to inform them that Williams had surrendered. McKnight, the lawyer, was still at the Des Moines police headquarters, and Williams conversed with McKnight on the telephone. In the presence of the Des Moines chief of police and a police detective named Leaming, McKnight advised Williams that Des Moines police officers would be driving to Davenport to pick him up, that the officers would not interrogate him or mistreat him, and that Williams was not to talk to the officers about Pamela Powers until after consulting with McKnight upon his return to Des Moines. As a result of these conversations, it was agreed between McKnight and the Des Moines police officials that Detective Leaming and a fellow officer would drive to Davenport to pick up Williams, that they would bring him directly back to Des Moines, and that they would not question him during the trip.

In the meantime Williams was arraigned before a judge in Davenport on the outstanding arrest warrant. The judge advised him of his Miranda rights and committed him to jail. Before leaving the courtroom, Williams conferred with a lawyer named Kelly, who advised him not to make any statements until consulting with McKnight back in Des Moines.

Detective Leaming and his fellow officer arrived in Davenport about noon to pick up Williams and return him to Des Moines. Soon after their arrival they met with Williams and Kelly, who, they understood, was acting as Williams' lawyer. Detective Leaming repeated the Miranda warnings, and told Williams:

> "(W)e both know that you're being represented here by Mr. Kelly and you're being represented by Mr. McKnight in Des Moines, and ... I want you to remember this because we'll be visiting between here and Des Moines."

Williams then conferred again with Kelly alone, and after this conference Kelly reiterated to Detective Leaming that Williams was not to be questioned about the disappearance of Pamela Powers until after he had consulted with McKnight back in Des Moines. When Leaming expressed some reservations, Kelly firmly stated that the agreement with McKnight was to be carried out that there was to be no interrogation of Williams during the automobile journey to Des Moines. Kelly was denied permission to ride in the police car back to Des Moines with Williams and the two officers.

The two detectives, with Williams in their charge, then set out on the 160-mile drive. At no time during the trip did Williams express a willingness to be interrogated in the absence of an attorney. Instead, he stated several times that "(w)hen I get to Des Moines and see Mr. McKnight, I am going to tell you the whole story." Detective Leaming knew that Williams was a former mental patient, and knew also that he was deeply religious.

The detective and his prisoner soon embarked on a wide-ranging conversation covering a variety of topics, including the subject of religion. Then, not long after leaving Davenport and reaching the interstate highway, Detective Leaming delivered what has been referred to in the briefs and oral arguments as the "Christian burial speech." Addressing Williams as "Reverend," the detective said:

> "I want to give you something to think about while we're traveling down the road....
> Number one, I want you to observe the weather conditions, it's raining, it's sleet-

ing, it's freezing, driving is very treacherous, visibility is poor, it's going to be dark early this evening. They are predicting several inches of snow for tonight, and I feel that you yourself are the only person that knows where this little girl's body is, that you yourself have only been there once, and if you get a snow on top of it you yourself may be unable to find it. And, since we will be going right past the area on the way into Des Moines, I feel that we could stop and locate the body, that the parents of this little girl should be entitled to a Christian burial for the little girl who was snatched away from them on Christmas (E)ve and murdered. And I feel we should stop and locate it on the way in rather than waiting until morning and trying to come back out after a snow storm and possibly not being able to find it at all."

Williams asked Detective Leaming why he thought their route to Des Moines would be taking them past the girl's body, and Leaming responded that he knew the body was in the area of Mitchellville a town they would be passing on the way to Des Moines.[1] Leaming then stated: "I do not want you to answer me. I don't want to discuss it any further. Just think about it as we're riding down the road."

As the car approached Grinnell, a town approximately 100 miles west of Davenport, Williams asked whether the police had found the victim's shoes. When Detective Leaming replied that he was unsure, Williams directed the officers to a service station where he said he had left the shoes; a search for them proved unsuccessful. As they continued towards Des Moines, Williams asked whether the police had found the blanket, and directed the officers to a rest area where he said he had disposed of the blanket. Nothing was found. The car continued towards Des Moines, and as it approached Mitchellville, Williams said that he would show the officers where the body was. He then directed the police to the body of Pamela Powers.

Williams was indicted for first-degree murder. Before trial, his counsel moved to suppress all evidence relating to or resulting from any statements Williams had made during the automobile ride from Davenport to Des Moines. After an evidentiary hearing the trial judge denied the motion....

* * *

II

* * *

B

There can be no doubt in the present case that judicial proceedings had been initiated against Williams before the start of the automobile ride from Davenport to Des Moines. A warrant had been issued for his arrest, he had been arraigned on that warrant before a judge in a Davenport courtroom, and he had been committed by the court to confinement in jail. The State does not contend otherwise.

There can be no serious doubt, either, that Detective Leaming deliberately and designedly set out to elicit information from Williams just as surely as and perhaps more effectively than if he had formally interrogated him. Detective Leaming was fully aware before departing for Des Moines that Williams was being represented in Davenport by Kelly and in Des Moines by McKnight. Yet he purposely sought during Williams' isolation from his lawyers to obtain as much incriminating information as possible....

---

1. The fact of the matter, of course, was that Detective Leaming possessed no such knowledge.

III

* * *

We conclude ... [that] the record in this case falls far short of sustaining petitioner's burden [for waiver]. It is true that Williams had been informed of and appeared to understand his right to counsel. But waiver requires not merely comprehension but relinquishment, and Williams' consistent reliance upon the advice of counsel in dealing with the authorities refutes any suggestion that he waived that right. He consulted McKnight by long-distance telephone before turning himself in. He spoke with McKnight by telephone again shortly after being booked. After he was arraigned, Williams sought out and obtained legal advice from Kelly. Williams again consulted with Kelly after Detective Leaming and his fellow officer arrived in Davenport. Throughout, Williams was advised not to make any statements before seeing McKnight in Des Moines, and was assured that the police had agreed not to question him. His statements while in the car that he would tell the whole story after seeing McKnight in Des Moines were the clearest expressions by Williams himself that he desired the presence of an attorney before any interrogation took place. But even before making these statements, Williams had effectively asserted his right to counsel by having secured attorneys at both ends of the automobile trip, both of whom, acting as his agents, had made clear to the police that no interrogation was to occur during the journey. Williams knew of that agreement and, particularly in view of his consistent reliance on counsel, there is no basis for concluding that he disavowed it.

Despite Williams' express and implicit assertions of his right to counsel, Detective Leaming proceeded to elicit incriminating statements from Williams. Leaming did not preface this effort by telling Williams that he had a right to the presence of a lawyer, and made no effort at all to ascertain whether Williams wished to relinquish that right. The circumstances of record in this case thus provide no reasonable basis for finding that Williams waived his right to the assistance of counsel.

* * *

IV

The crime of which Williams was convicted was senseless and brutal, calling for swift and energetic action by the police to apprehend the perpetrator and gather evidence with which he could be convicted. No mission of law enforcement officials is more important. Yet "(d)isinterested zeal for the public good does not assure either wisdom or right in the methods it pursues." Haley v. Ohio, 332 U.S. 596, 605 (Frankfurter, J., concurring in judgment). Although we do not lightly affirm the issuance of a writ of habeas corpus in this case, so clear a violation of the Sixth and Fourteenth Amendments as here occurred cannot be condoned. The pressures on state executive and judicial officers charged with the administration of the criminal law are great, especially when the crime is murder and the victim a small child. But it is precisely the predictability of those pressures that makes imperative a resolute loyalty to the guarantees that the Constitution extends to us all.

The judgment of the Court of Appeals is affirmed.

It is so ordered.

[The concurring opinions of Justice Marshall, Powell, and Stevens, as well as the dissenting opinions of Chief Justice Burger, Justice White, and Justice Blackmun are omitted.]

Notes and Questions

1. How many times did the officers read Williams his *Miranda* rights? One argument against the usefulness of *Miranda* is that suspects do not really listen to and internalize the warnings as they hear them. Could the same be true of the officers who are giving the warnings?

2. In an omitted dissenting opinion, Chief Justice Burger argued that the majority had "imprison[ed] a man in his privileges" by rejecting his ability to waive his *Miranda* rights. Is it possible that Williams did waive his *Miranda* rights on the drive from Davenport to Des Moines? Can you read the sequences of events in this case as anything other than a flagrant violation of Williams' rights?

3. Reconsider the scene following D'Angelo Barksdale's arrest, in *The Wire*, Season 1, Episode 12, at 43:10 minutes. D'Angelo unequivocally requests a lawyer four times before the officers end the interrogation, and even then they try to play on his sympathies by telling him that one of his friends was murdered by his Uncle's drug organization. Do you get the impression from this scene (and from *Brewer v. Williams*) that some police officers only comply with the *Miranda* warnings when it is convenient for them?

4. Do you have the impression that the police understand the *Miranda* warnings and can rigorously follow them if they choose to do so? Watch *The Wire*, Season 3, Episode 9, at 32:50 minutes. After Officer Pryzbylewski shoots another officer, he is locked in an interrogation room. Sergeant Landsman is standing outside and Lieutenant Daniels attempts to enter the room.

> Landsman: He's in a situation where you can't compel a statement out of him until we read him his rights, and we haven't done that yet.
>
> Daniels: I'm his commanding officer. I just want to know if he's alright.
>
> Landsman: … It's a legal question at this point.

Do you think Landsman and Daniels would have been as interested in the formalities of the *Miranda* doctrine if the person inside the interrogation room had not been a police officer?

5. The Court decided *Brewer v. Williams* roughly a decade after *Miranda*. More than 35 years have passed since then. Has police misconduct in the interrogation room become markedly less common? Can we really know if officers are behaving better? The next case explores that question.

United States v. DeLaurentiis

629 F. Supp.2d 68 (D. Me. 2009)

D. BROCK HORNBY, District Judge.

* * *

II. MOTION TO SUPPRESS

* * *

… DEA agents arrested DeLaurentiis as she got out of her car at her residence in Juno Beach, Florida around 6 p.m. There is some disagreement about what happened next at the residence, such as who suggested that a neighbor could care for her twelve pets, whether the neighbor was already at his door or had to be summoned by knocking, whether at arrest she had to place her hands on her car, and how it came about that agents removed her handcuffs while she cared for her pets. But the only material issue is what happened *after* DeLaurentiis was permitted to arrange for her pets' care and as agents were placing her in the DEA car to take her to the DEA office for questioning. Her neighbor testified by affidavit that it was then that DeLaurentiis asked him to "call her mother and have her uncle, *whom she stated specifically was a lawyer,* meet her." That statement is consistent with DeLaurentiis's testimony at the suppression hearing, where she testified: "I asked [Mr. Gannett] to call my mother to have her call my uncle, who is her brother, who I explained is an attorney, and to get him to meet me downtown because I needed help." Although the agents testified that they heard no such utterance and that DeLaurentiis's only reference to her uncle was earlier, as a possible caretaker for the pets, I find, in light of the neighbor's affidavit, that DeLaurentiis made the utterance as described and that the agents could hear her, since they were nearer to her than her neighbor. Nevertheless, DeLaurentiis's utterance at that time was not, alone, an unambiguous assertion of her right to counsel in connection with any questioning. It was not directed to the agents and nothing about it suggested that it was directed to questioning (as distinguished, for example, from assistance in posting bail).

At her residence and on the ride to the DEA office, DeLaurentiis made no statements that the government intends to use against her. It is undisputed that the agents administered *Miranda* warnings to DeLaurentiis upon arrival at the DEA office. But there are two flatly opposite versions of what happened thereafter, the time period of the incriminating statements that are the object of the motion to suppress.

DeLaurentiis testified that when agents told her at the DEA office that she could have a lawyer, "I said that I would like to phone my mother now to have her call my uncle, who is an attorney, and see if he can come down here." Under the caselaw, that statement alone is probably ambiguous as it relates to assertion of the right to counsel. *See Davis,* 512 U.S. at 462, (affirming the lower court's finding that the defendant's statement "Maybe I should talk to a lawyer" was not a sufficiently clear request for counsel)....

But DeLaurentiis also testified that she asked at least four times for her uncle the lawyer. In response to the question, "Did the officers say anything to you that made it clear that they knew you were asking for a lawyer?," DeLaurentiis testified:

> [T]he agent said, you do not want your attorney here.... They told me that if I asked for an attorney the conversation would be over and that I would go to the jail and I would be remanded there until trial. But if I cooperated with them and didn't ask for my attorney, that if I told them everything I already know — that they already know, they would tell the prosecutor that I was cooperative and tell her to tell the — the judge to get me on bail.

And later,

> After the first time I asked if I could get ahold of my mother again. We had a short conversation, and then I asked if I could call my uncle. And they said I couldn't call my attorney, they said that, again, if I asked for an attorney they would tell the judge I was uncooperative, that I was being charged with a conspiracy that held a ten-year-to-life sentence, and that if I was cooperative, even though they couldn't guarantee that I wouldn't do any jail time, that I would probably do less than what the sentence was.

The government argues that this DeLaurentiis account of her interrogation is wholly incredible. In doing so, the government does not contend that DeLaurentiis's references to a lawyer or to her uncle were ambiguous. Instead, the agents deny outright that during the interrogation (or at her residence) DeLaurentiis ever said anything even resembling reference to a lawyer and maintain that she never asked to speak with *anyone*. I must determine, therefore, which version is accurate.

The interview at the DEA office lasted between forty-five minutes and an hour. The agents then took DeLaurentiis to the local jail around 8 p.m. for booking and overnight custody before she could see a federal judicial officer in the morning. The testifying agent did not know what happened after she was taken to the jail, did not know if she then called a lawyer, and did not know if the jail had voice recording policies. Apparently, DeLaurentiis and her current lawyer here in Maine also did not know about recording policies until a couple of days before the suppression hearing. But then they discovered that the jail does record all phone calls. As a result, the defense introduced at the suppression hearing a CD of a jail-recorded phone call from DeLaurentiis to her uncle starting at 8:01 p.m. on the night of her arrest, a recording of which the prosecutor and testifying agent were previously unaware. I have listened to that CD many times. It is apparent that DeLaurentiis is very emotional at the beginning of, and at other times during, the phone call. I find that under the circumstances she had no reason to lie to her uncle at that stage or to create a false scenario, that at least her earliest statements on the phone call were uncoached, and that these statements made to her uncle in such close proximity to the DEA questioning persuasively confirm her version of the interrogation.

As the CD recording opens, DeLaurentiis's uncle calls her by name (Lisa) and tells her "Hey, don't talk to anybody, okay?" DeLaurentiis responds, "But I already talked to the DEA agent." Her uncle immediately says, "Well, don't say another word," and she responds, "I asked them if I could talk to you when they first brought me in the room. I said that I want to call my Uncle Steve who is an attorney, and they wouldn't let me do it." That was an emotional, unsolicited, utterance given to a trusted relative immediately after the interrogation, at a time when there is no reason to think that DeLaurentiis understood its significance or that she was being recorded. She then responds "yes" to her uncle's questions whether the agents told her that she was under arrest and that she had the right to an attorney. Next, she tells her uncle on the phone call that she told the agents, "'I want to call my Uncle Steve' and they said 'No you'll be better just to talk to us. You just sit and talk to us.'" ....

All of these contemporaneous statements, previously unknown to the government, are consistent with DeLaurentiis's, not the agents', testimony of what occurred at the interrogation.[9] ....

In light of all the evidence presented at the suppression hearing, I find that a reasonable officer would have understood DeLaurentiis to have made a clear, unequivocal request for counsel at questioning (*Davis*'s "requisite level of clarity") given her repeated requests and the agents' responses, and that the DEA agents instead actively dissuaded her from contacting a lawyer. I also find that the DEA threats to "tell the judge" if DeLaurentiis did not cooperate were coercive and that her resulting statements were involuntary.

Accordingly, the motion to suppress is GRANTED.

SO ORDERED.

---

9. As should be apparent, the existence of the contemporaneous recorded phone call has a major effect on the outcome of this motion. Without it, I would have been inclined to disbelieve DeLaurentiis's version of the interrogation.

Notes and Questions

1. In footnote 9, the judge indicates that he would have ruled differently if he had not heard the recording of DeLaurentiis's call from jail. In most suppression cases, evidence like this will not be available to help judges make their decisions. Does this make you concerned about whether judges can correctly determine whether it is the police or the suspect who is lying about what happened in the interrogation room?

2. How could the dispute about whether DeLaurentiis invoked her right to counsel have been avoided? Would video-recording the entire interrogation have been a preferable approach? *See* Commonwealth v. DiGimbattista, 813 N.E.2d 516 (Mass. 2004).

3. If DeLaurentiis's story is true, then the police violated her *Miranda* rights. But even so, if she had been a sophisticated suspect she still could have refused to confess. Would all suspects have been steamrolled by the officers the way DeLaurentiis was? Watch *The Wire*, Season 2, Episode 4, at 47:05 minutes. In that scene, the officers go to great lengths to get Thomas "Horse" Pakusa, one of the senior dock workers, to come to the police station for an interrogation about the dead women found in a shipping container, but they are unsuccessful:

Detective Bunk:	All right, let's take a ride downtown [to] clear this mess up.
Horse:	No.
Detective Bunk:	Get … in the car.
Horse:	Am I locked up?
Detective Bunk:	Get in the damn car.
Horse:	You want me in that car, you need to lock me up. And if that's the way it's going to be then I want to talk to my shop steward. And he can have a [union] lawyer go with me.

Detective Bunk gave Horse the impression that he had no choice but to go to the police station, but that was false. And Horse called Bunk's bluff. The scene suggests, perhaps correctly, that the Fifth Amendment protection against self-incrimination, like the Fourth Amendment's protection against unreasonable searches and seizures, is largely the province of the sophisticated.

5. While cases like *Brewer* and *DeLaurentiis* indicate that some police still disregard the *Miranda* doctrine, are physically coercive interrogations—beatings, torture, and threats of violence—a thing of the past? In thinking about that question, consider the two cases below—an infamous decision from decades past and a lesser-known case from just a few years ago.

Brown v. Mississippi
297 U.S. 278 (1936)

Mr. Chief Justice HUGHES delivered the opinion of the Court.

The question in this case is whether convictions, which rest solely upon confessions shown to have been extorted by officers of the state by brutality and violence, are consistent with the due process of law required by the Fourteenth Amendment of the Constitution of the United States.

Petitioners were indicted for the murder of one Raymond Stewart, whose death occurred on March 30, 1934. They were indicted on April 4, 1934, and were then arraigned and pleaded not guilty. Counsel were appointed by the court to defend them. Trial was begun the next morning and was concluded on the following day, when they were found guilty and sentenced to death.

* * *

... [The facts] are clearly and adequately stated in the dissenting opinion * * * [and] we quote this part of his opinion in full, as follows:

'The crime with which these defendants, all ignorant negroes, are charged, was discovered about 1 o'clock p.m. on Friday, March 30, 1934. On that night one Dial, a deputy sheriff, accompanied by others, came to the home of Ellington, one of the defendants, and requested him to accompany them to the house of the deceased, and there a number of white men were gathered, who began to accuse the defendant of the crime. Upon his denial they seized him, and with the participation of the deputy they hanged him by a rope to the limb of a tree, and, having let him down, they hung him again, and when he was let down the second time, and he still protested his innocence, he was tied to a tree and whipped, and, still declining to accede to the demands that he confess, he was finally released, and he returned with some difficulty to his home, suffering intense pain and agony. The record of the testimony shows that the signs of the rope on his neck were plainly visible during the so-called trial. A day or two thereafter the said deputy, accompanied by another, returned to the home of the said defendant and arrested him, and departed with the prisoner towards the jail in an adjoining county, but went by a route which led into the state of Alabama; and while on the way, in that state, the deputy stopped and again severely whipped the defendant, declaring that he would continue the whipping until he confessed, and the defendant then agreed to confess to such a statement as the deputy would dictate, and he did so, after which he was delivered to jail.

'The other two defendants, Ed Brown and Henry Shields, were also arrested and taken to the same jail. On Sunday night, April 1, 1934, the same deputy, accompanied by a number of white men, one of whom was also an officer, and by the jailer, came to the jail, and the two last named defendants were made to strip and they were laid over chairs and their backs were cut to pieces with a leather strap with buckles on it, and they were likewise made by the said deputy definitely to understand that the whipping would be continued unless and until they confessed, and not only confessed, but confessed in every matter of detail as demanded by those present; and in this manner the defendants confessed the crime, and, as the whippings progressed and were repeated, they changed or adjusted their confession in all particulars of detail so as to conform to the demands of their torturers. When the confessions had been obtained in the exact form and contents as desired by the mob, they left with the parting admonition and warning that, if the defendants changed their story at any time in any respect from that last stated, the perpetrators of the outrage would administer the same or equally effective treatment.

* * *

'All this having been accomplished, on the next day, that is, on Monday, April 2, when the defendants had been given time to recuperate somewhat from the tortures to which they had been subjected, the two sheriffs, one of the county where the crime was committed, and the other of the county of the jail in which the prisoners were confined, came to the jail, accompanied by eight other persons, some of them deputies, there to hear the free and voluntary confession of these miserable and abject defendants. The sheriff of the county of the crime admitted that he had heard of the whipping, but averred that he had no personal knowledge of it. He admitted that one of the defendants, when brought before him to confess, was limping and did not sit down, and that this particular defendant then and there stated that he had been strapped so severely that he could not sit down, and, as already stated, the signs of the rope on the neck of another of the defendants were plainly visible to all. Nevertheless the solemn farce of hearing the free and voluntary confessions was gone through with, and these two sheriffs and one other person then present were the three witnesses used in court to establish the so-called confessions, which were received by the court and admitted in evidence over the objections of the defendants....'

* * *

... It would be difficult to conceive of methods more revolting to the sense of justice than those taken to procure the confessions of these petitioners, and the use of the confessions thus obtained as the basis for conviction and sentence was a clear denial of due process.

* * *

[T]he judgment must be reversed.

It is so ordered.

Notes and Questions

1. Watch *The Wire*, Season 1, Episode 7, at 49:50 minutes. Sergeant Landsman photographs Bird, a member of the Barksdale drug gang, and explains to him that "we really wanted to show all the jurors that you left our little interrogation here without any more scuff marks than what you brought in." Four minutes later however, the officers beat Bird while he is handcuffed to the table. Did you find this scene believable?

2. Also consider *The Wire*, Season 1, Episode 5, at 17:05 minutes in which Officers Carver and Herc design a good-cop/bad-cop routine to get Bodie to give up information about Avon Barksdale. Carver begins by telling Bodie that Officer Herc can't wait to get in the interrogation room and beat him up. Thereafter, when Bodie is rude and uncooperative, Officer Carver loses his cool and begins beating Bodie himself, with Herc joining in shortly after that. The scene leaves the impression that Carver had not intended to assault Bodie but simply lost control because Bodie baited him. Do you think most cops would be able to restrain themselves better than Carver?

3. Finally, consider *The Wire*, Season 3, Episode 3, at 10:05 minutes. McNulty sees a suspect in an interrogation room who is bleeding and appears to have been beaten. Bunk informs McNulty that the suspect confessed to shooting a police officer. McNulty asks whether that was "before or after you knocked the shit out of him?" Bunk smiles and reads from the report: "injuries were sustained while patrol officers were effecting procedures and arrest of aforementioned suspect." When a suspect is believed to have shot a cop, do you think it is likely that the interrogating officers will use force or threat of force against the suspect?

4. Is police brutality like that in *Brown* and *The Wire* rare in the United States today? It is hard to know for sure. Many victims of brutality likely do not file complaints. Nev-

ertheless, Human Rights Watch was able to document numerous incidents of police brutality in cities across the country. HUMAN RIGHTS WATCH, SHIELDED FROM JUSTICE: POLICE BRUTALITY AND ACCOUNTABILITY IN THE UNITED STATES (1998), available at http://www.hrw.org/reports98/police/uspo06.htm.

5. Not surprisingly, the brunt of the police brutality problem is borne by minority victims. *See* I Bennett Capers, *Crime, Legitimacy, and Testilying*, 83 Ind. L.J. 835, 844–49 (2008). Does the police brutality problem seem like it is getting better? Or are law students—who are predominantly middle-class and white—not in a position to have any idea whether the problem is improving?

People v. Vigil

242 P.3d 1092 (Colo. 2010)

Justice MARTINEZ delivered the Opinion of the Court.

I. Introduction

Clovis Vigil was arrested and charged with possession of a controlled substance as well as possession with intent to distribute. At the time of his arrest, Vigil confessed to possession and indicated where he kept the drugs only after the arresting officers had used force against him, inflicting numerous injuries. The trial court held that Vigil was arrested without probable cause and that his various inculpatory statements were involuntarily given. The trial court suppressed those statements from admission into evidence as well as the bags of cocaine that were collected from Vigil's pocket. The People appeal the trial court's suppression order. We conclude that the trial court's suppression order was proper and affirm its decision.

II. Facts and Procedure

In July 2009, an off-duty Sheriff's Deputy witnessed what he believed to be an illegal drug transaction in the parking lot of a store in Walsenburg, Colorado. He observed Clovis Vigil, his dog leashed to one hand, approach a parked car with two occupants. After a short interaction, Vigil was handed something, which he placed in his pocket. Vigil then left the parking lot on foot. The off-duty Sheriff's Deputy reported his observations to the dispatcher, identifying Vigil and the two people he had interacted with as people he knew to be involved in drug deals. Dispatch then relayed this information to a Walsenburg police officer, who proceeded to locate Vigil while he was still walking through town.

While driving in his patrol car, the responding police officer spotted Vigil, activated his emergency lights, and pulled up next to him. Exiting his vehicle, the officer told Vigil that he needed to ask him a few questions. At the officer's request, Vigil stopped walking and listened to him. The officer told Vigil that he needed to speak with him because he had been named in a possible drug transaction in the parking lot of a nearby store. Vigil, through a string of profanities, clearly indicated that he did not want to answer any questions. The officer responded by saying that he wanted a brief explanation of Vigil's actions in the parking lot, as an off-duty officer had said that he had seen Vigil in a drug deal.

Vigil apparently grew agitated and flailed his arms, one of which was still tethered to his leashed dog. Although Vigil was not carrying anything and was dressed in jeans and a t-shirt, because of Vigil's agitated state, the officer asked him to put his hands on the hood of the police car and submit to a frisk "because of an officer safety issue." Vigil declined and apparently turned to leave the scene. At this time a second officer arrived.

As Vigil turned to leave, the first officer informed Vigil that he was under arrest for disorderly conduct. The officer slowed Vigil's attempt to leave the scene by grabbing his shirt. When Vigil attempted to shrug off the officer's grab, the first officer struck him with a martial arts "back fist" to his face, fracturing multiple bones in his face and dropping Vigil to his knees. The second officer attempted to spray Vigil's eyes with OC spray, a chemical repellant, and then struck him three times with a metal baton around the lower back and buttocks. Both officers then forced him against the ground, kneed him in the back, and handcuffed him. While being handcuffed, Vigil called out, "alright, alright, I'll give you the shit. It's in my left front pocket." The officers rolled him over and discovered baggies of cocaine in his pocket.

With Vigil's injuries both numerous and apparent, he was taken from the scene in an ambulance to a local hospital. Once at the hospital he received over six hours of medical treatment. Vigil's sinal and occipital bones were broken; his left eye was deeply bruised and bleeding; he had numerous lacerations on his face and side from being pushed against the ground, and welts from being struck with the baton were already evident. The medical staff recommended that Vigil be taken to Pueblo because of the severity of his injuries, but he refused and was instead taken directly to the police department by the same officers who had arrested him. There, he was interrogated beginning at 2:05 a.m. after signing a *Miranda* waiver form, and he gave various inculpatory statements.

Prior to trial, Vigil moved to suppress his confession at the scene of his arrest, the drugs found on his person, and the inculpatory statements he made during his interrogation. The trial court found it incredible that two trained and fully armed officers felt threatened by a man attempting to walk away from them with a leashed dog. Further, the trial court found that Vigil never posed a threat to officer safety and that the amount of force used was unreasonable and unnecessary. The court held that Vigil's initial confession at the scene of his arrest was an involuntary utterance as the result of the police officers' coercive use of physical force, and that the officers arrested Vigil without probable cause. The court also concluded that the prosecution had not met its burden of establishing that Vigil's subsequent confession at the police department was voluntarily made. As such, the trial court suppressed Vigil's statements as well as the baggies of cocaine.

The People filed this interlocutory appeal challenging the trial court's suppression order. After reviewing the record, we affirm the trial court's order.

III. Analysis

The People challenge the trial court's suppression order with respect to Vigil's first confession, the contraband discovered in his pocket, and his later confession after medical treatment. We conclude that the trial court's suppression order was appropriate.

A. Confession at Arrest

Although not clearly articulated in their brief, the People appear to challenge the trial court's determination that Vigil's original statement at the scene of his arrest was involuntary and so inadmissible. . . .

The People assert—though without argument—that Vigil's remarks of "alright, alright, I'll give you the shit, it's in my left front pocket" were spontaneous and voluntary. However, in the same sentence, the People admit that Vigil only made the statement after finding himself "under the firm control of the officers." It is apparent from the record that Vigil gave this statement immediately after being struck in the face, pushed to the ground, sprayed with chemical repellent, and hit several times with a metal baton. In fact, Vigil uttered these words of confession while being handcuffed and with both of the officers pushing their knees into his back. Vigil's protestations of "alright, alright" indicate that his comments were meant as a response to the officers' use of physical force following the attempt to question him about his activity. The officers' use of force played a significant role in procuring an answer for their original and repeated inquiry, which was an explanation of Vigil's involvement in a drug deal.

* * *

... [H]ere, the trial court found that Vigil posed no threat to the officers and that the amount of force the officers used against him was not only "wholly disproportionate to the circumstances involved," but rather coerced his statement. We agree with the trial court. Neither officer could articulate anything specific about Vigil's manner that imperiled their safety. Vigil was out walking his dog, dressed only in a pair of jeans and a t-shirt, carrying nothing. When the officer commanded Vigil to comply with a protective weapons search, he swore and just tried to leave.

We see no evidence in the record that supports the People's assertion that Vigil's statements were voluntarily given....

* * *

... [T]he record [also] supports the trial court's determination that the coercion of Vigil's first confession infected his subsequent confession. After being told to seek further medical attention for his rather serious injuries, Vigil was released into the hands of the same officers that had inflicted those injuries. The officers then immediately took him to the police department for interrogation at 2:00 a.m. On such facts, it is perfectly reasonable to conclude that the officers were the beneficiaries of their own coercive conduct when they received Vigil's subsequent cooperation and confession.... As such, we affirm the trial court's order suppressing Vigil's police department confession.

* * *

Notes and Questions

1. Did Vigil commit the crime of disorderly conduct or was he in violation of the unwritten law sometimes called "contempt of cop?"

2. Hopefully, the United States has progressed to the point where police brutality like that described in *Brown v. Mississippi* is extremely rare. But is the type of force used by the officers in *People v. Vigil* still common enough to be extremely worrisome?

3. Although the officers' actions in Vigil are disturbing, do they deserve credit for honesty? What was to stop the officers from claiming that they beat Vigil because he had attacked them or because they saw a bulge in his pocket that looked like a weapon? Is it possible for police to use physical force — particularly outside the interrogation room — by lying about the danger posed by the suspect? How can courts and legislatures stop police from engaging in this kind of brutality and dishonesty?

D. Are the Police Too Clever
for the Supreme Court?

Hopefully, most police officers do not engage in the type of lying and physical abuse detailed in Section C above. The average police officer — we hope — properly reads the

Miranda warnings before conducting a custodial interrogation, and the officer stops the interrogation when the suspect has invoked his right to counsel or silence. But in complying with the rules, do officers err on the side of caution and the spirit of the *Miranda* doctrine, or do the officers walk right up to the line of what is permitted? Put differently, do officers understand the complex Fifth Amendment law well enough to skirt the edges of what is permissible without committing a violation? And are courts willing to give the officers the benefit of the doubt in this regard? In thinking about the case below, ask yourself whether the officers understood the *Miranda* doctrine and whether they were intentionally pushing the envelope. Also ask yourself whether the court showed enough skepticism of the officers' story.

Rhode Island v. Innis
446 U.S. 291 (1980)

Mr. Justice STEWART delivered the opinion of the Court.

In *Miranda v. Arizona*, 384 U.S. 436, the Court held that, once a defendant in custody asks to speak with a lawyer, all interrogation must cease until a lawyer is present. The issue in this case is whether the respondent was "interrogated" in violation of the standards promulgated in the *Miranda* opinion.

I

On the night of January 12, 1975, John Mulvaney, a Providence, R.I., taxicab driver, disappeared after being dispatched to pick up a customer. His body was discovered four days later buried in a shallow grave in Coventry, R.I. He had died from a shotgun blast aimed at the back of his head.

On January 17, 1975, shortly after midnight, the Providence police received a telephone call from Gerald Aubin, also a taxicab driver, who reported that he had just been robbed by a man wielding a sawed-off shotgun. Aubin further reported that he had dropped off his assailant near Rhode Island College in a section of Providence known as Mount Pleasant. While at the Providence police station waiting to give a statement, Aubin noticed a picture of his assailant on a bulletin board. Aubin so informed one of the police officers present. The officer prepared a photo array, and again Aubin identified a picture of the same person. That person was the respondent. Shortly thereafter, the Providence police began a search of the Mount Pleasant area.

At approximately 4:30 a.m. on the same date, Patrolman Lovell, while cruising the streets of Mount Pleasant in a patrol car, spotted the respondent standing in the street facing him. When Patrolman Lovell stopped his car, the respondent walked towards it. Patrolman Lovell then arrested the respondent, who was unarmed, and advised him of his so-called *Miranda* rights. While the two men waited in the patrol car for other police officers to arrive, Patrolman Lovell did not converse with the respondent other than to respond to the latter's request for a cigarette.

Within minutes, Sergeant Sears arrived at the scene of the arrest, and he also gave the respondent the *Miranda* warnings. Immediately thereafter, Captain Leyden and other police officers arrived. Captain Leyden advised the respondent of his *Miranda* rights. The respondent stated that he understood those rights and wanted to speak with a lawyer. Captain Leyden then directed that the respondent be placed in a "caged wagon," a four-door police car with a wire screen mesh between the front and rear seats, and be driven to the central police station. Three officers, Patrolmen Gleckman, Williams, and McKenna, were assigned to accompany the respondent to the central station. They placed the respondent in the vehicle and shut the doors. Captain Leyden then instructed the officers not to question the respondent or intimidate or coerce him in any way. The three officers then entered the vehicle, and it departed.

While en route to the central station, Patrolman Gleckman initiated a conversation with Patrolman McKenna concerning the missing shotgun. As Patrolman Gleckman later testified:

> "A. At this point, I was talking back and forth with Patrolman McKenna stating that I frequent this area while on patrol and [that because a school for handicapped children is located nearby,] there's a lot of handicapped children running around in this area, and God forbid one of them might find a weapon with shells and they might hurt themselves."

Patrolman McKenna apparently shared his fellow officer's concern:

> "A. I more or less concurred with him [Gleckman] that it was a safety factor and that we should, you know, continue to search for the weapon and try to find it."

While Patrolman Williams said nothing, he overheard the conversation between the two officers:

> "A. He [Gleckman] said it would be too bad if the little—I believe he said a girl—would pick up the gun, maybe kill herself."

The respondent then interrupted the conversation, stating that the officers should turn the car around so he could show them where the gun was located. At this point, Patrolman McKenna radioed back to Captain Leyden that they were returning to the scene of the arrest and that the respondent would inform them of the location of the gun. At the time the respondent indicated that the officers should turn back, they had traveled no more than a mile, a trip encompassing only a few minutes.

The police vehicle then returned to the scene of the arrest where a search for the shotgun was in progress. There, Captain Leyden again advised the respondent of his *Miranda* rights. The respondent replied that he understood those rights but that he "wanted to get the gun out of the way because of the kids in the area in the school." The respondent then led the police to a nearby field, where he pointed out the shotgun under some rocks by the side of the road.

On March 20, 1975, a grand jury returned an indictment charging the respondent with the kidnaping, robbery, and murder of John Mulvaney. Before trial, the respondent moved to suppress the shotgun and the statements he had made to the police regarding it....

... It was the view of the state appellate court that, even though the police officers may have been genuinely concerned about the public safety and even though the respondent had not been addressed personally by the police officers, the respondent nonetheless had been subjected to "subtle coercion" that was the equivalent of "interrogation" within the meaning of the *Miranda* opinion.... Having concluded that both the shotgun and testimony relating to its discovery were obtained in violation of the *Miranda* standards and therefore should not have been admitted into evidence, the Rhode Island Supreme Court held that the respondent was entitled to a new trial.

We granted certiorari to address for the first time the meaning of "interrogation" under *Miranda v. Arizona.*

II

* * *

… The parties are in agreement that the respondent was fully informed of his *Miranda* rights and that he invoked his *Miranda* right to counsel when he told Captain Leyden that he wished to consult with a lawyer. It is also uncontested that the respondent was "in custody" while being transported to the police station.

The issue, therefore, is whether the respondent was "interrogated" by the police officers in violation of the respondent's undisputed right under *Miranda* to remain silent until he had consulted with a lawyer. In resolving this issue, we first define the term "interrogation" under *Miranda* before turning to a consideration of the facts of this case.

A

* * *

We conclude that the *Miranda* safeguards come into play whenever a person in custody is subjected to either express questioning or its functional equivalent. That is to say, the term "interrogation" under *Miranda* refers not only to express questioning, but also to any words or actions on the part of the police (other than those normally attendant to arrest and custody) that the police should know are reasonably likely to elicit an incriminating response from the suspect. The latter portion of this definition focuses primarily upon the perceptions of the suspect, rather than the intent of the police. This focus reflects the fact that the *Miranda* safeguards were designed to vest a suspect in custody with an added measure of protection against coercive police practices, without regard to objective proof of the underlying intent of the police. A practice that the police should know is reasonably likely to evoke an incriminating response from a suspect thus amounts to interrogation. But, since the police surely cannot be held accountable for the unforeseeable results of their words or actions, the definition of interrogation can extend only to words or actions on the part of police officers that they *should have known* were reasonably likely to elicit an incriminating response.

B

Turning to the facts of the present case, we conclude that the respondent was not "interrogated" within the meaning of *Miranda*. It is undisputed that the first prong of the definition of "interrogation" was not satisfied, for the conversation between Patrolmen Gleckman and McKenna included no express questioning of the respondent. Rather, that conversation was, at least in form, nothing more than a dialogue between the two officers to which no response from the respondent was invited.

Moreover, it cannot be fairly concluded that the respondent was subjected to the "functional equivalent" of questioning. It cannot be said, in short, that Patrolmen Gleckman and McKenna should have known that their conversation was reasonably likely to elicit an incriminating response from the respondent. There is nothing in the record to suggest that the officers were aware that the respondent was peculiarly susceptible to an appeal to his conscience concerning the safety of handicapped children. Nor is there anything in the record to suggest that the police knew that the respondent was unusually disoriented or upset at the time of his arrest.

The case thus boils down to whether, in the context of a brief conversation, the officers should have known that the respondent would suddenly be moved to make a self-incriminating response. Given the fact that the entire conversation appears to have consisted of no more than a few off hand remarks, we cannot say that the officers should have known that it was reasonably likely that Innis would so respond. This is not a case where the police carried on a lengthy harangue in the presence of the suspect. Nor does the record support the respondent's contention that, under the circumstances, the officers' comments were particularly "evocative." It is our view, therefore, that the respondent was not subjected by the police to words or actions that the police should have known were reasonably likely to elicit an incriminating response from him.

The Rhode Island Supreme Court erred, in short, in equating "subtle compulsion" with interrogation. That the officers' comments struck a responsive chord is readily apparent. Thus, it may be said, as the Rhode Island Supreme Court did say, that the respondent was subjected to "subtle compulsion." But that is not the end of the inquiry. It must also be established that a suspect's incriminating response was the product of words or actions on the part of the police that they should have known were reasonably likely to elicit an incriminating response. This was not established in the present case.

For the reasons stated, the judgment of the Supreme Court of Rhode Island is vacated, and the case is remanded to that court for further proceedings not inconsistent with this opinion.

It is so ordered.

[The concurring opinions of Justice White and Chief Justice Burger and the dissenting opinion of Justice Marshall and Justice Stevens are omitted.]

Notes and Questions

1. In his opinion for the Court, Justice Stewart remarks that "the entire conversation appears to have consisted of no more than a few off hand remarks" and that "we cannot say that the officers should have known that it was reasonably likely that Innis would so respond." Is it remotely plausible that the patrolmen in *Innis* were engaged in simple conversation, rather than a calculated effort to extract incriminating information from Innis? Do you think Justice Stewart and the rest of the majority truly believed the officers had simply made some off hand remarks? If so, are the justices naïve? If not, is the Court stretching the facts to uphold a conviction that seems to violate *Miranda*?

2. Watch *The Wire*, Season 1, Episode 2, at 26:00 minutes where Detectives Bunk and McNulty trick D'Angelo Barksdale into writing an apology letter to a homicide victim's young children. When D'Angelo's attorney arrives and sees D'Angelo writing, the lawyer complains that when "he calls his lawyer that's supposed to be the end of the interview." Bunk responds that "your client gave no statement, we took no statement. He just decided voluntarily to write a letter." Is Bunk correct about this under *Rhode Island v. Innis*?

3. Also consider again the photocopier ruse in the first scene of *The Wire*, Season 5, Episode 1, in which Detective Bunk Moreland and his partner conduct a fake polygraph examination by using an office photocopier. Does anything in this scene violate the *Miranda* doctrine or the protection against coerced statements?

4. Were the patrol officers in *Innis* simply too clever to be seriously limited by the *Miranda* doctrine or the Supreme Court? When the Supreme Court decided *Miranda* in an attempt to make interrogations less coercive, could they possibly have foreseen officers hooking suspects to copy machines for polygraph examinations or Neutron Proton Negligence Intelligence Tests that supposedly test for gunshot residue? Will the police—either through

watercooler discussions or trainings by prosecutors—always be able to figure out how to skirt judicial restrictions?

E. Recording Interrogations:
A Solution or an Empty Hope?

One solution that is widely endorsed by experts is for all custodial interrogations to be recorded. Does this solution seem plausible? Video-recording interrogations would not be particularly expensive. Yet, possibly because of the political power of law enforcement, only a handful of legislatures have passed laws requiring it. Could courts step in and require video-recording or would that exceed their authority? Is there a less invasive step courts could take? Consider the approach taken by the Massachusetts Supreme Judicial Court in the decision below.

Commonwealth v. DiGiambattista
813 N.E.2d 516 (Mass. 2004)

SOSMAN, J.

The defendant, Valerio DiGiambattista, was convicted of burning a dwelling house. That conviction rested, in large measure, on DiGiambattista's confession to the police during an unrecorded interrogation at a fire station. It is undisputed that, in an effort to obtain his confession, the interrogating officers resorted to trickery, falsely suggesting to DiGiambattista that his presence at the scene of the fire had been captured on videotape, while simultaneously expressing sympathy for his actions and opining that he needed counseling for his alcoholism. In his subsequent confession, DiGiambattista's version of how and where he started the fire was completely contrary to the forensic evidence, and other details of his confession were ultimately shown to be impossible.... For the following reasons, we conclude that the defendant's confession should have been suppressed, and we therefore reverse the defendant's conviction and remand the case for further proceedings. We also take this occasion to announce that, henceforth, the admission in evidence of any confession or statement of the defendant that is the product of an unrecorded custodial interrogation, or an unrecorded interrogation conducted at a place of detention, will entitle the defendant, on request, to a jury instruction concerning the need to evaluate that alleged statement or confession with particular caution.

... Facts

The evidence, viewed in the light most favorable to the Commonwealth, was as follows. DiGiambattista, Nicole Miscioscia (his girlfriend and later fiancée), and Miscioscia's children lived in a rented house at 109 Adams Street in Newton. The property was owned by Angelo Paolini, who had a construction company on the lot next door. During the final year of his tenancy, DiGiambattista withheld rental payments on account of Paolini's failure to make much needed repairs to the premises.

On March 7, 1998, buoyed by the receipt of a tax refund, DiGiambattista and his family moved out of the 109 Adams Street property and relocated to an apartment in Chelsea. A few days prior to their departure, DiGiambattista installed a new lock on the front door, keeping one key for himself and giving the other one to his mother. (A few of his mother's belongings remained on the premises, with the understanding that she would later retrieve them.) With that new lock in place, the only way to lock the door from the outside was by way of a key.

Shortly prior to midnight on Tuesday, March 10, 1998, a neighbor noticed smoke coming from the house at 109 Adams Street. When firefighters arrived at the scene, they found the front door locked, the other two doors boarded up, and the windows closed. Inspection of the scene and testing of samples revealed that the perpetrator had used gasoline as an accelerant and had started the fire in or near a closet underneath a stair landing. A second, but insignificant, fire had also been set in the kitchen sink, lighting a small amount of paper. Expert assessment was that the fire had been started sometime between 11:25 P.M. and 11:55 P.M.

The following evening, officers questioned DiGiambattista and Miscioscia concerning the fire. There were some inconsistencies in their versions as to DiGiambattista's whereabouts on the night of the fire, and inconsistent versions as to who still had a key to the new front door lock. During initial questioning, DiGiambattista suggested the possibility that Paolini had set the fire, mentioning that Paolini may have used gasoline. (At that point in the interview, the officers had not said anything about an accelerant being used to start the fire, and did not yet have expert analysis identifying the accelerant as gasoline.) Further investigation uncovered a witness who claimed that he had seen a man resembling DiGiambattista enter the 109 Adams Street property at around 6 or 6:30 P.M. on the night of the fire.

On April 10, 1998, one month after the fire, DiGiambattista voluntarily accompanied two officers (a State trooper and a Newton police officer) to a nearby fire station for further questioning. The trooper told DiGiambattista that he was free to leave, gave him Miranda warnings, and obtained his written waiver of rights. After an initial period of conversational, mild-mannered questioning, the officers changed tack and told DiGiambattista that he was their prime suspect, that his statements were inconsistent with those of other witnesses, and that they had a witness who placed him at the scene of the fire that night. DiGiambattista denied that he had been at the house that night and denied setting the fire. The officers inquired as to his willingness to take a lie detector test. After what the officers described as some hesitation and seeming reluctance, DiGiambattista agreed.[5]

At that point in the interview, another trooper came into the room carrying a thick folder and two videotapes. The folder was stuffed with blank paper and miscellaneous newspaper clippings having nothing to do with the case. One of the videotapes, marked "109 Adams Street," was a recording made at the scene the night of the fire. The other, labeled "Paolini Construction Worker's Comp Case," was blank. This fictitious folder and videotape had been prepared in advance, with a plan that the other trooper would bring them into the interview room at a designated time. With the folder and videotapes conspicuously placed on the table next to the interrogating trooper, the trooper asked DiGiambattista: "If I told you that somebody at Paolini Construction was under surveillance by an insurance company for a workers' comp fraud case, is there any reason you would show up on that videotape?" While confronting DiGiambattista with this ostensible evidence against him, the trooper simultaneously sought to "downplay the crime itself, and give [DiGiambattista] a way of saving face, to confess to this by downplaying it," pointing out that "no one was hurt" in the fire and that, in light of the deplorable condition of the premises, the trooper could "relate to" and "understand" his anger at the landlord and

---

5. No polygraph test was administered, and the officers had no intention of administering one. They posed the inquiry in order to gauge DiGiambattista's reaction to the suggestion.

the desire to "do something like that." DiGiambattista continued to deny that he had been at the scene.

The two officers left the room and were replaced by the trooper who had brought in the folder and tapes. That trooper repeated to DiGiambattista that they had a witness placing him at the scene, and that his own prior statement and the statements of witnesses contained inconsistencies as to the time he had left his new apartment that night. The trooper then expressed the view that DiGiambattista had not meant to hurt anyone, and that his lighting the fire was the product of stress, alcohol consumption, and understandable frustration with his living situation at 109 Adams Street. The trooper then gave DiGiambattista two proposals, that he had either done this "to hurt someone" or that he "had to be upset," under "stress," and that "when you add the booze in, you're going to make mistakes." During the trooper's explanation, DiGiambattista began nodding, and then acknowledged that he "was stressed" and had been drinking. The trooper asked him if he had used matches or a lighter. DiGiambattista replied that he had used both. The trooper asked him how he had lit the fire. DiGiambattista said that he used gasoline. After one more question and answer (which the trooper could not recall at trial), the trooper summoned the original interrogators into the room to take a more detailed statement because they were the ones "who had all the background knowledge of the case."[7]

DiGiambattista's detailed statement to the officers recounted that he had traveled from Chelsea to 109 Adams Street using public transportation, stopping at a named hardware store in Watertown to buy a two and one-half gallon gasoline can. He also identified the gasoline station where he bought one dollar's worth of gasoline. After a period of drinking beer, he proceeded to 109 Adams Street, let himself in the front door, and then poured gasoline in multiple locations in the house, "lighting the gas as [he] went along." He claimed to have done so "in almost every room in the house."

At the officers' request, DiGiambattista also drew a diagram of where he had spread gasoline and lit fires. On the diagram of one floor, DiGiambattista wrote that he "[p]oured gas almost everywhere," and on the diagram of the other floor, he indicated that he "[p]oured gas all over." The diagram identified four definite locations (and a fifth possible location) where he had started fires on both floors. None of the locations identified in the diagram corresponded with the closet area where the experts determined the fire had been started. Despite the officer's suggestion that DiGiambattista indicate the location of the kitchen sink in his diagram (an apparent attempt to jog his memory concerning the paper fire they had found in that location), DiGiambattista's confession and diagram made no reference to starting a fire in the sink (or anywhere else in the kitchen). Similarly, whereas DiGiambattista unambiguously confessed to pouring gasoline liberally throughout both floors of the house, examination of the scene revealed gasoline only in a few specific locations, notably in the vicinity of the closet fire (an area not designated by DiGiambattista as a place he had spread gasoline).

---

7. At the hearing on the motion to suppress and at trial, DiGiambattista testified that other pressures were brought to bear to obtain his confession, namely, that the troopers threatened to arrest both him and Miscioscia, warned that a high bail would keep him in custody over the weekend (with an even higher bail likely to be imposed at arraignment on Monday), and predicted that State officials would take their children away. He also testified that the officers told him that, if he confessed, the case could be resolved with his participation in counselling. He also claimed that he asked for an attorney, but was told that the involvement of any attorney would be the end of the "deal." The motion judge's findings (rendered on remand four and one-half years after the evidentiary hearing on the motion) did not credit DiGiambattista's testimony on any of these points.

In his confession, DiGiambattista said that he thought that he threw the gasoline can "in the back room," but he was "not 100 percent sure." He then "left out the front door and ran." However, when the officers informed DiGiambattista that they had not found any gasoline can in the house, he changed his statement to say that he had taken the can with him on the bus as far as Harvard Square and had thrown it in a dumpster. The officers expressed incredulity that anyone would carry a gasoline can on a bus, at which point DiGiambattista changed his statement again, claiming that he had thrown the can away at a picnic area along the Charles River not far from the fire scene. DiGiambattista also told the officers that he had thrown the key in the river, but then later told them that he still had the key at home. (At the conclusion of the interrogation, the officers took DiGiambattista home, whereupon he retrieved the key and gave it to them.)

There was no electronic recording or taping of any portion of the interrogation or of the confession that it ultimately produced. One of the officers took down the confession in written form, which DiGiambattista reviewed, corrected, and signed. DiGiambattista also drew and signed the two-page diagram of both floors of the house described above. Finally, at the officers' suggestion, DiGiambattista also composed a letter of apology for the fire, explaining that he had been "stressed out because of the conditions of the house" and "drunk," expressing that he was "happy that nobody got hurt," acknowledging that he "need[ed] help with [his] alcoholism problem," and agreeing "to get help with [his] alcohol problem and any stress related problems." The interrogation, lasting approximately two and one-half hours, was then concluded.

Subsequent investigation revealed that DiGiambattista could not have bought the gasoline can from the hardware store he had identified in his confession.[8] Similarly, the gasoline station that he had identified had no record of anyone buying one dollar's worth of gasoline that night. The officers later recovered a gasoline can from a back room at the house (on a different floor from the disposal location initially identified by DiGiambattista), but that can was a six gallon can (not the two and one-half gallon can described by DiGiambattista). There was no evidence of any gasoline can found in the picnic area where DiGiambattista had ultimately indicated he disposed of it.

* * *

... Electronic recording of interrogations

... As is all too often the case, the lack of any recording has resulted in the expenditure of significant judicial resources (by three courts), all in an attempt to reconstruct what transpired during several hours of interrogation conducted in 1998 and to perform an analysis of the constitutional ramifications of that incomplete reconstruction. Where, as here, it is the Commonwealth that bears the burden of proof, gaps in that reconstruction, and the inability to place the coercive features of the interrogation in their precise context, must result in suppression of the statement. We will never know whether, if able to hear (or even view) the entirety of the interrogation, the impact of the officers' trickery and implied offers of leniency might have appeared in context sufficiently attenuated to permit the conclusion that DiGiambattista's confession was nevertheless voluntary.... We therefore take this occasion to revisit the issue of electronic recording of interrogations.

Eight years ago, this court announced that, although failure to record an interrogation would not result in automatic suppression of a defendant's statement, the lack of a

---

8. That store had closed at 8 P.M. on the night of the fire (at which time DiGiambattista was undisputably still in Chelsea), and its records indicated that no one had bought a gasoline can that day.

recording was itself a relevant factor to consider on the issues of voluntariness and waiver. *Commonwealth v. Diaz*, 661 N.E.2d 1326 (1996)....

While we have to date stopped short of requiring electronic recording of interrogations as a constitutional or common-law prerequisite to the admissibility of any resulting statements by the defendant, this court has repeatedly recognized the many benefits that flow from recording of interrogations. Other jurisdictions, similarly reluctant to articulate a taping requirement as a matter of State constitutional law, have acknowledged that recording of interrogations would act as a deterrent to police misconduct, reduce the number and length of contested motions to suppress, allow for more accurate resolution of the issues raised in motions to suppress, and at trial on the merits, provide the fact finder a complete version of precisely what the defendant did (or did not) say in any statement or confession. See *People v. Raibon*, 843 P.2d 46, 49 (Colo.Ct.App.1992); *State v. James*, 678 A.2d 1338 (1996); *State v. Kekona*, 886 P.2d 740 (1994); *Stoker v. State*, 692 N.E.2d 1386, 1390 (Ind.Ct.App.1998); *People v. Fike*, 577 N.W.2d 903 (1998) (Fitzgerald, J., concurring in part and dissenting in part); *Williams v. State*, 522 So.2d 201, 208 (Miss.1988); *State v. Godsey*, 60 S.W.3d 759, 772 (Tenn.2001); *State v. James*, 858 P.2d 1012, 1018 (Utah Ct.App.1993); *State v. Kilmer*, 439 S.E.2d 881 (1993). Commentators endorse the recording of interrogations, urging courts to adopt a requirement by way of court rule or constitutional law. See Westling, Something Is Rotten in the Interrogation Room: Let's Try Video Oversight, 34 J. Marshall L.Rev. 537 (2001); Drizin, Let the Cameras Roll: Mandatory Videotaping of Interrogations Is the Solution to Illinois' Problem of False Confessions, 32 Loy. U. Chi. L.J. 337 (2001); Comment, False Confessions and Fundamental Fairness: The Need for Electronic Recording of Custodial Interrogations, 6 B.U. Pub. Int. L.J. 719 (1997); White, False Confessions and the Constitution: Safeguards Against Untrustworthy Confessions, 32 Harv. C.R.-C.L. L.Rev. 105, 153–155 (1997); Leo, The Impact of Miranda Revisited, 86 J.Crim. L. & Criminology 621, 681–691 (1996); Kamisar, Foreword: *Brewer v. Williams*—A Hard Look at a Discomfiting Record, 66 Geo. L.J. 209 (1977); Unif. R.Crim. P. 243(b), 10 U.L.A. 38 (Master ed.2001); Model Code of Pre-Arraignment Procedure § 130.4(3) (1975).

To date, only two State courts have imposed a requirement that interrogations be recorded. See *Stephan v. State*, 711 P.2d 1156, 1158 (Alaska 1985) (unexcused failure to record custodial interrogation violates due process clause of State Constitution); *State v. Scales*, 518 N.W.2d 587, 592 (Minn.1994) (exercising court's supervisory power to mandate suppression of unrecorded custodial interrogations). Meanwhile, three States and the District of Columbia have, by legislation, imposed a recording requirement for certain types of cases and interrogations. See 725 Ill. Comp. Stat. Ann. 5/103-2.1 (West 2003); Me.Rev.Stat. Ann. tit. 25, § 2803-B(1)(J), 2004 Me. Legis. Serv. 780 (West 2004); Tex.Code Crim. Proc. Ann. art. 38.22, § 3 (West 1999); D.C.Code Ann. § 5-133.20 (2003). Despite initial reluctance on the part of law enforcement personnel, actual experience with recording of interrogations has confirmed that the benefits expected from the procedure have indeed materialized, and most of those benefits ultimately inure to the prosecution, not to the defendant. Sullivan, Police Experiences with Recording Custodial Interrogations, Nw. U. Sch. Law, Center on Wrongful Convictions, Special Report (2004); Geller, Videotaping Interrogations and Confessions, National Institute of Justice, U.S. Dep't of Justice, Research in Brief (Mar.1993)....

The principal objection to recording of interrogations springs from the fear that suspects will refuse to talk at all, or will decline to make a full confession, if they know they are being recorded. Based on experience to date in other jurisdictions, those fears appear exaggerated. Moreover, what is posed as an objection to recording of interrogations is itself inherently contrary to our requirement of a knowing and voluntary waiver of the right to remain silent. We recognize that interrogating officers may prefer to lull suspects into the mistaken belief that they are having a confidential chat with a sympathetic listener, and thus do not want an ongoing audiotape or videotape recording that will serve to remind a suspect of the fact "that anything he says can be used against him in a court of law." *Miranda v. Arizona,* 384 U.S. 436, 479 (1966). A technique, like recording, that reinforces a suspect's understanding and appreciation of that portion of the Miranda warnings is not to be eschewed because it would have that desirable reinforcing effect.

* * *

Proponents of electronic recording of interrogations ask that we, like Minnesota, exercise our superintendence power to impose a bright-line rule refusing to admit in evidence statements and confessions obtained by way of unrecorded custodial interrogation. Although appealing in its superficial simplicity (and unquestionably an effective method of convincing law enforcement officials to adopt recording as a standard practice), we still decline to impose such a rule. Among other problems, adoption of a rule excluding evidence of unrecorded interrogations necessitates precise identification of what interrogations will be subject to that rule—does it cover only custodial interrogations, or should it also cover any noncustodial interrogation conducted in particular locations (e.g., at police stations)? If the requirement were to be premised on the custodial (as opposed to noncustodial) nature of the interrogation, what do we do with interrogations that start out as noncustodial but arguably become custodial at some later (and often disputed) point during questioning? A rule of exclusion would also have to allow for justifiable failures to record—e.g., equipment malfunction, or the suspect's refusal to allow recording (or insistence that the tape recorder be turned off at a particular point during the interrogation). With regard to a suspect who is willing to speak to the interrogator but initially unwilling to be recorded, would we need to impose some requirement that the interrogator make a good faith effort to convince the suspect to agree to recording, lest that ostensible "justification" for not recording too easily become the exception that swallows the rule? Notwithstanding predominantly positive experiences in those jurisdictions that have imposed recording requirements as a prerequisite to admissibility, we are hesitant to formulate a rigid rule of exclusion, and all its corollary exceptions and modifications (each of which would potentially spark new disputes in motions to suppress).

We are not, however, satisfied with preservation of the status quo, which amounts only to repeated pronouncements from the court about the potential benefits of recording interrogations. Just as we have advised judges of the significance they may attach to the lack of a recording when deciding motions to suppress, we believe it is appropriate to provide juries with that same advice.

* * *

Where, as here, there are grounds for questioning the reliability of certain types of evidence that the jury might misconstrue as particularly reliable, specific instruction to the jury may be appropriate. We recognize the exceptionally potent quality of a defendant's statement or confession, and that potency can only be magnified when the evidence of that statement or confession is presented by one or more of the interrogating officers. Where, however, those interrogating officers have chosen *not* to preserve an accurate and complete recording of the interrogation, that fact alone justifies skepticism of the officers' version of events, above and beyond the customary bases for impeachment of such testimony. We believe that a defendant whose interrogation has not been reliably preserved by means of a complete electronic recording should be entitled, on request, to a cautionary instruction concerning the use of such evidence.

Thus, when the prosecution introduces evidence of a defendant's confession or statement that is the product of a custodial interrogation or an interrogation conducted at a place of detention (e.g., a police station), and there is not at least an audiotape recording of the complete interrogation, the defendant is entitled (on request) to a jury instruction advising that the State's highest court has expressed a preference that such interrogations be recorded whenever practicable, and cautioning the jury that, because of the absence of any recording of the interrogation in the case before them, they should weigh evidence of the defendant's alleged statement with great caution and care. Where voluntariness is a live issue and the humane practice instruction is given, the jury should also be advised that the absence of a recording permits (but does not compel) them to conclude that the Commonwealth has failed to prove voluntariness beyond a reasonable doubt.

* * *

Where we now mandate a jury instruction, not a rule of exclusion, we think that the instruction is appropriate for any custodial interrogation, or interrogation conducted in a place of detention, without regard to the alleged reasons for not recording that interrogation. It is of course permissible for the prosecution to address any reasons or justifications that would explain why no recording was made, leaving it to the jury to assess what weight they should give to the lack of a recording. The mere presence of such reasons or justifications, however, does not obviate the need for the cautionary instruction.

* * *

... The judgment of conviction is reversed....

So ordered.

GREANEY, J., concurring in part and dissenting in part,

* * *

... The proposed instructions are far too intrusive on the Commonwealth's rights and of a nature that will tend to "dynamite" a jury into concluding that a defendant's statement should be rejected. The instructions appear to presuppose that many statements given by defendants are being obtained by police misconduct of a degree that renders them involuntary and that recording will expose widespread violations of defendants' rights. The opposite is the fact. Based on the countless number of statements each year that are held voluntary by judges (after hearing motions to suppress), and by juries (after hearing the evidence and the required instruction on voluntariness when that subject is in issue), the proof of police misconduct overbearing the will of defendants is virtually non-existent. In the absence of a firm basis to suspect police misconduct as widely prevalent, there is no reason to require jury instructions that will tilt the playing field unfairly against the Commonwealth....

* * *

SPINA, J., dissenting...,

* * *

... [The majority] asserts that recordings will "reduce the number and length of contested motions to suppress." However, the briefs of amici curiae in the law enforcement community, including veteran police investigators, argue that tape recording will result in far fewer confessions, because many suspects are unwilling to speak if their conversation is to be recorded. They contend that a tape recording requirement will compromise an investigator's ability to build trust with a suspect, "trust that can be used ... to gain information in an effort to solve crimes and to prevent future violence." The court gives short shrift to this concern....

* * *

Under our current law, judges may consider the lack of a recording as a factor bearing on the issues of voluntariness and waiver when ruling on a motion to suppress. See *Commonwealth v. Diaz,* 661 N.E.2d 1326 (1996).

Here, as the court points out, the defendant raised the Commonwealth's failure to record during the suppression hearing (by cross-examining the officers about it), and although the judge made no specific finding as to the question, he nevertheless concluded that the defendant's confession was made voluntarily.... It seems that rather than "not [being] satisfied with preservation of the status quo," the court is simply not satisfied with the result in this case.

... I respectfully dissent.

Notes and Questions

1. The Massachusetts Supreme Judicial Court extols the benefits of video-recording interrogations but only requires a jury instruction about the lack of recording, rather than mandating the recording itself. Will a jury instruction serve any real purpose though? Do jurors carefully pay attention to and understand instructions like the one the court has adopted? Social science evidence suggests the answer is "no." *See, e.g.,* Amiran Elwork et al., Making Jury Instructions Understandable 12 (1982).

2. The Court notes that a few states require, either by statute or court decision, that interrogations be recorded. Would this approach be preferable to the Massachusetts approach? If states required that all interrogation be videotaped in their entirety, would that eliminate most police coercion? Would police find ways to make threats and use force that would not show up on the videotape?

3. As of 2011, the law of eighteen states and the District of Columbia required or at least strongly encouraged that interrogations be recorded. More than 500 police departments record interrogations and officers are generally supportive. *See* Brandon L. Garrett, Convicting the Innocent: Where Criminal Prosecutions Go Wrong 248 (2011). Given that videotaping is inexpensive and prevents wrongful convictions, why don't most states require it?

4. Are you surprised that one of the state legislatures to mandate video-recordings of interrogations is Texas? If Texas is thought of as a conservative state and Massachusetts a liberal state, why does Texas have the more defendant-friendly rule? Perhaps Texas is not as tough as it appears. *See* Adam M. Gershowitz, *Is Texas Tough on Crime But Soft on Criminal Procedure?* 49 Am. Crim. L. Rev. 31 (2012).

5. In states that do require interrogations to be recorded, a crucial problem is ensuring that the entire interrogation is recorded. In some instances, police stop the videotape when a suspect's story ceases to be incriminating and restart it once it begins to sound inculpatory again. *See* Garrett, Convicting the Innocent, *supra* note 3, at 32. How do we ensure that the entire interrogation is recorded? Should police department interrogation rooms be subject to 24-hour video surveillance? And, if so, how do we ensure that the interrogations are actually conducted in those rooms?

6. Videotaping station-house interrogations seems like a plausible solution, but what about interrogations that happen on the street? New technology may improve this problem as well, assuming police departments can afford it. Some police departments now issue officers "body worn video" or helmet cams that record everything an officer sees during an encounter with a suspect. *See* David A. Harris, *Picture This: Body Worn Video Devices (Head Cams) As Tools for Ensuring Fourth Amendment Compliance By Police*, 43 Tex. Tech L. Rev. 357 (2010).

7. What other steps could courts and legislatures take to eliminate coercive interrogations and reduce wrongful convictions?

Chapter VI

Compstat: Crime Fighting Breakthrough or Invitation to Manipulation?

"Right now, my boss [Tommy Carcetti] needs the crime to go down. Not three years from now, not even a year from now. He needs a ten-percent drop in the next quarter.... Be creative, gentlemen."[1]

—Mayoral Aide Michael Steintorf to the
Chief of Police and Deputy of Operations

A. Introduction

Most people outside of the criminal justice system (and many who actually work in the system) have never heard of Compstat. The purpose of Compstat was to put statistical information about crime hot spots in the hands of police supervisors immediately so that they could target those areas and reduce crime. Before Compstat was introduced in New York City in the 1990s, police commanders had to wait months before receiving aggregated crime data about the areas they were patrolling. Compstat thus provided faster and better information that commanders could use to fight crime. The Compstat system quickly spread across the country and today it is used by hundreds of police departments. The conventional wisdom is that Compstat has been a huge success.

The Wire gives Compstat prominent—and almost exclusively negative—billing. The criticism of Compstat is consistent with a main theme of *The Wire,* that institutions often do not make the right choices. Rather, the key decision-makers in the institutions are interested in making life better for themselves, not in doing the right thing. While Compstat might provide more information to commanders, *The Wire* contends that the top brass in the police department are not using the data primarily to stop crime. Rather, they are manipulating the numbers to make themselves look good.

---

1. *The Wire,* Season 5, Episode 9, at 11:40 minutes.

B. Compstat: Good, Bad, or Misused?

In the first excerpt in this chapter, William Bratton extols the virtues of Compstat and related police techniques. Bratton was the Chief of Police in New York City during the 1990s and was a key figure in the introduction of Compstat and the dramatic decrease in New York City's crime rate. Not all criminologists buy the story that Bratton dramatically reduced crime and made New York City the nation's most liveable big city. Professors John Eterno (a former NYPD captain) and Eli Silverman maintain that Bratton and other high-ranking NYPD officials privileged arrests over civil liberties and actually caused harmful backlash in many New York neighborhoods. Moreover, they question Bratton's signature accomplishment—the enormous statistical drop in crime rates—contending that the numbers have been manipulated. Interestingly, they argue that the Compstat process, both intentionally and inadvertently, led NYPD officers from the top to the bottom of the chain of command to fudge the statistics and privilege numbers over crime-fighting. As you read the excerpts below, it should be easy to see whose view David Simon, the creator of *The Wire*, agrees with. Ask yourselves whether you agree with Simon's position and whether, perhaps, he is too quick to discount the benefits of Compstat.

William Bratton, Cutting Crime and Restoring Order: What America Can Learn From New York's Finest
The Heritage Foundation, Oct. 15, 1996

I am an optimist when it comes to the issue of crime in this country. I believe that over the last several years we have begun to find answers to a problem for which many felt there were no answers. We have begun to turn the corner, and American police forces are becoming better at what they do. I think society, in general, understands more significantly what causes crime, what can be done about it, and—most important, from my perspective as a former police official—what police departments can be expected to accomplish.

* * *

To understand fully the impact of what has happened in New York in the last few years, we need to take a walk back through time—to the late 1960s and early 1970s, to the time when I went into the police department in Boston as a young patrolman. To understand the impact of changes in New York City today, we need to have an appreciation of what policing and crime were like in the 1970s and the 1980s, and indeed what they *are* like as we move through the 1990s. But before I begin that walk back through time, you may be wondering: Where *is* New York City today with respect to crime? I will give you the end of the story before I tell you the beginning, so that you can appreciate how important the figures I am about to give you are, why so much attention is being paid to the New York City Police Department, and why its successes over the last few years have begun to generate such optimism in this country and around the world. Something *can* be done about crime.

"Miracle on 42nd Street"

By the end of 1996, recorded incidents in New York City of the seven top crimes measured by the Uniform Crime Reports will be down from their 1990 figures by almost 50 percent—a 50 percent decline in America's largest city, over a six-year period of time, in the seven major crime categories of murder, rape, robbery, aggravated assault, auto theft, larceny, and burglary.... Subway crime has continued to decline, and by the end of this year will be down 80 percent from what it was in 1990.

These percentages sound great, but what do they mean in terms of the actual number of people who have not been victims of crime this year in New York City?

- *Homicides:* In 1990, there were 2,246 homicides in New York City, a figure somewhat inflated because of 85 deaths in one fire. Even if you deduct those 85 deaths from the total, this was an historic all-time high for New York City—2,246 murders in one city, in one year. Yet by the end of 1996, New York City will report fewer than 1,000 homicides for the year—a decline of almost 55 percent.

- *Shooting victims:* In 1990, there were 6,000 shooting victims in New York City. By the end of 1996, there will be about 3,000. Shooting victims are a category that police have tended not to track, but one that we track very closely in New York City because of the many things that are done now to save lives, like quicker police response and improved medical services. To understand changes in the incidence of crime, we need to look at the larger issue of crime—not only at the number of homicide victims, but also at the number of people who may have been homicide victims and were not.

- *Auto thefts:* There were 143,000 auto thefts in New York City in 1990. In 1996, there will be about 65,000.

- *Robberies:* From approximately 85,000 robberies in 1990, it is estimated that the number will fall to the 50,000 range this year.

- *Victims of crimes:* Finally, when 1996 comes to a close, there will be approximately 200,000 fewer victims of crime in New York City than there were in 1990.

To understand the significance of these figures, we need to understand how New York got to the position it held in 1990, and then look at what began to happen in 1990 and accelerated in 1994 to allow New York to be able to claim now, without fear of contradiction, that it is definitely one of the safest cities in the United States with populations over 100,000 and, among the major cities of the world, one of the safest in the world.

Rethinking the Methods of Conventional Policing

In 1970, when I joined the Boston Police Department, the country had just begun to emerge from the civil rights era—an era of race riots and assassinations, if you will. The Kerner Report had come out on what to do about crime in the United States, and American police forces began to enter a new era—one that has been described as the professional or reform era of policing. This was an era marked by what I describe as the three R's:

- *Reactive policing:* In the 1970s, 1980s, and—unfortunately for many departments in this country—into the 1990s, policing consisted of something I have come to understand as reactive policing. In the 1970s the intention was to emphasize the ability of police to respond quickly to calls for assistance. The emergency number 911 came into being in the early 1970s and spread rapidly across the country, and police departments began to focus their attention on how quickly they responded to those calls.

- *Random patrols:* The principal means of policing city streets in the 1970s and 1980s became random, not targeted, patrol. When officers were not chasing 911 calls, they were expected to randomly patrol their assigned sector and, by the visibility and randomness of their patrol, deter criminals from committing other crimes.

- *Reactive investigation:* Lastly, there was a significant effort to improve the professionalism of our detectives to investigate—but this was reactive investigation.

What do all of these elements have in common? They are all actions taken after the fact. American police forces began to measure their impact, not on what crime they were preventing, but on how they were responding to crime — which was a sea change in terms of how the police were policing American cities and why they were invented in the first place. Sir Robert Peel and the Metropolitan Police in London in the early 1800s had officers in uniform — the British "bobbies" — patrolling their beats and preventing crime by their presence, by their activity. Somehow, in the 1960s and in the increasingly permissive society of the 1970s, we began to excuse police from having any responsibility for the prevention of crime. We began to espouse that there were so many causes of crime that were beyond the control of police: How could we hold the police accountable for preventing crime when so many of the things that we believed caused crime were beyond their control?

* * *

A City Falling Apart

To appreciate the sea change that has occurred in New York City, we should revisit the New York City of 1990.... I remember flying into New York City and the gauntlet I had to run at LaGuardia Airport. There were all these cab drivers and livery drivers; it was sheer chaos, like in a Third World country, with all of them haranguing, "Take my cab, take my cab!" Finally I found a cab, got in, and off we went. I was now in the hands of somebody I did not know, who did not speak a great deal of English, in a cab that literally did not look like it was going to make it, and we were traveling down roads that were by all accounts incredible — riddled with potholes, dirty, with graffiti everywhere, and with abandoned cars, litter, and rubber tires all along the highway from LaGuardia heading into Manhattan. "Welcome to New York."

And as we entered New York and the island of Manhattan through one of the over 15 ways to get onto the island, we encountered the notorious "squeegee pests," phalanxes of them with five, ten, and 15 at the intersection. One wondered if they were going to take the torch out of the Statute of Liberty's hand and replace it with a squeegee. This could be the official symbol of the city there; it had become that bad. This was everybody's first impression of New York: Whether you were a tourist, a visitor, a person on business, or anybody coming to the city strictly by car, people intimidated you into giving them money for what passed as washing the windshield. This was your "Welcome to New York."

I remember going down the "miracle mile," Fifth Avenue. Fifth Avenue is often described as one of the richest shopping areas in the world. Once again, I saw illegal peddlers, beggars, panhandlers, filth, graffiti, and no sign of police. The only police were riding by in police cars that looked as though they were in worse shape than the taxi I was riding in. There just did not seem to be any control, or any pride, or any sense of ownership in the streets of New York.

And then I toured the subway. If I thought the streets were bad, the subways were something else. There are 700 entranceways into the city's 450 or so subway stations. Every one of those entranceways seemed like a walk down into Dante's *Inferno*. They were dirty and grimy. The whole idea of walking below ground can be disheartening to the average person, but especially so when all the turnstiles are disabled. Vandals disabled the turnstiles so that they could stand at the entrance gates with their hands out like the squeegee pests. The only thing they offered you, though, was not to be spit upon or harangued. It was, simply, "Give me your money and I'll let you through this gate."

On every platform, there were encampments of homeless people in cardboard cities. In 1990 it was estimated that 5,000 homeless people were living in the subway system in New York City — a system that killed about 178 of them that year as they fell onto the trains, or were hit by trains, or were murdered in the system. Subways are not for sleeping, and we had to initiate a major campaign to deal with that issue. Then we stepped onto the subway cars, which were remarkably free of graffiti. They were probably the only public entity in New York that was not marked with graffiti because there had been a major campaign in the 1980s to get rid of the graffiti on the cars. But on every car, it seemed, there were aggressive beggars or, once again, homeless people who had taken up residence there. It was not a very encouraging environment.

* * *

The Rise of Community Policing in the 1990s

I have a simplistic definition of a community policing program: it must have three elements.... Partnership; Problem solving; and Prevention.

First, community policing involves something that American police lost sight of in the 1970s and 1980s—partnership. The police are the most effective when they work in partnership with the community and when they are of the community, not apart from it....

* * *

And what are they going to work on? Problems. Not 911 calls, the individual incidents, but the problems that generate all those calls, and problems that generate those signs of disorder in our streets. At one point, Lee Brown had advanced an idea that we should look at crime in a medical sense. I responded to this idea when I heard it described this way: Think of malaria; for years and years the response to malaria was to swat at all those mosquitoes. But we are never going to kill all those mosquitoes. What was generating all of those mosquitoes? Swamps. Not until people went in and drained the swamps did they start dealing effectively with the problem. We have developed an inoculation to help, but draining the swamps is something that is still done to this day to control mosquitoes. Problem identification, and going after the problem, is the second P of community policing. Policing must be more focused on the problems that generate crime, whether it is actual crime or the signs of crime—something we had not been doing well in the 1970s and '80s.

Partnership and problem solving are important, but for what purpose? Prevention—to prevent crime in the first place, and to prevent all those victims.... [W]e saved several hundreds of thousands of people from becoming victims of serious crimes....

* * *

Establishing Managerial Accountability

My form of community policing ... put less emphasis on the cop on the beat and much more emphasis on the precinct commanders, the same precinct commanders who met with community councils and with neighborhood groups. They were empowered to decide how many plain clothes officers to assign, how many to put in community policing, on bicycle patrols, and in robbery squads. They were empowered to assign officers as they saw fit—in uniform or in plain clothes—to focus on the priorities of that neighborhood. If it was a 75th precinct, they would focus on the shootings and the drug dealings. If the problem was the bicycle messengers on the sidewalks of Manhattan, they would go after that. Whatever was generating the fear in their precinct, they were empowered to address it by prioritizing their responses. We decentralized the organization, and I eliminated a few levels in the organization of the force and in the hierarchy as well.

Second, we put into place a system called COMPSTAT (for computer statistics) to manage our 38,000 police officers and a 44,000-person organization. When I began running the NYPD in 1994, the crime statistics were gathered only twice a year for the sole purpose of submitting the statistics to the FBI for their semiannual and annual reports. The NYPD did not use crime statistics to manage the routine assignment of resources. At first, they told us we could not get crime stats on a daily or weekly basis—there were just too many of them. Finally, with a lot of prodding, pushing, kicking, and replacement of personnel and the naysayers, we developed a system so that I could get crime statistics every day and, more important, every week to share with the rest of the department. It was timely, accurate intelligence. Imagine trying to run a business without timely, accurate information on where your customers are and where your markets are; it is not an efficient or profitable way to operate.

Using the Private-Sector Model

We began to run the NYPD as a private profit-oriented business. What was the profit I wanted? Crime reduction. I wanted to beat my competitors—the criminals—who were out there working seven days a week, 24 hours a day. I wanted to serve my customers, the public, better; and the profit I wanted to deliver to them was reduced crime. All of my franchises—my 76 precincts—were measured, not on how many calls they responded to, but on how much crime was reduced. And every one of the 76 precincts in New York City saw a double-digit decline in crime, so the results were not just happening in the war-torn neighborhoods. Crime reductions were happening throughout the city by our empowering the precincts to act. We were running the police department as a business, and we developed the COMPSTAT process to facilitate it.

The city of New York is divided into eight geographical areas, or boroughs. We call them patrol boroughs, and each one has 8 to 10 precincts. Once a month from 7:00 to 10:00 in the morning, we would have a borough come down with its precinct commanders and detective squad commanders to meet with all the headquarters specialized units, all the super chiefs in the departments, myself as Police Commissioner, probation, parole, and District Attorney representatives, crime analysis representatives, and representatives from each of the other seven boroughs. For three hours we would work on the issue of crime in that borough: Why is it up? Why is it down? What's happening? We utilized computerized statistics. Using very large computerized pin maps to show where the crime is occurring, we would ask ourselves: What are we doing about it? Where are we making arrests? Where are the parolees living? Large amounts of information were reduced to the simplest form by such computer analysis.

Sharing Information

Another major element of what we did in this new process at NYPD was inclusion, not exclusion. The NYPD had been run as an exclusive organization; it would exclude people from information. We approached it from the other direction—inclusion: Give everybody as much information as they need and want. The sharing went on in that room from 7:00 to 10:00 in the morning; everybody was sharing information. If an issue was raised, such as why someone could not make an arrest, and the answer came out that it was because the District Attorney would not give them the complaints, I could confront the District Attorney's representatives who were right there. Instead of spending three or four days trying to track the D.A. down, I could get answers directly from someone right there in the room. And if that representative did not have the answer, then I would call the D.A. Intimacy, the sharing of information in as wide a range as possible, inclusion, and COMPSTAT were important to this process.

It is my belief that the COMPSTAT process can be utilized effectively by any police department, in this country and abroad. The COMPSTAT process is made up of four very simple elements:

- *Timely, accurate intelligence.* What good is crime statistics information for preventing crime when it is gathered only twice a year?

- *Rapid response.* Using the COMPSTAT process, we could identify a trend developing with only two or three incidences, instead of waiting for 40 or 50 over six months. Sharing this information so that everybody is aware of a problem and works together on providing resources very quickly to address that problem allows us to rapidly respond to where the crime is happening—using plain clothes, uniforms, specialized units, or whatever is required.

- *Effective tactics.* We were able to ask ourselves: What works? The answer could be plain clothes, uniforms, or coordinated activity with the Feds or the D.A.

- *Relentless follow-up.* People in that meeting knew they were coming back the next month, and that next month we were going to talk about the same issues that were raised this month. The issues don't go away. We weren't discussing something that happened one time and then could be put on the shelf. In the COMPSTAT process, everyone knew they were coming back to explain why crime is up or why it is down. Over the last two years, every precinct commander in the police department has been replaced. Many of them have been promoted up because they were doing such a good job, but many others were moved out because they were not doing a good job. They were not moved out because they were not reducing crime. They were moved out because they didn't understand the problems in their community and they were not responding to these problems effectively; after several tries, if they still were not responding, they were replaced.

* * *

Getting Results

Similarly, in New York City, we now know where the enemy is, up to the minute; we know where the problems are, and we go after them. That COMPSTAT meeting room is a high-pressure environment, with 200 to 250 police officials and others looking at crime. It is show time. In one of our meetings, Jack Maple, my principal crime strategist, asked the commander of one of the east New York precincts to put on the map all of the drug complaints in that precinct; and up they went. The whole map was covered with complaints, but there were clusters, the hot spots. Then he asked the commander to mark where his drug units were making arrests last month. Those went up right off the bat. Interestingly, the complaints were on one side of the map; the drug arrests were on the other side. You would think they would overlap each other. This process graphically showed what was going on under the old system, where police were rated "effective" by the number of arrests they were making, not by the problems they were solving. They were rated on the incidents they responded to, not on the problems they were solving.

When we asked the drug unit commander why his officers were making arrests on that side of the precinct and not over where the complaints were, he responded that the complaints were coming from the public housing developments. When asked why they were not making arrests there if the drug complaints came from there, he responded that it was hard to make arrests there. Can you imagine what it is like to live there if the police will not even go there to make arrests? That was the mentality running the NYPD, and I guarantee it is still running many major police departments....

* * *

I believe that as a profession we found better ways of policing in New York City, and a lot of our success lies under the umbrella of community policing and the philosophy it espouses. You and I—you as the public and I in my former capacity as a member of the police force—can work together to deal with the problems that you and I identify. And we will work from the basic premise that it is much better to prevent a crime than to solve it after the fact.

———————

Notes and Questions

1. Are you astounded to hear that as recently as the 1990s, the New York City Police Department only gathered crime statistics twice per year?

2. In 1994, Compstat analyzed arrest statistics and determined that 28% of police officers in the Queens borough of New York City had not made a single arrest in the first half of the year. *See* Eli B. Silverman, NYPD Battles Crime 105 (1999).

3. Can the increase in information flow, officer accountability, and strategic planning explain, at least partly, the dramatic crime decrease that Bratton describes? Or are the numbers simply too dramatic to believe? Is it possible that violent crime could actually drop by fifty percent in a period of less than seven years as Bratton suggests? Even more stunningly, could the number of homicides in New York City drop by 1,000 (a fifty-five percent decline) in such a short period of time?

4. Commissioner Bratton describes the "relentless follow-up" of the Compstat process and how precinct commanders were "moved out" if they "were not doing a good job." Is the pressure Bratton describes necessarily a positive motivator? Doesn't pressure sometimes lead people to make bad decisions and cut corners? Watch *The Wire*, Season 3, Episode 11, at 11:10 minutes, in which Commissioner Burrell tells Councilman Carcetti about Major Colvin's Hamsterdam operation. Burrell explains:

> Major Colvin lost the necessary perspective that is required for command. Now, we were all under pressure to reduce crime before year end. And he responded poorly to that pressure.... The pressure was applied all the way down the line. From headquarters, to the district commanders, to the shift and sector supervisors.

As the one applying the pressure in New York City, do you think Commissioner Bratton understood how far down the chain that pressure reached? And do you think he contemplated the types of misconduct that lower ranking officers might have engaged in as a result?

5. At first glance, *The Wire* portrays Compstat in an exclusively negative light, but is it more nuanced than the first glance appears? Watch *The Wire*, Season 3, Episode 2, at 33:45 minutes, in which Deputy Rawls questions a district commander. Rawls elicits that the 278 officers under the commander's supervision made only 16 felony arrests and recovered zero handguns in the span of a month—an abysmal record. The commander is also unable to connect four homicides that occurred within blocks of each other in a single night. The scene ends with Rawls telling the commander that "you've got eight hours to get a grip on this mess or you're done." Thereafter, when the commander still has not cleaned up the drug corners in his district, the Commissioner demotes him on the spot. As the other district commanders sit stunned, the Commissioner asks them "anyone else having trouble with the writing on the wall?" *The Wire*, Season 3, Episode 3, Opening Scene. Isn't this type of accountability among the top level of the police department what we should expect? And doesn't Compstat make that accountability possible?

John A. Eterno & Eli Silverman, The New York City Police Department's Compstat: Dream or Nightmare?

8 International Journal of Police Science & Management 218 (2006)

Compstat tributes are extensive. Compstat has been described as 'perhaps the single most important organizational/administrative innovation in policing during the latter half of the 20th century.' A Criminology and Public Policy editor recently termed Compstat 'arguably one of the most significant strategic innovations in policing in the last couple of decades.' The authors of a major study note that Compstat 'has already been recognized as a major innovation in American policing.' In 1996, Compstat was awarded the prestigious Innovations in American Government Award from the Ford Foundation and the John F. Kennedy School of Government at Harvard University. Former Mayor Giuliani proclaims Compstat as his administration's 'crown jewel.'

Since Compstat was first unveiled by the New York City Police Department (NYPD) in 1994, a Police Foundation's 1999 survey for the National Institute of Justice (NIJ) revealed that a third of the nation's 515 largest police departments had implemented a Compstat-like programme and 20 percent were planning to do so by 2001. The same survey found that about 70 percent of police departments with Compstat programmes reported attending a NYPD Compstat meeting. Our own research indicates that very few of the over 250 outsiders who attended Compstat meetings between 1994 and September 1997 were exposed to any Compstat elements other than the meetings (with the exception of a NYPD booklet on Compstat). It is unlikely that the Police Foundation's 70 percent differed much in their exposure to Compstat. In fact, there may be some overlap between the two groups.

… Attendance at a Compstat meeting, while a useful introduction, does not provide adequate preparation for introducing and establishing Compstat. In fact, it may be misleading because attendees often become mesmerised by the flashy overhead display of multiple crime maps synchronised with technologically advanced portrayals of computerised crime statistics.

The comments and critiques in this paper are based on over 25 years of research of the NYPD. This understanding was developed using direct observations, interviews and experience. Over the years hundreds of Compstat meetings were attended. Interviews, both formal and informal, were conducted with leaders, managers, and supervisors as well as the rank and file. Field observations were conducted in numerous locales including precincts, the street, boroughs and headquarters.

A Critical Examination of Compstat

This in-depth understanding, based on information and data uniquely available to the authors, informs this paper which, while acknowledging Compstat's strengths, illuminates Compstat drawbacks. This approach can hopefully assist other law enforcement agencies as they implement Compstat.

Compstat is often associated with broken windows theory…. ['J]ust as a broken window left unattended was a sign that nobody cares and leads to more severe property damage, so disorderly conditions and behaviors left untended send a signal nobody cares and results in fear of crime, serious crime, and the "downward spiral of urban decay."' From this, [broken windows proponents] suggest that to influence crime rates, police need to be attentive to minor quality of life offences and use 'assertive policing' methods.

One may assume, therefore, that the underpinning of Compstat is the theory of broken windows. Based on our direct experience and knowledge of the development of

Compstat, we know that this, however, is *not* the case.... Rather, Compstat was designed as an innovation essentially to fix what Bratton felt was a dysfunctional organisation, that is the NYPD. Jack Maple, one of the key figures to develop Compstat, even stated that it was only years after Compstat's development that he had read the broken windows article and then realised how neatly Compstat might accommodate broken windows theory. Compstat was developed as a management tool, specific to the NYPD, in an attempt to bring down crime. The fact that certain aspects of the programme may fit with broken windows theory is merely an afterthought....

* * *

One of the more disturbing aspects of Compstat is an overwhelming focus on crime control....

* * *

What good do police departments do if they control crime but at the cost of violating citizens' fundamental rights? For example, controlling crime, maintaining order, and protecting life and property can be done very easily by enacting Draconian laws and aggressively and illegally enforcing them (eg, curfews, cruel and unusual punishments, disrespecting search and seizure guidelines, etc). If the cost of maintaining order is living under such conditions, the price is too high. One might retort that this has not happened and never will. Given the right conditions, however, such a horrid society can develop anywhere. In fact, as we shall see, the evidence from the New York City experience with Compstat — often cited as the pre-eminent example of the success of Compstat — suggests that some major concerns surrounded the programme especially during the initial years of deployment.

The relationship between Compstat and crime declines has been debated by scholars. Nevertheless crime downswings in Compstat police departments have also given rise to concern about due process. For example, civilian complaints during this early period of Compstat dramatically increased. [One scholar has explained that] 'Civilian complaints against police for allegedly illegal searches skyrocketed by 135% in the first two years illegal vehicle searches jumped ... 108% ... [and] allegations of illegal apartment searches shot up 179%.' Thus, as crime decreased, civilian complaints for abuse of authority increased. This negative relationship is certainly glaring but only one of several measures indicating a problem.

Self-report data during this same period also indicate that officers were abusing their authority. In 1997, a survey of 1,259 New York City officers who worked in all 76 of New York City's precincts was conducted. Eterno shows that officers who accepted the aggressive-policing paradigm are significantly more likely to violate the constitutional rights of citizens by conducting illegal searches and stops. When two separate methods, official data and self-report data, indicate abuse of authority by officers, one can be confident that a problem was occurring.

Additionally, anecdotal evidence from New York City communities — especially minority communities — suggests that they felt alienated, to say the least, by the police during the early years of Compstat. Minority communities were particularly outspoken about police abuse. They cited events such as the sexual abuse of a prisoner, Abner Louima, who had a stick placed up his rectum by the officers who had him in custody; the shooting of an unarmed black man, Amadou Diallo, 41 shots by police; and the shooting of another unarmed black man, Patrick Dorismond. These are just a few examples of incidents in which issues between police and minorities became tense. To some, especially those in minority communities, the police were like an army of occupation. During this time, citizens were quoted as stating that people, 'are locked up because of their race or their politics, as in Nazi Germany.'

... Prior to Compstat, NYPD had adopted a service style. The emphasis was on 'service and the beat cop.' After Compstat the focus was on formal sanctions: arrests and summonses to be reflected in the Compstat meetings so the commanding officer could defend him/herself.... This was a drastic change for NYPD: from 'service and the beat cop' to 'crime and commanding officers.' Another problem with Compstat is that the management style not only alienated some members of the community but also alienated some in the NYPD. Officers below the executive rank were frequently subjected to a top-down management style and alienated by Compstat.

* * *

... [One scholar] interviewed a recently retired NYPD captain, exposing this Compstat weakness. 'Captain Costello's primary complaint was not pay, but what he viewed as the numbingly relentless demand to top his own arrest or summons numbers.' Compstat was perceived as a legalistic-style numbers game combined with leadership by fear. Captains feared embarrassment during their presentations. On some occasions, high-level executives would berate them in public if their crime numbers were not decreasing. That is, commanding officers feared presenting at Compstat meetings and would do almost anything to escape the embarrassment of having crime statistics going up. In practice, fear was observed as a central aspect of Compstat in New York City.

In addition to leadership style and officer alienation, another Compstat weakness derives from the department's failure to motivate the vast majority of officers. Commentary on Compstat would have us think that it is an all-inclusive programme. That is, the rhetoric of Compstat suggests that commanding officers of precincts are able to change the behaviour of most officers under their command such that the vast majority of officers will work in unison to decrease crime.... Based on direct observations and numerous interviews with NYPD personnel, however, we can confidently state that this was not a common occurrence in the NYPD. Conversely, managers tended to guard their power jealously. Executives, at times, blamed the lower ranks for any increase in crime rates, to the point of occasionally yelling, screaming and publicly berating them at Compstat meetings. Additionally, executives took credit for decreasing crime rates, giving little or no credit to the rank and file.

The idea that commanding officers have enormous control over the officers under their command and that somehow the bureaucratic sanctions motivated many officers is not supported by research. In a 1997 survey ... NYPD officers indicated that very few at the precinct level were motivated by the Department's sanctions. In fact, the survey of 1,259 officers who worked in precincts suggests that commanding officers have very little influence on most officers. In the questionnaire, officers are placed into hypothetical situations and asked how they would respond. The questionnaire was scientifically designed so that the researcher could determine various influences on officers' stop-and-search behaviours. Influences included on the questionnaire were the police culture, the police bureaucracy, the community in which officers worked and the law. The bureaucracy was operationalised using commanding officers' statements at a roll call. Assuming the commanding officers were motivating officers, the statements that should have elicited more aggressive behaviour on the part of most officers did not have that effect on the vast majority of officers. In fact, bureaucratic sanctions were practically ineffectual indicating that Compstat has little or no effect on most officers. This is, of course, another weakness, namely, Compstat fails to motivate most officers. There were, however, some interesting exceptions in the results of the statistical analysis of the questionnaire that shows an even deeper weakness.

Officers were given four situations: car stop, person stop, weapon search and drug search. The only situation that had an effect on officers was the car stop situation in which the commanding officer stated at a roll call that, 'The precinct is down on felony arrests compared to last year's figures.' As officers are aware (and as Compstat works), the commanding officer is consistently compared with last year's arrest numbers. Assuming that the Compstat process is working, every officer in the precinct should immediately try to make more felony arrests when the commanding officer states he or she needs them. On the questionnaire, however, very few officers changed their behaviour and only did so for the car stop situation in which the commanding officer made the above statement. What is interesting about this is who changed their behaviour and how.

While most officers simply disregarded the commanding officers comments, two groups of officers were markedly influenced by the commanding officer's statement in the car stop situation. The first group was anti-crime officers. We expect them to be influenced since they are the most aggressive crime-fighting unit in the precinct. They work in plain clothes and may advance to the rank of detective after serving a period of time in the anti-crime unit. These officers are supposed to be proactive. One way to be proactive is to make car stops with the intention of finding a felony arrest. One would hope that these officers would only do legal, constitutional car stops in their search for an arrest. However, the results from the questionnaire indicate that when officers in this unit merely heard the commanding officer's request, approximately 45 percent did an illegal car stop! By way of comparison, generally in the questionnaire, only 15 percent of officers violated constitutional guidelines in the car stop situation. Anti-crime is an aggressive unit and we expect some increase in search behaviour, but the large increase from 15 percent to 45 percent in unconstitutional behaviour merely upon hearing the commanding officer's request, is quite unexpected. However, it gets worse.

As stated, there was a second group of officers influenced by the commanding officer's statement. These are officers who have 'inside the precinct assignments.' These officers are the ones who generally work in the station house, for example crime prevention officers, community affairs officers and domestic violence officers. These officers are appointed to their positions at the discretion of the commanding officer. These officers also responded to the commanding officer's statement by being proactive. Alarmingly, 60 percent of them indicated that they would do an illegal car stop merely on hearing the commanding officer's statement at a roll call. What does this mean?

Based on the questionnaire, it is likely that Compstat-driven activity is accomplished by very few officers who are most directly influenced by the commanding officer. In fact, most patrol officers do not react to Compstat or, for that matter, to most Department sanctions. Those officers who do the work for Compstat—who secure many of the arrests and summonses that are reflected in the Compstat figures—owe their assignments to the commanding officer. These results, perhaps alarming, make sense. That is, those officers who are directly influenced by the commanding officer respond to his or her needs. Most others disregard the comments. Thus, Compstat failed to motivate most NYPD officers. Contrary to the rhetoric of Compstat, few are actually involved in crime-fighting and doing the work necessary to help the commanding officer at Compstat meetings. Importantly, some of these officers are doing so at the cost of violating the Constitutional rights of citizens. Any level of illegal behaviour is unacceptable but this level is also unconscionable. This increase in illegal behaviour is apparently another by-product of the Compstat process as initially practised by the NYPD.

* * *

Even if we assume that fighting crime (or the numbers of crimes) is the key to polic-ing, we must ask if the aggressive police methods of Compstat are the most effective and efficient way to do it. Indeed, one weakness with Compstat is that officers will not ag-gressively seek victims (eg rape, domestic violence and child abuse victims who are less likely to report to the police) for fear of creating another 'number'! ...

Overall, the police in New York City using the Compstat process should be given at least some credit for decreasing crime. However, the concerns outlined in this paper require us to: (1) acknowledge that there are some weaknesses in the process as developed in New York City; (2) learn from those weaknesses; and (3) begin to develop models of policing that will take into account lessons learned.

Beyond Compstat: An Alternative Model

Compstat is an important innovation that should not be discarded. However, police managers need to understand the ramifications of merely emulating the NYPD method.... In this section, some suggestions are outlined on how Compstat could more properly be integrated into democratic policing.

... The positive aspects are: efficiency (effective at reducing crime); clarification of who is in command (high-ranking NYPD officials run the Compstat meetings and every-one is aware they are in charge); workers aware of expectations (officers know how many arrests and summonses are expected of them); and reduction of bias (everyone is treated equally, although the negative aspect of this is that everyone may be treated equally badly when the system is abused. The negative aspects are: depriving employees of a voice in decision-making (lower ranks are unable to innovate outside of getting fewer crime complaint numbers); serving the public receives little recognition; concealment of mistakes (lower ranks will rarely admit mistakes for fear of retaliation by senior of-ficers which will have the effect of maintaining non-working elements of the bureaucracy such as not being proactive in detecting victims of serious crimes and then taking po-lice reports for those crimes); discouraging loyalty to the organisation (many officers who have the skills and abilities to get other jobs will leave including officers such as Cap-tain Costello); feelings of alienation (the typical saying on the NYPD is 'twenty and out' meaning most officers will leave as soon as possible and many take jobs in the Fire De-partment or policing in the suburbs where pay is higher and, generally, the worker is treated with more dignity).

The first step that should be taken by an agency emulating Compstat is to borrow from the human relations management school. That is, management should consider the roles, feelings, frustrations and needs of those in the organisation. Commanders and lower ranking officers who are thought of as part of a 'team', rather than dispens-able instruments to be yelled at when numbers are not going down, are more likely to be productive, innovative, to fix and take responsibility for mistakes and, most im-portantly, treat the public with respect. This is directly related to the most important change (even paradigm shift) that needs to be taken by police organizations that adopt Compstat. Reducing crime, as admirable as that is, is not the most critical goal of policing in democracies; it is incomplete. The most critical goal is to protect Consti-tutional rights while, at the same time, attempting to reduce crime. This is what makes policing such a high calling and so difficult in a free society. It is easy to reduce crime without respecting rights: simply arrest, stop, search and generally disrespect those whom you merely suspect of doing a crime. Certainly, you will reduce crime, but at what price?

* * *

… Compstat is most frequently understood by its most visible elements. These include: up-to-date, computerized crime data, crime analysis and advanced crime mapping as the bases for regularised, interactive crime strategy meetings which hold managers accountable for specific crime strategies and solutions in their areas.

It is fair to say that the widespread diffusion of Compstat refers to these most noticeable elements. Too often, therefore, Compstat has been interpreted as primarily a meeting with a statistical computer program which, when it generates accurate and timely crime statistics, transforms a traditional bureaucracy into a flexible, adaptable police agency geared to effective crime control strategies. In the vernacular, it is only necessary to display computer generated crime maps and to pressure commanders in order to 'make the dots go away.' This superficial approach is emblematic of the quick managerial fix approach, thus contributing to the misunderstanding and misapplication of Compstat.

Compstat, however, was originally a far more complex product of changes in managerial and organisational arrangements including flattening, decentralisation, greater personal authority, discretion and autonomy, geographic managerial accountability and enhanced problem-solving. Compstat cannot be a fully viable entity if the above administrative, managerial and operational activities do not precede it.

* * *

… Compstat offers a mechanism by which many resources can be brought to bear on a problem. It is capable, as indicated above, of stressing and measuring citizen-police encounters as well as problem-solving activities. If Compstat meetings were to highlight these endeavours, they would be more central to the NYPD's mission.

Meetings, then, should involve commanding officers talking about crime problems and solutions to those problems, some being very innovative. However, it should be a team approach in which senior officers do not berate but rather offer assistance to the commander. If a commander is failing, he or she should not be publicly embarrassed but, privately and in a respectful way, reprimanded. If an officer needs to be removed from an assignment, it must be done in a way that is not demeaning to the person.… Police need to set an example by respecting members in their own ranks as well as community members. In this way, whatever resources or police behaviours are needed for an area (including long-term strategies) can be brought to bear on a problem. Idealistic and misleading depictions of Compstat are not helpful. We need to learn and embrace the lessons of Compstat, but modify it so that we focus on problem-solving, service and, most importantly, protecting the freedoms and rights that are part of the democratic society we so deeply cherish.

Notes and Questions

1. Watch *The Wire*, Season 3, Episode 1, at 44:40 minutes, in which Acting Commissioner Burrell meets with the Mayor to discuss how Councilman Carcetti is making waves about the Baltimore crime rate. The Mayor and his aide say the Commissioner should show a 5% drop in felonies and that he should get the total number of murders below 250 for the year. Commissioner Burrell says that number is not possible and the best he could do is possibly 275 murders for the year. The Mayor's aide responds, "that's a promise, right?" Shortly thereafter, Commissioner Burrell addresses his commanders at a Comp-

stat meeting and explains "the word from on high is that felony rates, district by district, will decline by 5% before the end of the year.... In addition, we will hold this year's murders to 275 or less." When an officer tries to challenge the feasibility of the numbers, Commissioner Burrell pointedly remarks "Any of you who can't bring in the numbers we need will be replaced by someone who can." Do you think this is what happens in the real world? Do politicians actually demand the crime statistics they want? And do police commissioners instruct their subordinates to make those numbers happen?

2. In more recent scholarship, Professors Eterno and Silverman contend that a substantial portion of New York City's decrease in crime has come from cooking the books. They explain that New York City has reported a decrease in crime for sixteen straight years and that from 1990 to 2009 the claimed decrease has totaled more than 77%. Moreover, they explain that the decrease came at the same time that the total number of officers employed had declined by thousands. As one example for the decrease, Etero and Silverman point to burglary statistics, which dropped by more than 40% from 2001 to 2009. They hypothesize that the decrease is primarily due to reclassifying burglaries as criminal trespasses, a lower level offense. During the same time period, the number of criminal trespasses in New York City rose by more than 70%, an enormous figure that Eterno and Silverman suggest cannot be a coincidence. *See* John A. Eterno & Eli B. Silverman, The Crime Numbers Game: Management by Manipulation 26–27, 43 (2012).

3. Given the strong criticism of Compstat in the Eterno & Silverman article, you might be surprised to know that one of the authors provided a very favorable picture of the initial use of Compstat. In a 1999 book about the New York City Police Department, Professor Silverman explained in detail how Compstat had encouraged police accountability and led to dramatic improvements in the flow of information. *See* Eli B. Silverman, NYPD Battles Crime 97–124 (1999). Are you surprised how Professor Silverman's opinion could change in such a short time? Is it the case that Compstat is effective if used correctly but a dangerous tool if police brass and supervisors send the wrong signals?

4. The manipulation of crime statistics can take many forms, including officers simply refusing to take police reports. For example, when a woman told police that a passing bicyclist had groped her two days in a row, an officer told her looking for the suspect "would be a waste of time because [she] didn't know who the guy was" and that she should ignore the incidents because "[t]hese things happen." *See* Al Baker & Joseph Goldstein, *Police Tactic: Keeping Crime Reports Off the Books*, N.Y. Times, Dec. 31, 2011.

5. In one brief scene, *The Wire* paints a picture of just how easy it is for police on the street to manipulate statistics. Watch *The Wire*, Season 3, Episodes 2, at 28:15 minutes in which senior commanders praise a junior officer who eliminated two auto thefts because it was "not impossible the car was borrowed" and two armed robberies because it was "too dark to ID the weapon—not impossible knife wasn't a comb."

6. Perhaps an even bigger problem is the manipulation of crime statistics by the commanding officers themselves. Watch *The Wire*, Season 3, Episode 3, at 23:10 minutes in which a police lieutenant and another supervisor sit in the major's office to figure out which felonies they can downgrade to misdemeanors to improve their division's statistics. The problem is nicely summed up when one commander asks Major Valcheck "How you gonna give Rawls his numbers?" Valcheck replies "flex squads on the corners, foot patrols ... overtime ... and if that don't work, cheat on the stats." *The Wire*, Season 3, Episode 3, at 28:05 minutes.

7. An interesting storyline of Season 2 of *The Wire* is Colonel Rawls' effort to avoid taking responsibility for the thirteen dead women found in the shipping container. Although

Compstat is not introduced until Season 3, it looms even if unnamed. Rawls wants to avoid any additional homicides that will harm his clearance rate. He tells an official from the Maryland State Police that "I have fought and scratched and clawed for four months to get my clearance rate up above 50%. And right now it stands at exactly 51.6%. Do you happen to know what my clearance rate will be if I take thirteen who-done-its off your hands? Thirty-nine point four percent...." Watch *The Wire*, Season 2, Episode 2, at 27:25 minutes.

8. Another way for police departments to manipulate their numbers is to file charges before a case is fully investigated so that they can remove the matter from the list of un-solved cases. For example, Watch *The Wire*, Season 1, Episode 6, at 26:20 minutes, in which Sergeant Landsman orders Detective Bunk to issue arrest warrants in a case McNulty and Bunk are still working on. Bunk tries to talk him out of it, saying "this weak ass shit is not going to get past a grand jury," but Sergeant Landsman refuses to back down. Although a weak case will cause problems for prosecutors once it advances to the next stage of the crim-inal justice process, that fact is of little concern to Major Rawls and Sergeant Landsman who simply want to improve their clearance rate. As Detective Freamon explains in the next scene, "[Rawls] can charge anything he wants and get credit for the clearance. The grand jury doesn't indict, [it] drops the case, [but Rawls] keeps the stats." *Id.* at 30:55 minutes.

9. *Telling the Truth Like Crazy*: Adrian Schoolcraft, an officer in NYPD's 81st Precinct, believed his colleagues were refusing to accept legitimate criminal charges in order to keep crime statistics low. After Schoolcraft met with investigators to level that accusation, he "was forcibly taken from his home in Queens by senior police officials and delivered to a hospital psychiatric ward." Jim Dwyer, *Telling the Truth Like Crazy*, N.Y. TIMES, Mar. 8, 2012. A New York newspaper, *The Village Voice*, undertook years of investigation into Schoolcraft's institutionalization and his underlying allegations. *The Voice*'s series, "The NYPD Tapes," prompted the NYPD Chief of Police to order an investigation, which re-sulted in a 95-page report. Although the NYPD refused to release the report, *The Village Voice* subsequently unearthed a copy, which found that there had been "a concerted ef-fort to deliberately underreport crime in the 81st Precinct." *See* Graham Rayman, *The NYPD Tapes Confirmed*, THE VILLAGE VOICE, Mar. 7, 2012.

10. Is the problem of statistical manipulation unique to law enforcement? Watch *The Wire*, Season 4, Episode 9, at 34:45 minutes, in which teachers are instructed to "teach to the test" to improve their school's statistics. Rather than teaching what the students should be learning, the teachers are instructed to teach the actual questions that will be on the statewide examination. Officer Pryzbylewski explains that the administrators are "juking the stats ... making robberies into larcenies ... I've been here before." Is the educational system comparable to the manipulation associated with Compstat?

11. Closer to home, is it possible that law schools have been manipulating their employ-ment numbers in order to enhance their *U.S. News and World Report* rankings? *See* Sophia Pearson & Phil Mitford, *New York, Chicago Law Schools Among Group Sued by Graduates Over Job Data*, BLOOMBERG, Feb. 1, 2012 (describing how more than a dozen law schools had recently been sued for "falsely inflating graduate employment rates"). Indeed, the lies are so overt that some criminal law experts believe that law deans and *U.S. News and World Report* committed felonies such as wire fraud, mail fraud, conspiracy, racketeering, and mak-ing false statements by providing false statistics. *See* Morgan Cloud & George Shepherd, *Law Deans in Jail*, available at http://papers.ssrn.com/sol3/papers.cfm?abstract_id=1990746/.

Chapter VII

Hamsterdam: How Should the Criminal Justice System Respond to Drugs?

"A brilliant idea. Insane and illegal, but ... brilliant nonetheless."[1]

—Deputy Rawls, upon learning about Hamsterdam

A. Introduction

The criminalization and punishment of drugs in the United States has an enormous impact on the entire criminal justice system. There are more than 2.3 million people currently incarcerated in the United States, making America the world's leader in incarceration. Roughly a quarter of American prisoners are incarcerated for drug offenses. Many others are serving time for theft, burglary, or prostitution, but were led to those crimes by the desire to satisfy their drug habit. The United States spends billions of dollars to lock up these drug dealers and users every year. But prisons and jails are not the only cost. Police officers must spend time arresting and processing offenders. Courts are clogged with drug cases. Parole and probation officers spend time monitoring offenders once they are released from prison or jail. Whatever your view of America's war on drugs—and some very smart people come out on different sides of the issue—there is no question that drug use and related crime is a costly and vexing problem in the United States. *The Wire* shows us the horror of drug use from many angles. Drug addiction destroys the lives of many characters in the series. The black market for drug distribution is responsible for dozens of murders and other violence that is committed in the name of fending off rival dealers, keeping soldiers in line, and ensuring profit for those at the top of the pyramid. And the incarceration of drug dealers removes many African-American men from their communities, leaving children without fathers. How do we weigh the costs and benefits of current drug policy? Is the status quo the necessary or best course of action? Should incarceration be the primary response to the problem? Would legalization of drugs, or partial decriminalization stop some of the violence? And, finally, is Deputy Rawls correct to say that the Hamsterdam experiment in Season 3 is "insane and illegal?" The materials below consider these questions.

---

1. *The Wire*, Season 3, Episode 10, at 48:05 minutes.

B. Should We Legalize, Decriminalize, or Ignore Ordinary Drug Use?

Perhaps no criminal justice problem has garnered as much attention as the legalization (or decriminalization) of drugs. Most people have very strong opinions about how society should handle drug use, and they are often very eager to share their views. But are most people's opinions on either side of the drug debate well informed? A full analysis of the legalization or decriminalization question is beyond the scope of this textbook. However, the excerpts below raise many of the most important questions that policymakers should ask in determining drug policy. The DEA, quite obviously, takes a position strongly opposed to drug legalization. Professor Steven Duke, on the other hand, describes a litany of social problems caused or at least exacerbated by current drug policy. Finally, Professor Steven Wisotsky contends that facts and evidence will never settle the legalization or decriminalization debate and that logic will never win the day. In reading the materials below, consider whether they have any impact on your pre-existing position on drug policy in the United States.

United States Drug Enforcement Agency, Speaking Out against Drug Legalization

4 (2003)

… We have made significant progress in fighting drug use and drug trafficking in America. Now is not the time to abandon our efforts.

Demand Reduction

Legalization advocates claim that the fight against drugs has not been won and is, in fact, unconquerable. They frequently state that people still take drugs, drugs are widely available, and that efforts to change this are futile. They contend that legalization is the only workable alternative.

The facts are to the contrary to such pessimism. On the demand side, the U.S. has reduced casual use, chronic use and addiction, and prevented others from even starting using drugs. Overall drug use in the United States is down by *more than a third* since the late 1970s. That's 9.5 million people fewer using illegal drugs. We've reduced cocaine use by an astounding 70% during the last 15 years. That's 4.1 million fewer people using cocaine.

Almost two-thirds of teens say their schools are drugfree, according to a new survey of teen drug use conducted by The National Center on Addiction and Substance Abuse (CASA) at Columbia University. This is the first time in the seven-year history of the study that a majority of public school students report drug-free schools.

The good news continues. According to the 2001–2002 PRIDE survey, student drug use has reached the lowest level in nine years. According to the author of the study, "following 9/11, Americans seemed to refocus on family, community, spirituality, and nation." These statistics show that U.S. efforts to educate kids about the dangers of drugs is making an impact. Like smoking cigarettes, drug use is gaining a stigma which is the best cure for this problem, as it was in the 1980s, when government, business, the media and other national institutions came together to do something about the growing problem of drugs and drug-related violence. This is a trend we should encourage—not send the opposite message of greater acceptance of drug use.

The crack cocaine epidemic of the 1980s and early 1990s has diminished greatly in scope. And we've reduced the number of *chronic* heroin users over the last decade. In addition, the number of new marijuana users and cocaine users continues to steadily decrease.

The number of new heroin users dropped from 156,000 in 1976 to 104,000 in 1999, *a reduction of 33 percent.*

Of course, drug policy also has an impact on general crime. In a 2001 study, the British Home Office found violent crime and property crime increased in the late 1990s in every wealthy country except the United States. Our murder rate is too high, and we have much to learn from those with greater success — but this reduction is due in part to a reduction in drug use.

There is still much progress to make. There are still far too many people using cocaine, heroin and other illegal drugs. In addition, there are emerging drug threats like Ecstasy and methamphetamine. But the fact is that our current policies balancing prevention, enforcement, and treatment have kept drug usage outside the scope of acceptable behavior in the U.S.

To put things in perspective, less than 5 percent of the population uses illegal drugs of any kind. Think about that: More than 95 percent of Americans do not use drugs. How could anyone but the most hardened pessimist call this a losing struggle?

Supply Reduction

There have been many successes on the supply side of the drug fight, as well. For example, Customs officials have made major seizures along the U.S.-Mexico border during a six-month period after September 11th, seizing almost twice as much as the same period in 2001. At one port in Texas, seizures of methamphetamine are up 425% and heroin by 172%. Enforcement makes a difference — traffickers' costs go up with these kinds of seizures.

Purity levels of Colombian cocaine are declining too, according to an analysis of samples seized from traffickers and bought from street dealers in the United States. The purity has declined by nine percent, from 86 percent in 1998, to 78 percent in 2001. There are a number of possible reasons for this decline in purity, including DEA supply reduction efforts in South America.

One DEA program, Operation Purple, involves 28 countries and targets the illegal diversion of chemicals used in processing cocaine and other illicit drugs. DEA's labs have discovered that the oxidation levels for cocaine have been greatly reduced, suggesting that Operation Purple is having a detrimental impact on the production of cocaine.

Another likely cause is that traffickers are diluting their cocaine to offset the higher costs associated with payoffs to insurgent and paramilitary groups in Colombia. The third possible cause is that cocaine traffickers simply don't have the product to simultaneously satisfy their market in the United States and their rapidly growing market in Europe. As a result, they are cutting the product to try to satisfy both.

Whatever the final reasons for the decline in drug purity, it is good news for the American public. It means less potent and deadly drugs are hitting the streets, and dealers are making less profits — that is, unless they raise their own prices, which helps price more and more Americans out of the market.

Purity levels have also been reduced on methamphetamine by controls on chemicals necessary for its manufacture. The average purity of seized methamphetamine samples dropped from 72 percent in 1994 to 40 percent in 2001.

The trafficking organizations that sell drugs are finding that their profession has become a lot more costly. In the mid-1990s, the DEA helped dismantle Burma's Shan United Army, at the time the world's largest heroin trafficking organization, which in two years helped reduce the amount of Southeast Asian heroin in the United States from 63 percent of the market to 17 percent of the market. In the mid-1990s, the DEA helped disrupt the Cali cartel, which had been responsible for much of the world's cocaine.

Progress does not come overnight. America has had a long, dark struggle with drugs. It's not a war we've been fighting for 20 years. We've been fighting it for 120 years. In 1880, many drugs, including opium and cocaine, were legal. We didn't know their harms, but we soon learned. We saw the highest level of drug use ever in our nation, per capita. There were over 400,000 opium addicts in our nation. That's twice as many per capita as there are today. And like today, we saw rising crime with that drug abuse. But we fought those problems by passing and enforcing tough laws and by educating the public about the dangers of these drugs. And this vigilance worked—by World War II, drug use was reduced to the very margins of society. And that's just where we want to keep it. With a 95 percent success rate—bolstered by an effective, three-pronged strategy combining education/prevention, enforcement, and treatment—we shouldn't give up now.

* * *

... Illegal drugs are illegal because they are harmful.

There is a growing misconception that some illegal drugs can be taken safely—with many advocates of legalization going so far as to suggest it can serve as medicine to heal anything from headaches to bipolar diseases. Today's drug dealers are savvy businessmen. They know how to market to kids. They imprint Ecstasy pills with cartoon characters and designer logos. They promote parties as safe and alcohol-free. Meanwhile, the drugs can flow easier than water. Many young people believe the new "club drugs," such as Ecstasy, are safe, and tablet testing at raves has only fueled this misconception.

Because of the new marketing tactics of drug promoters, and because of a major decline in drug use in the 1990s, there is a growing perception among young people today that drugs are harmless. A decade ago, for example, 79 percent of 12th graders thought regular marijuana use was harmful; only 58 percent do so today. Because peer pressure is so important in inducing kids to experiment with drugs, the way kids perceive the risks of drug use is critical. There always have been, and there continues to be, real health risks in using illicit drugs.

Drug use can be deadly, far more deadly than alcohol. Although alcohol is used by seven times as many people as drugs, the number of deaths induced by those substances are not far apart. According to the Centers for Disease Control and Prevention (CDC), during 2000, there were 15,852 drug-induced deaths; only slightly less than the 18,539 alcohol-induced deaths.

Ecstasy

Ecstasy has rapidly become a favorite drug among young party goers in the U.S. and Europe, and it is now being used within the mainstream as well. According to the 2001 National Household Survey on Drug Abuse, Ecstasy use tripled among Americans between 1998 and 2001. Many people believe, incorrectly, that this synthetic drug is safer than cocaine and heroin. In fact, the drug is addictive and can be deadly. The drug often results in severe dehydration and heat stroke in the user, since it has the effect of "short-circuiting" the body's temperature signals to the brain. Ecstasy can heat your body up to temperatures as high as 117 degrees. Ecstasy can cause hypothermia, muscle breakdown, seizures, stroke, kidney and cardiovascular system failure, as well as permanent brain damage during repetitive use, and sometimes death. The psychological effects of Ecstasy include confusion, depression, anxiety, sleeplessness, drug craving, and paranoia.

The misconception about the safety of club drugs, like Ecstasy, is often fueled by some governments' attempts to reduce the harm of mixing drugs. Some foreign governments and private organizations in the U.S. have established Ecstasy testing at rave parties. Once the drug is tested, it is returned to the partygoers. This process leads partygoers to believe that the government has declared their pill safe to consume. But the danger of Ecstasy is the drug itself—not simply its purity level.

Cocaine

Cocaine is a powerfully addictive drug. Compulsive cocaine use seems to develop more rapidly when the substance is smoked rather than snorted. A tolerance to the cocaine high may be developed, and many addicts report that they fail to achieve as much pleasure as they did from their first cocaine exposure.

Physical effects of cocaine use include constricted blood vessels and increased temperature, heart rate, and blood pressure. Users may also experience feelings of restlessness, irritability, and anxiety. Cocaine-related deaths are often the result of cardiac arrest or seizures followed by respiratory arrest. Cocaine continues to be the most frequently mentioned illicit substance in U.S. emergency departments, present in 30 percent of the emergency department drug episodes during 2001.

Marijuana

Drug legalization advocates in the United States single out marijuana as a different kind of drug, unlike cocaine, heroin, and methamphetamine. They say it's less dangerous. Several European countries have lowered the classification of marijuana. However, as many people are realizing, marijuana is not as harmless as some would have them believe. Marijuana is far more powerful than it used to be. In 2000, there were six times as many emergency room mentions of marijuana use as there were in 1990, despite the fact that the number of people using marijuana is roughly the same. In 1999, a record 225,000 Americans entered substance abuse treatment primarily for marijuana dependence, second only to heroin—and not by much.

At a time of great public pressure to curtail tobacco because of its effects on health, advocates of legalization are promoting the use of marijuana. Yet, according to the National Institute on Drug Abuse, "Studies show that someone who smokes five joints per week may be taking in as many cancer-causing chemicals as someone who smokes a full pack of cigarettes every day." Marijuana contains more than 400 chemicals, including the most harmful substances found in tobacco smoke. For example, smoking one marijuana cigarette deposits about four times more tar into the lungs than a filtered tobacco cigarette.

Those are the long-term effects of marijuana. The short-term effects are also harmful. They include: memory loss, distorted perception, trouble with thinking and problem solving, loss of motor skills, decrease in muscle strength, increased heart rate, and anxiety. Marijuana impacts young people's mental development, their ability to concentrate in school, and their motivation and initiative to reach goals. And marijuana affects people of all ages: Harvard University researchers report that the risk of a heart attack is five times higher than usual in the hour after smoking marijuana.

* * *

... Drug control spending is a minor portion of the U.S. budget. Compared to the social costs of drug abuse and addiction, government spending on drug control is minimal.

Legalization advocates claim that the United States has spent billions of dollars to control drug production, trafficking, and use, with few, if any, positive results. As shown in previous chapters, the results of the American drug strategy have been positive indeed—with a 95 percent rate of Americans who do <u>not</u> use drugs. If the number of drug abusers doubled or tripled, the social costs would be enormous.

Social Costs

In the year 2000, drug abuse cost American society an estimated $160 billion. More important were the concrete losses that are imperfectly symbolized by those billions of dollars—the destruction of lives, the damage of addiction, fatalities from car accidents, illness, and lost opportunities and dreams.

Legalization would result in skyrocketing costs that would be paid by American taxpayers and consumers. Legalization would significantly increase drug use and addiction—and all the social costs that go with it. With the removal of the social and legal sanctions against drugs, many experts estimate the user population would at least double. For example, a 1994 article in the *New England Journal of Medicine* stated that it was probable, that if cocaine were legalized, the number of cocaine addicts in America would increase from 2 million to at least 20 million.

Drug abuse drives some of America's most costly social problems—including domestic violence, child abuse, chronic mental illness, the spread of AIDS, and homelessness. Drug treatment costs, hospitalization for long-term drug-related disease, and treatment of the consequences of family violence burden our already strapped health care system. In 2000, there were more than 600,000 hospital emergency department drug episodes in the United States. Health care costs for drug abuse alone were about $15 billion.

Drug abuse among the homeless has been conservatively estimated at better than 50 percent. Chronic mental illness is inextricably linked with drug abuse. In Philadelphia, nearly half of the VA's mental patients abused drugs. The Centers for Disease Control and Prevention has estimated that 36 percent of new HIV cases are directly or indirectly linked to injecting drug users.

In 1998, Americans spent $67 billion for illegal drugs, a sum of money greater than the amount spent that year to finance public higher education in the United States. If the money spent on illegal drugs were devoted instead to public higher education, for example, public colleges would have the financial ability to accommodate twice as many students as they already do.

In addition, legalization—and the increased addiction it would spawn—would result in lost workforce productivity—and the unpredictable damage that it would cause to the American economy. The latest drug use surveys show that about 75% of adults who reported current illicit drug use—which means they've used drugs once in the past month—are employed, either full or parttime. In 2000, productivity losses due to drug abuse cost the economy $110 billion. Drug use by workers leads not only to more unexcused absences and higher turnover, but also presents an enormous safety problem in the workplace. Studies have confirmed what common sense dictates: Employees who abuse drugs are five times more likely than other workers to injure themselves or coworkers and they cause 40% of all industrial fatalities. They were more likely to have worked for three or more employers and to have voluntarily left an employer in the past year.

Legalization would also result in a huge increase in the number of traffic accidents and fatalities. Drugs are already responsible for a significant number of accidents. Marijuana, for example, impairs the ability of drivers to maintain concentration and show good judgment. A study by the National Institute on Drug Abuse surveyed 6,000 teenage drivers. It studied those who drove more than six times a month after using marijuana. The study found that they were about two-and-a-half times more likely to be involved in a traffic accident than those who didn't smoke before driving.

Legalizers fail to mention the hidden consequences of legalization. Will the right to use drugs imply a right to the access to drugs? One of the arguments for legalization is that it will end the need for drug trafficking cartels. If so, who will distribute drugs? Government employees? The local supermarket? The college bookstore? In view of the huge settlement agreed to by the tobacco companies, what marketer would want the potential liability for selling a product as harmful as cocaine or heroin — or even marijuana?

Advocates also argue that legalization will lower prices. But that raises a dilemma: If the price of drugs is low, many more people will be able to afford them and the demand for drugs will explode. For example, the cost of cocaine production is now as low as $3 per gram. At a market price of, say, $10 a gram, cocaine could retail for as little as ten cents a hit. That means a young person could buy six hits of cocaine for the price of a candy bar. On the other hand, if legal drugs are priced too high, through excise taxes, for example, illegal traffickers will be able to undercut it.

Advocates of legalization also argue that the legal market could be limited to those above a certain age level, as it is for alcohol and cigarettes. Those under the age limits would not be permitted to buy drugs at authorized outlets. But teenagers today have found many ways to circumvent the age restrictions, whether by using false identification or by buying liquor and cigarettes from older friends. According to the 2001 National Household Survey on Drug Abuse, approximately 10.1 million young people aged 12–20 reported past month alcohol use (28.5 percent of this age group). Of these, nearly 6.8 million (19 percent) were binge drinkers. With drugs, teenagers would have an additional outlet: the highly organized illegal trafficking networks that exist today and that would undoubtedly concentrate their marketing efforts on young people to make up for the business they lost to legal outlets.

Costs to the Taxpayer

The claim that money allegedly saved from giving up on the drug problem could be better spent on education and social problems is readily disputed. When compared to the amount of funding that is spent on other national priorities, federal drug control spending is minimal. For example, in 2002, the amount of money spent by the federal government on drug control was less than $19 billion in its entirety. And unlike critics of American drug policy would have you believe, all of those funds did not go to enforcement policy only. Those funds were used for treatment, education and prevention, as well as enforcement. Within that budget, the amount of money Congress appropriated for the Drug Enforcement Administration was roughly $1.6 billion, a sum that the Defense Department runs through about every day-and-a-half or two days.

In FY 2002, the total federal drug budget was $11.5 billion. By contrast, our country spent about $650 billion, in total, in 2000 on our nation's educational system. And most of us would agree that it was money well spent, even if our educational system isn't perfect. Education is a long-term social concern, with new problems that arise with every new generation. The same can be said of drug abuse and addiction. Yet nobody suggests that we should give up on our children's education. Why, then, would we give up on helping to keep them off drugs and out of addiction?

Even if drug abuse had not dropped as much as it has in the last 20 years—by more than a third—the alternative to spending money on controlling drugs would be disastrous. If the relatively modest outlays of federal dollars were not made, drug abuse and the attendant social costs ($160 billion in 2000) would be far greater.

On the surface, advocates of legalization present an appealing, but simplistic, argument that by legalizing drugs we can move vast sums of money from enforcing drug laws to solving society's ills. But as in education and drug addiction, vast societal problems can't be solved overnight. It takes time, focus, persistence—and resources.

Legalization advocates fail to note the skyrocketing social and welfare costs, not to mention the misery and addiction, that would accompany outright legalization of drugs.

Legalizers also fail to mention that, unless drugs are made available to children, law enforcement will still be needed to deal with the sale of drugs to minors. In other words, a vast black market will still exist. Since young people are often the primary target of pushers, many of the criminal organizations that now profit from illegal drugs would continue to do so.

Furthermore, it is reasonable to assume that the health and societal costs of drug legalization would also increase exponentially. Drug treatment costs, hospitalization for long-term drug-related diseases, and treatment of family violence would also place additional demands on our already overburdened health system. More taxes would have to be raised to pay for an American health care system already bursting at the seams.

Criminal justice costs would likely increase if drugs were legalized. It is quite likely that violent crime would significantly increase with greater accessibility to dangerous drugs—whether the drugs themselves are legal or not. According to a 1991 Justice Department study, six times as many homicides are committed by people under the influence of drugs as by those who are looking for money to buy drugs. More taxes would have to be raised to pay for additional personnel in law enforcement, which is already overburdened by crimes and traffic fatalities associated with alcohol. Law enforcement is already challenged by significant alcohol-related crimes. More users would probably result in the commission of additional crimes, causing incarceration costs to increase as well.

... Legalization of Drugs Will Lead to Increased Use and Increased Levels of Addiction. Legalization has been tried before, and failed miserably.

Legalization proponents claim, absurdly, that making illegal drugs legal would not cause more of these substances to be consumed, nor would addiction increase. They claim that many people can use drugs in moderation and that many would choose not to use drugs, just as many abstain from alcohol and tobacco now. Yet how much misery can already be attributed to alcoholism and smoking? Is the answer to just add more misery and addiction?

It's clear from history that periods of lax controls are accompanied by *more* drug abuse and that periods of tight controls are accompanied by less drug abuse.

During the 19th Century, morphine was legally refined from opium and hailed as a miracle drug. Many soldiers on both sides of the Civil War who were given morphine for their wounds became addicted to it, and this increased level of addiction continued throughout the nineteenth century and into the twentieth. In 1880, many drugs, including opium and cocaine, were legal—and, like some drugs today, seen as benign medicine not requiring a doctor's care and oversight. Addiction skyrocketed. There were over 400,000 opium addicts in the U.S. That is twice as many per capita as there are today.

By 1900, about one American in 200 was either a cocaine or opium addict. Among the reforms of this era was the Federal Pure Food and Drug Act of 1906, which required manufacturers of patent medicines to reveal the contents of the drugs they sold. In this way, Americans learned which of their medicines contained heavy doses of cocaine and opiates — drugs they had now learned to avoid.

Specific federal drug legislation and oversight began with the 1914 Harrison Act, the first broad anti-drug law in the United States. Enforcement of this law contributed to a significant decline in narcotic addiction in the United States. Addiction in the United States eventually fell to its lowest level during World War II, when the number of addicts is estimated to have been somewhere between 20,000 and 40,000. Many addicts, faced with disappearing supplies, were forced to give up their drug habits.

What was virtually a drug-free society in the war years remained much the same way in the years that followed. In the mid-1950s, the Federal Bureau of Narcotics estimated the total number of addicts nationwide at somewhere between 50,000 to 60,000. The former chief medical examiner of New York City, Dr. Milton Halpern, said in 1970 that the number of New Yorkers who died from drug addiction in 1950 was 17. By comparison, in 1999, the New York City medical examiner reported 729 deaths involving drug abuse.

The Alaska Experiment and Other Failed Legalization Ventures

The consequences of legalization became evident when the Alaska Supreme Court ruled in 1975 that the state could not interfere with an adult's possession of marijuana for personal consumption in the home. The court's ruling became a green light for marijuana use. Although the ruling was limited to persons 19 and over, teens were among those increasingly using marijuana. According to a 1988 University of Alaska study, the state's 12 to 17-year-olds used marijuana at more than twice the national average for their age group. Alaska's residents voted in 1990 to recriminalize possession of marijuana, demonstrating their belief that increased use was too high a price to pay.

By 1979, after 11 states decriminalized marijuana and the Carter administration had considered federal decriminalization, marijuana use shot up among teenagers. That year, almost 51 percent of 12th graders reported they used marijuana in the last 12 months. By 1992, with tougher laws and increased attention to the risks of drug abuse, that figure had been reduced to 22 percent, *a 57 percent decline.*

Other countries have also had this experience. The Netherlands has had its own troubles with increased use of cannabis products. From 1984 to 1996, the Dutch liberalized the use of cannabis. Surveys reveal that lifetime prevalence of cannabis in Holland increased consistently and sharply. For the age group 18–20, the increase is from 15 percent in 1984 to 44 percent in 1996.

The Netherlands is not alone. Switzerland, with some of the most liberal drug policies in Europe, experimented with what became known as Needle Park. Needle Park became the Mecca for drug addicts throughout Europe, an area where addicts could come to openly purchase drugs and inject heroin without police intervention or control. The rapid decline in the neighborhood surrounding Needle Park, with increased crime and violence, led authorities to finally close Needle Park in 1992.

The British have also had their own failed experiments with liberalizing drug laws. England's experience shows that use and addiction increase with "harm reduction" policy. Great Britain allowed doctors to prescribe heroin to addicts, resulting in an explosion of heroin use, and by the mid-1980s, known addiction rates were increasing by about 30 percent a year.

The relationship between legalization and increased use becomes evident by considering two current "legal drugs," tobacco and alcohol. The number of users of these "legal drugs" is far greater than the number of users of illegal drugs. The numbers were explored by the *2001 National Household Survey on Drug Abuse*. Roughly 109 million Americans used alcohol at least once a month. About 66 million Americans used tobacco at the same rate. But less than 16 million Americans used illegal drugs at least once a month.

It's clear that there is a relationship between legalization and increasing drug use, and that legalization would result in an unacceptably high number of drug-addicted Americans.

When legalizers suggest that easy access to drugs *won't* contribute to greater levels of addiction, they aren't being candid. The question isn't whether legalization will increase addiction levels — it will — it's whether we care or not. The compassionate response is to do everything possible to prevent the destruction of addiction, not make it easier.

… Crime, Violence, and Drug Use Go Hand-In-Hand

Proponents of legalization have many theories regarding the connection between drugs and violence. Some dispute the connection between drugs and violence, claiming that drug use is a *victimless crime* and users are putting only themselves in harm's way and therefore have the right to use drugs. Other proponents of legalization contend that if drugs were legalized, crime and violence would decrease, believing that it is the illegal nature of drug production, trafficking, and use that fuels crime and violence, rather than the violent and irrational behavior that drugs themselves prompt.

Yet, under a legalization scenario, a black market for drugs would still exist. And it would be a vast black market. If drugs were legal for those over 18 or 21, there would be a market for everyone under that age. People under the age of 21 consume the majority of illegal drugs, and so an illegal market and organized crime to supply it would remain — along with the organized crime that profits from it. After Prohibition ended, did the organized crime in our country go down? No. It continues today in a variety of other criminal enterprises. Legalization would not put the cartels out of business; cartels would simply look to other illegal endeavors.

If only marijuana were legalized, drug traffickers would continue to traffic in heroin and cocaine. In either case, traffic-related violence would not be ended by legalization.

If only marijuana, cocaine, and heroin were legalized, there would still be a market for PCP and methamphetamine. Where do legalizers want to draw the line? Or do they support legalizing all drugs, no matter how addictive and dangerous?

In addition, any government agency assigned to distribute drugs under a legalization scenario would, for safety purposes, most likely not distribute the most potent drug. The drugs may also be more expensive because of bureaucratic costs of operating such a distribution system. Therefore, until 100 percent pure drugs are given away to anyone, at any age, a black market will remain.

The greatest weakness in the logic of legalizers is that the violence associated with drugs is simply a product of drug trafficking. That is, if drugs were legal, then most drug crime would end. But most violent crime is committed not because people want to buy drugs, but because people are on drugs. Drug use changes behavior and exacerbates criminal activity, and there is ample scientific evidence that demonstrates the links between drugs, violence, and crime. Drugs often cause people to do things they wouldn't do if they were rational and free of the influence of drugs.

According to the 1999 Arrestee Drug Abuse Monitoring (ADAM) study, more than half of arrestees for violent crimes test positive for drugs at the time of their arrest.

For experts in the field of crime, violence, and drug abuse, there is no doubt that there is a connection between drug use and violence. As Joseph A. Califano, Jr., of the National Center on Addiction and Substance Abuse at Columbia University stated, "Drugs like marijuana, heroin and cocaine are not dangerous because they are illegal; they are illegal because they are dangerous."

There are numerous statistics, from a wide variety of sources, illustrating the connection between drugs and violence. The propensity for violence against law enforcement officers, coworkers, family members, or simply people encountered on the street by drug abusers is a matter of record.

A 1997 FBI study of violence against law enforcement officers found that 24 percent of the assailants were under the influence of drugs at the time they attacked the officers and that 72 percent of the assailants had a history of drug law violations.

Many scientific studies also support the connection between drug use and crime. One study investigated state prisoners who had five or more convictions. These are hardened criminals. It found that four out of every five of them used drugs regularly.

Numerous episodes of workplace violence have also been attributed to illegal drugs. A two-year independent postal commission study looked into 29 incidents resulting in 34 deaths of postal employees from 1986 to 1999. "Most perpetrators (20 of 34) either had a known history of substance abuse or were known to be under the influence of alcohol or illicit drugs at the time of the homicide. The number is likely higher because investigations in most other cases were inconclusive."

According to the 1998 National Household Survey on Drug Abuse, teenage drug users are five times far more likely to attack someone than those who don't use drugs. About 20 percent of the 12–17 year olds reporting use of an illegal drug in the past year attacked someone with the intent to seriously hurt them, compared to 4.3 percent of the non-drug users.

As we see in most cases, the violence associated with drug use escalates and, in many instances, results in increased homicide rates. A 1994 Journal of the American Medical Association article reported that cocaine use was linked to high rates of homicide in New York City.

As these studies, and others, prove—violence is the hallmark of drug abuse. Drug users are not only harming themselves, but as we can see, they are harming anyone who may have the misfortune of crossing their path. Dr. Mitchell Rosenthal, head of Phoenix House, a major drug treatment center, has pointed out that, "there are a substantial number of abusers who cross the line from permissible self-destruction to become 'driven' people who are 'out of control' and put others in danger of their risk-taking, violence, abuse, or HIV infection."

It is impossible to claim drug use is victimless crime or deny the relationship between drugs and violence, especially when looking at an Office of National Drug Control Policy (ONDCP) estimate for 1995, which estimates there were almost 53,000 drug-related deaths in that year alone, compared to 58,000 American lives lost in eight and a half years in the Vietnam War. The assertions dismissing the connection between drugs and violence by legalization proponents are simply not true. Drug use, legal or not, is not a victimless crime; it is a crime that destroys communities, families, and lives.

* * *

… Most non-violent drug users get treatment, not just jail time.

There is a myth in this country that U.S. prisons are filled with drug users. This assertion is simply <u>**not**</u> true. Actually, only 5 percent of inmates in <u>federal</u> prison on drug charges are incarcerated for drug possession. In our <u>state</u> prisons, it's somewhat higher — about 27% of drug offenders. In New York, which has received criticism from some because of its tough Rockefeller drug laws, it is estimated that 97% of drug felons sentenced to prison were charged with sale or intent to sell, not simply possession. In fact, first time drug offenders, even sellers, typically do not go to prison.

Most cases of simple drug possession are simply not prosecuted, unless people have been arrested repeatedly for using drugs. In 1999, for example, only 2.5 percent of the federal cases argued in District Courts involved simple drug possession. Even the small number of possession charges is likely to give an inflated impression of the numbers. It is likely that a significant percentage of those in prison on possession charges were people who were originally arrested for trafficking or another more serious drug crime but plea-bargained down to a simple possession charge.

The Michigan Department of Corrections just finished a study of their inmate population. They discovered that out of 47,000 inmates, only 15 people were incarcerated on first-time drug possession charges. (500 are incarcerated on drug possession charges, but 485 are there on multiple charges or pled down.)

In Wisconsin the numbers are even lower, with only 10 persons incarcerated on drug possession charges. (769 are incarcerated on drug possession charges, but 512 of those entered prison through some type of revocation, leaving 247 entering prison on a "new sentence." Eliminating those who had also been sentenced on trafficking and/or non-drug related charges; the total of new drug possession sentences came to 10.)

Policy Shift to Treatment

There has been a shift in the U.S. criminal justice system to provide treatment for non-violent drug users with addiction problems, rather than incarceration. The criminal justice system actually serves as the largest referral source for drug treatment programs.

Any successful treatment program must also require accountability from its participants. Drug treatment courts are a good example of combining treatment with such accountability. These courts are given a special responsibility to handle cases involving drug-addicted offenders through an extensive supervision and treatment program. Drug treatment court programs use the varied experience and skills of a wide variety of law enforcement and treatment professionals: judges, prosecutors, defense counsels, substance abuse treatment specialists, probation officers, law enforcement and correctional personnel, educational and vocational experts, community leaders and others — all focused on one goal: to help cure addicts of their addiction, and to keep them cured.

Drug treatment courts are working. Researchers estimate that more than 50 percent of defendants convicted of drug possession will return to criminal behavior within two to three years. Those who graduate from drug treatment courts have far lower rates of recidivism, ranging from 2 to 20 percent.

What makes drug treatment courts so different? Graduates are held accountable to the program. Unlike purely voluntary treatment programs, the addict — who has a physical need for drugs — can't simply quit treatment whenever he or she feels like it.

Many state governments are also taking the opportunity to divert non-violent drug offenders from prison in the hopes of offering treatment and rehabilitation outside the penal facility. In New York, prosecutors currently divert over 7,000 convicted drug felons from prison each year. Many enter treatment programs.

States throughout the Midwest are also establishing programs to divert drug offenders from prison and aid in their recovery. In Indiana, 64 of the 92 counties offer community corrections programs to rehabilitate and keep first time non-violent offenders, including nonviolent drug offenders, out of prison. Nonviolent drug offenders participating in the community corrections program are required to attend a treatment program as part of their rehabilitation.

In July of 2002, the Ohio Judicial Conference conducted a survey of a select group of judges. The results from the survey demonstrated that judges "offer treatment to virtually 100 percent of first-time drug offenders and over 95 percent of second-time drug offenders." According to the survey, these percentages are accurate throughout the state, no matter the jurisdiction or county size. The Ohio Judicial Conference went a step further, reviewing pre-sentence investigations and records, which demonstrated that "99 percent of offenders sentenced to prison had one or more prior felony convictions or multiple charges."

The assertion that U.S. prisons are filled with drug users is simply untrue. As this evidence shows, more and more minor drug offenders are referred to treatment centers in an effort to reduce the possibility of recidivism and help drug users get help for their substance abuse problems. The drug treatment court program and several other programs set up throughout the United States have been reducing the number of minor drug offenses that actually end up in the penal system. The reality is that you have to work pretty darn hard to end up in jail on drug possession charges.

––––––––––

Notes and Questions

1. Briefly into the Hamsterdam experiment, Detectives McNulty, Greggs, and Sydnor stop a car heading to the free zone. Major Colvin arrives on the scene and takes the other officers through his experiment. Detective Greggs is incredulous, saying, "You legalized drugs." *The Wire*, Season 3, Episode 7, at 36:40 minutes. Major Colvin does not explicitly dispute her statement, although earlier in the scene he claims that drugs are "not legal, we just look the other way is all." Later in Season 3, Major Colvin explains his approach at a Compstat meeting. Deputy Rawls is furious and yells, "he's legalized drugs." Major Colvin responds, "[a]ctually, I elected to ignore them." *The Wire*, Season 3, Episode 10, at 44:30 minutes. Are Greggs and Rawls correct that Hamsterdam is the equivalent of legalizing drugs? Or is Major Colvin correct?

2. What is the difference between legalizing drugs and decriminalizing drugs? Legalization is the simpler term; it means that drug use and distribution are not illegal. By contrast, decriminalization involves maintaining criminal penalties for manufacturing and selling drugs, but eliminating criminal penalties for using or possessing drugs. Individuals found in possession of drugs can still be subject to non-criminal penalties such as fines or being sent to drug treatment. Portugal adopted the decriminalization model in 2001. *See* Mark A. Kleiman et al., Drugs and Drug Policy: What Everyone Needs to Know 26–27 (2011). Does decriminalization make sense? How can it be possible to permissibly possess and use something that cannot be lawfully made or distributed?

3. Even if you agree that drugs should not be legalized, does the DEA take a position that is so hard-line as to cut off valuable areas of scientific research? For instance, some

European countries have had success with "heroin maintenance," a program in which heroin users who have tried and failed other kinds of treatment are provided heroin in a medically supervised facility. This approach reduces overdoses and minimizes the need to steal in order to get the money to pay for heroin. *See* Peter Reuter, Can Heroin Maintenance Help Baltimore?: What Baltimore Can Learn From the Experience of Other Countries (Abell Foundation 2009) (documenting positive results from studies in Switzerland, The Netherlands, and Germany). Can you imagine the DEA ever agreeing to a scientific study testing such a program in the United States? *See id.* at 36 ("Persuading the relevant agencies to grant a research license for the importation of heroin for this experiment would be difficult. It is likely that the DEA would be highly skeptical...."). How can the DEA confidently take a firm position against drug legalization without conducting such research?

4. Watch *The Wire*, Season 1, Episode 6, at 39:45 minutes. After Bubbles and Johnny sell stolen copper wire to get the money to buy drugs, we see the apartment where they have shot up the drugs. The apartment is filthy, with garbage strewn about. There is another man, who is never introduced to the audience, just sitting on the couch completely passed out. Is this what we should realistically expect in a nation that makes drug use illegal? In other words, is it false to say the choice is between allowing drug use or disallowing it? Is the real choice between allowing it publicly or pushing it into the dirtiest, least safe corners of the world? How do you think the authors of the DEA position paper would respond to this scene?

5. Also consider *The Wire*, Season 2, Episode 6, at 11:50 minutes, in which defense attorney Maurice Levy cross-examines Omar Little in Bird's murder trial.

> Levy: ... You are feeding off the violence and the despair of the drug trade. You are stealing from those who themselves who are stealing the lifeblood from our city. You are a parasite who leaches off....
>
> Omar: Just like you, man.
>
> Levy: Excuse me?
>
> Omar: I got the shotgun. You got the briefcase. It's all in the game though, right?

Is Omar correct? Are paid defense lawyers making a living off the drug trade? How about prosecutors, judges, police, and prison guards? Do those who work in the criminal justice system have the opportunity to make a nice living in part because the war on drugs — including the incarceration of hundreds of thousands of people — finances their lifestyle? How would the DEA respond to this question? How would they respond to Omar's more pointed question that a paid defense attorney is just as involved in the game as the drug dealers?

Steven B. Duke, Drug Prohibition: An Unnatural Disaster
27 Connecticut Law Review 571 (1995)

* * *

The idea that government should determine for its people which psychoactive drugs they are free to consume and jail them for using others is a fairly recent arrival in the United States. Except for an occasional fling with prohibition at the state level, Americans were free until 1914 to consume any drugs they chose and to buy from anyone who chose to sell them. Those rights were widely exercised. In addition to alcohol, tobacco, and caffeine, tens of millions of Americans consumed cocaine and opiates in the nineteenth century. Cocaine was even an ingredient in Coca Cola until 1905, and opium was included in nostrums fed to colicky babies. Heroin was originally sold as a cough suppressant. Although dependence on these drugs was not uncommon, it was never as serious a problem as alcoholism. Indeed, although the proportions of the population using these drugs in the late nineteenth century was probably higher than it is now, the problems associated with their use were less serious than they are today.

In 1914, Congress enacted the Harrison Act, which was designed to medicalize cocaine and heroin by confining their distribution to health professionals. In 1919, on the eve of alcohol prohibition and doubtless influenced by prohibitionist fervor, the Supreme Court converted the Harrison Act into a ban on the distribution of such drugs, holding that prescribing drugs to addicts was not the practice of medicine and was therefore criminal. Drug and alcohol prohibition then proceeded to wreck the country. Crime, corruption, and disrespect for law grew at unprecedented rates. Because of alcohol prohibition, many Americans replaced their appetite for beer with a newly discovered preference for the cocktail, containing distilled spirits, which poisoned thousands.

Thirteen years of alcohol prohibition was enough. It was repealed in 1933 by the Twenty-first Amendment, which left alcohol regulation to the states. The repeal of alcohol prohibition coincided with the depth of the depression, when unemployment reached record levels and millions of Americans were without food, shelter, welfare, or hope. Despite this widespread misery and despair, crime rates dropped precipitously after the repeal, as did alcohol poisoning and contempt for law. Hardly anyone considers the repeal of alcohol prohibition to have been a mistake. Why, then, did we not repeal the Harrison Act at the same time? Why don't we repeal its modern sequelae? We are addicted to drug prohibition.

* * *

I. SOME COSTS OF "DRUG WAR" PROHIBITION

A. *The Criminogenics of Drug Prohibition*

Contrary to what our government told us when it imposed drug prohibition, most illegal recreational drugs have no pharmacological properties that produce violence or other criminal behavior. Heroin and marijuana diminish rather than increase aggressive behavior. Cocaine—or cocaine withdrawal—occasionally triggers violence but usually does not. Very little crime is generated by the mere use of these drugs, especially in comparison to alcohol, which is causally related to thousands of homicides and hundreds of thousands of assaults annually. The major linkages between illegal drugs and crime must be found elsewhere—in prohibition.

1. *Prohibition Creates Motivation to Steal and Rob*

One of the main strategic goals of the drug war is to increase the costs of producing and distributing, and hence of buying, illicit drugs. As the price to the consumer is increased, demand can hopefully be curtailed and the number of users or the quantities of illicit drugs used can be reduced. The tactics for increasing producer and distributor costs include impeding production or distribution of the raw materials used in making drugs, attempting to interdict the products before they reach the consumer (with border searches, busts of stash houses, and the like), and putting smugglers and distributors of the illicit products in prison. Until recently, the strategy had considerable "success" in that prices for marijuana, heroin, cocaine, and other illicit drugs were quite high. A heroin addict would commonly need $200 or more per day to support a habit, and a cocaine user, before the era of cheap "crack," might need even more than that. Many cocaine users spent a thousand dollars a week on powder cocaine.

There is little evidence that demand is greatly reduced by jacking up the free market price of these drugs by a factor of 100 or more, but there is strong evidence that the consumers of these products increase their participation in acquisitive crimes in order to feed their habits. In a recent survey of persons in prison for robbery or burglary, one out of three said that they committed their crimes in order to get money to buy drugs. Those who commit crimes for drug money also seem to commit them at a much greater rate than less strongly motivated robbers, burglars, and thieves.

In a study of 356 heroin users in Miami, James Inciardi found that they admitted to committing nearly 120,000 crimes (an average of 332 per person) during a single year. In another study of 573 heroin users, Inciardi found them responsible for about 215,000 offenses during the previous year. Included were 25,000 shopliftings, 45,000 thefts and frauds, 6,000 robberies and assaults, and 6,700 burglaries. In another study of 459 nonnarcotic drug users (chiefly cocaine), Inciardi found them to have admitted to an average of 320 crimes apiece during the previous year. In a survey of callers to a cocaine hotline, 45% of the callers said they had stolen to buy cocaine. In a survey of adolescents, the 1.3% who admitted using cocaine accounted for 40% of the admitted crimes. In several studies of drug use by persons imprisoned, 65% to 80% have admitted regular or lifetime illicit drug use. All this data suggests that about 75% of our robberies, thefts, burglaries, and related assaults are committed by drug abusers. Some of the crimes committed by drug abusers—perhaps one-third—would be committed in any event, but numerous studies show that drug users commit far fewer crimes when undergoing outpatient treatment or even when the prices of drugs go down. Half of America's property crime, robberies, and burglaries are probably the result of the high costs of drug acquisition created by the drug war.

2. Systemic Causes

Creating an incentive to steal in order to buy drugs is only one of many criminogenic effects of drug prohibition. The illegal drug market is itself a cauldron of criminality. Murder is employed to protect or acquire drug-selling turf, to settle disputes among drug merchants and their customers, to enforce contracts, to remediate fraud, and to steal drugs and drug money from dealers. In many cities, such as New Haven, Connecticut, at least half of the killings are drug-business related. Nationwide, between 5,000 and 10,000 murders per year are systemic to the drug business. Thus, more people are killed by the prohibition of drugs than by the drugs themselves. Drug money is also the lifeblood of criminal gangs, members of whom kill members of rival gangs, and innocent bystanders, for almost any reason, including showing off.

3. Victimogenics

Another way in which drug prohibition causes crime is by making victims vulnerable to predators. Many drug customers have to enter crime-infested territory to get their supplies. Since they are criminals themselves, obviously in the neighborhood to "score," they have strong disincentives to complain to the police about having been robbed or assaulted. As such, they are prime targets.

4. Proliferation of Deadly Weapons

Drug prohibition also accounts for much of the recent proliferation of handguns and assault rifles (which are doubling every twenty years). Guns are essential to carrying on the drug trade, since drug dealers must enforce their own contracts and provide their own protection from predators. Even "mules" who deliver drugs or money need weapons. Due in part to its association with the glamorous drug trade, packing a gun, like fancy clothing or costly jewelry, has become a status symbol among many adolescents. In such an atmosphere, other youngsters carry guns in the hope they will provide them with some protection. As a result, disputes that used to be settled with fists are now settled with guns. A decade ago only 15% of teenagers who got into serious trouble in New York City were carrying guns. Now the rate is 60% to 65%.

* * *

5. Corruption Costs

Drug prohibition also fosters crime by producing police corruption. The news media are full of accounts of cops caught stealing money or drugs from drug dealers and re-selling the drugs, simply taking money from drug dealers in exchange for looking the other way, or providing tips about police raids or other plans. The recently released report of New York City's Mollen Commission provides chilling accounts of drug-prohibition-related corruption in that city. Such corruption denigrates and demoralizes all police. It spreads like cancer into all phases of police work.

6. Distraction of Law Enforcement

The distractive effects of the drug war on the police are also indirectly but profoundly criminogenic. In many cities, half or more of the arrests are for drugs or other crimes related to drug trafficking. The energy expended by the police on drug criminals is not available to be focused on domestic violence, rape, and other nondrug offenses. As a consequence, criminals who are not directly involved in drug trafficking have a much better chance of escaping detection and punishment than they would have otherwise.

If, as the just enacted Violent Crime Control and Law Enforcement Act correctly presumes, the number of police available to detect and prosecute crimes has a strong effect on the number of crimes committed, then wasting half of our available police resources on drug and drug-related crimes — effectively cutting our police forces in half-clearly causes crime. Repeal of drug prohibition would in effect add 400,000 police officers — at no cost. On that account alone, it would surely eliminate one-fourth or more of our violent and property crimes.

7. Paralyzing Our Courts

Our court system is on the verge of collapse, mainly because of drug-related cases. Criminal cases are not decided on their merits. In many cities, most people who are indicted end up having their cases dismissed. Only a fraction of the people charged with felonies are ever convicted of those felonies. There are simply too many cases for the system to handle, and at least half of them, in many courts, are drug cases or drug-prohibition-caused cases.

8. Dilution of Incarceration Resources

The drug war deeply undercuts the role of imprisonment in dealing with non-drug related crimes, such as child molesting, rape, and homicide. We now jail or imprison 1.3 million Americans, the second highest rate of incarceration in the world. Our prisons are filled beyond capacity even as our rates of incarceration are increasing faster than ever before. Forty states are under court orders for overcrowding. Funds are not available to build prisons fast enough to provide the needed space. Child molesters and kidnappers are being paroled early or having their sentences cut to make prison space for drug users and drug dealers. Many dangerous criminals don't even make it to prison because there is no room for them. Because many drug users and dealers — most of them nonviolent —

have mandatory sentences, they have priority for prison space. Repeal of drug prohibition would open up about 500,000 jail and prison spaces. The beneficial effects on crime rates can hardly be exaggerated.

* * *

It must be conceded that all of the prohibition-generated crime would not disappear overnight with the repeal of prohibition. Many of the street level drug dealers have no marketable skills in legitimate business and have been so corrupted by the lifestyle of drug dealing that they would be very reluctant to "go straight" even if they had the opportunity. Deprived of their income, such dealers would try to find alternative illegal methods of economic survival. A temporary surge in thefts and robberies might even occur if drug dealers were immediately deprived of their black-market livelihood. Former drug dealers would replace addicts as a cadre of predatory criminals. Theft and robbery, however, are not substitutes for drug dealing because they are not nearly as lucrative and more skill is needed to avoid getting caught. The markets for stolen cars, televisions, and hubcaps are limited, and few of our drug dealers are capable of stealing computer chips or trade secrets. That drug dealers will not simply replace their income with predatory crime will be even clearer when we have freed our police from prohibition and turned them loose on thieves and robbers. Over time, many former drug dealers will be absorbed into legitimate society (those that aren't will be imprisoned). How quickly and thoroughly the assimilation occurs depends on how committed we are as a society to providing the opportunities—the training and the jobs—to replace the fruits of crime. We will have plenty of money to spend on such opportunities when we repeal prohibition.

B. *Prohibition Wastes at Least $100 Billion Per Year*

The federal, state, and local governments spend about $75 billion a year on law enforcement and criminal justice programs. About $20 billion of that is directly related to drug law enforcement. Roughly another $15 billion is related to crimes committed to obtain drug money or is systemically related in some way to drug commerce. Hence, about $35 billion per year spent on law enforcement can be saved by repeal of drug prohibition.

* * *

The direct public expenditures on law enforcement of drug prohibition pale in comparison to the costs of the drug war borne by individual citizens. Estimates of the yearly earnings of the illicit-drug business range as high as $100 billion. Fifty billion dollars is a safe estimate. Pharmaceutical cocaine costs less than one percent of the price of street cocaine. The other 99% that users pay for street cocaine is attributable to drug prohibition. Thus, if the principal recreational drugs were legal, drug consumers could be expected to save nearly $50 billion each year (less taxes government might levy on drug sales).

Although nonusers may have difficulty sympathizing with a policy that would make drug use more economical, nonusers have a large financial stake in drug price reductions. Nonusers provide much of the money spent on drugs when they are innocent victims of crime. If $10 billion of the money spent to buy drugs comes from stolen property—a rough estimate—property owners may lose $50 billion worth of property to provide the thieves with $10 billion in cash or equivalents with which to buy drugs (stolen property is sold at steep discounts). Nonusers also indirectly bear much of the cost of high drug prices when they pay for theft insurance, when they purchase security systems, when they pay taxes for police protection, and when they pay a premium to live in gated communities or suburbs. Owners of property in the inner-city pay when their tenants move out to escape the horror of their surroundings or when businesses close because of drug-related crime. * * *

C. *Urban Blight*

Drug prohibition is a major contributor to the destruction of our inner-cities. In America's most disadvantaged neighborhoods, open-air drug markets and gang violence related to drug-turf battles make life miserable. Residents of neighborhoods where drug trade is concentrated also suffer disproportionately from the crimes generated by drug prohibition, such as crimes to get drug money. When the drug business leaves the cities, our homes, streets, and schools will become much safer. It may even become possible to educate children in urban public schools.

* * *

D. *Public Health Costs*

Drug prohibition makes the inevitable use of psychotropic drugs far more dangerous than would be the case under regulation. Most overdoses and drug poisonings are attributable to the operation of the illicit market. Drug analyst James Ostrowski concludes that 80% of drug-use-deaths are caused by prohibition, only 20% by the inherent qualities of the drugs. That estimate does not include the fact that needle sharing by intravenous drug users now does as much or more to spread HIV, hepatitis, and other deadly diseases as do unsafe sexual practices. Our drug war mentality has widely blocked the implementation of clean-needle programs that clearly reduce the spread of AIDS and other deadly diseases. Drug prohibition also deters drug users from seeking treatment for a myriad of other medical conditions, many of which are communicable. Ironically, the criminal status of drugs even deters drug abusers from seeking treatment for drug addiction.

* * *

If prohibition were repealed, the dangers to physical health to users and to third parties from heroin, cocaine, marijuana, or other previously illegal drugs would be *greatly* reduced. Also, the economic factors pushing producers, traffickers, and users toward more concentrated, more deadly, and more addictive drugs would be eliminated by repeal. Before prohibition, opium was a popular drug. Under prohibition, opium has disappeared and has been replaced by a far more potent, more addictive opiate-heroin. After repeal, we could expect many users to confine their drug consumption to highly diluted forms, just as consumers of alcohol more often drank beer before and after alcohol prohibition than they did during prohibition, during which they drank liquor. Opium should make a comeback and marijuana use should increase, both increases being offset by reductions in hard drug consumption. Crack might disappear. This alone would greatly reduce the health risks and the addictive potential of drug use. Under regulation, drug purities would also be standardized and clearly and accurately labeled. Adulterants, and their risks, would also be disclosed. The risks of accidentally overdosing or being poisoned would be a fraction of what they are under the present regime.

Relegalizing heroin, cocaine, and marijuana would probably produce a net reduction in the use of tobacco and alcohol, saving thousands of lives every year, perhaps tens of thousands. This reduction would come from several sources. Our present demonization of illicit drugs permits us to avoid confronting the realities of alcohol and tobacco—that they are our two deadliest popular drugs. Prohibition of some drugs encourages consumption of permitted drugs....

* * *

When heroin addicts are deprived of heroin, they become alcoholics. When drinkers are deprived of alcohol, they turn to opiates. If repeal were to cause more consumption of heroin (by no means certain), some of the increase would probably represent a substitution for alcohol. To the extent heavy alcohol drinkers were to substitute opiates for alcohol, that would create significant health benefits (opiates cause virtually no physical damage to the body). Despite common misconceptions about the relative health costs of using legal and illegal drugs, health benefits could even accrue if consumers were to switch from alcohol or tobacco to cocaine or heroin.

* * *

F. *Drug Prosecutions Destroy the Lives of Otherwise Productive Citizens*

Most users of presently illegal drugs, like most users of tobacco and alcohol, are productive and generally law abiding people. But treating their drug consumption as a serious crime makes it harder for them to be so and makes it impossible for some to be so—those who are socially and economically marginal to begin with. Legalizing drugs would greatly increase the capacity of the users of presently illicit drugs to be productive citizens.

I estimate that about 500,000 of our 1.3 million jail and prison inmates are there for illegal drug or drug-related offenses, and as many as 300,000 would not be there if drug prohibition were repealed because they would not be criminals. They would be available to their families and would have an opportunity to be useful members of society rather than embittered criminals enraged over their unjust punishment. No one who gets a prison term of any duration for using drugs or selling drugs to a willing adult buyer is likely to be persuaded that his punishment was deserved. Hundreds of thousands of Americans who might otherwise be integrated into the mainstream of society have that possibility virtually eliminated by a combination of embitterment and stigma, rendering their acceptance of and by the mainstream unlikely. This appalling waste of human lives, which itself far exceeds any plausible cost of illegal drug use, would be eliminated by repeal.

* * *

III. A NATION OF ZOMBIES?

* * *

During most of its history, this country had no drug prohibition, and drug abuse was never worse than it is now. There are few, if any, countries in the history of the world who ever had a majority of their adult populations addicted to any drug other than tobacco, and if any approached that condition, the drug was alcohol. Drugs are still at least *de facto* legal in much of the world, as they have been throughout most of human history, yet if there is or ever has been a country that has ten percent of its population abusing cocaine or heroin, I have not heard of it....

* * *

At various times, eleven American states more or less decriminalized the possession and use of marijuana. Yet marijuana consumption declined at approximately the same rate in the states that decriminalized it as consumption has declined elsewhere in the United States. It did not increase anywhere.

Marijuana use has decreased in the Netherlands and in other states that decriminalized its use for the same reasons it has declined in places that have retained prohibition. People stopped using marijuana, or use it to a lesser extent, because "pot smoking" is simply less fashionable than it once was, because recreational drug use in general has been declining for about fifteen years, and because other more harmful drugs have been substituted. What these experiences demonstrate is that extra-legal, psycho-social forces account for changes in patterns of drug consumption far more than do prohibition efforts, and that official suppression—or lack thereof—is a relatively uninfluential factor in drug use trends and patterns. This is corroborated by a random telephone survey of 1,401 American adults conducted in 1990. Of those Americans polled, fewer than 1 in 100 who had not tried cocaine would do so if it were legal.

Since greatly shrinking the black market in drugs is the main object of prohibition's repeal, drug prices under a system of regulation, even though taxed, must be kept much lower than they are now. When most commodities become cheaper, more people use them and those who used them before use more of them. That is true to some extent when the commodity is a pleasure drug. We observed that the invention of crack in the mid-1980s, which drastically reduced the cost of a cocaine high, brought in hordes of new users. In July 1992, the *New York Times* reported that due in part to the recent abundance of heroin and cocaine (despite decades of drug war aimed at preventing it), drug dealers had cut the price of a $10 or "dime" bag of heroin to $5 and, in some parts of the city, reduced the price of a dose of crack to an all-time low of 75 cents. New York authorities believed that the reduced prices also accompanied increases in the numbers of both new users and abusers of cocaine. Heroin use also increased as prices declined because users could afford to snort heroin rather than inject it and thus avoided the risk of AIDS and several other diseases related to intravenous drug use. Several studies show that the price of cigarettes — our most addictive drug — has a measurable impact upon consumption, especially long term: the higher the price, other things being equal, the less tobacco is smoked. Reducing the money it takes to buy a dose of a drug is not the only cost reduction to the user contemplated by legalization. The legal user will no longer be a felon for using drugs and will no longer feel the need to commit crimes in order to pay for the drugs used. Thus, in a broad sense, the "price" of drug use under legalization will be vastly reduced.

* * *

There is ... a substantial likelihood that, *all other things remaining equal*, legalization will be accompanied by an increase in the consumption of newly-legalized drugs. But there is also little reason, and no support in what followed the repeal of alcohol prohibition, to suggest that legalizing illicit drugs would produce a huge increase in the numbers of users of pleasure drugs. One who neither smokes tobacco nor drinks alcohol is extremely unlikely to be a user of any of the other pleasure drugs, caffeine aside, and even less likely to become an abuser. The major reasons why people desist from smoking tobacco and drinking alcohol — health concerns, social stigma, morality, aesthetics, etc. — are also applicable to other pleasure drugs.

The potential new users of legalized drugs are therefore people who are presently deterred by the price of these drugs or by the criminality of their use, but who nonetheless drink or smoke cigarettes. To the extent that such persons were to substitute newly-legalized pleasure drugs for tobacco or alcohol, they would improve their bodily health and the health of those with whom they come into contact. Cocaine or heroin users do not pollute the air and rarely beat their mates or children while intoxicated on those drugs.

Most people who would abuse cocaine or heroin if it were legalized, but who do not now use these drugs, are already abusing alcohol, killing themselves and others by the tens of thousands every year. They would be less likely to kill themselves with drugs if they used less alcohol, even if they used more cocaine or heroin, and would also be much less dangerous to the rest of us.

* * *

In sum, the drug market is already saturated with a combination of legal and illegal drugs. Virtually everyone who now wants to get high already does so. Legalization may significantly alter market shares among the now legal and illegal drugs, but it is unlikely to create a strong surge in *new* demand for psychoactive drugs. It is even less likely to create a new population of drug *abusers*. . . .

Thus, I conclude that while the use of drugs that are legalized will probably increase following repeal, especially in the short run, the increases will be mostly in the use of much safer, less addictive drugs like marijuana, and will be offset by reductions in the use of more dangerous drugs like alcohol. We will certainly not become a nation of zombies.

Notes and Questions

1. Professor Duke does not dispute that drug use can be harmful. Rather, he takes the position that drug prohibition causes more harm than drug use itself and should therefore be abandoned. Is that the only conclusion that could flow from Professor Duke's analysis though? Should we instead be asking how drug prohibition could be implemented more effectively rather than decriminalizing drug use?

2. Does Professor Duke oversell his case? For instance, he asserts that re-directing police resources away from drug crimes would "in effect add 400,000 police officers — at no cost" and "would surely eliminate one-fourth or more of our violent and property crimes." How can he say that with such certainty?

3. In another example, Professor Duke contends that "about 75% of our robberies, thefts, burglaries, and related assaults are committed by drug abusers" and that decriminalization would reduce that number dramatically, perhaps to one-third. How does Professor Duke know that? Is it possible to make such an assertion with any level of confidence?

4. Professor Duke does concede that legalizing drugs might result in a temporary increase in other crimes as out-of-work drug dealers look for other criminal work. Watch *The Wire*, Season 3, Episode 7, at 33:00 minutes. Sergeant Carver realizes that in a legalized drug zone, the drug dealers no longer need young children (the hoppers) to serve as runners and lookouts. Carver demands that the drug dealers "pay them hoppers for the week, whether you use them or not you pay this money out. This shit is like unemployment insurance. Every employer got to pay in. . . . The least you all can do is look after your own people a little bit." Carver's partner, Officer Herc, belittles the idea, calling Carver a communist. If drugs were legalized, would the average police officer go out of his way to look out for the unemployed youth like Sergeant Carver or leave them alone to delve into other criminal activity like Officer Herc?

5. Would drug dealers — including tough, aggressive drug dealers — be willing to trust the police if drugs were legal? Watch *The Wire*, Season 3, Episode 8, at 5:30 minutes. After a drug dealer is robbed of his drugs in Hamsterdam he begins to yell at the police for not protecting him. He says, "I wanna file a report." Detective Herc is amused and asks, "You want to make a complaint to us that you were selling drugs and someone took your money?" The idea of such a complaint is ridiculous in the United States today. Would it be realistic in a world where drug use was decriminalized?

6. As you surely noticed, Professor Duke's article is nearly two decades old, thus making many of the statistics outdated. In many areas, matters have gotten more extreme. For instance, Professor Duke noted that the United States had the second highest incarceration rate of any nation and locked up 1.3 million people. Today, the United States leads the world in incarceration and has more than 2.3 million people behind bars. Whereas

the United States was spending $13 billion per year on the drug war in the 1990s, today the amount is conservatively estimated at more than $30 billion. For these and other updated statistics, see Alex Kreit, *The Decriminalization Option: Should States Consider Moving from a Criminal to a Civil Drug Court Model*, 2010 U. Chi. Legal F. 299 (2010).

7. As Professor Duke notes, over thirty years ago, Professor James Inciardi attempted to gauge just how much crime heroin users commit to support their habit. In an unusual approach, he gained the confidence of some users and then simply asked them. The findings were startling. The 356 persons studied reported committing a total of 118,134 criminal offenses during a single year. While many of those offenses were victimless, the respondents admitted to committing more than 27,000 FBI "index crimes," serious offenses such as homicide, rape, aggravated assault, robbery, burglary, and theft. *See* James A. Inciardi, *Heroin Use and Street Crime*, 27 Crime & Delinq. 335, 344 (1979). How much of this crime would vanish if heroin use were decriminalized?

8. Watch *The Wire*, Season 3, Episode 7, at 45:45 minutes. Sergeant Carver is standing in Hamsterdam, watching the young children run past. He tells Major Colvin: "I don't know, boss. If there weren't so many … kids down here I might be okay with it." Obviously, Major Colvin's Hamsterdam is not a carefully regulated drug zone that has been planned in advance with the full support of the government regulatory apparatus. But what if it were? Would it be possible to operate a free zone in Baltimore and keep the children out? Alcohol is legal for adults over the age of twenty-one. How successful has the United States been about keeping alcohol out of the hands of children? Is that the relevant question, or is it more appropriate to ask how successful society has been at keeping children out of bars? Assuming the government's performance in keeping drugs from children were comparable to its success in keeping alcohol away from kids, would that leave you more or less confident in the concept of free zones?

9. Professor Duke makes a logical argument why the drug war has been a failure. Does logic have anything to do with drug policy though? The next excerpt makes the case that all the statistics and logic in the world will not change drug policy in the United States.

Steven Wisotsky, Drug Facts Don't Matter: A Brief Comment on Drug Prohibition: An Unnatural Disaster
27 Connecticut Law Review 639 (1995)

Professor Steven Duke's article *Drug Prohibition: An Unnatural Disaster* is an excellent restatement and updating of familiar arguments that have been made for many years. For readers coming to the issue for the first time or trying to get a sense of the "big picture," the article is a strong brief of the case against drug prohibition. In terms of its potential impact on attitudes or policy, however, it is the wrong argument at the wrong time.…

… He asserts that "[a] rational approach to the problem requires us to compare the costs or disadvantages of drug prohibition" with alternatives. The unstated, meta-premise is that "a rational approach" has the potential to make a difference. The experience of decades has taught the contrary. It's all been said many times before—the arguments based on (dis)utility—and to this jaded observer, it's Yogi Berra's "deja vu all over again."

* * *

… I was struck by the fact that the article is almost completely devoid of historical and epistemological context. From reading the article, one would never know that the issue of legalization or decriminalization of drugs has been hotly debated for at least three decades.… Nor is there any reference to a carefully researched drug policy monograph series by the RAND Corporation, nor any reference to the National Institute on Drug Abuse's monograph series. The extensive coverage and debate in popular magazines and journals including, *inter alia, The Atlantic, The Economist, Harper's, Time, Scientific American*, etc. are consigned to oblivion. There is not even mention of the list of pro-legalization celebrities such as Nobel laureate Milton Friedman or conservative gadfly William F. Buckley, Jr.

It is as though Duke were addressing the issue *de novo*. And yet he is obviously aware of that history, having recounted some of it in his book. Further, he has obviously read the work of many of the scholars listed above, also citing many of them in his book. Well, I've already said that there is only so much one can do in the confines of an article, and Duke has apparently decided that a weighing of the costs and benefits of drug prohibition is the crux of the issue.

That is where we part company. I think reliance on the analytical mode of discourse for drug reform is a major conceptual and strategic error. Conceptually, the weighing of social costs and benefits flowing from the war on drugs is not central to the fundamental questions of individual autonomy, privacy, and responsibility....

Strategically, exclusive reliance on utilitarian debate lends itself to Crossfire-style shouting matches based on half-truths, unprovable claims, and bogus statistics. For every assertion, there is a counter-assertion: drug prohibition causes crime? No, drug use causes crime. There are too many variables. Controlled experiments are nigh impossible. Further, utilitarian arguments appeal primarily to the already convinced and a tiny band of policy wonks.

If this be deemed an exaggeration, at least it can be said that the utilitarian mode of discourse is profoundly incomplete. It assumes that education is the complete answer — that all that is necessary is for people of good will and sound intellect to inform themselves in order to come to the correct conclusion, i.e., repeal. This is an understandable position for a Yale Law School professor to take. But the history of twentieth-century drug policy makes a powerful case to the contrary — that people, even policy makers, are not driven by fact and knowledge, but by values and symbols. One is reminded of Holmes's dictum that the life of the law has not been logic: it has been experience.

Scientific and medical knowledge about drugs are simply over-whelmed by the power of the metaphor, the power of the image, whether it be marihuana as the "gateway" drug to "hard" drugs, a fried egg as symbol of "your brain on drugs," or "live-at-five" video footage of crack-addicted infants writhing in their cribs. No matter what the National Commission or the National Academy of Sciences says about marijuana; no matter that follow-up studies show that most babies overcome their birth deficits, given proper neonatal care; no matter that fetal alcohol syndrome is far worse. No amount or quality of argument based on empiricism and utilitarian analysis has ever been able to budge federal policy in a reformist direction. In the last fifteen years, the anti-drug position has hardened into political and legal concrete. The possibility of drug law reform, from the perspective of 1995 (with a Baby Boomer President who did not inhale and in October 1994 firmly denounced all illegal drugs as dangerous) is not even a dream; it is an illusion. And even if the contrary were true, even if marginal reforms were politically possible, it would take a generation of struggle to de-escalate the War on Drugs to the "kinder and gentler" levels that prevailed in, say, 1979.

This is why I argue that Duke has made the wrong argument at the wrong time. His lawyerly marshalling of the arguments and supporting facts ignores the reality that dozens, if not hundreds, of virtually identical "briefs" have failed to advance the cause of sound drug policy. Why will this one, however well done, be any different? The answer, I think, is self-evident.

Arguments based on (dis)utility simply do not respond to the fear and other emotions that dominate the drug policy debate. You cannot "win" the argument about flag burning as constitutionally-protected speech by showing that it does not harm national security. You cannot "win" the argument about the right to abortion by showing that it is a very safe medical procedure. You cannot even "win" the argument about the aesthetic merit of Maya Lin's black monolith Vietnam memorial with the true believers who wanted, needed, and paid for an Iwo Jima (Marines-on-the-beach) style heroic statuary.

In each case, the "truth" is a matter of conflicting values and cannot be resolved by empirical inquiry. It is the wrong epistemology. The same is and has been true of drug law and policy for nearly a century. *The drug debate is not, and has never been, about facts or evidence.* The issue is debated metaphysically and metaphorically. Consider the power of First Lady Nancy Reagan's brilliant anthropomorphic slam-dunk that "drugs steal our children's lives" or a similar trope by President Bush in a televised speech to the nation's schoolchildren: "They [(drugs)] have no conscience. . . . They just murder people. Young and old, good and bad, innocent and guilty — it doesn't matter."

How can fine-tuned empirical analysis stand up to those images? How can it defeat the outright lies? For example, at Pennsylvania Governor Raymond Shafer's press conference in the 1960s, he announced that a youth had taken LSD and stared into the sun until he was blinded. He later explained that he had made up the story in order to scare off potential experimenters from the real (but unstated) dangers of LSD. Why did he knowingly propagate a falsehood? He was justifying a deeper "truth," one that was real for him regardless of any data concerning the psychopharmacology of LSD.

* * *

. . . It is not the case that politicians and the public are panicked while more deliberate decision-makers can get it right. Judges, for example, have an appalling track record in their treatment of drug-related issues. The factually based, closely reasoned decisions that are the hallmark of good judging are almost nonexistent in this realm, even in the U.S. Supreme Court.

* * *

Indeed, there is often little difference between what is said by politicians and what is written by judges. Compare, for example, President Bush's speech quoted above with the opinion of the Chief Judge of the Southern District of Florida, condemning in *obiter dictum* drug dealers as "merchants of misery, destruction and death" whose greed has wrought "hideous evil" and "unimaginable sorrow" upon the nation.

There are two primary images in the cases on drugs. The original and probably still dominant image is the addict as slave to drugs. The imagery is expressed with a dark verbal palette: "degradation"; "debasement"; "shameful"; "depravity"; and "evil." The second major theme is drug traffic as an "insidious crime" that reinforces the subjugation of the addict causing crime and violence and inflicting "unimaginable sorrow" on society as a whole. . . .

* * *

Against such powerful images, reinforced by "fried eggs" and writhing crack babies, what chance does mere empiricism have? It really does not matter that Drug Enforcement Agency Chief Administrative Law Judge Frances Young ruled in 1988 that marijuana is "far safer than many foods we commonly consume" and that its medical benefits are "clear beyond any question." Its many therapeutic applications include the relief of intra-ocular pressure in glaucoma sufferers and the relief of the nausea often suffered by chemotherapy patients. The reality is that marijuana has an outlaw legal status; it is listed along with heroin as a Schedule I drug and is thus completely outlawed in medical practice in the United States, except for extremely restricted experimental protocols. It doesn't matter that in 1982 the National Academy of Sciences reviewed the findings and recommendation of the National Commission on Marihuana and Drug Abuse and found no "conclusive evidence" of major long-term public-health problems caused by marijuana, only "worrisome possibilities." The National Academy of Sciences basically endorsed the position of the 1972 National Commission: "On balance ... we believe that a policy of partial prohibition is clearly preferable to a policy of complete prohibition of supply and use."

* * *

So, is there no hope? What exactly should scholars such as Duke do in lieu of sterile utilitarianism? They should seek to transform the terms of discourse, create new images for discussion of "drugs," and expose the anthropomorphic premises of present law. They must strive to create a breakthrough of some kind, instead of imitating intellectual hamsters running in a wheel to nowhere.

You may have heard this before, but what is needed is a new paradigm. The drug problem as presently formulated is insoluble. What we have is a radical disjunction between those who see drugs primarily as substances conceptually indistinct from alcohol and tobacco, and those who see drugs as both agents and symbols of evil. You cannot solve "the drug problem" from within this fractured framework. Instead of utilitarian arguments for repeal or legalization, we need a viable meta-argument about the context of and ground rules for the argument. It will take a major breakthrough before true dialogue can even begin. Failing that, it will be business (or drug war) as usual, *ad infinitum*.

Notes and Questions

1. Professor Duke responded to Professor Wisotsky, essentially arguing that he is too pessimistic about the prospects for change. *See* Steven B. Duke, *Facts Do Matter: A Reply to Professor Wisotsky*, 27 CONN. L. REV. 651 (1995). Given that nearly two decades has passed since the exchange, we are in a position to consider (although perhaps not definitively resolve) who was correct. In support of Professor Duke's position, we can see that the opposition to the War on Drugs is much stronger than it was in 1995. Indeed, in Maryland itself, policymakers have made an effort to divert drug offenders to treatment rather than jail. *See* KEVIN PRANIS, PROGRESS AND CHALLENGES: AN ANALYSIS OF DRUG TREATMENT AND IMPRISONMENT IN MARYLAND FROM 2000 TO 2005 (Justice Policy Institute Report Sept. 2006). On the other hand, Professor Wisotsky might still be correct. How much has really changed in the last two decades? Prisons are still overflowing with drug offenders and there has been no significant legalization of drugs in the United States.

2. Season 3 of *The Wire* graphically portrays the problems with America's War on Drugs. In a recent interview, David Simon made clear what was implicit to viewers of *The Wire*—that he would like to "decriminalize drugs in a heartbeat [and] ... put all the interdiction money, all the incarceration money, all the enforcement money ... into drug treatment." BILL MOYERS, BILL MOYERS JOURNAL: THE CONVERSATION CONTINUES 81 (2011). Yet, if Professor Wisotsky is correct, does the powerful imagery of *The Wire* actually hinder Simon's desire for legalization? Watch *The Wire*, Season 3, Episode 7, at

19:20 minutes. Bubbles walks slowly through Hamsterdam and watches addicts over-dosing on drugs, young children wandering the streets without supervision, a woman performing sex presumably in exchange for drugs, and other horrible things. While le-galized drugs need not look like this, is the imagery consistent with Professor Wisotsky's point?

3. What is the ultimate lesson of Hamsterdam? Is it that politics trumps public pol-icy? Is the lesson that simple slogans such as "drugs are bad" always win out over com-plicated concepts—such as the legalized drug zones in Hamsterdam—that are more nuanced and difficult to explain? *See* Lance McMillan, *Drug Markets, Fringe Markets, and the Lessons of Hamsterdam*, 69 WASH. & LEE L. REV. 849 (2012).

C. Is Hamsterdam Legal and Is It Sound Policy?

In 2012 the Governor of New York proposed decriminalizing small amounts of mar-ijuana in order to make it a violation (the equivalent of a traffic ticket) punishable by a $100 fine, rather than a misdemeanor.[1] The Mayor of New York City and the police com-missioner endorsed the proposal, but the majority leader in the New York State Senate im-mediately stated his opposition[2] and the proposal died in the State Senate a few weeks later.[3] But was this legislation even necessary at all? If the New York City police commis-sioner favored decriminalization of marijuana, couldn't he have simply ordered his offi-cers to cease conducting any arrests for that crime? Should it matter that in previous years, police had made roughly 50,000 arrests annually for low-level marijuana posses-sion?[4] What if the order to cease enforcing drug laws came from a lower ranking police officer—for instance, Major Bunny Colvin in the Fifth District of the Baltimore Police Department—rather than the police commissioner himself? Can a law enforcement of-ficer—whether it be the commissioner, a lower ranking officer, or a cop walking a beat—simply decline to enforce the law? And if it is permissible, is it a good idea?

United States v. Armstrong
517 U.S. 456 (1996)

Chief Justice REHNQUIST delivered the opinion of the Court.

* * *

In April 1992, respondents were indicted in the United States District Court for the Central District of California on charges of conspiring to possess with intent to distribute more than 50 grams of cocaine base (crack) and conspiring to distribute the same, in vi-olation of 21 U.S.C. §§ 841 and 846 (1988 ed. and Supp. IV), and federal firearms offenses. For three months prior to the indictment, agents of the Federal Bureau of Alcohol, To-

---

1. *See* Thomas Kaplan, *Cuomo Seeks Cut in Frisk Arrests*, N.Y. TIMES, June 4, 2012, at A1.
2. *See* Thomas Kaplan, *G.O.P Leader Says Senate Won't Pass Marijuana Plan Without Changes*, N.Y. TIMES, June 7, 2012, at A20.
3. *See* Thomas Kaplan & John Eligon, *Divide in Albany Kills Proposal on Marijuana*, N.Y. TIMES, June 20, 2012, at A21.
4. *See* Thomas Kaplan, *Police and Mayor Back Plan to Curtail Marijuana Arrests*, N.Y. TIMES, June 5, 2012, at A1.

bacco, and Firearms and the Narcotics Division of the Inglewood, California, Police Department had infiltrated a suspected crack distribution ring by using three confidential informants. On seven separate occasions during this period, the informants had bought a total of 124.3 grams of crack from respondents and witnessed respondents carrying firearms during the sales. The agents searched the hotel room in which the sales were transacted, arrested respondents Armstrong and Hampton in the room, and found more crack and a loaded gun. The agents later arrested the other respondents as part of the ring.

In response to the indictment, respondents filed a motion for discovery or for dismissal of the indictment, alleging that they were selected for federal prosecution because they are black. In support of their motion, they offered only an affidavit by a "Paralegal Specialist," employed by the Office of the Federal Public Defender representing one of the respondents. The only allegation in the affidavit was that, in every one of the 24 § 841 or § 846 cases closed by the office during 1991, the defendant was black. Accompanying the affidavit was a "study" listing the 24 defendants, their race, whether they were prosecuted for dealing cocaine as well as crack, and the status of each case.

The Government opposed the discovery motion, arguing, among other things, that there was no evidence or allegation "that the Government has acted unfairly or has prosecuted non-black defendants or failed to prosecute them." The District Court granted the motion. It ordered the Government (1) to provide a list of all cases from the last three years in which the Government charged both cocaine and firearms offenses, (2) to identify the race of the defendants in those cases, (3) to identify what levels of law enforcement were involved in the investigations of those cases, and (4) to explain its criteria for deciding to prosecute those defendants for federal cocaine offenses.

* * *

… When the Government indicated it would not comply with the court's discovery order, the court dismissed the case.

* * *

A selective-prosecution claim is not a defense on the merits to the criminal charge itself, but an independent assertion that the prosecutor has brought the charge for reasons forbidden by the Constitution. Our cases delineating the necessary elements to prove a claim of selective prosecution have taken great pains to explain that the standard is a demanding one....

* * *

Of course, a prosecutor's discretion is "subject to constitutional constraints." *United States v. Batchelder*, 442 U.S. 114, 125 (1979). One of these constraints, imposed by the equal protection component of the Due Process Clause of the Fifth Amendment, is that the decision whether to prosecute may not be based on "an unjustifiable standard such as race, religion, or other arbitrary classification," *Oyler v. Boles*, 368 U.S. 448, 456, (1962)....

… Judicial deference to the decisions of these executive officers rests in part on an assessment of the relative competence of prosecutors and courts. "Such factors as the strength of the case, the prosecution's general deterrence value, the Government's enforcement priorities, and the case's relationship to the Government's overall enforcement plan are not readily susceptible to the kind of analysis the courts are competent to undertake." *United States v. Wayte*, 470 U.S. 598, 607 (1985). It also stems from a concern not to unnecessarily impair the performance of a core executive constitutional function. "Examining the basis of a prosecution delays the criminal proceeding, threatens to chill law enforcement by subjecting the prosecutor's motives and decisionmaking to outside inquiry, and may undermine prosecutorial effectiveness by revealing the Government's enforcement policy." *Ibid.*

The requirements for a selective-prosecution claim draw on "ordinary equal protection standards." *Id.* at 608. The claimant must demonstrate that the federal prosecutorial policy "had a discriminatory effect and that it was motivated by a discriminatory purpose." *Ibid.* To establish a discriminatory effect in a race case, the claimant must show that similarly situated individuals of a different race were not prosecuted....

* * *

Having reviewed the requirements to prove a selective-prosecution claim, we turn to the showing necessary to obtain discovery in support of such a claim. If discovery is ordered, the Government must assemble from its own files documents which might corroborate or refute the defendant's claim. Discovery thus imposes many of the costs present when the Government must respond to a prima facie case of selective prosecution. It will divert prosecutors' resources and may disclose the Government's prosecutorial strategy. The justifications for a rigorous standard for the elements of a selective-prosecution claim thus require a correspondingly rigorous standard for discovery in aid of such a claim.

* * *

... The vast majority of the Courts of Appeals require the defendant to produce some evidence that similarly situated defendants of other races could have been prosecuted, but were not, and this requirement is consistent with our equal protection case law....

The Court of Appeals reached its decision in part because it started "with the presumption that people of *all* races commit *all* types of crimes—not with the premise that any type of crime is the exclusive province of any particular racial or ethnic group." It cited no authority for this proposition, which seems contradicted by the most recent statistics of the United States Sentencing Commission. Those statistics show: More than 90% of the persons sentenced in 1994 for crack cocaine trafficking were black; 93.4% of convicted LSD dealers were white; and 91% of those convicted for pornography or prostitution were white. Presumptions at war with presumably reliable statistics have no proper place in the analysis of this issue.

The Court of Appeals also expressed concern about the "evidentiary obstacles defendants face." But all of its sister Circuits that have confronted the issue have required that defendants produce some evidence of differential treatment of similarly situated members of other races or protected classes. In the present case, if the claim of selective prosecution were well founded, it should not have been an insuperable task to prove that persons of other races were being treated differently than respondents. For instance, respondents could have investigated whether similarly situated persons of other races were prosecuted by the State of California and were known to federal law enforcement officers, but were not prosecuted in federal court. We think the required threshold—a credible showing of different treatment of similarly situated persons—adequately balances the Government's interest in vigorous prosecution and the defendant's interest in avoiding selective prosecution.

In the case before us, respondents' "study".... failed to identify individuals who were not black and could have been prosecuted for the offenses for which respondents were charged, but were not so prosecuted. The judgment of the Court of Appeals is therefore reversed....

It is so ordered.

[The concurring opinions of Justices Souter, Ginsburg and Breyer, as well as Justice Stevens' dissenting opinion are omitted.]

_____

Notes and Questions

1. The majority opinion contends that "if the claim of selective prosecution were well founded, it should not have been an insuperable task to prove that persons of other races were being treated differently than respondents." Does that seem correct to you? Where would Armstrong have found white individuals who had been caught with crack but not charged? Could he have asked passersby at the local shopping mall? If he found any similarly situated white individuals, would he have been able to get them to sign affidavits swearing that they were caught with crack but not charged?

2. The vast majority of individuals arrested in *The Wire* are black and live in neighborhoods that are predominantly African-American. How would those defendants know if any similarly situated white individuals were not prosecuted?

3. The Court's decision in *Armstrong* is typically cited for the proposition that prosecutors have almost unlimited discretion in their charging decisions. Does it stand to reason that police have similarly broad discretion? What does the *Armstrong* decision tell you about the legality of Hamsterdam?

4. Is broad discretion — whether for prosecutors or police — a necessary evil in the criminal justice system? Can you imagine a framework that eliminates such discretion? In New Orleans, former District Attorney Harry Connick eliminated plea bargaining, instead relying on careful up-front charging. For a discussion, see Ronald Wright & Marc Miller, *The Screening/Bargaining Tradeoff*, 55 STAN. L. REV. 29 (2002).

5. Many people have driven past a police officer while exceeding the speed limit and not been stopped. Putting aside traffic violations however, do the police regularly ignore serious criminal violations? In the next article, Professor Alexandra Natapoff answers in the affirmative.

Alexandra Natapoff, Underenforcement
75 Fordham Law Review 1715 (2006)

The United States' criminal system is infamous for its excesses: too many laws, over-criminalization, and over-punishment. Our comprehensive criminal codes, staggering incarceration rate, and their heavy impact on communities of color have made charges of overenforcement pervasive. As the "politics of crime" generates new offenses and ever harsher punishments, the United States puts more people in prison than any other nation. Many scholars conclude that the criminal system occupies an increasingly central role as a general governance mechanism.

Criticisms of the U.S. system often revolve around the insight that a system as pervasive, harsh, and racially charged as ours requires serious rethinking. Indeed, much of the critical literature focuses on the disproportionate weight of overenforcement on minority communities. The overcriminalization and mass incarceration of so much of the black male population has created a visible legal underclass, and has perpetuated the destruction of families, economic opportunities, and other human capital. Overenforcement policies are also increasingly challenged as normatively counterproductive; with their draconian overkill and racial skew, they foster resentment and disrespect for the law among otherwise law-abiding members of the community and reduce social incentives to obey the law. For some, the racial inequalities created by overenforcement strike at the heart of the legitimacy of the entire system. In these ways, "overenforcement" has become one of the central lenses through which the racial imbalances, inegalitarianism, and other weaknesses of the criminal justice system are viewed and understood.

By comparison, underenforcement has been given short shrift, particularly in the area of street and violent crime....

Underenforcement deserves a more central role in the evaluation of the evenhandedness and democratic legitimacy of the criminal system. Underenforcement is a weak state response to lawbreaking as well as to victimization. It thus offers important insights into the government's relationship with vulnerable groups in the context of the criminal system. In practice, underenforcement is often linked with official discrimination, increased violence, legal failure, and the undemocratic treatment of the poor. Underenforcement can also be a form of deprivation, tracking familiar categories of race, gender, class, and political powerlessness. Conceived of as a form of public policy, underenforcement is a crucial distribution mechanism whereby the social good of lawfulness can be withheld.

Underenforcement is far from abstract: It embodies concrete relationships and experiences, often of violence or insecurity. Within certain communities or institutions—what I will call "underenforcement zones"—the state routinely and predictably fails to enforce the law to the detriment of vulnerable residents. Police concede that they will not arrest certain sorts of perpetrators; many victims expect that they will remain unprotected; and violators rest secure in the knowledge that their crimes are the sort that will go unpunished. This type of underenforcement deprives residents of personal and economic security, rendering calls to the police futile or even dangerous and victimhood a routine fact of life. For residents of these zones, lawfulness is spread unevenly throughout daily life and the legal system is at best unpredictable.

... When law enforcement fails to answer constituent needs, it devalues the security, property, and dignitary interests of those the law purportedly protects. More formally, such failure weakens the rule of law in those areas by neglecting the enforcement of existing legal rules. By failing to maintain an atmosphere of legality, law enforcement turns its back on victim classes twice: first, by denying them material protective resources, and second, by depriving them of a robust, responsive legal system.

* * *

I. The Spectrum: Examples of Underenforcement

* * *

A defining aspect of living in high-crime urban communities is that police often fail to respond to crime. Police openly let certain sorts of criminality slide, and residents know that their complaints may be responded to weakly or not at all. While it is commonplace to contrast official tolerance of "white-collar crime" with intolerance of "street" or traditional crime, this comparison elides the fact that in some neighborhoods, street crime is officially accepted as a fact of life....

... This urban underenforcement takes various forms, including unsolved homicides, permitted open-air drug markets, slow or nonexistent 911 responses, and the tolerance of pervasive, low levels of violence, property crimes, and public disorder. The sources of the phenomena are likewise diverse: inadequate funding for urban area services, official expectations about crime and disorder in politically weak neighborhoods, police hostility to and fear of residents, and residents' distrust of police.

It is also well recognized that poor urban communities of color suffer from higher crime and victimization rates than do more affluent white neighborhoods and that African

Americans (who tend to live in poor urban communities) are disproportionately victimized. But it is unclear precisely how law enforcement decision making contributes to these trends, in part because underenforcement is so often informal and unacknowledged by police themselves....

* * *

Received wisdom has it that police and prosecutors "invariably" or "almost always" pursue, arrest, and charge perpetrators for serious felonies. But this rule of thumb is imperfect. For a constellation of reasons, including under-funding, lack of political will, and poor police-community relations, serious crimes in inner cities often go unaddressed.

In Los Angeles, California, for example, of the 11,000 homicides since 1988, there are nearly 6000 for which no arrest was ever made; three-quarters of those homicides are concentrated in one-quarter of the city. In the neighborhood now known as South L.A. (formerly South Central), more than half of all killers are never caught. Unsolved homicide rates correlate not only to neighborhood poverty and racial segregation, but also to thinner police forces, reflecting the unequal allocation of public resources. For example, while the Compton area suffers the city's highest homicide rates, it has only seventy-five full-time police deputies, while the neighboring southeast division — with dropping homicide rates — employs more than 250 officers to patrol a comparable geographical area and has an only slightly larger population. Los Angeles Police Chief William Bratton criticized the city for devoting so few resources to policing "one of the most dangerous cities in America. Sorry, you get what you pay for," he said. "It's incredible what's going on over there."

Baltimore, Maryland, similarly suffers from a long history of underenforcement of serious crimes in its poorest and most dangerous neighborhoods. With an overall murder rate over seven times the national average, the 1998 murder rate for African Americans in Baltimore was six times higher than for whites. While there are numerous contributing factors, residents and officials alike blame these trends, at least in part, on police underenforcement. Some residents perceive the police as unresponsive or even indifferent to crime and victimization, asserting that "police have become reluctant in their desire to fight crime." One resident reported that she "called the police over twenty times to arrest known drug dealers in front of her house and the police still did not appear." Even the city's acting Police Commissioner, Edward T. Norris, recognized that police failure accounted for some part of the city's violence. "[Baltimore] is a city where many members of the general public have lost faith in the resolve, skill, and even integrity of their police," he said.

An infamous 2002 incident revealed the depths of police inattention to drug dealing and violence. Angela Dawson and her family had repeatedly called the police and 311 about drug dealing in their neighborhood, but the drug dealers about whom they complained were at best chased away, and often the police failed to respond at all. When threats against the family were relayed to the police, the police provided no additional protection. When an individual later assaulted Mrs. Dawson, he was arrested and released the next morning. Finally, after months of police inaction, drug dealers arranged a firebombing in retaliation for the family's complaints. Mrs. Dawson and five of her children died in the attack.

Other cities exhibit similar underenforcement tendencies. According to a study conducted by The Dallas Morning News:

> The murder rate in southern Dallas [a high-poverty section of the city] is twice as high as in the rest of the city. Assaults are nearly twice as likely.... Business or home burglaries are one and a half times higher in the south than in the north.

Police response times are slow citywide by national standards—and they're worst in the highest-crime areas. And the officers patrolling those neighborhoods are the department's least experienced …

… "We've abandoned the people and the neighborhoods," [says] Police Chief David Kunkle. The Dallas Police Department's own study indicated that "[r]andom gunfire, alleged prostitution, and other nuisance complaints get low priority and often no follow-up"; that "[p]roperty crimes are rarely investigated and are typically handled over the telephone by an expediter—most residents found this to be an unacceptable response by the police department"; and that "[t]he general feeling among members of the Hispanic community is to 'stay clear of officers.'"

* * *

Law enforcement unresponsiveness creates a vicious cycle: Criminals grow bold, while residents grow reluctant to cooperate with police, making serious crimes such as drug dealing and homicide harder to solve, and police more reluctant to work on them. In those "hardest-hit neighborhoods, people describe how fear, and the conviction that serious crimes are not solved, makes them reluctant to confront homicide, unwilling to cooperate with authorities or act as witnesses, and disinclined to place their faith in the police." Potential victims—mostly black and Latino young men—see the police as "unreliable and hostile," and conclude that the police will not protect them. Police likewise describe their alienation from residents, their fear of going into high-crime areas, and their conviction that "the people here hate us."

* * *

Prostitution

Prostitution is an infamous "underenforcement zone." Not only is the crime of prostitution itself routinely underenforced against prostitutes, and even more so against customers (so-called "johns"), but a constellation of other underenforcement practices spring up in association with the tolerance of the sex trade, including the under-protection of prostitutes from other crimes and the tolerance of criminality in prostitution-heavy areas. This underenforcement contributes to the lawlessness and violence that surrounds the prostitution industry, alienates prostitutes from legal institutions, and creates distrust of the police in surrounding communities.

Prostitution is in some ways a subset of the urban underenforcement phenomenon described above, often associated with urban decay and a frequent target of community policing programs. However, it has special characteristics that deserve additional attention. First, prostitution is a prime example of how underenforcement exacerbates lawlessness. Official toleration of prostitution is tied to the underenforcement of numerous other laws, driving a wedge between law enforcement and community residents, including prostitutes themselves. Prostitution also highlights the official tendency to withhold full legal protection from those who have broken the law in some way, a socially destructive and legally problematic aspect of underenforcement.

The criminal offense of prostitution is enforced infrequently and unevenly. Many prostitutes who work off the street are never arrested, while "streetwalkers," who are arrested more frequently, are often immediately released. Customers are arrested even more rarely. This high level of nonenforcement is also racially skewed: Prostitutes who are arrested are overwhelmingly minority women. This underenforcement is public and official: Police, prosecutors, and judges openly make resource allocation decisions based on the assumption that prostitution laws will remain underenforced.

At the same time, crimes such as assault, robbery, and rape against prostitutes are common, while police responses to prostitute victimization are weak. . . .

Above and beyond failing to protect prostitutes, police themselves often commit crimes against prostitutes. Common practices include demanding sex in return for the decision not to arrest, trading protection for sex, and raping prostitutes. Official harassment of prostitutes also correlates with racial harassment; some studies indicate that prostitutes of color are more likely to receive illegal police treatment. . . .

More broadly, underenforcement practices erode the lawfulness of the environments in which prostitution takes place. Nineteenth century red-light districts were neighborhoods officially set aside where prostitution, liquor, and gambling laws were relaxed, and other forms of criminality were notorious. Today, residents of prostitution-heavy neigh borhoods often complain that police do not enforce laws regarding alcohol, drugs, loitering, noise, and other public nuisances. In response, many communities have set up private police forces—surveillance teams, patrols, and websites—to deter and punish prostitutes themselves. Community members who take law enforcement matters into their own hands do so in recognition of the fact that the police function has failed them.

* * *

Current Underenforcement Doctrine

Jurisprudentially speaking, underenforcement is a non-issue. Two strands of jurisprudence render this so. First is the Supreme Court's highly deferential treatment of enforcement decisions—to arrest or not to arrest, to charge or not to charge—rendered by law enforcement officials. The Supreme Court consistently treats underenforcement of the criminal law as a necessary incident of law enforcement discretion, which in turn is practically unreviewable. Absent unconstitutional motivations, a single instance of non-enforcement triggers no cognizable legal concerns. Police may decline to arrest a person whom they have probable cause to believe has committed a crime. Likewise, prosecutors routinely and properly decide not to press charges that are legally supportable. Indeed, we recognize that police and prosecutors cannot and should not pursue every case they might, and the Supreme Court has made clear that individual police failures to enforce laws and even direct court orders are not actionable.

Even when nonenforcement decisions reach systemic proportions, law enforcement decision makers are well shielded from judicial scrutiny. In United States v. Armstrong, the Court declined to permit discovery regarding racially suspect prosecutorial charging patterns based in large part on the understanding that prosecutorial discretion is the "special province of the Executive," entitled to a "presumption of regularity." This sort of judicial cloaking of prosecutorial decisions tends to validate all under- and overenforcement policies; it also ensures that the public will rarely be able to obtain information about actual enforcement patterns. Even more definitively, in McCleskey v. Kemp, the Court declined to invalidate discretionary prosecutorial decisions that resulted in statistically significant racial disparities in the treatment of capital defendants. The decision reads like a treatise on discretion, in which the Court describes the near-sanctity of law enforcement choice and the central role that discretionary decisions by police, prosecutors, and juries play throughout the criminal system. Armstrong and McCleskey have been widely interpreted to preclude meaningful judicial review of the systemic impact of law enforcement discretion.

* * *

The second strand of jurisprudence that shields criminal underenforcement from review is the Court's long-standing commitment to a "negative" theory of constitutional rights, under which the state is not constitutionally obligated to provide for basic human needs, even when such needs are themselves necessary to preserve life, liberty, or material equality. This general approach characterizes the Court's treatment of a wide range of social services, from education to abortion. Absent any racial or other independently unconstitutional basis for the inequality, the state's failure to provide services, or even failure to provide them in equal measure, rarely triggers constitutional concern.

In the criminal law context, this negative rights philosophy is embodied in DeShaney v. Winebago County Department of Social Services, in which the Court held that the state's failure to protect an individual from private violence does not violate substantive due process....

More recently, the Court extended its position in DeShaney, holding in Town of Castle Rock v. Gonzales that even where a court orders police to perform a protective function—in that case by issuing a domestic violence protective order—and even where state law mandates police protection, this does not give rise to a protected property interest as a matter of procedural due process....

Together, DeShaney and Gonzales stand for the proposition that the Constitution does not mandate police protection. Even court orders and legislative enactments that call for police protection in specific instances will not give rise to constitutionally protected interests. In effect, police and prosecutors retain their discretion to underenforce the law and allocate resources as they please even in the face of judicial and legislative mandates to the contrary.

* * *

Conclusion

Our criminal system is rife with inegalitarian enforcement failures—pervasive, yet little-noticed ways that the state predictably abandons its constituents by failing to enforce the rules. In underenforcement "zones," social life vacillates between lawfulness and lawlessness: While some aspects of the law are enforced, others are not; some victims are protected while others are not. This is the lawlessness of the frontier and of fledgling democracies that makes people insecure and distrustful of government. It is the sort of localized unpredictability that implicates many of the same rule-of-law concerns associated with transitional justice, states of emergency, and other extraordinary circumstances where the law fails to operate in a coherent, rule-bound fashion. And yet it exists openly in well-lit places throughout American society.

Underenforcement casts a long shadow over the viability and legitimacy of our criminal system. Like overenforcement, rampant underenforcement makes the rule of law into a democratic luxury; it renders full, fair, and balanced law enforcement an experience limited to those who can bend the government to their will. To address this democratic deficit, underenforcement should be better recognized as a potentially destructive phenomenon in its own right. In recognition of the linkages between over- and underenforcement, underenforcement needs to be approached qualitatively, as a call not for harsher but for more responsive policing. Structural and doctrinal criticisms of our criminal system should better account for the role of underenforcement in eroding the system's efficacy, fairness, and democratic accountability. Perhaps most importantly, it demands that we attend more carefully to the experiences of the system's many clients, including the vulnerable and the disadvantaged, who, while sometimes criminals themselves, remain entitled to the protections of the law.

Notes and Questions

1. As Professor Natapoff notes, commentators have long bemoaned over-enforcement and mass imprisonment in the criminal justice system. Far less attention has been paid to the damage caused by under-enforcement. After watching *The Wire*, do you find this absence of scholarship surprising? Does the series vividly portray a problem that academia has missed? For instance, watch *The Wire*, Season 3, Episode 11, at 37:10 minutes, in which residents praise the police for the drop in crime and urge the officers to tackle additional problems, such as noise violations.

2. One of the more memorable scenes from *The Wire* comes when Officers McNulty and Greggs stumble across Hamsterdam and confront Major Colvin about it.

Greggs: And it's legal to sell here?

Colvin: It's not legal. We just look the other way is all.

Officer: But how can you?

Colvin: I know it hurts your head to think about....

The Wire, Season 3, Episode 7, at 37:00 minutes. Can Major Colvin exercise this much discretion without violating the law? Professor Natapoff's article suggests the answer is yes. Is there any argument to the contrary?

3. Is it unusual for a law enforcement agency to openly acknowledge that they are not enforcing the law as written? And if an agency does so, is it likely that another agency will be upset with that policy? In Texas, it appears clear that an individual caught with a crack pipe containing drug residue is guilty of felony drug possession. Yet, the Harris County District Attorney refused to charge any of those cases as felonies, instead handing out tickets for the misdemeanor offense of possessing drug paraphernalia. While many criminal justice experts applauded, the policy "infuriate[d] Houston police." Brian Rogers, *Crack Policy Puts Harris County DA at Odds With Police*, Hous. Chron., Dec. 5, 2011.

4. Assuming Hamsterdam is legal, is it a good idea? If Professor Natapoff is correct that underenforcing prohibitions against open-air drug markets and other criminal activity severely damages urban communities, would moving most drug operations to a single location allow police to better serve communities that are often ignored today? Consider the remainder of the scene where Detective Greggs incredulously asks if it is legal to sell drugs in Hamsterdam:

Greggs: And it's legal to sell here?

Colvin: It's not legal. We just look the other way is all.

Officer: But how can you?

Colvin: I know it hurts your head to think about. But before you decide to lose your mind on this, take a moment [and] ride around to my corners, my worst drug corners ... They're empty. All of them. District-wide, my crime is down 5%.

The Wire, Season 3, Episode 7, at 37:00 minutes. Interestingly, while the creator of *The Wire*, David Simon, is a proponent of legalized zones, his writing partner (and former Baltimore narcotics detective), Ed Burns, is more skeptical. *See* Rafael Alvarez, The Wire: Truth Be Told 205 (2009).

5. Assuming legislative bodies (or police exercising their discretion) decide to create free zones like Hamsterdam where it is permissible to buy and sell drugs, how would they deal with the transport of drugs into and out of the free zones? For instance, Watch *The*

Wire, Season 3, Episode 7 at 32:00 minutes, where officers conduct a traffic stop and find a large quantity of drugs in the car. One drug dealer objects that "Y'all can't do this, we're headed to Hamsterdam." If the government does not outrightly legalize drugs and instead only makes them available under limited circumstances, won't the government have to set up very clear regulations in advance? And won't those regulations be very difficult to draft?

6. Relatedly, some reformers propose decriminalizing personal quantities of drugs, but retaining laws against widescale drug trafficking or selling drugs to children. Are there bright line rules that can cover these situations, or will these be thorny, grey rules that will also be difficult to legislate?

D. Responding to Drug Offenders: Is Drug Court the Answer?

The previous section explored whether society should legalize personal drug use, decriminalize it, or quarantine drug distribution to small areas. Assuming the status quo and that none of those options take hold, how should the criminal justice system deal with offenders who are arrested for drug use? For decades, the answer has been that we treat drug offenders the same as other offenders by routing their cases through the adversary criminal justice system. Recently, however, an alternative approach has taken hold. An increasing number of jurisdictions are using drug courts to deal with a small subset of offenders who might fare better outside the standard plea bargaining and jury trial system. The article below explores the benefits and criticisms of drug courts.

The Honorable Peggy Fulton Hora & Theodore Stalcup, Drug Treatment Courts in the Twenty-First Century: The Evolution of the Revolution in Problem-Solving Courts
42 Georgia Law Review 717 (2008)

* * *

A. The Traditional Criminal Justice System and America's Drug Problem

The number of persons incarcerated in federal, state, and local correctional facilities across the nation has risen dramatically in the last decade. As of 2005, more than 2.1 million Americans were incarcerated, 4.1 million Americans were on probation, and over 700,000 were on parole. In all, nearly seven million people are under the control of the criminal justice system. If they were residents of a single U.S. state, the population would be larger than thirty-eight existing states in the United States.

Of these seven million or so people, eighty percent of adults incarcerated for felonies could be categorized in one or more of the following ways:

1. were regular alcohol or other drug abusers;

2. had been convicted of an alcohol or other drug violation;

3. were under the influence of alcohol or other drugs at the time of their crime;

4. committed a crime to support their drug use; or,

5. exhibited one or more elements of any of these categories.

Additionally, twenty-nine percent of state prisoners and twenty-five percent of federal prisoners have committed violent offenses, including homicides and sexual assaults, while under the influence of drugs. When alcohol is added to the mix, studies suggest that as many as thirty-seven percent of assault offenders and sixty percent of sexual offenders were drinking alcohol at the time of the offense.

Incarceration does little to change substance use patterns. Subsequent to release, ex-offenders continue to use alcohol or other drugs at alarming rates. In 2004, 19.1 million Americans, nearly eight percent of the total population, were users of an illicit drug. Among persons on probation, however, the rate was over twenty-six percent.

As previously stated, research shows that nearly seventy percent of all drug offenders are rearrested within three years of release from incarceration. Roughly forty-one percent are rearrested for a specific drug offense.

The costs associated with alcohol- or other drug-abusing offenders are staggering. The U.S. government is now spending upwards of $12.9 billion per year on illicit drug control, including police protection, the judiciary, corrections, and related costs. In 2003, alcohol and other drugs were responsible for roughly 628,000 emergency room visits in the United States. Moreover, the total impact on society of alcohol and other drug use is estimated to have cost the United States in excess of $180 billion in 2002, a 5.34% increase over the prior decade. Using U.S. Census data, this figure represents a burden of $642 for every resident of the country during 2002....

Striking disparities exist across ethnic lines between rates of drug use, rates of incarceration for drug-related crimes, and access to substance abuse treatment. Despite the fact that seventy-two percent of regular drug users are white, fifteen-percent are African American, and ten percent are Latino, of those incarcerated in state prisons on drug charges, forty-five percent are African American, twenty-one percent are Latino, and twenty-six percent are white. Not only are arrest rates higher for people of color, but access to treatment in this population is even more restricted than in the white population, and their treatment outcomes are poorer.

The impact of substance abuse on women and families also is profound. The number of women incarcerated continues to rise at a rate one-third higher than that of men. Nearly one-third of women report being victims of domestic violence and over 1,400 are killed by their partners each year, an average of three women each day. Between 1993 and 1998, nearly three out of every four victims who suffered violence by an intimate partner, such as a spouse, boyfriend, or girlfriend, reported that alcohol or other drug use had been a factor. More than half of men in treatment for alcohol dependence or abuse have inflicted violence on their intimate partners.

The cost of intimate partner violence exceeds $5.8 billion each year, with $4.1 billion in direct medical costs and mental health services. Intimate partner violence also leaves a legacy. Children who witness domestic violence are more likely to become users of alcohol and other drugs; experience educational, mental health, and behavioral problems; and perpetuate a generational tradition of violence by becoming perpetrators themselves.

With such sobering statistics, the important question to ask is how the criminal justice system handles this troubled population. Despite some innovative efforts, historically, the problem of substance abuse has been addressed by the criminal justice system with a combination of punishment and indifference. In 1997, only ten percent of drug abusers were given treatment while they were incarcerated in state prisons, a fall from twenty-five percent just six years earlier. The numbers are only slightly better when other resources such as self-help programs—with typically voluntary twelve-step attendance—

are included as options in the custody setting. Intervention while in custody can be effective when it incorporates not only substance abuse treatment during physical detention but also a transitional program for reentry into society that integrates an aftercare component. Prisoners receiving comprehensive treatment, transitional care, and aftercare have recidivism rates half that of untreated control groups. However, treatment in custody without the structured follow-up offered by the successful programs is only marginally effective. For those on probation, only seventeen percent of drug abusers receive treatment once sentenced.

Because addiction is a disease that most medical professionals agree cannot be overcome by self-will alone, merely incarcerating substance abusers or placing them on probation without treatment fails to treat the disease and invites the inevitability of recidivism. Perversely, lengthy incarceration is not only the most expensive response to drug crimes but also the option most likely to result in recidivism. While there are multiple, sometimes conflicting, theories of punishment in our criminal justice system — retribution, deterrence, rehabilitation, and incapacitation — it is naive to believe that merely incarcerating a substance abuser, that is, physically incapacitating them, will lead to recovery from addiction or cessation of alcohol or other drug use. Although prisons and jails, ostensibly, have procedures in place to prevent drugs from entering facilities, they are still readily available behind bars. As a result, drug use by individuals may continue while they are incarcerated, despite the best efforts of law enforcement to prevent it.

The correctional system consumes billions of dollars annually with few positive results. California, for example, spends $900 million annually to incarcerate parole violators. Although three quarters of California inmates have alcohol or other drug problems, only six percent receive treatment while in custody, and a positive drug test is often the sole reason these inmates are returned to prison while paroled. Because of overwhelming statistics like these, multiple jurisdictions across the nation have instituted problem-solving courts, specifically drug treatment courts, as a pragmatic yet innovative way to address the root cause of many recidivistic offenses: addictive disease.

B. Drug Treatment Courts and America's Drug Problem

In 1989, the first adult drug treatment court was established in Miami, Dade County, Florida. Since then, the number of drug courts has grown steadily. As of 2004, there were 1,621 operational drug treatment courts in the United States and 215 jurisdictions were formally involved in the process of planning such a court.

Drug treatment courts enable the criminal justice system to more effectively tackle the problem of addiction and the issues presented by substance abusers. Drug treatment courts are organized around a set of unifying principles called the "key components." These principles of drug treatment courts integrate the need to address addictive disease by enabling the traditional criminal justice system to use a non-adversarial approach. Participants are identified early in the criminal court process, placed quickly into a treatment program, and monitored frequently by the court and by the treatment provider with drug tests. Drug treatment courts may use a pre- or post-adjudication model. Pre-plea drug treatment courts operate as diversion programs in which the defendant is given the opportunity to participate without entering a plea of guilty or going through the trial process. The end result of successful participation is dismissal of the criminal charges. Post-plea courts require a finding of guilt, often by way of a guilty plea. In the post-plea model, the program is imposed as a condition of probation, and any sentence is suspended pending completion of the program.

Drug treatment court participants routinely interact directly with the judge and other members of the drug court team rather than speaking exclusively through counsel as in traditional court proceedings. The drug treatment court team generally is comprised of the judge, defense counsel, prosecutor, treatment providers, and community corrections personnel. Some courts also have team members who are probation officers, substance abuse counselors, or other helping professionals. In addition, some jurisdictions involve community policing representatives and concerned members of the public as part of the team. All team members work cooperatively with the drug treatment court participants to reduce their propensity to commit further crimes by treating their addictive disease. Team members focus on returning drug treatment court participants to productive, sober membership in society....

* * *

III. The Role of Coercion

According to Black's Law Dictionary, to coerce is to "compel by force or threat." In the drug treatment court context, it is more accurate to say that a bench officer, using "judicial leverage," "offers" or "suggests" the treatment option rather than "coerces" its selection. The drug court judge offers the defendant a choice of penal consequences where historically the available options were exceedingly narrow. As outlined above, these options without treatment are largely ineffective, while the less onerous option, drug treatment court, offers a program wherein the individual has the opportunity for rehabilitation and often the possibility of less onerous penal consequences.

Plea bargaining, which requires the defendant to waive many of his or her rights in exchange for conviction on a lesser charge and a diminished punishment, is the status quo for the overwhelming majority of criminal drug defendants in the United States. The drug treatment court model, which asks defendants to waive some of their rights in exchange for the opportunity to receive treatment and possibly avoid a criminal conviction, should be embraced as a natural extension of the plea bargaining process.

A. Coerced Versus "Voluntary" Treatment

Detractors of the treatment proffered by drug courts argue that the treatment is forced, and question whether courts should be in the business of coercing people accused or convicted of crimes into medical treatment. The implication is that by offering defendants a subjectively favorable sentence in exchange for their agreement to enter the drug treatment court program, the defendants' right to refuse treatment somehow has been violated.

Contrary to this assertion, drug treatment courts are voluntary programs that do not diminish the right to refuse treatment. In many models, a determination of eligibility to participate in treatment is made at the time of charging. In a drug treatment court context, an arrest is viewed as an "opportunity for intervention." Initially, the defendant is offered the choice of whether to participate in the drug treatment program or to receive traditional case processing, whether or not that commonly includes incarceration. In some models, post-conviction defendants are referred after sentencing to the drug treatment court for supervised probation. In any case, a full explanation is given to the offender by defense counsel or, if the person is unrepresented, by a court coordinator. The explanation must include a description of the program and the consequences that may result from each possible choice. This counseling represents an opportunity for the defense both to practice advocacy and to ensure the client understands the rights being extended or waived.

Although defendants often hope to avoid incarceration by voluntarily enrolling in drug treatment court programs, they must be, and are, informed that violation of the drug treatment court contract may result in short terms of confinement, sometimes called "smart punishment." Some programs allow participants to choose between jail time and a community work alternative program when there has been a breach of the drug treatment court contract.

If the defendant chooses the drug treatment program alternative, he may still, at any point in the process, decide to leave the program and enter the traditional criminal justice case processing system, with all the attendant rights, remedies, burdens, and consequences of that system.

The treatment option provided by drug treatment courts is synonymous with the practice of plea bargaining. Nationally over ninety-five percent of drug offenses are settled with a plea bargain; less than one in twenty is adjudicated by trial. Every day in courts across the nation defendants waive certain constitutional rights in order to receive a more favorable outcome, such as a reduced sentence or charge. In a plea bargaining situation, defendants who receive probation may be required to waive their right to be free from unreasonable search and seizure under the Fourth Amendment of the U.S. Constitution by accepting what is known as a "search clause," which may include their person, personal effects, automobile, and home. Defendants in drug treatment courts, like most criminal defendants, also relinquish the right to a speedy trial guaranteed by the Sixth Amendment. Similarly, drug court participants surrender various rights when agreeing to enter drug treatment court (for example, substance abuse treatment confidentiality), but also gain the benefits that go along with successful treatment.

*   *   *

Finally, although a defendant's participation in a pre-plea drug court is based on an informed decision to accept treatment, the defendant retains the right to subsequently refuse treatment, withdraw from the program, and face resumption of traditional criminal proceedings. The defendant's drug treatment court participation cannot be used adversely if he withdraws from the program and returns to traditional criminal proceedings. Those who elect to leave the program and have their case tried in a traditional court have all of their constitutional rights reinstated. Post-plea participants also are able to leave the program, although they may have to accept any conviction and its subsequent penal consequences based on the plea entered prior to beginning the program.

*   *   *

D. Drug Treatment Court Components

Short Jail Terms

Brief periods of incarceration for noncompliance with the terms of the treatment program are an integral part of drug treatment courts. The sanctions usually involve one or two days but no more than one week of jail time. "Smart punishment," as the short jail stays are sometimes called, is primarily criticized because of concerns about potential due process violations. When the drug court team determines that a remedial period of incarceration is necessary to facilitate recovery, there may be no formal hearing. A formal adversarial hearing is not required because the drug treatment court team has agreed in advance to the availability of this sanction, and the client has knowingly and voluntarily consented to this process upon enrollment in the program. A hearing may be granted, however, if specifically requested by the participant or defense attorney. In any court setting, constitutional principles are paramount, therefore the outcome goals of drug courts never trump a defendant's fundamental constitutional rights. It is the defendant, and never the court, who exercises the right to waive constitutional safeguards, and such waiver must be voluntary, knowing, and intelligent. Additionally, participants are forewarned of the consequences for failing to comply with the program's terms and are advised that the punishments may include short jail stays. Only after being advised of the terms can a defendant voluntarily and knowingly consent to such conditions and become a drug court participant.

Frequent Court Appearances

Frequent appearances before the same judge are a crucial component of drug treatment court. A survey conducted by the Drug Court Clearinghouse at American University found that "eighty percent of participants … would not have remained if they did not appear before a judge as part of the process." Involving the same bench officer in each of the defendant's appearances lessens the chance that inconsistent rulings and ignorance of a particular defendant's circumstances will interfere with the treatment program. The Criminal Justice Research Institute reported that drug treatment court participants hailed close supervision and encouragement by judges as among the top three factors that led to their success in drug court programs.

The direct involvement of the bench officer may be one of the reasons that drug treatment court programs are more successful than other methods employed by the criminal justice system in dealing with addicts. One study of high-risk drug addicts (those with previous treatment failures or mental disorders) found that eighty percent of participants who had frequent mandatory contact with the judge successfully graduated from the program. A comparison group that saw the judge only when requested by the treatment provider, much like California's Proposition 36 program, suffered from a completion rate of only twenty percent.

* * *

V. Ethical Issues of Collaboration Between Prosecution and Defense

Drug treatment courts are founded on a nonadversarial, collaborative approach that is focused on the participant's recovery rather than the minutia of the pending case. This is critical because drug addiction remains a unique and pervasive problem that cannot be adequately addressed by traditional case processing. The adversarial nature of traditional criminal courts may be a roadblock to open communication and thus a hindrance to the goal of recovery. As a result, the adversarial process is suspended in drug treatment courts in order to focus solely on the participant's recovery and law-abiding behavior.…

* * *

In drug treatment courts, practices of the criminal court system that otherwise would hinder recovery are suspended and replaced with less traditional roles for the defense and prosecution. For defense counsel, the drug treatment court process may be viewed as more cumbersome for the defendant. For example, the defendant may be required to spend (initially at least) more time in jail, to attend court more frequently, and to examine and address the root causes for his drug addiction. Additionally, in order to be effective, the prosecution must proceed less punitively and more constructively, a stance viewed by some as appearing "soft on crime." On the surface, these goals may raise some ethical questions. However, a closer look shows that the duties inherent to both defense counsel and the prosecution may successfully be carried out in a drug treatment court context.

* * *

Prosecutors in drug treatment court settings must redefine what it means to "win" a case. Putting defendants in jail only to have them return again and again protects public safety only during those times when prisoners are incarcerated. Providing treatment for the offender, however, costs less and removes many from an endless cycle of court involvement, thus resulting in a more lasting public benefit. When the criminal court process returns a now sober and productive offender to society, the prosecutor should consider it a positive outcome or win. Because the adversarial system hinders the treatment process by obstructing communication and encouraging denial, pure iterations of the adversarial system fail to effectively promote public safety.

Drug treatment courts also are proper forums for the defense attorney's primary responsibility: ensuring the protection of his clients' rights. One task of the defense counsel is to inform the client of all rights and available options, allowing the client to make informed decisions given the specific situation. Just as competent defense attorneys will advise their clients of the risks and benefits of accepting a plea, savvy defense counsel will familiarize themselves with at least the fundamentals of addiction, substance abuse treatment, and the options afforded by their jurisdiction's drug treatment court....

Once the client is in a drug treatment program, the concerns change from those found in the traditional court setting to a broader goal. In traditional courts, the defense counsel's main goal is to "beat" the charges or reduce the amount of time the client spends incarcerated. Although there is a possibility that drug court participants could spend more time in jail than they would have in the traditional court setting, participants may spend less time in jail over the course of their lives by becoming sober and not committing new crimes because of their addiction. This requires defense counsel to have a broader lens through which to view their client's "criminal lifetime" and best interests....

* * *

Encouraging a client to participate in a program even though the attorney knows it may or may not initially result in more jail time or require more effort from the client does not usurp the ethical duties owed to the client as long as the attorney provides all of the information needed to make a genuine choice. Presenting the client with an opportunity to lead a clean and sober life gives the client the chance not only of an improved legal outcome in the present case, but also enhances prospects for life in the future....

* * *

Participation in drug treatment court is consistent with a prosecutor's ethical obligations as well. First and foremost, a prosecutor is charged with protection of public safety. This duty is met by participation in drug treatment court because the prosecutor works to rehabilitate the defendant, thus making the community safe from continued lawlessness by that person. As a member of the drug treatment court team, the prosecutor is uniquely positioned to assess the participant's progress in the program and make recommendations that serve the goals of the community. If the participant has difficulties complying and fails to make sufficient progress towards rehabilitation, the prosecution can advocate for an alternative strategy. The prosecutor also may advance the goal of community safety by recommending that a participant be terminated from the program when it is clear that the client is not amenable to further interventions. Termination from the program would subject the defendant to his or her previously suspended sentence or allow the defendant to be brought to trial.

* * *

VI. Return on Investment and Other Economic Concerns

The traditional criminal justice approach to dealing with alcohol and other drug addiction is costly to the taxpayer. Incarceration of drug-using offenders costs between twenty thousand dollars and fifty thousand dollars per person per year, depending on the jurisdiction. The cell used to hold a drug-using offender can cost a state more than eighty thousand dollars to construct. Contrast these figures to the costs of a drug court system, which typically range from $2,500 to $4,000 annually for each offender. Even residential treatment, required only in rare cases, is less costly than incarcerating the offender.

The defendant is not the sole beneficiary of the drug treatment court process. A recent California study estimated that drug courts save taxpayers ninety million dollars annually. Additionally, the community experiences a reduction in crime, with an estimated monetary value of as much as twenty-four thousand dollars per drug court participant due to reduced future court costs and victim impact costs. This value may actually underestimate the financial benefit to society because it does not take into account the ability of the newly sober drug treatment court graduate to work, effectively parent, pay taxes, participate in commerce, and perhaps lead a healthier lifestyle, all of which would result in savings of future medical costs, including the costs of substance-exposed infants. A study of addicted California Medicaid recipients conducted by the Kaiser Permanente Foundation, found that addicts who underwent outpatient drug treatment reduced their overall medical costs by a third. The study found that the costs were truly reduced, not merely shifted from one area of care to another.

In the first year following graduation from drug treatment court, roughly eighty-five percent of offenders, measured nationally, will have no new arrests. Two years after leaving the drug treatment court program, nearly seventy-three percent of graduates will not have been rearrested....

* * *

With their substantial cost savings, described by one study as seven dollars saved for each dollar spent on treatment, and high success rates, demonstrated by much lower recidivism, drug treatment courts offer a win-win solution that cannot be ignored.

* * *

... As long as drug treatment courts are adequately funded, they will continue to serve the ultimate goals of the criminal justice system by taking in intransigent and recidivistic offenders and returning productive and sober members of society.

Notes and Questions

1. The authors note that since being introduced in 1989, the number of drug courts increased dramatically to 1,621 by 2004. The last decade has seen even further expansion. As of early 2012, there were about 2,600 drug courts in the United States. *See* Types of Drug Courts, National Association of Drug Court Professionals, http://www.nadcp.org/learn/what-are-drug-courts/models (last visited Aug. 22, 2012) Additionally, other specialty courts — such as veterans courts — have begun to take hold. *See* Judge Michael Daly Hawkins, *Accommodating the Special Needs of Military Veterans to the Criminal Justice System*, 7 Ohio St. J. Crim. L. 563 (2010).

2. Hora and Stalcup offer a vigorous defense of drug courts, and most criminal justice observers agree with them. There are critics however. For instance, Professor Mae Quinn has expressed concern that drug courts force defense counsel to abdicate their responsibility to vigorously defend their clients. *See* Mae C. Quinn, *Whose Team Am I On Anyway? Musing of a Public Defender on Drug Treatment Court Practice*, 26 N.Y.U. Rev. L. & Soc. Change 37, 57 (2000). Other scholars assert that drug courts have a poor track record in helping true addicts and members of disadvantaged groups such as the poor

and the uneducated. *See* Josh Bowers, *Contraindicated Drug Courts* 55 UCLA L. Rev. 783 (2008). Professor Eric Miller questions whether the existence of drug courts leads to more defendants being brought into the criminal justice system in the first place, rather than having prosecutors dismiss cases. *See* Eric J. Miller, *Embracing Addiction: Drug Courts and the False Promise of Judicial Intervention*, 65 Ohio St. L.J. 1479 (2004). Do Hora and Stalcup adequately address these objections?

3. Like most other major cities, Baltimore has a drug court program. The Baltimore City courts run 21 adult drug courts. At any given time, there are between 200 and 400 defendants in Baltimore drug courts, with about one-third of those individuals successfully completing the program every year. *See* Glynis Kazanjian, *Baltimore Judge Launching Nonprofit To Help Support Drug Courts*, The Daily Record, Oct. 16, 2011. Yet, David Simon does not devote a single scene of *The Wire* to drug court programs, instead mentioning it only in a passing reference in Season 1. Is this a fair decision given that drug court programs—even if successful—amount to only a tiny fraction of the criminal docket in Baltimore and elsewhere? Or should Simon have devoted some attention to a program that shows the criminal justice system making positive progress?

4. Are there any characters from *The Wire* who would be good candidates for drug court?

Chapter VIII

Prisoner Reentry:
The Cutty Dilemma

"Truth is, I don't know what I want. I know I'm looking for something, but I can't even tell you what it is."[1]

— Dennis "Cutty" Wise

A. Introduction

The vast majority of prisoners—over 93%—are released and eventually return to society. The number of inmates who return home each year—more than 600,000 nationally[2]—is staggering. Some of these offenders have stable families to return to; others have marketable skills or education that will help them to get a job. Most, however, have neither. After years or even decades "inside" without a glimpse of the free world, how will these ex-offenders adjust to society? Overwhelmingly, the answer is "not well." About 30% of those released re-offend within six months, and within a year that number rises to more than 40%.[3] The American criminal justice system is a revolving door. In *The Wire*, the corner boys—whether it be those like D'Angelo who are running the corners, the mid-level managers like Bodie and Poot, or the younger hoppers and runners—are in and out of jail repeatedly throughout the series. What can we do to stop this cycle of failure?

B. The Challenges of Transitioning from Prison to Society

We see the problem of prisoner reentry throughout *The Wire*, although it is most vividly portrayed by the dilemma of Dennis "Cutty" Wise. Cutty was incarcerated for fourteen years. Upon being released, Cutty turns back to his former life as a soldier and joins the Barksdale drug gang. But he is not sure the game is for him anymore. He tries to work as a day laborer doing landscaping work. He also turns to a church deacon in an effort to find a steady job. But the church does not simply give out jobs and Cutty must

---

1. *The Wire*, Season 3, Episode 7, at 42:30 minutes.
2. *See* Joan Petersilia, When Prisoners Come Home: Parole and Prisoner Reentry 3 (2003).
3. Bureau of Justice Statistics Special Report, Recidivism of Prisoners Released in 1994 (June 2002).

find work himself. The choice between going straight and returning to the drug trade is difficult for Cutty. It is much easier to go back to what he knows than to find employment with no education, no connections, and a felony record. Does it have to be this difficult? When a parolee like Cutty wants to go straight, shouldn't society know what to do to help make that happen? As you will read in the materials below, experts believe they know what will foster successful prisoner reentry. Making it happen, however, is no easy task.

Urban Institute, Understanding the Challenges of Prisoner Reentry: Research Findings From the Urban Institute's Prisoner Reentry Portfolio
2–19 (2006)

Introduction

The four-fold increase in incarceration rates in America over the past 25 years has had far-reaching consequences. In 2003 alone, more than 656,000 state and federal prisoners returned to communities across the country, affecting public safety, public health, economic and community well-being, and family networks. The impact of prisoner reentry is further compounded by the returning jail population with its unique set of challenges and opportunities.

Research in the last decade has begun to measure the effect of reentry on returning prisoners, their families, and communities. Two-thirds of released prisoners are rearrested within three years of release. One and a half million children have a parent in prison. Four million citizens have lost their right to vote. Men and women enter U.S. prisons with limited marketable work experience, low levels of educational or vocational skills, and many health-related issues, ranging from mental health needs to substance abuse histories and high rates of communicable diseases. When they leave prison, these challenges remain and affect neighborhoods, families, and society at large. With limited assistance in their reintegration, former prisoners pose public safety risks to communities, and about half will return to prison for new crimes or parole violations within three years of release. This cycle of removal and return of large numbers of adults, mostly men, is increasingly concentrated in communities often already deprived of resources and ill equipped to meet the challenges this population presents.

* * *

… The Urban Institute's cornerstone study is *Returning Home: Understanding the Challenges of Prisoner Reentry*, a multistate, longitudinal study that documents the pathways of prisoner reintegration, examines what factors contribute to a successful or unsuccessful reentry experience, and identifies how those factors can inform policy. The *Returning Home* study has been implemented in four states, including a pilot study in Maryland and full studies in Illinois, Ohio, and Texas. The goal in each state is to collect information on individuals' life circumstances immediately prior to, during, and up to one year after their release. *Returning Home* documents the challenges of reentry along five dimensions: individual, family, peer, community, and state.

* * *

Employment and Reentry

Finding and maintaining a job is a critical dimension of successful prisoner reentry. Research has shown that employment is associated with lower rates of reoffending, and higher wages are associated with lower rates of criminal activity. However, former pris-

oners face tremendous challenges in finding and maintaining legitimate job opportunities, including low levels of education, limited work experience, and limited vocational
skills. This is further compounded by the incarceration period, during which they for-
feit the opportunity to gain marketable work experience and sever professional connections and social contacts that could lead to legal employment upon release. In addition,
the general reluctance of employers to hire former prisoners serves as a barrier to job
placement.

* * *

Recent Findings from the Urban Institute on Employment and Reentry

- **While prisoners believe that having a job is an important factor in staying out of
prison, few have a job lined up after release.** The vast majority of *Returning Home*
respondents felt that having a job would help them stay out of prison; however,
on average, only about one in five reported that they had a job lined up immediately after release.

- **Despite the need for employment assistance, few prisoners receive employment-
related training in prison.** Several studies have shown that the vast majority of
prisoners cite assistance finding employment as one of their greatest needs after
release. However, only about one-third of Illinois and Maryland *Returning Home*
respondents reported participating in an employment readiness program while
in prison, and far fewer reported participating in a job-training program in prison
(one-quarter of Maryland respondents and only 9 percent of Illinois respondents).
One-quarter of prisoners in Virginia (2002) participated in vocational programs
while in prison, as did 6 percent in New Jersey (2001) and 1 percent in Georgia
(2002).

- **Participation in work release jobs in prison may have a positive impact on the
likelihood of finding full-time employment after release.** Respondents in the
Maryland and Illinois *Returning Home* sample who held a work release job in
prison were more likely to be fully employed and had worked more weeks after
prison.

* * *

- **Prisoners who *do* find work after release do not necessarily have full-time or consistent employment.** When interviewed four to eight months after release, 44 percent of Illinois *Returning Home* respondents reported having worked for at least
one week since their release. However, less than a third (30 percent) of respondents
were employed at the time of the interview, and just 24 percent of all respondents
were employed full-time (40 or more hours per week). At their first postrelease interview, 56 percent of Maryland respondents were either unemployed or were
working fewer than 40 hours a week.

- **Transportation is a significant barrier to employment** ... [M]ore than a third of
the respondents reported having difficulty obtaining a car for work or emergencies and nearly a quarter reported various difficulties accessing public transportation. Former prisoners in a focus group in Rhode Island also cited
transportation challenges as a barrier to employment as well as access to services.

- **Finding and maintaining employment may reduce recidivism** ... [A]n increase in
levels of employment was a predictor of reductions in drug dealing, violent crime,
and property crime. *Returning Home* findings show that Illinois respondents who
were unemployed were more likely to be reincarcerated after release.

Health and Reentry

The prevalence of severe mental disorders and chronic and infectious diseases among the prison population is far greater than among the general population. Even when individuals have received adequate physical and mental health services while in prison, they often face limited access and insufficient linkages to community-based health care upon release. Service providers have identified the lack of available resources for services and the competition for funding as significant problems in delivering services to former prisoners, especially those with the most serious health needs. In addition, incarceration disqualifies inmates from Medicaid eligibility. Restoring eligibility can take several months, interrupting access to prescription drugs and putting individuals at high risk of relapse.

* * *

Recent Findings from the Urban Institute on Health and Reentry

- **A substantial number of prisoners have been diagnosed with a physical or mental health condition.** *Returning Home* findings show that between nearly 30 and 40 percent of respondents reported having a chronic physical or mental health condition, with the most commonly reported conditions including depression, asthma, and high blood pressure. In New Jersey, about a third of prisoners released in 2002 had been diagnosed with at least one chronic and/or communicable physical or mental health condition.

- **More prisoners report being diagnosed with a medical condition than report receiving medication or treatment for the condition while incarcerated.** While 30 percent of Illinois *Returning Home* respondents reported having a physical or mental health condition, only 12 percent reported having taken medication on a regular basis while in prison. In a small study of prisoners in Ohio, over half reported being diagnosed with depression, but only 38 percent of the sample reported receiving treatment or taking prescription medication for depression. Similarly, 27 percent reported having asthma, yet less than 14 percent reported receiving treatment for asthma.

- **Many corrections agencies lack discharge planning and preparation for addressing health care needs upon release, making continuity of care difficult.** Less than 10 percent of prisoners in the Illinois *Returning Home* study reported receiving referrals to health care or mental health care services in the community. In fact, respondents who reported having *fair* or *poor* health were no more or less likely to receive referrals to health care in the community than those reporting to be in good general health.10 In addition, only 20 percent of respondents in the small study of Ohio prisoners reported programming or assistance to prepare them to address their health care needs upon release.

* * *

- **The vast majority of returning prisoners do not have any form of medical insurance.** *Returning Home* findings show that four to eight months after release, only 10 to 20 percent of respondents in Maryland and Illinois had private insurance. Sixteen months after release, the percentage of Illinois respondents who had private insurance dropped from almost 20 to 15 percent. In Maryland, only 5 percent of *Returning Home* respondents reported being recipients of Medicaid or Medicare, a disability pension, or Veteran's Administration health insurance.

Housing and Reentry

Securing housing is perhaps the most immediate challenge facing prisoners upon their release. While many returning prisoners have plans to stay with family, those who do not confront limited housing options. The process of obtaining housing is often complicated by a host of factors: the scarcity of affordable and available housing, legal barriers and regulations, prejudices that restrict tenancy for this population, and strict eligibility requirements for federally subsidized housing. Research has found that released prisoners who do not have stable housing arrangements are more likely to return to prison, suggesting that the obstacles to securing both temporary and permanent housing warrant the attention of policymakers, practitioners, and researchers.

* * *

Recent Findings from the Urban Institute on Housing and Reentry

* * *

- **The majority of returning prisoners live with family members and/or intimate partners upon release.** Three months after release, 88 percent of the *Returning Home* respondents in Illinois and nearly 60 percent of those in Maryland were living with a family member and/or intimate partner. Between 63 and 78 percent of respondents in Ohio and Texas anticipated living with a family member upon release.

- **Many former prisoners return home to living arrangements that are only temporary.** Overall, one-third of Illinois *Returning Home* respondents returned home to temporary living arrangements. About one in five reported living at more than one address after being in the community for one to three months, and by six to eight months after release, 31 percent had lived at more than one address. Furthermore, more than half of Illinois respondents believed they would not be staying in their current neighborhood for long. The Maryland *Returning Home* respondents reported similar expectations of relocating six months after release, with over half expecting to leave their current location within weeks or months.

- **Housing options for returning prisoners who do not stay with family members or friends are extremely limited.** Potential housing options for former prisoners include community-based correctional housing facilities; transitional housing; federally subsidized and administered housing; homeless assistance supportive housing, service-enhanced housing, and special needs housing supported through HUD; and the private market. However, most of these options are extremely limited and often unavailable to formerly incarcerated people. A Rhode Island focus group of service providers and former prisoners overwhelmingly agreed that the shortage of affordable and available housing is an enormous problem for returning prisoners.

- **Practitioners and researchers agree that there are few evidence-based reentry housing programs that target returning prisoners with mental illness.** Thousands of persons with mental illness exit prisons and jails each year, and research has found that adequate housing for this population can enhance their ability to become self-sufficient and avoid future justice system contact. However, few programs provide housing for releasees with mental health problems, and there is no body of compelling evidence regarding the most effective components of such housing programs.

Substance Use and Reentry

Substance use among former prisoners presents significant challenges to the reentry process. Studies have shown that while 83 percent of state prisoners have a history of drug use, only a small fraction receive treatment while incarcerated and after release. For example, while three-fourths of state prisoners have had some type of involvement with alcohol or drug use in the time leading up to their offense, only 15 percent of this group receives treatment in prison. Furthermore, for those who have access to and take advantage of treatment programs in prison, few continue to receive appropriate treatment once they return to the community. At the same time, prison-based drug treatment has been shown to reduce drug use and criminal activity, especially when coupled with aftercare treatment in the community.

* * *

Recent Findings from the Urban Institute on Substance Use and Reentry

- **A majority of prisoners have extensive substance use histories.** Similar to national statistics, most *Returning Home* respondents reported some drug use (between 66 and 80 percent) or alcohol use or intoxication (between 48 and 60 percent) prior to prison. Specifically, *Returning Home* findings show that in the six months before entering prison, 41 percent of Maryland respondents reported daily heroin use, and 57 percent of Texas respondents reported daily cocaine use (compared with less than 5 percent who reported daily heroin use).

- **Prisoners identify drug use as the primary cause of many of their past and current problems.** The Maryland *Returning Home* study found that nearly two-thirds of drug users reported arrests associated with their drug use, and about one-third reported missing school and/or losing their job as a result of drug use. In Illinois, 60 percent of respondents cited substance use as the cause of one or more family, relationship, employment, legal, or financial problem. Almost one-third of Ohio respondents reported experiencing problems in their relationships due to drug use.

- **Despite high levels of drug use, relatively few prisoners receive drug treatment while incarcerated.** Of all *Returning Home* respondents, between 21 and 27 percent reported participating in specific drug or alcohol treatment programs. In Illinois, only 42 percent of *Returning Home* respondents who reported drug use prior to prison also reported receiving drug treatment in prison. In 2002, New Jersey implemented a Substance Use Disorder Continuum of Treatment plan that included prison-based therapeutic communities; however, despite the fact that 81 percent of New Jersey inmates suffer from some type of drug or alcohol abuse problem, program capacity was limited to 6 percent of the 2002 state prison population. Similarly, in Texas, substance abuse program capacity can only serve 5 percent of the potential population in need.

- **Consensus in the field holds that individualized in-prison treatment in concert with community-based aftercare can reduce substance use and dependency.** Corrections and treatment researchers and practitioners agree that in-prison treatment is much more likely to effectively sustain a decline in substance use if it is tailored to an individual's need and level of risk, integrated across all stages of the justice system, and linked to drug treatment aftercare in the community.

- **Those with substance use histories and those who engage in substance use after release are at a high risk to recidivate.** *Returning Home* respondents who were rearrested after release had more extensive criminal and substance use histories and were more likely to have used drugs before prison as well as after release.

Families and Reentry

The impact of incarceration and reentry on children and families is significant, and in many respects difficult to measure. More than half of U.S. prisoners (55 percent of state male inmates and 65 percent of state female inmates) are parents of minor children. By the end of 2002, 2 percent of all minor children in America, and 7 percent of children of color, had a parent in prison. Including parents who are in jail, on probation and on parole, this number increases to 10 percent of all minor children. When a parent is sent to prison, the family structure, financial responsibilities, emotional support systems, and living arrangements are all potentially affected. Incarceration, as a result, can drastically disrupt spousal relationships, parent-child relationships, and family networks. Restoring these relationships, reunifying with the family, and undertaking these roles and responsibilities upon return also pose a unique set of challenges. In recent years, research has found that strengthening the family network and maintaining supportive family contact can improve outcomes for both family members and prisoners. In fact, maintaining family connections through letters, phone calls and personal visits has shown to reduce recidivism rates. Yet, given the challenges of maintaining this contact—including visiting regulations, transportation costs to distant corrections facilities, other financial barriers, and emotional strains—more than half of incarcerated parents report never having received a personal visit from their children. However, many social service providers and corrections departments across the country are working to overcome and address these barriers.

* * *

Recent Findings from the Urban Institute on Families and Reentry

* * *

- **Strong family support before prison may reduce the likelihood of recidivism.** Respondents in the Illinois *Returning Home* study who reported more positive family relationships were less likely to be reconvicted, while those with negative family relationships were more likely to be reconvicted or reincarcerated. Further, respondents in the Maryland *Returning Home* study with closer family relationships and strong family support were less likely to have used drugs since their release.

- **While most prisoners have some regular contact with family members during their prison term, relatively few ever receive visits.** The vast majority of respondents in the Illinois *Returning Home* study reported having had at least some telephone or mail contact with family members and intimate partners. However, only 13 percent of respondents had in-person contact with family members or children, and 29 percent had visits from partners.

- **One of the greatest challenges to maintaining contact with incarcerated family members is the distant location of the prison.** Three-quarters of family members identified by respondents in the Illinois *Returning Home* sample reported that it was a challenge to stay in touch with their incarcerated family members because the prison was located too far away. For the two-thirds who did not visit their family members in prison, the median estimated travel time to the prison was four hours longer than those who visited, a possible indicator of why they did not visit.

- **Close family relationships may improve employment outcomes for returning prisoners.** Respondents in the Maryland *Returning Home* study who had closer family and intimate partner relationships and stronger family support were more likely to be employed after release. In Illinois, respondents who had an intimate partner after release reported having been employed for more weeks on average (30 percent more) than those without a partner.

Communities and Reentry

Released prisoners are returning in relatively high concentrations to a small number of communities in America's urban centers, thereby having a profound—and disproportionate—impact on community life, family networks, and social capital in these neighborhoods. Social and economic disadvantage often characterize these communities, compounding the challenges and burdens that this population brings to bear when they return home. Research also suggests that high rates of incarceration and reentry of community residents through the revolving door of the criminal justice system may further destabilize these communities.

* * *

Recent Findings from the Urban Institute on Communities and Reentry

- **A relatively large number of prisoners return to a small number of cities in each state.** For example, Chicago and Baltimore received more than half of prisoners returning to Illinois and Maryland, respectively, in 2001. Houston received a quarter of all prisoners returning to Texas. In 2002, 2 of New Jersey's 21 counties accounted for nearly a third of returning prisoners. In 2002, more than one-third (37 percent) of adult prisoners returned to 2 of Massachusetts's 14 counties. Five of Idaho's 44 counties accounted for 73 percent of returning prisoners.

- **Returning prisoners are often clustered in a few neighborhoods within those cities.** In 2001, 8 percent of Chicago communities (6 of 77) accounted for 34 percent of all prisoners returning to Chicago. Thirty-six percent of respondents in the Maryland *Returning Home* study returned to 11 percent of Baltimore communities (6 of 55). In 2002, almost half of adult prisoners returning to Suffolk County, Massachusetts, returned to just 10 percent of Boston's 630 block groups. In Virginia, about half of all prisoners returning to Richmond in 2002 returned to 15 percent of the city's 163 block groups. In 2003, 7 percent of the Zip Codes (8 of 115) in Wayne County, Michigan, all of which are located in the city of Detroit, accounted for 41 percent of all prisoners released to parole in Michigan.

- **High levels of social and economic disadvantage often characterize the communities to which prisoners return.** The Chicago, Baltimore, Cleveland, and Houston communities that are home to the greatest concentrations of released prisoners have above-average rates of unemployment, female-headed households, and families living below the federal poverty level. In Virginia, New Jersey, and Massachusetts, the cities to which the greatest percent of prisoners return have poverty rates more than twice that of the state as a whole and are characterized by higher than average levels of unemployment and female-headed households.

- **Prisoners do not necessarily return to the communities from which they came.** About half of *Returning Home* respondents who returned to Chicago and Baltimore did not return to the neighborhood in which they lived prior to incarceration. These respondents reported that the principal reasons for relocation were either to avoid problems in their old neighborhood or because their families had moved.

- **Former prisoners who relocate after they are released tend to move to neighborhoods similar to the ones they left.** Illinois *Returning Home* findings show that prisoners who move at least once in the two years after their release move to neighborhoods with similar socioeconomic characteristics as the ones they left.

- Prisoners returning to neighborhoods perceived to be unsafe and lacking in social capital are at greater risk of recidivism. Illinois *Returning Home* respondents who viewed their communities as safe and good places to live were much less likely to return to prison and more likely to be employed than those who reported their communities were unsafe or characterized by low social capital. In addition, those who felt that drug selling was a problem in their neighborhood were more likely to have engaged in substance use after release than those living in neighborhoods where drug selling was not perceived to be a problem.

Public Safety and Reentry

Given the significant rates at which former prisoners recidivate, prisoner reentry presents a tremendous pubic safety dilemma. The Bureau of Justice Statistics estimates that within three years of release, more than two-thirds of prisoners are rearrested for a new crime—most within the first year out of prison. Forty-seven percent of all releasees are reconvicted for a new crime and more than half are reincarcerated for a new crime or parole violation. Released prisoners make a substantial contribution to new crime; one study estimates that recent prison releasees account for about one-fifth of all adult arrests made by police. This statistic likely understates the proportion of new crime for which former inmates are responsible because it includes neither those reentering from jails nor former prisoners who have been in the community for more than three years.

* * *

Recent Findings from the Urban Institute on Public Safety and Reentry

- Most returning prisoners have extensive criminal histories. Most *Returning Home* respondents (between 80 and 87 percent) had at least one prior conviction, and at least two-thirds had previously served time in prison. In Massachusetts, all but 1 percent of prisoners released from the Department of Correction in 2002 had been previously incarcerated in a Massachusetts state or county facility. Between 1996 and 2003, almost 80 percent of the individuals who were admitted and released to the Philadelphia Prison System had been previously incarcerated there.

- A substantial number of released prisoners are reconvicted or rearrested for new crimes, many within the first year after release. Illinois *Returning Home* findings show that one-fifth (22 percent) of released prisoners were reconvicted for a new crime within 11 months of release, and nearly one-third (31 percent) were returned to prison on a new sentence or parole revocation within 13 months of release. Maryland *Returning Home* findings show that within 6 months of release, roughly one-third (32 percent) had been rearrested for at least one new crime, 10 percent had been reconvicted for a new crime, and 16 percent had been reconfined to prison or jail for a new crime conviction or technical violation.

- Those with substance use histories and who engage in substance use after release are at a high risk to recidivate. *Returning Home* respondents who were rearrested after release had more extensive criminal and substance use histories and were more likely to have used drugs before prison as well as after release.

* * *

Community Supervision and Reentry

Nationwide, the vast majority (about 80 percent) of released prisoners are subject to a period of supervision in the community. There are now 765,000 released prisoners on parole, up from 220,000 in 1980. Resources have not kept pace with this increase. Most supervision officers are responsible for 70 parolees, about twice the volume experts recommend. Large numbers of parolees return to prison for new crimes or technical violations of their parole and account for 35 percent of new prison admissions nationally. While trends in community supervision are measured on a national level, there is extensive variation in release decisions and supervision practices across states.

* * *

Recent Findings from the Urban Institute on Community Supervision and Reentry

- **Nationally, parole violation rates have increased substantially over the past 25 years, and in many states, violators account for a significant number and share of state prison admissions.** The number of people returned to state prison for a parole violation increased sevenfold in the last two decades, from 27,000 in 1980 to 203,000 in 2000. Further, parole violators, who accounted for 17 percent of state prison admissions in 1980, accounted for over one-third of all admissions in 2000. In 2002, more than 40 percent of prison admissions in Virginia and Georgia were the result of probation or parole violations.

- **A significant share of prisoners is serving time in prison or state jail for parole or probation violations.** *Returning Home* findings show that about 4 in 10 respondents in Texas and Ohio had been serving their current term in prison or state jail because of a parole or probation violation. Of prisoners released in New Jersey in 2002, 39 percent were incarcerated for a violation of parole.

- **Many prisoners believe that it will be easy to avoid a parole violation after release.** The majority of *Returning Home* respondents (between 77 and 81 percent) believed it would be easy to avoid a parole violation. Nearly 60 percent of prisoners surveyed in the Philadelphia Prison System believed it would be *very easy* or *pretty easy* to avoid a parole or probation violation upon release.

* * *

- **Parole supervision appears to have little effect on the rearrest rates of released prisoners in some large states.** A study of 14 states indicates that mandatory parolees, the largest share of released prisoners, fare no better on supervision than similar prisoners released without supervision in terms of rearrest outcomes. Parolees released by a parole board were less likely to be rearrested; yet when taking into account personal characteristics and criminal histories, this difference narrows to about 4 percentage points. Despite this general finding, females, individuals with fewer prior arrests, public order offenders, and those in prison for technical violations were less likely to be rearrested if supervised after release.

* * *

Notes and Questions

1. The Urban Institute research excerpted above, along with numerous other studies, makes clear that employment, housing, drug treatment, and mental health counseling for ex-offenders is crucial for successful prisoner re-entry. How much money would it cost to do this correctly? Is there political will to spend the enormous amount of money necessary?

2. The study indicates that a huge percentage of incarcerated people (approximately 40% in some states) are there for violations of parole or probation. However, is this sta-

tistic deceptive? In many jurisdictions, when a parolee or probationer is caught committing a new crime, prosecutors move to revoke parole or probation, rather than prosecuting the new offense. Why would prosecutors do that? And if this occurs regularly, do
you see why it might be deceptive to suggest that prisons are filled with people who simply violated their parole? On the other hand, for individuals who only committed a technical violation of parole or probation, what should courts do with them?

3. If most ex-offenders must move in with their families upon release, and if those
families are in the same neighborhoods where the offender got into trouble in the first place,
isn't that a recipe for disaster? What could be done to end this cycle? Certainly, courts
cannot forbid a released inmate from returning to his old neighborhood entirely. If the
state spent tremendous amounts of money to provide housing for ex-offenders, would they
move into those housing units?

4. How hard is it to break free of old patterns? Watch *The Wire*, Season 3, Episode 4,
at 7:00 minutes. In that scene, Cutty is sitting uncomfortably in the back of a pickup
truck on the way to or from a landscaping job. At a red light, two young men, ostensibly
drug dealers, pull up in an expensive Range Rover and give him a dismissive look, as
though Cutty is totally insignificant. In a moment like that, how hard is it for Cutty to
resist returning to the drug game, where he is powerful and important? Is there anything
society can do to even the playing field and encourage ex-offenders like Cutty to resist
the temptation?

5. How is it possible that so many drug-addicted prisoners are released without receiving any drug treatment? Would it be constitutional for states to mandate that inmates
complete drug treatment programs before being released? Would it be plausible? Would
it be cost-prohibitive?

6. Once paroled, offenders are subject to supervision by parole officers. But how effectively do parole officers monitor parolees? Watch *The Wire*, Season 3, Episode 5, at
21:30 minutes. Cutty has to give a urine sample to test for drugs in his system. Before
walking into the office, he is able to buy clean urine for $5 from a man selling it on the
street. Is it this easy to beat drug testing in the real world? If so, how effective can parole
monitoring actually be?

7. According to the leading expert on prisoner reentry, "85 percent of all U.S. parolees
are supervised on regular caseloads, averaging 66 cases to one parole officer, in which
they are seen (face to face) less than twice per month." Joan Petersilia, When Prisoners Come Home: Parole and Prisoner Reentry 84 (2003). Are parole officers able to
have a positive impact with such a high caseload? How low would the ratio of parolees
to officers have to be for officers to have a major impact? Watch *The Wire*, Season 3,
Episode 7, at 6:00 minutes. Cutty explains to his boss: "Man, parole officers, employment agencies ... I just felt like I was an interruption to their lunch break." Do you think
that the parole officers and employment caseworkers didn't care about Cutty, or was it that
they had such an overwhelming caseload that they couldn't accomplish much for him?

8. One overriding (but unstated) theme of the Urban Institute report is that successful prisoner-reentry is expensive and politicians aren't interested in spending money on
job, housing, and treatment programs that will anger voting constituents who themselves
haven't gotten in trouble with the law. On the other hand, because most offenders recidivate, failure to spend the money on reentry likely means that the voting public pays
on the back end through higher crime. Is there a way to convince the law-abiding public that spending money on offenders before and at the time of their release is in society's interest?

9. Does prison actually cause crime that would have never occurred? On some level the answer would seem to be yes. For instance, some prisoners will meet other criminals and learn illegal tactics that they were not already aware of. And locking up fathers may leave their children unsupervised and push the children toward delinquency. The next question is how much crime do prisons cause. One author recently estimated that "incarceration causes about 7 percent of total crime: 1 percent because of in-prison crime, 2 percent because of prison-induced recidivism, and 4 percent because of the impact of incarceration on the delinquency of inmates' children." Martin H. Pritkin, *Is Prison Increasing Crime?* 2008 Wis. L. Rev. 1049, 1082. On the other hand, how much crime does incarceration prevent?

10. Watch *The Wire*, Season 4, Episode 6, at 32:15 minutes. It is election day. Cutty jogs through the city for exercise while the three mayoral candidates are voting in the primary. When an election worker asks him to vote, Cutty responds that he cannot because he has a felony conviction. Cutty's scenario is very common in the United States, and has resulted in the disenfranchisement of a large portion of the African-American population. An analysis by The Sentencing Project found that nearly 6 million felons or ex-felons have been disenfranchised because of their convictions. One in every thirteen African-Americans has been disenfranchised in the United States. That amounts to almost 7.7% of the African-American adults, compared to 1.8% disenfranchisement of non-African American adults. *See* The Sentencing Project, State-Level Estimates of Felon Disenfranchisement in the United States, 2010 1–2, 12 (2012). Should convicted felons be permitted to vote? Can we expect ex-felons to seamlessly re-enter society if we are simultaneously telling them that they are lesser citizens?

Harry J. Holzer & Steven Raphael, Urban Institute, Employment Barriers Facing Ex-Offenders
2–11 (2003)

INTRODUCTION

Over 600,000 people are now being released from prisons each year. Many suffer from a variety of serious difficulties as they attempt to reenter society. Among the most challenging situations they face is that of reentry into the labor market. Employment rates and earnings of ex-offenders are low by almost any standard—though in most cases they were fairly low even before these (mostly) men were incarcerated. Low employment rates seem closely related to the very high recidivism rates observed among those released from prison.

* * *

EMPLOYMENT AND EARNINGS AMONG EX-OFFENDERS

* * *

Using a variety of data sources and techniques, most studies find that employment and/or earnings are reduced by a spell of incarceration, relative to what they would be in its absence. In particular, earnings are reduced by anywhere from 10–30% by a spell of incarceration in these studies, while employment losses are generally smaller but can also be as high as 20–30% in some studies. . . .

BARRIERS TO SUCCESS AMONG EX-OFFENDERS IN THE LABOR MARKET

What are the factors that limit employment and earnings among ex-offenders? Below we separate factors that operate on the supply side of the labor market—through the attitudes, characteristics and behaviors of the individuals themselves—from those that operate on the demand side—through the attitudes and behaviors of employers, and the characteristics of jobs they seek to fill.

Supply-Side Barriers

Ex-offenders have a variety of characteristics that greatly limit their employability and earnings capacities. These include:

- Limited education and cognitive skills;
- Limited work experience;
- Substance abuse and other physical/mental health problems.

For instance, about 70% of offenders and ex-offenders are high school dropouts.

According to at least one study, about half are "functionally illiterate." Prior to incarceration, the employment rates of those involved in criminal activities are certainly not trivial in any sense, but they generally lag well behind those of other young men—even those who had similarly limited skills and also lived in poor inner-city neighborhoods. As a consequence, the work experience that they had accumulated prior to incarceration was generally well below what it might have been in the absence of their participation in crime. On top of that, the (often multiple) periods of time they have spent incarcerated have impeded them from gaining any additional private sector experience, and no doubt help erode whatever job skills, positive work habits or connections to employers they might have had beforehand. Thus, if and when they do attempt to reenter the labor market after incarceration, the poor skills and very limited work experience that they bring with them limits both employability and earnings potential.

In addition, a large fraction of these men suffer from substance abuse and other health problems. For instance, about three-fourths have had substance abuse problems; 2–3% have AIDS or are HIV-positive; 18% have hepatitis C; and 15–20% report emotional disorders. Among the small fraction of ex-offenders who are women, large numbers suffer from depression and/or past sexual abuse. All of these factors limit employability because they limit the basic "job-readiness" that employers almost universally seek as a precondition for employment, as we note below.

Besides these skill and health-related problems, most ex-offenders are minorities—nearly half are African-American, and nearly a fifth are Latino or Asian. To the extent that minorities continue to suffer labor market discrimination, this will further impede the ability of ex-offenders to gain employment or earn higher wages....

Furthermore, most return to low-income and predominantly minority communities that have relatively few unskilled jobs, and to peer groups who presumably provide relatively few contacts to the world of legitimate work. Thus, both "spatial mismatch" effects on employment and weak networks and contacts will continue to their employment difficulties. These difficulties are reinforced by parole restrictions that often require these men to live in the same communities from which they came, and by laws that prohibit ex-offenders in some states from obtaining driver's licenses.

In addition to the "barriers" these individuals face—over which they presumably have little control—the attitudes and choices that they make may also limit their employment outcomes. For instance, it is likely that a large number of these men might be able to find some kind of work if they search long enough, but at jobs that pay very low wages and provide few benefits or chances for upward mobility. In these circumstances, many ex-offenders may simply choose to forego these employment options, in favor of illegal opportunities or more casual work. Alternatively, they may accept these jobs temporarily, but may not retain them for very long. Their attachments to the legitimate labor market might be quite tenuous over the longer term—both as a result of these relatively unappealing options, or perhaps because of their own estrangement over several years from the world of work.

Thus, the limited employment outcomes that ex-offenders experience will at least partly reflect "barriers," perhaps compounded by their own attitudes towards and responses to these circumstances.

Demand-Side Barriers

The barriers faced by ex-offenders because of their very limited skills, poor health, and race or area of residence often reflect a "mismatch" between these characteristics and those sought by employers on the demand side of the labor market. We can also consider two kinds of barriers generated by employers: those relating to the general personal characteristics of ex-offenders vs. those that are explicitly related to their ex-offender status.

For instance, the poor skills and work experience of most ex-offenders generally conflict with the skills and credentials sought by employers, even when trying to fill relative unskilled jobs.... [I]n central-city labor markets, fewer than 5% of unskilled jobs (i.e., those that do not require college diplomas) require no high school diplomas, work experience, or other relevant skills. Even where little formal skill is required, basic "job readiness" is almost universally sought by employers. This personal quality involves the employer's expectation that the worker will show up every day and on time, will work hard and take some responsibility, will be generally trustworthy, etc. In fact, recent work on welfare recipients in the labor market indicates that their success in employment, once hired, often depends crucially on these types of variables. Unfortunately, those with substance abuse and/or other health problems (both physical or emotional) are the least likely to be job-ready, and will likely face few job offers or high discharge rates upon being hired.

In addition to these factors, the race/gender and geographic locations of potential job applicants also affect employer tendencies to hire and/or retain workers. For instance ... African-American men are the least likely job applicants to receive offers....

So ex-offenders will have some difficulty obtaining job offers from employers even in the absence of their criminal records. But the fact that they have criminal records will then further limit what is available to them, as most employers are very reluctant to hire those with such records.

Why do most employers hesitate to hire those with criminal records? To start, certain occupations are legally closed to individuals with felony convictions under state and, in some cases, federal law. Examples include jobs requiring contact with children, certain health services occupations, and employment with firms providing security services. In addition, employers may place a premium on the trustworthiness of employees, especially when the ability to monitor employee performance is imperfect. Jobs that require significant customer contact or the handling of cash or expensive merchandise will require dependable, honest employees. To the extent that past criminal activity signals something less, employers may take such information into account when making hiring decisions.

Furthermore, in many states employers can be held liable for the criminal actions of their employees under the theory of negligent hiring. Legally, negligence is premised on the idea that one who breaches a duty of care to others in an organization or to the public is legally liable for any damages that result. Under the theory of negligent hiring, employers may be liable for the risk created by exposing the public and their employees to potentially dangerous individuals....

* * *

... Currently, 23 states have some form of public access or freedom of information statutes that pertain to some aspect of criminal history record information. And the growing availability of this information over the internet, usually from private firms and at very low cost (e.g., $10–15 per person), makes it increasingly easy for employers to access these data.

* * *

To be sure, employers can try to avoid hiring ex-offenders even without background checks by screening job applicants on the basis of characteristics that seem to predict previous criminal activity. For example, if employers believe that African-Americans, welfare recipients, or workers with unaccounted-for breaks in their employment histories are more likely to have past criminal convictions, employers might "statistically discriminate" against such individuals.

While imperfect information will clearly lead to instances of "false-positive" and "false-negative" assessments of previous criminality, basing employment decisions on such discriminatory rules of thumb may minimize the likelihood of hiring ex-offenders.

Thus, the ability of ex-offenders to obtain job offers from employers will depend both on how averse employers are to hiring them and whether or not they actually check criminal backgrounds. In our previous work, we have documented stated employer preferences towards the hiring of ex-offenders and their tendencies to check criminal background using data from a series of employer surveys administered in various large metropolitan areas between 1992 and 2001. Among our findings are the following:

- Employers are much more averse to hiring ex-offenders than they are towards any other disadvantaged group, such as welfare recipients;

- Employers vary in their stated willingness to hire ex-offenders according to the characteristics of their establishments and the jobs they are seeking to fill;

- They also vary according to the offense committed by the offender and whether any meaningful work experience has been obtained since release; and

- Employer tendency to check backgrounds is far from universal, but has risen over the previous decade.

For instance, over 90% of employers surveyed are willing to consider filling their most recent job vacancy with a welfare recipient, while only about 40% are willing to consider doing so with an ex-offender. Willingness to hire ex-offenders is greater for jobs in construction or manufacturing than in retail trade and the service sector, and is strongly influenced by the extent to which a variety of tasks are required on the job—especially contact with customers. Employer reluctance is greatest when the offense in question was a violent one and least when it was a non-violent drug offense. The tendency of employers to check criminal records ("sometimes" or "always") in Los Angeles rose from under 50% in 1993–94 to over 60% in 2001, consistent with the growing ease and low cost of accessing these data that we cited above.

* * *

Notes and Questions

1. Season 3 of *The Wire* shows Cutty's struggle to readjust to life outside prison. How hard is it for him to find a job? What kind of employment is Cutty qualified for?

2. How difficult is it to convince a released prisoner to go back to school to further his education? Watch *The Wire*, Season 3, Episode 5, at 14:00 minutes, in which the deacon unsuccessfully tries to convince Cutty to pursue a GED. Should prisoners be required to earn a GED before being released from prison? Would conditioning parole on first receiving a GED be constitutional?

3. What is the purpose of imprisoning criminals? The most common answers are retribution (because the individual deserves punishment), general deterrence (to send a message to others not to commit crimes) specific deterrence (to incapacitate this offender from committing other crimes) and rehabilitation (to help the offender to improve himself and avoid criminal activity in the future). Which of these theories of punishment do you think the American criminal justice system accomplishes? In enacting the federal sentencing guidelines, Congress rejected rehabilitation and focused instead on retribution, deterrence, and incapacitation. *See* Mistretta v. United States, 488 U.S. 361, 367 (1989).

4. Is it possible to design a correctional system that will foster rehabilitation and successful prisoner reentry? Decades ago, the public believed rehabilitation could be achieved. By the 1970s, the public came to reject this theory and prominent scholars began to argue that there was no evidence that rehabilitation reduced recidivism. *See* Robert Martinson, *What Works? Questions and Answers About Prison Reform*, The Public Interest, vol. 35 (1974). Thereafter, America moved toward a tougher correctional system based on retribution.

5. Has the tough-on-crime model of the last four decades been successful? If not, should we give the rehabilitative model another try? Do you think social scientists are better today than they were four decades ago at risk analysis and determining which offenders can be rehabilitated and reintegrated into society? Should the limited resources of the criminal justice system focus on reentry programs for the offenders most likely to be successfully rehabilitated?

6. Cutty escapes the cycle of recidivism by opening a boxing gym with a $15,000 donation from Avon Barksdale. *See The Wire*, Season 3, Episode 11, at 24:00 minutes. Most offenders cannot count on any money when they leave prison, much less $15,000. How would Cutty's storyline have turned out without Barksdale's money? Consider Barksdale's response when Cutty said he wanted to get out of the drug selling game: "But you ain't done shit else ... so what you gonna do?" *The Wire*, Season 3, Episode 6, at 52:20 minutes.

7. Following the economic collapse that began in 2008, unemployment hovered around 9% for years. With unemployment that high, is there any plausible scenario in which most ex-felons find steady work? What job options are realistically open to ex-felons?

Nino Rodriguez & Brenner Brown, Vera Institute of Justice, Preventing Homelessness Among People Leaving Prison

1–6 (2003)

Thomas was serving the end of his sentence at New York State's Queensboro Correctional Facility in New York City. There were several places where he could live when he left prison, but none of them passed muster with his parole officer. His first choice was to live with his wife, but that was ruled out because she was the codefendant in his current conviction for selling drugs. He could have stayed with his mother, but that was ruled out because his brother was staying there while serving time on parole. With a homeless shelter his only alternative, Thomas met with a community coordinator for Project Greenlight, a prison-based program that could help him find a place to live.

Because Thomas would be under parole supervision for almost a year, he wanted to find a residential program that could keep him occupied. As Thomas saw it, he would rather be in a structured program that might help him successfully complete his parole than have the temptations of total freedom and risk going back to prison. Project Greenlight's community coordinator placed Thomas with an organization that provides housing as part of a yearlong employment program, and Thomas went there directly upon his release from prison.

Many people preparing to leave prisons and jails do not have a home. They often return to communities where persistent poverty and lack of jobs and affordable housing make finding a permanent home difficult. Even those like Thomas who have places to live face policies or practices, including restrictions on access to subsidized housing, that either inadvertently or intentionally eliminate these options.

Although there are no national statistics on homelessness among people leaving correctional facilities, and we know little about the true scope of the problem, figures from some major jurisdictions suggest a troubling picture. At any given time in Los Angeles and San Francisco, 30 to 50 percent of all people under parole supervision are homeless. In New York City, up to 20 percent of people released from city jails each year are homeless or their housing arrangements are unstable. One study found that at least 11 percent of people released from New York State prisons to New York City from 1995 to 1998 entered a homeless shelter within two years—more than half of these in the first month after release. Jeremy Travis, a senior fellow at the Urban Institute who studies reentry issues, notes that a "significant percentage" of the 600,000 people leaving state prisons each year are likely to be homeless. "Even if it's 10 percent of 600,000 a year, that's 60,000 a year coming out that have some serious housing issue."

* * *

Homelessness Among People Released From Prison

Three main factors contribute to and complicate homelessness among people leaving prison. First, ex-offenders face the same social and economic conditions that lead to homelessness among the general population. Ex-offenders returning to the community also confront barriers to housing associated with their criminal justice system involvement. Finally, there is a lack of ownership of the problem among government agencies and community organizations.

Homelessness has grown among the general population over the past 25 years for several reasons, including a widening gap between rich and poor and a growing shortage of affordable low-income housing in cities. A scarcity of well-paying jobs and limited access to education or training also contribute to the problem. People who lack independent living skills or have physical or mental disabilities may be even more vulnerable to becoming homeless. It is likely that ex-offenders face some or all of these problems as they seek housing after prison.

The barriers to housing associated with involvement in the criminal justice system are significant. Thomas's experience is an example of the effects of policies or practices that exist in many jurisdictions to restrict ex-offenders' exposure to people and situations that may place them at risk of reoffending. In addition, federally subsidized housing providers, such as local public housing and Section 8 programs, may—and sometimes must—deny housing to people with a criminal history involving drugs or violence.

Still other circumstances make finding a home difficult for people who recently have left prison. For example, someone who has been incarcerated for one or more years without access to employment at market wages may not have the financial resources to rent an apartment, particularly in large urban areas. Ex-offenders who live in a shelter or on the street don't have a fixed address or phone number where potential employers can contact them. They also may be unable to maintain personal hygiene and may not have clean, appropriate clothes to wear to interviews or at work.

Providing housing assistance to people leaving prison does not fall easily within the purview of criminal justice, homeless services, or housing development agencies. Corrections agencies are not necessarily responsible for inmates once they have been released. Parole agencies and other agencies charged with supervising offenders in the community, which are more directly affected by the problem than corrections agencies, typically are too small, with tight budgets and limited expertise in brokering housing or developing or managing residential facilities. Homeless services agencies may be wary of having ex-offenders funneled into their system. In a jurisdiction that does not have a homeless services agency, the responsibility of housing the homeless usually falls to a general social services agency, where it must compete with other priorities such as public assistance or child welfare.

These factors combined make it extremely difficult for ex-offenders to find a permanent home and establish stable lives in the community. They may also contribute to an offender's further involvement in the criminal justice system. Some of the men who participated in Project Greenlight, for example, had lived in shelters and reported that substance abuse, theft, and robbery commonly led to fighting and assaults.

Current research suggests that homelessness and incarceration are linked, though the nature of this relationship remains unclear. According to a study by the federal Bureau of Justice Statistics, 12 percent of state prisoners were homeless at the time of their arrest, and the

Interagency Council on the Homeless has reported that 18 percent of all homeless people have spent time in a state or federal prison. Moreover, among parolees who have been reincarcerated, 19 percent were homeless upon their arrest. A recent study of more than 48,000 people released from New York State prisons to New York City found an increased risk of reincarceration among people who had used shelters (either prior to or following their incarceration), compared with those who had not ... [T]his risk for reincarceration was highest for released prisoners with a pattern of long-term homelessness—defined as shelter use both before and after incarceration.

If homelessness increases the risk of recidivism, the implications for criminal justice agencies and communities could be substantial. In addition to costs associated with recidivism, criminal justice agencies could face increased costs related to the time parole officers spend locating parolees who do not have a permanent home. Homelessness makes standard community supervision techniques, such as unannounced late-night visits to confirm curfew compliance, nearly impossible.

* * *

Prohibiting Homelessness

... Hawaii does not release inmates to parole unless they have housing, and Illinois has a statewide goal of ensuring that everyone leaving prison has housing.

• The Hawaii Paroling Authority will not release an inmate to parole supervision without an approved place to live. Homeless shelters are not considered an approved residence. Inmates who are eligible for parole are released on furlough for short periods so that they can establish ties in the community, including a place to live, a job, and renewed connections with family. Max Otani, who worked as a parole officer and an administrator responsible for parole operations statewide during his 17 years with the Paroling Authority, says that it usually takes a couple of months for an inmate to find housing. For disabled inmates or high-risk inmates such as sex offenders and arsonists, finding housing can take up to a year. Parole officers sometimes refer inmates to services to help them with housing, but in most cases inmates are on their own in finding a place to live.

• The Illinois Department of Corrections has pledged to not release any prisoner to homelessness. Its Placement Resource Unit attempts to find transitional housing, as well as short-term employment, for those who would otherwise be homeless. In practice, though, the unit must focus most of its resources on the most difficult to place, many of whom are sex offenders. People leaving Illinois prisons with other criminal backgrounds may receive only very short-term housing. The unit plans to use a portion of its federal reentry funds to serve an additional 180 inmates over the next three years from the general prison population who do not have special needs. Each will receive between 70 to 90 days of either transitional housing or rental and utility assistance. However, in a state that released 25,302 inmates in 2001, the number of offenders receiving such assistance is small.

Providing Housing as Part of Drug Treatment or Employment Services

California and Maryland are examples of states that are focusing on the objective of providing housing as part of substance abuse treatment or employment programs.

• In California, inmates who participate in pre-release drug treatment programs are eligible for up to six months of housing linked to post-release drug treatment. Of the approximately 160,000 inmates statewide, 7,500 are in drug treatment programs. Vitka Eisen, associate director of criminal justice programs at Walden House, a San Francisco-based nonprofit health services organization that operates four in-prison substance abuse programs and three residential treatment facilities for parolees, estimates that 65 percent of inmates in drug treatment programs are required to participate and generally have low levels of motivation in the program. She says that motivation increases, however, when inmates learn that post-release services, including housing, are available. Participants must first complete a residential treatment program and later can become eligible for housing in privately run "sober living" residences while they participate in outpatient drug treatment.

• In Maryland, ex-offenders in Baltimore can enroll in job training and get help finding a job through the Re-Entry Partnership Initiative. The program provides two months of housing, which participants pay for with the stipend they receive while they're in job training. The goal is for ex-offenders to save money so that they can eventually live on their own. The program, a joint venture of the State Division of Correction and the Enterprise Foundation, began in 1999 and serves about 130 people per year. With the federal reentry funds, the program plans to expand its services to 325. Former Program Director Tomi Hiers says, "We thought that probably about a third of the overall population would need some sort of transitional housing support … but it's been roughly 50 percent."

Providing Housing as Part of Comprehensive Transition Planning

Rather than focus on one particular service to help ex-offenders return to the community, some programs focus on the third objective of providing an array of transitional services, including housing assistance. Hawaii, Massachusetts, Rhode Island, and Tennessee have such programs.

- Hawaii's Being Empowered and Safe Together (BEST) Reintegration Program is a small-scale program in Maui County supported by federal reentry funds. The program is designed to serve 225 people paroled to the island of Maui over three years. BEST provides transitional services such as substance abuse treatment, family reunification services, and cognitive skills training. The program employs a full-time housing coordinator and sets aside $200 for housing for each participant. Although the monthly rent of a studio apartment on Maui is about $765, program planners expect that even this small stipend will help ex-offenders find housing in the first few weeks they are out of prison.

- Massachusetts' Department of Corrections, like those in Hawaii and Illinois, has a policy of not releasing any inmate to homelessness or to a homeless shelter. According to Lisa Jackson, who heads the department's 20-person Reentry Unit, the department's system-wide approach to release planning addresses inmates' housing needs as they enter prison and as they are planning to leave. In addition, in 2002, the department contracted with the South Middlesex Opportunity Council (SMOC), a private human services organization, to provide housing with integrated social services for people leaving prison who are at risk of homelessness. From early July 2003, when it began providing services, until the end of September 2003, SMOC received referrals for 20 inmates, all of whom were placed. The department is evaluating the effectiveness of its reentry programming. The most recent data available suggest that, despite the state's policy to not release inmates to homelessness, some exoffenders are falling through the cracks. In 2001, the department released 2,692 inmates. According to the Massachusetts Housing and Shelter Alliance (MHSA), in the same year 365 people, or seven percent of those released in 2001, entered emergency shelters directly upon their discharge from a state correctional facility.

- Rhode Island Department of Corrections' COMPASS project (Challenging Offenders to Maintain Positive Associations and Social Stability), which began operations in February 2003, provides comprehensive transitional planning. The program will place 200 participants per year into its casemanagement program. Those who need housing must offset the cost of transitional housing subsidized by COMPASS with income from employment or another source, such as Supplemental Security Income disability insurance. Initial housing expenses will be treated as a loan that participants pay back as their earnings increase.

- In October 2002, the Tennessee Department of Corrections implemented Tennessee Bridges for up to 300 people as a transition between in-prison programming and post-release community supervision. The two-year program has three phases: six months of prerelease services including cognitive skills training, substance abuse treatment, and job readiness; six months of work-release; and a year of post-release case management. One of the program's goals is for participants to build savings for permanent housing during the work-release phase. Those who are unable to find housing while on work-release will receive assistance from case managers for placement in transitional housing. If an inmate does not have enough money saved and if the case manager determines that placement in a transitional residence is in the inmate's best interest, that inmate can receive a loan to cover the first week's deposit.

* * *

Notes and Questions

1. The Report notes that "[p]roviding housing assistance to people leaving prison does not fall easily within the purview of criminal justice, homeless services, or housing development agencies." How can it be the case in many states that no agency has primary responsibility for ensuring that prisoners have housing upon their release? If responsibility is split among different agencies, is that the same as if no one is in charge? Consider the famous case of Kitty Genovese, who was murdered while 38 witnesses listened but failed to call the police because they assumed someone else would do it. *See* A.M. Rosenthal, Thirty-Eight Witnesses (1964). Social scientists have recognized that when responsibility is diffused, action is not taken. *See, e.g.,* Bibb Latane & Steve Nilda, *Ten Years of Research on Group Size and Helping*, 89 Psychol. Bull. 308 (1981). Should there be a specific agency whose sole responsibility is to ensure that released prisoners have housing?

2. The Report makes a point of favorably noting that some states, such as Massachusetts, have "a policy of not releasing any inmate to homelessness or to a homeless shelter." Would it be reasonable for a state to have any other type of policy? Why would the criminal justice system—which is in the business of deterring criminal misconduct—even contemplate releasing a prisoner to the streets where he would almost certainly become the perpetrator or victim of crime?

3. Watch *The Wire*, Season 5, Episode 1, at 32:00 minutes. In an effort to kick his drug habit, Bubbles moves into his sister's basement. When she leaves for work, Bubbles' sister kicks him out because "you don't stay here when I'm not around, that's our rule." Bubbles pleads to stay, explaining that "I ain't got nowhere to go when I leave here." Later in the episode, Bubbles walks around town because he has no place to stay. He walks straight through drug corners where heroin is being sold. How much better of a chance would Bubbles have to kick his addiction if he had a steady place to live? Is the lack of funding for public housing for recovering drug addicts and parolees simply penny wise and pound foolish?

Department of Housing and Urban Development v. Rucker
535 U.S. 125 (2002)

Chief Justice REHNQUIST delivered the opinion of the Court.

With drug dealers "increasingly imposing a reign of terror on public and other federally assisted low-income housing tenants," Congress passed the Anti-Drug Abuse Act of 1988. The Act, as later amended, provides that each "public housing agency shall utilize leases which ... provide that any criminal activity that threatens the health, safety, or right to peaceful enjoyment of the premises by other tenants or any drug-related criminal activity on or off such premises, engaged in by a public housing tenant, any member of the tenant's household, or any guest or other person under the tenant's control, shall be cause for termination of tenancy." 42 U.S.C. § 1437d(*l*)(6) (1994 ed., Supp. V). Petitioners say that this statute requires lease terms that allow a local public housing authority to evict a tenant when a member of the tenant's household or a guest engages in drug-related criminal activity, regardless of whether the tenant knew, or had reason to know, of that activity. Respondents say it does not. We agree with petitioners.

Respondents are four public housing tenants of the Oakland Housing Authority (OHA). Paragraph 9(m) of respondents' leases, tracking the language of § 1437d(*l*)(6), obligates the tenants to "assure that the tenant, any member of the household, a guest, or another person under the tenant's control, shall not engage in … [a]ny drug-related criminal activity on or near the premise[s]." Respondents also signed an agreement stating that the tenant "understand[s] that if I or any member of my household or guests should violate this lease provision, my tenancy may be terminated and I may be evicted."

In late 1997 and early 1998, OHA instituted eviction proceedings in state court against respondents, alleging violations of this lease provision. The complaint alleged: (1) that the respective grandsons of respondents William Lee and Barbara Hill, both of whom were listed as residents on the leases, were caught in the apartment complex parking lot smoking marijuana; (2) that the daughter of respondent Pearlie Rucker, who resides with her and is listed on the lease as a resident, was found with cocaine and a crack cocaine pipe three blocks from Rucker's apartment; and (3) that on three instances within a 2-month period, respondent Herman Walker's caregiver and two others were found with cocaine in Walker's apartment. OHA had issued Walker notices of a lease violation on the first two occasions, before initiating the eviction action after the third violation.

United States Department of Housing and Urban Development (HUD) regulations administering § 1437d(*l*)(6) require lease terms authorizing evictions in these circumstances. The HUD regulations closely track the statutory language, and provide that "[i]n deciding to evict for criminal activity, the [public housing authority] shall have discretion to consider all of the circumstances of the case…." 24 CFR § 966.4(*l*) (5)(i) (2001). The agency made clear that local public housing authorities' discretion to evict for drug-related activity includes those situations in which "[the] tenant did not know, could not foresee, or could not control behavior by other occupants of the unit." 56 Fed.Reg. 51560, 51567 (1991).

After OHA initiated the eviction proceedings in state court, respondents commenced actions against HUD, OHA, and OHA's director in United States District Court. They challenged HUD's interpretation of the statute under the Administrative Procedure Act, 5 U.S.C. § 706(2)(A), arguing that 42 U.S.C. § 1437d(*l*)(6) does not require lease terms authorizing the eviction of so-called "innocent" tenants, and, in the alternative, that if it does, then the statute is unconstitutional. The District Court issued a preliminary injunction, enjoining OHA from "terminating the leases of tenants pursuant to paragraph 9(m) of the 'Tenant Lease' for drug-related criminal activity that does not occur within the tenant's apartment unit when the tenant did not know of and had no reason to know of, the drug-related criminal activity."

A panel of the Court of Appeals reversed, holding that § 1437d(*l*)(6) unambiguously permits the eviction of tenants who violate the lease provision, regardless of whether the tenant was personally aware of the drug activity, and that the statute is constitutional. An en banc panel of the Court of Appeals reversed and affirmed the District Court's grant of the preliminary injunction….

We granted certiorari and now reverse, holding that 42 U.S.C. § 1437d(*l*)(6) unambiguously requires lease terms that vest local public housing authorities with the discretion to evict tenants for the drug-related activity of household members and guests whether or not the tenant knew, or should have known, about the activity.

That this is so seems evident from the plain language of the statute. It provides that "[e]ach public housing agency shall utilize leases which ... provide that ... any drug-related criminal activity on or off such premises, engaged in by a public housing tenant, any member of the tenant's household, or any guest or other person under the tenant's control, shall be cause for termination of tenancy." 42 U.S.C. § 1437d(*l*)(6) (1994 ed., Supp. V). The en banc Court of Appeals thought the statute did not address "the level of personal knowledge or fault that is required for eviction." Yet Congress' decision not to impose any qualification in the statute, combined with its use of the term "any" to modify "drug-related criminal activity," precludes any knowledge requirement. As we have explained, "the word 'any' has an expansive meaning, that is, 'one or some indiscriminately of whatever kind.'" *United States v. Gonzales,* 520 U.S. 1, 5 (1997). Thus, *any* drug-related activity engaged in by the specified persons is grounds for termination, not just drug-related activity that the tenant knew, or should have known, about.

* * *

Comparing § 1437d(*l*)(6) to a related statutory provision reinforces the unambiguous text. The civil forfeiture statute that makes all leasehold interests subject to forfeiture when used to commit drug-related criminal activities expressly exempts tenants who had no knowledge of the activity: "[N]o property shall be forfeited under this paragraph ... by reason of any act or omission established by that owner to have been committed or omitted without the knowledge or consent of that owner." 21 U.S.C. § 881(a)(7) (1994 ed.). Because this forfeiture provision was amended in the same Anti-Drug Abuse Act of 1988 that created 42 U.S.C. § 1437d(*l*)(6), the en banc Court of Appeals thought Congress "meant them to be read consistently" so that the knowledge requirement should be read into the eviction provision. 237 F.3d, at 1121–1122. But the two sections deal with distinctly different matters. The "innocent owner" defense for drug forfeiture cases was already in existence prior to 1988 as part of 21 U.S.C. § 881(a)(7). All that Congress did in the 1988 Act was to add leasehold interests to the property interests that might be forfeited under the drug statute. And if such a forfeiture action were to be brought against a leasehold interest, it would be subject to the pre-existing "innocent owner" defense. But 42 U.S.C. § 1437(d)(*l*)(6), with which we deal here, is a quite different measure. It is entirely reasonable to think that the Government, when seeking to transfer private property to itself in a forfeiture proceeding, should be subject to an "innocent owner defense," while it should not be when acting as a landlord in a public housing project. The forfeiture provision shows that Congress knew exactly how to provide an "innocent owner" defense. It did not provide one in § 1437d(*l*)(6).

* * *

Nor was the en banc Court of Appeals correct in concluding that this plain reading of the statute leads to absurd results. The statute does not *require* the eviction of any tenant who violated the lease provision. Instead, it entrusts that decision to the local public housing authorities, who are in the best position to take account of, among other things, the degree to which the housing project suffers from "rampant drug-related or violent crime," 42 U.S.C. § 11901(2) (1994 ed. and Supp. V), "the seriousness of the offending action," 66 Fed.Reg., at 28803, and "the extent to which the leaseholder has ... taken all reasonable steps to prevent or mitigate the offending action," *ibid.* It is not "absurd" that a local housing authority may sometimes evict a tenant who had no knowledge of the drug-related activity. Such "no-fault" eviction is a common "incident of tenant responsibility under normal landlord-tenant law and practice." 56 Fed.Reg., at 51567. Strict liability maximizes deterrence and eases enforcement difficulties.

And, of course, there is an obvious reason why Congress would have permitted local public housing authorities to conduct no-fault evictions: Regardless of knowledge, a tenant who "cannot control drug crime, or other criminal activities by a household member which threaten health or safety of other residents, is a threat to other residents and the project." 56 Fed.Reg., at 51567. With drugs leading to "murders, muggings, and other forms of violence against tenants," and to the "deterioration of the physical environment that requires substantial government expenditures," 42 U.S.C. § 11901(4) (1994 ed., Supp. V), it was reasonable for Congress to permit no-fault evictions in order to "provide public and other federally assisted low-income housing that is decent, safe, and free from illegal drugs," § 11901(1) (1994 ed.).

* * *

The en banc Court of Appeals held that HUD's interpretation "raise[s] serious questions under the Due Process Clause of the Fourteenth Amendment," because it permits "tenants to be deprived of their property interest without any relationship to individual wrongdoing." 237 F.3d, at 1124–1125 (citing *Scales v. United States,* 367 U.S. 203, 224–225 (1961); *Southwestern Telegraph & Telephone Co. v. Danaher,* 238 U.S. 482 (1915)). But both of these cases deal with the acts of government as sovereign. In *Scales,* the United States criminally charged the defendant with knowing membership in an organization that advocated the overthrow of the United States Government. In *Danaher,* an Arkansas statute forbade discrimination among customers of a telephone company. The situation in the present cases is entirely different. The government is not attempting to criminally punish or civilly regulate respondents as members of the general populace. It is instead acting as a landlord of property that it owns, invoking a clause in a lease to which respondents have agreed and which Congress has expressly required. *Scales* and *Danaher* cast no constitutional doubt on such actions.

* * *

… Section 1437d(*l*)(6) requires lease terms that give local public housing authorities the discretion to terminate the lease of a tenant when a member of the household or a guest engages in drug-related activity, regardless of whether the tenant knew, or should have known, of the drug-related activity.

Accordingly, the judgment of the Court of Appeals is reversed, and the cases are remanded for further proceedings consistent with this opinion.

It is so ordered.

————————

Notes and Questions

1. The *Rucker* decision was not even close. The Court voted 8 to 0 (with Justice Breyer not participating) that innocent tenants can be evicted when other family members or even guests engaged in drug activity on the premises without the tenant's knowledge. Are you surprised that the decision was unanimous?

2. Do you think tenants in public housing are aware of the rule upheld in *Rucker*? If so, do you think it affects whom they will allow to live with them? If you lived in public housing and your brother or cousin were just released from prison after a drug conviction, would you allow him to live with you?

3. If families refuse to take in released offenders (either because of the risk of eviction or for other reasons), where are offenders supposed to go?

Chapter IX

Indeterminate Sentencing versus Sentencing Guidelines and Mandatory Minimums: Should Avon Barksdale Have Been Eligible for Parole?

"Society said I deserve another chance."[1]

— Poot

A. Introduction

When a defendant is sentenced to prison, how much of his sentence should he serve before being eligible for release? Should he have to serve the whole term or should we provide the option of early parole to inmates who behave well and appear to have a good chance of becoming productive citizens if they are released? Consider the following scene from *The Wire* where Poot is released from prison and immediately returns to a drug corner and encounters his friend Bodie and the police:

Bodie:	Hey, look, see this is what's wrong with the justice system right here. [People] get locked up and they don't stay that way. Damn, makes it hard to take this shit serious ... What you snitching [to get out]?
Poot:	No. They only gave me like 4 ... I already done 15 months. So with good time ...

[The police then arrive on the scene]

Officer Herc:	Didn't you get locked up ...?
Poot:	Society said I deserve another chance.

The Wire, Season 4, Episode 9, at 00:30 minutes.

Is Bodie right? Is it hard to take the justice system seriously when a convicted offender only serves a fraction of his sentence and can walk right back to the drug corner where he was arrested? Or is Poot correct that the criminal justice system is premised on the idea of giving second chances to offenders? In a nation where the public is split between

---

1. *The Wire*, Season 4, Episode 9, at 00:30 minutes.

agreeing with Bodie and Poot, how is the criminal justice system supposed to operate? Is it possible to satisfy both perspectives or do we have to choose one or the other?

B. American Sentencing Law in Historical Perspective

If you are like the average law student, you are in your mid-20s and have grown up in an America with very tough sentencing laws and very high incarceration rates. For the last few decades, long sentences, mandatory minimums, and restricted opportunities for parole have been the norm. It has not always been that way, however. Not long ago, indeterminate sentencing was the prevailing approach and the percentage of those incarcerated was much smaller. The excerpt below provides a historical overview of American sentencing. As you think about the different sentencing approaches, consider how the American incarceration rate has changed over the last four decades. In the early 1970s, the United States incarcerated about 160 inmates for every 100,000 people. By 1985, the incarceration rate was 313 per 100,000. In 1995, there were 601 people per 100,000 behind bars. In the beginning of the twenty-first century, the incarceration rate rose to 738 per 100,000 people.[1]

Judge Nancy Gertner, A Short History of American Sentencing: Too Little Law, Too Much Law, or Just Right?
100 Journal of Criminal Law and Criminology 691 (2010)

* * *

I. Colonial Juries and Sentencing

In colonial times, and particularly in the period before American independence, juries were de facto sentencers with substantial power. Many crimes were capital offenses. The result was binary — guilty and death, or not guilty and freedom. There were few scalable punishments, or punishments involving a term of years. This is so because penitentiaries were not common until the end of the eighteenth century. Jurors plainly understood the impact of a guilty verdict on the defendant because of the relative simplicity of the criminal law and its penalty structure, and often because of the process by which they were selected. They were picked from the rolls of white men with property. Indeed, steps were sometimes taken to secure better qualified people to serve on juries. Juries were hardly representative in the sense that we understand today. The substantive criminal law was the province of the states, and was, for the most part, state common law, often deriving from cases with which the jurors were familiar.

Like the modern jury, colonial jurors were authorized to give a general verdict without explanation, but unlike the modern jury, the colonial jury was explicitly permitted to find both the facts and the law. If capital punishment were inappropriate, they would simply decline to find guilt, or find the defendant guilty of a lesser crime in order to avoid the penalty of death. No one disparaged this as "jury nullification." Ignoring the law to effect a more lenient outcome was well within the jury's role. In fact, several colonies explicitly provided for jury sentencing.

---

1. *See* U.S. Dep't of Justice, Prison and Jail Inmates at Midyear 2005, at 2, tbl. 1 (2006).

Thus, in the colonial division of labor, juries had a preeminent role. There was no need for a priori punishment standards or rules, because there was, for the most part, a single punishment. Penal philosophy, at least as a formal matter, was retributive. There was little national federal law, even after independence. Most criminal law derived from the common law and in time, statutes from state legislatures—law with which jurors were familiar.

II. The Era of Indeterminate Sentencing

The turn of the nineteenth century brought scalable punishments—penitentiaries and, in time, reformatories—and thus, a more complex set of sentencing outcomes. The jury could no longer link conviction to a particular sentence even if it had the power to sentence or decide questions of law—and it did not. Now, they were explicitly instructed to find only the facts; judges determined the applicable law. Federal substantive criminal law began to evolve, although most criminal prosecutions were still state-based. And the jury changed: it was more diverse as barriers to serving as jurors were lifted for minorities and women, as were property restrictions. With more and more access to education, a professional class of judges and lawyers evolved, and with it, the power of the jury declined, including the power to affect the sentence.

Over time, a different division of labor evolved as between judges and juries: juries decided liability; judges sentenced. Selection procedures sought to insure that the jury would be selected in direct proportion to what they did not know about the issues, or the parties. And that was not too difficult in an urbanizing, diverse country. Juries became more and more passive, deferring to the professional judge.

This was especially true by the early twentieth century, when the dominant penal philosophy was rehabilitation and an indeterminate sentencing regime took hold. In indeterminate sentencing, the judge's role was essentially therapeutic, much like a physician's. Crime was a "moral disease," whose cure was delegated to experts in the criminal justice field, one of whom was the judge. Different standards of proof and of evidence evolved between the trial stage and the sentencing stage, reflecting the very different roles of judges and juries. The trial stage was the stage law students studied. It was the stage of constitutional rights, formal evidentiary rules, and proof beyond a reasonable doubt. At the sentencing stage, the rules of evidence did not apply; the standard of proof was the lowest in the criminal justice system: a fair preponderance of the evidence. The rationale was straightforward: it made no more sense to limit the kind of information that a judge should get at sentencing to exercise his or her "clinical" role than to limit the information available to a medical doctor in determining a diagnosis.

Unlike other common law countries, appellate review of sentences was extremely limited in American courts. In the federal system, the "doctrine of non-reviewability" prevailed until 1987, when the Federal Sentencing Guidelines became effective. Likewise, only a few states had appellate review of sentencing, and even then it was used "sparingly." A trial judge's authority to sentence was virtually unquestioned.

Consistent with this view of judges as the sentencing experts, Congress took a back seat, prescribing a broad range of punishments for each offense, and intervening only occasionally to increase the maximum penalty for specific crimes in response to public demand. Judges had substantial discretion to sentence, so long as it was within the statutory range. In effect, the breadth of the sentencing range left to the courts the task of "distinguishing between more or less serious crimes within the same category." While prosecutors had discretion to bring the charges, which, given the broad definitions of crimes, was not insubstantial, and defense lawyers could argue for creative "therapeutic" solutions, the judge had the final word. And even the judge's sentence did not fully determine the length of time a defendant would serve. Parole was available depending upon the defendant's conduct while incarcerated.

To sum up, judges and parole authorities had the most power relative to the other sentencing players. They were the acknowledged sentencing experts. There were few a priori rules or standards. Each case was resolved on its own merits; to the extent there were standards, they evolved from the day-to-day experience of sentencing individuals. There was little or no appellate review of sentencing. And the substantive law of sentencing was shaped by rehabilitation, a penal philosophy that necessarily reinforced the judge's role and limited Congress's and the public's. After all, neither was in a position to second guess the judge concerning what would rehabilitate an individual defendant. Finally, although federal criminal power was growing, most criminal law was state originated.

... [T]here were problems with indeterminate sentencing, problems that sowed the seeds of the next institutional shakeup. In fact, judges had no training in how to exercise their considerable discretion. Whatever the criminological literature, judges did not know about it. Sentencing was not taught in law schools; and to the extent there was any debate about deterrence and rehabilitation ... it was not reflected in judicial training. "It was as if judges were functioning as diagnosticians without authoritative texts, surgeons without Gray's Anatomy."

In the absence of any review, judges had little incentive to generate standards for sentencing which might be applied in future cases; few judges bothered to write sentencing opinions at all. Other efforts aimed at guiding judicial discretion, or even enhancing judicial decisionmaking, like sentencing councils, mimicking the clinical rounds of physicians, or sentencing information systems, were rejected.

Disparity was inevitable.... There was no common law of sentencing to create precedents to constrain discretion as exists in torts or contract. Without appellate review, no common law of sentencing could evolve. Constitutional review of sentencing decisions was limited; Eighth Amendment or due process review was rarely invoked, and even more rarely successful....

III. Guideline Movement

In response to widespread calls to reform the indeterminate system, a number of states implemented sentencing guidelines. The sentencing guideline approach introduced a new institutional player, an administrative agency—the sentencing commission—charged with generating sentencing standards. The role of the commission, its powers vis-à-vis the other sentencing players, and its animating penal philosophy varied from state to state.

In 1984, the federal government entered into the act with a version of sentencing reform that by the end of the decade would be widely criticized. Congress passed the Sentencing Reform Act of 1984 (SRA), creating the United States Sentencing Commission and abolishing parole. The Commission was supposed to do what Congress had been wholly unable to do, namely, to rationalize sentencing free of political influence, separate from the ever popular "crime du jour." At the same time, the dominant penal philosophy changed. The public, and certain members of the academy, gave up on rehabilitation as a central purpose of sentencing, instead championing a philosophy known as "limited" retribution. With that change, the locus of sentencing expertise moved from the judges and parole authorities to the Commission, Congress, and, to a degree, the public. Retribution made sentencing more accessible to the public and, ironically, to Congress. What the crime and the criminal deserved could be the subject of debate with the late night talk show host, or in time, the blogosphere.

To be sure, the institutional implications of the SRA were not immediately apparent. To some reformers, it was not clear whether the Guidelines would become a mandatory or an advisory system, or, put otherwise, whether they would supplement or supplant the judges. Where the system would land on the continuum from advisory to mandatory would have a substantial impact on the institutional division of labor.

Some who believed that the SRA would herald a truly advisory system pointed to such things as the fact that the Guidelines authorized a judge to depart from its confines whenever he or she concluded there was a factor "of a kind, or to a degree, not adequately taken into consideration" by the Commission. To others, the Guideline regime was unquestionably mandatory, underscoring the fact that the Guidelines were meant to determine sentencing outcomes in the vast majority of cases, and judges' power to depart was intended to be exercised sparingly.

As a result of various factors, many of which continue to shape the debate over sentencing today, the more onerous and mandatory vision of the system quickly took hold. Meanwhile, Congress, rather than taking a back seat to its newly created expert Commission, followed the passage of the SRA with a success of even more punitive mandatory minimum statutes and "three strikes and you're out" type sentencing enhancements. While cause and effect may not be clear, the following trends paralleled the Guideline movement.

A. POPULIST PUNITIVENESS

Crime became the fodder of political campaigns; "lenient" judges were parodied on the evening news and the burgeoning 24/7 cable outlets. But the popular rage went beyond judges who were supposedly "soft on crime." Efforts to restrict or even eliminate judicial discretion in sentencing paralleled efforts to strip judges of authority in a number of other areas. In 1981 and 1982 alone, more than two dozen bills stripping or altering federal courts' jurisdiction were introduced in the Ninety-Seventh Congress. And the anti-judge, significantly anti-federal judge language was vituperative.

B. MANDATORY MINIMUMS

Congress, propelled by this atmosphere, passed a succession of mandatory minimum statutes, statutes that were wholly inconsistent with the SRA's approach and surely with deference to the new "expert" Commission. Indeed, over time Congress directly intervened in Guideline determinations, ordering the Commission to increase this or that guideline. Congress's role grew as the criminal law became more and more federalized, now accounting for the prosecution of more and more local gun and drug offenses, the kind of street crime that had traditionally been the state's bailiwick.

C. THE COMPOSITION OF THE COMMISSION AND ITS GUIDELINES

The composition of the Commission and the guidelines it drafted exacerbated these trends. While the Commission was supposed to be made up of sentencing experts, the first Commission was not. Indeed, no one on the first Commission had experience in the day-to-day experience of sentencing offenders. It was, as many described it, political from the start and decidedly pro-prosecution. Without the patina of real sentencing expertise on the Commission, much less real independence, Congress had no problem regularly intervening in the Commission's decisionmaking and regularly ignoring it.

Additionally, the Commission made a number of problematic decisions in its initial drafting that had important institutional consequences. The Guidelines were complex and numerical. In an effort to minimize judicial discretion, they were keyed to the "objective" facts of the offense and the offender, such as the quantity of drugs or the amount of loss on the one hand and criminal record on the other. It rejected mens rea, the traditional basis for moral culpability, or other factors that judges had taken into account in the pre-Guidelines era.

And the Guidelines were severe, far more punitive than federal sentencing had ever been. While the Commission claimed to base the new Guidelines on existing practice, its data were limited and its analysis skewed. Moreover, it simply took existing sentencing lengths and then increased them. Notably, it chose to use Congress's mandatory minimum sentences as the base levels for the Guidelines, in effect requiring sentences even above the levels that Congress had set. Indeed, the Guidelines resulted in a marked increase in the percentage of all defendants sentenced to prison rather than probation, and for markedly longer terms of imprisonment. The severity of the Guidelines necessarily increased the power of the prosecutor who could now credibly threaten substantial sentences to extract guilty pleas.

The Commission chose to implement a "real offense" system, which allowed a judge to consider additional facts about the criminal conduct of the defendant, beyond the offense of conviction, and under the usual sentencing standard, a fair preponderance of the evidence. Moreover, the requirement to consider uncharged conduct that was part of the "real offense" led to the requirement that a judge consider even "acquitted conduct." While a judge, pre-Guidelines, had the discretion to consider uncharged conduct or acquitted conduct, post-Guidelines, it was mandatory, and that conduct came to have specific determinate consequences—an increase in one's sentencing score and a concomitant increase in one's sentence. And "real offense" sentencing also enhanced the prosecutor's power to determine what to charge and what to leave in reserve for sentencing, under a lesser burden of proof and few evidentiary standards.

* * *

D. THE FEDERAL JUDICIARY

… [F]ederal judges at both the trial and appellate levels could have played a critical role in mitigating the harsh effects of this Guideline system. They could have created a robust law of departures, or they could have critically evaluated them in formal opinions. Instead, the federal judiciary, which had overwhelmingly opposed the Guidelines, suddenly became wholly "passive" in their sentencing decisionmaking. They enforced the Guidelines with a rigor required by neither the SRA nor the Guidelines. This response was due in part to a continuation of conditions that existed prior to the promulgation of the Guidelines, the flaws of the indeterminate era. Judges still lacked training on how to sentence, and many did not have backgrounds in criminal justice. As a result, many judges—especially those who arrived on the bench after the Guidelines were promulgated—had no perspective independent of the Guidelines and no critical context within which to judge the Guideline outcomes. To them, the Guidelines seemed to define the fair sentencing outcome; it was the only one they knew. In part, judges mechanically followed the Guidelines because of how the federal guidelines were crafted and sold to them.… They believed that experts promulgated the comprehensive Guidelines, that they were based on empirical data, and that any gaps in their coverage were best filled by the expert Commission, rather than by the common law rulemaking of the federal bench. They believed this—and many still do—even though these assumptions were flawed.… The Guidelines' Introduction acknowledges that they are not comprehensive but rather have gaps intended to be filled in by judges' power to depart. Nor have they been drafted by sentencing experts, at least not the kind of experts envisioned by the SRA. Nor are they based on data or keyed to the purposes of sentencing.

In any event, even though the Guidelines were in fact enforced as if they were mandatory, that was not sufficient for some members of Congress. In 2003, Congress passed the PROTECT Act. The Act sought to eliminate virtually all departures from the Guidelines by creating a reporting mechanism for the judges who were not "compliant."

The result was a division of labor that gave extraordinary power to prosecutors who could effectively determine sentences, either by what they charged in the first instance or what they held in reserve for the sentencing "real offense" determination. It also gave power to Congress, which could also determine sentencing outcomes through mandatory minimum sentences or its edicts to the Commission. The power of judges to sentence was substantially diminished; parole had been abolished since the implementation of the Guidelines. Congress and the Commission became the exclusive source of sentencing rules. While the SRA was supposed to implement all of the purposes of sentencing, retribution was in fact the dominant philosophy. And with a growing federal criminal code, the federalization of crime, there were few external constraints on Congress. Unlike in the states, the federal correctional budget was a fraction of the total budget.

IV. United States v. Booker: Reenter the Jury

The implementation of the SRA sowed the seeds of a major constitutional challenge to the Guidelines. Under the still broad definition of crimes — the chaotic federal criminal code remained unchanged — the jury only found facts necessary to delineate the outer limits of punishments, facts that would trigger the application of the still broad statutory sentencing ranges. Then at the sentencing stage, the judge was obliged to make additional findings of fact in order to determine exactly where the offender fit in the sentencing grid. What was becoming more and more clear was that the judge was now nothing more than another fact finder, rather than a sentencing expert exercising any sentencing judgment, adding any kind of expertise. His or her job was to find facts with determinate numerical consequences under the Guidelines, a job which began to look more and more like the jury's.

In 2005, the United States Supreme Court handed down United States v. Booker, which held that the Guidelines were unconstitutional because of their impact on the jury. The Court found that the Guidelines violated the Sixth Amendment precisely because they obligated judges to find facts with the determinate consequences of increasing a defendant's sentence beyond the range required by a jury's verdict or a guilty plea. Suddenly, the jury was important in the sentencing division of labor, although as I have described, the jury of the twenty-first century looked nothing like the powerful colonial jury. This constitutional defect, according to the Court, required severance of the provisions of the SRA that made the Guidelines mandatory. The Court deemed the Guidelines to be "advisory," such that judges were to "consider" Guideline ranges but were permitted to tailor sentences in light of other statutory concerns.

* * *

At first, not much happened. The trends that predated the decision continued afterwards. Even after the Supreme Court declared mandatory application of the Guidelines to be unconstitutional, many judges continued to believe in the ideology of the Guidelines and urged continued deference. Many judges seemed to be uncomfortable exercising the discretion they now had. Many continued to use the numbers in the Guideline framework as a point of reference, illustrating the phenomenon known to cognitive researchers as anchoring.

But in a series of four cases after Booker, the Court made it quite clear that it meant what it had said. In Gall v. United States, the Court held that a judge could consider factors, such as offender and offense characteristics, regardless of whether they were allowable under the Guidelines. With Kimbrough v. United States and Spears v. United States, the Court indicated that a trial judge could even reject advisory Guidelines based solely on policy considerations, such as a conclusion that the applicable Guideline did not properly reflect national sentencing data and empirical research. And in Nelson v. United States, in a per curiam decision, the Court reversed a within-Guideline sentence, holding that "[t]he Guidelines are not only not mandatory on sentencing courts; they are also not to be presumed reasonable."

It is too early to say concretely what Booker and its progeny will do to the sentencing division of labor. It is clear that Booker has enhanced the position of the judge, whose sentencing expertise has been formally acknowledged again, at the cost of diminishing the position of the Sentencing Commission. Booker stripped the Guidelines of the force of law, transforming the Commission into a more traditional administrative agency, now subject to review akin to that required by the Administrative Procedure Act. Congress's role, to a degree, is unchanged, so long as it continues to legislate mandatory minimum statutes, although its influence on the Commission no longer translates into a direct influence on sentencing. The prosecutor's role is somewhat diminished to the extent that his or her charging decisions are no longer effectively outcome determinative. But given the remaining arsenal of federal offenses with mandatory minimum sentences, or enhanced penalties, that reduction is hardly substantial. And the role of the jury, whose diminished position was the initial concern of the Court in Booker, has effectively not changed.

While retribution remains an important purpose of sentencing, the other purposes of the SRA — including rehabilitation — have new importance in the federal sentencing scheme, making sentencing outcomes more complex and, I would argue, far more fair. Federal judges have an opportunity to participate in fashioning new sentencing standards, alongside the Sentencing Commission and Congress, although it is not at all clear how much they will use their power.

* * *

Notes and Questions

1. Congress abolished parole when it adopted the Federal Sentencing Guidelines. This is slightly misleading though. Federal prisoners are still eligible for "good time" credit — that is, reductions in their sentence of up to 54 days per year for good behavior. *See* 18 U.S.C. §3624(b). Additionally, non-violent inmates can earn a one-year reduction in their sentence by completing a drug treatment program. *See* 18 U.S.C. §3621(c)(2). Nevertheless, the opportunity for early release is very limited compared to the pre-Guidelines era.

2. Although Judge Gertner primarily focuses on the federal system, the trend she describes has taken hold in states as well. For an analysis of the sentencing guideline regimes adopted by other states, see Richard S. Frase, *State Sentencing Guidelines: Diversity, Consensus, and Unresolved Policy Issues*, 105 Colum. L. Rev. 1190 (2005).

C. The Risks of Indeterminate Sentencing

If Poot is correct that some inmates "deserve a second chance," who should have responsibility for making that decision? One approach could be to bring the inmate before the judge who had sentenced him and have the judge decide whether early release is appropriate. That is not how early release works in the United States, though. In states with indeterminate sentencing — that is, jurisdictions where it is not clear up front how long a defendant will actually serve — it is parole boards, not judges, who determine when release occurs. Although they are furnished with information — sometimes including statements from prosecutors, defense lawyers, or victims — the parole boards are further removed from the crime and the offender than the judge who sentenced the defendant. This might provide some beneficial objectivity. On the other hand, it carries risks that the parole boards will release inmates who should remain incarcerated.

Martinez v. California
444 U.S. 277 (1980)

Mr. Justice STEVENS delivered the opinion of the Court.

The two federal questions that appellants ask us to decide are (1) whether the Fourteenth Amendment invalidates a California statute granting absolute immunity to public employees who make parole-release determinations, and (2) whether such officials are absolutely immune from liability in an action brought under the federal Civil Rights Act of 1871, 42 U.S.C. §1983. We agree with the California Court of Appeal that the state statute is valid when applied to claims arising under state law, and we conclude that appellants have not alleged a claim for relief under federal law

The case arises out of the murder of a 15-year-old girl by a parolee. Her survivors brought this action in a California court claiming that the state officials responsible for the parole-release decision are liable in damages for the harm caused by the parolee.

The complaint alleged that the parolee, one Thomas, was convicted of attempted rape in December 1969. He was first committed to a state mental hospital as a "Mentally Disordered Sex Offender not amenable to treatment" and thereafter sentenced to a term of imprisonment of 1 to 20 years, with a recommendation that he not be paroled. Nevertheless, five years later, appellees decided to parole Thomas to the care of his mother. They were fully informed about his history, his propensities, and the likelihood that he would commit another violent crime. Moreover, in making their release determination they failed to observe certain "requisite formalities." Five months after his release Thomas tortured and killed appellants' decedent. We assume, as the complaint alleges, that appellees knew, or should have known, that the release of Thomas created a clear and present danger that such an incident would occur. Their action is characterized not only as negligent, but also as reckless, willful, wanton and malicious. Appellants prayed for actual and punitive damages of $2 million.

* * *

I

Section 845.8(a) of the Cal. Gov't Code Ann. (West Supp. (1979)) provides:

> "Neither a public entity nor a public employee is liable for:
>
> (a) Any injury resulting from determining whether to parole or release a prisoner or from determining the terms and conditions of his parole or release or from determining whether to revoke his parole or release."

The California courts held that this statute provided appellees with a complete defense to appellants' state-law claims. They considered and rejected the contention that the immunity statute as so construed violates the Due Process Clause of the Fourteenth Amendment to the Federal Constitution.

Like the California courts, we cannot accept the contention that this statute deprived Thomas' victim of her life without due process of law because it condoned a parole decision that led indirectly to her death. The statute neither authorized nor immunized the deliberate killing of any human being. It is not the equivalent of a death penalty statute which expressly authorizes state agents to take a person's life after prescribed procedures have been observed. This statute merely provides a defense to potential state tort-law liability. At most, the availability of such a defense may have encouraged members of the parole board to take somewhat greater risks of recidivism in exercising their authority to release prisoners than they otherwise might. But the basic risk that repeat offenses may occur is always present in any parole system. A legislative decision that has an incremental impact on the probability that death will result in any given situation—such as setting the speed limit at 55-miles-per-hour instead of 45—cannot be characterized as state action depriving a person of life just because it may set in motion a chain of events that ultimately leads to the random death of an innocent bystander.

* * *

We have no difficulty in accepting California's conclusion that there "is a rational relationship between the state's purposes and the statute." In fashioning state policy in a "practical and troublesome area" like this, the California Legislature could reasonably conclude that judicial review of a parole officer's decisions "would inevitably inhibit the exercise of discretion," *United States ex rel. Miller v. Twomey*, 479 F.2d 701, 271 (CA7 1973). That inhibiting effect could impair the State's ability to implement a parole program designed to promote rehabilitation of inmates as well as security within prison walls by holding out a promise of potential rewards. Whether one agrees or disagrees with California's decision to provide absolute immunity for parole officials in a case of this kind, one cannot deny that it rationally furthers a policy that reasonable lawmakers may favor. As federal judges, we have no authority to pass judgment on the wisdom of the underlying policy determination. We therefore find no merit in the contention that the State's immunity statute is unconstitutional when applied to defeat a tort claim arising under state law.

II

We turn then to appellants' § 1983 claim that appellees, by their action in releasing Thomas, subjected appellants' decedent to a deprivation of her life without due process of law....

Appellants contend that the decedent's right to life is protected by the Fourteenth Amendment to the Constitution. But the Fourteenth Amendment protected her only from deprivation by the "*State* ... of life ... without due process of law." Although the decision to release Thomas from prison was action by the State, the action of Thomas five months later cannot be fairly characterized as state action. Regardless of whether, as a matter of state tort law, the parole board could be said either to have had a "duty" to avoid harm to his victim or to have proximately caused her death, we hold that, taking these particular allegations as true, appellees did not "deprive" appellants' decedent of life within the meaning of the Fourteenth Amendment.

Her life was taken by the parolee five months after his release. He was in no sense an agent of the parole board. Further, the parole board was not aware that appellants' decedent, as distinguished from the public at large, faced any special danger. We need not and do not decide that a parole officer could never be deemed to "deprive" someone of life by action taken in connection with the release of a prisoner on parole. But we do hold that at least under the particular circumstances of this parole decision, appellants' decedent's death is too remote a consequence of the parole officers' action to hold them responsible under the federal civil rights law....

The judgment is affirmed.

So ordered.

Notes and Questions

1. What "requisite formalities" do you think the parole board failed to follow? Why does Justice Stevens' opinion not tell us what those formalities were?

2. What possible explanation could the parole board have given for paroling an attempted rapist after 5 years when the original recommendation was that he not be released before his maximum 20-year sentence expired?

3. Watch *The Wire*, Season 1, Episode 6, at 21:40 minutes and then at 23:25 minutes. Officers Carver and Herc are irate that Bodie has again managed to avoid incarceration for assaulting a cop. Previously, Bodie escaped from a juvenile facility. Carver and Herc grab Bodie on the street, assuming that he had escaped again, but Bodie is carrying papers showing that he has been released and been subjected only to home monitoring. Carver, Herc, and Bodie all agree that the juvenile system is a "big ... joke" for releasing him. Faced with a defendant who had a record for selling drugs, assaulted a police officer, and escaped from a detention facility, how could the judge have released him to home monitoring?

4. Watch *The Wire*, Season 3, Episode 7, at 52:00 and 53:30 minutes. Herc informs McNulty and Greggs that he saw Avon Barksdale riding on the street. Greggs doesn't believe him, explaining that he'll be in prison for at least four or five years of his seven-year sentence. Shortly thereafter, Greggs and McNulty check a database and discover Barksdale has already been released. How is it possible that no one in the police unit who worked Barksdale's case would be notified of his release? Is it because the real or fictional criminal justice system in Baltimore is more dysfunctional than the rest of the nation, or do you think information flow through most criminal justice systems is this bad?

5. The Court's unanimous opinion in *Martinez* seems unimpeachable as a matter of law. Like judges (and, to a lesser extent, police officers), parole officials must have immunity from civil liability in order to carry out their jobs based on their honest assessments, rather than based on the fear of reprisal. Yet, looking beyond the purely legal aspects, does the decision seem just? Can you see why the public might be angry at the idea that unelected officials can release criminals who later murder innocent children and that the officials face no repercussions?

6. Martinez killed his victim in 1975, after serving only ¼ of his maximum sentence. Could something like this happen today, or are inmates — even in indeterminate sentencing states — required to serve longer sentences before being eligible for parole? Consider Texas, which is supposedly America's most "tough on crime" state. For most felonies, Texas law requires the defendant to serve only one-quarter of his sentence before becoming eligible for parole. *See* Tex. Gov't Code Ann. § 508.145(f). And credit that prisoners receive for good behavior — days they did not actually serve — counts towards completing the one-fourth requirement. For the most serious felonies — murder, aggravated kidnapping, sexual assault, and a few others — Texas is slightly tougher and requires defendants to serve at least one-half of their sentences. *See* Tex. Gov't Code Ann.

§ 508.145(d). How do you explain that Texas, which is often referred to as the "capital of capital punishment," authorizes murderers to possibly be paroled after serving only half their sentence and sometimes frees other inmates after serving less than one-quarter of their sentences? Is Texas unique?

United States v. Golden

679 F.Supp.2d 980 (N.D. Iowa 2010)

MARK W. BENNETT, District Judge

* * *

Defendant Tony Terrell Golden came before me for sentencing on January 5, 2010, on his guilty plea to two crack cocaine charges....

I. INTRODUCTION

A. Indictment And Guilty Pleas

On July 23, 2009, a Grand Jury handed down an Indictment (docket no. 1) charging defendant Tony Terrell Golden with the following offenses: (1) conspiring, from about 2004 through June 26, 2009, to distribute 50 grams or more of crack cocaine in violation of 21 U.S.C. § 846 (Count 1); (2) possessing with intent to distribute 50 grams or more of crack cocaine on or about June 26, 2009, in violation of 21 U.S.C. § 841(a)(1) and (b)(1)(A) (Count 2); and (3) distributing 2.6 grams of crack cocaine within 1,000 feet of a public playground or school on or about June 3, 2009, in violation of 21 U.S.C. §§ 841(a)(1), 841(b)(1)(C), and 860(a) (Count 3). Although Golden had already been under investigation for drug trafficking, Golden was not arrested until he was stopped by an Iowa State Trooper for a traffic violation on June 26, 2009. A vehicle search after that stop revealed five individually-wrapped bags, four containing crack cocaine and one containing cocaine powder, underneath the rear seat of the vehicle that Golden was driving. During a post-Miranda interview, Golden reported that he purchased three and one-half ounces of crack cocaine and one ounce of powder cocaine in Arkansas, where he lived with his mother, for $1,200 per ounce, and that he planned to sell the drugs in Sioux City, Iowa, where his father lived, at a considerable profit. He also described to officers how he could either cook the powder cocaine into crack cocaine or sell it to customers in powder form. Further interviews and debriefing, as well as prior investigation, revealed that Golden had traveled from Arkansas to Sioux City on several occasions to sell crack cocaine that he had purchased in Arkansas. At least some of the drug-trafficking activity at issue occurred within 1,000 feet of a playground or school.

... On October 16, 2009, Golden entered a Consent To Plead Guilty Before A Magistrate Judge and Rule 32 Waiver. On October 16, 2009, Golden pleaded guilty to Counts 1 and 2 before Judge Zoss pursuant to a plea agreement providing, *inter alia*, for dismissal of Count 3....

B. The Presentence Investigation Report

Among other significant matters, the final Presentence Investigation Report (PSIR) ... summarized the relevant drug quantities in this case as 335.62 grams of crack cocaine (6,712.40 kilograms of marijuana equivalent) and 28.35 grams of powder cocaine (5.67 kilograms of marijuana equivalent), resulting in a converted combined weight of 6,718.07 kilograms of marijuana equivalent. Consequently, the PSIR calculated ... a Total Offense Level of 30.

The criminal history portion of the PSIR revealed no known juvenile adjudications, but four adult criminal convictions: (1) a conviction for "possession of cocaine" in Mississippi County, Arkansas, arising from an arrest on March 12, 1998, when the defendant was 17, and resulting in a sentence on April 24, 1998, to 3 years of probation; (2) a conviction for "failure to appear," also in Mississippi County, Arkansas, arising from an arrest on May 17, 2000, when the defendant was 19, resulting in a fine imposed on May 18, 2000; (3) a conviction for first-degree attempted murder in Mississippi County, Arkansas, arising from an arrest on November 16, 2000, when the defendant was 20, and resulting in a sentence on May 16, 2001, to 120 months of imprisonment, from which Golden was subsequently paroled three times; and (4) a conviction for third-degree burglary in Mississippi County, Arkansas, arising from an arrest on March 5, 2001, when the defendant was 20, and resulting in a sentence on March 14, 2001, to sixty days in jail.

Not surprisingly, the conviction for first-degree attempted murder drew my particular attention. The PSIR described that offense as follows:

> Osceola Police Department records indicate officers were called to a street intersection due to shots fired. It was reported that the defendant, Reggie Jackson, Marquette Smith, and Sedrick Askew were involved in an altercation with Scotty Ridley and Anthony Harris. The defendant and Ridley escalated into a physical argument. Ridley pulled a gun from the defendant's pocket; however, the defendant out muscled Ridley and took the gun back. As Ridley walked backwards from the defendant, he taunted the defendant. The defendant then fired the gun at Ridley. At the crime scene, officers recovered over 10 grams of crack cocaine but never located the firearm. Ridley was hospitalized for his injuries
>
> While incarcerated, the defendant received disciplinary action and/or loss of good time for: failure to obey staff (16 times), assault (six times), unexcused absence from work schedule (five times), battery (three times), abusive/obscene language (three times), out of place of assignment (three times), unnecessary noise (two times), interfering with count (two times), unauthorized presence, keep person/quarters within regulation, lying to staff member, indecent exposure, counterfeiting/forging, possession/introduction of clothing, and any felony act or misdemeanor. During a July 1, 2009, debriefing, the defendant admitted he purchased one ounce of marijuana from a prison guard while incarcerated.

The PSIR also explained that Golden was sentenced to 120 months of imprisonment on this offense on May 16, 2001; he was paroled on October 14, 2004; his parole was revoked on January 1, 2005; he was paroled again on March 1, 2006; his parole was revoked again on February 5, 2007; he was paroled for a third time on December 12, 2008; and a parole warrant, still active, was issued on July 30, 2009.

* * *

The criminal history calculation in the PSIR gave Golden a subtotal of six criminal history points: three for the first-degree attempted murder conviction, two for the burglary conviction, one for the possession of cocaine conviction, and none for the failure to appear conviction. The PSIR then gave Golden two points pursuant to U.S.S.G. §4A1.1(d) for committing the federal offenses while on parole for the attempted murder conviction, and one further point pursuant to U.S.S.G. §4A1.1(e) for commission of the federal offenses less than two years following Golden's most recent release from custody on the attempted murder conviction, resulting in a total of nine criminal history points, and a Criminal History Category of IV.

The PSIR concluded that, with a Total Offense Level of 30 and a Criminal History Category of IV, Golden's advisory guidelines sentencing range was 135 to 168 months....

* * *

II. LEGAL ANALYSIS

* * *

... [A] "standard" guidelines Total Offense Level of 30, which, with a Criminal History Category of IV, resulted in a "standard" advisory guidelines sentencing range of 135 to 168 months, with the sentence for Counts 1 and 2 to be imposed concurrently pursuant to U.S.S.G. §5G1.2(c).

* * *

In short, but for Golden's poor aim, he would likely be serving a life sentence for murder in circumstances in which 40 grams of crack cocaine were found at the scene of an argument and shooting. The assessment of a mere three criminal history points to such an attempted murder offense, even if it also resulted in the assessment of other criminal history points for commission of the present federal offense while on parole and within two years of Golden's most recent incarceration, is woefully inadequate. Pursuant to U.S.S.G. §4A1.1(a), the same three points would have been assessed for felony check fraud. I cannot conceive that a reasonable person would find equating attempted murder with felony check fraud makes sense in the assessment of criminal history for sentencing purposes.

I find it equally bewildering that the prosecution made no attempt to seek an upward variance based on this defendant's criminal history. Here, the prosecutor did not even suggest a sentence at the middle or the top end of the "standard" guidelines range, but was content to assert that a sentence anywhere within that guidelines range would be reasonable. When specifically asked, the prosecutor indicated that a sentence at the bottom of the advisory guidelines range would be reasonable in this case. I simply do not agree.

There are other aggravating factors in Golden's history and characteristics: his lack of employment history itself suggesting that he was making a living dealing drugs and his repeated parole revocations suggesting recidivism and the likelihood that he would reoffend unless incarcerated, all mitigated only by some inadequacies of his family relationships.[3] More specifically, I believe that an upward variance is also appropriate "to promote respect for the law," §3553(a)(2)(A), "to afford adequate deterrence to criminal conduct," §3553(a)(2)(B), and "to protect the public from further crimes of the defendant," §3553(a)(2)(C). For his attempted murder offense, Golden was sentenced to a mere 120 months in the first place and he was paroled, for the first time, after serving less than three-and-one-half years, then revoked twice and paroled twice more. The PSIR also indicates that Golden had a poor prison disciplinary record, including multiple disciplinary reports for assault and battery. Even if it was appropriate to parole a defendant convicted of attempted murder after only three-and-one-half years, it is clear from Golden's subsequent revocations of parole and his prison disciplinary record that he does not have any respect for the law or any ability to conform his conduct to its requirements. Thus, his ability to commit further crimes—which his record shows he assuredly will do if released—must be curtailed and the public must be protected from his further crimes.

A final aggravating factor relates to "the nature and circumstances of the offense." 18 U.S.C. §3553(a)(1). There is no indication in the PSIR that Golden's criminal conduct re-

---

3. The court also notes that Golden's lack of a father figure is potentially mitigating, but that lack is more than offset, in the court's view, by the presence of a hard-working mother. Thus, while I have considered Golden's family circumstances in my consideration of the §3553(a) factors, I do not find that they mitigate against an upward variance.

sulted from drug addiction. Rather, it appears to be the result of greed or at least a preference for making "easy money" dealing drugs rather than by working hard, as his mother clearly has done.

Upon consideration of the entire record and all pertinent sentencing factors.... I varied upward to 180 months of incarceration, with various other terms and conditions set out on the record at the sentencing hearing, as the sentence that, in my view, is sufficient, but not greater than necessary in this case.

* * *

III. CONCLUSION

Accordingly, defendant Gully was sentenced to 180 months of incarceration, with various other terms and conditions set out on the record at the sentencing hearing, as the sentence that, in my view, sufficient, but not greater than necessary in this case....

IT IS SO ORDERED.

Notes and Questions

1. Is a sentence of 180 months—that is, 15 years—a fair result for possession with intent to distribute drugs? Does it affect your answer to know that there is no parole in the federal system and the maximum credit Golden can receive for good behavior is 54 days per year?

2. Would it be reasonable for Judge Bennett to have assumed that Golden could not be rehabilitated and therefore needed to be locked up to incapacitate him? Consider that after being paroled for the attempted murder on October 14, 2004, Golden's parole was revoked less than three months later on January 1, 2005. When paroled again in March 2006, he lasted less than a year before being revoked again in February 2007. Finally, after being paroled for a third time in December 2008, Golden was arrested on the current charge only seven months later in July 2009.

3. Judge Bennett makes the assumption that Golden's lack of employment history indicates that he has been "making a living dealing drugs." Should Judge Bennett be allowed to make this assumption without additional facts? Is it a logical assumption? Put differently, do you think Golden was constantly involved in illegal activity during the times when he was not incarcerated? If Golden told the court that, for instance, he had gone almost a year without committing a violation between March 2006 and February 2007, would it be fair to respond that he was probably engaged in illegal activity but simply avoided getting caught?

4. How can it be that possession of less than half a kilogram of drugs can result in a 15-year sentence (with no possibility of parole and only 54 days per year of good time credit) while a conviction for attempted murder yields a 10-year sentence and parole after less than 4 years? Is either (or both) of these sentences out of line?

5. Are you surprised that Golden was paroled for his attempted murder conviction after less than four years? Given that he had other prior criminal infractions—drug possession, low-level burglary, and failure to appear—as well as a poor disciplinary record in prison, why would officials think Golden was a good candidate for parole?

6. Like many states, Iowa's prisons are overcrowded. As of April 2012, Iowa prisons had capacity for 7,209 inmates but actually held 8,478 inmates. *See* IOWA DEPARTMENT OF CORRECTIONS, DAILY STATISTICS (available at http://www.doc.state.ia.us/DailyStats.asp).

7. Another explanation for Golden's early release on the attempted murder charge is Iowa's good time system, which is more generous than most states. According to the Iowa Parole Board, "most offenders' sentences are also reduced by about half by good behavior in the prison system, so most ten-year sentences will expire in about five years." Iowa Board of Paroles, Annual Report for State Fiscal Year 2011, at 17 (2012). However, could Golden have qualified for good time credit given that he had dozens of disciplinary violations including six for assault and sixteen for disobeying staff?

8. On the other hand, perhaps there are facts that we (and Judge Bennett) do not know that would have explained Golden's early parole. In 2011, the only person paroled for attempted murder in Iowa had served 16½ years. See Iowa Board of Paroles, Annual Report for State Fiscal Year 2011, at 20 (2012). In 2010, two people convicted of attempted murder were paroled after serving 14½ and 15½ years. See Iowa Board of Paroles, Annual Report for State Fiscal Year 2010, at 21 (2011). These attempted murders served considerably longer sentences than Golden. Perhaps there was a good reason for Golden's quick parole.

9. Do you feel confident that the Iowa Board of Paroles knows what it is doing in deciding whether to release inmates? In 2004, the year Golden was originally paroled, the Board had five members serving staggered four-year terms. The members included a former administrative law judge, a licensed social worker who had previously worked in the Department of Corrections and as a rape counselor, and a lawyer who had served as a county attorney and as a magistrate. See Iowa Board of Paroles, Annual Report for State Fiscal Year 2004, at 4–5 (2005). Do you think individuals with those backgrounds would be good or bad arbiters in making parole decisions? Would they be in a better position than Judge Bennett to make determinations? Or would it be best if no one had authority to grant parole and that defendants simply would have to serve fixed sentences?

Bureau of Justice Statistics Special Report, Recidivism of Prisoners Released in 1994
1–11 (June 2002)*

This study of the rearrest, reconviction, and reincarceration of prisoners tracked 272,111 former inmates for 3 years after their release in 1994. The 272,111—representing two-thirds of all prisoners released in the United States that year—were discharged from prisons in 15 States: Arizona, California, Delaware, Florida, Illinois, Maryland, Michigan, Minnesota, New Jersey, New York, North Carolina, Ohio, Oregon, Texas, [and] Virginia.

* * *

Characteristics of the 272,111 released prisoners

Of offenders released from prisons in 15 States in 1994:

91.3% were male

50.4% were white

48.5% were black

24.5% were Hispanic

44.1% were under age 30.

---

* Editor's Note: All tables and highlight boxes have been removed from this edited version.

The 272,111 were in prison for a wide variety of offenses, primarily felonies:

22.5% for a violent offense (for example, murder, sexual assault, and robbery)

33.5% for a property offense (for example, burglary, auto theft, and fraud)

32.6% for a drug offense (primarily drug trafficking and possession)

9.7% for a public-order offense (roughly 33% driving while intoxicated/driving under the influence, 32% a weapons offense, 8% a traffic offense, 9% a probation violation, and the remainder, such crimes as escape, obstruction of justice, court offense, parole violation, contributing to the delinquency of a minor, bigamy, and habitual offender) 1.7% for some other offense (for example, an unspecified felony or misdemeanor).

The average prison sentence length was nearly 5 years. On average, the prisoners were released after serving 35% of their sentence, or about 20 months.

Seventy percent had 5 or more prior arrests (not including the arrest that brought them to prison), and half had 2 or more prior convictions (not including the conviction that resulted in their prison sentence).

For 56.4% of the released prisoners the prison sentence they were serving when released was their first-ever sentence to prison. Almost 44% had served a prior prison sentence.

Recidivism rates at different lengths of time after release

Within the first 6 months of their release, 29.9% of the 272,111 offenders were rearrested for a felony or serious misdemeanor.

Within the first year the cumulative total grew to 44.1% and within the first 2 years, 59.2%. Within the first 3 years of their release, an estimated 67.5% of the 272,111 released prisoners were rearrested at least once.

The first year is the period when much of the recidivism occurs, accounting for nearly two-thirds of all the recidivism of the first 3 years.

Within the first year of release, an estimated 21.5% of the 272,111 released offenders were reconvicted for a new felony or misdemeanor; within the first 2 years, a combined total of 36.4% were reconvicted; and within the first 3 years, a combined total of 46.9% were reconvicted.

Not all of the reconvicted prisoners were sentenced to another prison term for their new crime. Some were sentenced to confinement in a local jail. Some were sentenced to neither prison nor jail but to probation, which allowed them to remain free in their communities but under the supervision of a probation officer.

Within the first year of release, 10.4% of the 272,111 released prisoners were back in prison as a result of a conviction and prison sentence for a new crime; within the first 2 years, 18.8%; and within the first 3 years, 25.4%.

The number of crimes committed by the 272,111 released prisoners

How many crimes the 272,111 prisoners ever committed—both prior to and following their release—is unknown. The best estimate available from official sources is the volume of criminal charges found in arrest records. The volume of arrest charges is not the same thing as the volume of arrests.

The volume of arrests is the number of different times a person was arrested. The volume of arrest charges is the sum of the charges over all the different times the person was arrested.

Arrest records provide an incomplete measure of actual criminal activity. While people are sometimes arrested for crimes they did not commit, research indicates that offenders commit more crimes than their arrest records show.

New arrest charges following release from prison

The 67.5% of releases rearrested within 3 years, or 183,675 persons, were charged with 744,480 new crimes, or an average of 4 new crimes each. Over 100,000 were new charges for a violent crime, including 2,900 new homicides, 2,400 new kidnappings, 2,400 rapes, 3,200 other sexual assaults, 21,200 robberies, 54,600 assaults, and nearly 13,900 other violent crimes.

During the 3-year follow-up period, the released prisoners had new arrest charges for 40,300 burglaries and about 16,000 thefts of motor vehicles. They also had 79,400 new charges for drug possession, 46,200 new charges for drug trafficking, about 26,000 new charges for a weapons offense (such as illegal possession of a firearm), and approximately 5,800 new charges for driving while under the influence of drugs or alcohol.

The 744,480 new charges during the 3-year follow-up period consisted of 688,720 committed in the same State that released the prisoner plus 55,760 committed in other states.

Old arrest charges prior to their release from prison

Prior to entering prison, the 272,111 released prisoners had been arrested for about 4.1 million crimes, as indicated by the number of arrest charges in their criminal history files. The 4.1 million included the arrest charges that brought them to prison, plus all previous charges. Roughly 550,000 of the 4.1 million prior arrest charges were for a violent crime, including 18,000 prior charges for homicide, 10,700 prior charges for kidnapping, 44,400 prior charges for a violent sex offense (21,600 rapes and 22,800 sexual assaults), and 172,300 prior charges for robbery.

Combining new and old arrest charges

Over their adult criminal history (both prior to and following their release) the 272,111 offenders were arrested for nearly 4.9 million offenses altogether: 4.1 million prior to release plus nearly 0.8 million after release. That is an average of about 17.9 charges each.

A small fraction of offenders was responsible for a large number of the 4.9 million crimes. An estimated 6.4% of the prisoners were each charged with 45 or more offenses before and after their release in 1994. These high-rate offenders accounted for nearly 14% of all arrest charges.

Offenders with 25 or more charges represented nearly 24% of all offenders but about 52% of all charges.

By contrast, released prisoners with fewer than 5 arrest charges represented nearly 14% of all prisoners but accounted for about 6.4% of the 4.9 million arrest charges.

How many of the 272,111 were ever arrested for violence

Although 22.5% of the 272,111 were released from prison in 1994 following an arrest and conviction for a violent crime, 53.7% of all the prisoners had a prior arrest for violence, and 21.6% were arrested for a violent crime after their release. Altogether, 67.8% of the prisoners released in 1994 had a record of violence.

The 67.8% is less than the sum of three categories—22.5% in prison for violence plus 53.7% with prior violence plus 21.6% rearrested for violence—because some prisoners were in more than one category.

The fraction of all crimes that released prisoners accounted for

The study cannot measure precisely what fraction of all crime the former prisoners were responsible for during the 3 years following their release. The closest measure is the fraction of all arrests for seven serious crimes (murder, rape, robbery, aggravated assault, burglary, larceny, and motor vehicle theft). The number of "arrests" is not the number of "arrest charges" but the number of different days on which a person was arrested.

In 13 States (because of missing data Florida and Illinois could not be in this analysis) from 1994 to 1997, 234,358 released prisoners accounted for 140,534 arrests. During the period in the 13 States, 2,994,868 adults were arrested for the 7 serious crimes according to the FBI. Therefore, rearrests of the released prisoners were 4.7% of all arrests for serious crime from 1994 to 1997.

According to arrest records compiled in this study, of the 272,111 prisoners released in 1994, 719 were rearrested for homicide in the 13 States in 1995. The FBI reports that the number of adult arrests for homicide in the 13 States in 1995 was 8,521 altogether. The released prisoners accounted for 8.4% of all the homicides in the 13 States in 1995. Similarly, prisoners released in 1994 accounted for 5.4% of all the arrests for rape in the 13 States in 1994 and 9.0% of all the arrests for robbery in the 13 States from 1994 to 1997.

Although these percentages may seem small, they are actually the product of high rates of criminality. For example, to account for the 8.4% of 1995 homicides, the 234,358 released prisoners were arrested for homicide at a rate 53 times higher than the homicide arrest rate for the adult population. Note also that the 8.4% does not include homicides by (a) prisoners released in 1995, (b) prisoners released before 1994, or (c) released prisoners who had crossed State lines. The percentage of homicides attributable to released prisoners would be substantially greater if it included persons in categories a, b, and c.

* * *

Overall recidivism rate for the 272,111

Rearrest—An estimated 67.5% of the 272,111 released prisoners were rearrested for a new crime (either a felony or a serious misdemeanor) within 3 years following their release.

Reconviction—A total of 46.9% were reconvicted in State or Federal court for a new crime (a felony or misdemeanor).

Resentence—Over a quarter—25.4%—were back in prison as a result of another prison sentence. Sentences to State or Federal prisons but not to local jails are included in the 25.4%.

Return to prison with or without a new prison sentence—A total of 51.8% were back in prison because they had received another prison sentence or because they had violated a technical condition of their release, such as failing a drug test, missing an appointment with their parole officer, or being rearrested for a new crime. The percentage returned to prison solely for a technical violation, 26.4%, is approximated by taking the difference between the 51.8% and the 25.4%.

* * *

What they were in prison for

Of the 272,111 offenders, 1.7% were in prison for homicide. Following their release, 40.7% of these convicted homicide offenders were rearrested for a new crime (not necessarily a new homicide) within 3 years.

Convicted rapists made up 1.2% of the 272,111, and 46.0% of these released rapists were rearrested within 3 years for some type of felony or serious misdemeanor (not necessarily another violent sex offense).

Over a third of the released prisoners had been in prison for a property offense (for example, burglary, auto theft, fraud). Released property offenders had higher recidivism rates than those released for violent, drug, or public-order offenses. An estimated 73.8% of the property offenders released in 1994 were rearrested within 3 years, compared to 61.7% of the violent offenders, 62.2% of the public-order offenders, and 66.7% of the drug offenders. Property offenders also had higher rates of reconviction and reincarceration than other types of offenders.

Released prisoners with the highest rearrest rates were—

robbers (70.2%)

burglars (74.0%)

larcenists (74.6%)

motor vehicle thieves (78.8%)

possessors/sellers of
stolen property (77.4%)

possessors/sellers of
illegal weapons (70.2%).

What these high-rate offenders have in common is that they were all in prison for what are generally thought of as crimes for money. By contrast, many of those with the lowest rearrest rates—persons convicted of homicide (40.7%), rapists (46.0%), other sexual assaulters (41.4%), other violent offenders (51.7%), and those convicted of driving under the influence (51.5%)—were in prison for crimes not generally motivated by desire for material gain.

An exception to the pattern was drug traffickers. Their motive often is to make money, yet their rearrest rate (64.2%) was not above average.

What prisoners were rearrested for

Within the first 3 years of the release, of the 272,111 prisoners—

21.6% were rearrested for a violent offense

31.9%, for a property offense

30.3%, for a drug offense

28.3%, for a public-order offense.

These four percentages exceed 67.5% of released prisoners overall because some were rearrested for more than one type of offense. For example, a released Minnesota prisoner was rearrested for receiving stolen property (a property offense) in 1995 and for assault (a violent offense) in 1996. Similarly, a released Delaware prisoner was rearrested for cocaine trafficking (a drug offense) in 1995 and then for aggravated assault (a violent offense) in 1996.

Within the first 3 years of release, of the 272,111 prisoners—

0.8% were rearrested for homicide

0.6%, for rape

13.7%, for assault

9.9%, for burglary.

Within 3 years, 2.5% of the 3,138 released rapists were rearrested for another rape, and 1.2% of the 4,443 persons who had served time for homicide were rearrested for a homicide. Among other offenses, the percentages rearrested for the same category of offense for which they were just in prison were —

13.4% of released robbers

22.0% of released assaulters

23.4% of released burglars

33.9% of released larcenists

11.5% of released thieves of motor vehicles

19.0% of released defrauders

41.2% of released drug offenders.

Of the 3,138 released rapists —

overall 46.0% were rearrested for a new crime within 3 years

18.6% were rearrested for a new violent offense

2.5% were rearrested for another rape

8.7% were rearrested for a new non-sexual assault

11.2% were rearrested for a drug offense.

* * *

Number of prior arrests

The number of times a prisoner has been arrested in the past is a good predictor of whether that prisoner will continue to commit crimes after being released. Prisoners with just 1 prior arrest have a 40.6% rearrest rate within 3 years. With 2 priors, the percentage rearrested is 47.5%. With 3 it goes up to 55.2%. With additional priors, it continues to rise, reaching 82.1% among released prisoners with more than 15 prior arrests in their criminal history record.

The number of past arrests a prisoner has also provides a good predictor of how quickly that prisoner will resume his or her criminality after being released. A measure of how quickly prisoners resume their criminality can be constructed by combining information from 1-year and 3-year arrest rates.

To illustrate: Prisoners with 1 prior arrest have a 20.6% 1-year arrest rate and a 40.6% 3-year rearrest rate. The first-year rate (20.6%) is 51% of the cumulative rate at the end of the third year (40.6%). In other words, 51% of the recidivism of prisoners with 1 prior arrest occurs within the first year. The comparable figure for prisoners with 2 priors is 55%; 3 priors, 58%; 4 priors, 59%; 5 priors, 62%. Among those with 16 or more prior arrests, 74% of their recidivism occurs in the first year (61.0% / 82.1% = 74%). The pattern here is clear: the longer the prior record, the greater the likelihood that the recidivating prisoner will commit another crime soon after release.

Prior prison sentence

For 56% of the 272,111, the prison sentence they were serving when released in 1994 was their first-ever prison sentence (not shown in table). Of these "first-timers," 63.8% were rearrested following their release. Among those who had been in prison at least once before, a higher percentage — 73.5% — were rearrested.

Time served in prison

No evidence was found that spending more time in prison raises the recidivism rate. The evidence was mixed regarding the question of whether spending more time in prison reduces the recidivism rate.

Recidivism rates did not differ significantly among those released after serving 6 months or less (66.0%), those released after 7 to 12 months (64.8%), those released after 13 to 18 months (64.2%), those released after 19 to 24 months (65.4%), and those released after 25 to 30 months (68.3%).

Those who served the longest time—61 months or more—had a significantly lower re-arrest rate (54.2%) than every other category of prisoners defined by time in confinement.

Also, both those who served 31 to 36 months (62.6%) and those who served 37 to 60 months (63.2%) had a significantly lower rearrest rate than those who served 25 to 30 months (68.3%).

* * *

Notes and Questions

1. The Bureau of Justice Statistics is the research arm of the Department of Justice. It provides numbers and a statistical snapshot; it does not take a position on policy issues. Based on the data, what policy conclusions would you advocate?

2. Should the states studied in the Bureau of Justice Statistics Special Report abolish parole, as the federal government and a number of states have done?

3. In a more recent study, The Pew Center on States obtained recidivism data from states. Relying on data from 33 states from 1999 and 41 states from 2004, the Pew study found a fairly constant recidivism rate of roughly 43 to 45%. The data indicated that within three years of release, more than 43% of individuals were reincarcerated. *See* THE PEW CENTER ON THE STATES, STATE OF RECIDIVISM: THE REVOLVING DOOR OF AMER-ICA'S PRISONS 12–13 (2011). Recidivism rates vary between states for a variety of reasons. For instance, if states have shorter periods of post-prison supervision, they may have lower rates of individuals being revoked and sent back to prison. Another factor is the ability of supervising agencies to detect violations. Still another consideration is whether there is a culture of revoking offenders and returning them to prison for minor infractions. *See id.* at 18–19.

4. At the end of Season 1 of *The Wire*, Avon Barksdale was sentenced to seven years imprisonment. In Season 2 of *The Wire*, we see that he is paroled after serving only 26 months of his seven-year sentence. *See The Wire*, Season 2, Episode 5, at 30:25 minutes. Barksdale thus served only 31% of his sentence. When you watched the series, were you surprised by the low initial sentence and that Barksdale had to serve only about one-third of the sentence? The Bureau of Justice Statistics Report indicates that *The Wire* is realistic in this regard. The Special Report found that the average prison sentence of the parolees studied was 5 years and that the prisoners served an average of 35% of their sentences.

5. In Season 3 of *The Wire*, we see a difference of opinion between Stringer Bell (who had been leading the Barksdale gang while Avon was in prison) and Avon about how to handle conflict. Stringer wanted to run the operation as a Co-Op without fighting other gangs over territory. Avon didn't accept this approach, explaining "I ain't no suit man

businessman like you. You know, I'm just a gangsta, I suppose. And I want my corners." *The Wire*, Season 3, Episode 6, at 16:25 minutes. Avon prevailed and multiple murders ensued as a result. Consider what might have happened if Avon had not received parole after 26 months. Would there have been less violence?

6. Season 3 of *The Wire* introduces new characters, including Snoop, a key figure in Marlo Stansfield's gang. The woman who portrayed Snoop—Felicia "Snoop" Pearson— was no ordinary actress. Pearson was a foster child who ended up dealing drugs as a teenager. At 14, she killed another girl in a street fight. Only a few years after being re-leased, Pearson was discovered in a bar by Michael K. Williams, the actor who played Omar. Unfortunately, after the series ended, Pearson returned to criminal activity. In 2011, she was arrested in a major heroin and marijuana drug bust. *See* Justin Fenton, *More Than 60 People, Including "Snoop" of "The Wire," Arrested in Drug Raids*, Balt. Sun, Mar. 10, 2011. What is your reaction to this real-life tragedy? Does Pearson's real-life sit-uation better capture the parole and release issue than even *The Wire*'s brilliant story-telling about Avon Barksdale and his rivals? Does Snoop's recidivism make you think twice about an indeterminate sentencing regime?

7. Is a regime that requires tough mandatory minimum sentences and strict guideline calculations preferable to the discretionary parole system portrayed in *The Wire* and doc-umented by the Bureau of Justice Statistics?

8. *Revocation of Parole:* Watch *The Wire*, Season 3, Episode 12, at 36:00 minutes. After pursuing Avon Barksdale for most of the third season, the officers get a tip that Barksdale will be in a safe house with a large stash of automatic weapons and hand grenades. Being caught in the same room as the weapons is a big problem for Barksdale because some of these weapons, such as the hand grenades, are illegal for anyone to possess. Even the other lawful weapons are a problem because it is illegal for a convicted felon such as Barksdale to be in possession of any firearm. *See, e.g.*, Md. Public Safety § 5-133 (carrying a mini-mum sentence of five years for being a felon in possession of a firearm). When the po-lice raid the safe house, Detective McNulty arrests Barksdale and says: "You fall on the parole violation, no matter whatever else happens, you do every day of what's left of your seven, without seeing a jury." To translate, McNulty is saying that because it is a parole violation to be in possession of a firearm, Barksdale can be reincarcerated for that parole violation without a full jury trial. Prosecutors do not even have to file new criminal charges against Barksdale for being a felon in possession of a firearm; they can simply seek to have his pa-role revoked, a process that requires far less than proof beyond a reasonable doubt. If Barksdale's parole is revoked, he will likely have to serve the remainder of the original seven-year sentence that Judge Phalen imposed at the end of Season 1. For an overview of the Maryland rules governing parole and parole revocation, see Patuxent Inst. Bd. Of Review v. Hancock, 620 A.2d 917 (Md. 1993).

D. The Problems with Guidelines Sentencing and Mandatory Minimums

After reading the previous section, the problems with indeterminate sentencing should be clear. Because of a fear of crime, indeterminate sentencing and early release became very unpopular beginning in the 1970s. As a result, when Congress passed the Federal Sentencing Guidelines in 1984, it abolished parole in the federal system and enacted stringent guidelines that required a defendant to serve nearly the entire sentence imposed by the judge. Over the following years, Congress also imposed mandatory minimum sentences that further constrained judges' discretion to award lighter sentences. To many observers, this truth-in-sentencing and more stringent minimum punishments was a big improvement. Dangerous criminals would be sentenced to longer sentences and they would have to serve the time they received. However, just as there are problems with indeterminate sentencing, there are difficulties with one-size-fits-all mandatory minimums and rigid sentencing guidelines.

United States v. Hungerford
465 F.3d 1113 (9th Cir. 2006)

GRABER, Circuit Judge:

After a jury trial, Defendant Marion Hungerford was convicted of conspiracy, seven counts of robbery, and seven counts of using a firearm in relation to a crime of violence in violation of the Hobbs Act, 18 U.S.C. §§ 1951 and 1952, and 18 U.S.C. § 924(c)(1) and (c)(2). She appeals her conviction of four of the counts of robbery and the four related counts of using a firearm. She also appeals her sentence; she received 57 months of imprisonment for the conspiracy and robbery counts, to run concurrently, plus 60 months for the first firearm charge and 300 months for each of the other firearm charges, to run consecutively. We affirm.

FACTUAL AND PROCEDURAL HISTORY

Defendant met Dana Canfield in September 2001. In 2002, Canfield moved into her home. Neither was employed at the time. In order to get money to pay rent, Canfield and Defendant decided to rob a convenience store. At trial, Canfield testified, "Marion said that she was going to have to go on a crime spree. And since she has problems walking and stuff, I decided that I would do it." The pair drove around together looking at potential places to rob. They decided on a convenience store called 3-G's. In March 2002, Defendant dropped him off at the 3-G's and drove to a nearby laundromat. Canfield robbed the store at gunpoint, rendezvoused with Defendant at the laundromat, and gave her the money. The jury found Defendant not guilty of the 3-G's robbery.

The 3-G's robbery was the first in a series of Montana armed robberies carried out by Canfield at Defendant's instigation, the proceeds of which she received and spent. Next, Canfield testified to robbing a store called Bottles & Shots on April 6, 2002. He drove himself to the location while Defendant again waited for him at a laundromat. Again, he used a gun and delivered the proceeds of the robbery to Defendant. The jury found Defendant not guilty of the Bottles & Shots robbery.

Canfield testified that, after he told Defendant about the adrenaline rush that accompanied the robberies, "she wanted to be more involved in the crimes, so she wanted to be— she wanted to help participate." On May 6, 2002, Canfield robbed the Jackpot Casino, using a firearm. Defendant went into the casino ahead of Canfield and called to tell him how many people were inside and how many tills were operating. The jury found Defendant guilty of the Jackpot Casino robbery, a conviction that she does not challenge on appeal.

Canfield described similar involvement by Defendant in both the Alpine Casino and Cenex AmPride robberies. The two drove together to the Alpine Casino; Defendant entered, counted the number of employees who were working there, and returned to the car to report the information to Canfield. He then went inside, robbed the casino at gunpoint, returned to the car where Defendant was waiting, and gave her the money. Similarly, at the Cenex AmPride convenience store, Defendant went into the store first and signaled to Canfield that it was safe to proceed with the robbery. The jury convicted Defendant of both of those robberies, and she does not challenge those convictions here.

After the Cenex AmPride robbery, Detective Ewalt telephoned Defendant to ask questions about the Jackpot Casino robbery. Defendant and Canfield discussed the false statement that Defendant planned to give to the detective to impede his investigation. Further, they agreed that Defendant should establish an alibi during the next robbery. At the Jackpot Casino and Cenex AmPride robberies, she had been seen by employees when she entered the establishments just before the robber came in. Consequently, Defendant planned to remain at the home of the couple's landlord while Canfield committed the next robbery.

According to Canfield, Defendant did not help him "case out" the next location; she left "most … everything" up to him about where to go and what to do. Canfield robbed Magoo's at gunpoint on June 13, 2002. When he returned home afterward, Defendant was there and he gave her the money that he had stolen.

Canfield committed an armed robbery at the Second Shift Bar on June 25, 2002. Defendant did not help him case that establishment beforehand, nor did he tell her what business he planned to rob. Afterward, though, he gave all the proceeds to Defendant.

Canfield robbed the Winners Circle on July 2, 2002, using a firearm. Again, Defendant did not scout the location, and she stayed home during the robbery. She knew that Canfield was going to commit another robbery but did not know specifically where. Canfield gave the proceeds of this robbery, too, to Defendant.

Although her direct participation in these later robberies was minimal, Defendant did not ask Canfield to stop committing armed robberies. She accepted the proceeds, knowing their source, and the proceeds from these periodic crimes provided the only means the couple had to meet their financial needs.

After they had a chance meeting with Detective Ewalt, Defendant and Canfield decided that they ought to end the string of armed robberies. They mapped out a strategy to "leave a trail out of town" and then stop. The plan was to rob an establishment in Butte, Montana, then go to Missoula and rob another place there "using the same mask and MO" as had been used in the earlier robberies. They traveled to Butte, rented a hotel room, and together they scouted possible targets. They selected an establishment called Gramma's. When Canfield went there on July 27, 2002, he decided against robbing it and instead chose to rob Joker's Wild. Defendant remained in the hotel during this armed robbery. Afterward, Canfield gave Defendant the proceeds, and both of them together destroyed the checks, which they had obtained along with the cash. The police arrested Canfield that night at the hotel; Defendant was arrested later. Before being arrested, Defendant contacted an acquaintance and coaxed her to make a false statement to the Butte police concerning the identity of the Joker's Wild robber, to throw them off track.

* * *

DISCUSSION

* * *

B. *Title 18 U.S.C. § 924(c)(1) is not unconstitutionally vague.*

The jury convicted Defendant of seven counts of knowingly using or carrying a firearm in furtherance of a crime of violence, in violation of 18 U.S.C. § 924(c)(1) and (c)(2). The statute states, in pertinent part:

[A]ny person who, during and in relation to any crime of violence ... for which the person may be prosecuted in a court of the United States, uses or carries a firearm, or who, in furtherance of any such crime, possesses a firearm, shall, in addition to the punishment provided for such crime of violence ...—

(i) be sentenced to a term of imprisonment of not less than 5 years[.]

In the case of a second or subsequent conviction under this subsection, the person shall—

(i) be sentenced to a term of imprisonment of not less than 25 years[.]

Notwithstanding any other provision of law—

...

(ii) no term of imprisonment imposed on a person under this subsection shall run concurrently with any other term of imprisonment imposed on the person, including any term of imprisonment imposed for the crime of violence or drug trafficking crime during which the firearm was used, carried, or possessed.

Pursuant to the statute, the district court sentenced Defendant to five years for her first firearm conviction and 25 years for each of the other six firearm convictions, to run consecutively.

* * *

C. *The sentence violates neither the Fifth nor the Eighth Amendment.*

... Defendant brings two constitutional claims. She argues that the mandatory minimum sentence established by § 924 violates the Fifth Amendment's guarantee of due process by removing discretion from the judiciary and placing it in the hands of the prosecutor. We already have rejected the argument that mandatory minimum sentences established by statute violate due process. *United States v. Wilkins,* 911 F.2d 337, 339 (9th Cir.1990)....

Finally, Defendant argues that the Eighth Amendment precludes the lengthy consecutive mandatory minimum sentences imposed here under § 924. This argument also is directly precluded by our precedent. *United States v. Parker.* 241 F.3d 1114, 1117 (9th Cir.2001).

AFFIRMED.

REINHARDT, Circuit Judge, concurring in the judgment.

Although precedent forecloses Marion Hungerford's Eighth Amendment challenge to 18 U.S.C. § 924(c) (2006), under which she received almost all of her 159-year term of imprisonment, it cannot be left unsaid how irrational, inhumane, and absurd the sentence in this case is, and moreover, how this particular sentence is a predictable by-product of the cruel and unjust mandatory minimum sentencing scheme adopted by Congress. This court, along with many individuals, has previously urged Congress to "reconsider its harsh scheme of mandatory minimum sentences without the possibility of parole" [United States v. Harris, 154 F.3d 1082, 1084 (9th Cir. 1998)]; now, Hungerford's case serves as yet another forceful reminder that the scheme is severely broken and badly in need of repair. Although we lack the authority either to reform these statutes or to reconsider the Eighth Amendment principles adopted by the Supreme Court, those who have both the power and the responsibility to do so should return our federal sentencing scheme to a day in which the controlling principles are fairness, proportionality, prudence and informed discretion.

When we urged Congress to reform § 924 and other unnecessarily harsh mandatory sentencing laws, [Harris, 154 F.3d at 1084] each additional conviction for use of a firearm in connection with a crime of violence under §924(c) provided for a 20-year mandatory consecutive sentence. Months later, Congress amended §924(c)(1) to mandate 25-year mandatory consecutive sentences for such offenses. As a result, §924(c) now requires a 5-year sentence for a single conviction of use of a firearm and mandatory consecutive sentences of 25 years for each additional count. 18 U.S.C. §924(c)(1).

Although she never touched a gun, Hungerford, was convicted of one count of conspiracy, seven counts of robbery, and seven counts of use of a firearm in relation to a crime of violence. The district judge sentenced her to 5 years on the first count of use of a firearm and 25 years consecutively on each of six additional counts. In addition, the district judge sentenced her to serve 57 months for the conspiracy and 57 months for the robbery convictions, the sentences to run concurrently with each other. Because §924(c) gives the sentencing judge no choice or discretion, except to impose the statutory mandatory sentences, the judge was forced to sentence Hungerford, a 52 year-old mentally disturbed woman with no prior criminal record, to over 159 years in prison. What the judge was *not* permitted to take into account when sentencing Hungerford should shock the conscience of anyone who believes that reasonable proportionality between a crime and the sentence is a necessary condition of fair sentencing.

The judge could not consider myriad potential mitigating factors, including Hungerford's severe form of Borderline Personality Disorder, which can alter one's perception of reality in a manner similar to schizophrenia and has led to numerous suicide attempts on Hungerford's part. The judge could not consider a psychiatrist's testimony regarding Hungerford's very low capacity to assess reality, her low level of intellectual functioning, and the fact that she is "very easily victimized." Especially important, the court was prohibited from taking into account the fact that Hungerford was "a follower," was "susceptib[le] to outside direction" and suffered from "suggestivity." Also out of bounds was Hungerford's vulnerable and chaotic state. Shortly before the robberies her husband of 26 years, with whom she had four children, had moved out of their home, largely as a result of her deteriorating mental condition, and, Hungerford, finding herself impecunious and without a job or any prospects for employment, had begun living with a new male companion, on whom she became dependent, Dana Canfield, the principal in the robberies. Nor could the judge consider that Hungerford, at the age of 52, was a person with no criminal history prior to the string of armed robberies committed by Canfield, and that she had apparently led a spotless, law-abiding existence. The judge could not even take into account the significant facts that no one was physically injured in any of the robberies and that the total loss resulting from them was less than $10,000.

Most important, under the law, Hungerford's extremely limited role in the crimes of which she was convicted was also irrelevant to her sentencing. Although she conspired with and aided and abetted her new-found male companion, Canfield, in a string of armed robberies, her participation in the robberies themselves was quite limited, particularly when compared to Canfield's dominant role. During most of the robberies, Hungerford took no active part other than driving Canfield to or from the scene of the crime or casing the stores that Canfield later robbed. After a police detective contacted Hungerford, she did not participate whatsoever in any of the subsequent robberies and merely received money from Canfield following his commission of those robberies. It is worth noting that Hungerford's mental disorder likely impeded her ability to affirmatively opt out of the conspiracy after contact with the police, and even to accept the fact that she had been engaged in criminal conduct. Finally, at no time did Hungerford personally use or even carry a gun, or personally threaten anyone; yet, under §924(c), this fact, too, is deemed irrelevant. At the time of sentencing, Hungerford's counsel presented substantial evidence of her severe mental illness. Attached to this opinion is a summary of that troubling testimony.

Under a fair and proportional sentencing scheme, a judge would not just be *allowed* to consider these compelling mitigating circumstances, but rather he would be *required* to give them substantial weight in determining the proper sentence.... Here, it is difficult to escape the conclusion that the current mandatory sentencing laws have imposed an immensely cruel, if not barbaric, 159-year sentence on a severely mentally disturbed person who played a limited and fairly passive role in several robberies during which no one was physically harmed.[4]

Not only is the sentence cruel, it is absurd. It imposes a term of imprisonment of 159 years, under which Hungerford would be incarcerated until she reached the age of 208. The absurdity is best illustrated by the judge's reading to Hungerford the terms of supervised release which she would be required to undergo when she emerged from prison toward the end of the first decade of her third century. The judge told Hungerford that "[w]ithin 72 hours of release from custody," — in the year 2162 — she must "report in person to the probation office," and while on supervised release she must "participate in substance abuse testing to include not more than 104 urinalysis tests." He further ordered Hungerford to "participate in a program for mental health," and "pay part or all of the cost of this treatment, as determined by the U.S. probation officer." What Hungerford should do if she were too old or feeble to attend the mental health program, the judge failed to advise her. Certainly, requiring a defendant and a district judge to engage in a charade of this nature cannot increase respect for our system of justice.

* * *

Hungerford received her 159-year sentence because she refused to enter into a plea agreement with the government. Had she been able and willing to do so, she undoubtedly would have received a significantly lesser term than the principal's 32-year sentence. Hungerford tragically refused to cooperate with the government and plead guilty, most likely because her mental illness caused her to hold a fixed belief that she was innocent. Even after the jury convicted her, Hungerford repeatedly declared her innocence at sentencing, stating that "I have not done anything illegal. I did not go about with any gun. I don't like them.... I didn't take any money.... I honestly didn't do it ... So please don't do whatever you're going to do to me for what you think I did, because I didn't do it." Also in light of her mental illness, Hungerford may not have even understood the nature of the offenses for which she was convicted. Yet, incredibly, the prosecutor believed that Hungerford received a fair sentence, reflecting both her criminal acts and her refusal to cooperate with the government. He told the judge that

> counsel and the defendant can blame the prosecution, blame the Court, can blame the Congress. The jury convicted her. Early on in this process, the United

---

4. We are foreclosed from holding the sentence to be in violation of the cruel and unusual punishment clause because of its severity by *Harmelin* [*v. Michigan*, 501 U.S. 957 (1991)] and *Ewing v. California*, 538 U.S. 11 (2003). *Harmelin*, 501 U.S. at 995, (rejecting a requirement that the court consider mitigation or individual circumstances, and holding that a defendant's "sentence of life imprisonment without parole" for his first felony, possession of cocaine, "does not violate the Eighth Amendment"); *Ewing*, 538 U.S. at 30–31 (holding that a defendant's "sentence of 25 years to life in prison" for a third strike consisting of the theft of three golf clubs "is not grossly disproportionate and therefore does not violate the Eighth Amendment's prohibition on cruel and unusual punishments").

States went to her attorney. We have some credit on our side. We understood what the facts are. We suggested that cooperation would be there and that she cooperate against Mr. Canfield. She chose not to do that, Your Honor. Mr. Canfield chose another route. There is no one to blame here but Marion Hungerford herself....

But if Hungerford was in any way responsible for her absurd sentence, it was that her Borderline Personality Disorder prevented her from admitting her guilt and thus avoiding the imposition of a sentence of 159 years in prison. Surely, one cannot reasonably fault Hungerford for suffering from overwhelming and severe mental illness. Hungerford, in layman's terms, may have explained her predicament as well as anyone possibly could when she proclaimed her innocence at sentencing and explained that:

> my crime is not robbing, my crime isn't hurting anybody, because I don't do that, and my crime is not using a weapon to get money. *My crime is being stupid.* That's my crime. And it looks like I'm going to be faced with a lot of years for being stupid.

It is difficult to believe that anyone familiar with all of the facts and circumstances relating to Marion Hungerford's commission of the offenses of which she was convicted would believe that an appropriate sentence is 159 years in prison.... The only question, then, is whether this and future Congresses will choose to listen and take appropriate action to return reason and rationality to our currently malfunctioning sentencing system.

Because I am required to do so, I concur in the judgment, but nothing more.

This attachment summarizes the testimony of Dr. William David Stratford, a forensic psychiatrist, who evaluated Hungerford. He testified that

1. Having previously completed between 6,000 and 10,000 prior psychiatric evaluations, interviewing Hungerford was "one of the most arduous, painful experiences in my life." During the evaluation Hungerford was "very fragmented," had "fixed patterns," and she "[w]ould at times look at the floor and be unresponsive for periods of ten minutes or so."

2. Hungerford suffers from "severe borderline personality disorder," described as "a line between psychosis and other diagnoses. It is a varying diagnosis. It is pervasive in stability of mood, actions. A person can be delusional. They can have fixed ideas that are incorrect. They can often be suicidal, moody, and have difficulty integrating the big picture."

3. The psychological impairment which affected Hungerford is "one of the most severe psychological disorders. It's probably more severe than suffering from schizophrenia."

4. Hungerford's "mental state significantly diminishe[d] her capacity to appreciate criminality and conformed conduct."

5. Hungerford's belief that she was not guilty is "a product of her mental illness."

6. At sentencing, Hungerford did not have "a rational and factual understanding of what she's doing here" in the courtroom.

7. Hungerford is a "follower" whose behavior is marked by "susceptibility to outside direction," and suggestivity.

8. Hungerford does not presently constitute a danger to society, based on her 52 years in which she was not been hostile to others, and could benefit from treatment.

———————

Notes and Questions

1. Judge Reinhardt, who wrote separately in *Hungerford*, is considered to be one of the most liberal judges on the federal bench. Criticism of mandatory sentencing rules is not limited to liberal judges however. In 2004, Judge Paul Cassell—a very conservative and well-regarded former professor who has since returned to academia—imposed a fifty-five year sentence on a first-time drug offender because 18 U.S.C. § 924(a)—the same statute at issue in *Hungerford*—required that punishment. Judge Cassell wrote a lengthy opinion complaining that the sentence was "far in excess of the sentence imposed for such serious crimes as aircraft hijacking, second degree murder, espionage, kidnapping, aggravated assault, and rape" and that it even exceeded "what recidivist criminals will likely serve under the federal 'three strikes.'" United States v. Angelos, 345 F. Supp.2d 1227, 1230 (D. Utah 2004). As one author has explained, "Judge Cassell appears to have agonized over the decision, aching to strike down the fifty-five year sentence on Equal Protection and Eighth Amendment grounds ... [but he] believed that he was legally obligated to impose the sentence...." J.C. Oleson, *The Antigone Dilemma: When the Paths of Law and Morality Diverge*, 29 CARDOZO L. REV. 669, 682 (2007). Judge Cassell was so disturbed by the case that he wrote to the Office of the Pardon Attorney encouraging commutation and testified before Congress about the case. Neither the pardon attorney, the president, nor Congress has taken any action. *See id.* at 682–83. The Supreme Court denied certiorari. *See* United States v. Angelos, 549 U.S. 1077 (2006). Angelos will thus remain incarcerated until 2051.

2. Judge Reinhardt castigates the prosecutors for pursuing an enormous sentence against Hungerford while allowing the more culpable Dana Canfield to receive a sentence of 32 years in exchange for a guilty plea. Do the federal sentencing guidelines and other determinate sentencing regimes give prosecutors too much power? Do you understand the argument for why prosecutors actually hold much more sentencing power than judges in determinate sentencing systems?

3. At the end of his opinion, Judge Reinhardt attached the testimony of a psychiatrist who had examined Hungerford. The testimony paints a picture of a woman incapable of forming the mens rea for criminal misconduct. Why did the defense not argue the insanity defense?

4. Judge Reinhardt offers a long list of factors—for instance, Hungerford's limited involvement in the crimes, her lack of criminal history, and her mental illness—that the sentencing judge was not permitted to consider. Yet, the Federal Sentencing Guidelines takes into account most of the factors Judge Reinhardt mentioned. What did he mean when he said those factors could not be considered?

5. Assuming that Judge Reinhardt had his way and Congress abolished the mandatory minimum requirement, Hungerford's sentence still would have been determined by the federal sentencing guidelines. Is it possible for a list of rigid factors and a sentencing table to accurately capture the culpability of someone like Hungerford? Put differently, does a case like Hungerford's show that the federal sentencing guidelines cannot achieve a just outcome?

6. What do you think would be an appropriate sentence for Hungerford? On the one hand, she did assist in a string of robberies in which it was very possible a person could have been shot or even killed. On the other hand, her assistance was limited and, if you believe the psychiatric testimony, she suffered from mental illness. Many indeterminate sentencing states have wide sentencing ranges. For instance, in Texas, first-degree felonies are punishable by a range of five to ninety-nine years. *See* Tex. Pen. Code § 12.32. If you

had such a broad array of choices, what sentence would you impose on Hungerford? Would it bother you to learn that your classmates might impose a drastically different sentence?

United States v. Patillo

817 F. Supp. 839 (C.D. Cal. 1993)

LETTS, District Judge.

On April 14, 1992, the defendant Johnny Patillo pled guilty to a single count indictment that charged him with possession with intent to distribute approximately 680.7 grams of crack cocaine. On December 18, 1992, the court sentenced defendant, after orally making findings that it was compelled to impose a mandatory minimum sentence of ten years under 21 U.S.C. § 841(b)(1)(A). The Sentencing Guidelines called for a sentence of between 151 and 188 months (twelve years seven months to fifteen years), a range from which the court found departure appropriate. The court indicated that written findings would follow, which are set forth below.

I. MINIMUM SENTENCE

At least at the outset, this sentencing appeared to place me in the position of making the most difficult choice I have yet faced, between my judicial oath of office, which requires me to uphold the law as I understand it, and my conscience, which requires me to avoid intentional injustice. When I took defendant's plea of guilty in this case, he seemed to me to be the clearest possible example of everything that is wrong with guideline sentencing and statutorily imposed mandatory minimum sentences.

On January 16, 1992, defendant, a twenty-seven year old African-American man, brought a package containing approximately 681 grams of crack cocaine to a Federal Express office in Los Angeles and attempted to send the package to Dallas, Texas. According to defendant, he had never previously been involved in trafficking drugs, but had accepted a neighbor's offer of $500 to put the package in the mail. At the time, he was subject to extraordinary financial pressures, due to an accumulation of debt for student loans, credit cards, phone bills and rent. Defendant admits knowing that the package contained illegal drugs, but has steadfastly denied prior knowledge of the type of drug, or the amount of the drug the package contained. As far as the court can determine, defendant had never before been involved in any criminal activity. He had obtained a college education and held a steady job up until the time he was incarcerated.

The government's position is that the court cannot legally impose a sentence of less than ten years in this case, and it is correct. The ten year minimum is specifically mandated by a statute, 21 U.S.C. § 841(b)(1)(A), which has been upheld as constitutional by the Ninth Circuit Court of Appeals in decisions that bind this court. The court postponed sentencing several times in the hope of finding some reasoned basis for holding that precedent does not bind the court. This, however, has proved impossible. Defendant has argued that the mandatory minimum is unconstitutionally vague, that it is racially discriminatory, and that it violates due process and the Eighth Amendment. Ninth Circuit precedent rejects these arguments, and instead compels this court to apply the mandatory minimum.

I, however, will no longer apply this law without protest, and with no hope for change.

Statutory mandatory minimum sentences create injustice because the sentence is determined without looking at the particular defendant. Under 21 U.S.C. § 841(b)(1)(A), the mandatory minimum sentence is triggered by two factors only: (1) the type of drug and (2) the amount of drug. In this case, it is the fact that the package defendant brought to Federal Express contained 681 grams of crack cocaine which raises this offense to one in which the *minimum* sentence is ten years, *without possibility of parole.* If the package contained a different narcotic, or a lesser quantity of the same substance, defendant might have been sentenced to straight probation.

By agreement with the government, defendant's plea of guilty in this case rested upon his admission that he delivered a package to Federal Express which contained approximately 681 grams of cocaine base, and that at the time he made the delivery, he knew that the package contained an illegal substance. That is all his plea of guilty entailed. Defendant did not admit to knowing that the substance in the envelope was cocaine base, or to knowing that the package contained 681 grams of crack. In fact, he expressly denied any such knowledge.

Admittedly, the pre-sentence report ("PSR") filed by the Probation Office contains information which might cause one to speculate that defendant may have had a somewhat greater involvement in the business of drug trafficking than he has admitted. Any such information, however, is purely circumstantial. This court cannot form a reasoned conclusion based upon this information, and the government has made no effort to develop it. It has not been developed further because defendant's role in the business of drug trafficking is almost entirely irrelevant for sentencing purposes. The court considered information regarding the defendant's role in drug trafficking, but as explained below, only as a basis for departure.

The minimum ten year sentence to be served by defendant was determined by Congress before he ever committed a criminal act. Congress decided to hit the problem of drugs, as they saw it, with a sledgehammer, making no allowance for the circumstances of any particular case. Under this sledgehammer approach, it can make no difference whether defendant actually owned the drugs with which he was caught, or whether, at a time when he had an immediate need for cash, he was slickered into taking the risk of being caught with someone else's drugs. Under the statutory minimum, it can make no difference whether he is a lifetime criminal or a first time offender. Indeed, under this sledgehammer approach, it could make no difference if the day before making this one slip in an otherwise unblemished life, defendant had rescued fifteen children from a burning building, or had won the Congressional Medal Of Honor while defending his country.

I do not advocate giving up the attempt to rid our society from the evils of drug use. Drug crimes are not "victimless crimes," and it would be naive to suggest otherwise. Drug users use more than their share of many social benefits, and therefore victimize everyone who must pay for them. The need for money with which to buy drugs is the most frequent reason for committing crimes given by defendants convicted in this court. These crimes have victims. Drug users also have children, who suffer the effects of their parents' drug use.

I have no great difficulty imposing lengthy prison sentences upon proven high-volume drug merchants, and others proven to be high in the chain of drug distribution.[3] In some cases I would have imposed the same sentence in the exercise of pure discretion, not governed by any guideline. If, for example, defendant had admitted that he knew what was in the package he delivered to Federal Express, or if the government had been required

---

3. Unfortunately, in this court's experience, those high in the chain of drug distribution are seldom caught, and seldom prosecuted.

to prove it, this court could sentence him as the government recommends, with a clear conscience, although still not without misgivings.

Since the days when amputation of the offending hand was routinely used as the punishment for stealing a loaf of bread, however, one of the basic precepts of criminal justice has been that the punishment fit the crime. This is the principle which, as a matter of law, I must violate in this case.

Defendant could have been prosecuted for this offense by the state, rather than the federal government. A review of the relevant California state criminal statute suggests that had that occurred most likely he would have been incarcerated for a period of between one and two years. *See* Cal.Health & Safety Code § 11351.5 (West 1993) (possession of cocaine base for sale punishable by a term of imprisonment of three, four or five years, with eligibility for parole after half-time served).[5] Surely there are those who would say that this would be too short a period for the owner of drugs for distribution. I cannot imagine, however, those who would argue that such a sentence would be inadequate for a first time offender who merely delivered a package to a Federal Express office, knowing that it contained illegal drugs, but not knowing what drugs or the quantity.

I, for one, do not understand how it came to be that the courts of this nation, which stood for centuries as the defenders of the rights of minorities against abuse at the hands of the majority, have so far abdicated their function that this defendant must serve a ten year sentence.

No doubt there are civilized nations in which the penalty for crimes against the state, such as assassination and treason, are set in advance without reference to who does them and in what circumstances. There may even be some civilized nations in which the penalties for historic biblical offenses such as first-degree murder are set in advance. It is hard to imagine, however, that there is any other country in western civilization in which a crime such as this one—simply picking up an unknown quantity of an unknown illegal substance—is treated as the legal equivalent of the conscious commission of a capital offense. It is hard to imagine that there is any other nation in which a convicted rapist with a long and unsavory history of prior misconduct can be sentenced by the judge who presides over his trial to a sentence which will make him eligible for parole in a less than three years,[7] while defendant, a first time offender with a spotless prior record, stands to be sentenced by a Congress who has never seen him and never judged him to a minimum sentence of ten years, without the possibility of parole.

In my view a criminal justice system that does not require not only those who accuse a criminal, but also those who sentence him, to confront him and publicly acknowledge their acts as their own, to his face, is worse than uncivilized. It is barbaric.

II. DEPARTURE FROM THE SENTENCING GUIDELINES

Having reluctantly determined that the mandatory minimum applies, the court departs down to the mandatory minimum sentence of ten years. The Guidelines dictate an offense level of 36 for the 681 grams of cocaine base possessed by defendant. Sentencing Guidelines (U.S.S.G.) § 2D1.1(a)(3). The pre-sentence report ("PSR") subtracted two

---

5. Notably, in "unusual circumstances," a defendant such as Patillo, convicted on state charges of possession of 681 grams of cocaine base for sale could be sentenced to a term of probation, rather than imprisonment, "where the interests of justice would be best served." Cal.Penal Code § 1203.073(b)(5) (West 1993).

7. *See* Cal.Penal Code § 264 (West 1993) (rape is punishable by imprisonment for three, six or eight years).

points for acceptance of responsibility, resulting in an offense level of 34. Defendant has no criminal history, and therefore has a criminal history category of I; as noted above, the guideline range for sentencing is between 151 and 188 months incarceration and five years of supervised release.

The PSR did not identify any grounds for departure, although the Probation Officer recommended a sentence of 151 months, at the low end of the guideline range. The government requested that the court sentence defendant in accordance with the recommendation of the Probation Officer to a term of 151 months incarceration. Defendant maintained that a downward departure would serve justice.

Title 18 U.S.C. § 3553(b) allows a court to depart from the applicable guideline range where the court finds that "there exists an aggravating or mitigating circumstance of a kind, or to a degree, not adequately taken into consideration by the Sentencing Commission in formulating the guidelines." The court finds that defendant's crime presents several circumstances not adequately considered by the Commission.

A. *Defendant is a minor player in the drug trade*

First, defendant's minor role in the overall drug trade is a mitigating factor which warrants downward departure to the mandatory minimum. In *United States v. Valdez-Gonzalez*, 957 F.2d 643, 650 (9th Cir.1992), the Ninth Circuit affirmed the sentencing court's downward departure to account for the marginal roles defendants played in the drug trade. In that case, the defendants were Mexican nationals hired as day laborers to transport drugs across the border for one or two thousand dollars. The district court examined the socioeconomics and the internal politics of the drug trade along the Mexican border, and determined that the defendants were relatively blameless drug "mules," whose sentences should be mitigated to reflect their minimal roles.

The *Valdez-Gonzalez* court noted that to a limited extent, the Guidelines provide for downward adjustments in sentencing based on a defendant's role in an offense; defendants who are minimal participants in criminal activity may have up to four points subtracted from their offense level. *See* U.S.S.G. § 3B1.2. The Ninth Circuit recognized however that this downward adjustment only took into account the defendant's role in the charged activity. Where a defendant is the sole participant in the crime with which he is charged, the adjustment does not apply. 957 F.2d at 648. Since the Commission did not adequately take into consideration the need to make distinctions in all sentencings between the relative culpabilities of defendants who are mere drug "mules" and those who run drug operations, the Ninth Circuit concluded that a downward departure was appropriate to account for "defendant's role in conduct extending beyond the offense of conviction." *Id.* at 649.

The rationale of *Valdez-Gonzalez* compels this court to depart downward in this case to take into consideration the fact that defendant is a minor player in the drug trade which the federal laws aim to curb. Certainly defendant is not completely blameless. Arguably he is less sympathetic than the Mexican "mules" in *Valdez-Gonzalez* in that he had a steady job, is educated, and thus possibly was not subject to the same degree of socioeconomic pressures as Mexican couriers living in abject poverty on the border. On the other hand, defendant lived in a community where the opportunities to become involved in drug trafficking are rampant, and he was subject to tremendous financial responsibilities and other pressures that cannot be judged against those faced by a typical border "mule."

The Commission ignored the need for greater variations in sentencing to account for the vastly different culpabilities of the various players in the drug trade. Under the Guidelines, an owner of three tons (2500 kilograms) of cocaine would receive a sentence of thirty years in jail. Defendant, a first time offender, only minimally involved in the drug scheme, can receive up to fifteen years in jail under guideline sentencing. This court finds that the Commission could not have intentionally meant to create a mere two to one difference in the treatment of drug kingpins, who reap millions off the drug trade and destroy millions of people's lives, versus the treatment of low-level dealers, who themselves to a large extent have been victimized by the drug trade propagated by the kingpins. In the interest of justice, the court must depart to account for defendant's lower culpability in the drug trade.

B. *Defendant's Crime was Aberrant Behavior*

Second, this court finds that the aberrant nature of defendant's criminal act is another ground which justifies departure. In *United States v. Fairless,* 975 F.2d 664 (9th Cir.1992), the Ninth Circuit upheld a district court's departure based on defendant's aberrant act of armed robbery. Defendant committed his crime after a series of unfortunate circumstances in his life. He had lost his job, was under financial pressures, and was manic depressive; those who knew defendant described his crime as a "complete shock."

Like the crime committed by defendant in *Fairless,* defendant's crime is an act of aberrant behavior. Defendant is surrounded by family and friends, who say that this is the first time defendant has been in any kind of trouble. The Probation Officer has described defendant's crime as "out of character." Defendant held a well paid job, had a stable employment history, and only in a particular moment of financial weakness, committed this crime. Defendant had both unusual temptation and unusual opportunity to commit this crime—a crime for which he has demonstrated tremendous remorse. This court has confidence that if this defendant were not incarcerated, he would have learned enough from this criminal process not to make the same mistake again, and thus departs downward to the mandatory minimum.

C. *Departure is Necessary to Avoid Manifest Injustice*

Finally the unique circumstances of this case qualify as a combination of factors warranting departure to the level of the mandatory minimum. A "unique combination of factors may constitute a 'circumstance'" that justifies downward departure. *United States v. Floyd,* 945 F.2d 1096, 1099 (9th Cir.1991), (quoting *United States v. Cook,* 938 F.2d 149, 153 (9th Cir.1991)). The two factors already identified by this court as warranting departure together are part of a complex of mitigating factors which make departure necessary to avoid manifest injustice.

An additional factor separately influences the court's decision to depart. Defendant assisted his Probation Officer during the Los Angeles riots, in a way which speaks to his tremendous character, and which deserves award in sentencing. The government may move for departure below the mandatory minimum due to substantial assistance to authorities in the investigation or prosecution of another person who has committed an offense. U.S.S.G. § 5K1.1. In this case, defendant, an underling in the drug trade, does not appear to have been in a position to have identified the control persons in the chain of command in the drug trade. However, he provided substantial assistance to the authorities during the riots, ensuring the personal safety of the Probation Officer. The Guidelines do not adequately consider this type of assistance by defendants.

Whether this court is right that there are adequate grounds for departure from the Guidelines will be judged, as a matter of law, by judges of the Ninth Circuit. They will neither see defendant nor hear him, but they will decide his sentence. This is not to say or suggest, in any way, that any of the judges of the Ninth Circuit are unconscientious people, or are less sensitive to the problems of the "drug war" than the district court judges.

The truth is to the contrary. But they are bound by their own decisions and those of the Supreme Court.

IT IS SO ORDERED.

————————

Notes and Questions

1. Surely Judge Letts must be correct that a ten-year sentence for someone who simply delivered an envelope without knowing what quantity or type of drugs were inside seems overly harsh. Yet, are you sure that is what occurred in this case? The judge notes in passing that the pre-sentence report "contains information which might cause one to speculate that defendant may have had a somewhat greater involvement in the business of drug trafficking than he has admitted." Does it seem plausible to you that Patillo had no idea that the envelope contained a large quantity of crack? Would a rational person think they were being paid $500 to deliver an envelope unless there was a substantial amount of drugs inside?

2. Judge Letts concludes his opinion by saying that "[w]hether this court is right that there are adequate grounds for departure from the Guidelines will be judged, as a matter of law, by judges of the Ninth Circuit." Does the concluding paragraph give you the impression that Judge Letts expected to be reversed for giving a sentence below the guidelines range of 151 to 188 months?

3. At the time of the *Patillo* decision, federal judges faced two sets of constraints in drug cases: (1) a statutory mandatory minimum sentence (such as the ten-year minimum required by 21 U.S.C. § 841(b)(1)(A)); and (2) the minimum sentence calculated under the Federal Sentencing Guidelines (such as the 151 month period in this case). Getting around the mandatory minimum sentence was impossible. Getting around the minimum sentence under the guidelines was very difficult, although possible, if the judge could provide a reason to depart that was not already contemplated by the Guidelines. In *Patillo*, Judge Letts went to great effort to argue that the defendant should receive a sentence below the guideline range of 151 months because the Guidelines did not adequately account for (a) his minor role, (b) the aberrant nature of the crime given the defendant's other behavior, and (c) avoiding manifest injustice. Although the opinion does not make it particularly clear, trial judges faced an uphill climb to depart under these circumstances. Judges were not permitted to double-count factors that the Guidelines had already considered. Rather, they could depart if "the court finds that there exists an aggravating or mitigating circumstance of a kind, or to a degree, not adequately taken into consideration by the Sentencing Commission in formulating the guidelines that should result in a sentence different from that described." 18 U.S.C. § 3553(b). For instance, when the officers who beat Rodney King were convicted of civil rights violations, the trial judge departed below the guideline range because the officers had a low risk of recidivism. The Supreme Court rejected this argument, concluding that the Federal Sentencing Guidelines took account of the prospect of recidivism when they categorized defendants by their level of criminal history. *See* Koon v. United States, 518 U.S. 81, 111 (1996). Judge Letts departed downward for Patillo's sentence because his actions were "out of character" and "if this defendant were not incarcerated, he would have learned enough from this criminal process not to make the same mistake again...." Although *Koon* had not yet been decided when Patillo was sentenced, would Judge Letts' reasoning be upheld under *Koon*?

4. The Supreme Court's landmark decision in United States v. Booker, 543 U.S. 220 (2005) rendered the guidelines (but not the statutory mandatory minimums) advisory.

Thus, while judges are still bound by statutory mandatory minimums, they are not bound by the calculated guidelines ranges (such as the 151 to 188 month range in *Patillo*). So long as the judge acts reasonably, it is permissible to impose a sentence below the guidelines (as long as the sentence does not fall below the mandatory minimum. *See* Gall v. United States, 552 U.S. 38 (2007). Put simply, if *Patillo* were decided today, Judge Letts would not have had to engage in such intellectual gymnastics to impose a sentence below 151 months.

5. Regardless of whether you agree with Judge Letts' interpretation of the Guidelines, he was certainly wrong about one thing: Contrary to the final paragraph of the opinion, the Ninth Circuit never had the opportunity to decide Patillo's sentence. The Government never appealed Judge Letts' decision. Given that the probation office and the Assistant United States Attorney handling the case both suggested a 151-month sentence, why do you think the Government declined to push for the tougher sentence on appeal?

6. Looking at the bigger picture, what is your reaction to Judge Letts' comment that "I, for one, do not understand how it came to be that the courts of this nation, which stood for centuries as the defenders of the rights of minorities against abuse at the hands of the majority, have so far abdicated their function that this defendant must serve a ten year sentence"? Whose job is it to set sentencing policy in the United States? Should courts broadly defer to Congress and the Federal Sentencing Commission? Or should courts re-assert themselves in order to have a much more active role in determining sentences? Think back to your first-year Constitutional Law course and ask whether criminal defendants should be considered discrete and insular minorities in need of protection by the judicial branch from an elected Congress that benefits politically from being tough on crime. On that question of judicial review and the protection of discrete and insular minorities, see JOHN HART ELY, DEMOCRACY AND DISTRUST: A THEORY OF JUDICIAL REVIEW (1980).

7. Judge Letts seems to indicate that he might have imposed probation or a very short sentence on Patillo if he had not been constrained by the mandatory minimum. What sentence would you have imposed? If most of your classmates would impose a sentence of, for example, three years, does that suggest we should have a mandatory minimum of three years that prevents more lenient judges from arbitrarily giving Patillo a lighter sentence than that favored by the majority?

Chapter X

Race and Drugs: Mass Imprisonment of African Americans

A. An Introductory Note on Discussing *The Wire* and Race

The author of this book is white. Most of the students who use the book will be white. The creator of *The Wire*, David Simon, is white. Most of the viewers of *The Wire* were, are, and will be white. Yet, the show is predominantly about the life of urban, poor, African-American communities. And it paints a very bleak picture of those communities. How do we talk about race under these circumstances?

This territory is not entirely new to criminal law professors, although it is still uncomfortable. For example, most first-year criminal law classes read and discuss the Bernie Goetz case as part of the unit on self-defense. Goetz, a middle-aged white man, shot four black teenagers on a New York City subway train in 1984 and claimed he did it to prevent them from mugging him.

It is possible to clinically analyze the Goetz case without mentioning the race issue. Students can focus on the number of assailants in determining whether Goetz's actions were reasonable. Or they can discuss the fact that Goetz shot one of the teenagers a second time, well after he was immobilized and could not be a threat. Students can focus on the teenagers' criminal records or that Goetz bought a gun after being mugged previously. These facts are salient, but they are not really what the case was about. The Goetz case was about the fact that many people who travelled on the New York City subway in the 1980s were afraid of young black men. It is about the assumption that many white people (and some African-American people) have that a young black man who asks for money is not really requesting help, but instead is engaged in a prelude to mugging them. At its root, the Goetz case is about the assumption that young black men are criminals unless there is evidence to disprove that assumption.

Goetz's self-defense claim cannot really be analyzed without addressing these difficult questions about race. Yet, I am embarrassed to admit that in many semesters I do not ask my students these questions. The questions are uncomfortable. So I, and I suspect a number of other criminal law professors, avoid these questions and focus on a clinical assessment of the elements of self-defense.

The Wire is not about self-defense, but it does raise (often indirectly and implicitly) a host of questions about race in America. This chapter focuses on the mass incarceration of African-Americans — what Professor Michelle Alexander has called "The New Jim Crow."[1] Like the self-defense issues in the Goetz case, there may be some temptation to clinically focus on the reasons why imprisonment rates have skyrocketed in the last few decades without touching too closely on questions of race. But avoiding the race questions would be ill advised. A thorough discussion of the issues in this chapter asks us to consider whether drugs and drug laws are destroying black communities. Does fault lie primarily with the young men themselves who are violating the law or is it the criminal justice system that is targeting them for failure? Do the drug laws and their enforcement intentionally discriminate against African-Americans? And if the disparate treatment of blacks is unintentional, is it nevertheless racist anyway?

One final question is also crucial to consider. Is *The Wire* helpful or harmful in eliminating racism and stereotypes? *The Wire* is a story about the epic failure of institutions. Whether it is the police, the unions, the schools, or the media, David Simon sought to tell a story of institutional inertia and of individual actors putting their own interests above the common good. In the process, however, he spends dozens of hours showing black men selling drugs, murdering, thieving, and causing harm to their communities. There are certainly African-American role models in the show — Dennis Cutty opens a boxing gym to keep young men out of the drug trade; Major Colvin helps troubled high school students get back on track; Gus Haynes embodies the integrity and steadfastness we expect from journalists. But these positive portrayals are seemingly drowned out by the repetitive crime and violence committed by countless young African-American men in the show.

Is the brilliant storytelling and character development in *The Wire* worth the risk of reinforcing the myth that only blacks sell drugs and commit violent crime? Does David Simon raise awareness of the harm that United States drug policy is doing to African-American communities, or is he perpetuating the racial stereotypes that keep those policies in place?

B. The Scale of Imprisonment

Just how big is the United States prison population? The answer is staggeringly large. The United States incarcerates more than 2.2 million people. No other nation — past or present — comes anywhere close. It was not always like this. During a three-decade period from the 1970s until the turn of the century, the United States prison population quintupled. Minorities have borne the brunt of the impact. African Americans are incarcerated at nearly six times the rate of Whites. And young black men have fared worst of all. One in nine African-American men between the ages of 20 and 29 is currently incarcerated in the United States. How this staggering level of incarceration occurred over the last few decades is subject to some dispute. The excerpt below offers a starting point for analyzing the problem.

---

1. *See* MICHELLE ALEXANDER, THE NEW JIM CROW: MASS INCARCERATION IN THE AGE OF COLOR BLINDNESS (2010).

Adam M. Gershowitz, An Informational Approach to the Mass Imprisonment Problem
40 Arizona State Law Journal 47 (2008)

* * *

I. The Pervasive Problem of Mass Imprisonment

A. Imprisonment by the Numbers

At present, there are nearly 2.2 million people incarcerated in our nation's prisons and jails. Excluding children and the elderly, nearly one in fifty people in the United States wakes up behind bars each morning.

The United States incarcerates more offenders per capita than any industrialized nation in the world: three times more than Israel, five times more than England, six times more than Australia and Canada, eight times more than France, and over twelve times more than Japan. Given these ratios, it is not surprising that American prisoners convicted of violent crimes are incarcerated for five to ten times as long as their European counterparts. And while European nations rarely incarcerate nonviolent property and drug offenders, more than half of the people imprisoned in the United States have committed nonviolent crimes.

More telling than the total number of prisoners or the international comparisons is the upward historical trend in the United States. As Michael Jacobson has observed [in his book *Downsizing Prisons: How to Reduce Crime and End Mass Imprisonment*], "every state increased the size of its prison system over the last decade." Between 1972 and 2003, the national prison population rose by 500%. There were approximately 330,000 individuals in America's prisons and jails in 1973, which amounted to approximately 160 inmates per every 100,000 people in the United States. Over the next three decades, the number of inmates and the rate per 100,000 Americans steadily climbed. In 1985, 313 per 100,000 people were incarcerated. By 1995, the rate had risen to 601 per 100,000 people. In its most recent estimate at mid-year 2005, the Bureau of Justice Statistics placed the rate at 738 prison and jail inmates per 100,000 people.

The drastic increase in imprisonment has had significant financial consequences. As a result of the increase in the prison population, the United States was required to open the equivalent of one prison per week during the period from 1985 to 2000. The cost of locking up an offender for a single year exceeds $22,000. In some states, the cost is double that amount. All told, the United States spends approximately $60 billion annually on corrections.

And it is often questionable whether counties, states, and the federal government are spending enough money to keep up with the crushing number of incarcerated individuals. Many prisons and jails throughout the country are overcrowded. A recent study by the Bureau of Justice Statistics found that federal prisons held nearly 111,000 prisoners even though the facilities were only rated to handle approximately 83,000 individuals. On average, state prison facilities were also operating in excess of their capacity. And while the construction of new prisons across the country has reduced overcrowding, 145 of 1668 prisons in existence in 2000 were under court orders to reduce their populations. This is to say nothing of the overcrowding in hundreds of the nation's jails that are not analyzed by the Bureau of Justice Statistics.

B. The Roots of the Problem

It is undisputed that incarceration rates have exploded at the federal and state level over the last few decades. The harder question is: Why? Experts have long maintained that the increase in prison population cannot easily be tied to rising crime rates. Conversely, criminologists maintain the drastic increase in imprisonment has not led to a substantial decrease in crime rates. Instead, observers explain the incarceration expansion by pointing to certain criminal justice policies. The standard argument is that mandatory minimum statutes, three strikes laws, and the rise of determinate sentencing have resulted in a dramatic increase in the prison population. Other observers point to the reduction in the use of probation and parole. Still others raise concern about a variation of Parkinson's Law, whereby new prison construction inevitably leads to trial-level actors simply finding new occupants for those prison cells. Experts also point to the expansion of private prisons in recent years, explaining that prison companies have an incentive to expand the number of prisoners in order to provide a market for their services and that prison guard unions have a similar interest in seeing incarceration numbers climb. Finally, whether privately or publicly operated, prisons provide many local communities ravaged by the loss of industry with jobs and economic stimulus that the communities will fight hard to retain.

* * *

II. The Supreme Court's Failure to Step In

A. The Power to Criminalize Almost Anything

Although the Supreme Court heavily regulates the criminal justice system, its regulation focuses almost exclusively on criminal procedure, rather than the substance of criminal law. Accordingly, legislatures are free to enact virtually any laws they wish without interference from the courts.

In the late 1950s and early 1960s it looked as if the Supreme Court might be willing to engage in some regulation of substantive criminal law. In Lambert v. California, decided in 1957, the Court struck down a law making it a crime for a convicted felon to remain in Los Angeles for more than five days without registering with the police. The Court recognized that legislators have "wide latitude" to define criminal infractions, but explained that since Lambert had no knowledge of her duty to register and had been "wholly passive," it would violate due process to convict her of the offense. In dissent, Justice Frankfurter predicted that the Court's decision would turn out to be "an isolated deviation from the strong current of precedents — a derelict on the waters of the law."

Although Justice Frankfurter's prediction turned out to be correct, the Court did take one additional detour into the world of substantive criminal law a few years later. In Robinson v. California, the Supreme Court struck down a law making it a crime for a person to "be addicted to the use of narcotics." The Court concluded that it would be cruel and unusual punishment to convict someone for a "status" rather than a particular act. The Robinson decision seemed to signal that there would be constitutional scrutiny of criminal blameworthiness and more rigorous oversight of strict liability crimes. Yet, that rigorous oversight did not come to pass. Only a few years later, in Powell v. Texas, the Court refused to find unconstitutional a statute making it a crime to be "found in a state of intoxication in any public place." And since Powell, it is nearly impossible to find a non-capital case in which the Court has restricted legislatures' power to criminalize.

… In effect, the Supreme Court has completely abdicated the field of substantive criminal law. The reason for the abdication is less clear, though Professor Erik Luna may well be correct that the Court simply does not want to appear to be a "Lochner-esque super-legislature." And although scholars throughout the decades have been highly critical of the Court's failure to regulate the substance of criminal law and have proposed a number of ways to impose such limits, all evidence indicates that the Court will continue to ignore these suggestions.

B. The Power to Impose Almost Any Punishment

Just as the Court has refused to limit legislatures' power to criminalize behavior, it also has been extremely wary of meddling with the punishment decisions of legislatures and juries. As explained below, the Court has made clear that, with the exception of death-penalty cases, legislatures can punish defendants as harshly as they want without fear that courts will strike down the sentences as unconstitutionally excessive.

For over a century, the Supreme Court has wrestled with the question of whether the Eighth Amendment's prohibition against "cruel and unusual punishment" permits courts to strike down prison sentences simply because they are too long. In 1892, Justice Stephen Field contended that a fifty-four year sentence for selling liquor without authority violated the Eighth Amendment. Although Justice Field's position did not carry the day, a majority of the Court did subsequently find a sentence of fifteen years imprisonment at hard labor to be unconstitutionally excessive for the relatively minor offense of falsifying an official public document.

Several decades later, the Court struggled with the proportionality of long prison sentences for a series of very minor offenses. In 1980, the Court held that a sentence of life imprisonment for a recidivist who had committed three nonviolent property felonies involving less than $230 was constitutional because the "length of the sentence actually imposed is purely a matter of legislative prerogative." Yet, three years later, the Court seemingly reversed its position again by holding a sentence of life imprisonment without the possibility of parole for a recidivist who had committed seven nonviolent offenses to be excessive.

The Court's indecisiveness on the proportionality issue came to an end in the early 1990s. In Harmelin v. Michigan, the Court upheld a sentence of life imprisonment without the possibility of parole for the crime of possession of more than 650 grams of cocaine. While recognizing the existence of a "narrow proportionality principle," Justice Kennedy's plurality opinion made clear that successful challenges to long prison sentences would be extremely rare. And since Harmelin it is nearly impossible to find any federal court willing to strike down a prison sentence as disproportionate. As recently as 2003, the Supreme Court has reiterated its opposition to proportionality review when it upheld California's "Three Strikes and You're Out" recidivism statute.

In short, federal proportionality review of criminal punishments is all but dead. And while certain state courts have engaged in more rigorous proportionality review by looking to their own state constitutions, successful excessiveness challenges are still rare. As a result, when legislatures enact lengthy sentencing ranges, mandatory minimum statutes, three-strikes-and-you're-out-laws, and other tough-on-crime measures, trial judges are obligated to impose those stiff sentences irrespective of the circumstances. Because there is no judicial counterbalance to increasingly punitive laws, prosecutorial discretion becomes the main outlet for relief. And when political campaigns force each candidate or legislator to be tougher on crime than his opponent, the sentencing ranges and mandatory minimums become even longer. The result is more mass imprisonment.

C. Limited Oversight of Prison Condition Cases

Because so many defendants are sentenced to incarceration, prison officials are forced to scramble to find enough space to house them. Often there are simply not enough beds and prisons are forced to operate above capacity. This in turn leads to prison overcrowding, which in turn leads to litigation.

The litigation manifests itself in a variety of ways. Prisoners challenge the plain existence of the overcrowding. They also contend that the overcrowding has led to other problematic conditions of confinement, such as unsanitary facilities, inadequate staffing, poor medical care, heightened levels of tension and violence, and a higher incidence of sexual assault.

Unlike the areas of substantive criminal law and excessive punishments, the Supreme Court has not taken an entirely hands-off approach to the problem of prison conditions. Beginning primarily in the 1960s, the lower federal courts began to conclude that certain prison conditions were so egregious as to violate the Eighth Amendment's cruel and unusual punishment clause. While the lower federal courts were ahead of the Supreme Court in attacking egregious conditions, the high Court eventually followed suit. In the notable case of Hutto v. Finney, the Supreme Court found unconstitutional prison conditions in which as many as ten inmates were confined to unfurnished, "vandalized," eight-by-ten-foot cells for "months" while being given inadequate food and being punished with leather straps and electrical shocks.

Thus, in the 1970s and early 1980s, the federal courts, with the support of the Supreme Court, were actively supervising prison overcrowding through injunctions and court decrees. Interestingly, some wardens and corrections officials welcomed the litigation because federal court intervention slowed the flow of inmates into their facilities and mandated better, safer prisons.

The judiciary's involvement resulted in enormous improvements to prisons....

Yet, while the federal judiciary has fostered enormous improvements in prison and jail conditions through structural reform litigation, the conventional wisdom is that the period of rigorous judicial reform of prisons is over or, at minimum, substantially decreased. And with the judiciary's most rigorous period of reform behind it, it is noteworthy that the Supreme Court passed up the opportunity to attack the core problem of overcrowding. In Rhodes v. Chapman, the Court rejected a challenge to "double-celling" of prisoners because it did not lead to "deprivations of essential food, medical care, or sanitation. Nor did it increase violence among inmates or create other conditions intolerable for prison confinement." The Court made clear that the "Constitution does not mandate comfortable prisons," thus signaling that overcrowding alone would be insufficient to demonstrate an Eighth Amendment violation.

Moreover, in post-*Rhodes* decisions, the Court has heightened the standards to prove unconstitutional prison conditions. For instance, the Court's 1991 decision in Wilson v. Seiter demanded proof that poor prison conditions were the result of wanton behavior by prison officials, which in a typical situation amounts to "'deliberate indifference.'" Thus, while the judiciary's role in cleaning up egregious prison conditions has been substantial, and structural reform litigation continues to flourish in some areas, it is likewise clear that the Supreme Court has no appetite for eliminating the core problem of prison overcrowding except when it manifests itself in other appalling conditions.

* * *

Notes and Questions

1. The excerpt notes an incarceration rate in 2005 of 738 per every 100,000 in people. That number has climbed even higher. By 2008, the incarceration rate was 751 per every 100,000 people, far and away the highest rate in the world. The next closest country, Russia, imprisoned 627 per every 100,000 people. *See* Adam Liptak, *U.S. Prison Population Dwarfs That of Other Nations*, N.Y. Times, Apr. 23, 2008.

2. Why has the Supreme Court taken such a hands off role to key criminal justice questions, such as what behavior can be criminalized, the length of sentences, and (to a lesser extent) the conditions of confinement? By contrast, do you see how heavily the Supreme Court has regulated the field of criminal *procedure*? Does it make sense for the Court to be spending so much energy regulating procedural rules governing confessions, searches and other police tactics, but provide so little oversight of more substantive outcomes? For an argument critical of the Court's jurisprudence, see William J. Stuntz, *The Uneasy Relationship Between Criminal Procedure and Criminal Justice*, 107 Yale L.J. 1, 68–74 (1997).

3. The excerpt quickly dismisses the idea that mass imprisonment has decreased crime. How can we be sure though? Crime has declined substantially in recent years. Assuming the decline is real, rather than the product of statistical manipulation (see Chapter VI), can it be attributed to the fact that so many criminals have been locked up over the last forty years? In other words, is it possible that mass imprisonment   the so called ware housing of dangerous people—has made streets safer?

4. As the excerpt notes, the United States spends upwards of $60 billion per year on corrections. In recent years, as budgets have become tighter, states have declined to build new prisons and even closed some existing prisons and jails. The new conventional wisdom is that politicians may be more amenable to less punitive criminal justice policies if those policies will clearly save money. Indeed, even conservative politicians, who are traditionally the most "tough-on-crime" are supportive of such reforms. *See* Right on Crime, The Conservative Case for Reform: Fighting Crime, Prioritizing Victims, and Protecting Taxpayers (2012) (available at http://www.rightoncrime.com/). Do you think this trend is likely to be permanent? Is it possible that the United States will ever go back to an incarceration rate of 160 per every 100,000 people as was the case prior to the expansion of the last four decades? Or are we likely to be stuck at an incarceration rate of more than 700 per every 100,000 people?

5. What are the 2.2 million people incarcerated in prison and jail there for? Roughly a quarter of jail inmates are there for violent offenses, about 30% are there for drug offenses, and another 30% for non-violent property crimes. *See* Bureau of Justice Statistics, U.S. Dep't of Justice, Sourcebook of Criminal Justice Statistics: Online, at tbl.6.19 (2008).

6. The excerpt explains the reasons why mass imprisonment has occurred in the United States, but does not address how African-Americans have borne the brunt of the drastic increase in incarceration. Why have African-Americans and other minorities been disproportionately effected by mass imprisonment? The cases and materials below begin to provide an explanation.

C. Pretextual Stops and Unregulated Prosecutions

There is one crime that most African-American men have committed in their lifetime, although it is not a crime that you will find in the criminal code of any state. That crime is "driving while black." Police across the country — whether intentionally or subconsciously — stop African-American drivers in situations where they would not stop white drivers. Of course, these African-American drivers are not completely innocent. Police can point to roadway infractions such as speeding, changing lanes without signaling, or not coming to a complete stop at an intersection. Practically every American commits a traffic infraction of some type on his or her way to work or school in the morning. Police could not possibly stop everyone who commits these traffic infractions, so they must choose. If police subconsciously stop minorities more often, is there anything courts or society can do about that? What if police openly admit to pretextual stops in which they nominally stop a minority driver for a traffic offense, but acknowledge that they were really motivated by the driver's race? Is this illegal? What if African-Americans are prosecuted at much higher rates for certain crimes than non-minorities? Would that be an Equal Protection violation? Consider the cases below.

McCleskey v. Kemp

481 U.S. 279 (1987)

Justice POWELL delivered the opinion of the Court.

This case presents the question whether a complex statistical study that indicates a risk that racial considerations enter into capital sentencing determinations proves that petitioner McCleskey's capital sentence is unconstitutional under the Eighth or Fourteenth Amendment.

I

McCleskey, a black man, was convicted of two counts of armed robbery and one count of murder in the Superior Court of Fulton County, Georgia, on October 12, 1978. McCleskey's convictions arose out of the robbery of a furniture store and the killing of a white police officer during the course of the robbery. The evidence at trial indicated that McCleskey and three accomplices planned and carried out the robbery. All four were armed. McCleskey entered the front of the store while the other three entered the rear. McCleskey secured the front of the store by rounding up the customers and forcing them to lie face down on the floor. The other three rounded up the employees in the rear and tied them up with tape. The manager was forced at gunpoint to turn over the store receipts, his watch, and $6. During the course of the robbery, a police officer, answering a silent alarm, entered the store through the front door. As he was walking down the center aisle of the store, two shots were fired. Both struck the officer. One hit him in the face and killed him.

Several weeks later, McCleskey was arrested in connection with an unrelated offense. He confessed that he had participated in the furniture store robbery, but denied that he had shot the police officer. At trial, the State introduced evidence that at least one of the bullets that struck the officer was fired from a .38 caliber Rossi revolver. This description matched the description of the gun that McCleskey had carried during the robbery. The State also introduced the testimony of two witnesses who had heard McCleskey admit to the shooting.

The jury convicted McCleskey of murder. At the penalty hearing, the jury heard arguments as to the appropriate sentence.... The jury recommended that he be sentenced to death on the murder charge and to consecutive life sentences on the armed robbery charges. The court followed the jury's recommendation and sentenced McCleskey to death.

* * *

... [McCleskey's habeas] petition raised 18 claims, one of which was that the Georgia capital sentencing process is administered in a racially discriminatory manner in violation of the Eighth and Fourteenth Amendments to the United States Constitution. In support of his claim, McCleskey proffered a statistical study performed by Professors David C. Baldus, Charles Pulaski, and George Woodworth, and (the Baldus study) that purports to show a disparity in the imposition of the death sentence in Georgia based on the race of the murder victim and, to a lesser extent, the race of the defendant. The Baldus study is actually two sophisticated statistical studies that examine over 2,000 murder cases that occurred in Georgia during the 1970's. The raw numbers collected by Professor Baldus indicate that defendants charged with killing white persons received the death penalty in 11% of the cases, but defendants charged with killing blacks received the death penalty in only 1% of the cases. The raw numbers also indicate a reverse racial disparity according to the race of the defendant: 4% of the black defendants received the death penalty, as opposed to 7% of the white defendants.

Baldus also divided the cases according to the combination of the race of the defendant and the race of the victim. He found that the death penalty was assessed in 22% of the cases involving black defendants and white victims; 8% of the cases involving white defendants and white victims; 1% of the cases involving black defendants and black victims; and 3% of the cases involving white defendants and black victims. Similarly, Baldus found that prosecutors sought the death penalty in 70% of the cases involving black defendants and white victims; 32% of the cases involving white defendants and white victims; 15% of the cases involving black defendants and black victims; and 19% of the cases involving white defendants and black victims.

Baldus subjected his data to an extensive analysis, taking account of 230 variables that could have explained the disparities on nonracial grounds. One of his models concludes that, even after taking account of 39 nonracial variables, defendants charged with killing white victims were 4.3 times as likely to receive a death sentence as defendants charged with killing blacks. According to this model, black defendants were 1.1 times as likely to receive a death sentence as other defendants. Thus, the Baldus study indicates that black defendants, such as McCleskey, who kill white victims have the greatest likelihood of receiving the death penalty.

* * *

II

McCleskey's first claim is that the Georgia capital punishment statute violates the Equal Protection Clause of the Fourteenth Amendment. He argues that race has infected the administration of Georgia's statute in two ways: persons who murder whites are more likely to be sentenced to death than persons who murder blacks, and black murderers are more likely to be sentenced to death than white murderers. As a black defendant who killed a white victim, McCleskey claims that the Baldus study demonstrates that he was discriminated against because of his race and because of the race of his victim. In its broadest form, McCleskey's claim of discrimination extends to every actor in the Georgia capital sentencing process, from the prosecutor who sought the death penalty and the jury that imposed the sentence, to the State itself that enacted the capital punishment statute and allows it to remain in effect despite its allegedly discriminatory application. We agree with the Court of Appeals, and every other court that has considered such a challenge, that this claim must fail.

A

Our analysis begins with the basic principle that a defendant who alleges an equal protection violation has the burden of proving "the existence of purposeful discrimination." *Whitus v. Georgia,* 385 U.S. 545, 550 (1967). A corollary to this principle is that a criminal defendant must prove that the purposeful discrimination "had a discriminatory effect" on him. *Wayte v. United States,* 470 U.S. 598, 608 (1985). Thus, to prevail under the Equal Protection Clause, McCleskey must prove that the decisionmakers in *his* case acted with discriminatory purpose. He offers no evidence specific to his own case that would support an inference that racial considerations played a part in his sentence. Instead, he relies solely on the Baldus study. McCleskey argues that the Baldus study compels an inference that his sentence rests on purposeful discrimination. McCleskey's claim that these statistics are sufficient proof of discrimination, without regard to the facts of a particular case, would extend to all capital cases in Georgia, at least where the victim was white and the defendant is black.

* * *

... McCleskey's statistical proffer must be viewed in the context of his challenge. McCleskey challenges decisions at the heart of the State's criminal justice system. "[O]ne of society's most basic tasks is that of protecting the lives of its citizens and one of the most basic ways in which it achieves the task is through criminal laws against murder." *Gregg v. Georgia,* 428 U.S. 153, 226 (1976) (WHITE, J., concurring). Implementation of these laws necessarily requires discretionary judgments. Because discretion is essential to the criminal justice process, we would demand exceptionally clear proof before we would infer that the discretion has been abused. The unique nature of the decisions at issue in this case also counsels against adopting such an inference from the disparities indicated by the Baldus study. Accordingly, we hold that the Baldus study is clearly insufficient to support an inference that any of the decisionmakers in McCleskey's case acted with discriminatory purpose.

B

McCleskey also suggests that the Baldus study proves that the State as a whole has acted with a discriminatory purpose. He appears to argue that the State has violated the Equal Protection Clause by adopting the capital punishment statute and allowing it to remain in force despite its allegedly discriminatory application. But "'[d]iscriminatory purpose'... implies more than intent as volition or intent as awareness of consequences. It implies that the decisionmaker, in this case a state legislature, selected or reaffirmed a particular course of action at least in part 'because of,' not merely 'in spite of,' its adverse effects upon an identifiable group." *Personnel Administrator of Massachusetts v. Feeney,* 442 U.S. 256 (1979). For this claim to prevail, McCleskey would have to prove that the Georgia Legislature enacted or maintained the death penalty statute *because of* an anticipated racially discriminatory effect. In *Gregg v. Georgia, supra,* this Court found that the Georgia capital sentencing system could operate in a fair and neutral manner. There was no evidence then, and there is none now, that the Georgia Legislature enacted the capital punishment statute to further a racially discriminatory purpose.

Nor has McCleskey demonstrated that the legislature maintains the capital punishment statute because of the racially disproportionate impact suggested by the Baldus study. As legislatures necessarily have wide discretion in the choice of criminal laws and penalties, and as there were legitimate reasons for the Georgia Legislature to adopt and maintain capital punishment, we will not infer a discriminatory purpose on the part of the State of Georgia. Accordingly, we reject McCleskey's equal protection claims.

* * *

V

Two additional concerns inform our decision in this case. First, McCleskey's claim, taken to its logical conclusion, throws into serious question the principles that underlie our entire criminal justice system. The Eighth Amendment is not limited in application to capital punishment, but applies to all penalties. Thus, if we accepted McCleskey's claim that racial bias has impermissibly tainted the capital sentencing decision, we could soon be faced with similar claims as to other types of penalty. Moreover, the claim that his sentence rests on the irrelevant factor of race easily could be extended to apply to claims based on unexplained discrepancies that correlate to membership in other minority groups, and even to gender. Similarly, since McCleskey's claim relates to the race of his victim, other claims could apply with equally logical force to statistical disparities that correlate with the race or sex of other actors in the criminal justice system, such as defense attorneys, or judges. Also, there is no logical reason that such a claim need be limited to racial or sexual bias. If arbitrary and capricious punishment is the touchstone under the Eighth Amendment, such a claim could—at least in theory—be based upon any arbitrary variable, such as the defendant's facial characteristics, or the physical attractiveness of the defendant or the victim, that some statistical study indicates may be influential in jury decisionmaking. As these examples illustrate, there is no limiting principle to the type of challenge brought by McCleskey. The Constitution does not require that a State eliminate any demonstrable disparity that correlates with a potentially irrelevant factor in order to operate a criminal justice system that includes capital punishment....

... McCleskey's arguments are best presented to the legislative bodies. It is not the responsibility—or indeed even the right—of this Court to determine the appropriate punishment for particular crimes. It is the legislatures, the elected representatives of the people, that are "constituted to respond to the will and consequently the moral values of the people." *Furman v. Georgia,* 408 U.S. [238 (1972)] (Burger, C.J., dissenting). Legislatures also are better qualified to weigh and "evaluate the results of statistical studies in terms of their own local conditions and with a flexibility of approach that is not available to the courts," *Gregg v. Georgia, supra,* 428 U.S., at 186. Capital punishment is now the law in more than two-thirds of our States. It is the ultimate duty of courts to determine on a case-by-case basis whether these laws are applied consistently with the Constitution. Despite McCleskey's wide-ranging arguments that basically challenge the validity of capital punishment in our multiracial society, the only question before us is whether in his case the law of Georgia was properly applied. We agree with the District Court and the Court of Appeals for the Eleventh Circuit that this was carefully and correctly done in this case.

VI

Accordingly, we affirm the judgment of the Court of Appeals for the Eleventh Circuit.

It is so ordered.

[The dissenting opinions of Justices Brennan, Blackmun, and Stevens are omitted.]

Whren v. United States
517 U.S. 806 (1996)

Justice SCALIA delivered the opinion of the Court.

In this case we decide whether the temporary detention of a motorist who the police have probable cause to believe has committed a civil traffic violation is inconsistent with the Fourth Amendment's prohibition against unreasonable seizures unless a reasonable officer would have been motivated to stop the car by a desire to enforce the traffic laws.

I

On the evening of June 10, 1993, plainclothes vice-squad officers of the District of Columbia Metropolitan Police Department were patrolling a "high drug area" of the city in an unmarked car. Their suspicions were aroused when they passed a dark Pathfinder truck with temporary license plates and youthful occupants waiting at a stop sign, the driver looking down into the lap of the passenger at his right. The truck remained stopped at the intersection for what seemed an unusually long time — more than 20 seconds. When the police car executed a U-turn in order to head back toward the truck, the Pathfinder turned suddenly to its right, without signaling, and sped off at an "unreasonable" speed. The policemen followed, and in a short while overtook the Pathfinder when it stopped behind other traffic at a red light. They pulled up alongside, and Officer Ephraim Soto stepped out and approached the driver's door, identifying himself as a police officer and directing the driver, petitioner Brown, to put the vehicle in park. When Soto drew up to the driver's window, he immediately observed two large plastic bags of what appeared to be crack cocaine in petitioner Whren's hands. Petitioners were arrested, and quantities of several types of illegal drugs were retrieved from the vehicle.

Petitioners were charged in a four-count indictment with violating various federal drug laws, including 21 U.S.C. §§ 844(a) and 860(a). At a pretrial suppression hearing, they challenged the legality of the stop and the resulting seizure of the drugs. They argued that the stop had not been justified by probable cause to believe, or even reasonable suspicion, that petitioners were engaged in illegal drug-dealing activity; and that Officer Soto's asserted ground for approaching the vehicle — to give the driver a warning concerning traffic violations — was pretextual. The District Court denied the suppression motion, concluding that "the facts of the stop were not controverted," and "[t]here was nothing to really demonstrate that the actions of the officers were contrary to a normal traffic stop."

Petitioners were convicted of the counts at issue here. The Court of Appeals affirmed the convictions, holding with respect to the suppression issue that, "regardless of whether a police officer subjectively believes that the occupants of an automobile may be engaging in some other illegal behavior, a traffic stop is permissible as long as a reasonable officer in the same circumstances *could have* stopped the car for the suspected traffic violation." 53 F.3d 371, 374–375 (C.A.D.C.1995). We granted certiorari.

II

* * *

Petitioners accept that Officer Soto had probable cause to believe that various provisions of the District of Columbia traffic code had been violated. See 18 D.C. Mun. Regs. §§ 2213.4 (1995) ("An operator shall ... give full time and attention to the operation of the vehicle"); 2204.3 ("No person shall turn any vehicle ... without giving an appropriate signal"); 2200.3 ("No person shall drive a vehicle ... at a speed greater than is reasonable and prudent under the conditions"). They argue, however, that "in the unique context of civil traffic regulations" probable cause is not enough. Since, they contend, the use of automobiles is so heavily and minutely regulated that total compliance with traffic and safety rules is nearly impossible, a police officer will almost invariably be able to catch any given motorist in a technical violation. This creates the temptation to use traffic stops as a means of investigating other law violations, as to which no probable cause or even articulable suspicion exists. Petitioners, who are both black, further contend that police officers might decide which motorists to stop based on decidedly impermissible factors, such as the race of the car's occupants. To avoid this danger, they say, the Fourth Amendment test for traffic stops should be, not the normal one (applied by the Court of Appeals) of whether probable cause existed to justify the stop; but rather, whether a police officer, acting reasonably, would have made the stop for the reason given.

* * *

B

Recognizing that we have been unwilling to entertain Fourth Amendment challenges based on the actual motivations of individual officers, petitioners disavow any intention to make the individual officer's subjective good faith the touchstone of "reasonableness." They insist that the standard they have put forward—whether the officer's conduct deviated materially from usual police practices, so that a reasonable officer in the same circumstances would not have made the stop for the reasons given—is an "objective" one.

But although framed in empirical terms, this approach is plainly and indisputably driven by subjective considerations. Its whole purpose is to prevent the police from doing under the guise of enforcing the traffic code what they would like to do for different reasons. Petitioners' proposed standard may not use the word "pretext," but it is designed to combat nothing other than the perceived "danger" of the pretextual stop, albeit only indirectly and over the run of cases. Instead of asking whether the individual officer had the proper state of mind, the petitioners would have us ask, in effect, whether (based on general police practices) it is plausible to believe that the officer had the proper state of mind.

Why one would frame a test designed to combat pretext in such fashion that the court cannot take into account *actual and admitted pretext* is a curiosity that can only be explained by the fact that our cases have foreclosed the more sensible option. If those cases were based only upon the evidentiary difficulty of establishing subjective intent, petitioners' attempt to root out subjective vices through objective means might make sense. But they were not based only upon that, or indeed even principally upon that. Their principal basis—which applies equally to attempts to reach subjective intent through ostensibly objective means—is simply that the Fourth Amendment's concern with "reasonableness" allows certain actions to be taken in certain circumstances, *whatever* the subjective intent. But even if our concern had been only an evidentiary one, petitioners' proposal would by no means assuage it. Indeed, it seems to us somewhat easier to figure out the intent of an individual officer than to plumb the collective consciousness of law enforcement in order to determine whether a "reasonable officer" would have been moved to act upon the traffic violation. While police manuals and standard procedures may sometimes provide objective assistance, ordinarily one would be reduced to speculating about the hypothetical reaction of a hypothetical constable—an exercise that might be called virtual subjectivity.

Moreover, police enforcement practices, even if they could be practically assessed by a judge, vary from place to place and from time to time. We cannot accept that the search and seizure protections of the Fourth Amendment are so variable and can be made to turn upon such trivialities. The difficulty is illustrated by petitioners' arguments in this case. Their claim that a reasonable officer would not have made this stop is based largely on District of Columbia police regulations which permit plainclothes officers in unmarked vehicles to enforce traffic laws "only in the case of a violation that is so grave as to pose an *immediate threat* to the safety of others." Metropolitan Police Department, Washington, D.C., General Order 303.1, pt. 1, Objectives and Policies (A)(2)(4) (Apr. 30, 1992). This basis of invalidation would not apply in jurisdictions that had a different practice. And it would not have applied even in the District of Columbia, if Officer Soto had been wearing a uniform or patrolling in a marked police cruiser.

* * *

III

* * *

Where probable cause has existed, the only cases in which we have found it necessary actually to perform the "balancing" analysis involved searches or seizures conducted in an extraordinary manner, unusually harmful to an individual's privacy or even physical interests—such as, for example, seizure by means of deadly force, see *Tennessee v. Garner*, 471 U.S. 1 (1985) ... or physical penetration of the body, see *Winston v. Lee*, 470 U.S. 753 (1985). The making of a traffic stop out of uniform does not remotely qualify as such an extreme practice, and so is governed by the usual rule that probable cause to believe the law has been broken "outbalances" private interest in avoiding police contact.

Petitioners urge as an extraordinary factor in this case that the "multitude of applicable traffic and equipment regulations" is so large and so difficult to obey perfectly that virtually everyone is guilty of violation, permitting the police to single out almost whomever they wish for a stop. But we are aware of no principle that would allow us to decide at what point a code of law becomes so expansive and so commonly violated that infraction itself can no longer be the ordinary measure of the lawfulness of enforcement. And even if we could identify such exorbitant codes, we do not know by what standard (or what right) we would decide, as petitioners would have us do, which particular provisions are sufficiently important to merit enforcement.

For the run-of-the-mine case, which this surely is, we think there is no realistic alternative to the traditional common-law rule that probable cause justifies a search and seizure.

* * *

Affirmed.

Notes and Questions

1. What do *McCleskey* (a death penalty case) and *Whren* (a search and seizure case) have to do with this chapter's focus on mass imprisonment of African-Americans?

2. Consider the following statistics described by Human Rights Watch: In 1980 there were about 581,000 drug arrests in the United States; by 2006 that number had risen to nearly 1.9 million drug arrests. *See* Human Rights Watch, Targeting Blacks 8 (2008). "Between 1990 and 2000, drug offenses accounted for 27 percent of the total increase in black inmates in state prison and only 15 percent of the increase in white inmates." *Id.* at 10. From 1986 to 2003, "the rate of admission to prison for drug offenses for blacks quintupled; the white rate did not quite triple." *Id.* at 12. Drug offenses accounted for less than 24% of white men entering prison in 2003, compared with more than 38% of black men. *See id.* at 21. Most significantly, survey data has demonstrated that "whites and

blacks use illicit drugs at roughly the same rate." *Id.* at 41. In light of these figures, consider again the question in note 1: what do *McCleskey* and *Whren* have to do with the mass imprisonment of African-Americans?

3. A report published by the federal government in 2002 found that overall drug use varies little between whites and African-Americans: "Rates of current illicit drug use among the major racial/ethnic groups in 2001 were 7.2 percent for whites, 6.4 percent for Hispanics, and 7.4 percent for blacks. The rate was highest among American Indians/ Alaska Natives (9.9 percent) and persons reporting more than one race (12.6 percent). Asians had the lowest rate (2.8 percent)." Office of Applied Studies, U.S. Dep't of Health & Human Servs., 2001 National Household Survey on Drug Abuse (2002).

4. *Whren* was stopped for traffic violations and arrested for drug possession. However, many commentators would say that he was guilty of the crime of driving-while-black. What does that mean?

5. Would you be surprised to learn that *Whren* was decided unanimously? Did the Court's more liberal justices miss the significance of the decision?

6. *Whren* holds that pretextual arrests are constitutional so long as the officers have a legitimate reason to conduct the arrest. What are the ramifications of arresting African Americans, who are more likely to be poor? Unlike more affluent defendants who can afford to retain lawyers, poor defendants will have to rely on public defenders and appointed counsel. Studies have shown that defendants who are represented by public defenders and appointed counsel (who are more overburdened than private attorneys) are more likely to be detained pre-trial and more likely to be sentenced to incarceration. *See* Bureau of Justice Statistics Special Report, Defense Counsel in Criminal Cases (2000).

7. The Supreme Court rejected McCleskey's racial discrimination claims in part because, followed to their logical conclusion, they would throw "into serious question the principles that underlie our entire criminal justice system." If the Court had decided *McCleskey* differently, would it have had an effect on the imprisonment of drug offenders?

D. The Crack/Cocaine Disparity

From 1986 to 2010, possession with intent to distribute crack-cocaine was punished far more harshly in the federal system than possession with intent to distribute powder cocaine. Being caught with 50 grams of crack yielded the same sentence as being caught with 5,000 grams of powder cocaine. African-Americans were more likely to be convicted of offenses involving crack, whereas Whites were more likely to be convicted of offenses involving powder cocaine. Is this sentencing scheme racist? If so, is it unconstitutional? If a judge did not like it, was there anything he or she could do about it?

United States v. Clary
846 F. Supp. 768 (E.D. Mo. 1994)
FINDINGS AND CONCLUSIONS OF LAW

CAHILL, District Judge.

Defendant Edward Clary was arrested for possession with intent to distribute 67.76 grams of cocaine base. Clary pled guilty to possession with intent to distribute cocaine base ("crack cocaine"), pursuant to 21 U.S.C. § 841(b)(1)(A)(iii) (hereinafter referred to as the "crack statute"), punishable by a mandatory minimum sentence of 10 years imprisonment. Prior to sentencing, Clary, a black male, filed a motion challenging the constitutionality of the crack statute and contended, *inter alia,* that the sentence enhancement provisions contained in it and United States Sentencing Guidelines (U.S.S.G.) § 2D1.1 violated his equal protection rights guaranteed by the Fifth Amendment.

* * *

Specifically, defendant Clary asserts that the penalty differential of the "100 to 1" ratio of cocaine to cocaine base[1] contained in both the crack statute and the United States Sentencing Guidelines has a disproportionate impact on blacks because blacks are more likely to possess cocaine base than whites who are more likely to possess cocaine powder. Therefore, defendant's argument continues, providing longer sentences for possession of cocaine base than for the identical amount of cocaine powder treats a similarly situated defendant in a dissimilar manner, which violates his right to equal protection under the law.

THE PROBLEM BEFORE THE COURT

Before this Court are two different sentencing provisions contained within the same statute for possession and distribution of different forms of the same drug. The difference—the key difference—is that possession and distribution of **50** grams of crack cocaine carries the same mandatory minimum sentence of 10 years imprisonment as possession and distribution of **5000** grams of powder cocaine. Both provisions punish the **same** drug, but penalize crack cocaine 100 times more than powder cocaine!

Congress tells us that the rationale for this sentencing dichotomy which produces harsher punishment for involvement with crack cocaine is because it is so much more dangerous than powder cocaine. As "proof," Congress relied upon endless media accounts of crack's increased threat to society. While Congress may have had well-intentioned concerns, the Court is equally aware that this one provision, the crack statute, has been directly responsible for incarcerating nearly an entire generation of young black American men for very long periods, usually during the most productive time of their lives. Inasmuch as crack and powder cocaine are really the same drug (powder cocaine is "cooked" with baking soda for about a minute to make crack), it appears likely that race rather than conduct was the determining factor.

Although both statutory provisions purport to punish criminal activity for both crack and powder cocaine, the blacks using crack are punished with much longer sentences than whites using the same amount of powder cocaine. This disparity is so significantly disproportional that it shocks the conscience of the Court and invokes examination.

* * *

CRIME AND THE LEGISLATIVE RESPONSE

Crime!! The very word connotes fear and panic, resulting in a frenzied attempt to control and curtail criminal actions in today's violence-soaked world. Never before have Americans cringed at the thought of becoming victims of random, irrational assaults;

---

1. The enhanced penalty provisions of 21 U.S.C. § 841(b)(1)(A)(iii) provide that any person convicted of possession with intent to distribute "**50 grams** or more of a mixture or substance ... which contains cocaine base [crack]" shall be sentenced to no less than 10 years in prison. In contrast, the same penalty is imposed on a defendant only if he possesses with intent to distribute **5,000 grams** of cocaine [powder] in violation of 21 U.S.C. § 841(b)(1)(A)(ii)(II).

never before has the fear and frustration of average citizens grown to such a level that a "lynch mob mentality" becomes the common emotional reaction to crime.

Today there are so many senseless crimes whose gory details are displayed in living color on living room TVs in America that people, inured to the bloodshed, simply retreat in horror from the senseless details. Crime has always been an unpleasant but ever present segment of life in America, but never has it been so brutally and instantaneously reported in repetitive words and pictures from all segments of the media—print, audio, and video. So whether there is more violence, as most believe, or whether the ratio is about the same but appears greater because of the larger population and visual immediacy makes little difference. There is no doubt that the public's perception is so pronounced that the public is prepared—no, anxious—to pay *any* price to control crime even to the abandonment of traditional constitutional safeguards.

The media has for years kept up a drum beat of repetitive reporting of the most horrendous criminal actions, intruding upon the grief stricken victims, interrogating them while they are in shock and tears, further enraging the public against anyone even accused of a crime. The presumption of innocence is now a legal myth.

Of especial importance is the fact that crime is no longer segregated to the other side of town. People living in the "better parts" of the community are now subject to the random anger and uncontrolled hatred of psychopaths and weak, frustrated individuals unable to cope with the problems of life. When one reads of the brutal murder of elderly persons in the bedrooms of their ransacked homes, of gangland style executions and drive-by shootings, and ravishment of innocent children of tender years, it is understandable that anxious citizens demand action. Legislators, feeling the heat of the public's anger, scramble to comply with the demands of raging infernos caused by the citizens' ire.

For the last few years there has been a feeding frenzy of responses by lawmakers of every stripe and political persuasion, so that both Congress and state legislators fill the hoppers with proposed bills designed to curtail crime (each one more restrictive or Draconian than those before) in the misguided hope of reducing crime, but in the certainty that, effective or not, it will gain votes.

It is true we need the relief demanded by citizens. It is true that we need firm and stern punishment for many crimes, including life imprisonment in appropriate cases. It is true that the scourges of communities saturated with drugs must be corrected. It is true that the police alone cannot correct this destructive societal force. But it is also true that we cannot continue to ignore the "root causes" of crime, such as poverty, racism, unemployment, and poor education.

* * *

This Court recognizes that the control of crime is the most important goal of sentencing, and a firm and certain punishment must be the major goal in criminal justice. However, such punishment must be fair; it must fit the particulars of the offense and must acknowledge characteristics of individuals.

Let it be further understood that this Court would play no role in furthering the belief that drugs are to be condoned or ignored. Naturally, the greatest effectiveness would come from controlling those nearest the source of the drugs, but even the couriers and street peddlers facilitate the distribution of the deadly substances and they, too, must be punished—but to a degree commensurate with their culpability.

The "100 to 1" ratio, coupled with mandatory minimum sentencing provided by federal statute, has created a situation that reeks with inhumanity and injustice. The scales of justice have been turned topsy turvy so that those masterminds, the "kingpins" of drug trafficking, escape detection, while those whose role is minimal, even trivial, are hoisted on the spears of an enraged electorate and at the pinnacle of their youth are imprisoned for years while those most responsible for the evil of the day remain free.

* * *

A HISTORY OF RACISM IN CRIMINAL PUNISHMENT

That black people have been punished more severely for violating the same law as whites is not a new phenomenon. A dual system of criminal punishment based on racial discrimination can be traced back to the time of slavery. In order to understand the role that racism has played in enacting the penalty enhancement for using crack cocaine, one must first take note of America's history of racially tainted criminal laws, particularly drug laws. Race has often served as a significant contributing factor to the enhancement of penalties for crime.

Early in our nation's history, legislatures were motivated by racial discrimination to differentiate between crimes committed by whites and crimes committed by blacks. For example, "An Act Against Stealing Hogs" provided a penalty of 25 lashes on a bare back or a 10 pound fine for white offenders, while nonwhites (slave and free) would receive 39 lashes, with no chance of paying a fine to avoid the whipping. In 1697, Pennsylvania passed death sentence legislation for black men who raped white women and castrated them for attempted rape. White men who committed the same offense would be fined, whipped, or imprisoned for one year.

* * *

Prior to the civil rights era, Congress repeatedly imposed severe criminal sanctions on addictive substances once they became popular with minorities. Historically, a consortium of reactionary media and a subsequently inflamed constituency have combined to influence Congress to impose more severe criminal sanctions for use of narcotics once they became popular with minorities.

* * *

The Harrison Act of 1914, the first federal law to prohibit distribution of cocaine and heroin, was passed on the heels of overblown media accounts depicting heroin-addicted black prostitutes and criminals in the cities. The author of the Act, Representative Francis Harrison, moved to include coca leaves in the bill "since [the leaves] make Coca-Cola and Pepsi-Cola and all those things are sold to Negroes all over the South." At one point the bill appeared to be facing defeat until Dr. Hamilton Wright, the American delegate to the Hague Opium Conference, 1911–1912, submitted an official report in which he warned Congress of the drug crazed blacks in the South whose drug habits "*threaten[ed] to creep into the higher social ranks of the country*" [emphasis added]. The images of narcotics and a black rebellion in the South and images of black addicts involved with white women were central to the hysteria that motivated legislative enactments. His report, amplified and personalized by the news media and photographs, helped to shape public opinion regardless of the factual basis. True or not, the black addict became a stereotype not synonymous with most black men.

* * *

In later decades cocaine became associated with exotic groups such as Hollywood entertainers and jazz musicians. It earned the moniker of the "rich man's drug." In the early 1960s and 1970s, cocaine began to move into mainstream society, and became the "drug of the eighties." Even with the widespread use of powder cocaine, no new drug laws were enacted to further criminalize or penalize cocaine possession. The "war on drugs" with respect to powder cocaine was concentrated on impeding international import of the drug or targeted large scale financiers. The social history is clear that so long as cocaine powder was a popular amusement among young, white professionals, law enforcement policy prohibiting cocaine was weakly enforced.

Almost every major drug has been, at various times in America's history, treated as a threat to the survival of America by some minority segment of society. Panic based on media reports which incited racial fears has been used historically in this country as the catalyst for generating racially biased legislation. The association of illicit drug use with minorities and the threat of it "spreading to the higher ranks" is disturbingly similar to the events which culminated in the "100 to 1" ratio enhancement in the crack statute.

* * *

IMPACT OF THE 80s

The **1980s** were times of cataclysmic economic change in America. The smoke-stack industries which furnished considerable highly paid employment to many persons with limited formal education were dead, dying, or moving elsewhere. The major corporations were retreading and making more products with more machines but fewer humans, and finally, a pervasive opinion grew that government had to curtail spending for the poor in order to reduce its own budget deficit. Even the grants of the "military-industrial" complex were affected. Local and state governments were getting less and less money returned by the federal government, and therefore most community projects such as hospitals, playgrounds, emergency shelters, and food pantries were closed. Unemployment reached levels as high as 8 percent nationally but in the inner cities it hovered around 20 percent and in some cases soared to levels of 50 to 60 percent for young black men.

The 80s found many communities bereft of the assistance from institutions financed by the federal government, and with virtually no employment, many young residents of the inner cities lost hope and motivation. In their anger and frustration they turned to the most visible source of immediate financial reward—drug traffic. Because there were so few employment opportunities otherwise available, and because the immense drug market offered huge profits immediately, many persons were attracted to it. This, in turn, brought competition, and in the absence of regulation (usually enforced by government), turf competition developed which led to more and more gang wars in which the use of military type firearms flourished. Desperate to maintain their share of the obscenely lucrative profits from drug peddling, the gangs became more aggressive and exhibited little sympathy for bystanders caught in the crossfire. It must be noted that in the early years of the drug war few paid attention to the escalating violence among these competing gangs because they were then only killing each other or an occasional hapless victim who lived nearby. The media rarely did more than mention the victims who lived in the inner cities. It was only when suburbanites and European tourists became targets of these desperados that the government responded. Then did much of law enforcement concentrate on "controlling crime," mainly by keeping it boxed up in the ghettos.

Acrimonious relations began to grow in many communities, and a tendency simply to contain the crime in a designated area rather than to try to eliminate it began to form. Highways and fences were used to segregate the troubled zones, and police tried to isolate the residents of inner cities, many times by unjustified harassment and unfair arrests. In a recent 1987 incident, the residents of East St. Louis, Illinois, were blocked from crossing the bridge across the Mississippi River to prevent their attendance at the St. Louis

Fourth of July celebration until then Chief U.S. District Judge John F. Nangle, E.D. Missouri, ordered the police department to remove the barriers.

In the mid-1980s a sea change of attitudes toward crime itself had coalesced in America. Prior to this era, the predominant view was that crime was caused by deprivation or neglect and that rehabilitation was the main goal of incarceration. When the media (both press and electronic) became able to reveal instantaneously to the entire world graphic details of any crime occurring anywhere in this nation, the general public became aroused and angered as never before. The repetition of the stories on TV, cable, newspaper, and magazines, fanned the flames of anger into an inferno of fiery frenzy. This anger resulted in town hall meetings, TV crime dramas, pitiful photographs, all generating even more notoriety relating to crime and criminals. Most important of all, those parts of a neighborhood believed to be immune to the spread of crime now found that the plague was spreading, first to the edges of the inner cities and then to the affluent suburbs and even to the distant rural towns and villages.

∗ ∗ ∗

UNCONSCIOUS RACISM

Thus, the root of racism has been implanted in our collective unconscious and has biased the ideas that Americans accept about the significance of race. Racism goes beyond prejudicial discrimination and bigotry. It arises from outlooks, stereotypes, and fears of which we are vastly unaware. Our historical experience has made racism an integral part of our culture even though society has more recently embraced an ideal that rejects racism as immoral. When an individual experiences conflict between racist ideas and the social ethic that condemns those ideas, the mind excludes his racism from his awareness.

Unconscious racism existed in some limited form during slavery. As outright discrimination against blacks became increasingly politically and socially unacceptable, and, in 1954, in some measure *illegal,* racist actions metamorphosed into more subtle forms of discrimination. As more well-educated blacks flowed into America's mainstream, whites even began to differentiate between the kind of blacks who reflected white values and who were not like "those other" blacks akin to the inner city stereotype.

A benign neglect for the harmful impact or fallout upon the black community that might ensue from decisions made by the white community for the "greater good" of society has replaced intentional discrimination. In the "enlightened and politically correct 90s," whites have become indignant at the suggestion that they harbor any ill-will towards blacks or retain any vestiges of racism. After all, they have black friends. They work with black people every day. They enjoy black entertainers on their favorite television programs every night.

∗ ∗ ∗

… [T]he Court recognizes that while intentional discrimination is unlikely today, unconscious feelings of difference and superiority still live on even in well-intentioned minds. There is a realization that most Americans have grown beyond the evils of overt racial malice, but still have not completely shed the deeply rooted cultural bias that differentiates between "them" and "us."

The illustration of unconscious racism is patently evident in the crack cocaine statutes. Had the same type of law been applied to powder cocaine, it would have sentenced droves of young whites to prison for extended terms. Before the enactment of such a law, it would have been much more carefully and deliberately considered. After all, in these days when "toughness on crime" is a political virtue, the simplest and fairest solution would

have been to make the severe punishment for powder cocaine the same as for crack cocaine. But when the heavy punishment is inflicted only upon those in the weak and unpopular minority community, it is an example of benign neglect arising from unconscious
racism.

* * *

EQUAL PROTECTION ANALYSIS

A current equal protection analysis must therefore take into account the unconscious
predispositions of people, including legislators, who may sincerely believe that they are
not making decisions on the basis of race. This predisposition is a pertinent factor in determining the existence of a racially discriminatory motive. Racial influences which un-
consciously seeped into the legislative decision making process are no less injurious,
reprehensible, or unconstitutional. Although intent *per se* may not have entered Congress' enactment of the crack statute, its failure to account for a foreseeable disparate impact which would effect black Americans in grossly disproportionate numbers would,
nonetheless, violate the spirit and letter of equal protection.

* * *

ENACTMENT OF THE CRACK STATUTE

Crack cocaine eased into the mainstream of the drug culture about 1985 and immediately absorbed the media's attention. Between 1985 and 1986, over 400 reports had
been broadcast by the networks. Media accounts of crack-user horror stories appeared
daily on every major channel and in every major newspaper. Many of the stories were
racist. Despite the statistical data that whites were prevalent among crack users, rare was
the interview with a young black person who had avoided drugs and the drug culture,
and even rarer was any media association with whites and crack. Images of young black
men daily saturated the screens of our televisions. These distorted images branded onto
the public mind and the minds of legislators that young black men were *solely* responsible for the drug crisis in America. The media created a stereotype of a crack dealer as
a young black male, unemployed, gang affiliated, gun toting, and a menace to society.
These stereotypical descriptions of drug dealers may be accurate, but not all young black
men are drug dealers. The broad brush of uninformed public opinion paints them all as
the same.

Legislators used these media accounts as informational support for the enactment
of the crack statute. The *Congressional Record,* prior to enactment of the statute, is replete with news articles submitted by members for their colleagues' consideration which
labeled crack dealers as black youths and gangs. Members of Congress also introduced
into the record media reports containing language that was either overtly or subtly
racist, and which exacerbated white fears that the "crack problem" would spill out of
the ghettos.

These stereotypical images undoubtedly served as the touchstone that influenced
racial perceptions held by legislators and the public as related to the "crack epidemic."
The fear of increased crime as a result of crack cocaine fed white society's fear of the black
male as a crack user and as a source of social disruption. The prospect of black crack
migrating to the white suburbs led the legislators to reflexively punish crack violators
more harshly than their white, suburban, powder cocaine dealing counterparts. The ultimate outcome resulted in the legislators drafting the crack statute with its Draconian
punishment.

* * *

Defendant's evidence that the impact of the crack statute "bears more heavily" on blacks than whites is undisputed. 98.2 percent of defendants convicted of crack cocaine charges in the Eastern District of Missouri between the years 1988 and 1992 were black. Nationally, 92.6 percent of the defendants convicted during 1992 of federal crack cocaine violations were black and 4.7 percent of the defendants were white. In comparison, 45.2 percent of defendants sentenced for powder cocaine were white, as opposed to 20.7 percent of black defendants. All of the defendants sentenced for simple possession of crack cocaine were black. The national figures comport to essentially the same percentage as the Missouri statistics.

According to a *U.S.A. Today* report which investigated the racial disparity caused by the "100 to 1 ratio" and the mandatory minimum sentencing practices in the country, although only 12 percent of the population, blacks accounted for 42 percent of all drug arrests in 1991. The 1992 federal figures indicate that blacks comprise 1.6 million of the illegal drug use population while 8.7 million whites admit to illegal drug use. Yet, blacks are four times as likely as whites to be arrested on drug charges in this country. Notably, in the Eastern District blacks are eight times as likely to be arrested.

According to the U.S. Sentencing Commission, blacks receive sentences at or above the mandatory minimum more often than whites arrested on the same charge. The disparate application appears to be related to race, and the disparity is constant even when variables such as nature of the offense and prior criminal record are considered.

* * *

PROSECUTORIAL AND LAW ENFORCEMENT DISCRETION

The crack statute in conjunction with the resultant mandatory minimum sentence, standing alone, may not have spawned the kind and degree of racially disparate impact that warrants judicial review but for the manner of its application by law enforcement agencies. The law enforcement practices, charging policies, and sentencing departure decisions by prosecutors constitute major contributing factors which have escalated the disparate outcome.[68]

Prosecutors do have broad discretion in determining who will be charged with a crime. All that is required for the prosecutor to have probable cause is to believe that the accused committed an offense defined by statute. "The decision whether or not to prosecute, and what charge to file ... generally rests within his discretion." *Bordenkircher v. Hayes*, 434 U.S. 357, 364. While the prosecutor does have broad discretion, it is not unlimited. For example, the prosecutor may not base the decision to prosecute upon impermissible factors such as race, religion, or other arbitrary and unjustified classifications.

Prosecutorial discretion as it relates to crack cocaine cases should be exercised in a manner that is responsive to Congress' expressed intent to target "kingpins" and "high level traffickers." It would seem to be economically sensible to devote scarce government resources to reducing the large ingress and wholesale distribution of powder cocaine by

---

68. Despite the conviction rates, authoritative studies show that blacks and other racial minorities are less involved in crack use than whites. According to the National Institute on Drug Abuse, over 2.4 million whites have used crack, as opposed to 990,000 blacks and 348,000 Hispanics. National Institute on Drug Abuse ("NIDA"), *National Household Survey on Drug Abuse* (Nov. 20, 1992) at 38–39. In other words, the NIDA statistics show that of all individuals who have ever used crack in the United States, 64.4% are white, 26.2% are black, and 9.2% are Hispanic. In the past year before the survey, 540,000 whites used crack, as opposed to 334,000 blacks and 105,000 Hispanics. *Id.* at 38–39.

major traffickers which would consequently reduce the existence of crack as a derivative product. Without cocaine, there could be no crack.

However, both national and local statistical data do not show that the prosecution is targeting the upper echelons in the drug trade. Few kingpins are prosecuted. Review of the cases that have been prosecuted in this district reflects a clear pattern of disparate impact. Out of 57 convictions in the Eastern District of Missouri, 55 of the defendants were black, one was white, one was Hispanic, and not one kingpin among them. Three of the 56 defendants were jointly charged with having 944 grams, three others had 454 grams between them, and one had 451 grams. The other 50 had a total of less than 2000 grams, averaging less than 40 grams each. Eight defendants had less than 10 grams. Five of them had less than a gram, barely enough to detect or to utilize. The total amount of crack cocaine for 56 of the 57 defendants (the amount for one defendant was not determined) was less than 4,000 grams. Powder cocaine is usually imported into this country by boats, trucks, and planes, and in huge quantities. Kingpin dealers are then able to transport the drug in brick-like packages referred to as "kilos." A kilogram weighs 1,000 grams. Thus, it appears clear that the removal of this small quantity of drugs would hardly reduce the supply of crack cocaine in St. Louis or impede its flow.

* * *

… [W]hile the Eastern District of Missouri includes the City of St. Louis with its large black population, it also includes St. Louis County with a white population four or five times larger. Surely if the prosecution were really free of racism, unconscious or not, there would be more than one white defendant convicted for crack violations in the federal courts of the Eastern District of Missouri in three years.

Without explanation, the logical inference to be drawn is that the prosecutors in the federal courts are selectively prosecuting black defendants who were involved with crack, no matter how trivial the amount, and ignoring or diverting whites when they do the same thing.

There may be rational explanations for these disproportionate figures. That is why this Court repeatedly requested the U.S. Attorney's Office to make available its standards or principles for the selection of crack cocaine cases. But the prosecutor refused to divulge this information (an *in camera* submission would have been sufficient), citing prosecutorial discretion. The Court is not sure that it has the authority to demand such an explanation from the prosecutor. But failure to divulge the standards used during 1989–92 raises an inference that unconscious racism may have influenced the decision to severely punish blacks for violations involving their form of cocaine while hardly touching whites who utilize another form of the same drug—both are forms of cocaine.

* * *

THE JUDICIARY

This Court fully realizes the difficulties facing a court when it must modify or vacate a legislative act—especially when the Congress of the United States responds to the demands of its constituency to "do something" about the most pressing problem in America today—crime. This Court is fully aware of the fact that great deference must be given to such legislative expressions and only in the most extreme circumstances may the courts intervene. With full recognition of the limitations of judicial review, this Court, with reluctance, does act. It is the first and only time in more than 20 years of judicial responsibility that this Court has really seriously considered invalidating a federal criminal statute. Only the most extraordinary circumstances compel that action today.

* * *

The anomaly of modern political wisdom today is to recognize that any politician considered to be "soft on crime" will soon wear the wreath of defeat. Therefore, the immediacy of the problem requires expediency. While the fire is burning, no thought is given to the damage caused by high pressure water hoses, nor is there time to build a more resistant house. The Court recognizes all too well the difficulties before Congress, pressured to find a solution to quell the strident voices of citizens confronting crimes so intense in form and frequency, and so they are oblivious to the injustices occurring because of the rush to judgment.

But judges, by their temperament, experience, and exposure, are expected to weigh more carefully both the long and short range effects of policies and laws. More importantly, the shield of the Constitution gives them the insulation to withstand the firestorm of uninformed public opinion on emotional subjects such as crime. The courts have only one yardstick to measure equality — the Constitution.

* * *

The reason why we cannot wait for the congressional modification and changes that the Court believes will occur in time is that the horror of continuing is so very destructive. There are many prisoners serving 10-year sentences for possessing with intent to distribute 50 grams of crack. They are usually between 18–30 years of age and about 90 percent are black. Their absence in such numbers, if continued, threatens the possibility of the ultimate extinction of the black race in America.

It must be noted that the detection, arrest, prosecution, and conviction of these petty drug peddlers consumes so much of law enforcement's time and so many of the dollars of the criminal justice system that it makes it more difficult, if not impossible, to really stop the cancerous growth of drugs. The huge numbers of young, petty drug dealers serving long mandatory minimum sentences also use precious prison bed space that would better be reserved for the use of violent repeat offenders, the class of persons that society needs to be protected from most of all.

FINDINGS AND CONCLUSIONS

In summary, the Court, after careful consideration, reluctantly concludes that the pertinent sections of 21 U.S.C. § 841 which mandate punishment to be 100 times greater for crack cocaine than for powder cocaine are constitutionally invalid, both generally and *as applied* in this case. The Court finds that there is no material difference between the chemical properties of crack and powder cocaine, and that they are one and the same drug. The Court further finds that this defendant has been denied equal protection of the laws when the punishment assessed against him is 100 times greater than the punishment assessed for the same violation but involving powder cocaine.

The Court further finds that the "symbolic" action of the Congress in raising the original 50 to 1 ratio to 100 to 1 is yet another indication of its irrational and arbitrary actions, and further evidences the failure of the Congress to narrowly tailor its provisions as required by law in suspect class cases.

The Court further finds that the Congress enacted this law in an arbitrary and irrational manner, without the testimony of adequate scientific and professional advice, and without providing sufficient time for subcommittee hearings and debate.

The Court further finds that the statistics offered by the defendant, both local and national, show that the disparate impact upon blacks is so great as to shock the conscience of the court. Ratios as high as 55 to 1 appear in the Eastern District of Missouri; even greater disparities are evident on the national level. These ratios are apparent in arrest levels, convictions, and the prosecutorial acts which mitigate or eliminate punishment for whites while maximizing punishment for blacks. The Court finds that the actions of Congress and the prosecuting officials were influenced and motivated by unconscious racism, causing great harm and injury to black defendants because of their race inasmuch as whites are rarely arrested, prosecuted, or convicted for crack cocaine offenses.

The Court further finds that the Office of the U.S. Attorney for the Eastern District of Missouri only convicted one white person for crack cocaine violations during the years 1989–92 while convicting 55 blacks and one Hispanic. In the absence of explanation by the prosecutors, these disproportionate figures give rise to a strong inference that only blacks are being prosecuted in the federal courts for crack cocaine violations. Prosecution based on race is obviously discriminatory even if it is occasioned by *unconscious* racism.

INVALIDATION OF THE CRACK STATUTE

Therefore, this Court concludes that the disproportionate penalties for crack cocaine as specified in all of the pertinent sections of 21 U.S.C. §841 violate the Equal Protection Clause of the U.S. Constitution generally and as applied in this case. The Court further holds that the prosecutorial selection of cases on the basis of race is constitutionally impermissible as applied to this defendant in this case.

* * *

ADDENDUM TO MEMORANDUM RE: IMPOSITION OF SENTENCE

Defendant Edward Clary pleaded guilty to a charge of possessing with intent to distribute 67.76 grams of crack cocaine. He was sentenced to a four year prison term on January 26, 1994, prior to the processing of a lengthy legal memorandum which was filed on February 11, 1994.

The statute requiring a mandatory minimum sentence of 10 years for possessing with intent to distribute 50 grams of crack cocaine was coupled with a Sentencing Guideline Table fixing the range of punishment at 121 to 151 months. Had the cocaine been in powder form instead of crack or cocaine base, the Guidelines provided a punishment range of 21–27 months and even included the possibility of probation.

This defendant was 18 years of age at the time of the offense. He had no prior criminal convictions and therefore had a criminal history category of I per the Sentencing Guidelines.

Inasmuch as the Court has invalidated those pertinent sections of the statute fixing the punishment for crack cocaine offenses at a 100:1 ratio compared to powder cocaine, the 10 year mandatory minimum sentence was not applicable. The Court then decided to impose sentence in accordance with the range of the Sentencing Guidelines for powder cocaine, which would be for 21–27 months, with the possibility of probation.

However, the Court believed that there were aggravating circumstances which ought to be considered. Among those circumstances must be included the travel to California to purchase the cocaine and to return with it to St. Louis where he intended to sell it for profit. Because of this forethought and planning the Court departed upwards from the Sentencing Guidelines and imposed a prison sentence of four years followed by three years of supervised release.

United States v. Clary
34 F.3d 709 (8th Cir. 1994)

JOHN R. GIBSON, Senior Circuit Judge.

The United States appeals from the sentence imposed upon Edward James Clary for possession with intent to distribute cocaine base in violation of 21 U.S.C. §841(b)(1)(A)(iii). Clary entered a guilty plea to the charge which called for a ten-year mandatory minimum sentence. After conducting a four-day hearing, the district court sentenced Clary to four years. The court held that the 100 to 1 ratio for crack cocaine to powder cocaine was disproportionate and in violation of the Equal Protection Clause both generally and as applied, and that the selective prosecution of crack cases on the basis of race was constitutionally impermissible as applied to Clary. The United States essentially argues that these issues have been repeatedly decided and there was no equal protection violation or selective prosecution of Clary. We reverse and remand for resentencing in accord with the applicable statutes and guidelines.

* * *

The district court began its factual analysis by examining the role that racism has played in criminal punishment in this country since the late seventeenth century....

The district court also discussed the unconscious predisposition of legislators, and reasoned that although overt racial animus may not have led to Congress' enactment of the crack statute, its failure to account for a substantial and foreseeable disparate impact would violate the spirit and letter of equal protection. Accordingly, it concluded that the statute should be reviewed under strict scrutiny....

* * *

While the government directed the court to evidence that Congress considered crack to be more dangerous because of its potency, addictiveness, affordability and prevalence, the court found evidence in the record contradicting many of the legislators' beliefs. In particular, the court questioned Congress' conclusion that crack was 100 times more potent or dangerous than powder cocaine, referring to testimony that there is no reliable medical evidence that crack cocaine is more addictive than powder cocaine. In light of these factors, the court found the punishment of crack at 100 times greater than powder cocaine to be a "frenzied, irrational response." The court repeatedly stressed that "cocaine is cocaine."

* * *

We believe that this case could well be decided on the basis of past decisions by this court....

In [*United States v. Lattimore*, 974 F.2d 971 (8th Cir.1992)], Chief Judge Arnold carefully examined earlier authority holding that Congress clearly had rational motives for creating the distinction between crack and powder cocaine. Among the reasons were "the potency of the drug, the ease with which drug dealers can carry and conceal it, the highly addictive nature of the drug, and the violence which often accompanies trade in it." *Lattimore* squarely rejects the argument that crack cocaine sentences disparately impact on African Americans.... [W]e observed that even if a neutral law has a disproportionate adverse impact on a racial minority, it is unconstitutional only if that effect can be traced to a discriminatory purpose.... We concluded that there was no evidence that Congress or the Sentencing Commission had a racially discriminatory motive when it crafted the Guidelines with extended sentences for crack cocaine felonies.

* * *

We first question the district court's reliance on "unconscious racism." The court reasoned that a focus on purposeful discrimination will not show more subtle and deeply-buried forms of racism. The court's reasoning, however, simply does not address the question whether Congress acted with a discriminatory purpose....

We also question the court's reliance on media-created stereotypes of crack dealers.... Although the placement of newspaper and magazine articles in the *Congressional Record* indicates that this information may have affected at least some legislators, these articles hardly demonstrate that the stereotypical images "undoubtedly" influenced the legislators' racial perceptions. It is too long a leap from newspaper and magazine articles to an inference that Congress enacted the crack statute because of its adverse effect on African American males, instead of the stated purpose of responding to the serious impact of a rapidly-developing and particularly-dangerous form of drug use. Similarly, the evidence of the haste with which Congress acted and the action it took is as easily explained by the seriousness of the perceived problem as by racial animus.

* * *

We reverse and remand to the district court for resentencing consistent with this opinion.

Notes and Questions

1. Have you ever read a judicial opinion quite like Judge Cahill's district court opinion in *Clary*? Reconsider *McCleskey v. Kemp*, 481 U.S. 289 (1987). Is there any legal basis for Judge Cahill's opinion in *Clary* to stand on? If not, should a district judge strike down a federal statute (and offer such an opinionated view in the process) when higher courts had already clearly upheld the statute?

2. Does Judge Cahill make a compelling argument that the 100 to 1 ratio is terrible public policy and likely racist?

3. Many observers might say that Judge Cahill is correct as a matter of policy but that he dramatically overstepped his judicial authority. Do you agree with this? If Judge Cahill is correct as a matter of history and policy, are you concerned that the judiciary is powerless to change a statute that is having such a disparate and terrible impact on a large segment of the American population?

4. Are *McCleskey v. Kemp* and the cases that have followed it bad jurisprudence? Should it be possible for defendants to raise viable Equal Protection claims by pointing to a disparate impact rather than a discriminatory intent?

5. On remand, Clary's case was assigned to a new district judge. That judge imposed a sentence of 151 months (12 years and 7 months) as opposed to the four-year sentence imposed by Judge Cahill. The Eighth Circuit upheld the 151-month sentence. *See* United States v. Clary, 97 F.3d 1457 (8th Cir. 1996).

6. The district court opinion in *Clary* is not the only one rejecting the inconsistent treatment of crack and powder cocaine. In State v. *Russell*, 477 N.W.2d 886 (Minn. 1991), Minnesota's highest court struck down a 10 to 3 powder to crack ratio as unconstitutional under the state's constitution.

7. The district court opinion in *Clary* and the Minnesota Supreme Court's decision in *Russell* are outliers, however. For more than two decades, courts rejected Equal Protec-

tion challenges to the 100 to 1 ratio. For a list of dozens of decisions rejecting varied challenges to the constitutionality of the 100 to 1 ratio, see Thomas W. Hutchison et al., Federal Sentencing Law and Practice 478–79 (2012).

8. Although Judge Cahill's lengthy opinion was quickly reversed on appeal, it was not completely without impact. As Judge Jack Weinstein has explained, "[t]he fine opinion of the district court in United States v. Clary as well as other judicial and academic views, prompted Congress to act. In the Crime Bill enacted in September 1994, it directed the United States Sentencing Commission to study 'the differences in penalty levels that apply to different forms of cocaine.' The resulting report recommended lower sentences for offenses involving crack." Honorable Jack B. Weinstein, *Every Day Is a Good Day for a Judge to Lay Down His Professional Life for Justice*, 32 Fordham Urb. L.J. 131, 161 (2004).

9. The 100 to 1 ratio became law as part of the Anti-Drug Abuse Act of 1986. Drug and sentencing reformers spent many years unsuccessfully introducing legislation to undo the ratio. As Professor Kyle Graham recounts, reform bills were introduced in 1993, 1995, 1996, 1997, 1998, 1999, 2001, 2002, 2003, 2005, 2006, 2007, 2008, and 2009. *See* Kyle Graham, *Sorry Seems to be the Hardest Word: The Fair Sentencing Act of 2010, Crack, and Methamphetamine*, 45 U. Rich. L. Rev. 765 (2011).

10. Although the Supreme Court never struck down the 100 to 1 ratio as unconstitutional, it was eventually eliminated. In 2010, President Obama signed the Fair Sentencing Act of 2010, which eliminated the five-year mandatory minimum sentence for possession of five grams or more of crack cocaine. Rather than a 100 to 1 ratio, the new law imposed an 18 to 1 ratio. *See* 21 U.S.C. § 841(b).

11. Although the 100 to 1 ratio is no longer in effect, many defendants who were sentenced to long sentences under the old regime remain in prison. Years of tough sentencing policies in both the federal and state systems has led to an enormous number of African-American men being incarcerated. As the next excerpt describes, African-Americans and other minorities are disproportionately represented in prisons, although the degree varies widely by state.

E. Racial Disparities in Incarceration by the Numbers

As should be clear from the previous sections, the war on drugs has had a greater impact on minority communities than white communities. How much greater though? Are matters equally bleak throughout the country? And is the racial disparity improving or getting worse? The numbers tell a heart-wrenching story.

Marc Mauer & Ryan S. King, The Sentencing Project, Uneven Justice: State Rates of Incarceration by Race and Ethnicity
1–15 (2007)

INTRODUCTION

Since the early 1970s the prison and jail population in the United States has increased at an unprecedented rate. The more than 500% rise in the number of people incarcerated in the nation's prisons and jails has resulted in a total of 2.2 million people behind bars.

This growth has been accompanied by an increasingly disproportionate racial composition, with particularly high rates of incarceration for African Americans, who now constitute 900,000 of the total 2.2 million incarcerated population. The exponential increase in the use of incarceration has had modest success at best in producing public safety, while contributing to family disruption and the weakening of informal social controls in many African American communities. Overall, data from the Bureau of Justice Statistics document that one in six black men had been incarcerated as of 2001. If current trends continue, one in three black males born today can expect to spend time in prison during his lifetime. The prevalence of imprisonment for women is considerably lower than for men, but many of the same racial disparities persist, with black women being more likely to be incarcerated than white women.

While the disproportionate rate of incarceration for African Americans has been well documented for some time, a significant development in the past decade has been the growing proportion of the Hispanic population entering prisons and jails. In 2005, Hispanics comprised 20% of the state and federal prison population, a rise of 43% since 1990. As a result of these trends, one of every six Hispanic males and one of every 45 Hispanic females born today can expect to go to prison in his or her lifetime. These rates are more than double those for non-Hispanic whites.

* * *

Highlights of this analysis include:

- African Americans are incarcerated at nearly six (5.6) times the rate of whites;
- Hispanics are incarcerated at nearly double (1.8) the rate of whites;
- States exhibit substantial variation in the ratio of black-to-white incarceration, ranging from a high of 13.6-to-1 in Iowa to a low of 1.9-to-1 in Hawaii;
- States with the highest black-to-white ratio are disproportionately located in the Northeast and Midwest, including the leading states of Iowa, Vermont, New Jersey, Connecticut, and Wisconsin. This geographic concentration is true as well for the Hispanic-to-white ratio, with the most disproportionate states being Massachusetts, Pennsylvania, New York, New Hampshire, and New Jersey; and,
- States exhibiting high Black or Hispanic ratios of incarceration compared to whites fall into two categories: 1) those such as Wisconsin and Vermont which have high rates of black incarceration and average rates of white incarceration; and, 2) states such as New Jersey and Connecticut which have average rates of black incarceration and below-average rates of white incarceration. In both cases, the ratio of incarceration by race is higher than average.

NATIONAL PICTURE: SUBSTANTIAL RACIAL DISPARITY

The American prison and jail system is defined by an entrenched racial disparity in the population of incarcerated people. The national incarceration rate for whites is 412 per 100,000 residents, compared to 2,290 for African Americans, and 742 for Hispanics. These figures mean that 2.3% of all African Americans are incarcerated, compared to 0.4% of whites and 0.7% of Hispanics.

* * *

While these overall rates of incarceration are all at record highs, they fail to reflect the concentrated impact of incarceration among young African American males in particular, many of whom reside in disadvantaged neighborhoods. One in nine (11.7%) African American males between the ages of 25 and 29 is currently incarcerated in a prison or jail. Moreover, the uneven geographic distribution of incarceration in communities of color means that the effects of this situation radiate beyond the individual to the broader community. For example, criminologists James Lynch and William Sabol found that three percent of a single Ohio county's census block groups comprised 20% of the state prison population. This concentration among young males presents profound long-term consequences for employment prospects, family formation, and general quality of life.

Significant State Variation in Rates of Incarceration by Race

As is true for overall rates of incarceration, so too do racial and ethnic rates of incarceration vary significantly by state.... In addition to crime rates, the discretion of policymakers and practitioners in decisions related to arrest, conviction, sentencing, and severity of statutory punishment all play a key role in determining state rates of imprisonment. Moreover, it underscores the importance of where, and for what offense, a person has been convicted.

* * *

... [T]he black rate of incarceration ranges from a high of 4,710 per 100,000 (4.7% of the population) in South Dakota to a low of 851 (0.85% of the population) in Hawaii. Comparing the rates of incarceration for African Americans ... with those for whites ... reveals profound patterns of racial disparity. For example, the state with the lowest rate of incarceration for African Americans—Hawaii, at 851 per 100,000 population—maintains a rate 15% higher than the state with the highest rate for whites—Oklahoma, at 740 per 100,000 population. While more than 1% of African Americans in 49 states and the District of Columbia are incarcerated, there is not a single state in the country with a rate of incarceration that high for whites.

* * *

An examination of the ratio of black-to-white incarceration rates by state illustrates not only the heightened use of imprisonment for African Americans, but also regional differences in how incarceration policies produce disparities. While the national black-to-white ratio of incarceration is 5.6, among the states the ratio ranges from a high of nearly 14-to-1 in Iowa to a low of less than 2-to-1 in Hawaii.

In seven states—Iowa, Vermont, New Jersey, Connecticut, Wisconsin, North Dakota, and South Dakota—the black-to-white ratio of incarceration is greater than 10-to-1.

* * *

Hispanic Rates of Incarceration Higher Than Whites, Less Than African Americans

The national rate of incarceration for Hispanics—742 per 100,000—is nearly double that of whites, but considerably less than that of African Americans.... [T]he range of incarceration rates extends from a high of 1,714 per 100,000 in Pennsylvania to a low of 185 in Hawaii.... More than 1% of Hispanics in seven states are incarcerated, and 16 states have Hispanic rates of incarceration higher than the highest state rate (Oklahoma) for whites.

As with African Americans, there is broad variation among the states in the rate of incarceration compared to the non-Hispanic white population. A comparison of Hispanic rates of incarceration at the state level with those of whites reveals similar patterns of ethnic-based disparity to that between African Americans and whites. The Hispanic-to-white ratio of incarceration ranges from a high of 6.6 in Connecticut to an underrepresentation of Hispanics relative to whites in nine states....

* * *

Racial and Ethnic Disparities Produced in Diverse Ways

As is evidenced by the data presented in this report, there is substantial variation in both the overall rate of incarceration among states as well as the racial and ethnic differential in the use of incarceration. In addition, states with a high black-to-white differential in incarceration rates reflect one of two types of sentencing practices.

- In some states — Vermont, Wisconsin, South Dakota — the more than ten-fold difference in rates of incarceration is largely due to a high black rate of incarceration, double that of the national average.

- Other states — Connecticut, New Jersey, New York, Rhode Island — maintain black rates of incarceration that are near or below the national average, but have white rates of incarceration that are less than half the national average. Thus, an average black rate of incarceration and a low white rate of incarceration results in a high black-to-white ratio.

Conversely, some southern states — Alabama, Mississippi, Georgia — maintain black incarceration rates below the national average, but have a higher than average white rate of incarceration, thereby producing a lower black-to-white differential than other states.

A final note on the black-to-white differentials regards the relative mix of prison and jail populations in the overall data. At a national level, whites are more likely to be incarcerated in local jails (44% of the total population) than prisons (35% of the total). Since jail stays are relatively short compared to prison terms, the collateral consequences of incarceration — separation from family, reduced employment prospects — are generally less severe than for persons spending a year or more in state prison.

* * *

Notes and Questions

1. The Sentencing Project's report contains a lot of statistics including that "[t]he national incarceration rate for whites is 412 per 100,000 residents, compared to 2,290 for African Americans." Is it possible for America to move past its long history of racial tension while numbers like this remain?

2. Consider the following observation from Professor Michelle Alexander: "Although the majority of illegal drug users and dealers nationwide are white, three-fourths of all people imprisoned for drug offenses have been black or Latino." Michelle Alexander, The New Jim Crow: Mass Incarceration in the Age of Colorblindness 98 (2010). Can there be any legitimate explanation for this, or is the entire criminal justice system (perhaps unintentionally) racist?

3. Matters have improved somewhat since The Sentencing Project's 2007 report. With the Supreme Court's landmark decision in United States v. Booker, 543 U.S. 220 (2005), the Federal Sentencing Guidelines are no longer mandatory. And although most federal judges still follow the guidelines, there has been a slow movement toward departing downward to lighter sentences. Just before *Booker* was decided, federal judges departed below the guidelines in 7.5% of cases. The year after *Booker*, the number climbed to 12.1%. And by 2009 judges departed below the guidelines in 15.9 percent of cases. *See* Douglas A. Berman & Paul J. Hofer, *A Look at Booker at Five*, 22 Fed. Sent. R. 77, 77–78 (Dec. 1,

2009). Although small, in the long run these changes will result in a decrease in the prison population. Additionally, the Fair Sentencing Act eliminated the five-year mandatory minimum sentence for possession of five grams or more of crack cocaine. Now, the mandatory minimum applies only if the defendant possesses 28 grams or more of crack cocaine. *See* 21 U.S.C. § 841(b). This marked the first time in 40 years that Congress had eliminated a mandatory minimum sentence. *See* Kara Gotsch, *Breakthrough in U.S. Drug Sentencing Reform: The Fair Sentencing Act and the Unfinished Reform Agenda*, Washington Office on Latin America (2011). The United States Sentencing Commission estimated that about 3,000 defendants would benefit from the sentencing reduction each year, with an average reduction of two years' incarceration per defendant. *See id.* at 7. At the state level, many states sent fewer inmates to prison for new crimes or parole violations in order to cut costs. *See* Nicole D. Porter, *The State of Sentencing 2011: Developments in Policy and Practice*, The Sentencing Project (2012).

4. Partly as a result of the reforms and cost-cutting measures discussed in note 3, the state and federal prison population fell by about 9,000 inmates in 2010. *See* Bureau of Justice Statistics, Correctional Population in the United States 2010, at 7 (2011). This marked the first decrease in the United States prison population in forty years. Is there cause for optimism? Are legislators becoming less concerned about the political vulnerability of being seen a soft on crime? Will the pressure imposed by tight state budgets disappear once the economy improves?

Chapter XI

Informants and Snitching: The Bubbles and Randy Problems

A. Introduction

"They say a police is only as good as his informants."[1]

—Detective Bunk Moreland

The use of informants is pervasive in the criminal justice system. Police often rely on informants to serve as the basis for probable cause. Informants are therefore crucial to starting investigations, procuring search warrants, and turning investigations into convictions. And informants often receive very good deals in exchange for their cooperation. Given the importance of informants, the frequency of their use, and the opportunity for misuse, you might expect that police use of informants would be heavily regulated in the criminal justice system. You would be mistaken however. Courts talk about informants in assessing probable cause and the Federal Sentencing Guidelines take account of informants' cooperation in determining a sentencing range. But, for the most part, the "law" of informants is a free-for-all.

B. The Law and Rules Governing Informants

Informants appear all over judicial decisions. Appellate courts constantly have to assess whether an informant's tip provided enough suspicion to constitute probable cause for an arrest or search under the Fourth Amendment. But are there constitutional rules that govern when and how police can use informants? Are there constitutional restrictions on what informants can be paid or promised in exchange for their service? The answer to both questions is "no." Many jurisdictions and law enforcement departments have very few formal rules of their own that govern informants. And it is questionable whether police agencies enforce the rules they do have. The materials below begin with the most common scenarios in which courts talk about informants: probable cause and sentencing breaks. Thereafter, we turn to the FBI's in-house rules for dealing with informants and an independent assessment of how well the FBI complies with those rules.

---

1. *The Wire*, Season 2, Episode 5, at 27:30 minutes.

Illinois v. Gates
462 U.S. 213 (1983)

Justice REHNQUIST delivered the opinion of the Court.

* * *

… On May 3, 1978, the Bloomingdale Police Department received by mail an anonymous handwritten letter which read as follows:

> "This letter is to inform you that you have a couple in your town who strictly make their living on selling drugs. They are Sue and Lance Gates, they live on Greenway, off Bloomingdale Rd. in the condominiums. Most of their buys are done in Florida. Sue his wife drives their car to Florida, where she leaves it to be loaded up with drugs, then Lance flys down and drives it back. Sue flys back after she drops the car off in Florida. May 3 she is driving down there again and Lance will be flying down in a few days to drive it back. At the time Lance drives the car back he has the trunk loaded with over $100,000.00 in drugs. Presently they have over $100,000.00 worth of drugs in their basement.
>
> They brag about the fact they never have to work, and make their entire living on pushers.
>
> I guarantee if you watch them carefully you will make a big catch. They are friends with some big drugs dealers, who visit their house often.
>
> Lance & Susan Gates
>
> Greenway
>
> in Condominiums"

The letter was referred by the Chief of Police of the Bloomingdale Police Department to Detective Mader, who decided to pursue the tip. Mader learned, from the office of the Illinois Secretary of State, that an Illinois driver's license had been issued to one Lance Gates, residing at a stated address in Bloomingdale. He contacted a confidential informant, whose examination of certain financial records revealed a more recent address for the Gates, and he also learned from a police officer assigned to O'Hare Airport that "L. Gates" had made a reservation on Eastern Airlines flight 245 to West Palm Beach, Fla., scheduled to depart from Chicago on May 5 at 4:15 p.m.

Mader then made arrangements with an agent of the Drug Enforcement Administration for surveillance of the May 5 Eastern Airlines flight. The agent later reported to Mader that Gates had boarded the flight, and that federal agents in Florida had observed him arrive in West Palm Beach and take a taxi to the nearby Holiday Inn. They also reported that Gates went to a room registered to one Susan Gates and that, at 7:00 a.m. the next morning, Gates and an unidentified woman left the motel in a Mercury bearing Illinois license plates and drove northbound on an interstate frequently used by travelers to the Chicago area. In addition, the DEA agent informed Mader that the license plate number on the Mercury registered to a Hornet station wagon owned by Gates. The agent also advised Mader that the driving time between West Palm Beach and Bloomingdale was approximately 22 to 24 hours.

Mader signed an affidavit setting forth the foregoing facts, and submitted it to a judge of the Circuit Court of DuPage County, together with a copy of the anonymous letter. The judge of that court thereupon issued a search warrant for the Gates' residence and for their automobile. The judge, in deciding to issue the warrant, could have determined that the *modus operandi* of the Gates had been substantially corroborated. As the anonymous letter predicted, Lance Gates had flown from Chicago to West Palm Beach late in the afternoon of May 5th, had checked into a hotel room registered in the name of his wife, and, at 7:00 a.m. the following morning, had headed north, accompanied by an unidentified woman, out of West Palm Beach on an interstate highway used by travelers from South Florida to Chicago in an automobile bearing a license plate issued to him.

At 5:15 a.m. on March 7th, only 36 hours after he had flown out of Chicago, Lance Gates, and his wife, returned to their home in Bloomingdale, driving the car in which they had left West Palm Beach some 22 hours earlier. The Bloomingdale police were awaiting them, searched the trunk of the Mercury, and uncovered approximately 350 pounds of marijuana. A search of the Gates' home revealed marijuana, weapons, and other contraband. The Illinois Circuit Court ordered suppression of all these items, on the ground that the affidavit submitted to the Circuit Judge failed to support the necessary determination of probable cause to believe that the Gates' automobile and home contained the contraband in question. This decision was affirmed in turn by the Illinois Appellate Court and by a divided vote of the Supreme Court of Illinois.

The Illinois Supreme Court concluded — and we are inclined to agree — that, standing alone, the anonymous letter sent to the Bloomingdale Police Department would not provide the basis for a magistrate's determination that there was probable cause to believe contraband would be found in the Gates' car and home. The letter provides virtually nothing from which one might conclude that its author is either honest or his information reliable; likewise, the letter gives absolutely no indication of the basis for the writer's predictions regarding the Gates' criminal activities. Something more was required, then, before a magistrate could conclude that there was probable cause to believe that contraband would be found in the Gates' home and car.

The Illinois Supreme Court also properly recognized that Detective Mader's affidavit might be capable of supplementing the anonymous letter with information sufficient to permit a determination of probable cause. In holding that the affidavit in fact did not contain sufficient additional information to sustain a determination of probable cause, the Illinois court applied a "two-pronged test," derived from our decision in *Spinelli v. United States*, 393 U.S. 410 (1969). The Illinois Supreme Court, like some others, apparently understood *Spinelli* as requiring that the anonymous letter satisfy each of two independent requirements before it could be relied on. According to this view, the letter, as supplemented by Mader's affidavit, first had to adequately reveal the "basis of knowledge" of the letter writer — the particular means by which he came by the information given in his report. Second, it had to provide facts sufficiently establishing either the "veracity" of the affiant's informant, or, alternatively, the "reliability" of the informant's report in this particular case.

* * *

We agree with the Illinois Supreme Court that an informant's "veracity," "reliability" and "basis of knowledge" are all highly relevant in determining the value of his report. We do not agree, however, that these elements should be understood as entirely separate and independent requirements to be rigidly exacted in every case, which the opinion of the Supreme Court of Illinois would imply. Rather, as detailed below, they should be understood simply as closely intertwined issues that may usefully illuminate the common-sense, practical question whether there is "probable cause" to believe that contraband or evidence is located in a particular place.

III

This totality-of-the-circumstances approach is far more consistent with our prior treatment of probable cause than is any rigid demand that specific "tests" be satisfied by every informant's tip....

… [P]robable cause is a fluid concept—turning on the assessment of probabilities in particular factual contexts—not readily, or even usefully, reduced to a neat set of legal rules. Informants' tips doubtless come in many shapes and sizes from many different types of persons. As we said in *Adams v. Williams,* 407 U.S. 143 (1972), "Informants' tips, like all other clues and evidence coming to a policeman on the scene may vary greatly in their value and reliability." Rigid legal rules are ill-suited to an area of such diversity. "One simple rule will not cover every situation." *Ibid.*

* * *

Moreover, the "two-pronged test" directs analysis into two largely independent channels—the informant's "veracity" or "reliability" and his "basis of knowledge." There are persuasive arguments against according these two elements such independent status. Instead, they are better understood as relevant considerations in the totality-of-the-circumstances analysis that traditionally has guided probable cause determinations: a deficiency in one may be compensated for, in determining the overall reliability of a tip, by a strong showing as to the other, or by some other indicia of reliability.

If, for example, a particular informant is known for the unusual reliability of his predictions of certain types of criminal activities in a locality, his failure, in a particular case, to thoroughly set forth the basis of his knowledge surely should not serve as an absolute bar to a finding of probable cause based on his tip. Likewise, if an unquestionably honest citizen comes forward with a report of criminal activity—which if fabricated would subject him to criminal liability—we have found rigorous scrutiny of the basis of his knowledge unnecessary. Conversely, even if we entertain some doubt as to an informant's motives, his explicit and detailed description of alleged wrongdoing, along with a statement that the event was observed first-hand, entitles his tip to greater weight than might otherwise be the case. Unlike a totality-of-the-circumstances analysis, which permits a balanced assessment of the relative weights of all the various indicia of reliability (and unreliability) attending an informant's tip, the "two-pronged test" has encouraged an excessively technical dissection of informants' tips, with undue attention being focused on isolated issues that cannot sensibly be divorced from the other facts presented to the magistrate.

* * *

Finally, the direction taken by decisions following *Spinelli* poorly serves "the most basic function of any government": "to provide for the security of the individual and of his property." *Miranda v. Arizona,* 384 U.S. 436, 539 (1966) (WHITE, J., dissenting). The strictures that inevitably accompany the "two-pronged test" cannot avoid seriously impeding the task of law enforcement. If, as the Illinois Supreme Court apparently thought, that test must be rigorously applied in every case, anonymous tips seldom would be of greatly diminished value in police work. Ordinary citizens, like ordinary witnesses generally do not provide extensive recitations of the basis of their everyday observations. Likewise, as the Illinois Supreme Court observed in this case, the veracity of persons supplying anonymous tips is by hypothesis largely unknown, and unknowable. As a result, anonymous tips seldom could survive a rigorous application of either of the *Spinelli* prongs. Yet, such tips, particularly when supplemented by independent police investigation, frequently contribute to the solution of otherwise "perfect crimes." While a conscientious assessment of the basis for crediting such tips is required by the Fourth Amendment, a standard that leaves virtually no place for anonymous citizen informants is not.

For all these reasons, we conclude that it is wiser to abandon the "two-pronged test" established by our decisions in *Aguilar* and *Spinelli.* In its place we reaffirm the totality-of-the-circumstances analysis that traditionally has informed probable cause determinations.…

* * *

IV

The showing of probable cause in the present case was fully as compelling as that in *Draper.* Even standing alone, the facts obtained through the independent investigation of Mader and the DEA at least suggested that the Gates were involved in drug trafficking. In addition to being a popular vacation site, Florida is well-known as a source of narcotics and other illegal drugs. Lance Gates' flight to Palm Beach, his brief, overnight stay in a motel, and apparent immediate return north to Chicago in the family car, conveniently awaiting him in West Palm Beach, is as suggestive of a pre-arranged drug run, as it is of an ordinary vacation trip.

In addition, the magistrate could rely on the anonymous letter, which had been corroborated in major part by Mader's efforts — just as had occurred in *Draper.* The Supreme Court of Illinois reasoned that *Draper* involved an informant who had given reliable information on previous occasions, while the honesty and reliability of the anonymous informant in this case were unknown to the Bloomingdale police. While this distinction might be an apt one at the time the police department received the anonymous letter, it became far less significant after Mader's independent investigative work occurred. The corroboration of the letter's predictions that the Gates' car would be in Florida, that Lance Gates would fly to Florida in the next day or so, and that he would drive the car north toward Bloomingdale all indicated, albeit not with certainty, that the informant's other assertions also were true. "Because an informant is right about some things, he is more probably right about other facts," *Spinelli,* 393 U.S., at 427 (WHITE, J., concurring) — including the claim regarding the Gates' illegal activity. This may well not be the type of "reliability" or "veracity" necessary to satisfy some views of the "veracity prong" of *Spinelli,* but we think it suffices for the practical, common-sense judgment called for in making a probable cause determination....

Finally, the anonymous letter contained a range of details relating not just to easily obtained facts and conditions existing at the time of the tip, but to future actions of third parties ordinarily not easily predicted. The letter writer's accurate information as to the travel plans of each of the Gates was of a character likely obtained only from the Gates themselves, or from someone familiar with their not entirely ordinary travel plans. If the informant had access to accurate information of this type a magistrate could properly conclude that it was not unlikely that he also had access to reliable information of the Gates' alleged illegal activities. Of course, the Gates' travel plans might have been learned from a talkative neighbor or travel agent; under the "two-pronged test" developed from *Spinelli,* the character of the details in the anonymous letter might well not permit a sufficiently clear inference regarding the letter writer's "basis of knowledge." But, as discussed previously, probable cause does not demand the certainty we associate with formal trials. It is enough that there was a fair probability that the writer of the anonymous letter had obtained his entire story either from the Gates or someone they trusted. And corroboration of major portions of the letter's predictions provides just this probability. It is apparent, therefore, that the judge issuing the warrant had a "substantial basis for ... conclud[ing]" that probable cause to search the Gates' home and car existed. The judgment of the Supreme Court of Illinois therefore must be

Reversed.

[The opinion of Justice White concurring in the judgment, and the dissenting opinions of Justice Brennan and Justice Stevens are omitted.]

Notes and Questions

1. Does Illinois v. Gates adopt a test for probable cause that is too weak and easy to surmount? For an example of officers trying to follow the *Gates* formulation (although without specifically referencing *Gates*), watch *The Wire*, Season 3, Episode 12, at 21:00 minutes. Before applying for a warrant to search Avon Barksdale's safe house based on information from a confidential informant, Lieutenant Daniels asks: "what's the corroboration?" When Detective McNulty answers, Prosecutor Pearlman notes that the corroboration only relates to legal activity, not illegal criminal behavior, and is therefore insufficient. Only then does Detective McNulty give up additional information that confirms criminal activity. Are McNulty's additional details sufficient for probable cause? Does this scene show us that the *Gates* test can provide adequate Fourth Amendment protection and is not too easy for police to satisfy? Or are academic commentators correct when they contend that the *Gates* decision "drastically weakened the meaning of probable cause"? Thomas Y. Davies, *The Fictional Character of Law-and-Order Originalism: A Case Study of the Distortions and Evasions of Framing-Era Doctrine in Atwater v. Lago Vista*, 37 WAKE FOREST L. REV. 239, 381 (2002).

2. The *Gates* decision is primarily about the standard for determining probable cause, but it also tells us a lot about how the Supreme Court treats information from informants. What is your sense of the Court's view of the utility and accuracy of informants?

3. How much trust can we put in anonymous informants? Watch *The Wire*, Season 2, Episode 12, at 19:30 minutes. After Bubbles and Johnny are arrested for stealing syringes out of an ambulance, they are placed in an interrogation room and pressured by Detectives Greggs and McNulty. Detective Greggs says "c'mon Bubbs, you got to do better, you want to walk on this." Detective McNulty follows up by asking "How about some murders?" Bubbles is honest and does not make up a story to satisfy the officers. Would most drug users in Bubbles' shoes be so honest? Don't informants—particularly the anonymous informants the Supreme Court sanctions in *Illinois v. Gates*—have tremendous incentive to lie?

4. Subsequent to the Supreme Court's decision in *Gates*, the anonymous informant came forward and said she would have signed her name if she had any idea of the trouble her anonymity would have caused. *See* JOSHUA DRESSLER & GEORGE THOMAS, III, CRIMINAL PROCEDURE: PRINCIPLES, POLICIES, AND PERSPECTIVES 163 (4th ed. 2010). Although we now know the identity of the anonymous informant, how did the Supreme Court and the Illinois courts know it was a real informant? Couldn't Detective Mader or another officer in the case simply have made up the letter? Would the courts have any way of knowing whether the informant was a fake?

5. How much regulation does the *Gates* standard impose on law enforcement's use of informants?

Federal Sentencing Guidelines § 5K1.1

§ 5K1.1. Substantial Assistance to Authorities (Policy Statement)

Upon motion of the government stating that the defendant has provided substantial assistance in the investigation or prosecution of another person who has committed an offense, the court may depart from the guidelines.

(a) The appropriate reduction shall be determined by the court for reasons stated that may include, but are not limited to, consideration of the following:

(1) the court's evaluation of the significance and usefulness of the defendant's assistance, taking into consideration the government's evaluation of the assistance rendered;

(2) the truthfulness, completeness, and reliability of any information or testimony provided by the defendant;

(3) the nature and extent of the defendant's assistance;

(4) any injury suffered, or any danger or risk of injury to the defendant or his family resulting from his assistance;

(5) the timeliness of the defendant's assistance.

Commentary

Application Notes:

1. Under circumstances set forth in 18 U.S.C. § 3553(e) and 28 U.S.C. § 994(n), as amended, substantial assistance in the investigation or prosecution of another person who has committed an offense may justify a sentence below a statutorily required minimum sentence.

2. The sentencing reduction for assistance to authorities shall be considered independently of any reduction for acceptance of responsibility. Substantial assistance is directed to the investigation and prosecution of criminal activities by persons other than the defendant, while acceptance of responsibility is directed to the defendant's affirmative recognition of responsibility for his own conduct.

3. Substantial weight should be given to the government's evaluation of the extent of the defendant's assistance, particularly where the extent and value of the assistance are difficult to ascertain.

Background: A defendant's assistance to authorities in the investigation of criminal activities has been recognized in practice and by statute as a mitigating sentencing factor. The nature, extent, and significance of assistance can involve a broad spectrum of conduct that must be evaluated by the court on an individual basis. Latitude is, therefore, afforded the sentencing judge to reduce a sentence based upon variable relevant factors, including those listed above. The sentencing judge must, however, state the reasons for reducing a sentence under this section. 18 U.S.C. § 3553(c). The court may elect to provide its reasons to the defendant in camera and in writing under seal for the safety of the defendant or to avoid disclosure of an ongoing investigation.

Notes and Questions

1. Unless you have taken a separate course on federal sentencing law, it may be hard to grasp the significance and uniqueness of § 5K1.1. The first thing to notice is that a defendant cannot get the benefit of this sentencing departure without the prosecutor first making a motion to the court requesting the departure. The prosecutor thus has enormous power over a defendant who is cooperating with the government and hoping for a sentencing reduction. Is this kind of power over a criminal defendant a good thing or a bad thing? Does 5K1.1 unfairly pressure defendants?

2. The second important feature of the 5K1.1 departure is that it does not prescribe in advance how much of a sentencing reduction a defendant will receive for her cooperation. Under the federal sentencing guidelines, the two key factors that determine a defendant's sentence are his criminal history and his "base offense level." For example, a

crime may carry a base offense level of 32 and that number can be adjusted upward or downward for a variety of factors. The Federal Sentencing Guidelines provide for an enormous number of factors that can increase or decrease a defendant's base offense level. For instance, one of the most common ways to reduce a defendant's base offense level is under § 3E1.1 if the defendant demonstrates "Acceptance of Responsibility." By pleading guilty, the Guidelines prescribe that a defendant can receive either a two or three-level reduction in his base offense level. The 5K1.1 departure is similar in concept to 3E1.1 in that a defendant is given credit for providing assistance to the government, albeit by informing on other perpetrators, rather than informing on himself. Yet, the 5K1.1 departure does not specify in advance how much of a reduction the defendant will receive by providing assistance to the government. Unlike most other aspects of the Federal Sentencing Guidelines, this matter is left up-in-the-air and (primarily) within the discretion of the sentencing judge. Section 5K1.1 thus encourages the defendant to be extremely cooperative in turning on his former associates.

3. Many states do not have rigid sentencing guidelines. These states use an indeterminate sentencing approach in which judges have considerable discretion to sentence defendants within a wide range. Yet, cooperation and serving as an informant for the government is no less important in indeterminate sentencing regimes. For instance, in Texas, first-degree felonies are punishable by a range of five to ninety-nine years. *See* Tex. Pen. Code § 12.32.

4. Consider the sentencing reductions offered to D'Angelo Barksdale in Season 1 of *The Wire*. Prosecutors seemingly were willing to agree to a deal with no prison time if D'Angelo testified against Avon Barksdale and Stringer Bell. Ultimately, D'Angelo decides to "take the years" and not testify against others. He is sentenced to twenty years. Watch *The Wire*, Season 1, Episode 13, at 58:30 minutes. How can prosecutors in good conscience go from no prison time to twenty years?

5. Watch *The Wire*, Season 1, Episode 7, at 18:00 minutes. Detective Greggs, as a favor to her loyal snitch, helps Bubbles' friend Johnny get out of serious criminal charges. Before agreeing to help, the prosecutor reads Johnny's criminal history saying that he'd been convicted of "dope, coke, dope, theft, dope, loitering, coke, attempted theft, dope, dope, theft, dope, and the charge d'jour possession, to wit, cocaine ...." Despite this extensive criminal history, the prosecutor agrees to probation with ongoing treatment. The deal is so good that Detective Greggs actually asks the prosecutor "that's it?" Bubbles is a very valuable informant, but should the criminal justice system operate this way?

6. Judges' power to reduce sentences for cooperation is not unlimited however, particularly in the federal system. When judges depart downward, including under 5K1.1, they must still do so reasonably. Appellate courts are typically reluctant to overrule district judges' 5K1.1 reductions, but they do police against unreasonable departures. For example, in United States v. Martin, 455 F.3d 1227, 1232–33 (11th Cir. 2006), the Chief Financial Officer of Health South pled guilty to conspiracy to commit mail fraud and securities fraud. Thereafter he thoroughly cooperated with the government's efforts to prosecute other officials. The prosecutor made a 5K1.1 motion based on that substantial cooperation. Although Martin's original sentencing range was 108 to 135 months, the prosecutor recommended a sentence of only 62 months. The judge went even further though and imposed 60 months of probation. The court of appeals vacated that sentence because the judge failed to explain the reason for the extraordinary departure. The trial judge then held another sentencing hearing and this time imposed a sentence of only 7 days! On appeal, the Eleventh Circuit found that dramatic reduction to be unreasonable and transferred the case to a new judge for re-sentencing. Martin was eventually sentenced to three years. *See* Stephen Taub, *Former HealthSouth CFO Gets Three Years*, CFO.com, Sept. 12, 2006.

Office of the Inspector General, The Federal Bureau of Investigation's Compliance with the Attorney General's Investigative Guidelines
64–65, 75–77, 80–82, 90, 93, 96–98, 103–106 (Sept. 2005)

* * *

II. The Benefits and Risks of Using Confidential Informants in FBI Investigations

Since the inception of the FBI in 1908, informants have played major roles in the investigation and prosecution of a wide variety of federal crimes. The FBI's Top Echelon Criminal Informant Program was established in 1961 when FBI Director J. Edgar Hoover instructed all Special Agents in Charge (SACs) to "develop particularly qualified, live sources within the upper echelon of the organized hoodlum element who will be capable of furnishing the quality information" needed to attack organized crime. In 1978, the FBI replaced that program with the Criminal Informant Program. Its mission is to develop a cadre of informants who can assist the FBI's investigation of federal crimes and criminal enterprises. Informants have become integral to the success of many FBI investigations of organized crime, public corruption, the drug trade, counterterrorism, and other initiatives.

Directors of the FBI frequently make reference to the value of informants while acknowledging that they present difficult challenges. In a June 1978 article, Director William Webster stated:

> Not many people know very much about informants: and to many people, it's a queasy area. People are not comfortable with informants. There is a tradition against snitching in this country.

> However, the informant is THE with a capital "T" THE most effective tool in law enforcement today—state, local, or federal. We must accept that and deal with it.

> * * *

> We provide close supervision in the field at the special agent level. We have field and headquarters evaluation of what is going on in respect to our informants. We have inspectors ... who check each field office to be sure there is compliance with our regulations with respect to the use of informants. *And we have the attorney general's guidelines on when, and under what circumstances, we may use informants, and they are scrupulously observed.* [emphasis added]

* * *

III. Significant Requirements of the Guidelines

... [W]hen the FBI formalizes a relationship with a confidential informant, both the investigative benefits and the risks are substantial. Accordingly, the administrative and operational rules and procedures employed by the FBI ensure careful evaluation and oversight of informants and that appropriate expertise from both the FBI and DOJ is employed to evaluate informants who present the greatest risks and benefits to the interests of the government. The Confidential Informant Guidelines prescribe the process by which FBI Special Agents and their supervisors propose, approve, and operate confidential informants. We summarize below the major steps in that process.

A. Suitability Reviews

The Confidential Informant Guidelines prescribe how FBI agents are to obtain approval to evaluate and operate confidential informants. The period during which an individual is evaluated as a prospective informant is called the "Suitability Inquiry Period." During this period, the Guidelines require that a case agent proposing to operate a confidential informant complete an Initial Suitability Report & Recommendation (ISR&R). The ISR&R addresses 17 different factors, including the person's age, alien status, and the following particulars:

a. whether the person is a public official law enforcement officer, union official, employee of a financial institution or school, member of the military services, a representative or affiliate of the media, or a party to, or in a position to be a party to, privileged communications (e.g., a member of the clergy, a physician, or a lawyer);

b. the extent to which the person would make use of his or her affiliations with legitimate organizations in order to provide information or assistance to the [FBI], and the ability of the [FBI] to ensure that the person's information or assistance is limited to criminal matters;

c. the extent to which the person's information or assistance would be relevant to a present or potential investigation or prosecution and the importance of such investigation or prosecution;

d. the nature of any relationship between the CI and the subject or target of an existing or potential investigation or prosecution, including but not limited to a current or former spousal relationship or other family tie, and any current or former employment or financial relationship;

e. the person's motivation in providing information or assistance, including any consideration sought from the government for this assistance;

f. the risk that the person might adversely affect a present or potential investigation or prosecution;

g. the extent to which the person's information or assistance can be corroborated;

h. the person's reliability and truthfulness;

i. the person's prior record as a witness in any proceeding;

j. whether the person has a criminal history, is reasonably believed to be the subject or target of a pending criminal investigation, is under arrest, or has been charged in a pending prosecution;

k. whether the person is reasonably believed to pose a danger to the public or other criminal threat, or is reasonably believed to pose a risk of flight;

l. whether the person is a substance abuser or has a history of substance abuse;

m. whether the person is a relative of an employee of any law enforcement agency;

n. the risk of physical harm that may occur to the person or his or her immediate family or close associates as a result of providing information or assistance to the [FBI]; and

o. the record of the [FBI] and the record of any other law enforcement agency (if available to the FBI) regarding the person's prior or current service as a CI, Cooperating Defendant/Witness, or Source of Information, including, but not limited to, any information regarding whether the person was at any time terminated for cause.

... [I]f the case agent is satisfied that the person is suitable, the case agent may register the person as a confidential informant, subject to the field manager's approval. At this juncture, the case agent must document in the CI's files:

- a photograph of the CI;
- the [FBI's] efforts to establish the CI's true identity;
- the results of a criminal history check for the CI;
- the Initial Suitability Report and Recommendation;
- any promises or benefits, and the terms of such promises or benefits, that are given a CI by the [FBI] or any other law enforcement agency, if available to the [FBI];
- any promises or benefits, and the terms of such promises or benefits, that are given a CI by a federal prosecuting office or any state or local prosecuting office, if available to the [FBI]; and
- all information that is required to be documented in the CI's files pursuant to the CI Guidelines.

* * *

C. Authority to Engage in Otherwise Illegal Activity (OIA)

The Confidential Informant Guidelines permit the FBI to authorize confidential informants to engage in activities that would otherwise constitute crimes under state or federal law if engaged in by someone without such authorization. Such conduct is termed "otherwise illegal activity" or "OIA."

There are two types, or levels, of OIA: "Tier 1 OIA" and "Tier 2 OIA." Tier I OIA, the most serious, is defined as any activity that would constitute a misdemeanor or felony under federal, state, or local law if engaged in by a person acting without authorization and that involves the commission or the significant risk of the commission of certain offenses, including acts of violence; corrupt conduct by senior federal, state, or local public officials; or the manufacture, importing, exporting, possession, or trafficking in controlled substances of certain quantities. "Tier 2 OIA" is defined as any other activity that would constitute a misdemeanor or felony under federal, state, or local law if engaged in by a person acting without authorization.

Both Tier 1 and Tier 2 OIA must be authorized in advance, in writing, for a specified period not to exceed 90 days. Tier 1 OIA must be approved by an FBI SAC and the "appropriate Chief Federal Prosecutor," typically the U.S. Attorney in the district that is participating in the investigation utilizing the CI. Tier 2 OIA may be approved by a senior FBI field manager (usually an Assistant Special Agent in Charge (ASAC) or a Supervisory Special Agent (SSA)), but does not require the approval of the U.S. Attorney. The Guidelines state that the FBI is never permitted to authorize a CI to participate in an act of violence, obstruction of justice, or other enumerated unlawful activities.

* * *

Before either level of OIA may be authorized, the authorizing official must make certain findings as to why it is necessary for the CI to engage in the OIA and assess whether the benefits to be obtained from the FBI's authorization outweigh the risks. Specifically, the FBI must make a finding, documented in the CI's file, that the authorization for the CI to engage in the Tier 1 or Tier 2 OIA

(i) is necessary either to

(A) obtain information or evidence essential for the success of an investigation that is not reasonably available without such authorization, or

(B) prevent death, serious bodily injury, or significant damage to property, and

(ii) that in either case the benefits to be obtained from the CI's participation in the Tier 1 or Tier 2 OIA outweigh the risks.

If the OIA is approved, at least one FBI agent and an alternate agent must review special written instructions with the CI that the CI must sign or initial and date the form. The instructions must address the limits of the authority, the specific conduct authorized, the time period specified, prohibitions on certain behavior, including acts of violence and obstruction of justice, and the consequences to the CI of operating outside the authority granted. In addition, if the OIA is extended past the initial authorized time period, the informants must receive and sign the instructions pertaining to the OIA every 90 days.

* * *

V. The OIG Review of the FBI's Compliance with the Confidential Informant Guidelines

To test compliance with key provisions of the Informant Guidelines in the investigative files we reviewed, we selected a judgmental sample of 120 individual confidential informant files from 12 FBI field offices we visited between June and August 2004. The CI files we reviewed fit into at least one of four categories: long-term CIs, CIs authorized to perform otherwise illegal activity, privileged or media-affiliated CIs, and CIs who are not reviewed at FBI Headquarters....

* * *

VI. Compliance Findings

Overall, we found one or more Guidelines deficiencies in 104 of the 120 confidential informant files, or 87 percent of those we examined. The deficiencies included failure to document the agent's evaluation of one or more suitability factors in the initial or continuing suitability evaluations, failure to give the required instructions to CIs or to do so at the required intervals, failure to obtain proper authority to permit CIs to engage in otherwise illegal activities, issuance of retroactive approvals of otherwise illegal activities, failure to report unauthorized illegal activity in accordance with the Guidelines, and failure to document deactivation of CIs.

* * *

A. Initial and Continuing Suitability Reviews

Of the 120 CI files we reviewed, 44 required an Initial Suitability Report & Recommendation (ISR&R) during the period of our review. Of those 44 CI files, we found that:

- 15 of the 44 files, or 34 percent, did not contain documentation of at least 1 required suitability factor;
- the most frequently omitted suitability factors were the extent to which the CI's information or assistance could be corroborated (missing in 12 files); the extent to which the CI's information or assistance would be relevant to a present or potential investigation or prosecution and the importance of such an investigation or prosecution (missing in 11 files); and the nature of any relationship between the CI and the subject or target of an existing or potential investigation or prosecution (missing in 11 files);

* * *

Case agents who operate confidential informants are also required to make *continuing* suitability reviews at least annually and to forward their reports and recommendations to their field managers for approval....

We found that 2 of the 12 field offices we visited did not require case agents to perform the continuing suitability reviews required by ... the Confidential Informant Guidelines. Of the 120 CI files we reviewed, 96 required a Continuing Suitability Report & Recommendation.... [yet] we found that 57 of the 96 files, or 59 percent, did not contain 1 or more required [continuing suitability reviews].

* * *

C. Authority to Engage in Otherwise Illegal Activity (OIA)

... [U]nder some circumstances the Confidential Informant Guidelines permit confidential informants to engage in otherwise illegal activity (OIA). The most serious OIA is called "Tier 1 OIA," which must be authorized by the FBI Assistant Director in Charge or Special Agent in Charge of the Field Office or Division and the appropriate U.S. Attorney in advance and in writing. The authorization is effective for a period not to exceed 90 days. "Tier 2 OIA" may be authorized for a period not to exceed 90 days by a senior field manager and must also be in writing.

In order to be authorized to engage in either Tier 1 or Tier 2 OIA, the informant must be a fully operational CI, a status obtained only when the CI is "registered" at the conclusion of a successful suitability inquiry period. In addition, the authorizing official must make a finding that the authorization to engage in OIA is necessary either to obtain information or evidence that is essential for the success of the investigation and that is not reasonably available without the authorization, or to prevent death, serious bodily injury, or significant property damage, and that, in either case, the benefits to be obtained from the informant's participation in OIA outweigh the risks.

* * *

We surveyed Confidential Informant Coordinators to see if they believed case agents in their field offices were complying with the Guidelines' requirement to obtain the informant's written acknowledgement of instructions relating to authority to engage in otherwise illegal activity. Only 52 percent of the Coordinators reported that they believed agents in their field offices obtain the required written acknowledgements in all cases, and only 36 percent said they believed that agents in their field offices are conveying in all cases the instructions indicating that the CIs have not been authorized to engage in any criminal activity and have no immunity from prosecution.

* * *

We reviewed 25 informant files in which OIA was authorized, of which 2 included Tier 1 OIA and 23 were exclusively Tier 2 OIA. With respect to the Guidelines' requirements governing the authorization of OIA, our findings confirmed the views of the Confidential Informant Coordinators. We found that 15 of the 25 files, or 60 percent, reflected compliance deficiencies. The deficiencies included OIA authorizations for sources who had not yet been registered as CIs, retroactive authorizations of OIA, authorizations of Tier 2 OIA that should have been denominated as Tier 1 and therefore required DOJ approval, insufficiently specific descriptions of OIA, failures to obtain the CI's written acknowledgment of instructions regarding the limits of OIA activities, and failures to provide required instructions.

Four of the 25 files, or 16 percent, indicate that sources were authorized by field supervisors to engage in Tier 2 OIA from 45 to 154 days before the source was approved for conversion to a fully operational confidential informant. Although these four files do not indicate when the OIA was actually performed, we consider this to be a Guidelines violation since the period during which the CI was authorized to engage in OIA preceded the period for which the CI was eligible to engage in OIA under the Guidelines. The Tier 2 OIA that was authorized for these sources included making controlled buys of cocaine, paying over $10,000 to establish the CI's credibility in a racketeering investigation, and engaging in conspiratorial conversations relating to a drug trafficking investigation.

* * *

We also identified two instances in which the FBI failed to obtain proper authorization from the U.S. Attorney with respect to Tier 1 OIA. Both matters originated in the same field office, and the OIA in question was treated as Tier 2. In the first case, the FBI's authorization included conspiracy to commit robbery, a crime of violence. In the second case, the risk of violence justified the Tier 1 status.

* * *

Notes and Questions

1. The Attorney General's Confidential Informant Guidelines are actually much longer and more detailed than the excerpt above. The full guidelines include topics such as how to instruct informants, how to handle unauthorized illegal activity committed by informants, and the process of deactivating informants. Are you surprised by how detailed the FBI's informant guidelines are?

2. Do the informant procedures in *The Wire* in any way resemble the FBI's approach to handling informants?

3. The lack of informant guidelines in *The Wire* is not surprising. The Attorney General's Guidelines are much stricter and more detailed than other jurisdictions' guidelines. Indeed, many jurisdictions have virtually no restrictions on informant use whatsoever. *See* Michael L. Rich, *Brass Rings and Red-Headed Stepchildren: Protecting Active Criminal Informants*, 61 Am. U. L. Rev. 1433, 1479 (2012).

4. Are such strict procedures for the use of informants necessary? Are they feasible in the kind of investigations that Detectives McNulty, Bunk, and Greggs (and their real-life counterparts) conduct in homicide and drug distribution cases?

5. Do you think officers comply with the guidelines in the real world? For instance, the FBI guidelines require officers to register their confidential informants, including providing a photograph, a criminal history, and a list of promises and benefits. Is it easy for police to circumvent these rules? Watch *The Wire*, Season 2, Episode 7, at 48:00 minutes, and Season 2, Episode 8, at 22:15 minutes, in which Detectives Herc and Carver create a fake informant named "Fuzzy Dunlop" who they can claim provides probable cause and which they can use to embezzle cash from the police department.

6. As the Office of Inspector General Report details (in much greater detail than excerpted above), the FBI has failed to comply with the Attorney General's guidelines in an enormous percentage of cases. If elite FBI agents cannot comply (or choose not to comply) with the guidelines, is it likely that local police officers in Baltimore or other major cities will comply with their own internal procedures?

7. Are you surprised to read that law enforcement can pay informants thousands of dollars to buy drugs or otherwise "establish their credibility" with the targets of investiga-

tions? How about the fact that the FBI and other agents sworn to uphold the law can authorize informants to commit a wide variety of illegal activities in the name of providing valuable information?

C. The Ethics and Ramifications of the Use of Informants

Informants—particularly confidential informants—are very valuable to law enforcement. As Detective Greggs tells McNulty, "ain't nothing like a good C.I." *The Wire*, Season 1, Episode 5, at 15:30 minutes. But are informants getting as much out of the deal as the police? Surely some informants are making out extremely well. By snitching on their fellow criminals, informants get favorable plea bargains and shorter prison sentences. Some informants even manage to avoid being charged with crimes at all because of the information they provide to the police. And then there are the informants who snitch in exchange for money. The author of this textbook once met an undercover narcotics officer whose department was paying a confidential informant more than $300,000 per year because of the invaluable information the informant was providing. It is quite clear that some informants benefit tremendously by snitching. But do most informants benefit? And does snitching help or harm the larger community where the informant lives? Finally, should we be particularly concerned about using certain groups of people—such as juveniles—as snitches? The materials below look beyond the technical legal rules of informants to consider the ethical and social ramifications of police use of informants.

Alexandra Natapoff, Snitching:
The Institutional and Communal Consequences
73 University of Cincinnati Law Review 645 (2004)

I. Introduction

The use of criminal informants in the U.S. justice system has become a flourishing socio-legal institution unto itself. Characterized by secrecy, unfettered law enforcement discretion, and informal negotiations with criminal suspects, the informant institution both embodies and exacerbates some of the most problematic features of the criminal justice process. Every year tens of thousands of criminal suspects—many of them drug offenders concentrated in high-crime inner-city neighborhoods—informally negotiate away liability in exchange for promised cooperation. Law enforcement meanwhile recruits and relies on ever greater numbers of criminal actors in making basic decisions about investigations and prosecutions. While this marriage of convenience is fraught with peril, it is nearly devoid of judicial or public scrutiny as to the propriety, fairness, or utility of the deals being struck. Moreover, it both exemplifies and exacerbates existing problems with transparency, accountability, regularity, and fairness within the criminal process.

The caustic effects of the informant institution are not limited to the legal system; they can have a disastrous impact in low-income, high-crime, urban communities where a high percentage of residents—predominantly young African American men—are in contact with the criminal justice system and therefore potentially under pressure to snitch. The law enforcement practice of relying heavily on snitching creates large numbers of criminal informants who are communal liabilities. Snitches increase crime and threaten social organization, interpersonal relationships, and socio-legal norms in their home communities, even as they are tolerated or under-punished by law enforcement because they are useful.

The global contours of the informant institution are reflected both in the ways that the informant is created and managed by the government and how the informant in turn interacts with his community. The following example represents a classic drug informant scenario drawn from actual cases:

> Drew, a low-level drug dealer who is also an addict, is confronted by [federal Drug Enforcement Agency (DEA)] agents and local police on his way to make a deal. They offer to refrain from pressing charges at that moment in exchange for information and the active pursuit of new suspects. Drew agrees, immediately provides the name of one of his suppliers to whom he owes money, and is released. As an informant, Drew's investigative activities require him to meet with his police officer handler every two weeks to provide information and make a controlled buy every month or so. In the meantime, with his handler's knowledge, Drew continues to consume drugs and carries a gun illegally. Unbeknownst to (but suspected by) his handler, he skims drugs from his controlled buys and continues to deal drugs on the side. In the course of his cooperation he also provides the police with truthful incriminating information about a competing drug dealer, his landlord to whom he owes rent, and his girlfriend's ex-boyfriend whom he dislikes. The police arrest all three. When Drew is arrested in another jurisdiction for simple drug possession, his handler calls the prosecutor and those charges are dropped.

As the example demonstrates, not only do informants' past crimes go unpunished, but authorities routinely tolerate the commission of new crimes — both authorized and unauthorized — as part of the cost of maintaining an active informant. The phenomenon is particularly troubling because it represents under-enforcement and tolerance of criminality in high-crime communities. Authorities may also indirectly ratify the interests of informants when those informants provide information selectively and in self-serving ways. This scenario is repeated over and over, both within the criminal system and in the community, creating dynamics of scale. Within the system, the effect is a shift in the adjudicatory process whereby police and prosecutors informally adjudicate the criminal liability of informants based primarily on expediency and investigative usefulness. Within the community, large numbers of criminals remain active who, due to their role as government informer, obtain some degree of immunity (and, arguably, arrogance) even as they continue their antisocial behavior.

Many aspects of this type of informant practice are in obvious tension with principles of public accountability, consistency, predictability, and other "rule of law"-type precepts. In its most extreme form, bare-knuckled negotiations between suspect and agent take place unsupervised and unrecorded, without judicial or public review or even the presence of counsel. Informants consistently are treated differently from other equally culpable defendants, and informants themselves are routinely treated inconsistently. Similarly situated informants often receive widely disparate rewards for comparable cooperation. Although written cooperation agreements resemble contracts and formal plea bargains, they are generally vague and open-ended. The earlier and more informal the negotiation, the less is written down. Informant deals thus have become an all too common way of circumventing more formal adjudications of guilt and penalty, or even the counsel-dominated process of plea bargaining. Indeed, the use of informants can be seen as a relaxation of public, rule-bound decision-making in the most practical sense: secret negotiations lead to the application of secret rules in which crimes are forgiven, or resurrected, by state actors without defense counsel, judicial review, or public scrutiny.

The legal literature on snitching has not addressed its potential impact on high-crime, low-income communities in which the practice is common. The omission is glaring if only because of the potential scale of the phenomenon. Given rates of criminal involvement for some young black male populations at fifty percent or more, the predominance of drug-related arrests, and the pervasiveness of informant use in drug enforcement, the logical conclusion is that these communities are being infused with snitches and that informing has become part of the fabric of life. Active informants impose their criminality on their community, while at the same time compromising the privacy and peace of mind of families, friends, and neighbors. Informants also are a vivid reminder that the justice system does not treat suspects evenhandedly and may even reward antisocial or illegal behavior. In this scheme, the individual willing to sacrifice friends, family, and associates fares better than the loyalist; the criminal snitch is permitted to continue violating the law even as those on whom he snitches are punished.

Sociological studies have documented the harmful impact that pervasive informant presence can have on communities and individuals. In the context of poor, urban, American communities already suffering from high crime, reduced personal security, and distrust of law enforcement, the informant institution may function as a destructive social policy in ways that are not commonly recognized.

This Article is organized into five parts. Part II describes key features of the informant institution: it outlines the classic informant practice, surveys the limited public data on the scope and nature of the practice, describes the pervasive secrecy that surrounds the institution, and raises some theoretical difficulties with classic utilitarian justifications for the practice. This Part is not intended as an exhaustive description of informant practices; rather, it aims to identify the key features of the institution that render it systemically problematic in light of the analyses below.

* * *

II. The Informant Institution

* * *

B. Data on the Informant Institution

The informant institution is one of the most secretive aspects of the criminal justice system. Data on its key aspects simply do not exist. How many informants are there? What percentage of suspects become informants? How many are "flipped" without ever being arrested or formally charged? How many arrests or solved cases are due to informant tips? What types of crimes are tolerated when committed by active informants? We can only answer such questions partially and indirectly, based on general principles and the small percentage of informants who actually surface either because they eventually come to court or because some aspect of their cooperation becomes public.

It is undisputed that informant use is on the rise....

... Police and prosecutors rely on cooperation as a way of managing new suspects, conducting investigations, and resolving cases in court. Courts in turn see an increasing number of cases that involve informants, either as witnesses or—because trials are so rare—more often as defendants seeking a reduced sentence based on their cooperation.

* * *

The first clue to the empirical magnitude of informant use lies in the massive drug docket. There were approximately two million drug-related arrests in 2000, representing approximately thirty percent of federal arrests and ten percent of state arrests. Another type of case that commonly relies on informants is burglary, which accounts for another two million state arrests each year.

More explicitly, approximately twenty percent of federal offenders received on-the-record cooperation credit under USSG § 5K1.1, as did thirty percent of drug defendants. Those recorded percentages in turn represent less than half of defendants who actually cooperate: some cooperators receive no credit, while others escape the process altogether by having charges dismissed or never being charged at all.

Other indicia of informant use can be gleaned from warrant statistics. The San Diego Search Warrant Project found that the majority of the approximately 1,000 search warrants issued in 1998 were targeted to inner-city zip codes and that eighty percent of those warrants relied on a confidential informant. Studies in Atlanta, Boston, San Diego, and Cleveland produced comparable results, finding that 92 percent of the 1,200 federal warrants issued in those cities relied on an informant. It thus is reasonable to conclude that informants are involved in a high percentage of the hundreds of thousands of search warrants issued in inner-city communities every year.

Finally, additional factors suggest that standard data collection efforts are insufficient to determine the actual number of informants. Police jealously guard the identities of their informants, often failing to reveal that an informant has contributed to a case. Police and prosecutors will sometimes go so far as to drop cases or agree to reduced charges in efforts to maintain the confidentiality of informants who contributed to the investigation. In sum, the data suggest that there are hundreds of thousands of informants at any given moment, that informant use is concentrated around, although by no means limited to, drug enforcement in inner-city communities, and that public records severely understate the extent to which informants are used throughout the criminal process.

* * *

III. Doctrinal Problems with Informant Use

* * *

The Impact of Informant-Dependence on Law Enforcement

* * *

"You're only as good as your informant," explained the police officers to the sociology professor. "Informers are running today's drug investigations, not the agents," complained a twelve-year veteran of the DEA. "[A]gents have become so dependent on informers that the agents are at their mercy." "I can't tell you the last time I heard a drug case of any substance in which the government did not have at least one informant," related District Judge Marvin Shoob. "Most of the time, there are two or three informants, and sometimes they are worse criminals than the defendant on trial." Even prosecutors complain: "These [drug] cases are not very well investigated.... [O]ur cases are developed through cooperators and their recitation of the facts.... Often, in DEA, you have little or no follow up so when a cooperator comes and begins to give you information outside of the particular incident, you have no clue if what he says is true...." Another prosecutor revealed that "the biggest surprise is the amount of time you spend with criminals. You spend most of your time with cooperators. It's bizarre."

* * *

In relying on snitches, police and prosecutors receive information about the community of that informant, thereby ensuring a concentration of resources directed not by independent law enforcement decision, but by the identity and choices of the informant. To put it another way, snitches can only snitch on people they know. They are unlikely to know people outside their community or socio-economic group. The use of snitches thus becomes a kind of focusing mechanism guaranteeing that law enforcement will expend its resources in the snitch's community whether or not the situation there independently warrants it.... This is a particularly troubling development in the context of the war on drugs, which has led to disproportionate levels of drug-related arrests and law enforcement presence in black communities. The possibility arises that the concentration of law enforcement resources in black communities flows in part from law enforcement overdependence on informants.

* * *

By relying on informant tips in making their own investigative and prosecutorial decisions, police and prosecutors often inadvertently validate the interests of the informants who provide the information. When informants snitch on competitors or other enemies, the state effectively places its power at the disposal of criminals. The question is not whether those competitors and enemies are guilty: they often are. But the integrity of law enforcement discretion turns heavily on how the system selects among a vast pool of potentially culpable targets. Indeed, it is the quintessential role of the prosecutor to choose what crimes are to be prosecuted and how, in a way that validates broad public values of fairness and efficiency. The more reliant police and prosecutors become on snitches in the selection process, the more this aspect of the system's integrity is compromised.

* * *

IV. Community Harms

* * *

A. African American Community Vulnerability

Poor black urban communities suffer from a wide range of problems that make them likely loci of informant activity. First and foremost is the high rate of criminal exposure of African American men. Nationally, one in three black men between the ages of 20 and 29 are under some form of court supervision at any given time, while in poor urban neighborhoods the percentage can reach fifty percent or more. The nature of criminal involvement is also heavily weighted toward drug offenses, the type of offense most often associated with informant use. In particular, the trend toward high mandatory sentences for common drug offenses makes informing one of the only ways a drug suspect can avoid certain long-term incarceration. In addition, even where the individual's offense is not ostensibly drug-related, as many as seventy-five percent of offenders have a history of substance abuse; they routinely intersect with the drug trade in some way and are therefore potentially valuable drug-crime informants.

In this context, the routine law enforcement practice of pressuring drug offenders and users to cooperate has special significance for poor black communities. With half the male population under supervision at any given time, and with more than half of this group connected with the illegal drug trade, it is fair to estimate that more than one quarter of the black men in the community are under some pressure to snitch. Assuming that thirty percent of those succumb, approximately one in twelve men in the community are active informants at any given time. By way of comparison, at the height of its power the East German secret police—one of history's most infamous deployers of informants—

had 174,000 informants on its payroll, approximately one percent of the entire 16 million East German population.

The communal impact of these informants flows not only from their sheer numbers but from the social disarray and lack of resources in low-income urban communities, and the connectivity between criminal offenders and the communities in which they live. The combination of high rates of poverty, unemployment, single parent households, substance abuse, and involvement in the criminal justice system makes these communities uniquely insecure. Individuals not only lack material and educational resources but also are often related to someone who is incarcerated, a drug abuser, a parentless child, or otherwise needs special support. In addition, residents of high-crime, disadvantaged neighborhoods suffer psychological impacts such as high rates of depression and substance abuse.

* * *

Heavy pressure on large numbers of people to inform is taking place in communities that already are characterized by high levels of personal insecurity, fluid social relationships, and lack of private space. From this scenario several things can be inferred: informants can obtain information easily about a wide range of people; most residents are connected to someone who is vulnerable to law enforcement pressure; and it is common knowledge in the community that people are snitching. Social insecurities are thus being exacerbated by an undocumented but growing informant culture.

B. Increased Crime and Violence
1. Informants Generate Criminal Activity

… [A] central harmful aspect of informant use is the official toleration of crime. Ongoing crimes committed by active informants directly harm the communities in which they live. The crimes may involve violence, drug dealing, substance abuse, and other destructive activities that exact an immediate toll on their surroundings. The informant "revolving door," in which low-level drug dealers and addicts are arrested and released with orders to provide more information, arguably perpetuates the street-crime culture and law enforcement tolerance of it. At the very least, it violates the spirit of "zero tolerance" and "quality of life" community policing policies aimed at improving the communal experience in high-crime communities. Drug trafficking, for example, correlates highly with violence and petty theft, crimes that render the streets more dangerous, depress property values, and may compel those who can afford it to leave.

… For communities already suffering from high crime rates, criminally active informants exacerbate a culture in which crime is commonplace and tolerated.

… [T]he classic utilitarian justification for informants is that they enable the prosecution of certain types of crime that otherwise would be impenetrable to law enforcement, and therefore, that they produce a net crime-fighting benefit. Assuming for the sake of argument that this is true on average across the entire criminal justice system, it cannot be assumed in the context of high-crime urban communities. There, informants may well produce more criminal activity on any given day than they prevent. Informants participate in and facilitate ongoing crimes, generate crime, contribute to the tolerance of crime, and are forgiven for their crimes, all in their home communities. While providing information about an investigation, they are simultaneously participating in, even generating, a wide range of activities destructive to their surrounding community. A given informant, even a useful one, may be a neighborhood problem in his own right, a "broken window" that is tolerated by the authorities while his activities degrade his community.

* * *

2. Increased Gang Violence as a Response to Increased Snitching

Informant use also may cause increased violence within drug gangs and other illegal networks as a mechanism for ensuring loyalty. The use of violence against snitches is neither new nor surprising. Criminal gangs and organizations routinely use violence to prevent snitching and punish informants. More generally, widespread violence against informants has infected communities as diverse as the Palestinian territories and Northern Ireland.

... [T]he fact that drug-related violence is increasing raises the possibility that heavy informant use could be exacerbating violence in high crime areas. If so, this would be an extremely costly aspect of the informant institution.

* * *

D. Harm to Communal Faith in Law Enforcement and the Law

* * *

For high-crime communities, informant use sends problematic messages about the exercise of state power. First, it involves the official tolerance of crime, which can be seen as an abdication of the state's guardianship role in the very communities most in need of protection. Second, it sends the message that criminal liability is negotiable and rife with loopholes for those willing to betray others. In communities suffering from the collateral consequences of mass incarceration, the state-sponsored suggestion that this devastation is based on morally flexible standards adds insult to injury. Third, it institutionalizes secretive official decision-making and an arbitrary rewards system in which similarly situated individuals are treated differently depending on their personal relationships with and usefulness to law enforcement actors. For a population well acquainted with the dangers of unconstrained police authority and discretion, this might well be a fearsome state of affairs.

* * *

V. Proposals for Reform

* * *

A. Increase Openness in Individual Cases

Various commentators have called for increased disclosure of informant information in the context of litigation. Those proposals generally aim at increased fairness for individual defendants. They are appropriate here for a different reason: it is in individual litigation that informant excesses are most likely to be revealed by zealous defense counsel. That mechanism should be strengthened to serve both as an accountability check on the use of informants and a way of making public the extent and manner of informant use. To that end, specific reforms should include increased discovery, reliability hearings, and depositions.

1. Discovery

Defense counsel should have more and earlier access to information about informants, including their complete criminal records, any cooperation provided in or promised in any other cases, copies of any statements made regarding the case, and a description of all promises—implicit and explicit—made by the government. While such discovery is already provided to a limited extent, the government's ability to limit and postpone production of information should be curtailed....

2. Reliability hearings

In Daubert v. Merrell Dow, the Supreme Court held that expert testimony is at once so potentially powerful and so potentially unreliable that courts must act as "gatekeepers" of its admissibility.... [C]ourts should evaluate the reliability of informant witnesses in the same way that they evaluate experts. "Reliability hearings," comparable to Daubert hearings, should be used to help courts evaluate the likelihood that an informant is fabricating evidence or is otherwise so unreliable that his testimony should be excluded.

3. Depositions

Informant testimony is particularly hard to challenge on cross-examination, yet courts rely explicitly, sometimes exclusively, on cross-examination as the primary protection against fabrication and irregularity. Defendants should therefore have the opportunity to depose informants before trial. The more informal nature of depositions and the absence of the jury will permit defendants to expose inconsistencies and fabrications prior to trial in a way that in-court cross-examination does not allow. If depositions are not made available, courts should order them subsequent to or in lieu of reliability hearings where necessary.

B. Increase Democratic Accountability

Informants should no longer be treated as an exclusively law enforcement concern. Legislatures should expressly evaluate the practice and its impact on the judiciary and the community to determine appropriate regulations of the practice. In order to do this, legislatures need information. The following reforms are aimed first at increasing the information available to the legislative branch, and second, at suggesting ways in which legislatures might usefully impose limits on current executive informant practices.

1. Create Public Data

In order to permit legislatures and the public to evaluate the true costs and benefits of informant policies, the extent of informant use must be made public. Like tax information, law enforcement agencies could be required to provide annual compilations of redacted informant profiles, or perhaps aggregate statistics, so that public policies can be made on an informed basis. The types of information to be culled are: the actual number of informants created and maintained by police and prosecutors; the extent to which informants are not being formally charged (and therefore do not show up in public arrest records); the uses to which informants are being put; the number of arrests and convictions that arise, in part or in whole, from informant information; the race, gender, age, and location of informants; and the offenses that are being traded for information.

Although the production of such information would clearly impose an administrative burden on police and prosecutors, it would not jeopardize a single investigation, nor would it prevent the flipping of a single suspect. What it would do is provide a clear picture of the informant institution, its role in the criminal process, the concentration of informants in certain communities, and the types of liability decisions being made.

2. Restrict Informant Rewards

Legislatures should consider restricting informant compensation and lenience. These should take the form, not of mandatory informant guidelines, but rather restrictions on the types of criminal offenses that can be mitigated through cooperation. For example, legislatures could decide that liability for murder, rape, and other particularly heinous crimes could never under any circumstances be reduced as a result of a defendant's cooperation. That would insert a braking mechanism into law enforcement's consideration of using a particular informant if there was a possibility that he might be subject to such charges. It also would send an important expressive message to the public, namely, that certain crimes will not be tolerated even where the defendant is otherwise useful to the government.

Legislatures should also restore judicial oversight of sentencing for informants. The government motion requirement in USSG § 5K1.1 should be eliminated and judicial discretion restored in order to break the prosecutorial monopoly over cooperation-based rewards. Additional bases for departures below statutory minimums should also be created to reduce the pressure on defendants to inform.

* * *

VI. Conclusion

Recent developments in the law have placed excessive weight on the use of informants, damaging communities as well as the legal system. The heavy use of informants undermines fundamental principles of accountability, publicity, and regularity within the criminal system, and may well cause severe social and psychological damage in high-crime, low-income communities of color. It therefore is time to reevaluate the justice system's overreliance on the double-edged sword of the snitch. With better public disclosure, judicial and legislative oversight, limitations on rewards, and careful attention to community needs, the informant institution can be better regulated in order to mitigate the collateral damage that it now inflicts.

———————

Notes and Questions

1. Professor Natapoff highlights the serious problems with using informants. Has she given enough attention to the benefits that come from informants helping to stop crime?

2. Professor Natapoff explains how the mere use of informants may indirectly cause more crime by motivating higher-level drug dealers to murder any lower level gang member who might be suspected of snitching. This was certainly the case in *The Wire*. In Season 1, Stringer Bell ordered the murder of Wallace out of fear that he could talk to the police. In Season 4, Marlo ordered the murder of numerous people for the same reason. Do you think *The Wire* is realistic in this portrayal or does it exaggerate the number of homicides that occur because of snitching or just the risk of it?

3. Watch the opening scene of *The Wire*, Season 3, Episode 5, in which Johnny tries to talk Bubbles out of snitching to Detectives Greggs and McNulty in exchange for money. Johnny says, "there's got to be rules." Do you think Johnny's view is the prevailing view on the street? Put differently, do you think snitches like Bubbles are ashamed of what they do? Professor Natapoff would clearly like to see far less snitching. Do you think that is realistic? Will there come a time when Johnny's argument persuades Bubbles not to snitch?

4. Is there any political appetite for the reform measures Professor Natapoff proposes? If they were adopted, would law enforcement simply find ways to evade many of the reforms she suggests?

Andrea L. Dennis, Collateral Damage? Juvenile Snitches in America's "Wars" on Drugs, Crime, and Gangs
46 American Criminal Law Review 1145 (2009)

Introduction: Where's Wallace?

Sixteen-year-old drug dealer Wallace wants to get out of the Baltimore City drug trade. Orphaned and homeless, Wallace previously dropped out of school and now wants to go back. He's tired of the drug "game" and conflicted about his role in it. He tells this to D'Angelo, his boss and friend. Always supportive, D'Angelo gives Wallace some money to help him get out of the business.

Shortly thereafter, however, Wallace is arrested. Still eager to get out of the game, Wallace tells the arresting officer he is willing to give up information he knows. He identifies three of his drug crew members who were involved in the torture and murder of another teenager. He also explains his role as the one who pointed out the youth to the murderous thugs. To keep him safe before he testifies, the officers take Wallace to stay with his grandmother in the Maryland countryside.

Meanwhile, Wallace's and D'Angelo's bosses, who ordered the teenager's homicide, decide that Wallace needs to be eliminated because he can link them to the crime. When D'Angelo's bosses ask him where Wallace is, D'Angelo tries to protect Wallace. He assures them that Wallace is not a threat because he is no longer in the drug business and has moved out of town.

Out in the country at his grandmother's house, Wallace is homesick and bored. Not knowing that he's been tagged for elimination, he decides to go back to the city projects to ask for his "job" back. When he returns, he is immediately killed by the organization's "muscle." D'Angelo, unaware of Wallace's death, is later arrested by officers after completing a drug run. During interrogation, officers show D'Angelo pictures of Wallace's dead body and accuse him of not protecting his own. D'Angelo is upset but non-responsive to their accusations. Later, when D'Angelo's boss and the crew's lawyer visit him in jail, D'Angelo repeatedly implores them: "Where's Wallace?" He gets no answer to his question.

America has long had an ambivalent relationship with its children, especially regarding criminal and juvenile justice issues. On one hand, society views children as vulnerable incompetents requiring protection from themselves and others. Thus, the government invokes the doctrine of *parens patriae*, meaning the authority of the sovereign to protect vulnerable individuals, to create and maintain juvenile delinquency systems. On the other hand, at times, children are "adultified," i.e., viewed as miniature adults with similar abilities, obligations, and responsibilities. This contrasting view is exemplified when the government transfers juveniles to adult criminal court for prosecution, rather than adjudicating the matter in juvenile delinquency court.

America's "wars" on drugs, crime, and gangs have exacerbated this tension-filled relationship. The government has waged these "wars" to protect the public's safety from these perceived threats. To that end, it exercises its police power to adopt aggressive strategies and tactics to investigate and prosecute crimes. However, these strategies frequently clash with the government's long-standing commitment to protect children, pursuant to *parens patriae.*

One example of this clash is the government's use of juvenile informants in the investigation and prosecution of criminal and juvenile delinquency cases. Within the criminal justice system, a vibrant snitching institution operates to assist the government in its "wars" on drugs, crime, and gangs. Alongside adults, government officials enlist and conscript juveniles — some of whom are engaged in criminal activities and some who are not—to act as informants. As a result of their informant activities, some children have been killed. Others have suffered verbal and other non-physical intimidation or have been shunned by their peers. Even children who were simply suspected of being snitches have been killed.

The use of children as informants has been largely unacknowledged. Regulations of informants generally fail to distinguish between adults and juveniles. Similarly, legal scholarship discussing the use of informants primarily focuses on adult informants. Yet, the concerns respecting the use of juvenile informants are different from those of adult informants and require special attention. Because of their immaturity, underage informants raise special physical, psychological, ethical, and familial concerns.

Wallace's story, though fictional, dramatically demonstrates both the tension between *parens patriae* and police power, and the need for stricter regulation of juvenile informants. Wallace "worked" on the "front lines" in the streets of one of America's poor inner-cities rife with drugs and violence. He was orphaned, truant, and homeless. The government stood to gain substantially from his information and testimony. It would have closed a homicide case and obtained the arrest of several serious criminals long sought by the government. Wallace's motivations for informing were complex. He at once desired to get out of a criminal lifestyle, make amends for his involvement in a murder, and obtain criminal leniency. Without parents and legal counsel, however, his agreement to inform and actions thereafter were unguided and misguided. Ultimately, his decision cost him his street "family" and his life.

The police and prosecutor in Wallace's case, however, gave little weight to the particular vulnerabilities of child informants in comparison to their desire to investigate and prosecute crimes. In assuming a war-like approach to solving domestic social problems, the government abdicated its protector function vis-à-vis children and instead embraced a bunker, ends-justify-the-means mentality. To the government, Wallace was simply yet another crime-fighting weapon, and the government paid little regard to the harms such use posed to his life.

This Article contends that governments should temper the use of juveniles as informants by reliance on the doctrine of *parens patriae*. Doing so requires consideration of the harms that juveniles experience as a result of informing, rather than focusing solely on winning the "wars" for public safety. Consideration of the harms in turn dictates that governments adopt an extremely conservative approach to the use of juveniles as informants, thereby severely limiting and closely regulating their use.

* * *

I. Operating Off the Radar: the Regiment of Juvenile Informants

A. *Mission Defined*

An "informant" or "snitch" is any individual—whether a criminal, witness, victim, or tipster—who provides information to government authorities for use in investigating and prosecuting the illicit activities of another. The subject or target of information may be anyone, including, but not limited to, family members, friends, acquaintances, co-conspirators, or unrelated individuals. A "child informant" or "juvenile informant" is simply an informant who is under the age of eighteen years.

The government relies on child informants in an assortment of criminal cases ranging from the less serious to more serious. On one end of the spectrum, since the 1980s, children have been used to identify retailers who sell alcohol to minors. In the 1990s, the federal government's Substance Abuse and Mental Health Services Administration

("SAMHSA") expressly sanctioned the use of children as informants in the investigation and prosecution of tobacco cases.

At the other end of the spectrum, government officials use juvenile informants to investigate and prosecute more serious matters including gun, drug, burglary, sex abuse, and violent crime cases. For example, a South Carolina law enforcement official publicly acknowledged creating a program — "Gunstoppers" — designed to induce children to provide tips about individuals possessing guns and encouraged other law enforcement agencies to do the same. In Kentucky, a sixteen-year-old sued the City of Covington alleging that law enforcement officers forced him to engage in undercover acts of homosexual solicitation in furtherance of a law enforcement sting operation. He had been involved with drugs. He alleged that he was forced to participate in the sting without parental knowledge or permission and as a result "sustained severe psychological damage."

Some instances of the government using juvenile informants have had deadly results. In California, Chad MacDonald acted as an underage informant in a drug case. His mother unsuccessfully sued the City of Brea Police Department after Chad was tortured and killed by gang members upon whom he had informed. Police had arrested Chad on charges of drug distribution, and he offered to provide information to "correct" his mistakes. His arresting officer asked if he would identify his suppliers in exchange for dismissal of the pending charges. Chad's mother learned of this agreement only after it was made and Chad had already begun to provide information. Chad's mother faced a dilemma: on one hand, she was afraid that Chad would be incarcerated if he did not continue to cooperate, but she alternately feared that the individuals he informed on would seek retribution for his betrayal. Eventually, she acquiesced to the police using him as an informant, hoping that they would protect him on both accounts. To have his charges dismissed, Chad provided information regarding drug dealers and helped set up "drug busts." Eventually, individuals began to threaten Chad. About a month later, gang members tortured and killed him.

Seventeen-year-old Robbie Williamson contacted the City of Virginia Beach, Virginia, police department and volunteered to provide information regarding the illegal drug activities of others. The City accepted Robbie's offer and used him as an informant without obtaining parental permission or completing a background check. Robbie committed suicide after he was threatened by the individuals upon whom he had informed. His mother filed suit against the City of Virginia Beach, alleging claims based on the City's use of Robbie as an informant. The case reportedly settled.

Finally, when Virginia law enforcement officers arrested sixteen-year-old Brenda Paz, she began to inform on the Latin gang Mara Salvatrucha (MS-13), which eventually led to her death. Police arrested Brenda on car theft charges. Despite the relatively minor nature of that crime, she was able to provide information to federal law enforcement agents and police officers from other states regarding MS-13 gang leaders and members whom she had known intimately since she was a pre-teen. Slated to be a witness at a murder trial against MS-13 members, federal agents put her into the federal witness protection program. She did not remain there, however, as she later rejoined her gang family. After learning she had informed on them, MS-13 members killed her.

Ultimately, law enforcement and prosecutors use the information provided by child informants in a number of ways. Government officials may collect the information and place it in an investigatory case file to use it passively to identify other suspects or avenues of investigation or prosecution. More affirmatively, the police use the information for securing or justifying a search or arrest warrant. At the extreme, a child may be expected to perform undercover activities or testify in court proceedings.

B. Recruitment Efforts

Any number of concerns, working individually or collectively, may be influential in a child's agreement to inform. Children are often motivated by internal factors relating to their own criminal activity or victim-hood and external sources such as parents or law enforcement. Often their motivations are mixed and complex.

Parental input can play a factor in whether a child informs. A child who is accused of criminal activity may consult a parent when making decisions about a case, particularly whether to talk to the police. Such consultation offers parents the opportunity to approve a child's individual desire to inform and encourage or instruct a hesitant or unwilling child to cooperate. Some parents, however, will counsel their child not to inform.

Pressure from law enforcement is a significant factor in a child's decision to become an informant. Criminologist Dr. Mary Dodge collected qualitative social science data suggesting that the government's persuasive efforts can be characterized as undue influence, because of either the particular vulnerabilities of children or the nature of the efforts to convince children to inform. A study by law professor Barry Feld provides greater insight into the desire of law enforcement officials to convince juveniles facing criminal prosecution to act as informants and the lengths to which the officers will go to accomplish their goal. In 2006, Feld published a quantitative and qualitative study regarding routine law enforcement interrogation of juveniles sixteen years of age or older in Minnesota. The juveniles had been charged with felony offenses and had waived their *Miranda* rights. The aim of Feld's research was to produce empirical data regarding juvenile competence during police interrogations. The study also revealed, however, law enforcement efforts to recruit juvenile informants. In about thirteen percent of the interrogations reviewed, juveniles were reticent about, though apparently not adamantly against, informing on co-offenders. For those juveniles who exhibited a potential willingness to provide information, the interrogator engaged in a variety of tactics designed to overcome the hesitation.

Feld's study revealed that various types of reward and punishment were used to induce children to become informants. To reward potential juvenile informants, in one case, officers assured juvenile suspects that prosecutors and judges would react favorably if they cooperated and helped recover evidence. In another case, law enforcement offered an immediate release from pre-trial detention if the juvenile assisted. To punish a reticent juvenile informant, law enforcement threatened the juvenile with adult criminal charges. Even more extreme is the case involving an officer who threatened to detain the juvenile's sister if he did not cooperate with the investigation. Law enforcement pressure may be exerted in a more benign way. For example, in response to a juvenile's hesitation about providing information, an interrogator in Feld's study advised the juvenile that friendship should be put aside, that the juvenile had to take care of himself first because no one else would, and that failing to cooperate could result in more severe consequences for the juvenile.

The government also incentivizes children to inform by offering monetary payment for their information. For example, in 1996, Reuben Greenberg, then Chief of Police of the Charleston South Carolina Police Department, spoke publicly regarding his agency's efforts to reduce crime committed by and against juveniles. Among other programs, he described the Gunstoppers Program. Gunstoppers was a gun reporting program that provided one hundred dollars to individuals who provided law enforcement with detailed information regarding individuals carrying guns—a so-called "hot tip." Greenberg admitted the program was aimed at juveniles, whom he deemed "the greatest snitches in the world.... [Y]ou tell them they are going to get a hundred bucks, then they become super snitches with respect to other kids having guns and so forth." The juveniles wanted immediate compensation, so law enforcement developed a system to compensate them the same day they reported a hot tip.

Intangible personal desires can also factor into a child's reason for informing. Children are more likely than adults to engage in thrill-seeking behaviors, owing to decreased risk aversion. Such thrill-seeking may explain why juvenile informants who are not involved in criminal activity volunteer to act as informants. Moreover, redemption and the desire to change one's life may play a role in the decision. Thus, for example, the government suggested that Brenda Paz willingly informed in order to turn her life around and leave MS-13. A juvenile may also inform to avoid law enforcement retribution—that is, to keep law enforcement from harassing him either at the time or in the future. Finally, some—in particular the tipster, victim, or witness child informant—may inform out of a sense of civic responsibility or personal safety.

C. Deployment Levels

The extent to which the government uses juvenile informants is difficult to quantify for a number of reasons. First, law enforcement and prosecutorial communities disagree over whether the practice even occurs, and if so, with what frequency. Some law enforcement and prosecutorial agencies do not admit the practice occurs at all. Others say that the use of children is "negligible." In contrast, others willingly acknowledge that their use is "frequent" or "higher than many think."

More importantly, no government agency tracks the use of juvenile informants. Even if agencies tracked their use, however, government authorities may distort or conceal the number. The fact that law enforcement and prosecutors inconsistently define the term informant contributes to minimization. Some law enforcement officers distinguish the informal use of juveniles for information gathering from the formal use of them as informants by characterizing some juvenile informants as "friends" who voluntarily give information. In exchange, law enforcement may do "friendly favors" for the child (e.g., job placement; buy diapers, find babysitters). Confidentiality also imposes barriers to tracking the government's use of informants. Police are in general loathe to reveal the use of informants, preferring to keep their use a secret. Moreover, the use of child informants may remain concealed within the realm of highly discretionary and confidential juvenile court filings and proceedings that cannot be studied without special dispensation.

Despite the discrepant information regarding the scope of use of child informants, the practice exists in more than just a few, isolated instances. As early as the late 1960s, appellate courts in criminal cases have characterized children as informants. Since that time, opinions referencing juvenile informants can readily be found. Additionally, news reports confirm that their use is more than rare. Beginning in the late 1990s and continuing today, reporters have recounted stories of juveniles who were killed for informing. Finally, recent empirical studies have begun to confirm their more than infrequent use. Professor Dodge's qualitative study was directed at exploring the practice and revealed that it is occurring, although the levels may be debatable, and Professor Feld's data on police interrogation of juveniles revealed quantitatively and qualitatively that law enforcement officers interrogating juvenile suspects seek to convince the juvenile to act as an informant (i.e., "flip" the minor). While Dodge's study was limited in scope and Feld's study was both limited in scope and not focused on studying juvenile informants, it is reasonable to infer from their data that the attempted and actual use of child informants is more than minimal.

The lack of collected data regarding child informants creates difficulty in determining the characteristics of underage informants. Without study, the types of cases involving and endeavors undertaken by juvenile informants cannot be known. Additionally, the demographic characteristics of the group are unclear. The lack of social science studies of juvenile informants also makes it difficult to understand the actual impact of informing on juvenile informants. Further study is needed to develop these types of information.

D. Operating Procedures

There are no national guidelines on the use of juvenile informants by prosecutors. The United States Attorney General's guidelines for federal prosecutors do not specifically regulate the use of children as confidential informants in federal cases. The National District Attorneys' Association has not suggested the adoption of such guidelines.

Like prosecutors, law enforcement agencies as a whole have not established formal regulations on the use of juvenile informants. Some individual law enforcement agencies, however, have adopted regulations. Commonly, these regulations limit the use of children to "extraordinary" or "critical" circumstances, and require parental permission, waiver of liability, or approval by the supervisor of the law enforcement handler. At least one agency's guidelines require juvenile court approval or parental consent for juvenile informants who are granted anonymity or compensation, but the guidelines do not set out specifics for obtaining that approval.

Some jurisdictions have adopted state-wide guidelines particularly addressing the use of child informants. Unfortunately, they are anomalies. First, in 1997, the New Jersey Attorney General issued "Law Enforcement Guidelines on the Use of Juveniles as Informants" to supplement New Jersey's general guidelines on the use of informants. The juvenile-specific guidelines do not apply to underage witnesses, investigative targets, or operatives in tobacco stings, none of whom are considered informants. Further, under no circumstances may law enforcement use a child under twelve years of age as an informant. Law enforcement can use children under sixteen years of age a very limited basis. One exception arises when the "illegal activity is occurring regularly among a group of juveniles under the age of 16." In addition to age, other factors limit the use of juveniles. First, children undergoing drug and/or alcohol counseling may not be recruited. Second, children who have a mental or physical illness may not be used. Third, in recruiting juvenile informants, law enforcement officers may not "make any promises, express or implied, with regard to prosecution without first obtaining the express approval of the prosecutor or his designee." Fourth, a child may not make a controlled buy or act as an undercover operative unless law enforcement has "obtain[ed] written authorization from the county prosecutor, the Attorney General, or their designee." Finally, prior to acting as an informant, both the child and the child's parent must consent in writing, and waive liability.

The second set of statewide regulations came in 1998, when, after Chad MacDonald was killed by gang members on whom he had informed, the California legislature enacted a criminal procedure statute conditioning the use of minors as informants. California's statute defines a "minor informant" as a child who

> participates, on behalf of a law enforcement agency, in a prearranged transaction or series of prearranged transactions with direct face-to-face contact with any party, when the minor's participation in the transaction is for the purpose of obtaining or attempting to obtain evidence of illegal activity by a third party and

where the minor is participating in the transaction for the purpose of reducing or dismissing a pending juvenile petition against the minor.

Essentially, an informant is a juvenile who engages in undercover activities at the behest of law enforcement in exchange for criminal leniency for pending juvenile delinquency charges. A child who simply provides information without engaging in undercover activities is not a "minor informant." Neither is a child whose incentive is monetary or something other than criminal leniency for a juvenile petition. The statute does not regulate these types of informing. California absolutely bans government authorities from using children under the age of twelve years as informants. Children older than twelve years of age may be used only with prior court approval, unless they are involved in a tobacco sting program.

Before ordering that a child may act as a "minor informant," a court must consider the child's age and maturity, the gravity of the offense filed against him, the public's safety, and the "interests of justice." The court must also find that the child is voluntarily, knowingly, and intelligently agreeing to serve as an informant. In addition to consideration of the enumerated factors, the court must ensure several conditions have been satisfied. The court must find probable cause that the juvenile's charged offense was committed; advise the child of the mandatory minimum and maximum sentence exposures; and inform the minor of benefits he is to receive by cooperating. Finally, excepting instances in which the parent or guardian is the target of information, the court must confirm that the child's parent or guardian has consented to the informant activities.

* * *

II. Border Conflict: *Parens Patriae*, Police Power, and Juvenile Informants in the "Wars" on Drugs, Crime, and Gangs

* * *

Efficient and Necessary Crime-Solving Strategy

Law enforcement officers and prosecutors claim child informants are necessary and efficient. They claim that adults cannot penetrate the world of juveniles, law-abiding or otherwise. They suggest that adults cannot comprehend the sub-culture of juveniles, so the need for minors is greater when minors are being investigated. Finally, officials assert that when an adult criminal preys on juveniles or relies on juveniles to commit crimes, only juveniles will be close enough to the adult criminal to have incriminating information. Collectively, these justifications signify the belief that no "practical alternative" to using children as informants is available to achieve successful criminal prosecutions that protect public safety. Consequently, law enforcement officers are simply doing "good police work" when they vigorously recruit juveniles as informants.

Granted, testimonial witnesses are fundamental to the criminal justice system. Without information and testimony from witnesses, many criminal cases would not be solved, and the criminal justice system would come to a virtual standstill. The system's reliance on witnesses is not boundless, however. On occasion, prosecutors prioritize substantially competing interests over protecting public safety. One such instance involves the protection of child sexual abuse victim-witnesses. Children who have suffered sexual abuse can experience additional trauma, if required to testify in court in front of the alleged perpetrator. When handling child sex abuse cases, prosecutors weigh (1) the interest in not causing additional harm to the child by forcing her to testify against the defendant and (2) the desire to protect children and society from the defendant. The balancing is made all the more difficult because the child may be the only witness to the crime, and there may not be other admissible physical or corroborating evidence. The Supreme Court has authorized prophylactic measures aimed at preventing harm to the child victim while testifying in the defendant's presence. In some instances, however, the measure may be ineffective at preventing harm, or even if effective, the prosecutor may nevertheless choose not to call the child to testify. In such circumstances, if the child does not testify, a jury may acquit the defendant or the government may choose to dismiss the case against the defendant. The defendant remains free, possibly jeopardizing public safety.

Juveniles Are Miniature Adults

Some government agents claim that permitting children to act as informants respects the individual autonomy of children, particularly those children who are adolescents or are "mature." This justification suggests that child informants are no different from adult informants, whose use is generally accepted. In support of this rationale, many will point to data suggesting that adolescents as young as fourteen years of age engage in the same decision-making process as adults and are thus competent decision-makers and of equal culpability. Alternatively, in some instances, law enforcement will characterize particular juveniles as street-savvy, criminal-minded, *de facto* adults. It is proclaimed that because children with criminal histories have repeatedly engaged in criminal, i.e., adult behaviors, they should be treated as adults and allowed to inform without limitation.

* * *

The broad-sweeping adolescent maturity claim has been challenged by the Supreme Court. In *Roper v. Simmons*, the Supreme Court, citing scientific data, significantly undercut the rationale for treating juveniles as adults for criminal justice purposes. The Court's holding that invalidated laws authorizing the death penalty for children was premised in part on science demonstrating juveniles' immature decision-making capacity, limited life experience, low risk aversion, increased impulsivity, and emphasis on short term gains rather than a balancing of long and short term behavioral consequence.

Likewise, social science data undercut the claim that, by virtue of their criminal history and experience, some juveniles are as savvy as adults and should be treated as such in the criminal justice system. To varying degrees, juveniles have difficulty adequately understanding *Miranda* warnings to intelligently and knowingly waive their *Miranda* rights. With limited exceptions, they do not adequately understand the utility and import of the rights to counsel and silence. Children do not necessarily understand the, operation of the criminal adjudicatory process. Moreover, prior exposure to the justice system does not necessarily translate to greater understanding of the process. Thus, social science data suggests that even children who have experience with the juvenile or criminal justice system may lack adult levels of understanding regarding the criminal process.

Finally, the adultification of children also stands in tension with the general legal incapacity of children. Arguably, for children otherwise viewed as the equivalent of adults, many categorical, age-based restrictions should fall to the wayside, such as the minimum drinking age, voting age, age for military service, marital minimum age, contracting age, and age for jury service. Instead, regardless of their adultification in the criminal justice context, society maintains that children as a class should not engage in these activities because they are incapable of properly exercising these important privileges and rights.

* * *

Notes and Questions

1. Although not excerpted above, Professor Dennis's article discusses a number of possible solutions to the problem of juvenile snitching. One approach would be to categorically prohibit law enforcement from using juvenile informants. Another approach would be to require prior judicial approval that considers the best interests of the child, particularly physical, psychological, emotional, and developmental considerations. In a final possibility, Professor Dennis explores requiring police and prosecutors to obtain a judicial determination that a mature minor has given informed consent to act as an informant. Do you find any of these approaches compelling? Would they impose too great a burden on law enforcement's efforts to stop gang violence and other juvenile crime?

2. Watch *The Wire*, Season 4, Episode 11, at 24:20 minutes, in which Randy is beaten for having snitched. Then watch *The Wire*, Season 4, Episode 12, at 52:30 and 55:40 minutes in which Randy's house is torched for snitching and his foster mother is critically injured. Finally, watch *The Wire*, Season 4, Episode 13, at 1 hour, 14:30 minutes, in which Randy is beaten in his new group home because of his prior snitching. Is there any realistic possibility that police can protect juvenile snitches? Does the Randy storyline provide a compelling argument that police should not be allowed to rely on juvenile informants under any circumstances?

3. If you support Professor Dennis' last solution to require judicial approval for the use of juvenile informants, should that proposal also apply to other groups? Aren't the mentally ill and the drug-addicted as vulnerable in many cases as juveniles? *See* Michael L. Rich, *Brass Rings and Red-Headed Stepchildren: Protecting Active Criminal Informants*, 61 Am. U. L. Rev. 1433 (2012) (considering such a proposal).

4. The problem of juvenile snitching is particularly prevalent in season 4 of the series. For instance, watch *The Wire*, Season 4, Episode 6, at 24:45 minutes. The vice principal is interrogating Randy about his role as a lookout in a sexual assault. To stop her from calling his foster mother and the authorities, Randy offers to give information about a number of crimes—theft from the teacher's lounge, graffiti, slashing tires, and finally a murder. Can you see how the enormous pressure Randy is under leads him to snitch? Do you think he has any sense of his right to remain silent when questioned by the vice principal? Do you think he has any concept of the ramifications—both to himself and others—that will occur from his snitching?

Chapter XII

Distribution of Resources in an Overburdened System

"Embracing the hard choice. It's one of the burdens of command."[1]

—Mayor Tommy Carcetti

A. Introduction

Many government services are underfunded. Roads and bridges across the country are badly in need of repair. Lines are too long at the Department of Motor Vehicles. Teachers are underpaid. The situation in the criminal justice system is particularly dire, and most Americans do not realize it. A sizeable chunk of Americans have become frustrated with law enforcement when their cars have been broken into or, more rarely, when they have been the victims of violent crime. By and large however, most Americans become more annoyed when they are actually forced to interact with the police and the criminal justice system. Motorists stopped for speeding or charged with misdemeanor offenses often wish the police would just leave them alone. After getting a speeding ticket or being arrested for drunk driving, these citizens likely do not think to themselves that there are too few cops on the beat or that police departments are under-resourced. In fact, however, the criminal justice system is deeply under-resourced. From police on the front-end, to the prosecutors and public defenders who shepherd criminal cases through the system, to the correctional guards monitoring inmates, many parts of the criminal justice system subsist on shoe-string budgets and must cut more with each passing year.

B. Overburdened Police Departments

The Wire paints a vivid and dismal picture of the resources available to the Baltimore Police Department. Throughout the series, officers struggle to make do without computers, functional office space, working patrol cars, surveillance equipment, and—perhaps most importantly to the cops—overtime pay. Is the situation this dire in actual police departments across the country? The answer is, "it depends." In affluent communities with healthy tax bases, police might not have the latest and greatest technological gizmos, but it is a safe bet that their patrol cars work and that they can type their police

---

1. *The Wire*, Season 5, Episode 5, at 21:15 minutes.

reports on actual computers. In other cities—those where budges have been hit hard by falling tax revenues—the situation may be in the ballpark of what *The Wire* portrays. And with the impact of the Great Recession since 2008, funding problems have gotten worse. Consider the perspective of the police chiefs who are in the trenches.

Police Executive Research Forum, Is the Economic Downturn Fundamentally Changing How We Police?
(2010)

* * *

Newark, NJ Police Director Garry McCarthy:

Budget Cuts Are Resulting in More Violent Crime

We are preparing to lay off 167 police officers. We're also demoting 108 supervisors, and 211 civilians are being separated from the agency. It's unfortunate, because we've had a lot of success over the last few years in reducing crime in Newark. And we were way behind the curve....

You can only be as efficient as you can be. This year, I had almost a 10-percent cut in my budget. We were able to achieve that by collapsing bureaus, eliminating jobs, taking away detective stipends, moving people out of positions that weren't crime fighting positions and putting them back in uniform on patrol.

... This year, coming in to 2011, we were tasked with cutting another 12 percent out of our budget, which represents $17 million. We were able to knock out another $6 million by cutting out our traffic division, our mounted unit, our helicopter, everything. That left us $11 million short, and that $11 million is represented in the 167 layoffs, the demotions, and pay cuts for all 108 captains, lieutenants, and sergeants, and the layoffs of more than 200 civilians.

Philadelphia Commissioner Charles Ramsey:

We Expect to Be Down 200 People in a Year

Basically, we have a freeze on civilian employees. However, if there is a critical position vacant, I can argue to get that one filled....

My last two academy classes have been cancelled, and there are no plans to bring anyone in the academy anytime in the near future, certainly not in this fiscal year. So, with our rate of attrition, we should be down over 200 people by this time next year.

* * *

Baltimore Commissioner Fred Bealefeld:

Managing Internal Rifts Is a Balancing Act

... Our more serious staffing shortages are in the uniformed patrol division. And so when you talk to union guys or the rank and file, they're pushing radio cars. They have a solution: disband the warrant apprehension task force or the plainclothes detective squads, and put them back in uniform, and the situation is solved. So internally there are these splits between the "haves" and the "have nots." Last year, our union traded a work schedule for patrol members for furlough days, but the detectives didn't experience those furloughs. Patrol officers' morale is at all-time lows. So we challenge ourselves to find and cultivate the most highly-motivated people to go out and do some of these heavy-lifting operations. It's a very, very delicate balancing act.

Illinois State Police Director Jonathon Monken:

Cutting a Special Unit Brought a Spike in Highway Deaths

Out of a $450-million budget, we've been cut about $40 million over the last two years. I started with nearly 2,200 officers when I came in at the beginning of 2009, and we project we'll be at about 1,750 at the end of the next fiscal year. So we're going to lose more than 20 percent of our operational sworn force to retirements without cadet classes to replace them. And on the civilian side, the only exception we've seen in budget-cutting is for forensic scientists, because we can get funding for that from federal grant programs. Forensics is an area where the public outcry is significant because of backlogs in crime labs.

As a state police agency, we look at traffic fatalities as one way to gauge how we're performing. About five years ago we were at nearly1,450 fatalities a year, and last year was the first year in 88 years that we were below 1,000 deaths. This year we had to cut two-thirds of our motorcycle enforcement bureau to send the personnel back to district patrol. During the three months following this change we had 78 more fatal crashes than the previous year for the same time period....

* * *

Phoenix Chief Jack Harris:

We're Avoiding Layoffs by Holding Positions Vacant

* * *

One of the ways we've been able to cut our budget without resorting to layoffs is by holding positions vacant. Right now we have 400 vacant sworn positions, which accounts for about 11 percent of our authorized strength. To meet our budget goals during the slowed recovery, hiring is not planned to resume until late fiscal year 2013–14. Between now and then, we're projected to lose another 200–300 sworn positions through attrition. To put this in perspective, the impact of the recession on our sworn staffing will effectively set us back by about a decade because by the time we are able to start hiring, our sworn staffing levels are projected to be what they were in 2003–2004.

* * *

... A few years ago, we were competing with other law enforcement agencies across the country for qualified recruits and it was not uncommon for our Police Academy to be running five classes at the same time. Right now, we don't have any academy classes running and we haven't hired any sworn positions since late 2008. My concern is that when the economy turns around, it will take many years just to restore our staffing levels to where they were before the recession hit. And if the population rises, or if crime increases during this period, it will pose significant challenges for the Department.

Naperville, IL Chief David Dial:

Across-the-Board Cuts Have Changed the Department

Naperville is a suburb located about 35 miles west of Chicago.... We have a population of 145,000 people, and three years ago we had 189 sworn officers.

I've been the chief in Naperville for 20 years.... Until about 3½ years ago, our department grew commensurate with the community....

Then the economic downturn hit, and we started with some layoffs of civilians in the first year, and cutting police officers through attrition. Now, I'm down 28 employees and the layoffs of sworn officers have begun. We cut our crime prevention unit ... closed our front desk at nights and on weekends so we could send the officers out on the road, reduced our gang and narcotics unit, cut our records staff, cut some dispatchers, cut a property and evidence tech, cut a forensic tech, cut our Citizens Police Academy … reduced training, overtime and patrol staffing.

In November 2010, I had to lay off six more cops and cut two additional vacant positions. These cuts resulted in two fewer detectives, five less patrol officers, and one less patrol sergeant. Our authorized sworn strength is now down to 167, which is 22 fewer than it was 24 months ago.

* * *

Minneapolis Chief Tim Dolan:

We Rethought Narcotics Enforcement

… Every precinct has a plain-clothes group that handles chronic issues and does a lot of narcotics work. We also have the top-level work going on at the task force level with the federal agents and so forth. But we had to make budget reductions, and the bottom line when we looked at narcotics as a whole was that we weren't seeing a lot of bang for our buck in these mid-level narcotics arrests. Frankly people get more prison time for a misdemeanor domestic assault than a narcotics felony.

… The reality is that we figured we had adequate resources on drugs and could shut down the narcotics unit.…

* * *

Baltimore Commissioner Fred Bealefeld:

Cuts in Social Programs Will Impact Police

I think we need to remember that police departments don't exist in a vacuum. While we're gnashing our teeth about pensions and funding and budget cuts, the schools and other agencies are going through the same things. Baltimore is reducing drug addiction treatment, reentry programs, jobs programs for teenagers, funding to reduce teenage pregnancy. And while the national unemployment rate is 9 or 10 percent, in parts of Baltimore it's 40 to 50 percent. We learned hard lessons in the 1990s and built programs to help lead us out of some of these social problems. And now these programs are first on the chopping block.…

* * *

Notes and Questions

1. A general theme of the police chiefs' comments is that departments should cut everywhere possible before laying off officers and staff. Is that necessarily the best approach? Watch *The Wire*, Season 1, Episode 1 at 15:30 minutes in which Officer Greggs is filling out paperwork on a typewriter. Season 1 of *The Wire* was broadcast in 2002 and was set in present day. How is it possible that a big-city police department was using typewriters in 2002? On the other hand, watch *The Wire*, Season 5, Episode 6, at 23:25 minutes. Detective Bunk complains to the medical examiner that he still does not have laboratory reports for more than a dozen homicides a year after they occurred. The medical examiner responds "Cutbacks. You know that. We lost two or three trace examiners. Plus half of our clerical [staff] …" Is there any answer to this dilemma?

2. The surveillance equipment available to the Baltimore Police Department in *The Wire* is not much more advanced than the typewriters used to write police reports. Watch

The Wire, Season 1, Episode 3, at 14:15 minutes in which an officer is about to wear a wire in undercover surveillance but protests because the surveillance equipment is gigantic and would be obvious to any of the targets of the investigation. Have you ever seen a recording device as large as the one in this scene? How old do you think that piece of equipment was?

3. The final episode of *The Wire* aired on March 9, 2008, before the start of the Great Recession. Throughout all five seasons, the series demonstrates an incredibly dysfunctional police department that is hobbled by a lack of resources. How much worse would it have been if the series had been set after the recession?

4. Do most people realize that police departments are terribly underfunded? If not, is it because politicians are hiding, or at least obfuscating, the current state of affairs? Watch *The Wire*, Season 3, Episode 3, at 21:15 minutes. After a reporter learns that the police academy class was cancelled to save money, the Mayor refuses to honestly step forward and say that there are insufficient funds in the budget. Rather, he orders Acting Commissioner Burrell to take the blame by saying it was a personnel mistake or because there were not enough good recruits to generate a class. Why are politicians reluctant to speak up about underfunding?

5. *What about a natural disaster?* New Orleans has long had terrible police resource problems, but Hurricane Katrina made them dramatically worse. Almost two years after the Hurricane, the police force had fallen from 1,741 officers to 1,200. Criminal evidence was kept in the back of an 18-wheel truck and officers were still using FEMA trailers as police headquarters. *See* Gilbert Cruz, *New Orleans: Police Still Underfunded*, Time, June 20, 2007.

6. Does a lack of law enforcement resources sometimes lead to wrongful convictions? Consider the case of Cody Davis. In February 2006, a Caucasian man robbed a bar in West Palm Beach, Florida. Eyewitnesses told police that the robbery was committed by a man with a neck tattoo, and one witness remembered the perpetrator having a tattoo on his hand. Two witnesses subsequently picked Davis—who had a neck tattoo—out of a lineup. Police found a ski mask at the scene of the robbery, but did not consider it to be crucial evidence because none of the eyewitnesses reported the robber wearing a mask. The mask was turned over to the sheriff's laboratory for testing, but it was not given testing priority. Because of backlogs, the testing was not done before trial and Davis's lawyer was never told it was in line to be tested. In October 2006, a jury convicted Davis based on the testimony of the eyewitnesses and the informant. He was sentenced to three years' incarceration. However, four months into his sentence, the crime lab completed the testing on the ski mask and found the DNA profile of another man—Jeremey Prichard—on the mask. Prichard had both a neck tattoo as well as a hand tattoo that matched one witness' description. Davis did not have a hand tattoo. Officers questioned Prichard and he confessed to the robbery. About five months after his conviction and incarceration, Cody Davis was exonerated and released. *See* Susan Spencer-Wendel, Man, *Wrongfully Imprisoned in '06, Avoids Long Sentence for Latest Run-In*, Palm Beach Post, Dec. 27, 2008. If the sheriff's lab had been adequately staffed and was not backlogged by about a year, would Cody Davis ever have been convicted and incarcerated in the first place for the robbery?

7. Like many other governmental services, the resources of police departments vary widely depending on the jurisdiction. Some affluent cities and counties have state-of-the-art equipment and an adequate number of police officers to patrol the community. Other jurisdictions must make do with much less. And it seems that the rich get richer while the

poor get poorer. The Bureau of Justice Statistics reported in 2011 that 35 of the 50 largest police departments were able to employ more officers in 2008 than they had on staff in 2004. Yet, a number of cities were forced to cut officers, sometimes in large numbers. Between 2004 and 2008, Detroit cut the number of police officers by more than 35%; Memphis reduced its force by 23%; New Orleans cut more than 13% of its officers. *See* Bureau of Justice Statistics, Census of State and Local Law Enforcement Agencies, 2008 4–5 (July 2011).

8. Consider the situation in Oakland, California, where the homicide clearance rate is about 40 percent, which is about ten points below the rate in most large cities. In an interview conducted in December 2008—before the full force of the recession—Oakland's police chief contended that the department needed more than 300 additional officers and that 550 of the existing 800 officers were stuck in inflexible assignments because California legislation mandated it. *See* Mary Fricker, *Understaffed Oakland Department Behind Other Cities in Solving Homicides*, The Chauncey Bailey Project, Dec. 28, 2008.

9. And then there is Maryland, the subject of *The Wire*. A state audit in 2004 discovered a backlog of more than 8,000 cases from Baltimore City and Prince George's County that have unanalyzed crime scene DNA evidence. *See* Ralph Brave, *Legislative Audit Reveals Troubling Problems With Maryland State Police's Handling of DNA Database*, City Paper, July 28, 2004.

10. Even if a police department is adequately funded, its resources must be well distributed to be effective. Watch *The Wire*, Season 1, Episode 6, at 12:30 minutes in which police are waiting for the mobile crime scene unit to arrive to deal with a murdered and decomposing body. One officer explains that the city has only two mobile crime scene units working and that both of them are at the home a city councilman dusting for fingerprints after the councilman's law furniture was stolen. Even setting aside the outrageousness of this example, does it raise a larger problem about distribution of scarce resources? How do we ensure that police resources are distributed where they are most needed, as opposed to the areas of town that have the most political power?

11. Finally, watch *The Wire*, Season 5, Episode 1, at 7:35 minutes. At a morning meeting, officers angrily complain to Detective Carver—now a Sergeant in Charge in the Western Division—that they have not received their overtime pay for dozens of hours of work. Sergeant Carver tries to calm the officers by saying "the situation in the city right now is bad, but it won't stay bad forever." Can he say that with confidence? Following the 2008 recession that decimated city, county, and state finances across the country, how long will it be before police departments receive adequate levels (or even the levels from the recent past) of funding again?

C. Overburdened Defense Lawyers and Prosecutors

Although the goal of targeting drug offenders and other criminals in *The Wire* is ultimately to prosecute them, the series shows us relatively little about the prosecutors and defense lawyers who would handle such a trial. We get to know defense attorney Maurice Levy and prosecutor Rhonda Pearlman, but we do not see many other criminal lawyers. And what we see of Levy and Pearlman is not representative of the ethics, workload pressures, and responsibilities of lawyers in the criminal justice system generally.

At the most obvious level—and unlike Maurice Levy—most criminal defense lawyers do not participate in their clients' criminal conspiracies. They have little or nothing to do with their clients until after the crime is committed. Less obviously, the series does not show the audience how the vast majority of criminal defendants—upwards of 80%—are too poor to hire a private attorney like Levy and must instead rely on public defenders and appointed counsel. When we do see a public defender—for instance when D'Angelo Barksdale briefly decides not to be represented by Maurice Levy—the lawyer is attentive and has time to focus on the case. The real world of indigent defense is often very different and, as Professors Backus and Marcus describe below, much more disappointing.

The portrayal of prosecutors—primarily through Prosecutor Pearlman—is also incomplete. Many prosecutors in large cities are terribly overburdened and lack the time to dig into a case in detail the way Pearlman does. As Professors Gershowitz and Killinger discuss at the end of this section, the lack of funds for prosecutors can cause just as many systemic problems as the underfunding of police and indigent defense lawyers.

Mary Sue Backus & Paul Marcus, The Right to Counsel in Criminal Cases, A National Crisis
57 Hastings Law Journal 1031 (2006)

I. How Can This Be Happening?

A. The Examples Are Everywhere

In a case of mistaken identity, Henry Earl Clark of Dallas was charged with a drug offense in Tyler, Texas. After his arrest, it took six weeks in jail before he was assigned a lawyer, as he was too poor to afford one on his own. It took seven more weeks after the appointment of the lawyer, until the case was dismissed, for it to become obvious that the police had arrested the wrong man. While in jail, Clark asked for quick action writing, "I [need to] get out of this godforsaken jail, get back to my job … I am not a drug user or dealer. I am a tax-paying American." During this time, he lost his job and his car, which was auctioned. After Clark was released, he spent several months in a homeless shelter.

Two recent Georgia cases can only be seen as shocking, though in very different ways. Sixteen-year-old Denise Lockett was retarded and pregnant. Her baby died when she delivered it in a toilet in her home in a South Georgia housing project. Although an autopsy found no indication that the baby's death had been caused by any intentional act, the prosecutor charged Lockett with first-degree murder. Her appointed lawyer had a contract to handle all the county's criminal cases, about 300 cases in a year, for a flat fee. He performed this work on top of that required by his private practice with paying clients. The lawyer conducted no investigation of the facts, introduced no evidence of his client's mental retardation or of the autopsy findings, and told her to plead guilty to manslaughter. She was sentenced to twenty years in prison. Tony Humphries was charged with jumping a subway turnstile in Atlanta to evade a $1.75 fare. He sat in jail for fifty-four days, far longer than the sentence he would have received if convicted, before a lawyer was appointed, at a cost to the taxpayers of $2330.

A mother in Louisiana recently addressed a state legislative committee:

> My son Corey is a defendant in Calcasieu Parish, facing adult charges. He has been incarcerated for three months with no contact from court[-]appointed counsel. Corey and I have tried for three months to get a name and phone number of the appointed attorney. No one in the system can tell us exactly who the

court[-]appointed attorney is. The court told us his public defender will be the same one he had for a juvenile adjudication. The court[-]appointed counsel told me he does not represent my son. The court clerk's office cannot help me or my son. We are navigating the system alone. Eight weeks ago we filed a motion for bond reduction. We have heard nothing — not even a letter of acknowledgement from the court that it received our motion. Without a lawyer to advocate on Corey's behalf, we are defenseless. How many more months will go by without contact from a lawyer? How many more months will go by without investigation into the case?

Fifty-one criminal defendants in Western Massachusetts were arrested and jailed without any legal representation for many weeks at a time. As one government official stated, "One woman has been sitting in jail [for two months] without counsel and has not even been able to get a bail review. This is an embarrassment. How can we tolerate a system where people don't have lawyers?"

The Chief Public Defender of Fairfax County, Virginia (metropolitan Washington, D.C.) resigned in July 2005, after just ten months in the position. She said that even with legislative reforms in Virginia her office had so many clients and so few lawyers that the attorneys simply could not adequately represent the defendants at trials and on appeal. Last year, the twenty lawyers in the office defended more than 8000 clients.

A defendant in Missoula, Montana, was jailed for nearly six months leading up to his trial. During the months before his trial, the defendant met with his court-appointed attorney just two times. That attorney did nothing to investigate the defendant's allegations that police obtained evidence against him during an illegal search. A second court-appointed lawyer subsequently had the case dismissed.

* * *

III. The Basis of the Right to Counsel

In the early part of the 20th Century, little concern was expressed about the right to an attorney in criminal cases. The Supreme Court began a significant expansion of the right starting in the 1930s. In 1932, the Court decided in Powell v. Alabama that the Due Process Clause of the Fourteenth Amendment required that an indigent defendant on trial for a capital offense be provided counsel. While the facts there were extreme, the Justices' language, as noted earlier, was very broad. The Court expanded the right to representation when it later held in Johnson v. Zerbst that an individual accused of a felony in a federal court has a right to appointed counsel under the Sixth Amendment if he or she is unable to afford an attorney. In a major retreat, however, the Justices soon decided in the well-known case of Betts v. Brady that the right to counsel in the federal constitution could not be applied routinely to states through the Due Process Clause of the Fourteenth Amendment. The Betts decision lasted for two decades.

Finally, in 1963, the Supreme Court unanimously reversed Betts and ruled in Gideon v. Wainwright that the Sixth Amendment right to counsel applied to defendants charged with felonies in state court under the Due Process Clause. In oft-cited language, the Justices concluded that "any person haled into court, who is too poor to hire a lawyer, cannot be assured of a fair trial unless counsel is provided for him." Justice Black, writing for the Court, found that average citizens lack the necessary legal skills to be able to mount an effective defense. The result, he stated, is that indigent defendants cannot be ensured a fair trial without the guiding hand of counsel. The decision in Gideon was based on the principle that all individuals in the criminal justice system must be offered a fair opportunity to defend against charges brought against them....

* * *

Gideon certainly did not answer all the key questions involved with the Sixth Amendment right to counsel. Still, it set the principal benchmark against which the American criminal justice systems today must be measured.

* * *

V. The Crisis

A. Financial Support

By every measure in every report analyzing the U.S. criminal justice system, the defense function for poor people is drastically underfinanced. This lack of money is reflected in a wide range of problems, including poor people's limited access to attorneys and the resulting ineffective assistance of counsel, both of which are discussed later in this Article. Here, however, we examine the broader impact of inadequate funding, excessive public defender caseloads and insufficient salaries and compensation for defense lawyers.

* * *

2. Caseloads

In 1973, the National Advisory Commission on Criminal Justice Standards and Goals set forth recommendations for limits on public defender caseloads. The NAC stated that a single attorney in a year should not carry more than 150 felonies, or more than 400 misdemeanors, or more than 200 juvenile cases or more than twenty-five appeals. If an attorney handles the limit in one category then those are all the cases that person is to handle. Many lawyers throughout the nation do not come close to meeting that standard.

By 2001 the Clark County (Nevada) Public Defender Office had juvenile caseloads at about seven times the NAC recommended limit. Each of the two attorneys on the juvenile division staff had caseloads approaching 1500. A NLADA survey found that as the cases in the division increased from 1993 through 2001, the focus of the attorneys was not so much on representing their clients as it was "about processing cases." The evidence they present shows a more than 50% decrease in the amount of time available to the office to dispose of a case. In 1993, an average case took about sixty-three days to complete. By 2001, it was down to approximately twenty-six days.

In Louisiana, a public defender in Rapides Parish told the judge in a recent murder prosecution that she could not adequately defend the accused because she was so overwhelmed with cases that "if you divide the number of hours in a day by the number of cases ... I would be allowed ... to devote eleven minutes ... to each of the Public Defender files that I have.... [I]t's just not humanly possible for me to do that." Each defender there has a caseload of 472 clients. Because of the caseload burden, Rapides Parish public defenders began to refuse new clients, so a judge in Louisiana's Ninth Judicial District used the telephone book to call attorneys and appoint them to represent indigent defendants. Recognizing the situation as dire, the judge said, "We've run into a real crisis that we just can't address on the local level. What we need to do is hire more attorneys and pay them well, at least as much as the prosecutors are making."

The ninth Judicial District in Minnesota covers seventeen counties and has the highest caseload in the state. The chief public defender in the district has had to deal with lawyer resignations—eight within one year—and says that without additional funding the situation could be disastrous. On the whole, public defenders statewide each handle more than 900 cases a year.

* * *

3. Compensation

* * *

For court-appointed counsel, states or counties often set limits on the hourly rates and total compensation for the attorney. The most discussed, and criticized, system is Virginia's. Here there are "hard caps" on the amount a court-appointed attorney is to be paid, regardless of the length of the trial or the total hours she spent working on it....

While court-appointed attorneys in Virginia may claim up to $90 per hour in fees, they are faced with the lowest payment cap in the nation, $1235. But, that total is only for attorneys representing defendants who face twenty years to life in prison; if the potential sentence is for fewer than twenty years in prison the cap is $395. And, for a misdemeanor punishable by jail time the cap is $112. These caps are not waivable....

Caps exist elsewhere in the country, too, though they can be waived. In Ohio, a recent case highlights the inability of court-appointed attorneys to be compensated at levels that make it possible for them to offer an adequate defense. The caps, set by Miami County, limited the compensation for a death penalty case to $40,000, which was to be split between two attorneys and had to be used by them to pay support staff and take care of other expenses. This total compensation may be compared to the $40,000 spent by the prosecution in the same case merely to have one witness give expert testimony. However, Miami County is in the middle of the pack in terms of caps set by counties in Ohio. The caps range from $3000 in one county through a maximum of $75,000 set by two counties.

In Iowa, the former president of the Iowa State Bar Association decried the use of caps in paying for indigent defense. He asserted that the system actively discouraged competent attorneys from taking appointments. Recent law school graduates can no longer seek viable employment in the area because the debt loads from law school are too much and the compensation for indigent defense appointments is too little. "There is no chance," he wrote, "of servicing a $75,000 debt, let alone paying for a car, house and family, on the fees from indigent defense." In 2003, Iowa defenders could claim an hourly fee of $50 an hour for misdemeanor and some felony representation, but were faced with a $1000 cap for felonies and $500 for misdemeanors.

* * *

In addition to fees and flat contract rate payments, there are thousands of public defenders who receive annual salaries. Salaried public defenders sometimes face paychecks that are less than their counterparts in prosecutor offices, despite an ABA-adopted standard that public defenders and prosecutors be paid at "comparable" rates. In many states the parity does exist. In others, however, the defense lawyers receive lower salaries.

In Baton Rouge, the twenty-seven attorneys earn between $18,000 and $35,000 annually, figures that are about 30% less than the salaries in the district attorney's office. Public defender salaries in Alameda County, California ranged much higher than in Baton Rouge, anywhere in excess of $50,000 to greater than $130,000, but the top prosecutor salaries there far exceeded those of the public defender office. In Georgia, entry-level district attorney and public defender positions both start out at the same annual salary, but the upper limit on the public defender salary scale is lower than that of the district attorney salary. The average salary for a Portland, Oregon public defender in 2000 was $45,426 compared to $61,638 for a prosecutor there.

The key problem may not necessarily be a disparity in salaries between prosecutors and defense lawyers, though such a disparity certainly exists in many parts of our country. Rather, the more serious dilemma may be that both sets of lawyers, at the state level, are paid too little. In many states, including Alaska, Maryland, Idaho, Mississippi, Ohio, Illinois, California, Massachusetts, and New Mexico, prosecuting and defending lawyers are paid less than $40,000 per year.

The 2004 annual report by the Missouri Public Defender Commission cites low pay as one reason for the chronic problem of attorney retention. The current annual turnover rate in Missouri is more than 21%. Those leaving the system include entry-level attorneys and other more senior attorneys who depart for careers in the private sector. A targeted pay raise has not occurred there in ten years, and general state employee raises were not sufficient to retain attorneys. The high turnover rate resulted in a backlog of almost 22,000 cases.

* * *

G. Defender Resources

A lack of ancillary resources, critical to effective representation, plagues defender systems nationwide. The assistance of support staff, investigators, paralegals, social workers and independent experts is rarely available to the degree necessary to provide competent representation. The scarcity of defender resources usually stands in stark contrast to the prosecution's access to the additional resources and services of other governmental agencies, the costs of which are not reflected in their budgets. Although, as the United States Justice Department has suggested, it is difficult to measure accurately this disparity of resources, this gap undermines the validity and the effectiveness of the adversary system.

* * *

1. Investigators and Support Staff

Adequate investigation is the most basic of criminal defense requirements, and often the key to effective representation. An early study of public defender offices in the wake of the expansion of the right to counsel [for misdemeanor defendants] in Argersinger found that institutional resources were the most prevalent explanation for the variation in effectiveness scores among defender programs. Specifically, an in-depth analysis of nine urban public defender programs found that success in the courtroom was frequently tied to the availability of investigators. Investigators, with their specialized experience and training, are often more skilled than attorneys, and invariably more efficient, at performing critical case-preparation tasks such as gathering and evaluating evidence and interviewing witnesses. Without the facts ferreted out by an investigation, a defender has nothing to work with beyond what she might learn from a brief interview with the client. With such limited information regarding the strength and nature of the case, any attorney would be hard pressed to make the sensible strategic decisions necessary to adequately defend an accused or even have any leverage in plea bargaining.

Yet, all across the country, public defenders, appointed counsel and contract attorneys do not have access to appropriate investigative resources. A Montana public defender, with no investigative services, commented that he had to be a "private investigator ... in addition to being the attorney, [making it] difficult to juggle the time necessary to do that." In Pennsylvania, most public defenders and contract attorneys cannot recall the last time they used an investigator, and one desperate public defender admits he encourages his clients to conduct their own investigations. A part-time New York county assistant public defender's heavy caseload precludes him from spending any time on his assigned cases other than in court, so investigation is well beyond his reach. His frustration is shared by the full-time public defender who has neither the time nor the resources to investigate his cases either.

In many jurisdictions, appointed counsel and contract defenders must secure the approval of the court before incurring any fees for investigators or experts. Judges who have the authority to authorize such expenditures, however, are often reticent to expend taxpayer funds. In Virginia, judges so rarely approve funds for investigators or experts that defenders simply have ceased to ask. One Virginia attorney admitted that she does not use investigators because the state will not pay for them; shockingly, others confessed that they simply do not conduct investigations because they lack the time and resources. A similar situation existed in Georgia, where attorneys commented that getting investigators, even in death penalty cases, was like "pulling teeth." Hiring an investigator for a non-capital case in Mississippi is possible only if the lawyer pays for it herself. And, in Ohio a judge once refused to award funds for an investigator in a murder trial because one of the defense lawyers had been an investigator thirty years earlier.

A recent survey of nearly 2000 felony cases in four Alabama circuits vividly illustrates the chilling effect this kind of systemic denial of investigative resources has on future requests. The contract attorneys there did not request investigators or experts in 99.4% of the cases. As a Texas defense attorney explained, "Formal denials of specific requests are rare. But this is because of an unwritten understanding that requests will only be made in cases of extraordinary need. Hence, although virtually every case requires some sort of investigation, the attorney himself must perform these tasks in an uncompensated or under-compensated capacity."

One Pennsylvania public defender candidly admitted that the lack of investigator services available to defenders influences the outcome of cases. This is particularly true when the prosecution benefits from generally higher staffing levels and has the investigative resources of law enforcement available. In Kentucky, for instance, the chief public defender of a four-county area blamed insufficient staff for his office's inability to adequately represent clients. He pointed specifically to the state prosecutor's "huge investigative advantage" as a significant factor in the disparity and concluded that "[r]esources influence results." The lack of investigative services was identified as a major problem in Pennsylvania counties, particularly in light of the disparity of investigative resources available to the district attorneys and the public defenders. The 2002 evaluation concluded: "Juxtaposed with the vast resources of local law enforcement at the disposal of the District Attorney, the public defender who does not have investigative capabilities cannot put up a fair defense and begins at a disadvantage."

* * *

3. Other Resources: Support Staff and Technology

In addition to access to experts and investigators, defenders need the full complement of support services and technology that a modern law office would require. Secretaries and paralegals can assist with clerical and administrative tasks, client communication, and case preparation and free up time for legal work only the attorney can handle. In Lake County, Montana, neither of the two public defenders has a secretary or a paralegal, thus they either have to interrupt their work to answer the phone or ignore incoming calls. Alaska defenders complain of having their time consumed by filing, mailing, copying and other clerical tasks as a result of inadequate support staff. More than half of the defenders indicated that more than 10% of the tasks they routinely perform could be done by someone with less training, such as a secretary, paralegal, investigator, or other support staff. As one lawyer said, "I shouldn't be doing clerical work."

* * *

Defenders also need the proper tools to adequately represent clients, including the availability of legal research materials or electronic databases, computers and other equipment. However, equipment and resources that most law firms and prosecutor's offices take for granted are often denied to public defender offices. When the public defenders in Lake County, Montana need to do legal research, without the funds to subscribe to online legal research resources, they must drive seventy miles to the University of Montana Law School library. In Montgomery County, Ohio, the lack of basic equipment was so dire that some defenders resorted to bringing their personal computers to the office to prepare motions and memoranda. The lack of equipment also hinders the efforts of the few support staff available to defenders. Defenders must share county cars, and cell phones and digital cameras are just a few of the items denied to investigators from the San Bernardino County Public Defender Office, but provided to the investigators in the District Attorney's office. A recent assessment of Virginia's public defender offices found, for example, that the offices "lack the most basic equipment necessary to run a modern law office." These lawyers have outdated computers, limited printing capabilities, no capacity to take digital photos or even view those from the medical examiner's office, no ability to retrieve criminal history information on their clients and no access to the technology that would enable them to utilize the multimedia capabilities of the circuit court. The public defender cannot keep up with the prosecutor's office technology and, therefore, is greatly disadvantaged.

* * *

Notes and Questions

1. Professors Backus and Marcus report a bleak picture on the state of indigent defense. How can the situation be improved? Where will the money come from?

2. *The "Haves" and The "Have Nots"*: Watch *The Wire*, Season 5, Episode 7, at 6:25 minutes, in which Senator Clay Davis meets with a prominent attorney about his pending corruption trial. Senator Davis tries to convince the lawyer to take the case for $25,000 up front and $25,000 after trial. The lawyer refuses, explaining "I don't pick so much as a single juror without a full amount of my fee being paid." Davis responds "You['re] asking for me to pay a winner's fee right up front and you know what, I ain't a winner yet." The lawyer stands firm, saying "$200,000 is going to get you out from under this mess." This short scene perfectly encapsulates the way the criminal justice system works. Criminal defense lawyers typically demand their fees up front, and for good reason. If the defendant is convicted, he probably will not be able to pay his debts from prison. If the defendant is acquitted, he may lack the motivation to pay (after all, criminal defendants as a group are not noted for their honesty). Thus, defendants must pay up front. And to retain a high-powered lawyer, criminal defendants must pay a lot of money. How many people have $200,000 available to pay a lawyer? And what does it say about the criminal justice system when a defendant facing a relatively modest charge of political corruption pays $200,000 for his defense, while murderers and rapists are represented by appointed lawyers who can only earn a few thousands dollars per case? What does it say about our system when a defense lawyer earns $200,000 to work exclusively on one defendant's case, while public defenders earn roughly one-fourth of that amount per year to handle hundreds upon hundreds of cases? Is this simply the cost of capitalism? Or is something dreadfully wrong with our criminal justice system?

3. The Sixth Amendment only requires states to appoint counsel if an individual is sentenced to jail time. *See* Scott v. Illinois, 440 U.S. 367 (1979). Thus, for misdemeanor charges that do not carry jail time or cases where judges decide not to sentence defen-

dants to jail, could states and counties eliminate the right to an attorney and thus decrease defenders' caseloads? *See* Erica J. Hashimoto, *The Price of Misdemeanor Representation*, 47 Wm. & Mary L. Rev. 461 (2007). Is this a good idea? Are the collateral consequences of conviction—even for misdemeanors—so significant as to make lawyers essential? *See* Jenny M. Roberts, *Why Misdemeanors Matter: Defining Effective Advocacy in the Lower Criminal Courts*, 45 U.C. Davis L. Rev. 277 (2011).

4. Another way to reduce defender caseloads would be to decriminalize certain offenses. Fewer crimes on the books should mean fewer cases for defense lawyers to handle. Is this a realistic proposal? Would prosecutors simply charge different offenses rather than a fewer number of offenses?

5. Is there a role for the Supreme Court in fixing the underfunding of defense lawyers and prosecutors? Could the Supreme Court order that states and counties simply spend more money on indigent defense in order to satisfy defendants' Sixth Amendment right to counsel? How would the Court enforce such an edict? In the alternative, could the Court raise the standard of proof for states with inadequate defense funding to require proof beyond all doubt in order to convict, unless the state decides to improve its caseloads and funding? *See* Adam M. Gershowitz, *Raise the Proof: A Default Rule for Indigent Defense*, 40 Conn. L. Rev. 85 (2007).

6. Does *The Wire*—which offers a terrifically realistic picture of many criminal justice problems—do an adequate job of portraying criminal defense lawyers? Despite all of the arrests of indigent drug dealers, does *The Wire* ever show us more than a passing glance at public defenders? The only recurring criminal defense lawyer character in the show, Maurice Levy, is portrayed as both financially successful and dishonest. Watch *The Wire*, Season 1, Episode 11, at 31:55 minutes. In that scene, Detective McNulty and Prosecutor Pearlman threaten Levy with an investigation into his personal misconduct unless he identifies the person who shot Detective Greggs. Levy later complies to save himself at the expense of his clients. While this example might be extreme, is it similar in any fashion to appointed lawyers accepting payment for cases that they lack the time to adequately investigate and prepare? Put differently, are some of the defense lawyers quoted in Professors Backus and Marcus's article less upstanding than they portray themselves to be?

Adam M. Gershowitz & Laura R. Killinger, The State (Never) Rests: How Excessive Prosecutor Caseloads Harm Criminal Defendants

105 Northwestern University Law Review 261 (2011)

In recent decades, legal scholars have devoted enormous attention to two problems in the American criminal justice system: the appalling underfunding of indigent defense and intentional prosecutorial misconduct. Both problems are deeply troubling, and the academic literature helpfully serves to spotlight the problems and encourage reform. Remarkably, however, there is virtually no scholarship focusing on the opposite side of the coin. Scholars have failed to notice that prosecutors in large counties are often as overburdened as public defenders and appointed counsel. In some jurisdictions, individual prosecutors handle more than one thousand felony cases per year. Prosecutors often have hundreds of open felony cases at a time and multiple murder, robbery, and sexual assault cases set for trial on any given day. Prosecutors in many large cities have caseloads far in excess of the recommended guidelines that scholars often cite to criticize the caseloads of public defenders. Quite simply, many prosecutors are asked to commit malpractice on a daily basis by handling far more cases than any lawyer can competently manage.

Not only have scholars neglected to analyze excessive prosecutorial caseloads, they have also failed to consider how those caseloads result in inadvertent prosecutorial error. While there is an enormous (and important) literature analyzing intentional prosecutorial misconduct, the reality is that most prosecutorial misconduct is accidental. While some of these cases involve unscrupulous prosecutors, far more often the errors are inadvertent because prosecutors are too busy to properly focus on their cases or because they have not received proper guidance from senior lawyers who are terribly overburdened themselves.

The ramifications of excessive prosecutorial caseloads extend throughout the criminal justice system and, perhaps surprisingly, are most harmful to criminal defendants. Excessive caseloads lead to long backlogs in court settings, including trials, and bottom-line plea bargain offers. Defendants who have been unable to post bail thus remain incarcerated for months because overburdened prosecutors do not have time to focus on their cases. Jails accordingly remain overcrowded, resulting in not only great expense to taxpayers but also terrible conditions of confinement for defendants who are awaiting trial. Worse yet, excessive prosecutorial caseloads delay trials for months or even years, leading some defendants who would have exercised their trial rights to simply plead guilty and accept a sentence of time served. Some innocent defendants plead guilty to crimes they have not committed simply to get out of jail.

Because they are overburdened, prosecutors—who are sworn to achieve justice, not to win at all costs—lack the time and resources to carefully assess which defendants are most deserving of punishment. In rare cases, this means prosecutors will be unable to separate the innocent from the guilty. In far more cases, overburdened prosecutors will be unable to distinguish the most culpable defendants from those who committed the crimes but are not deserving of harsh punishment....

* * *

I. Prosecutors in Large Jurisdictions Often Have Excessive Caseloads

Although there are more than 2300 prosecutors' offices throughout the United States, a comparatively small number of district attorneys' offices in major cities handle a huge number of America's criminal prosecutions. Though these large district attorneys' offices are all organized somewhat differently, they have one thing in common: far too few prosecutors are tasked with handling far too many cases. As we explain in this Part, prosecutors in many large cities are asked to handle excessive caseloads that run afoul of advisory guidelines for criminal defense attorneys. Prosecutors are also asked to make do with grossly inadequate support staff. Unfortunately, tough economic times over the past few years have only made the situation worse.

A. Standards Suggest Prosecutors Should Not Handle More than 150 Felonies or 400 Misdemeanors per Year

In 1968, a national commission created by the Department of Justice studied the problem of excessive public defender caseloads and adopted a recommendation that defenders handle no more than 150 felonies or 400 misdemeanors in any year. In subsequent years, these guidelines have been widely endorsed by criminal justice organizations, the American Bar Association, and academic commentators. While the recommended caseloads are far from perfect, there is widespread agreement that, roughly speaking, limiting defense counsel to no more than 150 felonies or 400 misdemeanors ensures that they have sufficient time to devote to each of their cases.

In the over forty years since these guidelines for criminal defense caseloads were established, no organization has stepped forward with comparable caseload limits for prosecutors. It is beyond the scope of our project to offer an ideal caseload limit for prosecutors,
but it is quite plausible to suggest that the guidelines should be similar to those recommended for defense attorneys. Arguably, prosecutors are in a position to handle slightly more
cases than defense attorneys because they do not have to chase down leads in an effort to
establish an effective defense. On the other hand, prosecutors have many obligations, such
as handling arraignments or meeting with victims, which defense attorneys do not have
to shoulder. While we are not sure of the exact caseloads prosecutors should handle, we
are confident that it should be similar to the number recommended for defense attorneys.

* * *

B. Prosecutors in Large Counties Are Regularly Tasked with Hundreds or Even Thousands of Felony Cases per Year

In 2006, prosecutors in Harris County, Texas, surveyed the largest district attorneys'
offices in the nation to determine the sizes of their staffs and the numbers of cases they handle. Although the data showed that a few offices have reasonable workloads, many large
counties had caseloads far in excess of recommended guidelines for public defenders.

As Table 1 demonstrates, prosecutors in many large counties handle far more cases
than guidelines recommend. For example, although defense lawyer guidelines provide
that attorneys should handle no more than 150 felonies or 400 misdemeanors, the average caseload in Clark County, Nevada, was 166 felonies and 242 misdemeanors for every
prosecutor in the office. The workload for Harris County, Texas prosecutors was even
higher, with an average of 165 felonies and 292 misdemeanors for each prosecutor in the
office.

Unfortunately, the data in Table 1 vastly understate the scope of the problem by assuming
that every prosecutor in the office handles an equal number of cases. This assumption is
not correct. Each large district attorney's office has numerous prosecutors and attorneys
whose specialized roles leave them handling very small caseloads or no cases at all. In
turn, the overwhelming bulk of cases are handled by a smaller core group of "in-the-
trenches" prosecutors, whose case numbers are drastically higher than the averages listed
in Table 1. To put the actual workload of these prosecutors in perspective, consider all of
the attorneys in large district attorneys' offices who are not handling day-to-day cases:
First, there are management prosecutors who are responsible for supervisory functions
and do not personally handle many cases.... Second, in many large district attorneys' offices, there are line prosecutors, or assistant district attorneys, whose sole responsibilities include revoking bonds for defendants who have failed to show up for court or
performing "intake" by drafting warrants and answering police officers' questions. These
prosecutors handle isolated pieces of cases, but they do not have to prepare cases for trial.
Finally, there are prosecutors who exclusively handle complicated matters, such as white-
collar fraud or death-penalty cases and therefore have unusually low caseloads.

In sum, while large district attorneys' offices have hundreds of prosecutors on staff,
many of the prosecutors do not handle run-of-the-mill cases. The bulk of felony and misdemeanor cases are therefore left to a smaller group of prosecutors. For example, the
Philadelphia District Attorney's Office informed us that fewer than half of their prosecutors
(roughly 150 of 309 attorneys) handle pending cases that are set for trial. It is this group
of in-the-trenches prosecutors who are particularly overburdened. In some jurisdictions,
the workload of these prosecutors is truly staggering. One extreme example is Harris
County, Texas, where some prosecutors are handling upwards of 1500 felonies per year

Table 1 Cases per Prosecutor in Large District Attorneys' Offices in 2006

County	Pros- ecutors	Felonies	Misde- meanors	Felonies per Prosecutor	Misd. per Prosecutor	Total Filings per Prosecutor
Los Angeles, CA	1020	68,654	125,580	67	123	190
Cook, IL (Chicago)	800	60,000	265,000	75	331	406
New York, NY	532	11,190	111,055	21	209	230
Kings, NY (Brooklyn)	413	12,514	98,725	30	239	269
Maricopa, AZ	343	40,000	5000	117	15	132
San Diego, CA	310	18,888	27,654	61	89	150
Miami-Dade, FL	283	36,286	54,974	128	194	322
Philadelphia, PA	283	15,515	54,485	55	193	247
Queens, NY	276	5274	57,938	19	210	229
Orange, CA	249	19,011	50,233	76	202	278
Harris, TX (Houston)	238	39,154	69,494	165	292	457
San Bernardino, CA	219	20,187	38,459	92	176	268
Riverside, CA	217	15,518	21,197	72	98	169
Dallas, TX	217	24,251	53,637	112	247	359
Broward, FL (Ft. Lauderdale)	194	15,720	68,301	81	352	433
Wayne, MI (Detroit)	188	13,000	4000	69	21	90
Sacramento, CA	185	11,491	20,759	62	112	174
Santa Clara, CA	185	8729	25,164	47	136	183
Suffolk, NY (Long Island)	177	2930	33,889	17	191	208
King, WA (Seattle)	163	9815	16,000	60	98	158
Tarrant, TX (Fort Worth)	155	15,328	27,752	99	179	278
Alameda, CA (Oakland)	151	9731	26,165	64	173	238
Bexar, TX (San Antonio)	146	10,188	32,314	70	221	291
Clark, NV (Las Vegas)	135	22,420	32,678	166	242	408
Middlesex, MA (Cambridge)	113	720	38,000	6	336	343

and over 500 felonies at any one time. A brief description of the office's structure highlights the problem.

The Harris County District Attorney's Office assigns three felony prosecutors to each of its felony courts. On average, each felony court receives about 2000 new filings per year. The senior prosecutor in each court serves primarily in a supervisory role and personally handles only about a dozen of the court's most serious cases. Almost all of that court's 2000 felony cases are split between the other two prosecutors. The second-most senior prosecutor (the "number two prosecutor") is responsible for the more serious crimes: noncapital murders, sexual assaults, child abuse, robberies, and other serious felonies. These cases are the most complicated and therefore the most time-consuming. In a given year, the number two prosecutor handles about 500 serious felonies. The remaining 1500 felony cases—drug offenses, burglaries, assaults, and various other crimes—are assigned to the most junior prosecutor. At any one time, this junior prosecutor, who typically has about two years of prosecutorial experience under his belt, has about 500 open cases to handle. While these cases are less complicated, over the span of a year, a junior prosecutor in a felony courtroom handles ten times the number of felony cases than is recommended for public defenders.

The situation is similarly dire in other large district attorneys' offices. In Cook County, Illinois, the average felony prosecutor has 300 or more open cases at any one time. In a given year, many felony prosecutors there handle between 800 and 1000 total cases. In Tarrant County, Texas, home of Fort Worth, prosecutors handle upwards of 150 felony cases at any one time, and misdemeanor prosecutors juggle between 1200 and 1500 matters apiece. In Philadelphia County, Pennsylvania, prosecutors working in the Major Trials Unit or the Family Violence Sexual Assault Unit have open caseloads of 250 cases.

Although it may not be the most overburdened prosecutor's office in the country, the Clark County District Attorney's Office in Las Vegas, Nevada, truly puts the problem in perspective. The entire Clark County criminal justice system is terribly overburdened. In 2009, a report by an outside indigent defense consultant demonstrated that Clark County public defenders cleared 215 cases per year, in addition to dealing with other open cases. Almost any reasonable observer would conclude that Clark County public defenders are overburdened. The Nevada Supreme Court even contemplated imposing caps on public defenders' caseloads. Yet very little attention has been paid to the fact that prosecutors in Clark County have more cases than public defenders. In 2009, the District Attorney's Office filed more than 70,000 felonies and misdemeanors. After budget cuts and excluding attorneys whose sole job was to screen cases, the Clark County District Attorney's Office had only 90 prosecutors to handle those 70,000 filings, a ratio of nearly 800 cases per prosecutor.

* * *

... [Unfortunately,] the economic downturn has led a number of district attorneys' offices to reduce the number of prosecutors through hiring freezes or even layoffs. In Detroit, the Wayne County District Attorney's Office was forced to reduce its total number of prosecutors—through a hiring freeze and layoffs—by a stunning forty-eight people between 2008 and 2010, a 25% reduction. In Las Vegas, the Clark County District Attorney's Office suffered a similarly drastic cut from 135 prosecutors in 2006 to 102 prosecutors by 2010. Budget cuts forced the Cook County State's Attorney's Office to cut forty prosecutors and fifty staff in 2008. In Seattle, the King County District Attorney's Office was forced to cut eighteen prosecutor positions in 2008. In San Bernardino, California, the District Attorney's Office eliminated sixteen prosecutor positions between 2006 and

2010. In Phoenix, the Maricopa County District Attorney's Office has not replaced six-teen prosecutors who have left the office in the last two years. Other counties, including Harris County, Broward County, and Miami-Dade County, have also been forced to cut prosecutors in recent years.

C. Inadequate Support Staff

Although excessive caseloads are indefensible, the burden on individual prosecutors would be lessened if large district attorneys' offices had adequate support staff to help prosecutors handle the cases. For instance, paralegals are helpful in keeping track of files, drafting and responding to simple motions, and conducting legal research. Investigators are crucial in finding missing witnesses, serving subpoenas, and doing other background investigation. Victim-witness coordinators also serve a useful purpose in keeping victims apprised of court hearings and listening to family concerns. This is to say nothing of the secretaries and other basic support staff needed to answer phones, make copies, and keep the office running. It is well-known that public defender offices around the country must make do with inadequate support staff, but resources are also inadequate in district attorneys' offices.

For example, the four largest counties in Texas handle a combined total of more than 270,000 criminal cases per year. Yet, they have fewer than thirty-five paralegals combined to work on all of those cases. The Cook County District Attorney's Office is the second largest prosecutor's office in the nation and handles hundreds of thousands of cases per year with fewer than ten paralegals on staff.

Although large prosecutors' offices tend to have more investigators than paralegals, the numbers are still woefully inadequate. In 2006, the ten largest prosecutors' offices in the country represented a population of nearly forty million people and handled well over a million cases, but they had a combined total of only 1,043 investigators on staff. On average, then, in those ten district attorneys' offices, there were more than 1000 cases per investigator. In Clark County, Nevada—which had 29,308 felonies and 41,298 misdemeanors in 2009—there are only twenty investigators for the whole office, and most of their time is spent serving subpoenas because the office does not have enough process servers to contact all of the witnesses. In Seattle, the King County District Attorney's Office handled nearly 15,000 criminal cases without a single investigator on staff. And in Miami-Dade County, there were more than 4500 cases per investigator. Worse yet, the total number of investigators in Miami-Dade County has since dropped from twenty to fourteen, resulting in a ratio of more than 6100 cases for every investigator on staff in 2009.

* * *

II. Harm Caused by Excessive Prosecutorial Caseloads

* * *

A. Harm to Criminal Defendants

Conventional wisdom holds that defendants benefit when prosecutors have huge caseloads. The logic is simple: if prosecutors are overburdened, they will not have time to competently prosecute all of their cases and will not bring many cases to trial. By this logic, prosecutors accordingly must plea bargain cases on terms more favorable to defendants to shrink their dockets. To a certain extent, this conventional wisdom is correct. The entire class of criminal defendants—thousands of defendants in large jurisdictions—likely receives better plea deals from overburdened prosecutors. However, many other effects of excessive prosecutorial caseloads tend to harm criminal defendants, particularly those who are less culpable or even wholly innocent.

* * *

First, consider how excessive caseloads prevent prosecutors from giving sentencing breaks to the defendants who truly deserve them, while simultaneously giving discounts to the undeserving. In a jurisdiction where prosecutors are not overburdened, assume that the going rate for a run-of-the-mill armed robbery is ten years' imprisonment. Of course, not all robberies are the same. Prosecutors adjust the ten-year average sentence up or down depending on the facts they discover during their pretrial investigations. In the case of Robber A, prosecutors with adequate time and resources may learn that although police found him inside the bank while the crime was being committed, he was actually a minor player in the robbery who had fallen in with a bad crowd after having previously been a good student. The prosecutor might therefore be willing to offer Robber A a plea deal carrying five years' incarceration, well under the going rate of ten years. On the other hand, looking at Robber B's paper record, prosecutors might initially think he is entitled to a sentencing break as well; he is charged with stealing a relatively small amount of money and has only one prior criminal conviction for a simple assault that occurred over five years ago. If prosecutors had the time to conduct a proper investigation, however, they might discover that Robber B pointed his shotgun directly at the victims' heads and that he was the ringleader of the robbery. Moreover, the victim of Robber B's previous crime might inform prosecutors that Robber B had broken his nose and cheekbones and that the case was pleaded down to simple assault (rather than aggravated assault) only because Robber B had agreed to provide testimony against another perpetrator. With this information in hand, prosecutors might decide that Robber B should serve the going rate of ten years or perhaps more. In sum, with time and resources to investigate their cases, prosecutors are able to carefully differentiate between defendants and to tailor plea bargain offers accordingly.

Now consider what might have happened if the cases of Robbers A and B had been handled by overburdened prosecutors. Although the going rate for "average" robberies should be ten years, in jurisdictions with overburdened prosecutors the typical punishment may be closer to eight years because defense attorneys can bargain more aggressively knowing that trial is very unlikely. Even though they are overburdened, prosecutors nevertheless try to differentiate between offenders the best they can. But they must make do with less information. They will not have time to personally interview the bank tellers, meet with Robber B's previous victim, or learn that Robber A is regarded in the community as a good kid who was only a passive participant in the robbery. While Robber A's attorney may convey this information, prosecutors may discount the defense attorney's description as self-serving without neutral witnesses to attest to it. Accordingly, based primarily on the paper record in front of them, overburdened prosecutors might determine that both Robbers A and B are entitled to slight discounts on the going rate — say, seven years instead of ten. In the case of Robber A, the overburdened prosecutor will therefore offer a plea-bargained sentence in excess of what the defendant deserves. And in the case of Robber B, the prosecutor will offer a plea-bargained sentence that is far lower than what the defendant deserves. In both cases, overburdened prosecutors fail to achieve the most just result.

* * *

Perhaps more troubling than these failures of discretion is that excessive caseloads lead prosecutors to run afoul of their constitutional obligations and commit inadvertent prosecutorial misconduct. Overburdened prosecutors likely fail to comply with several constitutional and statutory obligations; as explained below, the most pervasive are so-called Brady violations.

Under the doctrine established in Brady v. Maryland, prosecutors are required to disclose favorable evidence that tends to either exculpate the defendant or impeach witnesses against him. This makes Brady at once one of the most important obligations imposed on prosecutors and one of the most common claims by criminal defendants in appealing their convictions. Academic commentators are critical of Brady violations, and when the violations are intentional, such criticism is justified. What most commentators fail to recognize, however, is that the overwhelming majority of Brady violations are unintentional and occur because prosecutors are overburdened or have received inadequate guidance from supervising prosecutors, who themselves are overburdened....

A few hypothetical, but all too common, situations illustrate the problem of inadvertent Brady violations. Imagine a felony prosecutor in a large district attorney's office with 200 open felony cases, four of which are set for trial each week. Though the prosecutor strives to give the defense attorney in each case notice of Brady material (and other more mundane matters a few weeks in advance of trial, it is difficult to keep up with the workload, and our prosecutor must make choices about which cases to prioritize. Believing that three of the four cases set for trial on, for example, June 1, will plea bargain, she focuses most of her attention on the case that she thinks is most likely to go to trial. Unfortunately, our prosecutor is not clairvoyant, and by the time May 28 arrives, one of the cases she thought would plea bargain fails to settle. The prosecutor is, of course, not totally unprepared. She has served subpoenas for likely witnesses and reviewed the other evidence in the file. But being prepared for trial requires much more than that. Our prosecutor must have in-depth meetings with the key witnesses and closely study the entire case file. With only a few days before trial, she must scramble to be ready in time. And in scrambling to get ready, the overburdened prosecutor can easily overlook Brady material that she should turn over to the defendant. Our overburdened prosecutor might fail to realize in her last-minute meeting that the witness's story now conflicts with something he said when speaking to the police many months ago. Or she may be fully aware of evidence that impeaches government witnesses and decide to delay producing it out of fear that disclosing witness identities too far in advance of trial will lead to witness tampering. In the hectic period before trial, prosecutors may simply forget to turn over evidence of which they are personally aware. The list of possible scenarios is endless, but the key point is the same in each permutation: prosecutors who have hundreds of open cases and are not sure which will actually go to trial will inadvertently overlook Brady material as they scramble to be ready for trial at the last minute.

More disturbing than simple oversights are instances in which junior prosecutors do not even realize they have a legal obligation to turn over evidence. In extremely busy district attorneys' offices, prosecutors are quickly saddled with enormous responsibilities very early on. While these young prosecutors surely learned about the Brady doctrine in law school, they may fail to recognize actual Brady obligations when they arise in the real world. For instance, a junior prosecutor who has tried only a few serious felonies may neglect to disclose that a domestic violence victim initially told a police officer that her bruises were from falling down rather than from being hit by her abuser. The junior prosecutor may simply not realize that such evidence is Brady material. In a properly staffed district attorney's office, a supervising prosecutor likely would catch the error and ensure that the State complies with the Brady doctrine's requirements. In overburdened prosecutors' offices, however, supervisors may fail to correct errors because they too are overwhelmed and lack the time to provide the hands-on guidance that is necessary to avoid inadvertent misconduct.

Excessive caseloads also prevent prosecutors from promptly dismissing cases with weak evidence or cases where the defendant is innocent. More crime is committed, and more suspects are arrested, than could possibly be processed through the criminal justice system. Most prosecutors' offices (even those that are overburdened) work hard to screen out weak cases early on before charges are filed. Still, prosecutors file charges against thousands of defendants each year only to later discover that the defendants are innocent or that the cases are too weak to bring to trial. While these defendants are certainly happy to have the charges against them dropped, for many defendants the dismissals do not happen until weeks or months after charges were initially filed. If the defendants are too poor to post bond, as more than 30% of criminal defendants are, they will be incarcerated for those weeks or months. With jails across the country overcrowded, these defendants are often forced to live in squalid conditions with poor medical care, awful food, and the risk of violence and death. While this problem is unavoidable to a certain extent, it is magnified in jurisdictions where prosecutors carry excessive caseloads.

The overarching story is fairly simple: when prosecutors carry excessive caseloads, they handle them in a triage fashion. Prosecutors do not look ahead to cases that will come to a boil in weeks or months; they live in the here and now. If evidence is lurking in a case file that will ultimately lead to a defendant's case being dismissed, it will linger there until the prosecutor has time to focus on the matter. The fewer cases the prosecutor has, the sooner the charges against innocent defendants will be dismissed.

The situation is more nuanced when prosecutors are pushed to dismiss cases by proactive defense attorneys. Often defense lawyers raise legitimate legal or factual questions about a case shortly after charges are filed. While a defense attorney's inquiries and concerns are not enough to justify outright dismissal of a case, they are sufficient to spur the prosecutor to investigate the facts and witnesses more closely. If the prosecutor has a manageable caseload, she will likely conduct this investigation very quickly. Ethical prosecutors have no interest in continuing to lock up innocent defendants. And efficient prosecutors have no desire to keep cases on the docket that could easily and justifiably be dismissed. If the prosecutor has an unreasonable caseload, however, she may not dig into the case until absolutely necessary, which may be just before the case is set for another status hearing or, worse yet, trial. Innocent defendants may thus languish in jail for longer than necessary.

* * *

Prosecutors lack the time and resources to discover who is innocent. Start with two basic truths about the criminal justice system: (1) most criminal defendants are guilty and (2) most criminal defendants lie to prosecutors and claim to be innocent. Understandably, prosecutors are skeptical of most claims of innocence. And because prosecutors are overburdened, they have little time to devote to each case. The little time prosecutors do have is strategically spent trying to convict defendants they firmly believe to be guilty rather than exploring undocumented theories that could exculpate other defendants. Moreover, even when prosecutors do take the time to inquire into defendants' claims of innocence, they may only have time to conduct cursory investigations that are unlikely to be successful. Prosecutors may try to track down alibi or self-defense witnesses that the defendant claims support his version of events, but when such witnesses have not come forward on their own, they are often hard to locate. Furthermore, because a considerable amount of violent crime is committed in minority neighborhoods where even law-abiding citizens fear the police, witnesses with helpful exculpatory information may be unwilling to come forward. This problem is even worse when the witnesses themselves are involved in criminal activity. And the problem is particularly vexing in border states where perfectly honest and otherwise law-abiding witnesses may be illegal immigrants afraid to speak with prosecutors out of fear of deportation. If prosecutors' offices had greater resources to hire investigators who could interact with the community and be seen as partners, then prosecutors might have a more realistic chance of finding witnesses to support the claims of innocent defendants.

Without sufficient time and resources, however, prosecutors often ask defense attorneys to shoulder the burden of investigating claims of innocence. Overburdened prosecutors who are skeptical of innocence claims (most of which are untruthful) ask defense attorneys to find the key witnesses that support their clients' claims and to have those witnesses sign affidavits swearing to the information. If the defense attorney is competent and not overburdened herself, there is nothing inherently wrong with this approach. The problem, of course, is that many public defenders or appointed counsel representing indigent defendants are overburdened as well. Worse yet, in some jurisdictions, compensation for appointed counsel representing indigent defendants is capped for each case, thereby encouraging defense attorneys to take more cases and creating a financial incentive to avoid spending much time working to prove their client's innocence. Overburdened, incompetent, or lazy defense attorneys are therefore unlikely to fare much better than overburdened prosecutors in uncovering compelling evidence that defendants are truly innocent.

⋆   ⋆   ⋆

Innocent defendants also plead guilty in exchange for sentences of time served and an immediate exit from jail. Most innocent defendants who are wrongfully convicted are not the victims of prosecutorial misconduct or inept defense lawyering. Rather, most innocent defendants are convicted because they knowingly and voluntarily pleaded guilty to offenses they did not commit. But why would an innocent defendant plead guilty? The simple answer is that excessive caseloads lead to long trial backlogs and short-sentence plea bargain offers. Innocent defendants thus can plead guilty to sentences of time served and simply leave jail.

When prosecutors have excessive caseloads, it is logistically impossible for every defendant who asserts his innocence to be afforded a timely, quick jury trial. Excessive prosecutorial caseloads therefore lead to many poor defendants who cannot afford bail, including innocent defendants, languishing in jail for months or even years awaiting trial. When innocent defendants are charged with the most serious crimes and face decades in prison, it makes sense for them to wait their turn for trial. If a defendant is found not guilty at trial, the time he spent in pretrial detention will be nowhere close to the sentence he would have received had he pleaded guilty and been convicted.

But when innocent defendants are charged with misdemeanors or low-level felonies, the time in jail while waiting for trial may actually exceed the sentence they would receive if they pleaded guilty. For example, imagine that a defendant is charged with burglary for breaking into a garage and stealing tools. The defendant has no resources with which to post bond. Although prosecutors do not know it, the eyewitness placing the defendant at the scene is mistaken. Moreover, the case against the defendant is so weak that if it proceeded to trial, a decent defense attorney would rip it apart: there was only one eyewitness, it was nighttime, police presented the mug shots in a suggestive fashion, and the defendant was found blocks away from the scene and was not in possession of any of the stolen property. If the defendant wants to continue waiting for a trial, he will almost certainly be acquitted. However, the defendant has already been in jail for a month, and the prosecutor is willing to offer a plea bargain for the one month the defendant has already served. While the innocent defendant does not want to admit to a crime he did not perpetrate, he ultimately pleads guilty simply to get out of jail.

Moreover, the collateral consequences of pleading guilty, such as stigma or harm to employment prospects, are unlikely to deter innocent defendants from pleading guilty. If an individual has already spent weeks in jail awaiting trial, any stigma or embarrassment has probably already attached. While pleading guilty may require the defendant to meet with a parole officer or undergo random urinalysis, the added stigma of conviction is likely of little consequence when his family and friends already knew that he was locked up in jail. Perhaps more importantly, defendants who are too poor to post bond are not likely to have their career prospects hindered by pleading guilty to a crime. They are unlikely to apply to medical school or law school, and in most instances they are not concerned that elite Fortune 500 companies are unlikely to hire individuals with burglary convictions. Instead, because these individuals are likely competing for manual labor jobs or low-paying employment in the service industry, pleading guilty to a crime they did not commit, particularly a misdemeanor, will not have much effect on their employment prospects. Innocent defendants thus have good reasons (and few obstacles) to plead guilty to crimes they did not commit.

* * *

Although it is counterintuitive, excessive prosecutorial caseloads are very damaging to criminal defendants. Overburdened prosecutors have trouble exercising their discretion as effectively as they might like. Less culpable defendants therefore do not receive sentencing discounts that they would receive from less-burdened prosecutors. Candidates for drug treatment courts may not be transferred to those courts because overburdened prosecutors fail to recognize worthy defendants. Well-meaning but overburdened prosecutors fail to disclose Brady material to defendants and likely run afoul of other constitutional and statutory obligations. Excessive caseloads hinder prosecutors from promptly dismissing weak cases, leaving innocent defendants imprisoned for far longer than necessary. And overburdened prosecutors may unknowingly offer too-good-to-refuse plea bargain offers to innocent defendants, encouraging the innocent to plead guilty to crimes they did not commit. While the entire class of criminal defendants might receive some plea bargaining benefit from overwhelmed prosecutors, excessive prosecutorial caseloads may well cause more harm than good to a host of criminal defendants.

* * *

_____

Notes and Questions

1. As with criminal defense lawyers, *The Wire* gives short shrift to the caseload pressures plaguing big-city prosecutors. Instead, *The Wire* repeatedly shows Prosecutor Pearlman spending time with the police officers in their office. *See, e.g., The Wire,* Season 3, Episode 1, at 49:00 minutes, in which Pearlman is having coffee and a bagel while discussing case strategy with Detective McNulty and Lieutenant Daniels. In many big cities, prosecutors rarely set foot in police stations (because the officers come to the District Attorney's Office) and they almost certainly do not spend the amount of time with the officers that Pearlman does. Most prosecutors simply lack the time to do so. There is one scene that alludes to caseload pressure though. Watch *The Wire,* Season 4, Episode 9, at 5:50 minutes, in which the newly elected district attorney explains how he will not have money to pay twelve prosecutors once a federal grant expires at the end of the year.

2. If Gershowitz and Killinger are correct that excessive prosecutor caseloads harm criminal defendants, what should be done about it? Would appropriating more money

for prosecutors be a good solution? Or would that simply create a further imbalance that would handicap criminal defense attorneys?

3. Is there a role for the Supreme Court to indirectly fix the system's problems? As Professor William Stuntz pointed out, the Supreme Court has carefully regulated criminal procedure, but has largely abdicated the role of regulating the substance of what criminal laws legislatures can enact. *See* William J. Stuntz, *The Uneasy Relationship Between Criminal Procedure and Criminal Justice*, 107 YALE L.J. 1 (1997). What would happen if the Supreme Court did an about face and began to rigorously review the substance of criminal laws?

4. In total, the articles in this section about underfunded police, defense lawyers, and prosecutors paint a dire picture of the criminal justice system. Big cities like Baltimore need an infusion of tens of millions of dollars to make their criminal justice systems functional. If that money is unlikely to be appropriated, are we simply stuck with sub-standard public safety and justice?

Chapter XIII

Problems of Policing

A. Introduction

Police officers have an enormous amount of power to make a positive impact. They can choose to patrol their beat vigorously. They can arrest the bad guys and release marginal suspects who may not truly deserve to become embroiled in the machinery of the criminal justice system. They can set a positive tone and good relations for the community by being respectful and professional, even when the suspects and citizens they encounter are not. One would hope that most officers embody these qualities and handle their responsibilities in an admirable way.

But where there is enormous power and responsibility, there is opportunity for mischief. And in the case of police officers there can be a lot of mischief. As we see throughout *The Wire*, officers can behave like "humps" and collect a paycheck for doing nothing. The humps might get drunk on duty or simply sit around without making any effort to do actual police work. Worse than that are officers who violate the Fourth or Fifth Amendments to secure evidence and then lie about it to make sure it is admissible. Some police behave more invidiously by using their authority to target minorities or particular individuals they do not like. Other officers intentionally use excessive force because they know they can get away with it. Finally, there are the officers who lie and thieve. As we see in *The Wire*, police can steal from drug dealers or threaten violence or arrests unless they are paid off.

How does society in general, and the criminal justice in particular, deal with these problems of policing? Should we look at these officers as bad apples who need to be weeded out, or is the problem more systemic with blame lying at the top of police organizations? How can courts and legislatures clean up this misconduct without stigmatizing and harming the good officers who do their jobs properly?

B. Police Brutality

In many communities across the country—particularly minority communities—the most pressing issue between police and citizens is the prevalence of police brutality. Residents feel that force is used too frequently, that it is sometimes used without any justification at all, and that police respond disproportionately even when some force is necessary. In some minority communities, residents' first reaction upon seeing the police is to flee, not because they have done anything illegal but because they believe they will be wrongfully arrested or beaten.

When excessive force is obvious, the situation is troubling but hopefully fixable. The problem, however, is that it is not always obvious whether the police were justified in using force or whether their use of force was excessive. Police officers on the street are often called to respond to confusing and dangerous situations. Looking backwards in retrospect, it is possible that the suspect might have posed no threat to the officer and that force was not necessary. On the other hand, matters might have escalated and endangered the officers and citizens on the scene. For instance, when confronted with what seems like a mentally ill man screaming and waving his arms erratically, should police be allowed to use force to restrain him? When a suspect believes he is being arrested unjustifiably and will not put his arms behind his back, how hard can the officer pull the suspect's arms to subdue and handcuff him?

Are you confident that you would know how much force is permitted in a particular situation? Do you think it is possible for courts to design rules that provide guidance to officers on the street about what they can and cannot do? And can we trust juries to decide most claims of excessive force, or do we need to provide police with additional protection against burdensome litigation and the possibility of monetary damages? In short, how do we balance the very serious problem of police brutality with the need to let police do their jobs safely and effectively?

United States v. Ankey

502 F.3d 829 (9th Cir. 2007)

OPINION

GRABER, Circuit Judge:

Defendant Kelly David Ankeny, Sr., was indicted on four counts of being a felon in possession of a firearm and one count of possession of an unregistered sawed-off shotgun. The district court denied his motion to suppress and, reserving the right to appeal that decision, Defendant pleaded guilty. The district court sentenced him to 262 months' imprisonment....

* * *

FACTUAL AND PROCEDURAL HISTORY

On October 21, 2003, Michele Rayley reported to the Portland police that Defendant, with whom she has an 18-year-old son, had choked and kicked her. The altercation with Defendant took place when Rayley went to the house where their son was living, located at 936 N.E. 94th Avenue in Portland, and found that Defendant was living there. She confronted Defendant about her belief that he was supplying drugs to their son, at which point Defendant became angry and attacked her. He then ran to another floor of the house and returned waving a semi-automatic handgun. Rayley told police that she believed Defendant was using methamphetamines and that he might flee or shoot at police.

The case was referred to Officer Rhodes of the Domestic Violence Reduction Unit. In ongoing conversations, Rayley reported to Rhodes that several other people, including an infant and a prison associate of Defendant, also were living in the house. Rayley told Rhodes that, on October 31, 2003, she and Defendant had another argument during which he displayed a handgun.

Officer Rhodes conducted a background check on Defendant and found that he had several outstanding arrest warrants and an extensive criminal history, including convictions for possession and delivery or manufacture of controlled substances, attempting to elude a police officer, escape, felon in possession of a firearm, and robbery. He also had been charged with, but not convicted of, assault on a police officer and aggravated assault.

The police considered various options for how to proceed, including arresting Defendant during a traffic stop, and ultimately decided that it was necessary to arrest Defendant at the house. The police believed that a street arrest would pose a risk to public safety because Defendant had a lengthy record of violence and hostility toward the police. Further, the police believed that an arrest outside the house would be risky because there was evidence of drug and firearm activity inside the house, in addition to the presence of a prison associate of Defendant.

A warrant was authorized on November 18, 2003, and executed on November 20, 2003, at around 5:30 a.m. The house was dark, and there was no noise or movement from within. The Special Emergency Reaction Team ("SERT") led the operation. Thirteen officers were assigned to enter the home and, in total, 44 officers participated in the execution of the warrant.

Officer Stradley yelled "police, search warrant" while pounding on the door and, about one second later, officers used a battering ram to break open the door. Officer Wilcox entered and directed a light-mounted weapon into the house. Defendant had been sleeping on a recliner near the front door; he stood up as the officers broke down the door. Officer Wilcox instructed Defendant to show his hands and get down. Officer Forsyth then threw a flash-bang device into the center of the room. Officer Forsyth testified at the suppression hearing that he heard Officer Wilcox tell Defendant to show his hands; he did not recall hearing him tell Defendant to get down. The flash-bang device had a fuse delay of one to one-and-a-half seconds. Officer Forsyth stated that Defendant went down to the floor during that delay, and the device exploded near his upper body. Because of his proximity to the flash-bang device when it exploded, Defendant suffered first- and second-degree burns to his face and chest and second-degree burns to his upper arms.

Meanwhile, officers stationed outside the house shot out the second-story windows with rubber bullets. Officers securing the second level of the house threw a second flash-bang device into an open area. A man and a woman were lying in bed in that area, and the explosion caused the bed to catch fire. After attempting to extinguish the fire, officers threw the mattress and box spring out of a window.

Extensive damage was done to the house during the entry. The police shot out approximately ten windows, kicked in many doors, burned carpet, and made holes in the walls and ceilings with the rubber bullets.[1]

Thereafter, the police recovered a 9mm semiautomatic handgun from the crack between the arm and the bottom cushion of the chair in which Defendant was sitting when the police entered the house. They also recovered a semiautomatic handgun on an adjacent chair. The police found a 12-gauge sawed-off shotgun and a .22-caliber long rifle in a closet in an upstairs bedroom and another .22-caliber rifle in the basement of the house. The police seized approximately $3,000, ammunition, and suspected drugs and drug paraphernalia.

Defendant was indicted on four counts of being a felon in possession of a firearm and one count of possession of an unregistered sawed-off shotgun.... Defendant moved to suppress the evidence seized during the search. After an evidentiary hearing, briefing, and ar-

---

1. The owner of the house estimated that the damage cost him $14,000 to repair. He filed a claim against the City of Portland for the loss, received $10,000, and decided, after consulting a lawyer, not to pursue a civil suit for the remainder.

gument, the district court denied the motion. Defendant entered a conditional guilty plea, reserving the right to appeal the denial of his motion to suppress.

* * *

DISCUSSION
A. *Motion to Suppress*

We first address Defendant's contention that the evidence found in the house should have been suppressed because the police failed to knock and announce their presence, a failure not justified by exigency, and because the extent of force used by the police rendered the search unreasonable.

* * *

1. *Knock and Announce*

Turning first to the alleged knock-and-announce violation, *see Wilson v. Arkansas*, 514 U.S. 927, 930 (1995) ("[The] common-law knock and announce principle forms a part of the reasonableness inquiry under the Fourth Amendment."), we hold that suppression is foreclosed by the Supreme Court's decision in *Hudson v. Michigan*, 547 U.S. 586 (2006).

In *Hudson,* police entered a suspect's home, with a warrant, after announcing their presence and waiting three to five seconds. The state conceded that there was a knock-and-announce violation. The Court held that violation of the knock-and-announce rule did not merit suppression of evidence found in the search, because the purposes of the knock-and-announce rule—to protect bodily safety, property, and privacy—are not vindicated by excluding evidence obtained after the rule has been violated. The Court emphasized that the knock-and-announce rule does not protect "one's interest in preventing the government from seeing or taking evidence described in a warrant" and that the social costs of exclusion for knock-and-announce violations out-weigh the benefits of deterrence. Thus, we need not resolve whether the knock-and-announce rule was violated and, if so, whether the violation was justified by exigent circumstances. Under *Hudson,* the evidence should not be suppressed in any event.

* * *

2. *Manner of Entry*

Defendant contends that, beyond the alleged knock-and-announce violation, the police's manner of entry violated the Fourth Amendment. He urges us to hold that the overall violence and destructiveness of the officers' actions were unreasonable and, thus, that suppression is warranted.

It is true that "the manner in which a warrant is executed is subject to later judicial review as to its reasonableness." *Dalia v. United States,* 441 U.S. 238, 258 (1979). Unnecessary destruction of property or use of excessive force can render a search unreasonable. Deciding whether officers' actions were reasonable requires us to balance "the nature and quality of the intrusion on the individual's Fourth Amendment interests against the countervailing governmental interests at stake." *Graham v. Connor,* 490 U.S. 386, 396 (1989).

Whether this entry and search were conducted reasonably is a close question. The police had legitimate concerns about their safety in entering and searching the house. Defendant had a substantial criminal record, which included violent crimes; there was reliable evidence that he was armed and aggressive; there were several other people in the house, including a former prison inmate; and certain physical characteristics of the house made it difficult to secure. Officers testified at the suppression hearing that the element of surprise was very important due to those factors and that they used the battering ram, rubber bullets, and flash-bang devices in order to surprise and distract the occupants of the house. Thus, the destruction of property and use of force arguably were necessary to carry out the search safely and effectively. The fact that a gun was found stuffed into the cushions of the chair in which Defendant was sitting when the police entered suggests as much: if officers had entered more gently, perhaps Defendant would have had a chance to draw his weapon and injure or kill an officer or be injured or killed himself.

Further, the search did not exceed the scope of the warrant, which weighs in favor of a conclusion of reasonableness. The warrant authorized officers to search the house for guns, ammunition, and associated documents and paraphernalia, and they did just that.

On the other hand, the extent of the property damage, and particularly the use of two flash-bang devices, one of which seriously injured Defendant, weigh in favor of a conclusion of unreasonableness. The record is unclear with respect to whether and why it was necessary to shoot out so many windows and break down so many doors.... It is not clear that the officers took all appropriate and available measures to reduce the risk of injury here. For instance, Officer Forsyth testified at the suppression hearing that he was trained to deploy the flash-bang device away from the outer walls of rooms and away from furniture and curtains that could catch on fire, so he aimed for the center of the room. Although his concern for fire safety was valid, Forsyth threw the flash-bang close to Defendant.

Ultimately, we need not determine whether the entry was unreasonable because we agree with the district court that suppression is not appropriate in any event. The alleged Fourth Amendment violation and the discovery of the evidence lack the causal nexus that is required to invoke the exclusionary rule.

The principle that the exclusionary rule applies only when discovery of evidence results from a Fourth Amendment violation is well-established. *See, e.g., Hudson,* 126 S.Ct. at 2164 ("[B]ut-for causality is ... a necessary ... condition for suppression.").

United States v. Ramirez, 523 U.S. 65 (1998), is instructive. There, the police obtained a no-knock warrant to search a home. Approximately 45 officers gathered, announced by loudspeaker that they had a search warrant, broke one window in the garage, and pointed a gun through the opening. The Supreme Court noted that "[e]xcessive or unnecessary destruction of property in the course of a search may violate the Fourth Amendment, even though the entry itself is lawful and the *fruits of the search are not subject to suppression." Id.* at 71 (emphasis added). Although the Court concluded that the police conduct in that case did not violate the Fourth Amendment, the Court noted that, had the search been unreasonable, it then would have had to determine "whether ... there was [a] sufficient *causal relationship* between the breaking of the window and the discovery of the guns to warrant suppression of the evidence." *Id.* at 72 n. 3 (emphasis added).

Here, the discovery of the guns was not causally related to the manner of executing the search. The police had a warrant, the validity of which is not questioned, and the guns, money, and other contraband were not hidden. Even without the use of a flash-bang device, rubber bullets, or any of the other methods that Defendant challenges, "the police would have executed the warrant they had obtained, and would have discovered the [evidence] inside the house." *Hudson,* 126 S.Ct. at 2164. Accordingly, we affirm the district court's denial of Defendant's motion to suppress the evidence.

* * *

REINHARDT, Circuit Judge, dissenting:

I. Introduction

I agree with the majority that the law enforcement officers' entry into David Kelly Ankeny's home without complying with the constitutional "knock and announce" requirements does not necessitate suppression of the evidence. After *Hudson v. Michigan,* 547 U.S. 586 (2006), such a knock-and-announce violation no longer justifies the remedy of suppression. Because I conclude, however, that the intensive and violent search that ensued was unreasonable due to the extreme use of excessive force and that the evidence seized during the unlawful search should be suppressed, I am compelled to dissent.

The majority avoids determining whether the military-style invasion of Ankeny's home, with the concomitant destruction of physical property and infliction of serious personal injuries, violated Ankeny's Fourth Amendment rights. It does so by holding that regardless of how unlawful the law enforcement officers' actions may have been, "suppression is not appropriate," because "[t]he alleged Fourth Amendment violation and the discovery of the evidence lack the causal nexus that is required to invoke the exclusionary rule."

Contrary to the majority's view, however, the remedy of suppression is hardly inappropriate in a case such as this, where a search executed with excessive and unreasonable force *directly* results in the discovery of the seized evidence. Because the unlawful search *was* causally related to the discovery of the evidence, and because our prior cases hold that suppression may be appropriate when the *manner of the search*—and not just the initial entry or a "preliminary mis-step,"—exceeds the terms of the warrant, I would hold that suppression is the proper remedy in Ankeny's case and therefore reverse his conviction.

* * *

III. Evidence May Be Suppressed Where, As Here, Officers Seize it as a Direct Result of a Search Executed with Unlawful Excessive Force

Although the majority correctly recognizes that "[u]nnecessary destruction of property or use of excessive force can render a search unreasonable," and states that "[w]hether this entry and search were conducted reasonably is a close question," it ultimately avoids deciding that issue by holding that "[t]he alleged Fourth Amendment violation and the discovery of the evidence lack the causal nexus that is required to invoke the exclusionary rule." After citing several cases for the proposition that causality is a necessary condition for applying the exclusionary rule, the majority concludes that "the discovery of the guns was not causally related to the manner of executing the search," because "[t]he police had a warrant" and "[e]ven without the use of a flash-bang device, rubber bullets, or any of the other methods that Defendant challenges, 'the police would have executed the warrant they had obtained, and would have discovered the [evidence] inside the house.'"

By holding that the exclusionary rule does not apply to searches conducted with excessive force, the majority overlooks our prior decisions that have applied or assumed the appropriateness of suppression when a "warranted search" is nevertheless rendered unreasonable because "it exceeds in scope or intensity the terms of the warrant." *United States v. Becker,* 929 F.2d 442, 446–47 (9th Cir.1991) (quoting *United States v. Penn,* 647 F.2d 876, 882 n. 7 (9th Cir.1980) (en banc)); *see also United States v. Chen,* 979 F.2d 714, 717 (9th Cir.1992). "[W]here there is a 'flagrant disregard' for the terms of the warrant, the district court may suppress all of the evidence, including evidence that was not tainted by the violation." *Chen,* 979 F.2d at 717 (quoting *United States v. Medlin,* 842 F.2d 1194, 1199 (10th Cir.1988)). These cases have never been overruled and they are in no respect inconsistent with *Hudson*. Because the intensity of the violent search of Ankeny's home demonstrated a "flagrant disregard" for the terms of the warrant, thereby turning it into a general warrant, it is necessary and appropriate to suppress the evidence that the officers seized pursuant to that warrant.

A. Discovery of the Guns is Causally Related to the Unlawful Search

Contrary to the majority's conclusion, the substantial Fourth Amendment violation in this case—the use of extreme and excessive force in the *search* (not merely the existence of an initial unlawful entry or a "preliminary mis-step," *Hudson*, 126 S.Ct. at 2164)—was the *direct* cause of the discovery of the guns. Under the controlling law, where, as here, the discovery of the evidence is the "direct result of an unconstitutional search," the evidence is subject to exclusion. *Segura*, 468 U.S. at 804 ("Evidence obtained as a direct result of an unconstitutional search or seizure is plainly subject to exclusion.").

In *Hudson*, as I have noted, the Court wrote that the knock-and-announce violation concerned only the "manner of entry" or a "preliminary misstep," 126 S.Ct. at 2164, which was followed by an "ensuing, lawful search...." *Id.* at 2171 (Kennedy, J., concurring). As Justice Kennedy explained, when "a violation results from want of a 20-second pause but an ensuing, lawful search lasting five hours discloses evidence of criminality, the failure to wait at the door cannot properly be described as having caused the discovery of evidence." *Id.* In this case, however, law enforcement officers executed the overall search that led directly to the seizure of the evidence with extreme and excessive force; indeed, the search was permeated with illegality. Given that the excessive force employed in this case rendered the entire search unlawful under the Fourth Amendment, the search bears no resemblance to the "lawful search" that followed the initial "entry" in *Hudson*. Indeed, the facts and circumstances in this case are the polar opposite of those in *Hudson*. In short, *Hudson* is entirely inapplicable.

Moreover, the majority's own description of the events belies its conclusion that the unlawful search was not the cause of the discovery of Ankeny's weapons. After explaining how the police broke down the door and entered the home, the majority then describes what happened inside the house subsequent to the unlawful entry. The law enforcement officers threw a flash bang device at Ankeny that exploded and badly burned him, secured the second floor, and threw a second flash bang device into an open area on that floor, setting on fire a bed in which two people were lying. Meanwhile, the officers shot bullets into the second story windows—indeed shot out ten windows. The majority then states that "[t]hereafter, the police recovered" two semiautomatic guns in the living room, a shotgun and a rifle in the upstairs bedroom, and another rifle in the basement. Because the immediate direct result of the violent search at issue here was the discovery of the guns, it follows that the discovery of the guns was causally related to the unconstitutional search....

B. The Benefits of Excluding the Evidence Outweigh the Costs in Cases in Which Excessive Force Renders a Search Unconstitutional

In addition to the presence of causality, in this case the cost-benefit rationale, which was critical to *Hudson*'s rejection of the exclusionary rule for knock-and-announce violations, strongly favors the suppression of the evidence directly obtained by a search conducted with unlawful, excessive force.... [T]he benefits of suppressing the fruits of military-style searches conducted with excessive force that may cause serious destruction to the home and serious injuries and the risk of death to occupants and guests, both adults and children, far outweigh the costs.

* * *

Although the fear of a lawsuit under 42 U.S.C. § 1983 may deter some officials from engaging in such dangerous and warlike conduct, I do not believe that the potential for civil damages would sufficiently deter law enforcement officers from using the type of excessive force at issue here. It is the official for whom the fear of civil liability is not ordinarily an effective deterrent that suppression is a necessary remedy in order to ensure compliance with the Fourth Amendment. One would expect that only the most belligerent of law enforcement officials, at whatever level, or those most disdainful of individual rights, would employ the type of force applied by the officers in this case. It is such officials, however, who are least likely to be deterred by civil liability alone, especially in light of the general practices regarding indemnification.[3] Moreover, informing law enforcement officials *a priori* that suppression will *never* be an available remedy if they first obtain a warrant, regardless of how excessive or destructive the invasion and search of the house, would serve only to encourage some individuals to unleash overwhelming force on our citizens in contravention of the Fourth Amendment.

Finally, the facts of this case demonstrate a lack of professionalism and disdain for the rights of individuals on the part of some law enforcement officers that is not likely to be cured by the possibility of a § 1983 action. The officers who executed the search were anything but professional in how they described, in text messages, "the fun" and the "good time had by all" when they caused Ankeny to suffer serious burns. In three text messages, officers wrote to each other:

> (1) "SORRY TIM, WE WERE JUST JUMPING OFF ... IT WAS 936 NE ... BIG FUN!"; (2) "IT WAS CRAZY ... FUN HAD BY ALL ... WELL EXCEPT FOR THE GUY WHO LAID ON THE FLASHBANG ... 2ND DEGR BURNS ... MISSING HALF A MUSTACHE"; (3) "BIG TIME FUN!! LOTS OF BROKEN GLASS, BAD GUY JUMPED ON THE FLASHBANG, GOOD TIME HAD BY ALL."

In sum, the costs of suppressing evidence in cases of excessive force are far less substantial than those in *Hudson,* whereas the benefits of deterrence, namely the protection of human life and property, are far more significant. Indeed, our analysis confirms that the exclusionary rule is not only appropriate, but absolutely necessary, to protect men, women, and children whose physical well being and very lives may be placed in jeopardy by the intentional and calculated use of excessive force in violation of the Fourth Amendment.

C. The Majority's Holding Will Lead to Unacceptable Results and is Unsupported by the Cases Upon Which It Relies

Although the majority does not explicitly state or hold that suppression may *never* be a remedy for the use of excessive force while executing a warrant, its causality argument followed to its logical conclusion does just that—it creates a blanket exception to the exclusionary rule for unreasonably executed searches *whenever* the officers possess a valid search warrant. This, of course, will inevitably lead to most unfortunate consequences, because under the majority's approach even the most outrageous methods employed by invading officers would be irrelevant so long as the officers had obtained a warrant....

* * *

---

3. "[P]olice officials are usually insulated from any economic hardship associated with lawsuits based on conduct within the scope of their authority.... Police officers are generally provided free counsel and are indemnified for conduct within the scope of their authority." *Briscoe v. LaHue,* 460 U.S. 325, 366 & n. 38 (1983) (Marshall, J., dissenting).

D. The Search of Ankeny's Home Was Unreasonable

Having determined that suppression may be an appropriate remedy in an excessive force case, I would hold that in this case the "intolerable intensity" of the force employed rendered the search unreasonable.

Ankeny contends that the tactics employed by officers constitute excessive force, including the deployment of 44 officers in the military style operation, the forcible entry of the home by means of a battering ram, the kicking down of the doors of every room in the house, the firing of myriad rubber bullets into the house shattering all the upstairs windows, and above all, the throwing of two "inherently dangerous" flash-bang devices towards three individuals, all with knowledge that a one year old infant was among the residents of the house. In this case, it is unnecessary, however, to look beyond the officers' use of the two flash-bang devices to hold that their "use of force was constitutionally excessive." In that respect, our decision in *Boyd* controls. There, we held that officers used excessive force when they threw a flash-bang device "'blind' into a room occupied by innocent bystanders, absent a strong government interest, careful consideration of alternatives and appropriate measures to reduce the risk of injury." [Boyd v. Benton County, 374 F.3d 773, 779 (9th Cir. 2004)] Here, one of the devices was hurled in Ankeny's direction as he was complying with the officers' instruction to him to get down on the floor. The other was then thrown toward a bed occupied by two individuals.

Compared to the deployment of the single flash-bang device in *Boyd,* the officers' use of two such devices in the instant action and the deliberate throwing of them in the direction of Ankeny and the two other occupants of the house whom the officers had no reason to believe had committed any offense was far more excessive. After breaking down the door with a battering ram, an officer demanded that Ankeny, who had been sleeping in a recliner in his living room, lie down on the floor. Although Ankeny did not resist or act in a threatening manner, an officer lobbed the flash-bang device towards him; as a result, the device exploded and caused first-and second-degree burns to his face and chest. Similarly, an officer who proceeded to an upstairs bedroom tossed a second device onto the floor by the edge of the bed where a man and a woman were lying, setting the bed on fire. If throwing a flash-bang device blindly into a room without warning is excessive, it is unquestionable that tossing these "explosive, incendiary weapon[s]" directly at three human beings without any notice, as the officers did here, constitutes constitutionally excessive force. *Id.* Also, as in *Boyd,* in which officers knew there were five to eight people sleeping in the apartment, officers here knew that at least four to seven adults and a one-year-old child resided at Ankeny's home.[5] Moreover, the evidence of severe property destruction noted by the majority—the breaking of many windows and doors without

---

5. The potentially dangerous circumstances that officers faced in searching the home in *Boyd* were also remarkably similar to—and if anything more perilous than—Ankeny's case, where police believed that Ankeny possessed a semi-automatic handgun. In *Boyd,* the officers believed that the armed robbery suspect might be in the apartment, that a stolen .357 magnum might be there as well, that another potential occupant had tried to buy an assault rifle, and two "armed individuals" were witnessed leaving the apartment. 374 F.3d at 777. The danger created by these weapons was heightened by the fact that "the apartment had a loft from which a shooter could have placed the officers in a vulnerable position as they entered the apartment...." *Id.* Despite such potential dangers, we held that the officers did not demonstrate the strong government interest that would permit officers to blindly deploy such an inherently dangerous device.

a clear explanation as to any necessity—strengthens the conclusion that the search was unreasonable due to its "intolerable intensity." Certainly, there is no evidence in the record that suggests that the officers took any substantial steps to reduce the risk of injury. In my view, a military style invasion of the type that occurred here is justified only in rare circumstances and only as a last resort, at least where innocent civilians and children are known to be present in the house.

IV. Conclusion

… I cannot agree that the mere fact that the police had a lawfully obtained search warrant bars this Court from suppressing the evidence directly discovered during the violent and unlawful search that actually occurred. Accordingly, I dissent.

———————

Notes and Questions

1. Do you agree with the majority that it was a "close question" whether the police acted reasonably? Was this a military-style invasion, as Judge Reinhardt contends in his dissent?

2. Despite Judge Reinhardt's passionate dissent, claims of excessive force almost never result in the suppression of evidence in criminal proceedings. Should the rule be otherwise? Isn't the exclusionary rule designed to deter police misconduct generally? Does it make sense to exclude evidence seized when police fail to follow the warrant procedures or very complicated rules governing warrantless searches, but not when they utilize excessive force?

3. Do you think Ankeny should have received a lighter sentence (he was sentenced to more than twenty years) because of the physical injuries and damage to his home? Would it be preferable to give defendants sentencing discounts when police violate the Fourth and Fifth Amendments, rather than excluding perfectly accurate evidence? For a discussion of this idea in the context of prosecutorial misconduct, see Sonja B. Starr, *Sentence Reduction as a Remedy for Prosecutorial Misconduct*, 97 GEO. L.J. 1509 (2009).

4. As Judge Reinhardt notes, the absence of an exclusionary rule for defendants subjected to excessive force pushes litigation into the civil justice system. In the federal system, Ankeny could bring a suit under 42 U.S.C. § 1983, alleging that the officers, acting under color of state law, violated his federal constitutional rights. How do you think Ankeny would fare in such a lawsuit before a jury of law-abiding citizens? Would they have much sympathy for a plaintiff who "had several outstanding arrest warrants and an extensive criminal history, including convictions for possession and delivery or manufacture of controlled substances, attempting to elude a police officer, escape, felon in possession of a firearm, and robbery" and who had "been charged with, but not convicted of, assault on a police officer and aggravated assault"? United States v. Ankeny, 502 F.3d 829, 833 (9th Cir. 2007).

5. Does the fact that many victims of excessive force are career criminals affect how the Court shapes § 1983 law? Consider one commentator's explanation:

> [T]he litigation of excessive force almost exclusively in the civil context skews lawmaking by focusing courts' attention on innocent plaintiffs—who may be unrepresentative of all those on whom force is used—and on law enforcement interests relating to civilian violence and officer safety—which may fail to capture many significant law enforcement interests. The result is an excessive force

analysis that engages a relatively small subset of the circumstances involving the use of force.

Nancy Leong, *Making Rights*, 92 B.U. L. Rev. 405, 452 (2012). Do you agree with Professor Leong's analysis?

6. In addition to the problem of being unattractive litigants (because they are criminal defendants), § 1983 plaintiffs must also contend with a challenging standard for determining excessive force. Consider the case below.

Graham v. Connor
490 U.S. 386 (1989)

Chief Justice REHNQUIST delivered the opinion of the Court.

This case requires us to decide what constitutional standard governs a free citizen's claim that law enforcement officials used excessive force in the course of making an arrest, investigatory stop, or other "seizure" of his person. We hold that such claims are properly analyzed under the Fourth Amendment's "objective reasonableness" standard, rather than under a substantive due process standard.

In this action under 42 U.S.C. § 1983, petitioner Dethorne Graham seeks to recover damages for injuries allegedly sustained when law enforcement officers used physical force against him during the course of an investigatory stop. Because the case comes to us from a decision of the Court of Appeals affirming the entry of a directed verdict for respondents, we take the evidence hereafter noted in the light most favorable to petitioner. On November 12, 1984, Graham, a diabetic, felt the onset of an insulin reaction. He asked a friend, William Berry, to drive him to a nearby convenience store so he could purchase some orange juice to counteract the reaction. Berry agreed, but when Graham entered the store, he saw a number of people ahead of him in the checkout line. Concerned about the delay, he hurried out of the store and asked Berry to drive him to a friend's house instead.

Respondent Connor, an officer of the Charlotte, North Carolina, Police Department, saw Graham hastily enter and leave the store. The officer became suspicious that something was amiss and followed Berry's car. About one-half mile from the store, he made an investigative stop. Although Berry told Connor that Graham was simply suffering from a "sugar reaction," the officer ordered Berry and Graham to wait while he found out what, if anything, had happened at the convenience store. When Officer Connor returned to his patrol car to call for backup assistance, Graham got out of the car, ran around it twice, and finally sat down on the curb, where he passed out briefly.

In the ensuing confusion, a number of other Charlotte police officers arrived on the scene in response to Officer Connor's request for backup. One of the officers rolled Graham over on the sidewalk and cuffed his hands tightly behind his back, ignoring Berry's pleas to get him some sugar. Another officer said: "I've seen a lot of people with sugar diabetes that never acted like this. Ain't nothing wrong with the M.F. but drunk. Lock the S.B. up." Several officers then lifted Graham up from behind, carried him over to Berry's car, and placed him face down on its hood. Regaining consciousness, Graham asked the officers to check in his wallet for a diabetic decal that he carried. In response, one of the officers told him to "shut up" and shoved his face down against the hood of the car. Four officers grabbed Graham and threw him headfirst into the police car. A friend of Graham's brought some orange juice to the car, but the officers refused to let him have it. Finally, Officer Connor received a report that Graham had done nothing wrong at the convenience store, and the officers drove him home and released him.

At some point during his encounter with the police, Graham sustained a broken foot, cuts on his wrists, a bruised forehead, and an injured shoulder; he also claims to have developed a loud ringing in his right ear that continues to this day. He commenced this action under 42 U.S.C. § 1983 against the individual officers involved in the incident, all of whom are respondents here, alleging that they had used excessive force in making the investigatory stop, in violation of "rights secured to him under the Fourteenth Amendment to the United States Constitution and 42 U.S.C. § 1983." The case was tried before a jury. At the close of petitioner's evidence, respondents moved for a directed verdict. In ruling on that motion, the District Court considered the following four factors, which it identified as "[t]he factors to be considered in determining when the excessive use of force gives rise to a cause of action under § 1983": (1) the need for the application of force; (2) the relationship between that need and the amount of force that was used; (3) the extent of the injury inflicted; and (4) "[w]hether the force was applied in a good faith effort to maintain and restore discipline or maliciously and sadistically for the very purpose of causing harm." 644 F.Supp. 246, 248 (WDNC 1986). Finding that the amount of force used by the officers was "appropriate under the circumstances," that "[t]here was no discernable injury inflicted," and that the force used "was not applied maliciously or sadistically for the very purpose of causing harm," but in "a good faith effort to maintain or restore order in the face of a potentially explosive situation," *id.*, at 248–249, the District Court granted respondents' motion for a directed verdict.

A divided panel of the Court of Appeals for the Fourth Circuit affirmed. The majority ruled ... that the District Court had applied the correct legal standard in assessing petitioner's excessive force claim.... We granted certiorari and now reverse.

Fifteen years ago, in Johnson v. Glick, 481 F.2d 1028 (2d. Cir, 1973), the Court of Appeals for the Second Circuit addressed a § 1983 damages claim filed by a pretrial detainee who claimed that a guard had assaulted him without justification. In evaluating the detainee's claim, Judge Friendly applied neither the Fourth Amendment nor the Eighth, the two most textually obvious sources of constitutional protection against physically abusive governmental conduct. Instead, he looked to "substantive due process," holding that "quite apart from any 'specific' of the Bill of Rights, application of undue force by law enforcement officers deprives a suspect of liberty without due process of law." As support for this proposition, he relied upon our decision in *Rochin v. California,* 342 U.S. 165 (1952), which used the Due Process Clause to void a state criminal conviction based on evidence obtained by pumping the defendant's stomach. 481 F.2d, at 1032–1033. If a police officer's use of force which "shocks the conscience" could justify setting aside a criminal conviction, Judge Friendly reasoned, a correctional officer's use of similarly excessive force must give rise to a due process violation actionable under § 1983. Judge Friendly went on to set forth four factors to guide courts in determining "whether the constitutional line has been crossed" by a particular use of force — the same four factors relied upon by the courts below in this case. *Id.*, at 1033.

In the years following *Johnson v. Glick,* the vast majority of lower federal courts have applied its four-part "substantive due process" test indiscriminately to all excessive force claims lodged against law enforcement and prison officials under § 1983, without considering whether the particular application of force might implicate a more specific constitutional right governed by a different standard. Indeed, many courts have seemed to assume, as did the courts below in this case, that there is a generic "right" to be free from excessive force, grounded not in any particular constitutional provision but rather in "basic principles of § 1983 jurisprudence."

We reject this notion that all excessive force claims brought under § 1983 are governed by a single generic standard.... In addressing an excessive force claim brought under § 1983, analysis begins by identifying the specific constitutional right allegedly infringed by the challenged application of force. In most instances, that will be either the Fourth Amendment's prohibition against unreasonable seizures of the person, or the Eighth Amendment's ban on cruel and unusual punishments, which are the two primary sources of constitutional protection against physically abusive governmental conduct. The validity of the claim must then be judged by reference to the specific constitutional standard which governs that right, rather than to some generalized "excessive force" standard.

Where, as here, the excessive force claim arises in the context of an arrest or investigatory stop of a free citizen, it is most properly characterized as one invoking the protections of the Fourth Amendment.... Today we make explicit ... and hold that *all* claims that law enforcement officers have used excessive force—deadly or not—in the course of an arrest, investigatory stop, or other "seizure" of a free citizen should be analyzed under the Fourth Amendment and its "reasonableness" standard, rather than under a "substantive due process" approach. Because the Fourth Amendment provides an explicit textual source of constitutional protection against this sort of physically intrusive governmental conduct, that Amendment, not the more generalized notion of "substantive due process," must be the guide for analyzing these claims.

... Our Fourth Amendment jurisprudence has long recognized that the right to make an arrest or investigatory stop necessarily carries with it the right to use some degree of physical coercion or threat thereof to effect it. Because "[t]he test of reasonableness under the Fourth Amendment is not capable of precise definition or mechanical application," *Bell v. Wolfish*, 441 U.S. 520, 559 (1979), however, its proper application requires careful attention to the facts and circumstances of each particular case, including the severity of the crime at issue, whether the suspect poses an immediate threat to the safety of the officers or others, and whether he is actively resisting arrest or attempting to evade arrest by flight.

The "reasonableness" of a particular use of force must be judged from the perspective of a reasonable officer on the scene, rather than with the 20/20 vision of hindsight.... With respect to a claim of excessive force, the same standard of reasonableness at the moment applies: "Not every push or shove, even if it may later seem unnecessary in the peace of a judge's chambers," *Johnson v. Glick,* 481 F.2d, at 1033, violates the Fourth Amendment. The calculus of reasonableness must embody allowance for the fact that police officers are often forced to make split-second judgments—in circumstances that are tense, uncertain, and rapidly evolving—about the amount of force that is necessary in a particular situation.

As in other Fourth Amendment contexts, however, the "reasonableness" inquiry in an excessive force case is an objective one: the question is whether the officers' actions are "objectively reasonable" in light of the facts and circumstances confronting them, without regard to their underlying intent or motivation. An officer's evil intentions will not make a Fourth Amendment violation out of an objectively reasonable use of force; nor will an officer's good intentions make an objectively unreasonable use of force constitutional.

Because petitioner's excessive force claim is one arising under the Fourth Amendment, the Court of Appeals erred in analyzing it under the four-part *Johnson v. Glick* test. That test, which requires consideration of whether the individual officers acted in "good faith" or "maliciously and sadistically for the very purpose of causing harm," is incompatible with a proper Fourth Amendment analysis. We do not agree with the Court of Appeals' suggestion that the "malicious and sadistic" inquiry is merely another way of describing conduct that is objectively unreasonable under the circumstances. Whatever the empirical correlations between "malicious and sadistic" behavior and objective unreasonableness may be, the fact remains that the "malicious and sadistic" factor puts in issue the subjective motivations of the individual officers, which our prior cases make clear has no bearing on whether a particular seizure is "unreasonable" under the Fourth Amendment....

Because the Court of Appeals reviewed the District Court's ruling on the motion for directed verdict under an erroneous view of the governing substantive law, its judgment must be vacated and the case remanded to that court for reconsideration of that issue under the proper Fourth Amendment standard.

It is so ordered.

[The opinion of Justice Blackmun concurring in the judgment is omitted.]

Notes and Questions

1. Professor Rachel Harmon contends that the Court has offered little guidance for police to determine when force is reasonable as opposed to excessive. *See* Rachel A. Harmon, *When Is Police Violence Justified*, 102 Nw. U. L. Rev. 1119, 1132 (2008) ("[T]he lower federal courts have recited *Graham* as if it were a mantra and then gone on to try to make sense of the facts of individual cases using intuitions about what is reasonable for officers to do."). Does the *Graham* decision offer helpful guidance?

2. One particularly troubling problem is the use of deadly force by police. Nearly thirty years ago, the Supreme Court held that police may not use deadly force to prevent the escape of a fleeing suspect unless the officer has probable cause to believe that the suspect poses a significant threat of death or serious physical injury to the officer or others. *See* Tennessee v. Garner, 471 U.S. 1 (1984). The *Garner* decision is cited often, but does it actually give police on the street much guidance about when it is permissible to use deadly force?

3. One scholar has remarked that "in applying the *Graham* objective reasonableness standard, the benefit of the doubt goes to the defendant police officer. If there is any way his actions could have been believed to be a reasonable response to the situation, as perceived by the officer at the time, the Fourth Amendment is not violated." Diana Hassel, *Excessive Reasonableness*, 43 Ind. L. Rev. 117, 122 (2009). Is Professor Hassel correct that the *Graham* standard imposes an impossibly high burden?

4. Plaintiffs face another obstacle in § 1983 litigation. State actors, including police officers, generally have qualified immunity from being sued as long as they did not act in violation of clearly established law. *See* Harlow v. Fitzgerald, 457 U.S. 800, 818 (1982). This means that state actors named as defendants can move to dismiss an excessive force lawsuit before a trial ever occurs. At first glance, it might seem harder for police officers to assert qualified immunity in excessive force cases. The reasonableness test for demonstrating a Fourth Amendment violation is very similar to the standard for establishing qualified immunity, so it would seem like a rare case where a plaintiff would be able to assert a viable Fourth Amendment excessive force claim for which the officer nevertheless has qualified immunity. In practice, however, successful civil rights suits alleging excessive force are fairly rare. One possible reason, as Professor Nancy Leong has explained,

is that "the qualified immunity determination exerts a gravitational pull on the constitutional merits determination, rendering courts more skeptical of the merits of plaintiffs' constitutional claims in cases where they intend to grant qualified immunity." Nancy Leong, *Making Rights*, 92 B.U. L. Rev. 405, 448 (2012).

5. One positive point for § 1983 plaintiffs is the way courts must look at the facts when a police officer moves for summary judgment on qualified immunity grounds. For many years, the law has been clear that a court is obligated to construe the facts in the light most favorable to the plaintiff who is alleging excessive force. Thus, when the plaintiff's story differs from the police officer's description of events, the court is required to assume the plaintiff's story is correct in a motion for summary judgment. *See* Saucier v. Katz, 533 U.S. 194, 201 (2001). But in an increasingly digital world, the court has scaled back this procedural rule. In Scott v. Harris, 550 U.S. 372 (2007), Harris was rendered a quadriplegic after an officer rammed his car and caused the vehicle to drive over an embankment and overturn. Harris contended that he was driving reasonably and did not pose a risk to any other drivers on the road. Officer Scott claimed that Harris was fleeing, driving at a high rate of speed, weaving in and out lanes, and posing a great danger to other motorists. Under the standard procedural posture, the court would be required to take Harris's statement of the facts as true in deciding whether Scott was entitled to qualified immunity. Yet, there was "an added wrinkle in this case: existence in the record of a videotape capturing the events in question." *Id.* at 378. According to the majority, the videotape unquestionably supported Officer Scott's claim. As such, the Supreme Court majority concluded that the summary judgment motion should be decided based on the videotape, not the "visible fiction" asserted by Harris, *id.* at 380–81, and that Officer Scott was entitled to summary judgment. Only Justice Stevens dissented, contending that the majority had "usurped the jury's factfinding function." *Id.* at 395. According to Justice Stevens (and the lower federal judges who sided with Harris in denying qualified immunity) it was possible for jurors to conclude that Harris's driving was not nearly as egregious as Officer Scott and the majority claimed and that it was possible to see Officer Scott's actions as unreasonable. How could Justice Stevens say this when his eight colleagues were so clearly convinced to the contrary? A group of professors studied this question by showing the videotape to a sample of 1350 Americans. Although a substantial majority came to the same conclusions as the eight Supreme Court justices, it was far from unanimous. As the authors explained, "African Americans, low-income workers, and residents of the Northeast, for example, tended to form more pro-plaintiff views of the facts than did the Court. So did individuals who characterized themselves as liberals and Democrats." Dan M. Kahan et al., *Whose Eyes Are You Going to Believe? Scott v. Harris and the Perils of Cognitive Illiberalism*, 122 Harv. L. Rev. 837, 841 (2009). You can watch the video and judge for yourself: http://www.supremecourtus.gov/opinions/video/scott_v_harris.html. Regardless of whether you think the majority was right or wrong to find Harris's story to be "visible fiction," the Court's opinion has made it more difficult for excessive force plaintiffs by giving judges an option in some instances to reject claims based on their interpretation of the facts.

6. *The Wire* shows a tremendous amount of police brutality. In some instances, as when Officer Walker breaks Donut's fingers out of spite because Donut had damaged property with a stolen car and created a lot of paperwork, it is clear that there has been unnecessary and unreasonable force. *See The Wire*, Season 4, Episode 10, at 2:20 minutes. But in other instances, it is far less apparent that officers used excessive force. Consider another scene from Season 4, Episode 10. Based on false information from Bubbles, Detective Herc pulls over a minister thinking that he is a member of Marlo's drug gang. Herc never punches

or kicks the minister, but he does forcefully shove his legs apart and push him to the ground during a frisk for weapons. Watch *The Wire*, Season 4, Episode 10, at 45:10 minutes. Did Detective Herc use excessive force? Do you think your conclusion is based on how Detective Herc has behaved in other instances throughout the series? Given the conclusions of Professor Kahan and his colleagues, is it possible that what seems like obvious police brutality in some scenes of *The Wire* is actually reasonable conduct?

7. Police officers have very dangerous jobs and thus need a certain amount of latitude to deal with unruly arrestees. On the other hand, police brutality is a terrible offense that harms not just the individuals who are beaten but also the community's confidence in the police. Are you confident from the law above that you could determine whether something constitutes excessive force? Do you think police are in a position to clearly know how far they can go in using force? Do you think lower federal courts have a clear view of the boundaries? Consider the cases below.

Crehan v. Davis

713 F. Supp.2d 688 (W.D. Mich. 2010)

PAUL L. MALONEY, Chief Judge.

Matthew Joseph Crehan ("Crehan") has asserted a Fourth Amendment excessive-force claim against City of Norton Shores, Michigan police officer James Davis ("Davis"), as well as claims arising under Michigan state law. Davis has moved for summary judgment on the federal claim on the basis of qualified official immunity, and he has moved to dismiss the state-law claims on different grounds....

BACKGROUND

On April 13, 2007, a police patrol car activated its overhead lights while driving behind plaintiff Crehan after Crehan had turned from westbound Norton Street onto northbound Davis Street. After the vehicles turned westbound on Kloap Street, the police car shined a spotlight on Crehan's vehicle. Then, after the vehicles turned northbound onto Glenside Street, the police car activated its siren. Crehan acknowledges that he was aware that a police vehicle was behind him at that time with its lights and siren activated while he was driving northbound on Glenside, and that nonetheless he did not pull over and stop the car. Instead, Crehan turned westbound on Summit, while the police car still had its overhead lights and siren activated.

At the time of the incident, Crehan was driving with a suspended driver's license, he knew that there was an outstanding civil bench warrant for his arrest, and the license plate on the car he was driving (588D32) was not registered to that car. But Crehan states, without contradiction from Officer Davis, that when Davis employed force against him, Davis did not yet know Crehan's identity and so did not know about the suspended license or the outstanding warrant. Crehan also points out, again without contradiction from Officer Davis, that the vehicle he was driving had not been reported lost, missing, or stolen as of April 13, 2007.

In any event, Crehan continued driving with knowledge that there was a police car running its overhead lights and blaring its siren behind him, not stopping until he reached his home at 1519 West Summit Road. According to Crehan, when he stopped in his driveway, he put his vehicle in "park", shut it off, opened the door, exited the car, and put his hands up in the air. Crehan heard shouts of "get on the ground", then felt his arm twisted behind his back and his body jammed into the cement driveway, inflicting chest contusions and a broken kneecap.

Crehan has submitted an affidavit which provides additional allegations "fleshing out" the incident from his perspective. Namely, Crehan attests that "as [he] was getting on the ground, while [already] in the 'push-up' position, defendant twisted affiant's arm behind his back, then forcefully slammed his body into the cement driveway." Significantly, Crehan also attests that Davis "never gave [him] the chance to completely 'get on the ground' before he inflicted chest contusions and a broken kneecap on [him]...."

Crehan was convicted of Fleeing and Eluding-Third Degree in violation of MICH. COMP. LAWS §750.479a(3). Section 750.479a, which is entitled Failure to Obey Directions of Police or Conservation Officer [and] Other Offenses, provides as follows, in pertinent part:

> (1) A driver of a motor vehicle who is given by hand, voice, emergency light, or siren a visual or audible signal, by a police or conservation officer, acting in the lawful performance of his or her duty, directing the driver to bring his or her motor vehicle to a stop[,] shall not willfully fail to obey that direction by increasing the speed of the vehicle, extinguishing the lights of the vehicle, or otherwise attempting to flee or elude the police or conservation officer. This subsection does not apply unless the police or conservation officer giving the signal is in uniform and the officer's vehicle is identified as an official police or department of natural resources vehicle.
>
> (2) Except as provided in subsection (3), (4) or (5), an individual who violates subsection (1) is guilty of fourth-degree fleeing and eluding, a felony punishable by imprisonment for not more than 2 years or a fine of not more than $2,000.00, or both.
>
> (3) Except as provided in subsection (3), (4) or (5), an individual who violates subsection (1) is guilty of third-degree fleeing and eluding, a felony punishable by imprisonment for not more than 5 years or a fine of not more than $5,000.00, or both, if 1 or more of the following circumstances apply:
>
> (a) The violation results in a collision or accident.
>
> (b) A portion of the violation occurred in an area where the speed limit is 35 miles an hour or less, whether that speed limit is posted or imposed as a matter of law.
>
> (c) The individual has a prior conviction for fourth-degree fleeing and eluding, attempted fourth-degree fleeing and eluding, or fleeing and eluding under a current or former law of this state prohibiting substantially similar conduct.

MICH. COMP. LAWS §750.479a(1)-(3). By contrast, Crehan notes, he was not prosecuted, let alone convicted, for resisting arrest or the like. Crehan seems to imply that if he had actually posed a threat to Officer Davis at the time Davis forcefully pushed him down to the ground, he would have been charged with such an offense, not merely fleeing and eluding from continuing to drive the car to his home.

* * *

LEGAL STANDARD: QUALIFIED OFFICIAL IMMUNITY

"The purpose of the qualified-immunity defense is to protect government officials from undue interference with their duties and from potentially disabling threats of liability." Binay v. Bettendorf, 601 F.3d 640, 646 (6th Cir. 2010). Absent such immunity, the "'prestige and pecuniary rewards'" of government employment might "'pale in comparison to the threat of civil liability,'" Smith v. Jefferson Cty. Sch. Bd. Of Comm'rs, 549 F.3d 641, 660 (6th Cir. 2008), deterring able people from serving in such positions.

Under the doctrine, a government employee performing a discretionary function generally is shielded from civil liability 'insofar as their conduct does not violate clearly established statutory or constitutional rights of which a reasonable person would have known.' Harlow v. Fitzgerald, 457 U.S. 800, 818 (1982). Moreover, qualified immunity is "'an immunity *from suit* rather than a mere defense to liability; and like an absolute immunity, it is effectively lost if a case is erroneously permitted to go to trial.'" Scott [v. Harris, 550 U.S. 372, 376 n.2 (2007).

Once the defendant asserted the defense of qualified immunity, the burden shifted to the plaintiff to show that he is *not* entitled to qualified immunity. To carry this burden, Crehan must show that a reasonable person in Officer Davis's position would have known that employing this type and degree of force under the circumstances alleged violated his Fourth Amendment rights under U.S. Supreme Court or Sixth Circuit precedent as it stood on April 12, 2007 (the day before the incident).

Although it is not always necessary to find a case where identical conduct had previously been determined to be unconstitutional, in light of preexisting law, the unlawfulness must be apparent.

Unpublished Sixth Circuit decisions cannot "clearly establish" a principle or the proper application of a principle to a set of facts, because such decisions are not binding; the same is true of district-court decisions, whether published or unpublished.

This means that Crehan cannot defeat Officer Davis's qualified-immunity defense with pre-April 13, 2007 precedent "clearly establishing" her *general* Fourth Amendment right to be free from excessive force at the hands of the government: "A constitutional right must be clearly established *in a particularized sense.* The contours of the right must be sufficiently clear that a reasonable official would understood that what he is doing violates that right." Garrison v. Glentz, 2005 WL 2155936, *5 (W.D. Mich. Sept. 5, 2005) (Miles, J.)

If a reasonable police officer in Davis's position "could disagree on the issue" of whether Davis's use of force violated his right to be free from excessive force *in this specific context and these specific circumstances,* immunity should be recognized. Key v. Grayson, 179 F.3d 996, 1000 (6th Cir. 1999)....

DISCUSSION: Federal Excessive-Force Claim

* * *

Under these circumstances was it excessive force for officer Davis to perform a takedown move to immediately bring this tense situation to a close and to ensure that the plaintiff did not decide to flee again? Clearly it was not. This is the quintessential situation where not every push and shove should be second-guessed in the safety and security of a court's chambers.... Officer Davis was faced with a choice: he could see if the plaintiff was sincere about ceasing flight and submitting to arrest, thereby risking another flight on foot or worse, or he could ensure that there would be no additional flight by forcefully taking custody of the plaintiff and putting the episode to an end. It was reasonable under the Fourth Amendment for Officer Davis to choose the latter course.

* * *

The court need not decide whether Officer Davis's use of force was reasonable for Fourth Amendment purposes, and it intimates no opinion on that issue. Even assuming *arguendo* that Davis's use of force against Crehan was *un*reasonable, the court determines as a matter of law that such unreasonableness was not necessarily apparent to a reasonable officer in Davis's position on April 13, 2007. Crehan's account may or may not be accurate, but the court is obligated to accept his version of the facts because he is opposing summary judgment. According to Crehan, Davis gave a command to "get down" on the ground, but never afforded him an opportunity to comply before employing force severe enough to break his kneecap and cause chest contusions. Even taking this as true, however, Crehan identifies no Supreme Court or published Sixth Circuit decisions predating April 13, 2007 which *clearly established* that performing this move under those circumstances (or materially similar circumstances) constituted excessive force.

As Officer Davis notes, he was faced with a difficult choice between only *two* options — force Crehan onto the pavement to minimize the risk that he would suddenly attack or again flee, or wait to see if he was indeed going to get all the way down to the ground (thereby "risking another flight on foot or worse", as Davis aptly puts it). The court agrees with Davis's reasoning that for purposes of qualified immunity, while he "might have misapprehended the amount of force called for under the circumstances", nonetheless "[if] he did so ... that mistake was reasonable."....

* * *

It is true, as Crehan notes, that it is excessive as a matter of law (and was recognized as excessive in April 2007 in our Circuit) to use force after the suspect has already been subdued, incapacitated or "neutralized."

But Crehan fails to explain what legal authority *compelled* Davis to conclude that Crehan was completely and safely neutralized, with no possibility of attack, resistance or further flight. The alleged fact that Crehan was starting to get down would not *conclusively* establish, beyond a doubt, that Crehan was not using the seeming start of compliance as a ruse to get the officer to momentarily "let his guard down." The court finds no binding precedent then in existence which would have clearly alerted a reasonable police officer that he was constitutionally required to wait — possibly at grave risk to his life, the life of other officers who would pursue if Crehan again fled, and members of the public — to see whether Crehan would, for the first time during the incident, begin to cooperate with lawful commands rather than using the appearance of compliance as a chance to surprise the officer by attacking him or running away.

Lastly, there is no allegation that Officer Davis made any comments to or about Crehan which suggest that he employed force out of malice rather than a belief — mistaken or not — that such force was necessary to minimize the still-lingering risk of attack or further flight. Contrast Baker v. City of Hamilton, 471 F.3d 601, 607 (6th Cir. 2006) (denying qualified immunity) (when striking plaintiff in the head with baton after plaintiff put his hands in the air in the "surrender" position, police officer yelled "that's for running from me"); Pigram v. Chaudoin, 199 Fed.Appx. 509, 513 (6th Cir. 2006) (police officer's slap of plaintiff "cannot be reasonably be construed as a means of subduing Pigram" where the officer told plaintiff contemporaneously that the slap was because plaintiff had a "smart-ass mouth").

For purposes of qualified immunity, then, Davis's conduct *at worst* falls within the doctrine's contemplated "ample room for mistaken judgments." Even with the benefit of the factual assumptions made on behalf of all parties opposing summary judgment, then, Crehan has not carried his burden of showing that Davis is not entitled to qualified immunity.

* * *

Summary judgment is **GRANTED to defendant** on the federal excessive-force claim.

* * *

Notes and Questions

1. Based on your understanding of the law of excessive force under the Fourth Amendment and qualified immunity, did the court reach the correct conclusion?

2. One reason the court finds qualified immunity for the officer is because he did not make "any comments to or about Crehan which suggest that he employed force out of malice." Should the absence of this factor matter at all in determining whether the officer complied with clearly established law? If so, how much or how little?

3. Assuming the court is correct that clearly established law allows an officer to immediately slam a suspect into the ground hard enough to break his kneecap following a police chase, does that rule make sense? Should police be obligated to give the suspect time to get down onto the ground? If so, how much time should be allowed before force can be applied? What are the countervailing considerations?

4. Crehan makes the point that he was not charged with resisting arrest, just fleeing from an officer. What is the significance of this? Does it show that Crehan posed a lesser threat to the officer and was engaged in a relatively low-level violation of the law? The *Graham* factors require courts to consider force in relation to the severity of the crime. Should we determine the controlling crime based on what prosecutors ultimately charged, what the officer subjectively believed at the time of the incident, or something else?

Jennings v. Jones
499 F.3d 2 (1st Cir. 2007)

LIPEZ, Circuit Judge.

Appellant Adam Jennings, a member of the Narragansett Indian Tribe, worked at a "smoke shop" operated by the tribe and located on Indian tribal land in Charlestown, Rhode Island. The smoke shop sold an array of cigarettes to members of the tribe and the general public. During a search of the smoke shop by the Rhode Island State Police, Jennings was arrested for disorderly conduct. Jennings initially resisted the arrest, requiring the use of force by state police officials to subdue him. As a result of that confrontation, appellee Kenneth Jones used an "ankle turn control technique" which broke Jennings' ankle. Jennings brought suit under 42 U.S.C. § 1983 against Jones and other officers, claiming that they had violated his Fourth Amendment rights by using excessive force to restrain him. Jennings also brought a claim under state law for battery.

Although a jury found in favor of most of the defendants, it ruled for Jennings on his excessive force and battery claims against Jones and awarded compensatory damages of $301,100. The district court then granted Jones' post-verdict motion for judgment as a matter of law, ruling for Jones on all three prongs of the qualified immunity inquiry. It first held that there was no constitutional violation because there was no evidence from which a reasonable jury could have concluded that the force used to subdue Jennings was excessive. It then concluded that, even if there had been a constitutional violation, Jones was entitled to qualified immunity because the relevant law was not clearly established and a reasonable officer would not have believed that the force was excessive and thus in violation of the Fourth Amendment....

On appeal, Jennings challenges the court's determinations on his Fourth Amendment claim. After careful review, we conclude that the court erred in granting qualified immunity to Jones. First, viewing the evidence in the light most favorable to the jury verdict, we conclude that the record establishes that Jones violated Jennings' constitutional right to be free of excessive force. Second, we find that this right was clearly established at the time of Jennings' injury. Third, we conclude that a reasonable officer in Jones' position would have believed that his actions violated Jennings' constitutional right. Consequently, we vacate the judgment of the district court and order reinstatement of the jury award....

I.

A. Factual Background

* * *

On July 14, 2003, Jennings was at work in a trailer referred to as the "smoke shop" owned and operated by the Narragansett tribe and located on tribal land in Charlestown, Rhode Island. The tribe and the State of Rhode Island were engaged in an ongoing dispute about whether the tribe could sell cigarettes tax-free. Pursuant to this dispute, the Rhode Island State Police had obtained a warrant to seize the cigarettes at the smoke shop, and several plain clothes officers were stationed inside the shop. After uniformed officers arrived in marked cars in the parking lot, the undercover officers inside the shop instructed Jennings to take a seat behind the sales counter. Jennings initially grabbed onto the counter, but then complied and seated himself behind the counter. He also complied when the state police asked him to move to a different seat.

Jennings testified that he was "upset" during these events. He complained loudly that the Rhode Island police had no right to be on his property, and he expressed concern over their treatment of his mother, who was also in the shop. He repeatedly used profanity in his comments.

Eventually, Officer Ken Bell asked Jennings to leave the shop without informing him that he was under arrest for disorderly conduct. A video taken by the state police shows that as Jennings was leaving the shop, an officer issued an order to handcuff him, and Jennings responded, "I'm not getting arrested." The video also shows that Jennings resisted handcuffing and that several officers subsequently wrestled him to the floor. Jones was one of the officers involved in subduing Jennings. He used an ankle restraint technique called the "ankle turn control technique" to control Jennings' leg.

During this conflict, the officers repeatedly instructed Jennings to stop resisting and to show them both of his hands because they were concerned that he might have a weapon. Jennings was initially unable to produce his left hand for handcuffing because it was trapped underneath his body. Officer Hill, one of the officers who was attempting to subdue Jennings, testified that he pulled Jennings' left arm out from under his body. The video shows that Hill then got up and walked away.

Jennings testified that he had ceased resisting before his arm was pulled out from underneath his body. About sixteen months prior to the smoke shop confrontation, Jennings had broken the ankle that Jones was restraining and had surgery performed on it. The officer's use of the "ankle turn control technique" caused Jennings considerable pain. Jennings informed Jones that the force Jones was using was hurting his previously injured ankle. Jones then increased the amount of force he was using and broke Jennings' ankle.

On the video, several seconds elapse from the time that Hill got up and left to the time that Jennings yelled in pain as his ankle was broken.[2] Within seconds after Jennings' in-

---

2. There is some uncertainty as to the precise length of time that elapsed between the time that Hill got up and the time that Jennings yelled in pain. In his closing argument to the jury, Jennings'

jury, the officers brought Jennings to his feet, already handcuffed, and escorted him out-side the smoke shop.

B. Procedural History

Jennings brought this action against Jones and several other police officers seeking damages under 42 U.S.C. § 1983 for excessive use of force and for battery under state law....

* * *

The case was submitted to the jury, which awarded Jennings $301,100 in compen-satory damages for his claims against Jones. Following the verdict, Jones moved for judg-ment as a matter of law ... on the ground that he was shielded from liability by the doctrine of qualified immunity....

The district court granted Jones' motion for judgment as a matter of law, concluding that it had erred in submitting the case to the jury to determine whether excessive force was used and ruling for Jones on all three prongs of the qualified immunity inquiry. It first held that there was no constitutional violation because there was no evidence from which a reasonable jury could have concluded that the force used to subdue Jennings was excessive. It then concluded that, even if there had been a constitutional violation, Jones was enti-tled to qualified immunity because the relevant law was not clearly established and a rea-sonable officer would not have believed that the force was excessive and thus in violation of the Fourth Amendment....

II.

The issue before us is whether the district court properly found appellee Jones entitled to qualified immunity from damages. When a defense of qualified immunity is pressed after a jury verdict, we have determined that "the evidence must be construed in the light most hospitable to the party that prevailed at trial." *Iacobucci v. Boulter,* 193 F.3d 14, 23 (1st Cir.1999)....

In this case, we must take this approach with respect to a critical factual dispute: whether Jones *increased* the force he applied after Jennings already had ceased resisting for several seconds. Jennings' claim of excessive force does not rest on the allegation that Jones merely *used* the ankle turn control technique, but rather that Jones *increased* the amount of force he applied after Jennings had stopped resisting and stated that Jones was hurting his previously injured ankle. Indeed, this theme of increased force by Jones with-out justification was the core of Jennings' case.

Jennings' opening statement immediately described this version of events to the jury. His attorney stated: "[O]ther witnesses will say that [Jennings] was warning [Jones] that he was breaking his leg. The evidence will show that ... the way [Jones] responded to that information was to twist harder, even though there was no reason to be twisting at all." At trial, three witnesses testified about Jones' restraint of Jennings. Jennings himself testified: "It was almost, not just incremental ... I'm telling the guy, look, you're going to break my ankle and so forth, and he twisted it more." Similarly, Domingo Monroe, who was seated across the room when the struggle occurred, testified: "Adam Jennings said,

_____

attorney described the interval as "twelve seconds at least," while Jennings' appellate brief describes the interval as eighteen seconds, citing only to the videotape of the incident. Although the videotape was played for the jury several times at trial and the jury also viewed the videotape during its deliberations, no one actually testified to the length of time that elapsed. Jones' appellate brief describes the time as "12–15 seconds" without citation....

you're hurting my ankle, it was already injured at one point in time … and then the officer said, well … if you wouldn't resist, then your ankle … wouldn't be hurting, and then as he said that, he cranked down harder on the ankle." Finally, Daniel Piccoli testified that he observed the struggle through the open door of the smoke shop:

> Q: Mr. Piccoli, could you describe the movements, if any, of the person who was on the floor?
>
> A: There weren't any.
>
> …
>
> Q: Did there come a point in time when you heard the person on the floor say something?
>
> A: Yes.
>
> Q: What did you hear him say?
>
> A: He said something in regard to, "let go, you're going to break my ankle."
>
> Q: And what, if anything, did the officer who was holding onto his ankle do?
>
> A: Just twisted more.

* * *

Near the end of the closing argument, Jennings' attorney returned to this theme:

> [Jones] never increased his force, he said, never decreased it. Now you tell me, if you've got constant force on somebody's ankle and their foot, why at some point does it break?… [D]id Trooper Jones who had Adam Jennings totally under control, lose it and just decide that because this guy was still complaining, that he was going to teach him a little bit of a lesson and put a little bit more pressure on.

As highlighted by the arguments of counsel, the consistent testimony from Jennings and two eye-witnesses would allow a reasonable jury to conclude that Jones *increased* the force he used to restrain Jennings after Jennings had already ceased resisting.…

* * *

The [district] court acknowledged that it could not supplant the jury's view of the facts with its own. Assessing credibility was the jury's role, and, as the court also acknowledged, the evidence permitted a reasonable finding by the jury that Jones increased the force he used after Jennings had ceased resisting. Yet the district court's qualified immunity analysis incorporated its skepticism about the jury's fact-finding on the critical issue of whether Jones increased his use of force. At one point, the court stated in its decision that "the jury determined that Jones' *use* of the ankle turn control technique amounted to excessive force." (Emphasis added.) Later, it referred to Jones "maintaining" the ankle hold after Jennings ceased resisting. Given the witness testimony discussed above, the district court's characterization is incomplete. Jennings and his two witnesses testified that Jones *increased* his force after Jennings ceased resisting, and we adopt this view of the evidence in accordance with the principle that we take facts in the light most favorable to the verdict.

* * *

In this case, the only view of the evidence consistent with the principle that we take the facts in the light most favorable to the jury verdict is that Jones increased the force he used to restrain Jennings after Jennings had ceased to resist and after Jennings had announced his prior ankle injury. That increased use of force broke Jennings' ankle. Our acceptance of these facts is no legal fiction. It is an acknowledgment of the deference that we must give to juries in the performance of their fact-finding role.

With this controlling legal principle in mind, and the view of the evidence required by that principle, we turn to the legal question of Jones' entitlement to qualified immunity. Our review is de novo.

III.

* * *

A. Prong One: The Constitutional Violation

In granting Jones' motion for judgment as a matter of law, the district court indicated that Jennings had not presented sufficient evidence for a reasonable jury to find that Jones had used excessive force in violation of the Constitution. To explore this question, we must first examine what constitutes excessive force under the Fourth Amendment, and then determine whether the evidence presented here was sufficient to support the jury verdict.

To establish a Fourth Amendment violation based on excessive force, a plaintiff must show that the defendant officer employed force that was unreasonable under the circumstances. *See Graham v. Connor,* 490 U.S. 386, 397 (1989). Whether the force used to effect a particular seizure is reasonable "must be judged from the perspective of a reasonable officer on the scene, rather than with the 20/20 vision of hindsight." *Id.* at 396. The reasonableness inquiry is objective, to be determined "in light of the facts and circumstances confronting [the officers], without regard to their underlying intent or motivation." *Id.* at 397. There must be "careful attention to the facts and circumstances of each particular case, including the severity of the crime at issue, whether the suspect poses an immediate threat to the safety of the officers or others, and whether he is actively resisting arrest or attempting to evade arrest by flight." *Id.* at 396.

We recognize the difficult situation confronting the police. It is undisputed that Jennings was challenging authority and resisting arrest. For much of the struggle, the police could not see Jennings' hands, and they reasonably could have believed that he might have a weapon. In making an arrest, a police officer has "the right to use some degree of physical coercion or threat thereof to effect it." *Id.* The fact that Jennings' ankle was broken does not, in itself, prove a constitutional violation: "[T]he use of force is an expected, necessary part of a law enforcement officer's task of subduing and securing individuals suspected of committing crimes." *Lee v. Ferraro,* 284 F.3d 1188, 1200 (11th Cir.2002).

However, the focus of Jennings' excessive force claim was not merely Jones' use of force, but rather Jones' *increased* use of physical force after Jennings had ceased resisting for several seconds and stated that the force Jones was using was hurting his previously injured ankle. Jennings used one of Jones' own witnesses to help establish that such force was unreasonable. Defendants initially called Officer Delaney, an instructor at the Rhode Island State Police Training Academy, to provide testimony about the training of officers and the use of various restraint techniques. During Jennings' cross-examination the parties agreed to treat Delaney as an expert witness. Delaney testified that the ankle turn control technique is taught to police officers as "a compliance technique and a restraint technique devised to control somebody from kicking." These techniques are taught in conjunction with the "Use of Force Continuum," a chart explaining that the degree of force that an officer uses should correlate with the degree of resistance offered by the arrestee. On cross-examination, Delaney testified that it was appropriate for an officer to continue to apply the ankle turn control technique after a suspect stops kicking:

> Q: [If] Adam Jennings is not kicking and his hands have been put behind his back and officers are attempting to put the flex cuffs on him ... would it be appropriate for an officer in the position of Trooper Jones to still be twisting his ankle?
>
> A: It would be appropriate for him to *maintain* that control over the leg.

(Emphasis added.)

However, Delaney's testimony about the continuum of force also supports the view that it would be unreasonable for an officer to *increase* his use of force when an arrestee has ceased to resist. Delaney testified during cross-examination that the continuum of force was a "two way street," meaning that, if the level of resistance changes, the level of force should be adjusted upward or downward correspondingly:

> Q: [E]ven if an officer feels at one point in time that one level of force is appropriate, he is supposed to adjust the amount of force he uses in response to a lessening of the arrestee; isn't that true?
>
> A: Yes. That would be the Trooper's own assessment of where that lies, yes, sir.

* * *

The district court's jury instructions noted that a factor in determining excessive force is whether "the degree of force used and also whether the degree of force was proportional to what was appropriate under the circumstances." Moreover, Jennings' closing argument specifically connected the content of Delaney's testimony to Jones' increased use of force:

> Now, the Judge is going to instruct you that, as does the Use of Force Continuum ... what goes up can come down and should come down if there's no need any longer to be applying that kind of force. Now, Adam Jennings himself has testified that he was on the floor, he was saying to somebody ... you're breaking my ankle or I just had surgery. And you heard testimony that the immediate response was [ ] a greater application of force than there already had been....

Thus, guided by the court's instructions on proportional force, the jury could conclude from Delaney's testimony that it would have been unreasonable for an officer to *increase* the pressure on Jennings' ankle several seconds after Jennings stopped resisting arrest and, moreover, stated that the pressure already applied was hurting his previously injured ankle.

* * *

... [A] reasonable jury could have exercised its common sense, informed by Officer Delaney's expert testimony, to find that Jones used excessive force by increasing pressure on Jennings' ankle after Jennings stopped resisting for several seconds and stated that Jones was using force that hurt his previously injured ankle. Consequently, we conclude that Jones violated Jennings' Fourth Amendment right to be free from an unreasonable seizure.

B. Prong Two: Whether the Law Was Clearly Established

The second prong of the qualified immunity analysis asks "whether the constitutional right ... was 'clearly established' at the time of the incident such that it would 'be clear to a reasonable officer that his conduct was unlawful in the situation he confronted.'" *Riverdale Mills Corp. v. Pimpare,* 392 F.3d 55, 65 (1st Cir. 2004). We consider whether existing case law gave the defendants "fair warning that their conduct violated the plaintiff's constitutional rights." *Suboh v. Dist. Attorney's Office of Suffolk,* 298 F.3d 81, 93 (1st Cir. 2002). In other words, the law is clearly established either if courts have previously ruled that materially similar conduct was unconstitutional, or if "a general constitutional rule already identified in the decisional law [applies] with obvious clarity to the specific conduct" at issue. *United States v. Lanier,* 520 U.S. 259, 271 (1997). We therefore consider whether materially similar cases or general Fourth Amendment principles gave Jones fair warning that it was unconstitutional for police officers to increase their use of physical force after an arrestee who has been resisting arrest stops resisting for several seconds and warns them that they are hurting his previously injured ankle.

We conclude that Jones had such notice. In *Smith v. Mattox,* 127 F.3d 1416 (11th Cir.1997), the Eleventh Circuit denied qualified immunity to a police officer accused of breaking the plaintiff's arm while putting on handcuffs. According to the plaintiff, he was at his mother's house when a uniformed police officer, acting on a tip from an informant, entered the yard. The plaintiff then "raised [a] baseball bat in a threatening posture" and ignored the officer's order to drop it. *Id.* at 1418. When the officer threatened to shoot, the plaintiff fled. He soon encountered the police officer again, and then plaintiff "docilely submitted to arrest upon [the officer's] request for him to 'get down.'" *Id.* In the process of putting on handcuffs, the officer bent the plaintiff's arm in a way that caused discomfort. When the plaintiff complained, the police officer, "with a grunt and a blow — but no sign of anger," broke his arm so severely that it required surgery for multiple fractures. The court concluded that such use of force would be excessive and that the officer was not entitled to qualified immunity.

Although *Smith* helps to demonstrate that the law protecting Jennings from Jones' increased use of force was clearly established, our conclusion does not depend on this strikingly similar case. Instead, *Smith* emphasizes the obvious unconstitutionality of increasing the force used on an arrestee to such a degree that a broken ankle results, after the arrestee has ceased resisting for several seconds and stated that the force already used is hurting his previously injured ankle.... Accordingly, we conclude that Jones' conduct was such an obvious violation of the Fourth Amendment's general prohibition on unreasonable force that a reasonable officer would not have required prior case law on point to be on notice that his conduct was unlawful. Indeed, even in *Smith,* which was decided six years before the incident at issue here, the court concluded that the law was clearly established against the use of increased force on a suspect no longer offering resistance because "the unlawfulness of the conduct is readily apparent even without clarifying caselaw." 127 F.3d at 1420.

* * *

Although the dissent professes to accept, arguendo, that Jones increased the force he used to restrain Jennings after Jennings had ceased resisting for several seconds, it continues to describe a different version of events with the cases it cites to show that the law was not clearly established. Some of these cases involve the use, rather than the increase, of force.[19] Others are inapplicable because the arrestee was still resistant.[20] Critically, these cases do not address the key conduct at issue here: the increased use of force on a previously resisting but now non-resisting arrestee. The dissent's reliance on such cases demonstrates its refusal to acknowledge that Jones' increased use of force was integral to Jennings' excessive force claim and that, consistent with our obligation to take the facts in the light most favorable to the jury verdict, we must accept this version of the facts in evaluating qualified immunity.

---

19. *Rodriguez v. Farrell,* 294 F.3d 1276, 1278–79 (11th Cir.2002); *Jackson v. City of Bremerton,* 268 F.3d 646, 650–53 (9th Cir.2001); *Eberle v. City of Anaheim,* 901 F.2d 814, 820 (9th Cir.1990).

20. *Huang v. Harris County,* No. 00-20806, 2001 WL 822534 (5th Cir. June 22, 2001) (unpublished disposition); *Brownell v. Figel,* 950 F.2d 1285, 1288, 1293 (7th Cir.1991).

When an individual has been forcibly restrained by several officers, has ceased resist-ing arrest for several seconds, and has advised the officers that the force they are already using is hurting a previously injured ankle, we cannot think of any basis for increasing the force used to such a degree that a broken ankle results. At the time of Jones' action, both existing caselaw and general Fourth Amendment principles had clearly established that this use of force was excessive in violation of the Constitution.

D. Prong Three: Whether a Reasonable Officer Would Have Believed a Violation Occurred

The final prong of the qualified immunity analysis is "whether an objectively reason-able official would have believed that the action taken violated that clearly established constitutional right." *Starlight,* 253 F.3d at 141. As we have previously explained, "[i]t is not always evident at the time an official takes an action that a clearly established right is involved. For example, the factual situation might be ambiguous or the application of the legal standard to the precise facts at issue might be difficult." *Riverdale Mills,* 392 F.3d at 61. Thus, even if an officer's conduct violated clearly established Fourth Amendment law, he may still be eligible for qualified immunity if he was reasonably mistaken as to the degree of force he should have used.

* * *

Again, we are sympathetic to the situation that Jones confronted. Jennings had to be subdued while he was resisting arrest, and the chaos caused by his struggle may have made it difficult for Jones to gauge the appropriate level of force. These circumstances would arguably allow a reasonable officer in Jones' circumstances to believe that it was law-ful to *maintain* the level of force he used even after Jones ceased resisting.

However, we reiterate that we must take the facts in the light most favorable to the jury verdict. Thus, we accept that Jones increased, rather than merely maintained, the force he applied to Jennings' ankle, even after Jennings had ceased resisting and stated that Jones was hurting his previously injured ankle.

Under such circumstances, even the "added measure of protection" provided by the third prong of the qualified immunity analysis does not insulate Jones from damages. *Cox v. Hainey,* 391 F.3d 25 (1st Cir. 2004). We find that an objectively reasonable officer in Jones' circumstances would not have believed that it was lawful to *increase* the amount of force that he used after Jennings ceased resisting and stated that Jones was hurting him.

* * *

IV.

We conclude that the district court erred in granting judgment as a matter of law to appellee Jones based on qualified immunity. Jones' use of increased force after Jennings ceased resisting violated the Fourth Amendment, the law was clearly established, and a reasonable officer in Jones' circumstances would have believed that his conduct was a vi-olation. Therefore, we vacate the district court's decision on that motion and reinstate the jury verdict.

* * *

So ordered.

LYNCH, Circuit Judge, dissenting. With respect, I dissent.

* * *

The majority reasons that the jury, by its general verdict, necessarily found that (1) Jennings had stopped resisting and had announced his prior ankle injury, and (2) Jones

nonetheless increased the twisting pressure on Jennings' ankle and broke it. The majority's reasoning entails a bit of legal fiction, since we do not know what the jury found and
these facts certainly were not necessary to the verdict. On this record, there is considerable ambiguity and no certainty about what underlying factual conclusions motivated
the *general* verdict.

Further, the facts themselves provide alternatives, and it is far from obvious on what
subsidiary facts the verdict rested. The jury could have found that the seriousness of the
injury, a broken ankle, was not justified by the charges Jennings was arrested on—disorderly conduct. This theory was argued by plaintiff's counsel at closing, and was consistent with the jury instructions. Or the jury could have concluded that the application
of force sufficient to break Jennings' ankle was itself excessive, whether or not Jennings
had continued to resist, and whether or not Jones increased the amount of force. The
jury could have concluded that it was unreasonable for Jones to maintain the same force
once Jennings said something about his ankle. Or it could have concluded that Jones
maintained the same level of force when, in its view, that level was excessive to begin
with. It may also be, as the district court noted, that the jury concluded that Jones "continued to twist Jennings' ankle *after* Jennings had stopped resisting." That is not a conclusion
that Jones "increased" the pressure, and again shows that the jury did not necessarily find
the facts as the majority assumes.

There is another reason not to conclude that the verdict against Jones necessarily entailed the majority's two factual findings. At the start of trial, there were seven individual defendants. There were also three plaintiffs, including Jennings' mother. These plaintiffs
asserted twenty-one different claims. On the six claims that went to the jury, the jury
ruled against plaintiffs on all claims except for the excessive force claim against Jones. Jurors sometimes reach compromise verdicts.

* * *

These are important issues ... [b]ut ultimately this case need not resolve those issues
because I believe the majority is wrong, even within its own set of assumptions. Even if
we assume, arguendo, that the rule that facts must be taken in support of the verdict permits the majority to assume its two facts, the district court's finding of qualified immunity must nonetheless stand....

B. *Second Prong: Clearly Established Law*

Officer Jones was undisputably acting within the scope of his authority and his discretion.
The burden then is on plaintiff to demonstrate the existence of clearly established constitutional law which the officer is said to have violated.

The second prong of the qualified immunity test asks whether the constitutional right
in question was "'clearly established at the time of the alleged violation' such that a reasonable officer would 'be on notice that [his] conduct [was] unlawful.'" *Riverdale Mills Corp.
v. Pimpare*, 392 F.3d 55, 61 (1st Cir.2004)....

In the end, the majority's holding that the law was so clearly established as to put the
officer on clear notice that his overall use of force, even increasing force, when the detainee
had stopped struggling (regardless of other circumstances) was unconstitutional rests on
two propositions. The first is that clear notice is established by a single case from the
Eleventh Circuit which is said to be so close to this case as to have put Jones on appropriate notice. The second is that there is no need for particularized notice because notice
of general principles is enough. Indeed, the majority goes so far as to reason that it should
have been perfectly obvious to Jones that his use of force was excessive, despite the fact

that the only expert testimony was directly to the contrary and the district court, which heard the case, concluded otherwise. The jury verdict made no conclusion on this issue, nor could it have.

1. *Lack of Prior Case Law*

There is no First Circuit case which gave Jones appropriate notice, nor is there a clear consensus of other persuasive authority giving such notice.

To start, a single opinion from another circuit is not, as a matter of law, sufficient to meet the plaintiff's burden of showing the law is clearly established. In *Wilson v. Layne*, 526 U.S. 603 (1999), the Supreme Court concluded that the law on a particular issue was not clearly established, and stated:

> [Plaintiffs] have not brought to our attention any cases of *controlling authority* in their jurisdiction at the time of the incident which clearly established the rule on which they seek to rely, nor have they identified a *consensus* of cases of *persuasive authority* such that a reasonable officer could not have believed that his actions were lawful.

Id. at 617 (emphases added). *Wilson* rejected reliance on one case as sufficient....

* * *

Further, *Smith* [*v. Mattox*, 127 F.3d 1416 (11th Cir.1997)] does not provide such fair notice to the officer, but supports the view that immunity was correctly granted. *Smith* merely affirmed the district court's *denial of summary judgment* on qualified immunity grounds because inferences, just barely, could be drawn that the force used was obviously and patently excessive....

Other court of appeals cases, in addition to *Smith*, tend to support the constitutionality of Jones' actions and so undercut plaintiff's claims that Jones was on clear notice from prior case law that his particular application of force was unreasonable. Many of these cases involve situations, as here, where officers were attempting to handcuff an individual who had been resistant. *See Rodriguez v. Farrell*, 294 F.3d 1276, 1278–79 (11th Cir.2002) (finding no excessive force, and noting that an officer need not credit an arrestee's claims of pain, especially when the arrestee is in the process of being handcuffed); *Jackson v. City of Bremerton*, 268 F.3d 646, 650–53 (9th Cir.2001) (finding no excessive force where plaintiff suffered a fractured finger after officer pushed plaintiff to the ground for purpose of handcuffing her despite being told of preexisting back and shoulder injuries, and where plaintiff had earlier posed a threat to officers' safety and ability to control a crowd); *Huang v. Harris County*, No. 00-20806, 2001 WL 822534, at *10 (5th Cir. June 22, 2001) (holding that force was reasonable where officer broke resisting arrestee's thumb by twisting her wrist, in an effort to "prevent her from kicking him ... and place her in handcuffs"); *Brownell v. Figel*, 950 F.2d 1285, 1288, 1293 (7th Cir.1991) (finding no constitutional deprivation where officers employed two different pain techniques, application of pressure on the plaintiff's knuckles and on a nerve behind his jaw); *Eberle v. City of Anaheim*, 901 F.2d 814, 820 (9th Cir.1990) (upholding the use of a "finger control hold" to remove a belligerent spectator from a sports arena). Under these cases, an officer in Jones' position could reasonably have concluded that his conduct was not unconstitutional.

2. *Need for Particularity and Obviousness*

For a variety of Fourth Amendment claims involving reasonableness and judgment calls, this circuit has required that plaintiff refer to particularized prior cases with similar facts. *E.g.*, *Buchanan v. Maine*, 469 F.3d 158, 168–69 (1st Cir.2006); *Riverdale Mills*, 392 F.3d at 65–66; *Napier v. Town of Windham*, 187 F.3d 177, 189 (1st Cir.1999)....

In excessive force cases, our rule is that there is an even greater emphasis on the requirement of particularity, where officers act under pressure and must make very quick judgments.... Jennings has not provided any such particularized prior case.

There is an exception to the need for particularized prior law where the police conduct is so excessive and lies so obviously at the core of what the Fourth Amendment prohibits that the unlawfulness of the conduct would have been readily apparent to an officer. The majority tries to fit within this exception. It reasons that it was so obvious that the use of force was excessive that Jones was clearly on notice for purposes of the second prong. The majority attempts to justify its obviousness conclusion by saying there is a clear and obvious dividing line between use of force and increased use of force. It cites no cases for that point, and the case law, described earlier, goes the other way. The majority's conclusion is not supported by the facts or by the case law.

As the district court pointed out, there are no cases holding that the use of the ankle turn control technique, which itself involves the use of varying degrees of force, is unconstitutional. Indeed, the use of pain, even when an individual complains of pain, is an established technique to bring an arrestee under control and to prevent possible injury to an officer. Case law has clearly established that the use of similar application-of-pressure techniques, even those involving increasing amounts of pain, does not amount to excessive force. There certainly are cases in which an officer's use of force is so obviously excessive that the officer is on clear notice; this is not one of them.

C. *Third Prong: Whether an Objectively Reasonable Officer Could Have Concluded that Jones' Actions Were Lawful*

The third prong of our qualified immunity test asks "whether a reasonable officer could have concluded that his actions did not violate [the] plaintiff ['s] constitutional rights." *Tremblay v. McClellan*, 350 F.3d 195, 199 (1st Cir.2003). This inquiry acknowledges that "law enforcement officials will in some cases reasonably but mistakenly conclude that [their conduct] is ... lawful." *Anderson v. Creighton*, 483 U.S. 635, 641 (1987). In *Saucier*, the Supreme Court explained how the third prong applies in excessive force cases:

> It is sometimes difficult for an officer to determine how the relevant legal doctrine, here excessive force, will apply to the factual situation the officer confronts. An officer might correctly perceive all of the relevant facts but have a mistaken understanding as to whether a particular amount of force is legal in those circumstances. If the officer's mistake as to what the law requires is reasonable, however, the officer is entitled to the immunity defense.

533 U.S. at 205.

Under the third prong, an officer who makes "a reasonable judgment call" is entitled to qualified immunity. *Buchanan*, 469 F.3d at 170. "The calculus of reasonableness must embody allowance for the fact that police officers are often forced to make split-second judgments—in circumstances that are tense, uncertain, and rapidly evolving—about the amount of force that is necessary in a particular situation." *Graham*, 490 U.S. at 396–97. On these facts, an objectively reasonable officer could have believed that Jones' use of force—and its degree—was lawful.

First, this was an instance of quick judgment by an officer in a chaotic situation. The district court stated that the entire series of these events took place in a chaotic scene over the course of about one minute. The key events, from when Officer Hill got up from the floor to when Jennings shouted in pain, took place within "several seconds." Jennings has represented the time in question to last anywhere from twelve to eighteen seconds. In this short time frame, a reasonable officer easily could have made mistakes as to Jennings' degree of resistance, the degree of risk Jennings posed to the officers, and the appropriate level of force to employ.

Concern over the safety of the officers and others was entirely reasonable. Jones testified he tried to secure Jennings' ankle both for his own safety, to prevent Jennings from kicking him while he was kneeling next to Jennings, and to lessen Jennings' resistance to arrest. He was also concerned that Jennings might have a weapon because he could not see Jennings' hands. Jennings himself acknowledged that at least one of his hands was not visible for a time. There is no doubt Jennings was resisting the officers earlier in the encounter. That was shown in the videotape.

Even if Jennings had just stopped kicking and flailing, the undisputed evidence demonstrates that (1) Jennings was not totally secured at the time his ankle was broken, (2) Jennings had posed a threat to the safety of the officers and others just seconds before, (3) the officers were having a difficult time getting the flex cuffs on Jennings, and (4) Jones' overall use of force was, in the opinion of the expert, reasonable under the circumstances. Delaney, the only expert witness on use of force, testified that *until* Jennings was "totally cuffed up and secured," it was appropriate for Jones to continue using the same compliance technique as he had, and alternative compliance techniques were not acceptable. Not even Jennings asserts that he was secured in handcuffs at the time his ankle was broken. Nor did any of his witnesses. Jennings asserted only that he had stopped moving and was not resisting arrest. And Officer Hill was clear that Jennings was not in cuffs when Hill stood up. Indeed, Hill got out of the way because other officers were having trouble cuffing Jennings.

The majority says it is irrelevant that Jennings was not handcuffed; the only important consideration is that Jennings had stopped struggling. Not so. Jennings had just been subdued by Hill; Hill then got up and Jennings could, until he was cuffed, have started up again at any time. An officer could reasonably view this as a time of great risk, and even greater risk than when Hill had subdued Jennings. The majority claims that expert testimony supports its view that any increase in force once Jones stopped struggling was unreasonable. The expert said just the opposite. Delaney testified that the degree of force was a judgment call, and that resistance was one factor and risk was another. Even if Jones were wrong about the degree of risk, his judgment was not unreasonable.

Jennings' argument is that regardless of whether he was cuffed, and even if the ankle turn control technique is acceptable, Jones applied the technique with too much force. But that is precisely in the area of judgment calls which are protected by qualified immunity....

* * *

For the reasons stated above, I respectfully dissent as to the majority's holdings.

Notes and Questions

1. Unlike many police brutality cases, in which qualified immunity stops the case before it gets to a jury, this case went to trial and was decided by a jury. As the court notes, the jury found in favor of the other police officers involved in the incident but found against Officer Jones. The jury awarded more than $300,000 in damages. Given that the

jury was willing to reject liability for most of the officers, does that make their decision against Officer Jones seem more or less reasonable?

2. The majority in *Jennings* relies on *Smith v. Mattox,* 127 F.3d 1416 (11th Cir.1997) for the proposition that there was clearly established law that forbids Officer Jones conduct. Do you find the *Smith* precedent persuasive?

3. In dissent in *Jennings,* Judge Lynch argues that an Eleventh Circuit case could not put Officer Jones (who works in the First Circuit) on notice. Do police officers read appeals court decisions at all, even from their own circuit? Do you think officers receive enough legal training from instructors to be aware of the court of appeals' views on how much force is appropriate? How many officers in the Untied States do you think are aware of the rules set forth in *Jennings* or *Crehan*?

4. The majority and the dissent in *Jennings* have very different views of what facts the jury did or might have found. And in rejecting the *Smith* decision as precedent, Judge Lynch points out that the district judge in that case had actually rejected qualified immunity, rather than granted it. How much deference should be given to trial judges who sat through the entire trial? Are judges on the court of appeals—who did not view the trial or even lay eyes on the arrestee or the officer—in any position to assess whether qualified immunity is appropriate? The law requires appellate courts to view the facts in the light most favorable to the plaintiff, but is that a plausible command? Can different judges apply the "light most favorable" rule and still reach different conclusions as to what the controlling facts are? If so, what can be done about that?

5. Do you think it is hard or easy for police officers to successfully claim qualified immunity? Do you think courts have set the standard in about the right place? Or should they be more or less willing to let excessive force cases go to trial by jury?

6. Can you reconcile the 1st Circuit's decision denying qualified immunity in *Jennings* with the Western District of Michigan's decision granting qualified immunity in *Crehan*?

7. Do you think it is clear to police officers on the street—who are called upon to use their hands, batons, handcuffs, and sometimes even their firearms to subdue suspects— how much force they can use without violating the Fourth Amendment or losing qualified immunity? Consider Rachel A. Harmon, *When Is Police Violence Justified,* 102 Nw. U. L. Rev. 1119 (2008) (contending that the Supreme Court has not offered adequate guidance).

8. How common is it for police officers to use excessive force? As a starting point, the Bureau of Justice Statistics estimates that only one percent of police encounters involve the use of any force at all. *See* Bureau of Justice Statistics, Contacts Between Police and the Public: Findings From the 1999 Survey (2001). Yet, one percent of all encounters amounts to about 500,000 events per year. Scholars estimate that about one-third of those encounters involve excessive force, meaning that excessive force "does not appear to be a rare occurrence." Ronald Weitzer & Steven A. Tuch, Race and Policing in America 28 (2006).

9. Why did Jennings initially resist the police? Although we cannot know for sure, one possibility is that he felt he was being targeted because he was Native American (and because his tribe was in a dispute with the State of Rhode Island). Social science evidence has long indicated that minority groups, particularly African-Americans, distrust the police to a greater degree than whites. *See* Tom R. Tyler, *Policing in Black and White: Ethnic Group Differences in Trust and Confidence in the Police,* 8 Police Quarterly 322, 323 (2005).

Susan Bandes, Patterns of Injustice:
Police Brutality in the Courts
47 Buffalo Law Review 1275 (1999)

Introduction

Legal consequences often hinge on whether events or incidents are categorized as isolated or connected, individual or systemic, anecdotal or part of a larger pattern. Courts tend to portray incidents of police brutality as anecdotal, fragmented, and isolated rather than as part of a systemic, institutional pattern. Though numerous doctrines—including federalism, separation of powers, causation, deference, discretion, and burden of proof-provide partial explanations for the judicial fragmentation of police misconduct, it seems clear that courts cannot or do not choose to see systemic patterns for reasons that transcend doctrinal explanations....

* * *

There are many such factors that lead courts to mask or discount systemic harm. Sometimes, courts cannot see connections because of conscious or preconscious assumptions and expectations about how the story should be told, what ought to be part of the story, or how the characters will behave. This article will seek to explore some of those assumptions.

The question I want to address is why this particular story, the story of police brutality, is so often anecdotalized. Police brutality is different in kind and degree from police misconduct, examples of which include conducting an unlawful search or using unnecessary force. Police brutality is conduct that is not merely mistaken, but taken in bad faith with the intent to dehumanize and degrade its target.... Police brutality is longstanding, pervasive, and alarmingly resilient. Perhaps the most puzzling aspect of its resilience is the extent to which it depends on the complicity of multiple governmental actors, including the courts.

Consider the example of ongoing police torture in the City of Chicago. During a period of at least thirteen years, more than sixty men, all of them black, have alleged that they were physically abused, and in fact, tortured, by several named officers in the Area Two Violent Crimes Unit on Chicago's South Side. Certain types of torture, by certain officers, were alleged repeatedly, including suffocation with a typewriter cover, electroshock with a specially constructed black box, hanging by handcuffs for hours, a cattle prod to the testicles, and Russian roulette with a gun in the suspect's mouth. The allegations were corroborated not only by defense attorneys and emergency room physicians, but by several other respected groups including a broad-based Chicago citizens' coalition, an investigative group from the internal police review agency, and Amnesty International. In a number of cases, defendants alleged that they were tortured into confessing. Yet despite the fact that the same group of Area Two officers was named again and again, and despite the startling similarity in methods alleged, the courts, with few exceptions, failed to see a pattern. Indeed, appellate courts upheld several rulings that prevented the identification of just such a pattern. Ten of the defendants are on death row today. In civil cases against the officers and the City of Chicago, the failure to introduce prior acts of brutality paved the way for a rejection of a finding of municipal liability. Although one of the officers, Commander John Burge (the creator of the infamous black box), was ultimately expelled from the force, other officers involved continued to progress through the ranks, garnering nothing but commendations and promotions.

It would be comforting to dismiss the story of Area Two as unusual, anecdotal, and unrepresentative. Unfortunately, in many significant respects, what happened at Area Two represents business as usual in Chicago and throughout the United States. Official reactions to police brutality fall into a familiar pattern. The violence inflicted on Rodney King, Malice Green, Abner Louima and Amadou Diallo (the unarmed West African immigrant in New York City who died in a hail of 41 police bullets) was, predictably, followed by police assurances that it was an aberration, the work of a few rotten apples, a criminal act rather than routine police conduct.

In most cases, the view of police brutality as aberrational (or even justified) shapes the conduct of every institution responsible for dealing with the problem, including police command, review boards, administrative agencies, city, state and federal government, and the courts. This view allows police brutality to flourish in a number of ways, including making it easier to discount individual stories of police brutality, and weakening the case for any kind of systemic reform. The fragmentation of systemic police brutality needs to be addressed at many institutional levels. This article is particularly, though not exclusively, concerned with how and why that fragmentation occurs in the courts.

The fragmentation takes several forms and is accomplished through numerous doctrinal means. Often, police engaged in incidents of brutality have a history of such incidents, departments house several officers engaged in similar types of brutality or corruption, or the brutality is concentrated in a single neighborhood. However, there are innumerable hurdles to identifying or documenting such patterns. Complaints are discouraged, confessions are not videotaped, record keeping is lax or nonexistent, records are sealed or expunged, patterns are not tracked, and police files are deemed undiscoverable. If a history of past incidents does exist and, despite these hurdles, becomes known to the brutality victim, he faces additional hurdles introducing evidence of the brutality in court, including restrictive evidentiary rulings, protective orders, judicial toleration of police perjury or of "the blue wall of silence," assumptions about credibility that favor police officers, the absolute immunity of testifying officers, substantive constitutional doctrines insulating failures to act or demanding an exceptionally high level of proof of wrongdoing, restrictive municipal liability standards coupled with a lack of receptivity to evidence of systemic wrongdoing, and standing doctrines that make injunctive relief nearly impossible to obtain.

In police brutality cases, the routine categorizing of incidents as isolated rather than systemic has had terrible consequences. Systematic police brutality has been masked, insulated, and implicitly condoned because courts have failed to make connections among incidents; failed to make causal links between police conduct and the injuries and confessions of suspects; denied litigants or juries access to information which would enable linkages to be discovered; and in general persisted in defining encounters as separate from — and irrelevant to — any overarching systemic patterns that need to be addressed.

* * *

I. Police Brutality: The Irrelevant Is That Which Fails To Preserve Our Laws

* * *

A. The Story of Chicago's Area Two Violent Crimes Unit

* * *

Consider the story of the Area Two Violent Crimes Unit, located in an overwhelmingly poor, black area of the South Side of Chicago. For years, stories trickled out of Area Two into the surrounding community that within that building, police officers were torturing people. The problem was getting anyone outside the community to believe the stories. Beginning in the early 1970's, numerous complaints were filed with the applicable administrative agencies, the mayor, the state's attorney, and the United States Attorney, and there were allegations raised in numerous judicial proceedings. These complaints and allegations came from numerous unconnected sources, described alarmingly similar acts of torture, and named the same men over and over. But the scandal is not only that no action was taken for so long. It is also that men continued to be convicted, imprisoned and—in ten cases—sent to death row (where they remain today), based on confessions they alleged were elicited by torture. The alleged torturers and those who supervised them continued to be commended and promoted through the ranks, never eliciting the slightest hint of official disapproval.

It eventually became known that over a period of at least thirteen years, starting in the early 1970's, more than sixty men, all of them black, had been systematically tortured by members of a group of approximately fifteen Area Two officers, all of them white. The Office of Professional Standards [OPS] did not investigate the complaints until 1990, and the city suppressed its report finding systemic torture in Area Two until 1992. The unit commander and ringleader, John Burge, was not fired until 1993. No criminal proceedings were ever instituted. Only two other officers (both of whom have been reinstated) were disciplined for any of the incidents, and many of them have been promoted, commended, and allowed to retire with full benefits. No effort has been made to identify or address systemic problems in Area Two, or higher up the chain of command. The story is presented as closed, and even given a happy ending: the ringleader was ferreted out. As far as we know, there is no more police torture in Chicago.

A close examination of the Area Two story yields insight into the ways in which interlocking institutions, including state and federal courts, enable police brutality to thrive within the contours of existing law and social policy. The examination will also provide a concrete illustration of the assumptions that help government officials, including judges, accept and in many respects condone official brutality, and the way those assumptions work.

When suspects were tortured in Area Two, many of them sought to file complaints. Some may have attempted to complain at Area Two itself. If so, there is no record of what occurred. The failure of police personnel to log complaints against their colleagues is a common problem, and one cause of the lack of data on police wrongdoing. But most suspects filed complaints with the OPS. In this venue, the complaints were dismissed as "not sustained," a fate that befalls the vast majority of the complaints filed with OPS. "Not sustained" usually means that the only witnesses to the incident were the police and the victims, and that OPS cannot figure out whom to believe. One journalist described "not sustained" as "a shrug that says 'who knows?'" A finding of "not sustained" also reflects the presumption, automatically employed as a matter of OPS policy, that in an uncorroborated swearing contest, the officer's word must be believed. When corroboration is available, it often comes from people whose credibility is questioned, such as other suspects, friends or family, people with criminal records, or gang members.

Brutality and its culture create many of these conditions. Brutality is, by definition, concealed. The torturer usually attempts to leave no marks. Many of Commander Burge's techniques, including suffocating the suspect, placing a revolver in the suspect's mouth, squeezing the suspect's testicles, and playing Russian roulette, leave no physical trace. When there is visible injury, unless there is corroboration, it becomes the officer's word against the suspect's as to how and where it occurred.

The swearing contest is stacked by two other essential characteristics of brutality. One characteristic is that it is concealed not only by the officer inflicting it, but by the officer's colleagues and supervisors. The nationwide code of silence is well documented, pervasive, and crucial to the continuation of official brutality. In Area Two, no officer ever publicly stepped forward to corroborate the existence of torture, or even intervened at the stationhouse itself.

The second characteristic is that brutality is practiced against members of marginalized groups living in marginal neighborhoods. In Area Two, for example, all of the 65 known torture victims were black. One Philadelphia cop describing the widely known rules stated: "The first is, keep it in the ghetto. In the good areas, you don't go stopping people without cause." One byproduct of this rule is that brutality will seem unbelievable or aberrant to decisionmakers who tend to hail from more privileged backgrounds — it will not correspond to their experience. Another is that those who can corroborate it are too easy to dismiss — they are more likely to have criminal records, to be associated with gangs, and to be less articulate, sophisticated, and educated. They are less likely to evoke the empathy of decisionmakers with whom they have little in common.

Whether a complaint is found sustained or unsustained, OPS makes no attempt to place it in any larger context. OPS files are not computerized. Due to police union complaints, in 1992 a five-year statute of limitations on administrative proceedings was established, with complaints over five years old held inadmissible in internal investigations. Thus police, attorneys, and the community were deprived of another avenue for tracking individual or precinct-wide patterns of brutality. In ruling on a complaint, OPS does not consider (or even ascertain) whether there were past complaints against the officer. No effort is made to discern patterns of complaints regarding particular officers, particular precincts, or certain types of conduct (such as discharging a firearm or searching without a warrant). This is particularly unfortunate since in Chicago, as nationwide, a vastly disproportionate amount of the brutality is committed by a small group of officers, each of whom may have many complaints in his file. Even multiple sustained complaints have no negative effect at all on the officer's career — they are not even entered in his personnel file.

Even when the rules permit, OPS has not usually been a zealous investigative agency. Since 1985, three internal audits have accused the agency of losing investigative files and failing to interview key witnesses. Even when a former Chief of Police asked the agency to look into allegations against Burge, it took an inordinate amount of time to do a slipshod and incomplete investigation. OPS' performance is consistent with that of many internal police divisions, stemming largely from the unwillingness of police officials to identify corruption in their ranks....

In the meantime, many of the torture victims confessed, and were charged with crimes. Thus individual complaints of torture at Area Two were making their way to the Illinois courts in suppression motions during the 1980's and early 1990's. For example, in 1982, Andrew Wilson said that he was repeatedly punched, kicked, smothered with a typewriter cover, electrically shocked, and forced against a hot radiator. In October 1983, Gregory Banks said he confessed to murder after Burge, John Byrne and other Area Two detectives beat him, suffocated him, and subjected him to Russian roulette. In November 1983, Darryl Cannon said Byrne, Peter Dignan, and others subjected him to electroshock with a cattle prod and played Russian roulette with him, placing the gun in his mouth. In 1985, Lonza Holmes said that Burge and Detective Madigan severely beat him. In 1986, Aaron Patterson said that Area Two officers placed a typewriter cover over his face, beat him, choked him, and threatened him.

In each case, the trial court denied a motion to suppress the confession. In many of the cases, the court denied the defendant access to police department brutality records on the officers involved. If the defendant had such evidence in his possession, and sought to introduce evidence of similar acts of brutality by Area Two officers, or even by the same Area Two officers, the trial court barred such evidence—granting the state's motion in limine on grounds that the evidence of prior beatings was irrelevant and immaterial. In all but the Banks and Wilson cases, the Illinois appellate courts initially affirmed the trial courts' rulings. The courts ruled that there were no visible bruises, or that the bruises could have been inflicted earlier or by the defendant himself. Contemporaneous written statements by one defendant chronicling his abuse were barred, and dismissed as self serving; the testimony by another defendant's brother regarding bruises was found insufficiently credible. The trial courts' decisions to suppress evidence of prior acts of brutality were upheld. The courts ruled, in case after case, that they would defer to the trial courts' factual conclusions.

Patterson's motion to introduce prior OPS files regarding brutality by Area Two detectives met the fate that has been, until quite recently, typical of such motions OPS had found the prior allegations "not sustained" which the Illinois courts transformed to "unfounded." The Illinois Supreme Court declined to second guess the trial court's decision to exclude the OPS evidence, stating: "A mere unfounded accusation that these officers beat someone who was arrested at Area Two one year previously, without more, does not tend to make it more probable that they coerced defendant's confession."

Given that holding, the Supreme Court had little trouble, only one year after rejecting Patterson's claim, in rebuffing Hobley's attempt to introduce testimony of several others who claimed to have been abused by Area Two detectives in similar fashion. The court found that the three years between Hobley's interrogation and the alleged incidents made the prior allegations too remote to be relevant.

* * *

The Illinois Supreme Court's peculiar notions of relevance may explain why the state's attorney was comfortable arguing, in the Cannon case, that the testimony of twenty-eight other arrestees who claimed to have been tortured at Area Two was irrelevant to Cannon's claim of torture. The testimony of the prior arrestees included claims that Dignan, Byrne, Grunhard, and others had suffocated them with plastic bags, shocked them in the testicles, beaten them with a flashlight, held a gun in their mouths, and hanged them from handcuffs, among other allegations. The State argued that the prior evidence was irrelevant because it differed from that at Cannon's trial. For example, whereas Cannon alleged that officers placed a shotgun in his mouth and pulled the trigger, these arrestees alleged that officers placed a handgun in their mouths. And whereas Cannon alleged the use of a cattleprod, other arrestees alleged that they were beaten with a flashlight. The Illinois Appellate Court rejected the argument, finding that the prior evidence was relevant to the intent, motive, and course of conduct of the officers, and also could be used to impeach their credibility. It remanded the case to the trial court, directing the judge to permit evidence of the prior brutal acts.

How did Darryl Cannon learn of twenty-eight prior incidents? Although he was first interrogated in 1983, and tried in 1984, his conviction was reversed on grounds unrelated to the conduct of his interrogation. By the time he was retried in 1994, information was available that had been nonexistent or inaccessible ten years earlier. It began with the 1982 interrogation of Andrew Wilson and his brother Jackie, who had been arrested for killing two police officers. . . .

In 1986 Wilson, represented by a small, highly committed group of veteran police misconduct litigators, filed a federal civil rights suit against the individual officers and the City of Chicago. Wilson's testimony is described in excruciating detail in three articles by

John Conroy, House of Screams, Town Without Pity, and The Shocking Truth. For example, from Wilson's testimony:

> Detective Yucaitis entered the room ... carrying a brown paper bag from which he extracted a black box. Yucaitis allegedly pulled two wires out of the box, attached them with clamps to Wilson's right ear and nostril, and then turned a crank on the side of the box.
>
> 'I kept hollering when he kept cranking,' Wilson said, 'but he stopped because somebody come up to the door.'... Burge returned with the black box about an hour later. He said 'fun time.'... Burge put one clip on each of his suspect's ears and started cranking.... 'I was hollering and screaming. I was calling for help and stuff. My teeth was grinding, flickering in my head, pain and all that stuff.... That radiator ... it wouldn't have mattered. That box ... took over. That's what was happening. The heat radiator didn't even exist then. The box existed.'

Photos taken the next day at the request of Wilson's lawyer showed burn marks where Wilson claimed to have been held against a radiator, and a pattern of scabs on his ears that "seemed inexplicable unless one believed that alligator clips had indeed been attached to Wilson's ears."....

The first trial ended in a hung jury. Toward the end of the first trial, Wilson's lawyers fortuitously began learning of other victims of torture at Area Two. The information came, at the beginning, from the anonymous letter mentioning Melvin Jones, who led the lawyers to other victims. At Wilson's second trial, District Judge Brian Duff excluded the testimony of Jones, who claimed to have been subjected to electroshock by Burge and other officers nine days before the interrogation of Wilson, in an investigation of the same crime. He also excluded the testimony of Donald White that he was arrested in the same investigation shortly before Wilson was, and was beaten for several hours by Burge and other Area Two officers. Judge Duff held Jones' and White's testimony irrelevant....

The jury thus heard no evidence of Burge's prior conduct. The resulting highly confusing jury verdict was that Wilson's constitutional rights had been violated, that the City of Chicago had a de facto policy authorizing its police officers to physically abuse persons suspected of having killed or injured a police officer, but that this policy had not been a direct or proximate cause of the abuse to Wilson.

In 1987, the Illinois Supreme Court overturned Wilson's criminal conviction, finding that he had visible injuries, such as burns on his chest and thigh, a black eye, cuts requiring stitches, and bleeding on the eye surface. It found he had been injured while in police custody, and remanded for a new trial because the state had not met its burden of explaining the injuries.

At the same time, public awareness of Wilson's allegations about Burge was beginning to grow. In 1989 — one year after Burge was promoted from lieutenant to commander — a local watchdog group called Citizens Alert asked OPS to reopen Wilson's 1982 investigation as well as some other files in which Burge was mentioned. Citizens Alert formed a special Task Force to Confront Police Violence, which created a coalition of more than fifty community organizations to lobby the police board. The coalition began an intensive campaign of letter writing, speeches, articles, marches and rallies. They spoke at every police board meeting until the board agreed to have OPS reopen the case. Protests escalated as other men began stepping forward with similar allegations of torture. In 1990, Amnesty International issued a report finding that systematic torture had occurred in Area Two. That same year, OPS began its new investigation.

OPS filed two reports in 1990. The first found that John Burge had applied electroshock to Wilson and had burned his face, chest, and thigh by holding them against a radiator. The second found that Burge and others had engaged in systematic abuse, including planned torture, for at least thirteen years, claiming at least fifty victims. It concluded that command members were aware of the systematic abuse and had perpetuated it, either by participating or by failing to take any action. The city immediately had the reports sealed, and they were not released until 1992, by the order of a federal judge in a related case. Upon the report's release, Police Superintendent Leroy Martin called it "statistically flawed." Martin reportedly claimed that "to believe the department has a brutality problem is to smear the sacrifices of officers who have died in the line of duty." Mayor Daley said, "These are only allegations ... allegations, rumors, stories, things like that. This is a report by an individual. It is not fully documented."

Although neither Daley nor Martin took action at the time, public pressure continued. Burge was eventually fired by the Police Board in 1993. Two other men were disciplined for fifteen months each and then reinstated. The president of the Police Board emphasized that the Board's findings were based on the Wilson case alone, stating "[w]e did not make findings on any other cases. This is not an indictment of the entire police department."

... No criminal charges were brought against Burge or any of the other Area Two officers. No federal investigation was undertaken. The other Area Two officers, like Peter Dignan, continue to be decorated and promoted. In 1995, Dignan was promoted to the rank of lieutenant for meritorious service. Police Superintendent Matt Rodriguez was quoted as saying he was unaware of the allegations against Dignan when the selection was made. The Mayor's spokesman said "the Police Department obviously had all sorts of information at its fingertips when it made these promotions, and is standing behind the promotion, and so are we."

* * *

III. Conclusion

The courts, like all the other institutions that have allowed police brutality to flourish, seem to believe that inaction is not only an option, but an ethically neutral one — a choice to opt out of the whole unpleasant situation. Or perhaps, on some levels, these institutions have made a choice, and are comfortable with it. The decision to maintain the status quo is unlikely to be made by police, or even judges, in a vacuum. Much of the police brutality literature suggests that many societal forces converge to encourage the existing order. To the extent that low level police officers, unhindered or condoned by supervisors, the chief, the local political structure, and the courts, are brutalizing minority residents of poor neighborhoods, it may be that these actions are part of an implicit bargain with society — at least that part of society that has political and economic power. Such brutality is often implicitly approved by majority residents of stratified, segregated societies who value law and order, who want the boundaries between black and white neighborhoods policed, and who will put up with the infliction of a substantial amount of brutality on others as long as it is not made impossible to ignore. The treatment of police brutality as aberrational and anecdotal is an essential though largely invisible part of the bargain.

———————

Notes and Questions

1. Professor Bandes paints a bleak picture of police brutality in Chicago. *The Wire* paints a similarly bleak picture of Baltimore. Do you assume the problem is similar in

every major American city? Is it worse in smaller towns, where there are likely to be fewer internal procedures and oversight in place?

2. Professor Bandes' article is nearly fifteen years old and the article chronicles conduct from decades ago. Does police brutality on this scale still exist in the United States? If it took so long to uncover the pattern of brutality in Area 2, how would you know if similar misconduct was occurring right now in your hometown?

3. Conventional wisdom is that tort suits against police officers and departments (whether under the federal § 1983 or state law) are fairly rare and very difficult to win. *See* Alison L. Patton, Note, *The Endless Cycle of Abuse: Why 42 U.S.C. § 1983 Is Ineffective in Deterring Police Brutality*, 44 HASTINGS L.J. 753 (1993). Is that correct though? Professors Marc Miller and Ron Wright looked behind the reported caselaw to analyze settlements reported in newspapers. They found that plaintiffs do file and settle tort suits against the police with some frequency. *See* Marc L. Miller & Ronald F. Wright, *Secret Police and the Mysterious Case of the Missing Tort Claims*, 52 BUFF. L. REV. 757 (2004). If many lawsuits alleging police brutality are settled, does that make you more comfortable that the system is working to remedy police violence?

4. *The Wire* portrays a considerable amount of police brutality. Much like Area 2, many of these officers work together in the same precinct. How difficult would it be for a plaintiff to unearth evidence of brutality against other victims? In theory, all of this information could be found during the pre-trial discovery process. But expecting that the information will turn up may not be a correct assumption. First, plaintiffs must have a capable lawyer who files discovery requests. Second, the attorney needs to know what kind of information to look for. Third, and possibly most important, the lawyer must be very persistent. Police departments typically fight hard to avoid turning over disciplinary records and personnel files. *See* Patton, *supra*, at 761–62. A lawyer must therefore request discovery, ask for the right types of information from the right precincts, and then persistently fight back against efforts from the police departments' attorney to deny that information. There are likely many instances in which plaintiffs never lay eyes on valuable information that would help their cases. Do you find this troubling? On the other hand, if it were much easier to seek discovery against police departments, would officers have to spend their time responding to document requests and interrogatories, rather than policing the streets to keep society safe?

Barbara Armacost,
Organizational Culture and Police Misconduct
72 George Washington Law Review 453 (2004)

Introduction

The events of September 11, 2001 have left us forever changed. We feel more vulnerable, we are more suspicious, and we are torn in new ways about the balance between vigorous law enforcement and cherished, individual rights of privacy and liberty. In the immediate aftermath of 9/11, the law enforcement community got very high marks. New York City Police officers and their brethren who poured in from all over the country were rightly hailed as heroes for their role in rescuing the injured, recovering the dead, protecting property, and helping to restore order. It was almost hard to remember the charges of overaggressive policing that had plagued the New York Police Department ("NYPD") during most of the pre-9/11 Giuliani administration.

When tightly knit service organizations such as police, firefighters, and rescue workers act courageously as they did following 9/11, we (and they themselves) attribute their sacrificial conduct not only to personal heroism, but also to the values of their service culture. The cultural self-definition of policing is exemplified by such terms of solidarity as the "brotherhood in blue" and the "thin blue line." As a result of their organizational cohesiveness, officers are quick to ostracize colleagues who let them down, but they (and their departments) view successful or heroic interventions as collective achievements.

When police officers are accused of misbehavior, however, police solidarity has the opposite effect. In the face of outside criticism, cops tend to circle the wagons, adopting a "code of silence," protecting each other, and defending each other's actions. If the misconduct is found to be true, moreover, their departments deem the miscreants "rogue cops" whose conduct does not reflect negatively on the organization from which they came.

The truth, however, is that the same organizational culture that produces extraordinary heroism also facilitates shocking misconduct, sometimes by the very same actors. One need look no further than the popular press to see that, alongside the high marks for heroism on 9/11, the NYPD is continually dogged by allegations of misconduct and brutality. Moreover, the NYPD is not alone. It is hard to think of a big city police department that has not been investigated by multiple commissions and task forces for charges of corruption, brutality, or other serious unlawful acts....

Despite all of the attention that has been paid to this issue in recent years — the news coverage, lawsuits, task forces, commissions, and congressional hearings — recurring incidents of police brutality have led many citizens to wonder why very little seems to change. Over the years, a number of prominent police departments have made efforts toward reform, often in response to the recommendations of independent commissions convened to investigate incidents of alleged wrongdoing by police. Still, misbehavior by law enforcement officers seems ubiquitous, and serious, lasting reform appears illusory. As one Los Angeles Times reporter observed in a story about the LAPD:

> Often, an investigation is undertaken, followed by recommendations for sweeping change, which are ignored or halfheartedly implemented. The cycle is so habitual that one steadfast aspect of each new report is a section wondering why the recommendations in past reports haven't been carried out.

What accounts for this lack of success in achieving lasting police reform? The answer I want to explore is that reform efforts have focused too much on notorious incidents and misbehaving individuals, and too little on an overly aggressive police culture that facilitates and rewards violent conduct. Real reform requires police organizations to accept collective responsibility, not only for heroism, but for police brutality and corruption as well.

Consider the way in which police departments describe and defend controversial actions by individual cops: either as well-intentioned but unfortunate responses to dangerous and ambiguous situations, or as the aberrant behavior of rogue cops. The first kind of explanation — the kind that police departments offered to justify the Rodney King beating and the more recent shooting of Amadou Diallo — seeks to place the incident in question outside of the category of police wrongdoing. Occasional beatings or shootings of suspects whom police reasonably believed were armed and dangerous are regrettable, but not culpable. They are the unavoidable consequences of the job that we ask police officers to do in a dangerous and unpredictable world. The second explanation, by contrast, accepts certain police actions as unquestionably wrong, but attributes them to a small minority of police officers gone bad. Thus, these incidents tell us little or nothing about the experience or motivation of the well-behaved and well-intentioned majority.

These explanations are powerful and important because they frame the way police departments — and ultimately the legal system — respond to police brutality. Every prescription for controlling police violence is based on a theory of why police officers behave the way they do. This article argues that, because the stories police departments tell themselves (and us) about the causes of police violence are flawed, it is not surprising that judicial, administrative, and departmental responses to police violence have been notoriously unsuccessful.

The primary defect in these explanations (and the solutions that go with them) is that they view police misconduct as resulting from factual and moral judgments made by officers functioning merely as individuals, rather than as part of a distinctive and influential organizational culture. The regrettable-accident explanation asks whether the officer's judgment about whether to shoot, or how much force to apply, was reasonable under the circumstances as known or perceived by the officer at the time of the incident. This explanation deems an officer not morally or legally culpable for a reasonable, though erroneous, decision. Thus, police departments view the regrettable-accident scenario as requiring no corrective intervention, except, perhaps, an official expression of regret for harm caused. What this explanation fails to consider, however, is how the officer came to be in that particular situation in the first place and whether there is anything to be learned by examining the organizational norms and policies that framed his judgment.

The officer-gone-bad explanation is flawed in a similar way. It assumes that the misbehaving cop is off on a "frolic and detour" for which he alone is accountable. This explanation allows the department to distance itself from incidents of misconduct by labeling the perpetrators "rogue cops," deviants who are wholly unlike their fellow officers. Moreover, it allows police leadership to declare to the rest of the rank and file, "this incident is not about you," as Los Angeles Mayor Riordan proclaimed to the rest of the police force in the aftermath of the recent Rampart scandal. All of this allows the police organization to absolve itself of any responsibility for the officer's wrong-doing.

By contrast, theoretical and empirical scholarship on policing strongly suggests that the police organization bears significant responsibility for police misbehavior. My goal in this Article is to explore the understudied and underappreciated link between organizational culture and police misconduct. Punishing individual cops will not cure the problem of police violence if systemic features of the police organization permit, sanction, or even encourage the officers' violent behavior. Like the individual-specific explanations that police departments offer for the misbehavior of their members, current remedies are inadequate to the extent that they ignore or undervalue institutional and organizational factors.

… [This article] demonstrate[s] the limitations of existing legal remedies for addressing police misconduct. The flaw is that these remedies focus almost exclusively on individual culpability for particular, isolated incidents. This individual-specific and incident-specific approach seriously underestimates the power of the police organization in shaping the conduct of street-level cops. Moreover, not only is individual-specific liability ineffective, it is perverse. It creates scapegoats that may satisfy society's moral outrage while deflecting attention away from the institutional structures that lie at the root of the problem of police brutality.

* * *

I. Police Brutality: Rotten Applies or a Rotten Barrel?

* * *

B. Individual-Specific Remedies and Systemic Harms

… Behavioral theories of civil and criminal liability posit that individuals who suffer negative consequences for their conduct will think twice before repeating their acts (specific deterrence), and observing others' punishments will discourage potential wrongdoers from engaging in similar acts (general deterrence). Putting aside the question of whether tort and criminal liability actually deter bad conduct, it is clear that civil and criminal sanctions have had only limited effect in curbing police brutality.

Section 1983 provides a federal civil cause of action for damages or equitable relief in circumstances where state or local governmental officials have deprived citizens of rights secured by the United States Constitution or federal law. Section 242 authorizes criminal prosecutions against government officials under similar circumstances. On both the criminal and civil side, the prosecuting or complaining party ordinarily frames civil rights actions as Fourth Amendment claims of excessive (unreasonable) force during a search or arrest.

A number of scholars have written extensive analyses explaining why civil and criminal liability under the federal civil rights statutes have had only limited success in curbing governmental misconduct. The conventional arguments fall into two main categories: practical obstacles—difficulties resulting from the characteristics of the typical litigant and the circumstances in which civil rights cases arise—and doctrinal obstacles—immunities and other features of the civil rights laws that make it difficult for plaintiffs to prevail. This article adds a third obstacle, namely the individual-specific and incident specific nature of civil rights litigation, which limits its ability to address institutional causes.

The primary mechanism for constitutional criminal prosecution of police officers who use excessive force is 42 U.S.C. § 242. Criminal prosecutions can also be brought under generally applicable state laws such as laws against assault, aggravated assault, manslaughter, and murder. Some states also have civil rights statutes, which, like § 242, make excessive force in violation of the federal or state constitution a distinct crime. Others have extensively catalogued the arguments for why criminal liability is not a very effective tool against police brutality, and I will review them only briefly.

First, it bears noting that criminal standards define the absolute minimum of socially-acceptable conduct. Thus, even when criminal laws are enforced effectively, they do not describe sufficiently high norms of behavior to constrain police discretion within professionally acceptable boundaries.

Second, and relatedly, the government brings criminal prosecutions against police officers only rarely and only in the most egregious cases. There are a number of reasons for the low prosecution rate. One set of explanations arises from the nature of the American penal system, in which the accused enjoys certain "procedural advantages" that make criminal cases more difficult to investigate and win. Moreover, governmental officials enjoy the benefit of additional immunities from prosecution under state and federal criminal law. These features reduce the number of prosecutions that are likely to be brought and won. In addition, prosecutors may view criminal sanctions as unjustifiably harsh when used against a police officer who is "just trying to do his job." The criminal sanction has an all or nothing quality that exposes the offending officer to the risk of prison, as well as job loss and public humiliation. A second reason for the low prosecution rate is that police and prosecutors have an identity of interest in investigating and prosecuting crime and an accompanying need to maintain good professional relationships, which may create disincentives for filing criminal cases against cops. A third explanation is that some jurisdictions have inadequate systems for tracking, monitoring, and investigating complaints of misconduct. Critics also charge that there are inadequate mechanisms for oversight and accountability outside of the law enforcement community to ensure that prosecutors bring the right cases.

Third, even when prosecutors bring excessive force cases, other factors make them difficult to win. In particular, juries are unlikely to be particularly sympathetic to civil rights victims, who are usually criminal suspects. When it comes down to whose story to believe—the criminal suspect or the police officer—in situations unlikely to involve other witnesses, the officer has a distinct advantage. The fact that the victim is viewed as unsympathetic and unreliable contributes to jurors' natural reluctance to brand a police officer a criminal and to send him to prison for doing his job.

Finally, federal prosecution under § 242 presents two additional impediments that limit its reach in police brutality cases. The first is that courts have interpreted § 242 to require "specific intent" to violate the victim's constitutional rights, which has confused many courts and made prosecution more difficult. In addition, to the extent that § 242 (like its civil counterpart) permits prosecution of ordinary torts and crimes—conduct otherwise under state jurisdiction—it raises issues of federalism that may lead prosecutors to err on the side of underenforcement.

While there is much more that could be said about criminal prosecution in the law enforcement context, there is virtually unanimous agreement that it cannot serve as a first-line offense against police brutality. As a practical matter, the government will not, and probably should not, employ criminal sanctions except in the clearest and most egregious cases of police brutality.

On the civil side, the practical obstacles to bringing and winning a § 1983 case are many. First, many damages suits are simply never brought at all because plaintiffs are ignorant of their substantive legal rights. In addition, they may lack ready access to legal representation, or may fear retaliation from police for bringing suit. Second, even when they are brought, § 1983 suits alleging excessive force are particularly difficult to win. This is due both to the nature of the legal standard, and to the kinds of situations that give rise to such suits. Recall that police may use only the level of force that was reasonable under all the circumstances, including, among other things, the seriousness of the crime at issue, whether the suspect's conduct threatened the safety of the officer or others, and whether the suspect was actively resisting or seeking to evade arrest. In addition, the standard is to be construed "from the perspective of a reasonable officer on the scene, rather than with the 20-20 vision of hindsight." In sum, excessive force determinations involve a fact-intensive balancing of the government's interest in crime control against the citizen's interest in safety and bodily integrity, which gives the benefit of the doubt to the governmental actors. Moreover, the end result often boils down to whose story the judge or jury believes—the suspect's or that of the officers who stopped, arrested, or questioned her.

This puts the civil rights plaintiff at a distinct, practical disadvantage. The typical complainant in an excessive force case is a criminal suspect from a poor, minority neighborhood, often with a criminal record—not a very credible witness in the eyes of the jury. In addition, the plaintiff's witnesses—who are likely to be family, friends, or acquaintances from the same neighborhood—will not be viewed as disinterested witnesses and may suffer from some of the same credibility problems as the plaintiff. The only other witnesses are likely to be other police officers who, perhaps understandably, will give their fellow officers the benefit of any doubt. More troubling, however, a widely documented norm known as the "code of silence" may lead officers to stonewall (or even lie) about the compromising details of the alleged abusive interaction. Thus, even where the plaintiff can prove serious injury, police officers may be able to allege facts—such as that the plaintiff was resisting arrest or appeared to be reaching for a gun—that would support the officers' use of force.

Moreover, despite the fact that the code of silence is a well known phenomenon, and despite evidence that police officers sometimes lie about police-citizen encounters, courts tend to give the officers' stories the benefit of the doubt. Judges and juries (and most ordinary citizens) view police officers as public servants who work under difficult, dangerous, and uncertain conditions to maintain the "thin blue line" between order and chaos. Moreover, the tendency by judicial decision makers to favor police officers over alleged victims of excessive force is reinforced by a widely held public view that a little bit of police brutality is simply the price we pay for crime control. All of this puts the injured plaintiff at a practical disadvantage in making out her case.

In addition to the practical difficulties, there are doctrinal obstacles as well. First, state police agencies are absolutely immune from civil damages liability under the Eleventh Amendment. Moreover, while courts have construed the Eleventh Amendment to permit injunctive relief against state agencies by the fiction of naming state officials in their individual capacities, the Supreme Court has effectively foreclosed this avenue of relief for victims of police violence through the application of standing rules that are virtually impossible to satisfy in the law enforcement context.

Second, although state and local police officers, in their individual capacities, have no Eleventh Amendment immunity, they are shielded by qualified immunity, which abrogates liability for unconstitutional conduct if a court finds that the offending officer could "reasonably have believed" his actions were justified under the circumstances. Moreover, recall that courts evaluating the officer's beliefs and action are not to engage in 20-20 hindsight, but to give the benefit of the doubt in close cases to the police. This follows from the very nature of police work, which requires quick thinking in rapidly changing, sometimes dangerous circumstances involving substantial uncertainty. In many cases, the events surrounding police-citizen encounters will be difficult to reconstruct, and the question of whether an officer applied reasonable force under the circumstances as he reasonably believed them to be will not be easy to answer. Thus, while qualified immunity does not protect police officers who engage in the worst sorts of police brutality, some amount of excessive—and unconstitutional—force will escape civil liability.

By these observations, I do not mean to suggest that qualified immunity is not justified in many instances. It stands to reason that even the very best police officers will make judgments or take actions that turn out, in hindsight, to have been mistaken. Immunity from damages liability in such cases is necessary and defensible. My point is, rather, that in cases where officers are immune from liability, there is no legal incentive for police departments to engage in self-criticism and self-review that could lead to insights about how to avoid potentially harmful police-citizen encounters in the future. By definition, however, these are instances in which self-review could be beneficial. Qualified immunity applies where the officer got it wrong but where his mistakes, either factual or legal, were reasonable. Police departments could use review and retraining to help officers identify and avoid some of these mistakes in future interactions. It bears noting, for example, that young recruits are more likely to resort to using force in police-citizen encounters than older, more experienced officers, who are more skilled in avoiding confrontations. Moreover, while uses of force that are immune from liability are not the most egregious cases, there is reason to think that unnecessary but low-level force is as troubling as outright brutality in creating police-community friction. Yet, this kind of conduct is likely to slip under the radar screen of existing civil and criminal regulation and thus be ignored by police administration.

A third limitation on the scope of civil liability for excessive force results from the narrow way in which the excessive force inquiry is ordinarily defined. In making the determination of whether the officer used reasonable force, only the circumstances immediately surrounding the violent encounter enter into the fact-finder's determination of whether the officer acted appropriately. Thus, the inquiry includes no consideration of whether the officer acted unreasonably in creating the confrontation or causing it to escalate to a point that required the application of force. Limiting the temporal definition of the claim in this way has a profound effect on how police officers will view their responsibility for avoiding excessive force. As long as the focus is on whether the circumstances justified the use of force at the moment it was applied, officers have no legal incentive to step back and ask themselves whether they could have avoided the entire situation without a violent confrontation. Like qualified immunity, limiting the temporal definition of the claim not only narrows liability, but also reduces incentives for constructive review and training to avoid excessive force in future police-citizen interactions.

Finally, while municipalities, unlike states, have no Eleventh Amendment immunity, their liability is limited in ways that make it especially unsuited to addressing police misconduct. Municipalities are liable only when the officer's harm-causing actions can be deemed a "custom or policy" of the entity itself. The easiest case for governmental liability is when a statute or regulation actually enshrines a facially unconstitutional policy, or when a very high-ranking official, such as a chief executive, has formally represented a particular approach as the official policy of the government. The easy cases, however, rarely arise precisely because very little misconduct is sanctioned ex ante by high-level officials, at least not formally. The only other way to satisfy the custom or policy requirement is to show a pattern of repeated incidents of similar misconduct. Where there is such a pattern, the locality is deemed to have an official policy of failing to train its employees to act lawfully.

Unfortunately, however, failure to train claims are very difficult to bring, and even more difficult to win. As an initial matter, the evidence necessary to make out a pattern of repeated instances of police brutality involving different victims is all in the hands of the government, and such information is available only through extensive discovery. Moreover, the sheer volume of factual evidence that is necessary to make out such a pattern makes failure to train cases very expensive to litigate. In addition, the doctrinal showing requires that the discrete instances that make up the pattern be similar enough, and distinctive enough, for a fact-finder to conclude that the misconduct resulted from an identifiable defect in the training program, rather than from some other factor such as the individual characteristics of the wrongdoers. The paradigmatic case for failure to train, according to the Supreme Court, is a series of instances of unjustified police shootings by police officers whose departments issued them dangerous firearms without any instruction on how to use them. As usual, however, the easiest cases do not arise. Most failure to train cases involve less concrete kinds of dangers than mishandled firearms, and correspondingly less clear implications for training. If experience is any indication, very few failure to train cases are ultimately successful in obtaining damages recovery against municipalities.

In sum, it is fair to say that practical and doctrinal obstacles make it relatively difficult for plaintiffs to win excessive force cases. Still, police brutality suits make up a large proportion of the total number of § 1983 suits filed each year, and the worst cases can lead to large damages awards, sometimes combined with criminal sanctions. Indeed, some big city police departments routinely pay out a seemingly enormous amount in liability costs every year.... In light of this pattern of significant liability costs in many major city police departments, the question remains, "why aren't these suits more effective in rooting out police brutality?"

There are at least two answers to this question: one that has received a significant amount of attention in recent scholarship, and one that has received very little. The first answer has to do with how police officers and their departments view the costs and benefits of police brutality. It goes without saying that liability only serves to punish and deter if defendants experience damages liability as a significant loss that outweighs any benefits from their harm-causing actions. Individual officials, however, almost never reap the financial consequences of § 1983 suits that are brought against them because the government handles their legal defense and indemnifies them for any damages assessed against them. Thus, although officials testify that lawsuits in which they are defendants cause them fear and anxiety about possible consequences, they virtually always come out of suits financially unscathed.

Of course, this only means that the municipality is footing the bill for individual as well as entity suits, which should give the government an incentive to discipline, or even fire, the wrongdoers who drive up their liability costs. It was certainly the Supreme Court's assumption ... that governmental liability would result in entities monitoring and sanctioning individual misconduct. Unfortunately, at least in the law enforcement context, civil rights suits that cost the government significant amounts of money do not necessarily, or reliably, result in negative consequences for the individual officers involved. First of all, § 1983 suits often involve protracted litigation over many years. By the time a plaintiff wins a judgment in the case, the passage of time has diminished greatly the connection between the events that gave rise to the suit and any sanction against the officials involved. It is a commonplace that the deterrent force of a sanction is heavily dependent on fostering a close link between deed and punishment. Second—and quite surprising—many (perhaps most) police departments do not keep records in a form that encourages or even permits supervisors to review reports of lawsuits, citizen complaints, and use-of-force reports on individual officers whose performance they are evaluating. Relatedly, many departments do not use these materials to track broader patterns and trends that might reveal problem officers or trouble spots in the police force. In some cases, this failure results simply from disorganized or fragmented record keeping or lack of computer capability. In others, it is more deliberate, flowing out of concerns that statistics about misconduct could be used in litigation against the police department. Whatever the cause, one result is that officers who are the subject of lawsuits, and other forms of citizen complaint alleging police brutality, are often the same ones who the department rewards with commendations and promotions. Obviously, when supervisors do not discipline officers, despite lawsuits or complaints involving police brutality, and those officers' personnel files remain exemplary, the officers have no incentive to change their behavior. Indeed, to the extent that police departments promote problem officers, they are actually rewarding their aggressive conduct.

More broadly, many police departments apparently consider the money they pay out in damages and settlements as simply a "cost of doing business"....

Moreover, governmental actors, unlike private actors, are much more likely to be motivated by political incentives than by purely financial ones. While police departments get negative publicity for the worst police abuses that become public—and they reportedly fear scandal more than the monetary liability that might accompany it—they also score political points for real or perceived success in fighting crime in their jurisdiction. Political accolades also turn into bigger budgets for crime fighting. To the extent that chiefs of police view a little bit of brutality as an effective law enforcement tool, they will balance the costs of liability against the perceived gains of aggressive policing. If police leadership views the use of force in this way, then it is not surprising that departments are lax in record keeping on such incidents, that they sweep evidence of police brutality under the rug, and that they do not sanction—and may even reward—police officers for engaging in aggressive conduct.

The second answer to the puzzle of why large damages awards seem to have so little effect on police brutality is related to the first. Assuming indemnification, both individual and entity suits depend for their success on the notion that the governmental entity, in the form of the police organization, will put pressure on misbehaving officers to change their behavior. But, if police leadership is tolerating, even sanctioning, a kind of aggressive conduct that leads to abuses and police leaders are willing to absorb the costs of liability, then the organization itself is part of the problem. My thesis ... is that police departments that have chronic problems with police brutality are implicitly or informally sanctioning police violence through their organizational culture. If I am correct, then the rogue cop story that police departments routinely offer in the face of allegations of police brutality is, at best, incomplete and, at worst, simply false. Moreover, police departments get off too easy when they claim that incidents of brutality have nothing to say about the police organization of which the offending officers are a part. Perhaps rotten apples are coming from a rotten barrel, which is not to say that all the cops in the barrel are "rotten," but only that the defective barrel is partially responsible for the ones that are! If so, the solution has to go beyond the misbehaving cops in order to address the organization that had a role in producing them.

The above observation suggests that, in addition to the doctrinal and practical limitations on civil rights liability as an answer to police brutality, there is a third, less appreciated limitation: available remedies rely on a remedial model that ignores or undervalues the power of the police organization as a cause of police misconduct. The § 1983 remedy, which is the primary legal tool available to victims of police misconduct, is both individual-specific and incident-specific. It is individual-specific in the sense that it views police officers as autonomous moral agents who are expected to adjust their conduct in response to the pressures of external sanctions. It is incident-specific in that cases only resolve single, isolated occurrences of police misconduct. The policing literature, however, paints a very different picture. In the real world, cops are far from independent agents. Rather, they act within the constraints of a very powerful organizational culture that significantly influences and constrains their judgments and conduct. For similar reasons, viewing police brutality as a string of unrelated incidents belies reality. Police officers who misbehave are often part of a larger pattern of misconduct involving multiple incidents and multiple actors. Such patterns cannot be attributed solely to the misbehaving individuals. Individual officers are behaving as their departments have trained them to behave—whether explicitly or implicitly—and the organizational culture that cultivated and sustained them must also bear some responsibility. To the extent that civil rights law is not equipped to capture these institutional realities, its utility in addressing the problem of police brutality is similarly limited.

One practical consequence of the individual-specific and incident-specific model is that judges and juries never get the information that would be most helpful in identifying sick police departments. In particular, they do not hear any comparative data on police shootings or brutality complaints more generally, including comparisons with other departments. They do not learn whether the cop standing before them has a long history of similar incidents or how his complaint history compares to that of his colleagues. They do not know whether the officer's complaint record is unusual or if it is part of a pattern of similar misconduct that includes other officers in the department. And finally, they do not hear any comparative data that would provide insight into how the officer's employing agency compares with other, similarly situated departments.

This leads to two problems. First, judges in § 1983 and § 242 cases have no organizational context. They have no way of knowing whether the occurrence that they are reviewing is an isolated incident or the natural and predictable product of a diseased organization. This distinction matters because these are two very different problems requiring very different solutions. It is possible to address isolated brutality by weeding out the bad apples, but sick organizations need organization-wide (systemic) solutions. The [Supreme Court's] "custom or policy" doctrine ... was supposed to provide a forum for considering evidence that suggests a pattern of misconduct, but it simply does not.

Second, and perhaps more important, without an organizational context, judges—and juries even more so—have no good way to draw lines separating bad police violence from police violence that is regrettable but justified. Incidents involving the use of force virtually always occur under circumstances that are fast-moving, confusing, and ambiguous. Sometimes suspects incur injuries as a result of their own actions, or because police misread the circumstances. Other times, police officers are also at fault for contributing to the escalation of a potentially violent situation. Unfortunately, there are often no other witnesses, save for the officers involved and the victim, who is usually a criminal suspect. If so, it may boil down to the cops' word against the suspect's. Comparative data—such as whether an involved officer has a complaint history that differs radically from his fellow officers or whether the entire police agency has a higher-than-average level of violent confrontations—could provide important clues for resolving these kinds of ambiguities. Although pattern evidence does not necessarily resolve the case at bar, it raises the question of why this officer finds it necessary to employ more force, in more situations, than colleagues in his own or other departments. If the officer is out of sync with his colleagues, it may suggest that his uses of force are "excessive." Similarly, if an entire police department is plagued by significantly more charges of excessive force than effective departments in comparable jurisdictions, the comparison could suggest that the level of force police officers are applying in the more violent department is needlessly excessive.

* * *

III.

* * *

B. Dealing with Police Culture: Changing the Message

... [W]hile the oft-repeated "bad apple" explanation for police brutality has focused attention on identifying problem officers, the real story is that organizational factors interact with individual propensities to produce police brutality. Cops do not arrive at the police department door as fully formed brutalizers; they are created, in some part, by features of organizational culture that enable (or incite) them to act on their violent propensities. Thus, police departments must supplement strategies that seek to identify violence-prone officers with measures aimed at changing features of police culture that encourage officers to act on their violent propensities.

Second, it follows that no legal strategy that ignores the power of the police organization will have any lasting success in addressing police brutality. Moreover, strategies to change the behavior of individual cops must include some way of controlling the informal, as

well as the formal, messages that frame the way they view their world. While the conclusion that changing the police requires a change in police culture is well-established in
the policing literature, it has not found its way into the legal regime that seeks to regulate police brutality. Of course, one possibility is that police culture is not amenable to change
by legal mechanisms. Perhaps change will require administrative reform, for example,
away from the "professional model" emphasizing aggressive crime control, and toward
community policing or problem-oriented policing....

A third and related conclusion is that thoroughgoing organizational change—the
kind that is necessary to alter entrenched patterns of thinking and conduct—will require top-down pressure, including strong police leadership at the highest levels. The
only way that individual cops will change is if the organizational culture changes, and
the only way that the organization will change is if high-level officials are held accountable for the actions of their subordinates. As long as police administrators can
chalk up misconduct to a few rotten apples and absolve themselves of any responsibility for the barrel out of which those rotten apples came, there will be no lasting reform....

... [P]olice managers articulate their policies most clearly by the personnel decisions
they make, i.e., by ensuring that disciplinary actions actually reinforce spoken and written norms, policies, and values ... [P]olice management "must accept responsibility for
moulding the organization's occupational culture. When misconduct occurs, blame must
not fall exclusively on the rank and file but must be shared by managers for failing to prevent misconduct from occurring."

* * *

Notes and Questions

1. Professor Armacost makes a compelling case that the Supreme Court has interpreted
§ 1983 and other federal statutes so as to render them woefully inadequate in deterring police brutality. While the Court surely intended to limit the scope of § 1983 liability faced
by individuals and municipalities, do you think it had any idea that doing so might have
such a significant impact on deterring police brutality? Do you think Congress has any
idea that it could amend § 1983 to allow pattern or practice claims to be more easily asserted and proved? If the Court and Congress were aware, how would they explain their
decisions? Do they see police brutality as "someone else's problem" that should be fixed
by police officials and local leaders?

2. As Professor Armacost notes, in the rare § 1983 case that goes to trial and in which
the officers lose, they rarely suffer any financial harms because the municipality typically
pays for the legal costs and the judgment itself. Why do municipalities do this though?
Wouldn't police officers behave much more carefully if they knew they were on the hook
for a financially ruinous monetary judgment? Would such a scenario make officers too
cautious in fighting crime? Would police departments have serious recruiting difficulties
if they did not provide indemnification?

3. Professor Armacost strongly opposes the term "bad apples" because it excuses the
police organization itself from taking responsibility for misconduct. But do you think
high-ranking officials in the police department know who the bad apples are? How far down
the organizational chain would you have to go to find officials who know of officers with
a reputation for using excessive force? Surely the Chief of the New York City Police De-

partment, which has more than 35,000 officers, probably has no personal knowledge of who the bad apples are. But what about captains or precinct commanders?

4. Watch *The Wire*, Season 5, Episode 10, at 1 hour and 5:20 minutes. After manufacturing a serial killer (including inventing crimes, tampering with crime scenes, and running an illegal wiretap), Detective McNulty is driven out of the Baltimore Police Department. Yet, the homicide detectives hold a huge party for him — a "detective's wake" normally reserved for detectives who have died — and wish him well. If the police culture were truly hostile to misconduct would such an event ever occur? Does this scene show Professor Armacost to be correct?

5. Watch *The Wire*, Season 1, Episode 11, at 24:50 minutes. After Bubbles pages Detective Greggs (who is in the hospital after having been shot by the Barksdale gang), officers pick up Bubbles and a large officer beats him in the interrogation room while Bubbles is chained to the desk. When other officers hear the beating, they immediately stop the rogue officer. Does this show that police will stop misconduct when it is patently obvious? On the other hand, do you think the department will discipline the officer who beat Bubbles for no reason?

6. In Season 1 of *The Wire*, why didn't the Baltimore Police Department fire Officer Pryzbylewski after his repeated and unjustified use of excessive force? Watch *The Wire*, Season 1, Episode 2, at 50:30 minutes, in which Lieutenant Daniels dresses down Officers Herc, Carver, and Pryzbylewski for going to The Terrace in the middle of the night, inciting violence, and brutally assaulting a juvenile, causing him to go blind in one eye. Does the following exchange exemplify the organizational misconduct problem?:

Lt. Daniels: Why [did you hit the kid with the gun]?

Pryzbylewski: He pissed me off.

Lt. Daniels: No, Officer Pryzbylewski, he did not piss you off. He made you fear for your safety and that of your fellow officers. I'm guessing now, but maybe he was seen to pick up a bottle and menace Officers Hauk and Carver both of whom had already sustained injury from flying projectiles.... Go practice [the story].

After Officer Pryzbylewski again finds himself in legal trouble in Season 3, Lieutenant Daniels again tries to coach him about how to present his story in the best light. Watch *The Wire*, Season 3, Episode 9, at 33:05 minutes.

7. Watch *The Wire*, Season 1, Episode 3, at 49:30 minutes. During a mass arrest, Bodie punches an older officer. Immediately thereafter, Officer Carver, Detective Greggs, and other police brutally punch and kick Bodie, even though he is no longer a threat. As the police beat Bodie repeatedly, you can hear Detective Greggs yelling "hold him down ... you can't hit a cop." Interestingly, the officer who Bodie hit was a lousy cop who was often drunk on the job and did not command respect from his colleagues. If police officers will engage in excessive and unjustifiable force to avenge an officer they do not even like, is there any real prospect for ending systemic organizational misconduct?

8. Will officers turn each other in for blatant misconduct? Watch *The Wire*, Season 5, Episode 3, at 1:00 minutes, in which Detective Bunk confronts McNulty about manufacturing murder cases to get increased department funding. After unsuccessfully trying to reason with McNulty, Bunk threatens him: "I'll tell [Sergeant] Landsman. You keep on with it, I'm going to rat you out." When you watched Bunk threaten to turn McNulty in, was your initial reaction that he might actually do it? McNulty saw it as a bluff and immediately dismissed Bunk's threat. And McNulty was correct, because Bunk backed

down and simply asked to have his name kept out of the file. Why was McNulty so quick to dismiss Bunk's threat? It is it because he is hard-headed or because he knows that cops don't turn each other in?

9. Can we realistically expect officers to turn in their fellow officers when people from other professions fail to do so as well? Consider the Penn State child abuse scandal. Legendary Penn State football coach Joe Paterno had a reputation for integrity and running an ethical football program. Yet, when informed that one of his key assistants was seen sexually assaulting a young boy in the shower, Paterno never called the police. *See* Mark Viera, *Paterno Ousted With President by Penn State*, N.Y. TIMES, Nov. 10, 2011, at A1. If a well-renowned football coach (who was incredibly powerful on campus) does not turn in his subordinates for misconduct, is it realistic to expect that police officers will?

10. Does *The Wire* present us some cause for optimism? Watch *The Wire*, Season 5, Episode 4, at 25:30 minutes. After Officer Colicchio beat an innocent driver for beeping his horn, Sergeant Carver dresses him down. Carver then coaches Colicchio about how to avoid trouble with internal affairs, but Officer Colicchio still demonstrates a bad attitude. Carver then decides to write up Colicchio for excessive force and conduct unbecoming an officer. Through five seasons of *The Wire*, we have never seen a supervisor discipline a subordinate like this and Officer Colicchio is outraged. He says: "You charge me, you're a f------g rat." Carver does not back down though. Is this cause for optimism, or was Colicchio's attitude so bad that the ordinary norms simply did not apply to him?

C. Police Corruption, Police Lies, and What to Do about It

"Lying cops don't automatically kill a case."[1]

— Prosecutor Rhonda Pearlman, responding to allegations that her evidence was tainted

Although police brutality and excessive force receive the most attention, there are other troubling types of police misconduct. As we see repeatedly in *The Wire*, police officers are in a position to steal from drug dealers and other criminals. They can lie to establish probable cause or to convict a defendant at trial. That certain police officers engage in this misconduct is not a new phenomena and it is not surprising. Officers have considerable power and are subject to fairly limited oversight as they perform their responsibilities. The temptation to engage in misconduct—either for personal gain or to convict defendants who might escape justice if police played by the rules—is substantial. As with police brutality, the first question is how pervasive the problem of police corruption and lying actually is. And the second question is whether anything can be done to limit the misconduct. The two excerpts below address those questions in order.

---

1. *The Wire*, Season 5, Episode 10, at 47:00 minutes.

The Mollen Commission Report [on] Allegations of Police Corruption and the Anti-Corruption Procedures of the Police Department

[10–11, 13–15, 17–20, 22–25, 27–28, 31–34] (July 7, 1994)

* * *

The new nature of police corruption this Commission observed shatters many of the traditional, and more comforting, notions of police corruption that existed at the time our investigation began. When former police officer Michael Dowd was arrested in May 1992, the Department maintained that he was an aberration and that corruption was limited to a few "rogue cops." Police corruption was said to be a matter of isolated and sporadic opportunities, rather than planned or organized group efforts. It was said to be motivated solely by greed, nothing more. The Commission found that these notions of police corruption were wrong and vastly underestimate the serious nature of present-day corruption.

Today's corruption is far more criminal, violent and premeditated than traditional notions of police corruption suggest and far more invidious than corruption of a generation ago. Testimony and field investigations demonstrated that its most salient forms include groups of officers protecting and assisting drug traffickers for often sizable profits—stealing drugs, guns and money—and often selling the stolen drugs and guns to or through criminal associates; committing burglary and robbery; conducting unlawful searches of apartments, cars and people; committing perjury and falsifying statements; and sometimes using excessive force, often in connection with corruption. Greed is the primary motive behind these activities, but a complex array of other powerful motives and conditions also spur corruption.

How widespread this corruption is in the New York City Police Department is difficult to gauge. With a staff of under twenty investigators and attorneys it was, of course, impossible to determine the full scope of the problem in the Department's seventy-five precincts and other commands. What we have concluded, however, is that in precincts where certain conditions exist—in particular an active and open narcotics trade and high crime—pockets of corruption are likely to exist in varying degrees of seriousness, frequency and size.

I. THE COMMISSION'S INVESTIGATIONS

The Commission's findings are based on the consistent and repeated results of our field investigations; on information from hundreds of sources both in and out of the Department; and on an extensive analysis of patterns of corruption complaints. While we cannot disclose the full details of certain Commission field operations that are still under investigation, we can disclose that in every high-crime precinct with an active narcotics trade that this Commission examined, we found some level of corruption to exist For example, the Commission's investigation into Manhattan North's 30th Precinct, which has thus far resulted in the arrest of fourteen police officers, revealed that a significant percentage of the precinct routinely engaged in some form of corruption. It further revealed that numerous other officers were complicit through their silence and protection of these corrupt cops.

* * *

… Our first sources of information came from within the Commission and its staff. Our senior investigators were former police officers with long and varied experience within the Department They were thoroughly familiar with the operations of the Department, its culture, and the likely sources of corruption facing officers today....

... At the same time, Commission staff members conducted over one hundred private hearings or informal interviews with current and former members of the Department, including Internal Affairs officers of all ranks....

* * *

One critical point is that our investigative approach vastly differed from the Department's limited approach to the investigation of police corruption. Instead of focusing simply on the single corrupt cop, we designed our investigations to gain evidence of broad patterns of criminal conduct and conspiratorial wrongdoing. In essence, we approached our investigation as the Department would typically approach any investigation of organized and continuing criminal activity—except for police corruption. That the Department did not apply these basic approaches to their own corruption investigations speaks volumes about its past reluctance to uncover the full extent of police corruption in our City.

Our methods and philosophy in investigating police corruption are best illustrated by our investigation into the 30th Precinct....

* * *

In December 1992, approximately three months after the Commission staff was assembled, Commission investigators began a series of proactive investigative tactics that had been sorely lacking from the Department's internal investigations for years. Before long, our investigation identified a group of police officers who we suspected were engaged in drug corruption. Within a month, Commission investigators developed a confidential informant who confirmed that a number of police officers in the 30th Precinct were accepting payoffs from drug dealers in bodegas and various other storefront locations in the neighborhood. We immediately put our informant to work in an undercover capacity. Wearing a body recorder under the Commission's supervision, the informant was able to engage in a number of criminal transactions with an individual we suspected of paying off police officers to protect drug operations....

In the Summer of 1993, Commission investigators arrested a civilian targeted in our undercover operations who acted as the intermediary for drug dealers who were paying off police officers for protection of their drug operations. After his arrest, this individual agreed to cooperate with the Commission and the United States Attorney's Office.

His cooperation allowed us to develop substantial evidence of drug-related corruption against a police officer who had approximately seventeen corruption allegations already filed against him at Internal Affairs, most of which involved narcotics. None of these allegations had ever been substantiated by Internal Affairs.

* * *

In the Fall and Winter of 1993, the investigation developed sufficient evidence to arrest two 30th Precinct police officers on charges of narcotics conspiracy. When faced with these charges, both officers agreed to cooperate with the investigation. Over the past months, these officers have worked in an undercover capacity, wearing recording devices, under the supervision of the Commission, the United States Attorney and selected members of the Police Department's Internal Affairs Bureau.

We discovered that the Department's past belief that corrupt officers will not cooperate or turn against fellow officers was wrong. When confronted with serious criminal charges, corrupt cops—like most other criminals—are often eager to assist prosecutors in exchange for consideration....

The fruits of this investigation have thus far resulted in the arrest of fourteen police officers and ten of their drug dealer associates—one of the largest, and most serious, police corruption cases in a generation. The investigation is still continuing at the time of the publication of this Report and additional arrests are anticipated.

* * *

Corruption and Drugs

Most serious police corruption today arises from the drug trade. And, not surprisingly, it is most prevalent in drug-infested precincts where opportunities for corruption most abound—and the probabilities of detection have been slim. The explosion of the cocaine and crack trade in the mid-1980s fueled the opportunities for corruption by flooding certain neighborhoods with drugs and cash, and created opportunities for cops and criminals to profit from each other. It also eliminated the unwritten rule of twenty years ago that narcotics graft is "dirty money" that is not touched even by corrupt officers. With that change in attitude and opportunity came a wide spectrum of drug-related corruption ranging from opportunistic thefts from street dealers, to carefully planned group assaults on drug locations, and long term partnerships with narcotics traffickers.

The seriousness of drug-related corruption must not be minimized. Many have mistakenly characterized today's corruption as cops "merely" stealing from drug dealers—or, in other words, punishing those who deserve to be punished. This is wrong. Today's narcotics corruption involves not only cops stealing from dealers, but cops using their authority to permit dealers and narcotics enterprises to operate freely and flourish on the streets of our City. Even worse: today's corruption involves officers using their police powers to actively assist, facilitate and strengthen the drug trade. Thus, the victims of corruption are not the drug dealers on the streets of East New York. Indeed, they are often corruption's beneficiaries. The victims of today's corruption are the thousands of law-abiding individuals who live in the high-crime, drug-ridden precincts of our City....

* * *

"Crew" Corruption: The New Organization of Corruption

* * *

Virtually all of the corruption we uncovered, however, involved groups of officers—called "crews"—that protect and assist each other's criminal activities. This was accomplished in a variety of ways, including: identifying drug sites; planning raids; forcibly entering and looting drug trafficking locations; and sharing proceeds according to regular and agreed-upon principles. These crews vary in closeness, purpose and size. In the 30th Precinct, a large group of cops worked in quasi-independent groups of three to five officers, each protecting and assisting the other's criminal activities. In the 73rd Precinct, a tightly knit group of eight to ten officers who worked together on steady tours of duty, routinely conducted unlawful raids on drug locations while on duty from 1988 to 1992. Sometimes most of the squad, ten to twelve officers, would attend clandestine meetings in desolate locations in the precincts—like one known as "the Morgue," an abandoned coffin factory—to drink, avoid patrol duties and plan future raids.

The 75th Precinct had a similar gathering location known as "the Pool"—an isolated inlet near Jamaica Bay—where Michael Dowd and as many as fifteen other officers from his crew would meet while on duty, to drink, shoot their guns, meet their girlfriends and plan future criminal activities. Another former police officer ... told the Commission how he and various members of his crew of approximately twelve police officers routinely burgled drug locations and beat local residents as well as suspected criminals. In the 9th Precinct, groups of officers would meet in a local store to drink, use cocaine, and avoid their duties.

This "crew" corruption displays a new and disturbing form of organization.... [C]rews are more akin to street gangs: small, loyal, flexible, fast moving, and often hard hitting. They establish areas to plan and discuss their operations. They often structure their legitimate police work to generate the leads they need to locate promising targets. They use the police radio network, and code names, to mount and coordinate operations. They often use Department equipment to force entry. They manipulate fellow officers, their supervisors, and the courts to their advantage. And they fuel each other's corruption through their eagerness to prove their loyalty and toughness to one another.

There is another feature of today's corruption that reflects planning and organization among officers: corruption pacts. Engaging in open criminality safely requires an agreement among the officers involved. Having such an agreement was critical to their corrupt conduct because it was a way to doubly insure that fellow officers witnessing their crimes would not report them....

* * *

Methods to Create Corruption Opportunities

We also found that corrupt cops did not just stumble upon opportunities for corruption, they sought them out. Numerous corrupt cops told us how they would elicit information from street dealers and other civilian accomplices on where large quantities of money and drugs could be found and when they would be transported. They would then attempt to steal from these "stash houses· or "bag men" transporting large quantities of cash. [Former police officer Michael] Dowd told us how he would "sniff out" potentially profitable radio runs—and respond to those calls to be the first to arrive on the scene and fill his pockets freely. In the 30th Precinct, a group of cops devised a way to identify drug locations and stash houses based on the type of keys in a suspect's possession. Cops would unlawfully frisk suspected dealers and search known hiding places in apartment buildings for what they called "felony keys"—keys to expensive locks. Since most residents in this low-income precinct had standard locks on their doors, a high security lock indicated a drug location, which the cops would then find and raid. Once inside a drug location, dealers usually hid their goods in floor tiles or other areas known as "traps" out of fear of rival dealers, robbers, and law enforcement. This did not hinder cops in pursuit of profit they would climb into crawl spaces and rip out wall panelling or floor tiles—often with the aid of devices like bathroom plungers—until as Dowd put it the "gold mine" was hit.

Methods To Escape Detection

Methods for evading detection often were similarly sophisticated and premeditated. In the 30th Precinct there was a highly organized method of regular protection payments from dealer to cop. Cops were too clever to accept payments directly from dealers. Instead, dealers would leave cash in brown paper bags for their police accomplices in neighborhood stores. The cop would then visit the location, and walk out with a brown bag filled with cash. Some of these payment schemes were fairly systematic, others were more opportunistic. One 30th Precinct officer allegedly picked up $2,000 in cash each week, off-duty, at a local shop. Michael Dowd picked up $8,000 in cash every Tuesday from an auto stereo shop that was a known drug location in his precinct, while on duty and in uniform.

To further insure their protection, corrupt—and even honest—cops would warn each other when Internal Affairs or a law enforcement "outsider" was in the precinct. They would transmit code words over their police radios—like "WO-IO" which meant "watch out 7 + 3" or 73rd Precinct—to warn of "unfriendlies" in the area. In the 73rd Precinct, corrupt cops would use code names to identify each other and certain locations over police frequencies to carry out corrupt activities.

They also employed a division of labor in carrying out corrupt acts. While committing an unlawful raid, for example, cops would regularly assign each other specific roles for carrying out the raid and insuring that they were protected from other cops and supervisors. To keep their victims quiet, they would employ a variety of schemes including leaving the dealer with some of his money or drugs, foregoing arrests, or threatening them with the consequences of making a report.

Other conditions also protected corrupt cops. First, victims of police corruption did not need much prodding to remain silent. They are often reluctant to report corruption. Internal Affairs' reliance on complaints for investigations meant that not only were officers safe from detection, but that the Department's official corruption statistics vastly underestimated the extent of the corruption problem in its precincts. More important, corrupt officers were typically protected by the silence of their fellow officers, and often the willful blindness of supervisors.

* * *

Thefts From Street Dealers: "Shake Downs"

The most common and simplest form of narcotics corruption is "shaking down" street dealers. According to a number of corrupt police officers and informants, officers would approach drug dealers operating on the streets of their precincts, force them to an alleyway, behind a building, or some other secluded location, and steal whatever drugs or money they found in their possession. If the dealer kept his drugs and money hidden somewhere nearby, some officers would threaten the dealer with arrest or with violence unless he revealed its location. Officers involved in the shakedown would sometimes split their "score" or proceeds in the patrol car or elsewhere. If drugs were stolen by the officer, they were usually concealed in a location to which the corrupt cop would return on his way home.

The size of scores from shakedowns varied depending on the dealer and the nature of the drug trade in a particular precinct. Most scores were not very large, ranging from a few dollars to a few hundred dollars. Nonetheless, even a high volume of small shakedowns could substantially contribute to an officer's income. Dowd and his partner set shakedown goals of $300 to $500 a day—and more in the holiday season—which totaled approximately $1,500 to $2,500 a week. Scores in the heaviest narcotics precincts like the 30th Precinct, however, could bring in thousands of dollars, from the seizure of drugs and cash. One former 30th Precinct officer, for example, chased a dealer into an apartment building, and stole a bag of crack and cocaine, which he later sold to another dealer for $8,000.

Even this most simple form of narcotics corruption was not without premeditation and planning. For example, to avoid complaints, officers typically let drug dealers go free after their scores, or left them with some cash and drugs. As [Officers] Dowd, Hembury, Cawley and others explained, if you left a drug dealer happy after stealing from him, he would not only be unlikely to complain, but would come to accept police shakedowns as a routine "tax" or cost of doing business. In many cases, officers would pretend to take drugs and money for vouchering as forfeited property and were doing the drug dealer a favor by letting him go unarrested. Far from considering himself the officers' victim, the dealer would then consider himself their friend. Officers could then use him to gain information about other dealers' lucrative drug locations.

These shakedowns were motivated primarily by greed—but not entirely. Corrupt officers said they would sometimes steal ten or fifteen dollars from dealers, just to show who was boss in their precincts.

* * *

Thefts From Radio Runs

Calls for service or radio runs are the everyday business of patrol officers. In busy, high-crime precincts, some officers respond to twenty or more radio runs each day. These calls for service—to the scenes of robberies, burglaries, domestic disputes, assaults, and murders—afford the enterprising corrupt officer with numerous opportunities for gain by providing a legitimate reason for entering a premise. These opportunities are, of course, particularly abundant in high-crime drug precincts, where large amounts of cash, drugs, guns, jewelry, or other expensive property are often stashed in apartments, stores and other locations.

Police officers, especially those assigned to busy precincts, come to know their precincts extremely well and can immediately identify a location where the opportunity for a score exists. Corrupt cops told us that they became expert at sensing corruption opportunities and would race to certain locations to search for money, drugs or other valuables before other officers arrived. Dowd, for example, testified that he and his partner would speed to what they called "rare locations", places not often the subject of radio runs—even if it was miles outside their assigned sector—because they were often stash houses used by drug rings, or private residences, where money or other valuables were likely to be kept.

* * *

Radio runs provided yet another avenue for corruption. In the 75th Precinct, for example, corrupt officers generated their own radio runs to specific locations by calling 911 with manufactured complaints. This practice provided a cover to justify an unlawful presence or entry into a location. In another precinct, which we are not at liberty to identify, police officers' used civilian accomplices, such as drug dealers, to call 911 with false complaints about locations where cash or drugs were stored. After receiving the radio runs generated by their associates, corrupt officers had an apparent justification to enter the premises to steal the contraband.

* * *

Theft From Unlawful Searches and Seizures:
"Raids," "Doing Doors," "Booming Doors"

* * *

To plan and carry out raids, officers in the 73rd Precinct arranged clandestine meetings in desolate locations within the precinct by calling each other over the Department radio on an unused frequency. To mask their communications, officers used code names to call each other and to identify the place they arranged to meet....

Although there was no consistent number of sector cars or officers who would join the meetings, on occasion most of the 73rd Precinct evening tour attended these secret rendezvous—four to seven sector cars with two officers in each car. Once at the meeting place, the officers discussed their plans for a raid, selected a location and assigned themselves various roles. Some officers would be responsible for breaking through the front door—often with Department issued hammers and crowbars—while other officers covered the rear of the building, the roof or other escape routes. The patrol cars then approached the location in tight formation, with radios and headlights off to escape detection and gain the element of surprise over dealers inside the premises they were about to assault.

Once inside it was every officer for himself. The officers stole whatever valuables they could find in the premises or on the people inside. Drug dealers within the building were typically let free, unless one of the officers wanted to make an arrest for overtime reasons. In that case, some of the money and drugs was vouchered, or recorded as evidence, to sustain the basis for the arrest.

* * *

Officers disposed of stolen drugs in one of three ways. The drugs were discarded or destroyed, kept for personal use, or sold to officers who had connections with drug dealers. If the drugs were sold, the profits were divided between the officer who stole the drugs and the officer who arranged the sale.

Stolen handguns were always a prize commodity. They provided several hundred dollars if sold. While some officers sold their stolen guns—sometimes to criminals—most officers either threw them away or brought them home. One officer even told us that stolen guns could be used as a "throw away" to plant on a suspect in the event of a questionable police shooting.

* * *

… COPS PROTECTING AND ASSISTING NARCOTICS TRAFFICKERS

Some corrupt police officers went so far as to conspire with drug dealers to protect, assist, and strengthen their drug operations. They worked hand-in-hand with drug traffickers and other criminals to thwart law enforcement efforts. Narcotics protection schemes existed twenty years ago, but on a much more limited scale. As the narcotics trade has grown, so too have the opportunities for this form of corruption not only for officers in special narcotics units as was exclusively the case in the past, but for much of the patrol force which now has regular contact with drug operations.

There is one motive only for this form of corruption: money, and often much of it. Some drug organizations are willing to pay handsomely for the power, prestige and protection of having a New York City police officer on their payrolls. The most notorious case of police officers assisting large-scale drug rings was Michael Dowd and his partner, Kenneth Eurell, who from 1987 through 1988 received $4,000 a week each to protect drug organizations operating in their precinct. Their Department paychecks: $400 a week—ten times less than their illicit profits. In fact, Dowd's weekly narcotics profits were so high that, as he testified at the public hearings, he sometimes forgot to collect his Department paycheck. Officers in the 30th Precinct also collected thousands of dollars a week each for protection—generally several hundred dollars from various small dealers in exchange for immunity from arrest.

There are many ways cops use their powers to assist drug traffickers—and many levels of involvement and assistance that can be provided. As the 30th Precinct case shows, "protection" ranges from cops providing permission to operate, to facilitation of operations; from occasional assistance, to long-term agreements for regular protection services. The most basic level of assistance is cops stealing drugs and money from street dealers in return for letting them operate freely on that day. The protection is immediate: no long-term relationship or promises are made. No active facilitation is involved. The protection offered dealers often was more long-term, organized and systematic. Cops and dealers entered into agreements whereby cops would allow dealers to operate freely and openly in their precincts, in exchange for regular, set payments that would be dropped off for cops at a specified location. The drop-off was usually at neighborhood stores to avoid direct contact and suspicions.

Some officers were paid not only to permit, but to facilitate drug operations. The most extreme level of facilitation is when the corrupt cops themselves become an integral part of the operation of the narcotics enterprise; when the corrupt cops themselves become dedicated drug traffickers. Such was the case with Michael Dowd, who when asked at the public hearings if at the height of his career he considered himself to be a cop or a drug dealer, he replied that he was "both." When asked whether he owed his allegiances as a New York City cop to the community he was supposed to be policing or the drug traffickers he was protecting, he replied, "I guess I'd have to say the drug traffickers."

* * *

The 30th Precinct investigation unearthed several cops who spent much of their days with their drug dealer friends rather than policing the streets. While Dowd was the most extreme case of police officer turned drug trafficker, he was not alone. The Commission observed numerous ways other corrupt officers actively assisted and facilitated the drug trade in New York City. First, officers provide dealers with confidential information about such things as narcotics raids and undercover operations to protect them from detection by the police. Sometimes the information was real, sometimes not. Sometimes it was provided regularly, sometimes only when the opportunity arose. Dowd and Eurell for example, were once offered $8,000 to provide information on planned police activity in a drug area in their precinct over the July 4th weekend. As patrol officers, they had no specific information on the narcotics division's planned activities, but based "just on common sense" as Dowd testified, they told the dealers their operations would be safe that weekend. Dowd and Eurell spent the weekend at home and made $4,000 each. They were later put on retainer by a major drug ring to regularly provide intelligence on narcotics operations.

Officers, however, also provide genuine information on planned raids to thwart law enforcement efforts. On one occasion, Dowd testified that he learned that narcotics officers planned to raid a bodega under his protection. While in uniform, he immediately entered the bodega, pretended to buy two beers and signalled that a raid was imminent. When the raid took place a short time later, all operations had been shut down as Dowd had instructed. Law enforcement efforts to shut down an active drug location were blocked, because of a corrupt cop.

Police officers also provide another valuable commodity to drug traffickers: armed police protection. This is typically done by protecting the transportation or transfer of large quantities of narcotics and cash. Officers do this by escorting a car transporting drugs or cash and intervening if the dealer's car is stopped by the police or rival dealers—a practice known as "riding shotgun." In June 1993, for example, the Queens District Attorney's office charged officer Andre McDougal from Queens' 101st Precinct with accepting $10,000 to escort and protect a drug dealer's delivery of $100,000 in illicit drug proceeds. The officer's role was to intervene in the event the delivery car was stopped by the police. As recently as May 1994, the Brooklyn District Attorney's Office charged Sergeant Robert Santana of the 71st Precinct in Crown Heights with conspiring with a drug dealer to provide him armed protection during a narcotics transaction.

Having a cop on the payroll provides drug organizations with another valuable asset: power, or "juice" as Dowd put it. Corrupt officers and dealers who provided information to the Commission reported that traffickers sometimes paid officers to simply watch, while in uniform or in their patrol cars, while drugs or cash were being transported or loaded into a car. The key was the cop's visibility. This protected an organization from rival dealers by signaling to them—and possibly to any law-abiding citizens watching—that this drug ring has the power of a cop behind it.

Corrupt cops also used their police powers to strengthen the powers and profits of protected dealers by harassing and intimidating their competition. Some officers, for example, would get information from "friendly" dealers about rival dealers' well-stocked stash houses. They would then raid these locations, keep the cash, and sell any stolen drugs back to their dealer-associates at cheap prices. Dowd also testified that he and others would sit in his police car outside a rival dealers' sale location to disrupt his business. On other occasions, officers would submit narcotics intelligence reports on a rival's operations to instigate enforcement activities against them.

What these various forms of protection reveal is far more than cops merely making money off drug traffickers. They reveal cops actively using their authority to facilitate and strengthen the drug trade and to thwart law enforcement efforts in the war against drugs. They reveal how easily narcotics corruption turns corrupt cops into criminals.

* * *

Notes and Questions

1. In a few scenes in *The Wire*, characters say "It's Baltimore, people," suggesting that typical problems such as police corruption are worse there than in other cities. After reading the Mollen Commission Report, do you feel as pessimistic about New York City as you do about Baltimore after watching *The Wire*?

2. The Mollen Commission report focused exclusively on police misconduct in New York City. Sociologists have documented the same type of misconduct in other cities, such as Chicago. *See* Sudhir Venkatesh, Gang Leader for a Day 233–36 & 267 (2008) (describing corrupt cops in the infamous Robert Taylor housing units in Chicago). Does (or did) the same type of misconduct occur in other police departments around the country, or are New York and Chicago (perhaps because of their size) somehow worse?

3. *The Wire* does not focus as much on police graft and theft as it does on the institutional failures of the police department as a whole. Still, David Simon does vividly portray the incentive of officers to steal drug money. Watch *The Wire* Season 1, Episode 9, at 18:30 minutes. Officer Herc suggests pocketing some drug money that he and Carver seized from the Barksdale drug gang. Carver talks him out of it, not because it is illegal or immoral, but because they might get caught if supervisors heard conversations on the wiretap discussing how much money was actually seized. Later in the series, Carver and Herc succumb to the temptation and steal cash during a drug raid. Watch *The Wire*, Season 1, Episode 11, at 52:40 minutes.

4. How do you solve the problem of police stealing drugs and money from drug dealers? Consider the incentives: First, everyone knows that drug dealers are not in a position to file police reports. Second, the average starting salary for police officers across the country is roughly $40,000. *See* Bureau of Justice Statistics, Local Police Departments, 2007 12 (Dec. 2010). Short of being clairvoyant about which prospective officers will be ethical hires, how are police supervisors supposed to prevent police corruption and shakedowns?

5. In Season 2, we see repeated abuse of power when Major Valchek settles a personal vendetta against Frank Sobotka. Valchek orders a subordinate to ticket all of the union workers' cars and to set up a DWI checkpoint near their favorite bar. Even worse, he pushes the Deputy Commissioner to create an entire police detail to investigate Sobotka and the union even though Valchek has no particular reason to believe illegal activity has occurred or is about to occur. Watch *The Wire*, Season 2, Episode 2, at 12:00, 22:00, and 27:00 minutes. Hopefully, opening a criminal investigation without basis is rare in the real world. But how often do you think police abuse their authority to ticket and harass individuals?

6. Corruption and abuse of power is not limited to the police. Watch *The Wire*, Season 4, Episode 3, at 9:00 minutes. Facing a tough re-election battle, Mayor Royce orders his staff to have the Department of Public Works tear down all of Councilman Carcetti's political signs. He also orders that any vehicles near Carcetti's headquarters with any technical violations be ticketed or towed. Listening to this, the District Attorney is visibly uncomfortable, yet he says nothing about the flagrant abuse of power.

Christopher Slobogin, Testilying: Police Perjury and What to Do About It

67 University of Colorado Law Review 1037 (1996)

O.J. Simpson's trial for the murders of Nicole Brown Simpson and Ronald Goldman provided the nation with at least two pristine examples of police perjury. First, there was the exposure of Detective Marc Fuhrman as a liar. While under oath at trial the detective firmly asserted, in response to F. Lee Bailey's questions, that he had not used the word "nigger" in the past decade. The McKinny tapes and assorted other witnesses made clear this statement was an untruth. That proof of perjury, together with the defense's innuendo that Fuhrman had planted a glove smeared with Nicole's blood on Simpson's property, severely damaged the prosecution's case.

Second, and less well known, is Judge Lance Ito's finding that Detective Philip Vannatter had demonstrated a "reckless disregard for the truth" in the warrant application for the search of Simpson's house. Among other misrepresentations, Vannatter insinuated that Simpson had suddenly taken flight to Chicago when in fact police knew the trip had been planned for months, and unequivocally asserted that the substance found on Simpson's Bronco was blood when in fact it had not yet been tested.

A third possible series of perjurious incidents occurred at the suppression hearing, when both Fuhrman and Vannatter stated that police investigating Simpson's compound had not considered O.J. a suspect, but rather had entered the premises solely out of concern for the athlete's welfare (and therefore had not needed probable cause or a warrant). Although both Judge Ito and Magistrate Kathleen Kennedy-Powell accepted these assertions, most who have considered the matter believe otherwise, on the common sense ground that police who knew that O.J. had beaten Nicole on past occasions, found what appeared to be blood on his car, and were unable to locate him after the murders would zero in on him as a possible culprit.

If one believes the defense theory of the case, Fuhrman's and Vannatter's deceitful exploits were a racist attempt to send an innocent person to jail, as well as a form of protective lying, meant to prevent discovery of their own criminal activity in planting evidence. If one believes the prosecution's theory, these lies were merely a well-intentioned effort, albeit an improper one, to ensure conviction of a guilty person. On the latter theory,

Fuhrman's denials at trial were meant to avoid a topic that would only have distracted the jury from the "real" issue. Similarly, Vannatter's lies in the warrant application and Fuhrman's and Vannatter's probable dissembling at the suppression hearing were designed to cover up irregularities in the evidence gathering process that, if discovered, might have lead to exclusion of crucial incriminating information.

We may never know with certainty the reason for the perjury in the Simpson case. But we do know that, whatever the motivation, the perjury was wrong. If the lying occurred to frame an innocent person, it was clearly corrupt. If instead it was meant to facilitate conviction of a person the police witnesses thought to be guilty, it was also reprehensible. Although, as we shall see, many police and even some attorneys and judges seem to think otherwise, lying to convict a guilty person is wrong for several reasons. It is wrong because it involves lying under oath to judicial officers and jurors. It is wrong because it keeps from those fact finders information relevant to constitutional and other issues. And it is wrong because the police cannot be counted upon to get guilt right.

Perhaps most importantly, police lying intended to convict someone, whether thought to be guilty or innocent, is wrong because once it is discovered, it diminishes one of our most crucial "social goods"—trust in government. First, of course, the exposure of police perjury damages the credibility of police testimony. As the aftermath of the Fuhrman debacle has shown, the revelation that some police routinely and casually lie under oath makes members of the public, including those who serve on juries, less willing to believe all police, truthful or not. One comment that a New York prosecutor made about the impact of the Simpson case illustrates the point: "Our prosecutors now have to begin their cases defending the cops. Prosecutors have to bring the jury around to the opinion that cops aren't lying. That's how much the landscape has changed."

Police perjury can cause other systemic damage as well. Presumably, for instance, the loss of police credibility on the stand diminishes law enforcement's effectiveness in the streets. Most significantly, to the extent other actors, such as prosecutors and judges, are perceived to be ignoring or condoning police perjury, the loss of public trust may extend beyond law enforcement to the criminal justice system generally.

Although both lying to convict the innocent and lying to convict the guilty thus deserve condemnation, this article will focus on the latter because it is the more resistant to change and the more prevalent (two traits that are not unrelated). Lying to convict the innocent is undoubtedly rejected by most police, as well as by others, as immoral and unjustifiable. In contrast, lying intended to convict the guilty—in particular, lying to evade the consequences of the exclusionary rule—is so common and so accepted in some jurisdictions that the police themselves have come up with a name for it: "testilying."

* * *

I. The Nature of Testilying

Whether it is conjecture by individual observers, a survey of criminal attorneys, or a more sophisticated study, the existing literature demonstrates a widespread belief that testilying is a frequent occurrence. Of course, there is Alan Dershowitz's well-known assertion (made long before his participation in the O.J. Simpson case) that "almost all" officers lie to convict the guilty. Dershowitz may have been engaging in hyperbole, but his claim is not as far off as one might think. In one survey, defense attorneys, prosecutors, and judges estimated that police perjury at Fourth Amendment suppression hearings occurs in twenty to fifty percent of the cases.... Even prosecutors—or at least former— use terms like "routine," "commonplace," and "prevalent" to describe the phenomenon. Few knowledgeable persons are willing to say that police perjury about investigative matters is sporadic or rare, except perhaps the police, and, as noted above, even many of them believe it is common enough to merit a label all its own.

Although testilying can occur at any stage of the criminal process, including trial, it usually takes place during the investigative and pretrial stages, since it is most frequently an attempt to cover up illicit evidence gathering. One of the best descriptions of such perjury comes from the Mollen Commission, named after Judge Milton Mollen, who led an investigation into corruption in the New York City Police Department in the early 1990s:

> Officers reported a litany of manufactured tales. For example, when officers unlawfully stop and search a vehicle because they believe it contains drugs or guns, officers will falsely claim in police reports and under oath that the car ran a red light (or committed some other traffic violation) and that they subsequently saw contraband in the car in plain view. To conceal an unlawful search of an individual who officers believe is carrying drugs or a gun, they will falsely assert that they saw a bulge in the person's pocket or saw drugs and money changing hands. To justify unlawfully entering an apartment where officers believe narcotics or cash can be found, they pretend to have information from an unidentified civilian informant or claim they saw the drugs in plain view after responding to the premises on a radio run. To arrest people they suspect are guilty of dealing drugs, they falsely assert that the defendants had drugs in their possession when, in fact, the drugs were found elsewhere where the officers had no lawful right to be.

As this excerpt suggests, the most common venue for testilying is the suppression hearing and the most frequent type of suppression hearing perjury is post hoc fabrication of probable cause....

The Mollen Report excerpt also refers to testilying during the warrant application process, which the Fourth Amendment requires take place under oath. Although estimating its prevalence is difficult, police misrepresentation on the application form and in oral testimony to the warrant magistrate has been recounted by numerous observers. Most frequent, it seems, is the invention of "confidential informants" (like the "unidentified civilian informant" referred to in the excerpt), a ploy that allows police to cover up irregularities in developing probable cause or to assert they have probable cause when in fact all they have is a hunch.

Finally, police perjury also occurs in connection with the fabrication of their reports. Although not technically testimony, police know these reports may be dispositive in a case resolved through plea bargaining, and can be compared to testimony in cases that aren't. As a result, "reportlying" also appears to be pervasive in some jurisdictions. The Mollen Commission, for instance, described how narcotics police "falsify arrest papers to make it appear as if an arrest that actually occurred inside a building [in violation of departmental regulations] took place on the street."....

The most obvious explanation for all of this lying is a desire to see the guilty brought to "justice." As law enforcement officers, the police do not want a person they know to be a criminal to escape conviction simply because of a "technical" violation of the Constitution, a procedural formality, or a trivial "exculpatory" fact.... A related reason for police dissembling is the institutional pressure to produce "results," which can lead police to cut corners in an effort to secure convictions....

These motivations are probably not the whole explanation, however. The police officer who lies to convict a criminal is generally lying under oath in a public legal forum. Thus, the lying officer is exposed to criminal charges in a proceeding involving a legally trained adversary and open to—indeed, usually directed against—those who can prove the perjury.

That perjury persists despite these risks can be explained by one simple factor: police think they can get away with it. Police are seldom made to pay for their lying. To some extent, this immunity may be due to their own expertise at deceit. Many prosecutors and judges believe perjury is systematic and often suspect it is occurring in individual cases. But they also frequently claim that they are not sure enough to do anything about it; after all, the typical situation pits a police officer, well trained on how to "constitutionalize" a case, against a person charged with a crime, who is decidedly less aware of the relevant law.

* * *

Probably the most stunning evidence of prosecutorial and judicial nonchalance toward police perjury is Myron Orfield's study of the Chicago system. His study is stunning because, unlike many of the comments on this issue, Orfield's findings are based on the views of prosecutors and judges as well as those of defense attorneys. In his survey of these three groups (which together comprised twenty-seven to forty-one individuals, depending on the question), 52% believed that at least "half of the time" the prosecutor "knows or has reason to know" that police fabricate evidence at suppression hearings, and 93%, including 89% of the prosecutors, stated that prosecutors had such knowledge of perjury "at least some of the time." Sixty-one percent, including 50% of the state's attorneys, believed that prosecutors know or have reason to know that police fabricate evidence in case reports, and 50% of the prosecutors believed the same with respect to warrants (despite the fact that many prosecutors refused to talk about this latter area). While close to half of all respondents believed that prosecutors "discourage" such perjury and fabrication, a greater percentage believed that they "tolerate" it, and 15% believed that prosecutors actually "encourage" it. One former prosecutor described what he called a "commonly used" technique of steering police testimony by telling officers "[i]f this happens, we win. If this happens, we lose." Most amazingly, 29% of the respondents did not equate lying at a suppression hearing with the crime of perjury. Although the respondents' views on judicial, as opposed to prosecutorial, attitudes toward testilying were not as directly plumbed in this survey, when asked whether Chicago's criminal justice system effectively controls policy perjury at suppression hearings, 69% of the respondents answered "no."

* * *

III. Reducing the Pressure to Lie and to Ignore Lying

* * *

… Changing the Remedy

… [The] most controversial suggestion for minimizing testilying is to abolish the exclusionary rule. While the first two proposals attempt to accommodate the police by trying to siphon off the pressure to lie, this proposal is meant to change the behavior of prosecutors and judges by reducing the urge to wink at such lying. As … [scholars] have observed firsthand, for people in the latter positions, "instrumental adjustments" by police hoping to convict guilty people are very hard to fault, much less prosecute and punish, when the result is the dismissal of worthy charges. If the rule were abolished, on the other hand, prosecutors would be more willing to expose and prosecute such perjury, and judges more willing to conclude that it occurred, especially if, as suggested above, a successful perjury prosecution meant the prosecutor and judge would never have to work with the officer again.

Further, abolition of the exclusionary rule does not have to mean the Constitution will become a dead letter. A liquidated damages remedy … may well provide a more than adequate substitute.... [One scholar's proposal] would authorize a government ombudsman to receive and investigate complaints against the police and to assign private counsel to sue the individual officer and the government in front of a judge. The officer found in bad-faith violation of the Constitution would be liable for a certain percentage of his salary, while the government would pay an equivalent sum for good-faith violations. Because such a system makes the officer liable for unreasonable mistakes, it is clearly a better individual deterrent than the rule, which is not very effective in this regard. Because it holds the department liable for reasonable mistakes of law made by its officers, this type of damages action also provides a strong incentive for training programs, and thus would probably not diminish the institutional compliance that is the one proven effect of the exclusionary rule.

* * *

Conclusion

Police, like people generally, lie in all sorts of contexts for all sorts of reasons. This article has focused on police lying designed to convict individuals the police think are guilty. Strong measures are needed to reduce the powerful incentives to practice such testilying and the reluctance of prosecutors and judges to do anything about it. Among them might be the adoption of rewards for truth telling, the redefinition of probable cause, and the elimination of the exclusionary rule and its insidious effect on the resolve of legal actors to implement the commands of the Constitution.

Ultimately, however, the various proposals set forth in this article are merely suggestive, meant to stimulate debate about how to curtail testilying at suppression hearings. There is strong evidence to suggest that police in many jurisdictions routinely engage in this kind of deceit, and that prosecutors and judges are sometimes accomplices to it. Even if it turns out that this evidence exaggerates the problem, the fact remains that, because of the O.J. Simpson trial and similar events, more people than ever before believe it exists. To restore trust in the police and the criminal justice system, we need to take meaningful steps against testilying now.

Notes and Questions

1. Because *The Wire* revolves around the streets and not the courtrooms, it contains only a handful of references to the suppression of evidence under the exclusionary rule. Yet, as Professor Slobogin rightly points out, a large percentage of police lying occurs in suppression hearings. Is this an oversight by the writers of *The Wire*, or does it indicate that the average police officer does not give much thought to whether evidence might be suppressed?

2. *Small Lies*: Although *The Wire* does not show us suppression hearings and courtrooms, it is replete with the kinds of search and seizure lies that Professor Slobogin describes. For example, watch *The Wire*, Season 1, Episode 9, at 37:40 minutes. While listening to the wiretap, McNulty hears incriminating information. But McNulty should not have been listening to the call in the first place because no officer was monitoring the payphone to see that one of the targets was making a call. Nevertheless, McNulty writes down in the log that Detective Sydnor was on the roof and saw the payphone. When Officer Pryzbylewski tries to challenge McNulty and stop him from lying, McNulty refuses to back down. Do you think this scene is realistic? Can you imagine something similar happening in a police department in the real world?

3. *Bigger Lies*: Watch *The Wire* Season 3, Episode 9, at 43:40 minutes, in which Detectives Herc and Carver are called to the scene of a murder. In order to keep the Hamsterdam operation quiet, Carver moves the body and gun casings out of the free zone. This tampering is done with the best of intentions, but of course is outrageously impermissible. Do you think officers regularly tamper with crime scenes or lie about the way events occurred—albeit in less blatant ways than Detective Carver—in order to convict a defendant they know to be guilty? In his "Rules of the Justice Game," Professor Alan Dershowitz famously offered 13 rules that participants in the criminal justice system well understand. Rule IV provides "[a]lmost all police lie about whether they violated the Constitution in order to convict guilty defendants." Rule V then explains that "[a]ll prosecutors, judges, and defense attorneys are aware of Rule IV." ALAN M. DERSHOWITZ, THE BEST DEFENSE xxi (1982). Is Professor Dershowitz too cynical? Or are most police willing to lie to convict a guilty defendant? In answering that question, consider the story of Melvin Williams, who portrayed "The Deacon" in *The Wire*. In his past life, Williams was arrested for drug trafficking. As a result of David Simon's investigative reporting in 1987, a former federal agent admitted manufacturing probable cause to arrest Williams and planting drugs on him during the arrest. The agent explained that "Williams was a large scale trafficker who could not be caught fair-and-square." *See* RAFAEL ALVAREZ, THE WIRE: TRUTH BE TOLD 106 (2009).

4. *Enormous Lies*: Season 5 of *The Wire* depicts the biggest lie of them all. Detective McNulty invents a serial killer, manipulates crime scenes, manufactures evidence, and tells explicit lies to his supervisors, colleagues, and the media. Put together, this elaborate plan seems far-fetched and unrealistic. But considered individually, how often does each type of lie occur? Do officers invent crimes (though less serious ones than murder) to get dangerous people off the street? Do officers tamper with crime scenes or manufacture evidence to help convict defendants who the officers believe to be guilty? Do officers lie about these actions when questioned by their supervisors or colleagues? The answer to all of these questions is almost certainly "yes." The harder question is how often does this occur? Does the average police department have ten officers like Detective McNulty, or just one officer, or none?

5. *The Power of Suggestion*: Watch *The Wire*, Season 1, Episode 13, at 1:00 minutes. When Detective Greggs starts to recover from being shot, Detective Bunk shows her a photo array of suspects who could be the shooter. As he holds the photo spread, Bunk points at one of the suspects and taps his finger over the suspect's picture. Bunk is clearly suggesting who Greggs should pick out of the photo spread. Later in the episode (at 11:00 minutes) Bunk calls this "the fat finger." Assuming Greggs followed Bunk's lead (which she refuses to do) would a judge or jury ever have found out about the suggestiveness?

6. What do you think of Professor Slobogin's proposal to replace the exclusionary rule with a damages remedy that officers would have to pay (at least part of) out of their own pocket? Would prosecutors and judges be more willing to stop and report police perjury if it would have no effect on the defendant's guilt? Or would prosecutors and judges still be reluctant to turn in people who they work with on a daily basis and expose them to potentially ruinous financial consequences?

Chapter XIV

The Influence of the Media

A. Introduction

Reporter: This serial killer is making [Clay Davis] ... very very happy ... One news cycle and his indictment is going to be off the front page.

Gus Haynes: Well, if it bleeds, it leads.[1]

We are all familiar with Gus Haynes' comment that "if it bleeds it leads." On most nights, the local news is overwhelmingly dominated by crime stories. It is easy to find fault with the exploitation of this violence and tragedy. The problem is much deeper though. While many viewers are disappointed or even disgusted by the media's crime coverage, few go the step further and consider the effects of "if it bleeds it leads." Is media coverage shaping public opinion of crime? Do people have any idea that violent crime coverage may be warping their viewpoints on a host of issues? Does the media drive criminal justice policy? Are politicians making bad policy and resource decisions because of a fear of simplistic news headlines? Is the focus on bleeding crime stories distracting our attention from important criminal justice issues? The sections below attempt to shed light on these difficult questions.

B. Does the Media Drive the Criminal Justice Train?

"Wrong zipcode. They're dead where it doesn't count. If they were white [in a different neighborhood] you'd have had 30 inches on the front."[2]

—Mike Fletcher (explaining why a triple murder got minimal coverage)

Who holds the true power in the criminal justice system? At the broadest level, legislatures decide what behavior is prohibited and they appropriate resources to combat crime. Police commissioners decide how best to allocate those resources, and police officers have at least some discretion in determining which criminal activity to focus on. District attorneys have considerable power in determining which cases to dismiss and the

---

1. *The Wire*, Season 5, Episode 5, at 36:05 minutes.
2. *The Wire*, Season 5, Episode 3, at 12:40 minutes.

types of plea bargains to offer. Wardens and sheriffs have wide authority in the day-to-day handling of jails and prisons. And parole boards have power to set and apply the criteria for releasing hundreds of thousands of inmates each year. Is one of these entities the dominant power in the criminal justice system? Or is possible that an outside player—the media—holds the real power? Although reporters and commentators lack the authority to make a single criminal justice decision, they have the power to shape every aspect of the process—from criminalization, through arrest, prosecution, incarceration, and release—with their coverage. When the media highlights an issue, legislators, police, prosecutors, wardens, and a variety of other stakeholders in the criminal justice system must be responsive. The question is whether the media helps to keep these powerful actors honest, or whether the media itself is driving the criminal justice train.

Sara Sun Beale, The News Media's Influence on Criminal Justice Policy: How Market Driven News Promotes Punitiveness
48 William & Mary Law Review 397 (2006)

Introduction

At the end of the twentieth century the criminal justice system in the United States underwent a major change, a shift toward more punitive policies, that has had a profound impact. Every U.S. jurisdiction adopted and implemented a wide range of harsher policies. In the federal system and in every state, sentences for adult offenders were substantially increased and in many instances made mandatory. Policies were adopted to make the conditions of incarceration more onerous for adult offenders, and every state adopted provisions allowing more juvenile offenders to be prosecuted and punished as adults. The result is a system that is significantly more punitive than that of any other Western democracy, and an incarceration rate that is—by a large margin—the highest in the world. Throughout this period crime was a highly salient political issue, and the policies in question had widespread public support.

Not surprisingly, there is a good deal of scholarship seeking to explain this fundamental shift in American criminal justice policy. There have almost certainly been multiple causes....

... [This] Article explores the news media's treatment of crime during the 1990s and into the new century, the reasons for that treatment, and the question whether the treatment of crime-in addition to or instead of the crime itself, or other factors such as partisan politics-may have had a significant role in reshaping public opinion, and ultimately criminal justice policy. I begin with the question of how the news media treats crime, focusing on economic factors and changes in media coverage. The news media are not mirrors, simply reflecting events in society. Rather, media content is shaped by economic and marketing considerations that override traditional journalistic criteria for newsworthiness. This trend is apparent in local and national television's treatment of crime, in which the extent and style of news stories about crime are adjusted to meet perceived viewer demand and advertising strategies, which frequently emphasize particular demographic groups with a taste for violence. In the case of local television news, this trend results in virtually all channels devoting a disproportionate part of their broadcast to violent crimes, and to many channels adopting a fast-paced, high-crime strategy based on an entertainment model. In the case of network news, this strategy results in much greater coverage of crime, especially murder, with a heavy emphasis on long-running, tabloid-style treatment of selected cases in both the evening news and newsmagazines. Newspapers also reflect a market-driven reshaping of style and content, accompanied by massive staff cuts, resulting in a continued emphasis on crime stories as a cost-effective means to grab readers' attention. These economic and marketing considerations shape the public's exposure to crime in the news media.

Turning next to the question of how the news media's market-driven treatment of crime may influence public opinion and bolster support for punitive penal policies, I survey research in the social sciences and media studies. Two key points emerge from this survey. First, through agenda setting and priming, the news media's relentless emphasis increases public concern about crime and makes it a more important criteria in assessing political leaders. Once the issue has been highlighted, the news media's emphasis appears to increase support for punitive policies.... Finally, media appears to influence public attitudes about criminal justice policies by instilling and reinforcing racial stereotypes and linking race to crime....

... My claim here is not that the news media is the sole or even the most important cause of America's uniquely punitive criminal justice policies, but rather that worrisome evidence suggests that it is playing a significant role in shaping- or distorting-public opinion.

* * *

IV. Public Opinion, Punitiveness, Politics, and the News Media

... [F]alling crime rates seems to have had little effect on public opinion in the United States. Public opinion polls in the United States throughout the 1990s and into the current decade demonstrated high levels of anxiety about crime, a persistent unawareness of the drop in crime rates, and strong support for more punitive measures. National polls identified crime as the most important problem facing the nation each year from 1994 to 1998, and in 1999 and 2000 crime was selected as the second- or third-most important national problem. In one 2000 survey, crime issues topped Americans' list of the worst problems facing their local communities. Only the attacks of September 11, 2001, and related concerns about war, terrorism, and the economy, finally pushed crime out if its lead position in 2002.

Moreover, national polling indicates that a majority of the public is not aware that crime has decreased dramatically. Although there was a slight dip in 2000 and 2001, ... [there has been] a widespread belief that crime in the United States has been rising rather than falling.

* * *

Perhaps this result should not be surprising. Numerous studies have indicated that only a small fraction of the U.S. public is knowledgeable about public affairs, and this state of political ignorance has changed little since social scientists began to measure it in the 1940s.

Public opinion also provides strong support for more punitive policies. For twenty years a random nationwide public opinion poll has asked, "In general, do you think the courts in [your] area deal too harshly or not harshly enough with criminals?" In every year from 1980 to 1998, more than 74% of those polled have responded "[n]ot harshly enough." Although the percent of respondents who say sentences are not harsh enough fell to 67% in 2002, that is still a very high level of agreement.

The general consensus that sentences are not harsh enough has persisted despite the major increases in both sentence length ... as well as the record-high rates of incarceration. What explains the persistence of public anxiety and support for punitiveness in light

of current conditions in the United States? Although public opinion likely will lag behind events, and thus concern about crime might persist for some time after crime rates
have fallen, other factors likely are enhancing public concern, and punitive attitudes,
about crime. This Article seeks to explore the role played by the media in shaping public opinion about crime and criminal justice. In so doing, I do not mean to suggest that
the news media are the only or even most important factor. The story of cause and effect
is much more complex. Some of the changes in media noted below occurred after the
punitiveness movement was well underway.

A. How the Media Portray Crime and the Criminal Justice System

* * *

1. Network News

Despite the falling crime rates, the networks dramatically increased the coverage of
crime in their dinner-hour newscasts in the 1990s. In 1990 and 1991, the three major networks aired an average of 557 crime stories per year in their evening newscasts. For the remainder of the decade, they aired an average of 1,613 stories per year. In 1995, the peak
year, the networks presented 2,574 crime stories in their dinner-hour broadcasts. Indeed,
crime was the leading topic the networks covered in their evening news shows in the 1990s.
Some of the increase was driven by the extraordinary coverage given to the O.J. Simpson
story, but a much more general trend was at work. Excluding the Simpson case, the focus
on murder increased steadily throughout the decade, even as the murder rate declined
precipitously. In the first third of the decade (1990 to 1992), the networks' evening news
averaged fewer than 100 murder stories each year. During the middle period (1993 to
1996), the networks broadcasted an average of 352 murder stories per year. In the last third
of the decade (1997 to 1999) they broadcasted an average of 511 murder stories per year-
five times as many as at the beginning of the decade, when the murder rate was highest.

During the 1990s the three networks' coverage of criminal investigations and trials,
such as those of O.J. Simpson, the Menendez brothers, and JonBenet Ramsey, frequently
overshadowed hard news on meaningful political and social issues, and this trend has
continued. A snapshot analysis of the programming schedules of three nightly newscasts
when a tabloid case was covered revealed that CBS spent 46% of its broadcast on the
tabloid crime, and NBC and ABC spent 45% and 31%, respectively. In a more extensive
study of all the news segments on the three networks in 1997, tabloid crime stories received
more attention than public policy topics. For example, there were eighty-six news segments
on the JonBenet Ramsey murder investigation, compared to nineteen segments on campaign finance reform and thirty-five segments on health care. Medicare received the highest amount of coverage among public policy topics at fifty-eight segments, compared to
ninety segments on the O.J. Simpson trial. Not even the events of September 11, 2001
changed the crime-laden news landscape. Although crime coverage dropped from 11.7%
of total stories in June 2001 to 3.5% in October 2001, it was back at its pre-September 11
level by 2002. In fact, crime was the only "soft news" topic other than religion that re-
gained the same level of prominence in network news that it had before the terrorist attacks. Between 2000 and 2003, crime remained the second or third most frequent topic
on the network news, with an average of 1,137 crime stories per year. There was, however, a significant reduction in crime stories in 2004, when crime news fell to fifth place,
trailing the war in Iraq, the presidential election, the economy, and terrorism.

What explains the growth and prevalence of crime stories in the network news, particularly when crime rates were falling? The answer is that the economic pressures facing
the networks changed, and a drive for profits in this new environment pushed the net-

works away from hard news and toward a greater emphasis on tabloid-style crime stories. Twenty years ago, network news was not expected to make money; in 1986, NBC News was losing "as much as $100 million a year." At that time, the big three networks earned enough money from entertainment programming to carry their news operations, and they provided hard news for their own prestige, their self-perceived journalistic responsibility to provide information that would promote an educated citizenry, and the Federal Communications Commission's (FCC) public service requirement. The environment today is quite different. The FCC no longer polices the public service requirements, and networks are now owned by corporate conglomerates less likely to tolerate losses or place a great deal of value on traditional journalistic criteria of newsworthiness. For example, ABC is now owned by Disney, and NBC by General Electric. Equally important, the network nightly news programs lost up to one-half of their audience during the 1990s, and the remaining viewers were generally older and hence less valued by many advertisers. During this period the networks had to compete with a multiplicity of new competitors, including all-news networks and the Internet, while also accommodating lifestyle changes that interfere with regular viewing habits at the dinner hour.

As the networks' profit margins eroded, corporate owners pressured their news divisions to become more efficient. The networks have acknowledged "that competition from increasing media rivals—cable news, Fox, and now the Internet—are forcing them to find new formulas to attract and keep viewers." A strategy emerged for making network news into a profitable business: (1) make the product more entertaining; (2) generate more news programming; and (3) cut the cost of hard news. The networks cut back on gathering information on various forms of hard news—most notably eliminating their foreign news bureaus—while increasing their focus on what has been called "infotainment," "soft news," and "news lite." The Project for Excellence in Journalism compared network news coverage in 1977, 1987, and 1997. It found a dramatic increase in scandal stories, from less than 0.05% in 1977 to 17.1% in 1987 and 15% in 1997. Similarly, human-interest stories and quality-of-life stories (or "news-you-can-use") doubled from 8% in 1977 to 16% in 1997. By contrast, straight news or in-depth analysis fell from seven in ten stories in 1977 to four in ten in 1997.

Sensational crime stories also fit this strategy. Focusing on the investigation and trial of a single criminal case gives the networks the opportunity to provide prolonged, detailed, and relatively inexpensive coverage. As cases drag on for weeks, months, or even years, they become national melodramas, and the networks and other media try to develop suspense and interest in cases such as O.J. Simpson, the Menendez brothers, JonBenet Ramsey, and Louise Woodward (the British nanny tried for murder of the child for whom she cared). Some cases, such as O.J. Simpson and William Kennedy Smith, involve wealthy or famous defendants. Others, such as the Lorena Bobbitt mutilation case, involve sexual titillation. Although a few cases, such as those involving Timothy McVeigh and the officers who beat motorist Rodney King, seem to involve broader public policy issues, the majority of cases covered in great detail by the networks had little traditional news value, and they exemplify the shift in content away from hard news. In fact, the networks have come increasingly to cover human-interest trials that would formerly have been left to the tabloid press.

Another key development altering network news programming has been the development of the television newsmagazines Dateline NBC, 20/20, 48 Hours, and 60 Minutes, which have proliferated since 1993. These shows, which air on the networks during primetime, present true crime stories as dramatic entertainment. The percent of broadcasts of these shows that included a crime story varied from roughly 20% on some shows to more than 40% for others. The existence and prominence of these newsmagazines have played a significant role in moving network news away from hard news and toward a focus on news as entertainment....

... Entertainment increasingly means crime and justice. In the fall of 1997, 60 Minutes covered no stories about government or foreign affairs, but allocated 27.8% of its show to segments on crime and law/justice. Government issues hardly fared better on Dateline NBC with only 1.4% of the stories, and with no stories on foreign affairs and 26% dedicated to crime and law/justice. A 1998 study examined the percent of news magazine broadcasts that contained a tabloid-style crime story and found it ranged from a low of 19% of programs on 20/20 to 47% of the airings of 48 Hours.

The coverage of crime on television newsmagazines is the epitome of "commodification—'the packaging and marketing of crime information for popular consumption.'" The show format presents crime as an unfolding mystery story, beginning with the main players' character profiles, then the crime itself (typically murder), the investigation, and finally the trial. These true crime stories are presented as dramatic entertainment, and rarely is there in-depth analysis of the legal, criminal justice, or societal issues that are implicated. The crime drama's unfolding nature is economically attractive to the shows' producers in two ways. First, it is relatively cheap to produce: a small crew can be dispatched to the crime scene for an extended period of time to cover the police bulletins, attorney press conferences, the courtroom activity, and interviews with friends, neighbors, and family of the victim and perpetrator. Second, the length of these proceedings allows for suspense to mount among the public, and for growing interest to translate into higher ratings as new developments emerge.

* * *

2. Local News

Various studies in the 1990s found that crime is the number one topic on local television news. One recent study also shows that the events of September 11 have not changed this trend; in fact, crime accounted for one-quarter of all stories on local television news both before and after the terrorist attacks. Crime coverage dominates local news programming, and local stations manipulate crime and violence as a marketing strategy. Viewers with a taste for violent entertainment media also have a taste for local news with an emphasis on crime, and stations treat local news, like entertainment programming, as a commercial product that they adjust to meet their target audience's interests....

* * *

High-crime coverage by a station did not reflect high crime in the local area. James Hamilton showed that the number of crimes occurring in a given market did not have a significant statistical impact on the proportion of crime stories. Instead, the characteristics of the viewing market determined whether a local news station would choose crime as a top story. For example, a one-point ratings increase in Cops, a quasi-reality crime show, was associated with a 5% increase in proportion of lead stories on crime. By contrast, a one-point ratings increase for the network nightly news, thought to indicate a greater interest in hard news, correlated with a 1.5% drop in lead crime stories. The larger the percentage of adult women in a viewing market, the lower the fraction of news devoted to crime. Similarly, a one-point ratings increase in Melrose Place, an evening soap popular among women between the ages of 18 and 34, correlated with a 2% decrease in lead crime stories.

* * *

C. How the Media Treatment of Crime Affects Public Opinion and Criminal Justice Policy

Americans report that they get critical information about crime from the media. For example, in one national survey, 81% of respondents said that they based their view of how bad the crime problem is on what they have read or seen in the news, rather than on their personal experience. In an American Bar Association poll asking respondents to identify "extremely or very important" sources of information on the criminal justice system, 41% of respondents identified television news, 37% identified primetime newsmagazines, and 36% identified local newspapers. Most people also trust the accuracy and fairness of the information received from these sources. But how does the information gleaned from the news media affect public opinion about criminal justice policies?

Although the news media is certainly not the only influence on public opinion, the media interacts with and reinforces other key influences, such as American culture and politics, to increase punitiveness.

1. Mechanisms that Increase Crime Salience

Data collected from hundreds of experimental simulations and surveys have confirmed the media's "agenda-setting" and "priming" effects. Agenda setting refers to the media's ability to direct the public's attention to certain issues, whereas priming describes the media's ability to affect the criteria by which viewers judge public policies, public officials, or candidates for office. When combined, the two phenomena show that the media's emphasis on crime makes the issue more salient in the minds of viewers and readers, which causes the public to perceive crime as a more severe problem than real world figures indicate.

* * *

Recent surveys verify ... that the media's agenda-setting and priming effects have directed public attention to the issue of crime. One study conducted during a period when local crime rates were falling found a .70 correlation between elevated public concern about crime and crime stories in the local newspapers, and an even higher correlation when the stories appeared on the front page. Additionally, the influence of media coverage of tabloid crime cases has been found to affect public confidence in the criminal justice system. Researchers found that respondents who had been primed with reminders of high-profile cases, such as the O.J. Simpson trial or the JonBenet Ramsey murder investigation, expressed lower levels of confidence in the criminal justice system as a whole; and less confidence in individual actors within the system, such as the police, judges, juries, and prosecuting attorneys, than in those who had not.

2. Mechanisms that Produce Increased Punitiveness

* * *

b. Fear

* * *

... [S]everal recent studies have linked increased fear to exposure to the news media. These studies buttress an earlier hypothesis that linked the reiteration of violent episodes in the media to the public's exaggerated view of crime, and suggest that high television viewing may actually be the cause of excessive fear. For example, recent research found a positive correlation between frequency of television watching and fear, though only for certain program types. These studies found fear levels were heightened among viewers who watched more local news, reality, and tabloid programs, though consumption of national news and news magazine were not related to fear. The researchers attributed this result to both the low rates of violence depicted in national news and the low level of proximate relevance in national stories.

The media's ability to instill fear in viewers varies from person to person. For example, one researcher found that local news consumption impacts the fear levels of women and blacks much more than it impacts the levels of men and whites. Other factors may also influence the link between fear and the media. Measuring the effects of the "reality of crime," researchers discovered that local news consumption has a statistically significant relationship to fear for individuals who live in high-crime areas, for viewers with recent victim experience, and for those who view local news as realistically portraying crime. These findings suggest that local news consumption raises fear levels regardless of direct experience with crime....

* * *

c. Racial Typification

Other scholars in the disciplines of media studies and criminology have identified racial typification as a cause of increased punitiveness. Racial typification refers to the media's stereotypical portrayal of crime as a minority phenomenon. Initial studies of media coverage found skewed crime content portraying some groups, such as juveniles and minorities, as more criminally dangerous than others. For example, researchers have found that media coverage exaggerates the prevalence of juvenile crime, provoking increased fear of youth "predators." Although juveniles were arrested for only about 9% of homicides in 1999, in one survey the public estimated this figure to be 43%.

Other research found that distorted crime coverage along racial lines causes viewers to link the threat of crime to minorities. A study of Chicago local television news broadcasts revealed an overrepresentation of white victims as opposed to black victims, as well as a discrepancy in the amount of screen time the average story devoted to victims of different races (185 seconds for white victims compared to 106 seconds for black victims). This resulted in a 3:1 disparity in total time devoted to white as opposed to black victims. Similar studies have confirmed that minorities appear more frequently on the news as criminal suspects than they do as crime victims, police officers, or role models. Evidence also suggests that local news disproportionately portrays minorities in menacing contexts, with blacks more likely than whites to be shown in mug shots, in the physical custody of law enforcement, and in street or prison clothing. Additionally, minorities are shown more often victimizing strangers and members of different races or ethnicities. These findings have led some scholars to conclude that unequal media representations cause the public to exaggerate the number of blacks arrested for crimes, overestimate the likelihood that they will be victimized by minorities, and attribute the crime problem to blacks as a group.

Some evidence suggests a positive correlation between racial typification of crime and punitive attitudes, which suggests that skewed crime coverage may contribute to increased punitiveness. Researchers who surveyed attitudes about punishment and black involvement in crime found that white individuals who associated crime with blacks held more punitive attitudes. This finding is broadly consistent with earlier studies finding negative perceptions of blacks and minorities to be related to various punitive attitudes. However, the perception that crime is disproportionately committed by blacks correlated with punitiveness only for whites who rated relatively low on the measure of concern for crime—which the researchers defined as a cognitive expression of the crime issue's importance, not an affective measure of fear. This finding raises interesting questions about the relationship between different factors associated with punitiveness, such as holding conservative attitudes and living in the South. Some scholars have suggested that racial typification of crime can substitute for heightened crime salience caused by other factors—such as conservatism and southern residence—provoking similar punitive attitudes. At some point, however, punitiveness reaches a high enough level that media exposure and racial stereotypes produce no increase. On the other hand, viewers who are not already concerned with crime may develop more punitive attitudes when they see distorted crime coverage.

* * *

Conclusion

Fundamental economic forces have reshaped the news media in the United States, and market forces are determining to a substantial degree the extent and content of the news media's treatment of crime and the criminal justice system. Evidence that these changes are not neutral is accumulating. My focus has been on the media's treatment of crime from 1990 onward. During that period, crime fell, but the news media's focus on crime, especially violent crime, increased. Remarkably, at least half of the public remained ignorant of the reduction in crime, and a large majority continued to rate crime as one of the nation's most serious problems and to support even harsher measures. During the same period, a wide range of punitive laws and policies were promulgated, and recently adopted laws were implemented with a vengeance, leading to unprecedented rates of incarceration. Although the research discussed above is not definitive, it supports the view that the news has been playing an important role in increasing both the political salience of crime and public support for punitive policies, and doing so in a manner that activates racist attitudes. According to this analysis, the news media are playing a critical—though unplanned and largely unexamined—role in the formulation of criminal justice policy. Though it does not address the origins of the swing toward punitiveness in the 1970s, the present research does suggest that the news media's treatment of crime has amplified or bolstered other forces, and has retarded responses that might have mitigated these policies.

Although news coverage may improve with awareness of the trends described, the changes are likely to be minimal absent a shift in market pressures. In light of the First Amendment and the values it reflects, it is unlikely that Congress or the FCC would seek to regulate the content of news media, or that such regulation would be valid if adopted. Some media self-monitoring, however, may occur. For example, the news media's awareness of the significant differences in treatment of black and white victims might spur greater efforts at evenhandedness. In addition, various groups of journalists, as well as policy centers and institutes, have attempted to articulate standards and provide background materials that encourage journalists to write thematic stories or add thematic elements to stories whose main focus is episodic. Journalists might also find preparing thematic stories about crime, and a variety of hard news stories, easier and less expensive if government or private institutions made more of an effort to provide information. Finally, some media outlets may even try, from time to time, to decrease their focus on crime. But given market forces, these changes are likely to be on the margins as long as graphic, episodic, tabloid-style crime stories increase viewers or readers and thus revenues.

* * *

Profound changes are also underway within news media. The traditional news sources—newspapers, newsmagazines, local and network television, and radio—have all continued to lose readers or viewers, while the Internet has become an increasingly important

source of news and twenty-four hour cable news networks have proliferated. Will less exposure to the news mean less fear and less punitiveness? Or will media outlets try to lure
back viewers with even more crime and violence? Further research is necessary to explore
the implications of these changes, particularly in light of research indicating that various
demographic groups tend to have different media preferences.

* * *

Notes and Questions

1. Watch *The Wire*, Season 5, Episode 5, at 14:15 minutes. Mayor Carcetti holds a second press conference of the day. At the earlier event — the unveiling of a major water-
front development project — only a few reporters attended. At this second event — a
briefing about a serial killer targeting the homeless — the room is packed with reporters.
Mayor Carcetti castigates the media for focusing only on the negative. A newspaper reporter rolls his eyes in response. Is this simply a case of the adage "if it bleeds it leads"?
Who is to blame here? Why is the Mayor holding a press conference if he doesn't want crime
stories to predominate?

2. In addition to driving crime policy generally, does the media have a dramatic effect
on death penalty cases in particular? Professor Susan Bandes argues yes:

> The death penalty is especially susceptible to the influence of media, at a num-
> ber of crucial pressure points. The feedback loop is especially visible at the leg-
> islative juncture, when crime control policies are made; at the prosecutorial
> juncture, when discretion about capital charging is at work; and at the adju-
> dicative juncture, when both judge and jury must make difficult decisions about
> sentencing.

Susan Bandes, *Fear Factor: The Role of the Media in Covering and Shaping the Death
Penalty*, 1 Ohio St. J. Crim. L. 585, 591 (2004). Do you agree with Professor Bandes that
the media perpetuates fear and thus leads the public and legislators to call for harsher
laws and sentences?

3. On the flip side of Professor Bandes' article, is it possible that the media is responsible for fewer death sentences being handed down in recent years? In 1996, there
were 315 death sentences handed down in the United States. By 2011, the number had
fallen to under 80. *See* The Death Penalty Information Center, The Death Penalty
in 2011: Year End Report. Over the last few decades, the media has given considerable
coverage to wrongful convictions and exonerations from death row. Scholars suggest
that this "innocence framing" and focus on the imperfections of the criminal justice
system may have shaped public attitudes and made jurors less willing to impose the
death penalty. *See* Frank R. Baumgartner et al., *The Decline of the Death Penalty: How
Media Framing Changed Capital Punishment in America* in Winning With Words: The
Origins and Impact of Political Framing (Brian F. Schaffner & Patrick J. Sellers
eds. 2010).

4. Does saturated media coverage of crime sometimes shake loose crimes that prosecutors otherwise would have ignored? Consider the Trayvon Martin case, in which a
young African-American man was shot and killed by a neighborhood watch captain
named George Zimmerman. Zimmerman claimed he shot Martin in self-defense, and
for weeks after the shooting Zimmerman was not arrested. Yet, after a firestorm of na-

tional media coverage, an independent prosecutor was assigned and Zimmerman was eventually charged. Does the Trayvon Martin case show the media harnessing its power for good, or is it yet a further example of the media having undue influence on what should be neutral decisions based on the law and the facts?

5. Does it make sense that we elect prosecutors? Do elections actually make prosecutors accountable, or do they simply sensationalize cases? And if elections fail to constrain prosecutors, who is ensuring that they handle their jobs honestly and effectively? For a discussion of these problems and other issues with elected prosecutors, see Ronald F. Wright, *How Prosecutor Elections Fail Us*, 6 Ohio St. J. Crim. L. 581 (2009).

6. Is there anything to be gained by having *local* as opposed to statewide prosecutors? If we eliminated local prosecutors and made charging decisions at the state level, would decisions be less influenced by local media coverage? *See* Adam M. Gershowitz, *Statewide Capital Punishment: The Case for Eliminating Counties' Role in the Death Penalty*, 63 Vand. L. Rev. 307 (2010) (advocating the elimination of local control of death penalty cases). Other scholars assert that there are benefits to local control. *See* Stephen F. Smith, *Localism and Capital Punishment*, 64 Vand. L. Rev. En Banc 105 (2011).

7. *The Perp Walk*: In an age where local news is dominated by crime stories, the news media (and sometimes the police) love the "perp walk," in which a suspect is arrested in front of the cameras. Watch *The Wire*, Season 2, Episode 11, at 10:45 minutes. After police handcuff Frank Sobotka and other union officials, the officers leave them sitting in the union hall until an FBI agent comes into the room and says "They're out there now." Major Valchek then says "Showtime, Franky" and brings Sobotka out the front door where many reporters are waiting with their cameras rolling. Fans of *The Wire* will notice that the series creator and former Baltimore Sun reporter, David Simon makes a cameo in this scene as a reporter. How often do you think Simon witnessed the perp walk in real life? Is there any legitimate purpose for the police engaging in the perp walk spectacle?

8. *Is the Perp Walk Legal*: In Lauro v. City of New York, 219 F.3d 202, 213 (2nd Cir. 2000), the court held a perp walk to be a Fourth Amendment violation because, while it was reasonable to arrest the defendant, the perp walk "was unrelated to the object of the arrest," "had no legitimate law enforcement justification," and invaded his "privacy to no purpose." What is the remedy for such a violation, however? An unconstitutional perp walk will not result in suppression of evidence. At best, a defendant subjected to a perp walk can file a civil rights lawsuit in federal court under 42 U.S.C. § 1983. Assuming the defendant was charged with a serious or salacious crime—after all, what would be the purpose of the perp walk otherwise—is a jury likely to award damages in a § 1983 suit?

9. *The Grand Jury Walk*: While the legality of the perp walk may be debatable, it is quite clearly illegal to alert the media to matters before the grand jury. Nevertheless, *The Wire* beautifully illustrates how politicians can violate this rule and leak grand jury matters to the media for political gain. Watch *The Wire*, Season 5, Episode 4, at 30:00 minutes.

10. Consider the quote at the beginning of this section: "Wrong zipcode. They're dead where it doesn't count. If they were white [in a different neighborhood] you'd have had 30 inches on the front." *The Wire*, Season 5, Episode 3, at 12:40 minutes. Is this true? If so, what can we do about it?

C. The Decline of Newspapers and the Death of Investigative Journalism about the Criminal Justice System

"Just because [of] a little belt tightening is no reason for us to fall down. Whatever cutbacks there are shouldn't affect our ability to put out an excellent product. We simply have to do more with less."[1]

— Thomas Klebanow, Baltimore Sun Managing Editor

When your parents grew up, did they have a home subscription to the local newspaper? Do you have a subscription today? When was the last time you sat at the kitchen table and physically read a newspaper? Chances are, your answers to those questions are "yes," "no," and "years ago." Industries come and go. As we saw in Season 2 of *The Wire*, the once robust shipping industry in Baltimore has fallen on hard times. When an industry declines or disappears, there are often secondary effects. Closing an automobile plant in Michigan harms not just the autoworkers in Detroit, but also the manufacturing employees in Indiana who make car parts. The same dynamic is true with the decline of newspapers. A generation ago, newspapers were the watchdogs of the criminal justice system. They reported on egregious prison conditions, patterns of prosecutorial misconduct, systemic police brutality, and ineffective defense counsel. With the decline of newspapers, how much of that investigative journalism has disappeared? What has it been replaced with? And is there any chance that new media will step in to fill the gap?

William R. Montross, Jr. & Patrick Mulvaney, Virtue and Vice: Who Will Report on the Failings of the American Criminal Justice System?
61 Stanford Law Review 1429 (2009)

Introduction

Above the fold:

HUNTSVILLE, Texas—Texas executed [name of inmate or description of inmate as a killer] on [day of week] for [brief description of crime for which inmate was sentenced to death].

"[Final statement of inmate, made from lethal injection gurney]," [name of inmate] said. He was pronounced dead at [time], [number] of minutes after the lethal drugs began to flow.

[Inmate's victim's family members' names] [and/or] [inmate's family members' names] watched through a window. "[Comment on execution]" they said/[they declined to speak to reporters]/[there was or was not eye contact between inmate and victim's family members].

[More detailed description of inmate's crime, perhaps explaining aggravating circumstances such as prior crimes.]

[Whether [name of inmate] maintained his innocence/said the killing was accidental.]

[Name of inmate] was the [ordinal number] person executed this year in Texas, the nation's most active death penalty state.

---

1. *The Wire*, Season 5, Episode 1, at 35:00 minutes.

Insert the name of the condemned man and some facts about the crime; add a paragraph quoting the victim's family; note any last-minute protestations of innocence or expressions of remorse on the part of the defendant; and update the execution tally. In a matter of grave national importance—the execution of Americans by this country's most notorious killing state, Texas—this formulaic ritual constitutes American crime reporting. After a brief suspension during the United States Supreme Court's consideration of the constitutionality of lethal-injection procedures in Baze v. Rees, Texas resumed executions in June 2008. From that point until the end of the year, it executed eighteen people. Each of the eighteen men killed by the state of Texas raised substantial questions about the fairness and validity of their convictions and death sentences: representation by ineffective trial counsel, mental illness, violations of international covenants, and failures by state and federal appellate courts to reach meritorious issues because of procedural bars. But such information has no place in the fill-in-the-blanks template employed by the newspapers providing coverage of the executions....

* * *

At a time when the attention of the citizens of Texas, and the whole nation, is most focused on Texas's death machine—as the act of execution occurs—the articles [reporting the death of inmates], constitute the near totality of information reported on these men and their cases. Nothing in these articles suggests that there was any reason not to kill these men. Almost entirely absent from the stories is any mention of the defense case or the defendant, other than a voyeuristic fascination with the condemned's last words. The above are examples of American crime reporting. They are succinct, superficial, and devoid of context.

There is also criminal justice reporting. Where crime reporting purports to answer the questions, "Who? What? When? and Where?," criminal justice reporting attempts to initiate conversation and debate about the far harder question of "Why?" Why is this man on death row? Why are people who kill a white person 400 to 500 percent more likely to receive the death penalty than people who kill a black person? Why do courts seem more concerned with protecting a death verdict than ensuring that justice was done? Criminal justice reporting is the opposite of crime reporting. Where crime reporting is salacious, criminal justice reporting is reasoned; where crime reporting ignores nuance, criminal justice reporting is full of complexity. Crime reporting appeals to a limited range of base emotions; criminal justice reporting elicits a far more complex emotional response, and, more importantly, it engages the intellect. Unfortunately, crime reporting increasingly dominates the American newspaper and criminal justice reporting has become an endangered species. The future of newspaper reporting on complex matters of crime and criminal justice is not in-depth investigative reporting, but superficial and callous treatment of complicated issues.

We are not journalists. Nor do we profess to be experts on journalism. Both of us are attorneys whose practice is devoted exclusively to representing individuals who face execution in the Deep South. We represent clients on death row. We do not have the ear of the American public. But if the public has learned and come to understand critical information about the criminal justice system—its inequities, its biases, its failures—it has done so because newspapers provided that information.

Our concern is that criminal justice reporting is appearing less and less in American newspapers. In its place, crime reporting is on a steady ascent. Our concern is for our clients and other people like our clients. Who will tell the American public about the generally abhorrent quality of representation afforded indigent persons accused of crimes in this country? Who will inform the American public about a criminal justice system more concerned with procedure and technicalities designed to streamline executions than the actual merits of a case? Who will reveal to the American public cases in which the defense attorney was drunk during his client's capital trial, or the attorney slept through his client's capital trial, or the attorney presented no evidence or testimony to the jury to attempt to save his client's life? In the past, American newspapers told these stories; we fear that in the future, they will not be able.

We would have fewer concerns if an alternative medium existed where issues of criminal justice could be reported. We recognize that many Americans receive their news from television, but our focus remains on written work in recognition of its unique ability to transcend sound bites, as well as the reality that written work so often serves as "the source from which other media draw." In the words of Henry Weinstein, "[a]n awful lot of the reporting, to the extent there is any, on television about criminal justice is very derivative from newspapers." And as we look around the media landscape, particularly at the proliferation of new media, we see no forum where criminal justice reporting and writing can continue to exist, never mind flourish.

To pursue the information necessary to publish credible, detailed, and compelling stories about this country's criminal justice system — its courts, its jails and prisons, its methods of execution — enormous resources must be expended. For all the virtues of new media, they do not possess either the resources or institutional power that newspapers once did. And to the extent that new media offer a participatory process — in effect, a democratization of the journalistic endeavor — the very community on which it relies excludes individuals immersed in the criminal justice system: those awaiting trial in jails throughout the country, those serving sentences in state and federal prisons, those awaiting the date of their execution on death row. In such a climate, "what will become of those people ... who depend on ... journalistic enterprises to keep them safe from various forms of torture, oppression, and injustice[?]" For our clients and people like them across the country, it is the answer to this question we fear.

* * *

I. The Virtues of Criminal Justice Reporting

On June 11, 2000, the Chicago Tribune published the first of a two-part series examining the death penalty system in Texas. The impetus for the investigation was the pending candidacy of George W. Bush for the presidency of the United States. During Bush's six years as governor, 150 men and 2 women were executed in Texas; far and away, Bush presided over more executions than any governor in the modern era of capital punishment.

Setting the stage for the Chicago Tribune's Texas series, well-documented and highly publicized flaws in the death penalty system in Illinois, also exposed in part by the Tribune, had resulted in Governor George Ryan's moratorium on executions in the state on January 31, 2000. Those flaws also led to Ryan's subsequent commutation of all 167 death sentences in the state on January 11, 2003....

However, Bush refused to acknowledge a similar problem in Texas. When asked if a moratorium was necessary in Texas, he responded that he was certain that the infirmities of the Illinois system had not infected Texas's death penalty process. "Maybe they've had some problems in their courts.... Maybe they've had some faulty judgments. I've reviewed every case, ... and I'm confident that every case that has come across my desk ... I'm confident of the guilt of the person who committed the crime." In June 2000, Johnny Sutton, Bush's criminal justice policy director, stated:

> We have a system in place that is very careful and that gives years and years of super due process to make sure that no innocent defendants are executed and that the defendant received a fair trial.... We think we have a good criminal justice system in Texas. It's not perfect, but it's one of the best around.

The Chicago Tribune disagreed. In the course of conducting the "first comprehensive examination of every execution during [Bush's] administration [,]" Tribune investigative reporters Steve Mills, Ken Armstrong, and Douglas Holt "examined trial transcripts, legal briefs, appellate rulings and lawyer disciplinary records, and ... interviewed dozens of witnesses, lawyers and judges." Extensive time and money were expended on the investigation, thousands upon thousands of pages of documents and transcripts were reviewed, and months were spent talking to sources. The result was an incisive series that belied the claim that Texas provided "years and years of super due process" to condemned men and women on Texas's death row. The Tribune's examination of the Texas death penalty system uncovered and presented evidence that defense attorneys in forty cases "presented no evidence whatsoever or only one witness during the trial's sentencing phase." Examining the prosecution practice of presenting evidence of an individual's "future dangerousness" at the penalty phase of a capital trial, and particularly focusing on Texas's prosecutors' reliance on a psychiatrist known as "Dr. Death" for these suspect assessments, the Tribune found that in at least twenty-nine cases, the prosecution presented "damaging testimony from a psychiatrist who, based upon a hypothetical question describing the defendant's past, predicted the defendant would commit future violence." In most of those cases, the Tribune continued, "the psychiatrist offered this opinion without ever examining the defendant. Although this kind of testimony is sometimes used in other states, the American Psychiatric Association has condemned it as unethical and untrustworthy." Confirming the suspicion that the death penalty is not reserved for those who commit the worst crimes, but for those who have the worst attorneys, the Tribune concluded: "While capital cases make the greatest demands on defense attorneys, the lawyers in these cases do not always represent the legal community's best." Specifically:

> In 43 cases, or one-third, a defendant was represented at trial or on initial appeal by an attorney who had been or was later disbarred, suspended or otherwise sanctioned. Though most were punished after they handled these cases, their disciplinary records raise questions about their suitability for such a complex job.

* * *

The Chicago Tribune series is only one example of comprehensive and detailed reporting on issues of criminal justice. In November 2005, the Birmingham News conducted a six-day exploration of the death penalty in Alabama. In September 2006, the New York Times, in a series entitled "Broken Bench," detailed the absence of both process and law in the town and village court systems of the state of New York. In September 2007, investigative reporters for the Atlanta Journal-Constitution authored a comprehensive and authoritative four-day series, entitled "A Matter of Life or Death," on Georgia's death penalty system. There are others. In a morass of crime reporting that was too often either dull and uninformed or sensationalist and misleading, the occasional presence of criminal justice reporting of the type published by the Chicago Tribune, the Birmingham News, the New York Times, and others demonstrated that newspapers could serve to initiate and ignite public debate about this country's criminal justice system. As the editors of the Birmingham News noted at the very beginning of their series, "[w]e are not telling you how to think; we are just challenging you to think."

This type of comprehensive, engaged reporting on matters of criminal justice cannot continue much longer. This is not because American newspapers have purposefully abandoned their conscience, their "moral imperative," or even their mythologized role as keepers of the public trust. It is because, in the past few years alone, the financial fragility of America's newspapers has worsened to the point where they simply cannot afford to choose "rational tempered stories that might help explain the vexing crime problem" over simplistic and salacious crime reporting.

What is different now — from ten years ago, from only a few years ago — is that newspapers today have very little choice in deciding whether to conduct criminal justice reporting or succumb to tabloid-style crime reporting. America's newspapers are in dire financial straits. The explosive availability of information from alternative sources, declining circulation, and diminishing advertising revenue have all contributed to extreme cost-cutting tactics undertaken by publishers. The result of cost-cutting tactics is a lesser paper — fewer reporters and less reporting....

* * *

The financial crisis facing American newspapers is not limited to small-town and mid-size dailies — papers of all sizes and stature are struggling. Even the New York Times reported in early 2008 that it would cut approximately 100 jobs as the company came "under increased pressure from shareholders — notably two hedge funds that recently bought almost 10 percent of the common stock — to do something significant to improve its bottom line." In the same article, the Times' editor-in-chief "suggested that the cuts could not help but affect the newspaper's journalism." The Chicago Tribune is currently suffering a worse fate. On December 9, 2008, the Los Angeles Times reported that its parent company, which also owns the Chicago Tribune, filed for bankruptcy protection....

* * *

Newspapers will continue to report on crime. Crime sells, as do scandal, sex, and celebrity. But it will continue in a form and manner devastating to the development of an intelligent and rational discourse on the failings of this country's criminal justice system. The tragedy lies not only in the absence of extensive reporting in the manner once conducted by the Chicago Tribune, but also in the continuing rise and dominance of a form of crime reporting that discourages any nuanced public discussion.

II. The Vices of Crime Reporting

* * *

As financially troubled newspapers cut costs to stave off extinction — eliminating reporters, editors and staff members — [sensationalist] crime reporting is not only a possible option; it is increasingly the only financially feasible option. As crime reporting becomes more and more prevalent in the daily press, newspapers are turned into tabloids. But so severe are the financial constraints facing newspapers that the ability of newspapers to engage even in crime reporting has also been compromised. Papers have increasingly become passive recipients and distributors of "facts" rather than active gatherers of information. Increasingly unable to conduct their own independent fact-finding investigations, newspapers rely more and more on subjective sources such as law enforcement agencies, which provide packaged "stories" readily convertible to newsprint, or on news services such as the Associated Press, which produces a generic product suitable for inoffensive publication. The local crime reporter does not even need to wallow in dirty police stations to procure his stories; the stories now come to him as an attachment to an email sent from the local district attorney's office. Crime reporting was never very probing or analytical in the first place, but the forms of crime reporting currently being practiced simply do not permit a perspective that is not superficial or prosecution-biased.

Nearly every police department, district attorney's office, or attorney general's office regularly produces press releases that praise the professionalism and thoroughness of the investigation, assert the certainty of the defendant's guilt, and proclaim the need for harsh punishment. These releases are produced by experts in media relations, and are consumed and republished, more or less verbatim, as stories by newspapers. The ability of local law enforcement to generate prepackaged stories in this form is a relatively recent development. But it is one that has proven of great benefit to the newspaper executives. The repackaging of law enforcement press releases relieves the newspaper of enormous financial costs that would be borne if the newspaper itself actively investigated the facts and wrote the story.... But the releases, and consequently the repackaged versions of the releases as they appear in the newspapers, uniformly fail to offer any reason to doubt the guilt of the accused and rarely present any mitigating information about the defendant that might warrant anything less than society's ultimate approbation. The press releases, and the newspaper stories they become, fail to suggest that there might be any explanation for the crime other than the monstrosity of the defendant. The releases rarely provide information that the accused suffers from a severe mental illness, or is cognitively impaired, or was the victim of horrific physical or sexual abuse. By stressing individual culpability, the press releases produced by law enforcement, and therefore the news stories, neglect the greater factors present in the lives of many criminal defendants: abject poverty, institutional failure, crumbling social structures, or widespread drug infestation throughout whole neighborhoods. Of course, the criminal justice system is adversarial, and it is unreasonable to expect that partisan advocates will publicly sow seeds of doubt as to their own positions. But as newspapers become more and more dependent for their crime stories on press releases generated by law enforcement, crime reporting becomes more and more a simple matter of prosecution propaganda.

It is becoming increasingly difficult to determine whether what is printed in the newspaper is the work of a journalist or the media specialist at the local law enforcement agency. Conversely, law enforcement agencies have designed their press releases to appear as articles contained in newspapers....

* * *

Before the state of Texas executed Larry Donnell Davis, Denard Manns, and Derrick Sonnier ... the Texas Attorney General issued comprehensive press releases concerning the "facts of the crime" and the "procedural history" of each case. The packages prepared by the Texas Attorney General provide enough information for newspapers which cannot afford to investigate to create an article. Detailed in the Attorney General's press release on Larry Davis are not only the facts of the crime, but summations of the state's case at the penalty phase of the trial. The reporter can learn that the state presented "evidence of Davis' abusive treatment of women[,]" that Davis's wife "finally left him when Davis became abusive toward their children[,]" and that while awaiting trial, Davis had an altercation with jail officials where Davis "was holding an uncapped Bic pen (considered a weapon in this context) in his fist in a 'stabbing' manner." Also contained in the press release is an exhaustive history of Davis's prior contact with the criminal justice system. Not surprisingly, there is nothing in the press release about what, if anything, was presented by the defense at any stage of Davis's capital murder trial. If the defense presented mitigating evidence, there is no mention of it in the press package. It is not the responsibility of the district attorney or the attorney general to present the position of the defense. But there is no countervailing press package from the defense. The vast disparities between the resources available to the government for purposes of prosecution and the resources available to defense counsel for the representation of indigent defendants so often mean that defense attorneys cannot afford the services of professionals to "package the facts." If a reporter wanted to include perspectives from the defense, the reporter would have to actively seek out the defense lawyer; however, that would entail switching from a passive recipient of "facts" to an active gatherer of information. That costs money. Therefore, it likely will not occur.

* * *

III. The Limitations of New Media

* * *

The national analysis of the developments in and advantages of new media is an ongoing process, and much of it centers on a single question: whether the new, democratized media have the ability to fill the gaps created by the fall of the institutional newspaper—a fall to which new media have obviously contributed. Stalwarts of traditional newspapers contend that bloggers and other nontraditional journalists merely repackage news rather than discover it, and as such they are dangerous parasites who reap the reporting benefits of the traditional newspaper while simultaneously destroying it. Of course, defenders of new media have a response. From their standpoint, the stalwarts' claim that new media lack the very essence of reporting—reporters—is a fallacy. The web has millions of reporters: ordinary people conducting their own investigations and sharing their own experiences.

Unfortunately, criminal justice reporting presents unique problems which the new, democratized media appear ill-suited to handle. The first is that effective criminal justice reporting takes serious money up front, not only to investigate but also to engage in the litigation that is often a necessary component of such investigation. The second issue is that the very strength of new media trumpeted by their adherents—the citizen as journalist—ends at the prison walls. New media rooted in citizen participation have yet to showcase a sustainable strategy for confronting either of those challenges, let alone the two challenges operating in concert.

The financial costs of effective criminal justice reporting are enormous.... The fact that launching and conducting journalistic investigations into the criminal justice system is so expensive poses a problem for the basic concept underlying the democratization of the media. It is true that many people can take some time out of their lives to contribute to blogs. But for the most part such people do not have the resources to spend days upon days observing court proceedings, more days sifting through legal documents, more days interviewing witnesses, and more days doing it all again....

In addition, investigating criminal justice is a minefield for litigation—both litigation concerning information access and litigation concerning the final product. Lawsuits over access to information are especially likely in the context of criminal justice reporting, as prisons and law enforcement agencies often stonewall prying outsiders until the officials are literally hauled into court.

Defenders of new, democratized media contend that what they lack in resources, they gain through citizen participation. Whereas traditional newspapers can only report on events where they have reporters on the scene, new media can capitalize on the insight of ordinary people—regardless of whether those people have a day's worth of journalism experience. As one media veteran observed, "Traditional journalism provides the view from the outside looking in, and citizen journalism provides the view from the inside looking out."

* * *

There are more than 2.2 million people in jails and prisons across the United States. They include people recently arrested for the first time and people wondering when, if ever, they will see an attorney. They include people serving nine-year prison terms and ninety-nine year prison terms, people with mental illness and mental retardation, people abused as children at home and abused as adults in prison. They include people languishing on death row and people nearing execution by lethal injection. None of those people can own a computer, and none have access to the Internet....

The reality is that the "inside looking out" view does not exist in the context of criminal justice news. People entangled in the criminal justice system cannot share their real experiences with the citizenry without a gatekeeper, and the citizenry cannot absorb those experiences. This is a problem not because people in jails and prisons have some legal right to unimpeded access to the Internet, but because society's increasing reliance on ordinary people to contribute to news coverage means that the perspectives of those in jails and prisons are featured even less by new media than by the traditional newspaper.

In short, the fall of the traditional newspaper has left people entangled in the criminal justice system to rely on participatory media to play the watchdog role of the "Fourth Estate." Alas, those people are not participants in the new participatory media.

If engaged citizens cannot conduct their own criminal justice reporting because it is too expensive and the participatory new media exclude people in jails and prisons, our fear is that new media—however valuable in other areas—cannot ride to the rescue as the traditional American newspaper abandons serious reporting of criminal justice.

Conclusion

The collapse of criminal justice reporting as an endeavor that newspapers today can undertake is more than a crisis of information. It is a moral crisis. Americans are not apathetic about the great issues of the day. The presidential election of 2008 demonstrated the opposite: Americans want to know what is being done in their name and what is happening in their own backyard. To a large extent, media—both traditional and new— met this demand for knowledge. If a citizen wanted to understand the candidates' differing positions on health care reform, he could read newspapers, and he could also wade through dozens of new media sources providing detailed analysis of the candidates' proposals and the perspectives of people without access to doctors.

We do not see such availability of information in matters of criminal justice. What is happening to our children when they are placed in delinquent institutions in faraway states? Why are poor people spending months in jail because they cannot afford the fees of private probation companies while rich people literally escape because they could afford the initial traffic fine? Why do courts tolerate such abysmal attorneys for poor people accused of criminal offenses? If such information is not available, the American public cannot be expected to react and demand change or reform. What is happening to our children, to poor people charged with crimes, and to the condemned and institutionalized in this country are critical questions that define who we are as a nation. But where do Americans get the information to answer these questions? In the past, newspapers could and at times did provide this information, but we do not see newspapers being able to perform this critical function moving forward. And we do not see new media filling the vacuum. "[W]hat will become of those people ... who depend on ... journalistic enterprises to keep them safe from various forms of torture, oppression and injustice"? They will be tortured; they will be oppressed; they will be victims of injustice. And Americans will not know.

Notes and Questions

1. Do you have a newspaper subscription that is delivered in hard copy to your doorstep each morning? If not, where do you get your news from? If it is from the internet, have you considered how those internet sites turn a profit?

2. When was the last time you read an investigative journalism piece like the *Chicago Tribune* or *Birmingham News* pieces the authors praise? If you have read one recently was it in a newspaper? The authors, who are death penalty lawyers, do not discuss whether magazines can replace (or even partially replace) the investigative journalism previously practiced by newspapers. For instance, in 2003, *The Atlantic Monthly* ran an in-depth piece on the shoddy clemency reviews conducted by then-Governor George W. Bush. *See* Alan Berlow, *The Texas Clemency Memos*, THE ATLANTIC, July 2003. In 2009 *The New Yorker* ran a compelling investigation into the execution of Cameron Todd Willingham and highlighted the deep flaws in arson investigation techniques. *See* David Grann, *Trial by Fire*, THE NEW YORKER, Sept. 7, 2009. The article caused a huge uproar and Texas subsequently established a forensic science commission to investigate. In 2010, Texas Monthly ran a lengthy story questioning the guilt of Anthony Graves, who had been on death row for eighteen years and was facing a retrial. *See* Pamella Colloff, *Innocence Lost*, TEXAS MONTHLY, Oct. 2010. One month later, the district attorney dropped the charges against Graves, citing a complete lack of evidence. Aren't these the types of investigative journalism that Montross and Mulvaney praise? Can magazines fill the shoes of newspapers in keeping the criminal justice system honest? Or are magazines soon to go the way of newspapers?

3. Can professional or semi-professional blogs fill at least part of the vacuum left by the decline of newspapers? For instance, in Texas the influential "Grits for Breakfast" blog analyzes a host of criminal justice issues specific to Texas. *See* http://gritsforbreakfast.blogspot.com/. On a national level, the Sentencing Law and Policy Blog run by Ohio State Law Professor Douglas Berman tracks and consolidates important information about the Federal Sentencing Guidelines, capital punishment, clemency, and a host of other important issues. *See* http://sentencing.typepad.com/. There are many similar local and national blogs focusing on other criminal justice topics. While these blogs do not have nearly the readership that newspapers once had, they are widely read by practitioners, academics, and even legislators and judges. Can the internet's ability to aggregate, summarize, and quickly disseminate information into the hands of powerful decisionmakers help to offset the decline of investigative journalism? Do Montross and Mulvaney take account of this phenomenon?

4. Assuming Montross and Mulvaney are correct about the internet killing investigative journalism, can we take some solace in the power of the internet and social media to actually effect change? Put differently, while print journalism might have kept the general public more informed a generation ago, did investigative journalism actually succeed in accomplishing much change? By contrast, do you think social media creates more change, whether it be democratic uprisings in Egypt or petitions to save death row inmates from execution in the United States? Does the power of facebook, twitter and other social media to spur change make up for the damage it has caused to investigative journalism?

Index